DANCING
IN THE PATHS
OF THE
ANCESTORS

Books on Native America by Thomas E. Mails

THE MYSTIC WARRIORS OF THE PLAINS

THE PEOPLE CALLED APACHE

THE PUEBLO CHILDREN OF THE EARTH MOTHER

DOG SOLDIERS, BEAR MEN, AND BUFFALO WOMEN

SUNDANCING AT ROSEBUD AND PINE RIDGE

THE CHEROKEE PEOPLE

SECRET NATIVE AMERICAN PATHWAYS

FOOLS CROW

FOOLS CROW: WISDOM AND POWER

HOTEVILLA

DANCING IN THE PATHS OF THE ANCESTORS

BOOK TWO OF
THE PUEBLO CHILDREN OF THE EARTH MOTHER

*The culture, crafts, and ceremonies of the Hopi, Zuñi, Acoma,
Laguna, and Rio Grande Pueblo Indians of yesterday and today*

Thomas E. Mails

MARLOWE & COMPANY
NEW YORK

To my wife, Lisa,
my daughter, Allison,
and my sons, Ryan and Andrew

Published by
Marlowe & Company
841 Broadway, Fourth Floor
New York, NY 10003

DESIGNED BY LAURENCE ALEXANDER

Dancing in the Paths of the Ancestors [ISBN 1-56924-689-0] formerly titled
Pueblo Children of the Earth Mother Volume II.

Library of Congress Cataloging-in-Publication Data

Mails, Thomas E.
    Pueblo children of the earth mother / by Thomas E. Mails.
        p.   cm.
    Originally published: Garden City, N.Y. : Doubleday. 1983.
    Includes bibliographical references and index.
    ISBN 1-56924-669-6
    1. Pueblo Indians.   I. Title.
E99.P9M225   1993
978.9'004974—dc21   98-27441
                                                                  CIP

CONTENTS

BOOK TWO

Preface

The Pueblo Indians living in Arizona and New Mexico are a remarkable people. For more than two thousand years they and their ancestors, the Anasazi, have walked the centuries warily, finding peace with the spirits to which they reverently entrust themselves, overcoming incredible hardships, tilling their beloved soil as part of a ritual of life, creating ingenious art and architecture, working hard and venerating tranquility, and seldom turning to wrath or rebellion. The Pueblos have also retained more of their traditional ways than any native peoples in North America. In both the topographical and human landscapes they have changed the least. Because of this, the Pueblo Indians provide a unique doorway through which an observer can step directly into unbroken history.

My telling of the Anasazi and Pueblo story in words and pictures has required two large and detailed books:

Book I describes the history, customs, and accomplishments of the Neighbors of the Anasazi; the Basketmaker Anasazi; and the Virgin, Chaco Canyon, Kayenta, Mesa Verde, and Little Colorado Region Anasazi.

Book II describes the history, customs, and accomplishments of the Hopi, Zuñi, Acoma, Laguna, and Rio Grande Pueblo Indians from their beginnings to the present.

Except for studies of a few Anasazi ruins, the color plates are portrayals of present-day Pueblo Indians. My purpose in this is twofold: to provide a constant reminder of the firm connection between the living Pueblos and their Anasazi ancestors, and also to emphasize the brilliant and symbolic color that has attended the culture throughout its history.

List of Color Plates

All color plates and drawings are original works of art by the author.

Chapter 1

THE HOPI—
PUEBLO V

HOPI LIFEWAY

Toward the end of the nineteenth century, and especially after 1882, when the Hopi Reservation was founded, Americans began to visit the Hopi on their sun-drenched mesas. To their surprise and delight the visitors discovered that life there appeared to be about what the first emissaries of Coronado experienced when they arrived in A.D. 1540. Although the Hopi had been exposed for a time to some of what the Spanish called "civilization," after more than three centuries all but a few of them continued to love their own culture better than anything "civilization" had to offer. A century under U.S. Government control, and life in the midst of the white race, would alter the situation somewhat. Yet half of the twentieth century would pass before inroads were made at Hopi and distinct white influences could be seen in their country. Even now, the customs and architecture existing at the turn of the century are present to an astonishing degree.

Close behind the earliest explorers came four extremely talented men whose contributions to the ethnology of the Hopi are of prime importance, and something needs to be said about each one of them. They, along with the superb later scholars Elsie Clews Parsons and Mischa Titiev, will be cited frequently in the Hopi material to follow.

Alexander M. Stephen was a Scotsman who, from 1881 until his death in 1894, lived at Keams Canyon with the trader Thomas Keam. Nearly all his years in Hopi country were devoted to a study of Hopi life, especially to its ceremonial aspects. He spent a great deal of time with the people, mainly on First Mesa, where he was respected and loved. He kept a series of superb notebooks that he profusely illustrated with eyewitness sketches and filled with minute descriptions of everything he saw. These notebooks were later edited by Elsie Clews Parsons and were published by the Columbia University Press in 1936. They are by far the most authoritative and exhaustive compendium of data ever assembled concerning any Pueblo group, and repeated reference is made to them in the literature.[1]

The Reverend Heinrich R. Voth made his first visit to Hopi country in 1892 and returned in 1893 with his wife to establish a Mennonite mission near Old Oraibi. Of late he has been blamed, unfairly, in the estimation of Fred Eggan and Harry C. James, for many of the difficulties experienced by the Hopi of Third Mesa.[2]

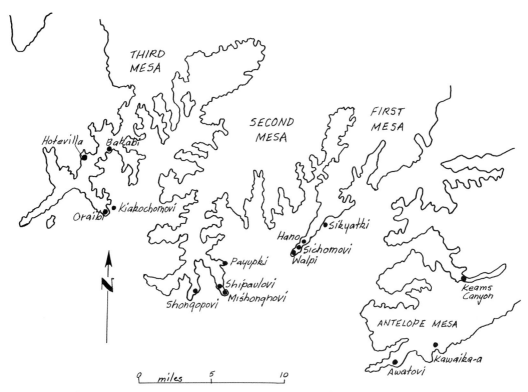

Top, map of the present Hopi reservation and mesas in relation to nearby cities and sites. *Bottom,* map of the Hopi mesas showing locations of the villages and also sites on Antelope Mesa.

The Voths entered into every phase of Hopi life and learned the language in order to convert more quickly what Voth called "immortal souls needing to be saved." However, in his writings one finds no evidence of contempt for the Hopi religion. On the contrary, there is great respect, and it may be assumed that Voth sought to convert only those he felt needed his help. In any event, the Voths had little success, and when his wife died in childbirth in 1901, he decided to leave the mission field. At this time a relationship with George A. Dorsey flowered, and Voth began to make artifact collections for the Field Columbian Museum.

When successors came to replace Voth at the mission, a few Hopi converts were at last gained, but, along with government interference, the successes fueled a fire already kindling a division of Old Oraibi that took place in 1906. After thirty years the converts numbered only about forty, and today the mission is no larger. Laura Thompson thinks that the Mennonites undermined the Hopi priesthood, converted priests, and caused thereby the general lapse of the ceremonies, "which together upset the organic balance of the social system." This, she argues, was the cause for the breakdown of the Oraibi ceremonial organization.[3]

Eggan believes she overstates the influence of the Mennonites and that she neglects the contributions to the demise of Old Oraibi made by environmental factors and overt government influences. The fact that Oraibi chiefs allowed Voth to enter their kivas and to witness rituals also calls Thompson's thoughts into question.

In any event, Voth was on his way to becoming an ethnologist. Even though he at first questioned the reasons for and effectiveness of the Hopi practices, Voth at the same time was powerfully intrigued. During the 1890s he undertook a systematic study of Hopi social and ritual life to understand their religious beliefs better.[4] In time he would admit that, as a whole, the ceremonies were devotional and serious. But he considered the "shows" of the clowns "degrading and filthy," and he thought the whipping of the children in the initiation ceremony was a travesty. In consequence, Voth asked the government to prohibit some features of certain ceremonies.

By 1897, Voth was so deeply into collecting lesser material culture objects and information about the Hopi that he was able to provide Dorsey with about four hundred well-documented specimens for an exhibit. These included twenty-four masks. From this point on, Voth provided Dorsey with a series of magnificently written and illustrated accounts of Hopi secular and ceremonial customs. The work in this instance was supported by the Stanley McCormick Hopi expedition, and it is published under that name. Included in Voth's contributions were a number of first-rate altar reproductions he created for displays at the Field Columbian Museum. Hopi who saw the displays were astonished at their accuracy. When one uninstructed society member had to succeed his brother as kiva chief after the brother's sudden death, he had no recourse but to follow Voth's account, translated by the new chief's grandson, to clarify details essential to the carrying out of the rituals.

In his final analysis of Voth, Eggan concludes, "For all his interest in Hopi religion he never attempted to understand it in its own terms because he had already defined it as false,"[5] adding, however, that as an ethnologist of Hopi life Voth had no peers.* The task of interpretation, however, "has had to be carried out by others, and particularly Mischa Titiev for Third Mesa."[6]

---

*Among those who benefited greatly from Voth's Hopi collections was Fred Harvey, who obtained in 1912 a superb display for his Hopi House at Grand Canyon. Although it lacked some culture items, it was a representative assortment, and in 1979, Northland Press, of Flagstaff, Arizona, published Barton Wright's *Hopi Material Culture*, which illustrates and describes the collection. It is a "must" book for any Hopi student.

Voth left Hopi in 1902 and became a home mission worker in Oklahoma. He died in 1927.[7]

Jesse Walter Fewkes was an extraordinary man. Despite the hazards of travel in the back country in the late 1890s and early 1900s, during his years with the U.S. Bureau of American Ethnology in the Smithsonian Institution he seems to have been everywhere at once, looking, listening, digging, recording, and speculating. He spent parts of many summers with the Hopi, mainly on the First and Second mesas; he was there while Alexander Stephen was alive, and the two shared notes. Voth was at Oraibi during this time, and Fewkes went there to gather information, but I do not know what contact the two men had. Eggan says that Fewkes wanted comparative data from Voth, but that Voth was reluctant, since it might weaken interest in his own accounts. Voth was probably right. Fewkes would have had it in print while Voth was still mulling over his introductory material.

What I admire most about Fewkes was his willingness to express openly his thoughts regarding the purpose and meaning of what he found, and to speculate about its historical development. This has never been a popular pursuit among archaeologists, since it is guaranteed to bring sharp criticism from other experts who dispute the views according to what they have decided about the same things, but hesitate to say so until another is bold enough to open the door in print. Fewkes put it all down, and he argued eloquently in his own behalf. Readers will find more than forty of his books and articles listed in my bibliography, and he is regularly cited in the footnotes.

As to his accuracy in what he deduced from his marvelous experiences, a few notes in regard to the Hopi are in order. Many honors were bestowed upon Fewkes by foreign countries and at home, but those he prized most were his initiations into the Antelope and Flute societies of Walpi. Both Fewkes and Stephen were permitted to witness, record, and participate in many ceremonies in the kiva and in the public performances.

Albert Yava was born in 1888 in the Tewa village of Hano, on First Mesa. He grew up in the context of both the Tewa and the Hopi worlds, coming to know the Hopi lifeway almost as well as any Hopi. He was initiated into the One Horn Kiva fraternity, where he learned the traditions of the clans and the essences of the ceremonial cycle upon which Hopi life is based.

Yava is a sensitive and perceptive man, and the superb story of his life, *Big Falling Snow,* published in 1978, is most informative. Among other things, he speaks now and then of certain anthropologists, ethnologists, and archaeologists who worked among the Hopi. As a rule, Yava is not especially kind to these. But Fewkes is an exception. "What he tells is absolutely true,"[8] Yava writes. In regard to the One Horn ceremonies, Yava says that, while he is "honor bound" to keep the rituals secret, Fewkes was the only white man who became an initiate, and none of the One Horns "could find any fault" with what Fewkes wrote about the society. The One Horn people even suggested that Yava should get rid of his copy of Fewkes's book because it was so accurate. "Fewkes," says Yava, "had a brilliant mind,"[9] a fitting tribute, I think, to one of the great archaeologists. Fewkes retired in 1928 and died in 1930.

A towering work on Hopi and Zuñi is *A Study of Pueblo Architecture*, Tusayan and Cíbola, by Victor Mindeleff, published as the BAE 8th Annual Report of 1886–87, although the field work was done in 1881–83. This astonishing collection of maps, sketches, commentary, and photographs presents a comprehensive display of the architectural accomplishments of the western Pueblo peoples as they existed before white influences began to change them. Some of these I have redrawn, or drawn from Mindeleff's photographs, to augment the descriptions I give of the Hopi lifeway.

At the time these four intellectual giants lived and studied at Tusayan, Stephen, Voth, Fewkes, and Mindeleff found about two thousand Hopi living in seven villages in an austere environment that formed the basis for their entire social and religious life, and we can turn now to a closer examination of its details.

Some of the Hopi men of A.D. 1900 were beginning to wear the white man's style of clothing, but others clung to the old-style homemade cotton trousers and either plain white or brightly colored shirts of calico or velvet. The trousers usually extended no lower than the shin, and they were split open at the seam on the outer side for about the lower half of their length. Footless stockings, homespun, dyed, and knitted were sometimes worn. These were held up by woven garters at a point just below the knee. A colorful bandanna was wrapped around the head at forehead level to hold the hair in place. At work in the fields or while hunting, the men wore considerably less, only a G-string made of hide or cloth and a pair of plain moccasins. It was comfortable attire for the Southwest climate, and the hot desert sun did not burn their dark skins so easily as it did that of white men. During ceremonies the Hopi men wore traditional moccasins and apparel, described further on.

Most of the women, especially the older ones, still dressed just as their immediate ancestors did. They wore beautiful woven blanket dresses, generally blue with a white border, or white with a red and blue border. A shawl of calico or of native weave was thrown over the shoulders to complete the outfit. The dress itself was made so that the left shoulder was left uncovered, and the hem came a little below the knee. A woven belt pulled the dress in at the waist. By 1900, though, many of the women and girls were being encouraged by the government and missionaries to wear a calico slip under the dress, so that arms and shoulders were well covered.

Women did not wear stockings, and it was common for them to go about barefooted. But buckskin moccasins with rawhide soles were worn now and then. There was a plain white high-topped style for daily wear in the village that sometimes had a black sole, and there was a white wraparound legging-moccasin combination whose primary use was for weddings and ceremonies. For travel and field work, some women topped their daily-wear moccasins with a separate buckskin leg-wrapping, so that the combination looked about like the one-piece wraparound type just described. It was left a natural color and offered protection when it was necessary to go to the desert where cacti, chollas, prickly shrubs, sharp rocks, and reptiles abounded.

Further on, exact details as to clothing styles and manufacture are given.

Hopi maiden in handwoven dress, blanket, and wraparound boots. Native costume of 1900. From a Museum of Northern Arizona photograph.

Jewelry in the year 1900 consisted of earrings, bracelets, necklaces, belts, and rings. Earrings of pure turquoise were common, but there were also wooden disks and rectangles with turquoise and shell mosaics appended on one side. Necklaces were fashioned of silver, turquoise, coral, shell, glass, and amber. Belts, rings, and bracelets were adorned with silver obtained in trade, although limited work had recently begun in copper.

Before they were eligible for marriage, girls wore their hair loose and much in the manner of boys, except that it was parted. Girls of marriageable age had their hair done up in traditional large whorls called *nash-mi,* with one whorl on each side of the head. Some say this was an imitation of the squash blossom, the Hopi symbol for purity, and that after marriage the hair was hung in two side coils to represent the long squash, a coiffure intended to symbolize fruitfulness. Others describe the whorls as representing butterflies, which they say is a symbol of virginity. But in the light of certain courtship practices that are treated further on, the suggestion of "virginity" becomes somewhat suspect.

To make the whorl, the hair was parted in the middle and then gathered into long rolls at the side. Each roll was wound over either a corn-husk form or a large U-shaped branch of wood, forming two semicircles that joined to produce a single disk with a diameter of approximately eight inches. Whorls like this were depicted in ancient pictoglyphs and in the murals at Awatovi.

Married women parted their hair in the middle, cut it fairly short, and then gathered it into two thick queues or rolls, one at each side of the head.

The "whorl" or "squash-blossom" manner of dressing the maiden's hair to indicate that she is eligible for marriage. *Top left,* winding the hair around a wooden U-shaped form and tying it with yarn. *Top right,* side view. *Bottom right,* front view.

The queues were then wound with a hair string for approximately four inches, and the ends were left loose in a fan shape. The methods of winding varied slightly.[10] Polingaysi Qoyawayma says that when she was a child in the 1890s, hair combings and cuttings were saved and made into a hair cord to be employed ceremonially, as in tying the maiden's whorl.

The hair style of the Hopi male child of 1900 was the same as that of his father, except that the father's was washed and combed oftener. Men did not part their hair, letting it fall long and loose to flow down their backs and trimming it across the forehead to make bangs. Sometimes they pulled it into a bun at the back of the head and wrapped it with yarn in the *chongo* style. Those influenced by whites began to crop the sides evenly just above the shoulders, and then fixed it in place with a cloth band.

Outside persuasion has changed Hopi attitudes somewhat, but in 1900 it was still a serious offence for men or women to cut their hair in any way not prescribed by ritual rules. Babies received a first, strange ritual haircut at the time of the February Powamû, and there are many symbolic references to hair in the myths and customs. For instance, the silken strands that lay across the ripened corn husks are really "hair" that will fall away when the life cycle of the ear is completed.[11]

Life was a cycle and the year was a cycle. For all things in the universe there was no beginning and there was no end. A Hopi died, but only to be born again in an Underworld where life went on much as it did on earth. In this comforting knowledge the Hopi found a general security, and every reason to follow month by month the ancient Way that promised them always a fulfilling existence. Things were never easy, but it seemed that even that was best, for comfort brought pride, and pride brought dissension, and dissension assured division. The welfare of the village came first, the individual came last, and each village had the strength of its whole upon which any one Hopi could depend. Prayers and acts were multiplied by the number present, and even those who lived "below" had ways of adding their strength to that of the people on earth. Deities watched over every aspect of life, and they provided man with all he needed to know toward obtaining their help in proper season. It was and still is a good Way, and outsiders who went to Tusayan at the turn of the century were profoundly impressed by people immersed in an existence that had continued without serious deviation for untold centuries.

After the harvest, when "Indian summer" was gone and the cold winds began to buffet the mesas, the Hopi stayed in their houses and moved close to their fireplaces. The change of season brought a kind of reunion, for until this moment the entire family had been preoccupied with the concerns and pleasures of outdoor summer life. Now the men had time to repair their Katcina masks and costumes. There were always moccasins to be made. The woodcarvers spent more time on their Katcina dolls, and the weavers were at their looms. The basketmaker took out her stock of split yucca leaves, twigs, and grass. Only the potter looked for other things to do. Her craft awaited the coming again of warmer months.

At the mesa-top pueblo of Walpi, women filled their earthenware jars at water holes and then carried the heavy load on their backs up the steep foot trail to their homes.

In general, the woman's daily work remained the same in all seasons. There was always corn to grind, food to be prepared, water to be carried up the steep trails, and walls to be whitewashed. Food for the coming winter had to be protected against mice and vermin. Whenever possible it was moved onto the roof to be sunned. But women could take their time, and everyone from the littlest child to the oldest grandparent lent a helping hand.

Late fall in Hopi country was enjoyable in many ways, for the sun was often bright and the sky was often clear. Snowfalls were as rare as the rains of summer. The cold at night might be intense, but the days were crisp or mild. There was little change in the landscape. Few trees were around to lose their leaves, and the desert plants seldom altered the appearance of the earth. Their tiny, thin leaves and somber colors were most often lost among the painted rocks and sweeping plains. Now and then the winds roared and whirlwinds undulated across deserted cornfields. The sun sank lower in the southwest until at last the Hopi grew properly concerned lest it depart entirely and leave them forever in the grasp of a winter hard at hand. But they also knew that the societies had the rituals to draw the sun back. They "owned" the ways, and after the Soyaluña Ceremony at winter solstice anyone with "eyes to see" acknowledged that the sun wandered no farther away.

Before September ended, the Lakon would perform their ceremony, and those errant Hopi who had not laid in a sufficient supply of wood went to gather it in a hurry. Usually they regretted their delay, for the trees were far off, and the day was hardly long enough to go there, load a burro, and return home. Each morning, also, the sheep and goats had to be prodded out of their corrals under the mesa ledges to feed on leafless brush.

October was called the "Harvest moon," and it was the time of the Marau and Oaqöl. Crops were gathered, and everyone feasted and rejoiced in the village. In November, called the "Neophyte moon," youths of proper age were initiated into the Katcina societies. In even years the great ceremony of the

A wood-bearer of 1890.

New Fire was enacted, with its enthralling rites of fire worship that had been handed down for centuries. In odd years the Na-a-ish-nya Ceremony was performed by the New Fire Society.

By December, Hopi country was held tightly in the grip of winter, but as the spirits were also held fast beneath the frozen ground, they could not do harm to anyone who mentioned them. So, many legends and stories were told around the glowing piñon fires that warmed the Hopi houses. Meanwhile, anticipation began to grow for Soyaluña, in many respects the most important ceremony in the Hopi calendar, for it marked the time when the Katcinas would return from resting and sleeping. December was called the "Hoe moon," because tradition dictated that in this month the farmlands were to be cleared and leveled for spring planting. The wind had already done its share in removing debris from the fields, but men must cooperate by smoothing over the surface.

January, called the "Prayer-stick moon," brought the ceremony of the Horn society with their great horned headdresses. More and more Katcinas arrived at Hopi from their homes in the towering peaks of the San Francisco Mountains. It was an exciting and promising time.

February was called the "Getting-ready moon," and weatherwise it was the hardest month of the winter season, although it was in this very month that the Katcina people had found melons and green corn growing near the San Francisco Mountains. So the Powamû Ceremony was held to celebrate what could not be seen, yet was known, and beans were planted in the kivas.

In March, the first shoots of green appeared. This month was called the "Prickly-pear moon," and it was the only month named for a natural object. March weather was often the most disagreeable of the year, for fierce winds came laden with dirt and sand to pile in great heaps against the mesa sides and to penetrate every crack in the houses on the mesa tops. Still, it was part of the Plan, and the Hopi made the most of it. Important ceremonies were enacted by the societies, and leaders met to discuss how things were going and what needed to be done. Kivas were places where agreeable company could be found to work and talk with. At home around the fireside there was always good company, and enthralling stories were told and told again. Men hunted if it was necessary and sometimes made journeys to trade or to observe ceremonies in other places, such as the Zuñi Shalako. Usually the Hopi disdained the cold. Their clothing remained the same as for other seasons, except that a blanket or robe might give added protection. If a man had an outdoor errand, he simply ran all the way there and back. When kiva ceremonies ended, the men usually climbed from the subterranean chamber wearing little more than a breechclout or G-string. In consequence, pulmonary diseases were common and were often made worse by the close, overheated, and badly ventilated dwellings.

Most visitors to Tusayan saw it at its best season—April. The cornfields were green, and the few cottonwoods were in full leaf. The desert was glowing, the people were well fed, and everyone was happy. A rebirth of Nature occurred every April, just when the farmers were cutting away the last of the brush and establishing windbreaks to protect the new crops. Sometimes a capricious Nature sent frosts and lashing winds to destroy all but the native plants, which had some special concert with her that granted them immunity. Even the precious peach crops would be lost. Yet the people had prepared for just such a time, and emergency stores put aside in other years were called upon to fill the gap.

May was known as the "Waiting moon," and the fields hummed with activity and anticipation. The sweet corn was planted, and the Hopi became once again an outdoor people. The cycle had returned to where we first encountered it. The winds were slacking off, and the sun was moving closer day by day. Despite the unceasing work to be done, there were countless minor celebrations by masked Katcinas and great ceremonies to be performed. After all, this was the season of awakening life.

June and July were especially happy times for the Hopi. Now more than ever it was clear to them that animal life was inseparably linked with growing things, and every word and act illustrated the oneness of mankind with an unseen but living world of mind and matter.

When the sun paused in its path at the summer solstice, the Hopi in gratitude spent the time making prayer sticks of thanksgiving to send with the Katcinas as they returned to their Underworld home. Now a new segment of ceremonies would get underway. The same dancers who had previously appeared in awesome Katcina masks and costumes would perform unmasked dances at this time, and the splendid and awesome Katcina paraphernalia was laid away. The Flute or the Snake-Antelope rituals and the ceremonies of the three women's societies would now take place, and everyone in the village prepared to enjoy them in a special way.

By late August the pueblo was settling down again. If all had gone as it should, the moon of September watched over a scene of tranquility in Tusayan. Once the crops were harvested, when "Indian summer" was gone, and the cold winds began to buffet the mesas, the Hopi stayed in their houses and moved closer to their fireplaces . . . and the yearly cycle unfolded once more.

All this sounds quite ideal, and when kept in its proper context it is. But no visitor to Hopi in 1900 could avoid some negative aspects of its life. The Hopi lived blithely in sanitary conditions not many of us would feel comfortable with today. The people relieved themselves wherever and whenever they wanted to, without the least concern for whoever was present. None of the villages had the equivalent of an outhouse, nor did they have adequate water—let alone running water. With all water having to be hauled on the back up a five- or six-hundred-foot cliff, it was always a scarce commodity. So the people followed a rule I once heard comedienne Lily Tomlin express: "Don't wash too often, and then only where it is dirty."

When John Bourke visited Mishongnovi in 1881, he reported, "The town was decidedly filthy. There were the usual piles of vegetable garbage and animal offal and ordure to be expected in places as small and poor and low in the social scale."[12] The situation is appreciably better today, but standards are still very low compared to the average urban situation.

Hopi children seen by the early visitors were described as excellent examples of adaptation to environment. Like wild animals adjusting to their habitat, they learned to care for themselves in most ways as soon as they were able to crawl. The manner in which tiny children could climb up and down ladders to their homes was marvelous. They played on the roofs, and they sat on the brinks of the mesa precipices hundreds of feet high without exciting the least fear in their mothers. Their canine pets, of which there were a great number, could easily run up and down the ladders with them.

Until 1920 or so, boys and girls at home wore only nature's clothing up to about the age of twelve. Generations of desert-and-mesa-bred ancestors, plus an active life in the open, endowed them with figures rivaling those of young Greek gods.

Hough says that as of 1896, the children seemed to deserve no correction, and it was rare to see a parent strike a child. Instead, there was kindness and affection worthy of the highest praise. It was refreshing to observe the close association of children with their parents or near relatives, and how quiet and obedient they were.[13]

The Hopi children had teachers at home or in the fields who explained to them the things they needed to know to become essential members of the community. It surprised visitors to discover how much small children had learned about birds, plants, and other aspects of nature, and about duties at home, in the fields, and in the village. Through "play-work" had come a kind of "know-how."

Little boys scarcely able to walk had tiny bows and arrows pressed into their hands, and were encouraged to shoot at brush targets by adults, who applauded heartily whenever they knocked one over. It was common to see several little armed "warriors" on the rooftops guarding the pueblo. Girls played house with the aid of a few stones and considerable imagination. When rain fell and filled the water holes, the children dived immediately into these, splashing around and immensely enjoying the rare treat.

Wherever the adults went, the children followed along, searching for the seeds of wild plants or for berries, gathering grass and yucca for baskets, watching the cornfields, gathering the crops, and always having some small share in the work. When a house was being built, they worked almost as hard as their elders, carrying in their little baskets loads of earth or stones with an earnestness that could only be admired.[14]

After the government school was established at Keams Canyon in 1887, the training methods were affected as attempts were made to compel attendance. For a time many Hopi elders, and particularly some at Oraibi, refused to cooperate in the move to turn their children into whites—especially when unspeakable devices were inaugurated, such as tying the children's hands with barbed wire while their hair was cut[15]—with Christian missionaries standing by and approving. An inevitable division began among the Hopi, leading eventually to the rending of Old Oraibi in 1906. Over the years thereafter the secular-education pattern of the Hopi was considerably transformed, while the religious-education pattern was buffeted, but remained intact.

Left, a Hopi girl in 1930 attire. From an E. B. Sayles photograph. *Right*, young Hopi hunters as photographed by Frederick Monsen in 1907.

In their contacts with government agents and schoolteachers, the Hopi soon learned that whenever questions arose concerning differences in moral behavior, their position would invariably be adjudged wrong, and severe punishment would follow. In the matter of sexual behavior this became a particular problem, for while modesty prevailed in public, sex was an open aspect of Hopi life. With everyone sleeping in the same room, marital relations were neither concealed nor embarrassing. Clowns performed obscene acts as an instructive device, and Katcinas feigned copulation with women of all ages. Premarital affairs were taken for granted and readily condoned.[16] Because of all this the Hopi opted for a dual manner of life, behaving one way for the whites and secretly continuing the old preferred ways at home.

Many of the Hopi religious ceremonials afforded the diversion that other peoples sought in athletic sports. Their racing was purely religious, and George Wharton James reports that they got "much fun out of some of their semi-religious exercises." A game they were very fond of, and one that required considerable skill to play, was wē-la. Several players, each armed with a feathered dart, or ma-te'-va, would rush after a small hoop made of corn husks or broomcorn well bound together—the wē-la—and throw their darts so that they stuck in it. The hoop was about a foot in diameter and two inches thick, the ma-te'-va nearly a foot long. Each player had his own color of feathers on his dart, so that he could tell when he scored. "To see a dozen swarthy and almost nude youths darting along in the dance plaza, or streets, or down

Games. *Top left*, shinny stick and balls. The ball is of hide filled with seeds. *Top right*, wooden tops and whipping sticks. The top is spun with a hide thong, and then kept in motion by whipping. *Bottom*, boy whipping a top.

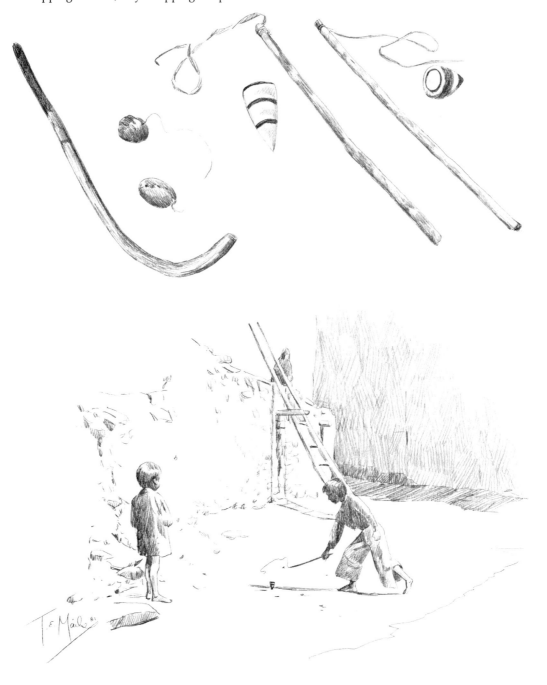

in the valley on the sand, laughing, shouting, gesticulating, every now and then stopping for a moment, jabbering over the score, then eagerly following the motion of the thrower of the wē-la so as to be ready to strike the ma-te'-va into it, and then, suddenly letting them fly," was a picturesque and lively sight.[17]

In 1921, however, Earl Forrest was able to photograph boys about the age of twelve playing with large homemade wooden tops, which they spun in the manner followed by all boys with tops and kept in motion by whipping.[18] The Voth items in the Fred Harvey collection include such Hopi tops and whips, a ring-and-dart game, and counters and gaming pieces.[19]

The Pueblos in other areas, particularly the Zuñi, played a number of games that are described in the chapters that relate to each of them. Quite probably the Hopi enjoyed some of the same games, but records of them were not made. When Wayne Dennis made his study of the Hopi child in 1937 and 1938 in New Oraibi, he found that after the children's assigned work was finished, they were free to amuse themselves. Evenings especially were times for play, and on moonlight nights it went on long after sunset. Play was always carried on outdoors, wherever in the village the children chose. However, girls and boys seldom played together, and initiated children did not play games with the uninitiated.[20]

There were unorganized play and organized play. The former consisted of girls playing "house," and boys playing "farmer" and "hunter." Makeup games with odd items fitted also in this category. Organized games included shinny, a kind of hockey game; tops; a stick-throwing game; a snake game employing a long twisting line of children; a girl's grinding party; archery; darts; pachisi; a gambling game; a hidden-object game.[21]

Foot racing still plays an important part in the religious life of the Hopi. Males are trained for this from childhood, and they often run for miles across the broiling desert without resting. Many of the fields are long distances from the villages, and although pickup trucks are in vogue, some farmers still make the round trip there and back on foot in a single day. In former times, a sixty-year-old citizen of Old Oraibi had a cornfield forty miles away. During the planting and growing season he camped at the field, and whenever he made the journey home for supplies he ran the entire distance, going both ways in less than twenty-four hours. George Wharton James on several occasions engaged a young man to take a message from Old Oraibi to Keams Canyon, a distance of seventy-two miles. The youth ran all the way, delivered the message, and brought back an answer within thirty-six hours. One Old Oraibi man of James's acquaintance ran over ninety miles in one day.[22] Fred Volz, a trader at Canyon Diablo and Oraibi, once hired a number of the best Hopi runners to round up wild horses for him. They gathered in not only the horses, but also deer and antelope.

As has been seen, the Anasazi compiled no books or written language; only the petroglyphs found on the cliff faces, the paintings on pottery, and the wall murals. Perhaps this explains why the Hopi begin the education of their children in the customs and beliefs of their people at an early age. In the ceremonial sphere, from the time the children are a few months old they are taken to see every public ritual that takes place in the village. The child grows up with the Katcinas, and the Katcinas and life are always one.

Hopi history is told in traditions and myths that describe life before emergence from the Underworld, the manner of the exit through the sipapu itself, the long years of wandering before they settled permanently, and finally the origins of their many religious ceremonies. These are handed down by word of mouth from one generation to another by elderly men versed in the lore of the Anasazi. Children are taught until they can repeat each legend with amazing accuracy. Some stories told recently have been compared with those recorded by the Spanish in the sixteenth century and found to be the same, even in the minutest details.[23]

From earliest childhood the Hopi were taught to be honest, obedient, and industrious. As a result, visitors in the year 1900 found their ethical standards to be extremely high. Murder was almost unknown among them. They were scrupulously honest. Robbery was very rare, and a liar was held in contempt by everyone. No judicial courts were needed.

With the advent of government schools and other white influences the behavior and belief situation changed appreciably, but in the Hopi mind the most important phase of the child's education still commences before the age of ten, when boys and girls are initiated into the tribe's Katcina Cult. A few years later the second step is taken as they join one or more of the several secret societies. Then, on achieving adolescence, the boy takes the third and climactic step by passing through the Tribal Initiation and being admitted to the Soyal Rite, which opens the annual cycle of ceremonial observances. All these occasions are treated in detail further on.

The steady immersion into the religious life infused and circumscribed Hopi existence. Within this sphere the major portion of adult education would take place, and an encompassing and wondrous education it was, full of the unexpected, the mysterious, and the miraculous. Yet it was not an aspect the Hopi asked questions about, for its efficacy lay in the fact that it had always been done in a prescribed way; through this Way the people had survived from their beginning.

In the Hopi view, nature and god are one, and according to Stephen there are seven principal deities who possess the root power that regulates and sustains life. Co-tuk-inung-wa is the all-powerful one who created the earth. Muingwas is the one who controls germination, lives in the Underworld, and is the guardian of life. Gna-tum-si is the creator of life. Baho-li-konga is a great serpent who controls life blood, vegetal sap, and especially water. Masau'u is the one who controls death. Omau is the force that controls clouds and rain. Dewa is the sun, or father.[24] The Katcinas are intermediaries, serving as messengers and as bearers of blessings. Some nonhuman beings serve as messengers, as do pahos, or prayer sticks, and other ritual paraphernalia.

Stripped to its essence, the Hopi religious position is that all created

18

things, human and nonhuman, have individuality, and each "individual has its proper place in relation to all other phenomena, with a definite role in the cosmic scheme." But, whereas the nonhuman individuals fulfill their obligations more or less automatically under the law, man has specific responsibilities that must be learned and fulfilled in the traditional Way, and much of the child's training is devoted to learning this Way.[25]

The Way consists of the manner of acting, feeling, and thinking in every role that a human being is required to assume in the life cycle from birth to death; the welfare of the tribe and the individual, in that order, depends upon the responsible and whole-hearted fulfillment of the role. Responsibilities increase with age, and they reach their peak in ceremonial participation, with the heaviest burden being carried by the village chief, and the next heaviest by the clan chiefs, although the matriarch plays her consistently vital role in the all-important matrilineal lineage system.[26] As one might assume, the Way teaches young people to respect their elders and to look to them for the solutions to a happy and productive existence. Elders are not "put out to pasture." They are essential to the fulfillment of life.

According to George Wharton James, the religious life of the Hopi in 1900 consumed anywhere from two to sixteen days out of every month.[27] It still does. Besides the ceremonies, there are the countless individual religious acts that accompany the major events in life and the conduct of life each day.

An acquaintance of mine once went to Hopi country with a Hopi artist friend. They were speeding along in the latter's car, it was still dark, and the Hopi was regaling him with stories of his various secular adventures to keep him amused and awake. Just as the sun made its first appearance the Hopi slammed on the brakes, leaped from the car, went off a short distance, and spent some time in prayer. This done he returned to the car, and in a moment it was roaring along again while he continued with his stories as if nothing had happened. This, I think, is an excellent example of how ingrained and automatic the Hopi religion continues to be.

As Thompson and Joseph point out, the rules for ritual observance have two aspects, the physical and the psychical. "If either aspect is neglected, or any regulation broken, failure will result."[28] Participants in ceremonies must perform the proper acts and observe the tabus, and they must exercise control over their emotions and hearts, keeping a good heart, and exulting only at those moments when it is traditionally appropriate, as when the snakes are ritually purified in the Snake Ceremony. Such control comes to a person through a life of ceremony and prayer.

In the scheme of control, prayer is thought of as a form of willing something into being. Hence by ritual acts that include prayer, the Hopi believe that human beings, in conjunction with the Katcina spirits, can control nature to a limited extent, and that if man fails to carry out his responsibility in this wise the universe may cease to function. The movement of the sun, the coming of the rain, crop growth, and reproduction as a whole are all linked to man's "correct, complete, and active carrying out of the rules."[29] If the Hopi wish these things to happen, they must fulfill their roles individually and collectively.

In this connection, Mischa Titiev mentions that while particular emphasis is placed upon individual freedom, Hopi behavior is checked by fear of nonconformity. Public opinion is so important in the closely grouped villages that a person seldom dares to depart from the conventional modes of behavior.

An interesting sidelight on behavior patterns is witchcraft. Whenever failure assumes the proportions of a crisis, such as a drought or an epidemic, the Hopi assume that one or more individuals have, for personal reasons, worked against the common good. These individuals are considered to be witches who are allied with ants, owls, crows, and the like. They have an animal heart and a human heart. They are organized into a secret society, and they even seek to recruit sleeping children.[30] Witches are greatly feared, even though difficult to identify. But manufactured charms and certain colors, such as turquoise, can turn witches away, and such charms and colors are always present in the home and on the person.

Very little is known about the medical practices of the Hopi outside the fact that each society has its cure for a specific illness. Early visitors to the reservation found that children were being educated in the use of herbs for medicinal purposes, and some of the ethnologists who lived among the Hopi were themselves treated by medicine men, usually not because they believed the medicine men could really heal them, but out of sheer curiosity.

When Caucasian doctors and nurses first arrived at the reservation in conjunction with the agency, they were met with mixed reactions, and they still are, although health conditions among the Hopi have never been good. Sanitation has been a persistent problem, and drought and famine have made their sporadic contributions. European invaders brought entirely new diseases, leading to several epidemics already mentioned. The combination of all these factors, plus the ordinary risks of daily life on the high mesas, keep the Hopi ever mindful of the perils of life, and they fear illness more than death. Death is only a transition from life in one world to life in the next, but illness can reduce the victim to a state of utter dependency; even worse, his failure to fulfill his role might disrupt the organized household group in all its aspects.[31]

Once their fears had been allayed somewhat, the younger Hopi responded reasonably well to the medical offerings of the government, but the conservative elders remained firm in their adherence to ancient curing ways.*

Walter Hough says there were few Hopi who did not know the "herbs and simples," and that even the children knew many of the herbs. The plants they used in medicine "would stock a primitive drug store." Bunches of dried herbs, roots, and other plants hung from the ceiling beams of every house and were made into teas and powders for every sort of illness. Hough encountered medicine women as well as medicine men, the best known of the women being Saalako, the mother of the Snake priest. She brewed the dark medicine for the Snake Dance and, Hough asserts, guarded the antidote for snakebites.

As Hough saw it, the Hopi theory of medicine was that "like cures like."

*The finest overall treatment of this facet of Hopi life that has come to my attention is found in *The Hopi Way*, by Laura Thompson and Alice Joseph, and I heartily recommend the book for its keen and general treatment of the Hopi as a whole.

Thus, hairy seeds would make hair grow. The leaves of a plant named for the bat, who sleeps in the daytime, would induce a child to sleep during the day. A tickling sensation in the throat was cured by a tea made from a hairy thistle.[32] Even today, two plants growing close together are believed to be related, and one is spoken of as the child of the other. Plants are also known as male and female, and each is associated with a cardinal direction. Many plants play a role in religious ceremonies, some of which are placed on altars, and others tied to prayer sticks.

Fewkes and Hough gathered extensive information on the plants used by the Hopi for various medicines. For headache the leaves of the *Astragalus mollissimus* are bruised and rubbed on the temples; tea is made from the root of the *Guara parviflora* for snakebite; women boil the *Townsendia arizonica* into a tea and drink it to induce pregnancy; a plant called by the Hopi *wütakpala* is rubbed on the breast or legs for pain; *Verbesina enceloides* is used on boils or for skin diseases; *Croton texlusis* is taken as an emetic; *Allionia linearis* is boiled to make an infusion for wounds; the mistletoe *(Phoradendron juniperinum)* that grows on the juniper makes a beverage which both Hopi and Navajo say is like coffee, and a species called *le mapi,* which grows on the cottonwood, is used as medicine; the leaves of *Gilia longiflora* are boiled and drunk for stomach ache; the leaves of the *Gilia multiflora* (collected forty miles south of Walpi at an elevation of six thousand feet), when bruised and rubbed on ant bites, is said to be a specific; *Oreocarya suffruticosa* is pounded up and used for pains in the body; *Carduus rothrockii* is boiled and drunk as tea for colds that give rise to a prickling sensation in the throat; the leaves of *Coleosanthus wrightii* are bruised and rubbed on the temples for headache, as is the *Artemisia canadensis.*

Curings by society officers ordinarily took place in the kivas, and if the cure was successful, males and females were expected to join the respective societies that cured them.

Individual treatments by medicine men usually occurred in the home. Alexander Stephen tells about a healing experience that took place at his home in 1894.[33] He had been ill with a severe sore throat and fever for some time, and Sikya'honauûh, a healer, came to visit him. After smoking and visiting for a while, the priest inquired about Stephen's illness. Upon learning he had taken some American medicine and Hopi herbs, the healer asked whether Stephen would like him to determine what ailed him, and Stephen agreed. As it was customary to give a preliminary gift to the healer and more substantial gifts when he was done, a Hopi friend of Stephen's obtained some calico from his house and offered this to Stephen to give to the healer.

The healer filled a bowl with water and placed it between Stephen and the fire. He then sat down and opened his medicine pouch, extracting four small quartz pebbles, and other pebbles whose colors represented the cardinal directions. Beginning with a yellow pebble he dropped them one by one into the bowl, all the while muttering prayers to Bear, Badger, Porcupine, Horned Toad, and Broad Star. The prayers requested that he be shown the nature of Stephen's illness, which had "cut off his voice."

The healer then crushed a small fragment of dry herb root between his fingers and sprinkled it in the bowl to make what he said was "charm water." Next he took a beautiful willow-leaf-shaped, pale-green stone knife and a lump of quartz crystal from his pouch, and had Stephen remove his shirt so that he could "see" what made Stephen ill. For four or five minutes he looked intently through the crystal at the ethnologist, swaying back and forth and moving his arms toward and away from Stephen. Suddenly he pressed the crystal against Stephen's right breast, at a place that elicited "severe pain."

He at once put the crystal back in his pouch and told Stephen to lie down. He took the green knife and began to saw on the skin over the place where the pain was. He scarified it only enough to draw blood, returned the knife to the pouch, and sipped a little of the charm water. Then he bent over Stephen, placed his lips on the wound, and exhaled twice upon it. As he did this, an icy chill ran through Stephen from head to foot. After each of the exhalations, the healer raised himself to his knees and breathed forcibly away from Stephen. He repeated the procedure, pulled Stephen's hand to his mouth, and spat into it "an abominable-looking, arrow-shaped, headless sort of centipede." Its legs moved and it seemed to be a living insect. "This," said the healer, "is the sorcerer's [witch's] arrow that causes sickness." As Stephen understood him, such an arrow could come to one through mishap, but usually it was sent, or shot, by a witch. It bored through the flesh until it reached the heart, which it also bored, and thus caused death.

The healer permitted Stephen to look at the insect only briefly and immediately went alone with it to the mesa's edge to perform an exorcising rite. Upon his return he had Stephen drink some of the charm water and gave the rest to two of Stephen's Hopi friends who had witnessed the entire affair. "They," says Stephen, "sat awestruck, and afterward confessed they were badly frightened."

The healer munched on the dried roots of four herbs (called Bear Charm) and spat them into a bowl of water to make a fragrant compound. Stephen was to drink this brew from time to time for four days. He did so, and the pains in his chest "ceased from that day" (the fourth day).

According to Stephen, Sikya'honauûh of Walpi, Kucha'koyo'ño (a blind man) of Mishongnovi, and Patü'ba of Oraibi were the only surviving members of the once numerous Po'boshtü, or medicine men's society. Stephen adds that there was one other medicine man who was not a full-fledged member because he had never had his head washed and he was married. The real Po'boshtü should lead an ascetic life and at least be a celibate, "which was probably why the society had diminished."

Voth knew a certain "Hómikini who was probably the best Indian physician in Oraibi. He is a splendid botanist, and has good knowledge of the medicinal properties of the various herbs, viewing the matter from the Hopi standpoint."[34]

Fewkes describes another society, the Yayawimpkia, or Yaya, as fire priests who heal by fire. They were experts in the art of making fire by drilling with a stick on a bit of wood, and they performed this act in the Sumaikoli or Little New Fire Ceremony. Few of them remained, however. Their services were sometimes called for when a burn or some such matter was to be treated. One woman whose breast had been blistered by a too-liberal application of kerosene was healed by a Yaya, who filled his mouth with soot and spurted the sooty saliva over the burn. The theory was that wounds made by fire should be stopped by fire or the products of fire.

The Yaya priests were supposed to be able to bring back to life people who had been killed in accidents. There was a story about a man who was pushed off a high mesa upon the rocks below, and who was restored to his friends by the magical power of the Yaya. "Other fabulous stories," Fewkes says, "always placed among the happenings of the past, tell of the wonderful doings of the Yaya. The Hopi relate that one Yaya standing at the edge of the mesa said: 'Do you see that butte over yonder (the Giant's Chair, thirty miles distant); it is black, is it not? I will paint it white.' So with a lump of kaolin the Yaya made magical passes skyward, and behold, the mountain was white! A brother Yaya said, 'I will make it black again!' So with soot he made magical passes horizonward, and behold, the butte resumed again its natural color!"

Fewkes learned that the fire priests did perform wonderful feats of juggling and magic, especially in winter, when abbreviated ceremonies were held. In consequence, the Hopi were renowned as jugglers and have a reputation extending far and wide over the Southwest.

Fewkes speaks also of other medicine men, or shamans, "who relieve persons afflicted by sorcerers."One sufferer believed that a sorcerer had shot with his span-long bow an old turquoise bead or arrowhead into his body. He summoned one of his medicine men to relieve him. This healer was called Tu-hi-ky-a, "the one who knows by feeling of touching." His first treatment was to pass an eagle feather over the body of the afflicted person until the healer asserted he had found and felt the missile.

The term applied to more than one medicine man is Poboctu or eye-seekers. In the concluding part of their conjuring, in which more than one healer usually engaged, they moved around, peering and gazing everywhere, until they determined the direction in which the malign influence lay. Fewkes was informed by Stephen that, when he saw them engaged over a victim in Sitcumovi many years ago, they cleverly pretended to take out of the sufferer's breast a stone arrowhead half the size of a hand.[35]

Hough reports that in 1896 one might see a patient being treated for headache or some minor ailment. The method was very like massage; the eyebrows, forehead, temples, and root of the nose were rubbed with straight strokes or passes, with occasional pressure at certain points, while a preternatural gravity was maintained by the operator.[36]

Certain Katcina impersonators at Hopi, as well as non-Katcina Buffalo and Snake dancers, use what is called a "lightning frame." It is constructed of the wood of a pine or spruce that has been struck by lightning. The frame is built of a series of hinged angles that open and fold accordion-style when the handles are worked. The Snake men "shoot" the frame toward the east where the sun rises as they make ritual circuits. They also use it in their kiva, where they shoot it four times up toward the hatchway, swinging at the same time the rhombus, or bull-roarer, to call the thunderclouds that bring rain. Parsons says that Flint doctors, who cure lightning-sent disease, strike initiates over the heart and on the back with a frame "in order to impart the power of lightning."[37]

Stephen also describes a time in August 1893 when severe illness was present among the children. In this instance the three previously mentioned medicine men made an altar in their kiva and placed prayer sticks on it at about sunset. All the women with ailing children assembled that night in the kiva, sitting on the north side while the men sat on the south. Tawi'moki, a priest who made the final preparations on the altar, remained in his assumed position until about 10 P.M., at which time he and Sikya'honauûh led in the singing of songs.[38]

Despite the demise of the medicine society, the healers at Hopi by no means became extinct. A few years ago I listened to a television interview in which a Hopi medicine man described his approach to healing. He explained that, if time permitted, he took four days to prepare himself for the actual healing. Over this time he ritually purified his person, so as to become a fit channel through which the spirit powers would perform the cure.

It appears that Hopi medical practices, including their views and approaches, closely parallel those I have experienced personally with Sioux, and in a lesser way with Apache, medicine men. Perhaps most of the native cultures, working in like environments, developed similar thoughts and procedures.

Judging from the few cryptic accounts that have appeared in publications, not many Caucasians have witnessed the burial of a Hopi.

H. R. Voth, who had the opportunity to do so, wrote a short paper on his reactions, providing a number of photographs of Hopi burial places. While some of the family and close relatives might cry and mourn over a death, he says, they do not lament and scream. Moreover, in many cases there is an appalling lack of concern. The Hopi do not care to talk about the deceased, no matter how much they may have loved them.[39] Later pages, on the way in which Hopi view death, will, to some extent, help to explain this.

The remains are immediately prepared for burial, and there is no embalming. Nor is there any rule as to who does the preparation, although it is most often the father and a relative. A prayer offering is tied to the hair in front, and the face is covered with a masklike layer of cotton. Openings are provided for eyes and nose, and the mask is tied on by a string that passes around the head at forehead level, "to hide themselves in." To this string are fastened a number of prayer feathers that the deceased will wear in the Underworld. Fewkes states that, as the mask is put on, the deceased is addressed as follows: "You have become a Katcina. Aid us in bringing the rain, and intercede with the gods to fertilize our farms."[40] Black marks are made under the eyes, on the lips, forehead, cheeks, the palms of the hands, and the soles of the feet. Prayer feathers, sometimes a little food, and a small container of drinking water are placed on the chest. The body is then wrapped in several blankets, which are secured by ropes. It is then carried on the back of the father, some relative, or on a horse or burro, to its final resting place.[41] Fewkes says it is carried by the oldest man in the clan.[42]

Helen Sekaquaptewa says that when a death occurs at Old Oraibi, all the family leave the house except the two older men who will prepare the body. The hair of the deceased is ritually washed, and the face is heavily dusted with cornmeal and covered with a layer of cotton, into which the eye and nose holes are cut. Clothing is put on, and the body is fixed in a seated position and bound securely with yucca strips before it is wrapped in the blankets. Fewkes confirms this procedure.[43] Also, a downy feather is tied to the hair at the top of the head and another one to an ankle to symbolize the flight of the spirit. When those who carry the body to the grave return home, they move all of the personal belongings of the deceased outside the home and burn them. Next they purify the house with burning cedar branches and pitch, bathe themselves in water in which cedar twigs have been boiled, and finally dress in clean clothes. After all this the family can use the house again.[44]

As to burial places, Voth informs us that dead children who had not yet been initiated into any religious society are placed in one of the numerous crevices along the edge of the mesa on which the village is located. A covering of stones is placed over the body. If the burial site has been used before for children belonging to the family, the stone covering is removed, the new bundle is placed in the hole, and the stones are replaced. For each child thus buried, a stick from one to two feet long is thrust between the rocks. This is the only marker.[45]

The bodies of grown persons who have been members of societies are buried in a graveyard that is usually situated on the slope of a mesa or on a hilltop. Graveyards are scattered around the mesas and are neither marked nor taken care of. A hole from five to seven feet deep is dug and, according to Voth and Fewkes, the body is lowered into it in a sitting position, with the face turned toward the east. The hole is filled with the excavated earth, and a pile of stones is laid on top to prevent animals from digging into the grave. However, windstorms and erosion often combine forces to strip away the covering and expose the bones. There are no tombstones, but insignia indicating the society to which the deceased belonged are sometimes placed on the graves.[46]

On the third day after the burial, a last meal and the final prayer offerings are prepared. The meal is fixed by the mother, wife, aunt, or other near relative, and it consists of piki, cooked beans, corn, meat, herbs, and other foods. All this is put in a bowl. The one who has prepared the body for burial makes a double-stick paho with painted green sticks and black points, one single black paho, and a *pühu,* or road, consisting of an eagle-breath feather. To this are tied two cotton strings. Six other prayer offerings are also fashioned. In the evening the paho maker takes these and the bowl to the grave site, placing

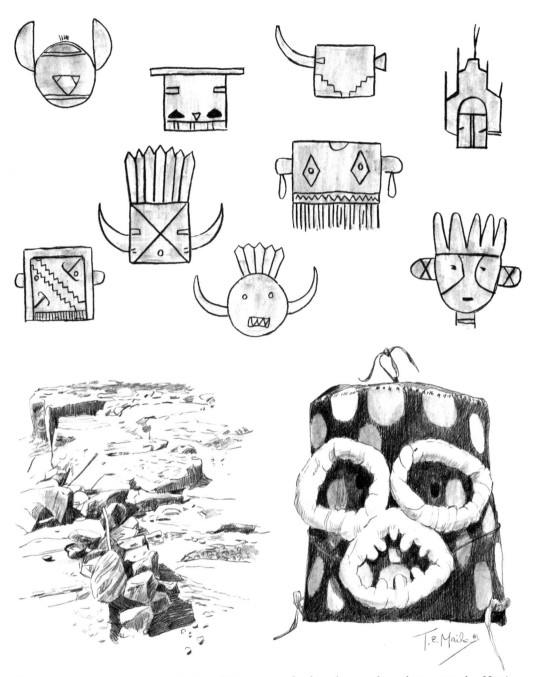

Top, some of the many petroglyphs of Katcina masks found on rock surfaces near the Hopi villages. From Fewkes and Stephens. *Lower left,* children's burial places in crevice graves. The piles of stones, sticks, and food bowls mark the places. From Dorsey and Voth, 1901. *Lower right,* mask of Masau'u, god of death and one of the war gods.

everything except the *pühu* on top of the grave. At a place west of the grave he places the "road" pointing westward. Then he sprinkles a cornmeal line farther westward, denoting the continuation of the road.[47]

The Hopi believe that at sunrise the next morning the breath or soul of the deceased rises from the grave, partakes of the food in the bowl, mounts the single black paho, and then travels along the "road" to the Underworld carrying the double-stick paho with him.[48] According to Fewkes, the reason the body faces east is that the deceased will see the sun when it rises and be able to emerge from the grave in time for the journey.[49]

The exception to the making of this journey is the uninitiated child. In this case the string-and-meal road points toward the child's former home, to which the soul of the child returns and where it is reincarnated in the next child born in the family. Until then, the little soul is believed to hover above the house. Whenever the family hears an unusual noise it thinks the little soul is moving about, and the mother may secretly deposit a pinch of food for the soul to eat. In the event no other child is born to the mother, when she dies and goes on her journey to the Underworld she takes the little soul with her.[50]

As a final note, Voth states that the dead are sometimes remembered by prayer offerings and food in such ceremonies as the Soyal and Marau. More information about this practice is given further on.[51] He also says that offerings prepared for ceremonial use are afterward deposited in shrines and other places "where the dead come and get them." Those who find none are said to be very sorry and cry. In one legend, a visitor to the Underworld received complaints that certain of the prayer feathers hanging before the faces of the dead were very old and that their friends were forgetting to prepare new ones for them.[52]

Death and healing are accepted facts in the lifeway of the Hopi. Whatever happens, education and growth continue. Initiation into the Katcina Cult is considered a point of maturity for the Hopi youths, who are expected then to give up childish ways and to take their place in adult society. After all, they know now that the awesome Katcinas they see dancing in the villages are actually being impersonated by their own fathers and male relatives. For girls, marriage is not far off. In former days, virtually all would be wives by the time they were fifteen (it is now seventeen), and some would have their own homes to care for as early as the age of twelve. Accordingly, their training to be mothers and housewives intensifies as they become older. They are taught to grind corn perfectly and to prepare foods with it and other items particular to the Hopi diet. Some girls become potters and basketmakers, and all share in the raising of younger children and in house building and repair. Boys spend more time in the fields, some learn to weave, others to craft tools and weapons, and some still hunt. Until the Navajo were subdued, the young men were expected to join the Momcit, or Warrior, Society, and to become the defenders of the village. Some went on trade missions, others went to gather salt. After the Tribal Initiation, the youth was a man, and that is still the case. There is no avoiding it, and he does thereafter only what Hopi men do.

Until the 1940s, elementary day schools were located near the villages but below the mesas. Children could walk to them and then return home to be with their families. The parents were also able to visit the schools, and thus they had a part in the educational system. More recently, modern educational facilities and teachers' quarters have been built at points far enough away to require bussing. Thus the bond between home and school no longer exists. Teachers seldom visit the homes, and the consequences have been serious for the Hopi, who center all in communal living. There is no high school on the

Reservation, and Hopi youth who wish to continue their education are forced to leave home during this critical period and live in boarding schools, although excellently furnished ones, in places like Phoenix, Arizona, and Riverside, California.

BIRTH

Dennis found that American medicine had influenced scarcely at all the old Hopi practices in regard to childbirth. Although free medical care was available to Keams Canyon, and Hopis were encouraged by government workers to use it, no women from Hotevilla, and few from New Oraibi, went there unless they had been too long in labor and were near death, nor was a doctor called to the home until then. The customs being followed in 1938 at the two villages just named were the same as those seen by Voth at Old Oraibi between 1901 and 1905.[53] In the last forty years, more use has been made of the Public Health Service, and the extremely high infant-mortality rates have been reduced.

In his research, J. G. Owens, who assisted Fewkes at Tusayan, discovered that a mother carried out her daily tasks until labor started. Then she called upon a weasel skin that hung from the ceiling to aid in making the delivery quick and easy.[54]

Helen Sekaquaptewa named her first child Joy, because the baby girl "opened a door of joy" for her mother and father. Helen explains that when a birth is imminent, everyone leaves the house except the mother and a male relative who will help her with the delivery.[55] (Dennis states that the woman's mother and father, and sometimes her husband, stay to help.)[56]

A place is prepared in the corner of the room, consisting of a sheepskin on the floor (others say sand), some clean cloth, and a chair or a stool to rest on. If it is winter, the place is made next to the stove. When labor reaches its precipitous point the mother squats or kneels on the sheepskin. The helper stands behind her, places his arms around her body, and supports her. She folds her arms across her body, and together they exert a slight downward pressure. She is cautioned not to scream, and to hold the air in to help expel the baby. Between pains the mother may rise and walk about, but no one is to touch her internally. Once the baby drops, they both work to get the placenta, and the cord is not cut until it is out. The mother now bathes in cedar water, and hot sand is placed on the sheepskin for her to rest on while the sand absorbs any liquid.[57]

A midwife then comes and cuts the cord. She ties it with hair taken from the mother's head. Then she washes the baby and sprinkles it with sacred ashes found at a certain point south of Oraibi. The ashes are obtained by the father and are applied daily as a skin treatment for twenty days.[58]

Hough says that, when a Hopi baby is delivered, the head is washed with amole suds and the body is rubbed with ashes by its paternal grandmother or by one of her sisters.[59] This person also makes four marks with cornmeal on the four walls of the birth room and puts lines on the ceiling and floor. A blanket is hung over the doorway for the first five days, during which time the mother must not be touched by the sun, nor may she put on her moccasins, for this act will assuredly bring bad luck.[60] Two ears of white corn are placed near the baby, and it is carefully wrapped and placed in the cradleboard. For the next nineteen days the mother is to avoid eating salt, fresh fruits, and vegetables, since these may affect breast milk adversely.[61] One of the wall marks is erased on the fifth, tenth, fifteenth, and twentieth day of the child's life. On each of these days the baby and its mother will have their heads washed with yucca suds. On the nineteenth evening a family feast is held.

On the twentieth day, before sunrise, the grandmother comes. She draws four cornmeal lines on the floor, places a prayer feather tied to a cotton string on top of these, and on the string sets a bowl filled with amole soapsuds. The mother kneels before the bowl. The grandmother dips an ear of corn in the suds four times, each time touching the mother's hair with it. Then she bathes the mother's head. The mother's arms and legs are bathed in juniper tea, and when some of the tea is thrown on heated stones, she stands over the steam to complete the purification. The grandmother then sweeps the room, and another woman sprinkles water on the floor while she says, "Clouds and rain."[62] Now the grandmother bathes the baby, rubs it with white cornmeal, and places some sacred cornmeal on its lips. She offers a prayer in which she requests that the child reach old age, and in this prayer she gives it a name. Some of the women members of the father's clan come also, one at a time, bathe the baby by touching it with dipped corn, and give it additional names. Each name has a relation to the clan of the one who bestows it. Of the various names, the infant's family chooses one that will be retained until the child is initiated into a society.[63] At that time a new name is given by the ceremonial mother or father. The person never speaks his new name for fear of "giving himself away" and suffering bad consequences for doing so.[64]

After the original names have been given, the mother puts on her wedding robe, the father notifies the paternal grandmother when it is time, and she goes with the mother and child to the eastern edge of the mesa, arriving there just as the sun begins to show itself. The two ears of corn are brought along, and now the grandmother touches them to the infant's breast and waves them toward the east. She also tosses cornmeal toward the sun, and places a little in the child's mouth. As she is doing these things she also prays aloud, speaking in the course of the prayer the names that have been given to the baby. The mother then repeats the actions and offers a similar prayer.[65]

Formerly, the Hopi used two kinds of cradleboards. People on the First and Third mesas wove an oval-shaped cradleboard from wooden rods, with the upper portion being narrowed and looped over to be attached to a woven hoop that provided a crownlike head protector. At First Mesa a hole was provided in the cradleboard at the appropriate location to insert an absorbent pad of bark. People on Second Mesa used a flat, rectangular board with holes burned into the sides to receive lashing thongs and into the top to secure a head-protector attachment.[66]

Today, babies are wrapped in a blanket with their arms at their sides and are then lashed tightly to the cradleboard. A cloth draped over the head protector shades the child's face while it is in the sun or sleeps. Wright describes a butterfly cocoon pacifier that is filled with cornmeal and tied to the wrist to keep the child's fingers out of its mouth.[67] The cradleboard is usually carried in the mother's arms, seldom hung on her back.

According to Hough, custom formerly required that a certain swift insect

Top left, girl carrying child in traditional manner. *Top right*, mother and child, 1900. *Bottom right*, mother holding infant in wickerwork cradleboard. *Bottom left*, mother and child in a Hopi doorway, 1905.

be tied to a boy's wrist to make him a runner, and the cocoon of a butterfly be tied to a girl's wrist to make her strong for grinding corn. Later, for some reason not known, a band of yucca was placed on the child's wrist and ankle and left on for several days. Then the child was held over an anthill, and the bands were removed and left to the ants.[68] Hough also says, in quoting J. G. Owens, that the Hopi were good to the elderly. In the birth ceremony, for example, the elderly were given special gifts of cornmeal and food, and if the grandmother was an invalid, she was "tenderly carried to the dedication" at the mesa's edge.[69] What Owens actually says is that since the paternal grandmother in a certain case was an invalid, her sister filled the office of godmother. The paternal grandmother was present, being carried by her husband like a water jug in a blanket that hung from his forehead. When the presents were distributed in the morning both the grandmother and her sister received "an unusually large amount of meal."[70]

By now, the impression may be forming that the Hopi Way begat and fostered children who were akin to "angels" in their behavior. No one really knows how Anasazi children behaved in former times, but the studies of Dennis caused him to conclude that, overall, Hopi children and young people behaved about as rural white children did in similar circumstances. This fact, however, should not obscure the important differences that have always existed.[71]

Owens found in 1891 that even very little girls were being given a large share of responsibility in the care of their younger brothers and sisters. They were required to carry babies in the same manner as their mothers did, and it was common for a child of six or seven to haul a child of one or two years on her back. Mothers and daughters never carried babies in their arms. They stooped forward, placed the little one on their back, threw a blanket over it, and then as they straightened up drew the blanket tightly in around the waist so that the baby was held in a kind of bag, usually to one side and facing forward. Owens thought the load was far too great for little girls, a hindrance to their physical development, and undoubtedly the reason why so many of the women were bow-legged.[72]

He also thought that three other factors made particular contributions to early aging in the women. The first was their grueling work at the grinding mills. At least three of every twenty-four hours were spent at this task, which was injurious to the lower limbs, back, and arms. The second was the heavy burdens the women carried up to the mesa tops almost daily, particularly water jugs holding about three gallons each. Owens considered the sight of eight or ten women wearily struggling up the steep and rocky trail with water jugs a picturesque sight but a sad one. The third cause of aging was early marriage.[73]

Hopi mothers lavished a great deal of affection on their children. Babies were nursed openly and without any show of mock modesty in the presence of white visitors.[74]

MARRIAGE

I have mentioned earlier that the Hopi find it necessary to keep their sexual behavior patterns a secret from the whites. This is not because they feel what they do is wrong. On the contrary, their practices seem healthy, entertaining, anticipatory, and productive for them. Nowhere is this seen better than in the matter of courtship.

According to Titiev, as soon as a girl "comes of age" she moves her bed to a place some distance from that of her parents or, if possible, to a different room, and she also undergoes an adolescence ritual. At the age of twelve or thirteen, boys begin to spend their nights in the kiva, where they are free from parental supervision and can roam at night wrapped in blankets so that their identities are concealed. Sometimes by prearrangement, sometimes in hope, they enter silently into the homes of girls, find them, and if accepted spend the remainder of the night, departing before daybreak. Of course, the parents know the custom, and they sanction it. It is considered courtship, the manner of bringing marriages to pass.[75]

A girl might have several such visitors, but if the affair settles down to one consistent caller, the parents begin to consider his suitability as a bridegroom. They may discuss it with her, mentioning their approval or disapproval and citing the reasons for feeling as they do. In any event, the girl makes the final choice and the parents accept it. The choice may be solidified by a premarital pregnancy, in which case the girl is free to name her favorite visitor as the father of her child. He might agree to marry her, or he might not. Usually he does, but a girl who bears a child out of wedlock is by no means frowned upon by the community. In time, another male will take her for a wife. In all instances, the marriage must occur between persons of different clans, and anything to the contrary is branded as incest.[76] In addition, a formerly married man is not allowed to court a single girl who has not been married, and a youth who has not been married cannot marry a widow or a divorcée. Titiev sees this as "an age grading factor," adding that it is an offense punished in the afterlife.[77]

I think it only fair to note that Albert Yava makes no mention of the courtship custom just given. Nor does Helen Sekaquaptewa or Polingaysi Qoyawayma (Elizabeth Q. White) in her story of a Hopi woman's struggle to live in two worlds.[78]

Courtship also has its place in the religious sphere. During night dances held in the kivas and during the ninth-day public ceremonies, there are, according to traditional practice, specific opportunities for young men and women to make their feelings for one another plain through gift exchanges and the like. On the final evening of the Powamû rite, an unmarried girl dressed in her traditional costume and whorl hairdo can even offer a loaf of qömi as a proposal of marriage to a young man she loves.[79]

Although there are certainly exceptions, marriage usually takes place in the fall or winter, and it begins when the mother of the girl goes with her to the young man's house to deliver a tray of white cornmeal. The tray is given to the prospective husband's mother, and the girl's mother returns home while the girl remains and grinds corn for three days. Titiev says that during this period the boy's paternal aunts "punish" the bride for "stealing" their sweetheart. They announce their attack in advance, and then foster an all-out mud and recrimination battle, all done in good fun and with damage recompensed.[80]

Before dawn on the morning of the fourth day, the relatives of the couple gather at the bridegroom's house. The two future mothers-in-law prepare two large bowls of yucca suds. The mother of the girl washes the boy's head with one, and the mother of the boy does the same for the girl with the other. Female relatives assist in rinsing the suds from the hair.[81] Titiev adds that, during the washing, the hair of the bride and that of the groom are mingled or actually knotted to symbolize the union taking place.[82]

When the hair washing is finished, the bridal couple take a pinch of cornmeal and quietly walk to the eastern edge of the mesa. As the sun rises they breathe on the cornmeal, throw it toward the sun, and offer a short prayer. When they return to the bridegroom's house the marriage is considered complete, even though the ceremony is actually just beginning, and from this time on the pair can sleep together as husband and wife.[83] The bride and her mother-in-law prepare a breakfast that is eaten by both families. Afterward, the bridegroom's father races out of the house and distributes bolls of cotton to friends and relatives, who are expected to separate the seeds from the cotton.[84]

A few days later, the village crier announces that the spinning of the cotton is to take place. The male relatives and their friends gather in their kivas and spend the day carding and spinning. That evening they bring their yarn to the bridegroom's house, where everyone shares in a feast of mutton and corn.

Using the cotton yarn, the father of the bridegroom, assisted by the bridegroom and other men of the family, weaves two white robes, one a little smaller than the other, and a white fringed sash. A pair of traditional women's moccasins is made of deerskin, and both the robe and the moccasins are coated or saturated with white clay. The manufacturing process usually takes six or seven weeks, and when it is done the bride is dressed by her mother-in-law in one of the robes. The other robe and the bride's broad white rain-belt are rolled up in a specially made reed mat. She holds this bundle horizontally in her outstretched hands and goes alone to her mother's house, where she awaits the arrival of the bridegroom. They then live with the girl's family until a new home can be built. In former times the bundle was suspended from the roof beams, but today the garments are placed in a bag or suitcase.[85]

The preparation of clothing for the bride by the men of the bridegroom's family is an ancient custom; Castañeda mentions the practice by the Rio Grande Anasazi in the 1540s.[86]

Hopi bride, 1930. She carries the reed mat, which is wrapped around the rain sash and white robe. Behind her are an oval ceramic jar with a Polik Mana (Butterfly) Katcina design and a metal wash bucket. Both are filled with cornmeal, which serves as part payment for her bridal outfit. Adapted from a Southwest Museum photograph.

According to Barton Wright, who quotes from other authorities also, the bride wears her wedding costume at the next Niman ceremony to be held and at the naming ceremony for her firstborn child on the twentieth day. The larger robe's final use is as her burial shroud, and it is considered her only means of transportation to the Underworld.[87] Thus the robe and marriage become absolutely essential in the Hopi mind, and if any untoward happening prevents the fulfillment of the entire wedding ceremony, the Hopi have a set of contingency acts that can be performed to make the girl's entrance into the Underworld still possible.[88] The smaller robe may be embroidered with symbolic designs of rain clouds, flowers, and butterflies, and then worn by men in certain Katcina rituals.[89]

The Hopi have no formal procedure for divorce, and Hopi marriages are not stable today. Whether this was always true is not known. Infidelity is reasonably common, as is incompatibility. The situation is one that in a general way the outside world can identify itself with completely. But whereas we divide property and provide alimony, the Hopi wife in all instances retains possession of the home. All the husband gets as he is "shut out" is his personal effects. In line with the principle of matrilineal descent, children remain with the mother. She is also entitled to a section of her clan's land, and life goes on as usual.[90]

HOUSE BUILDING

As I have said, a newly married couple usually lives with the bride's mother and father until, with the help of relatives and friends, they can build a house of their own. How soon that happens depends upon the ambition of the young husband, and upon how anxious the parents are to be rid of them. Ordinarily, the youngest daughter and her husband will stay and take over the mother's household. A few years later it will become the daughter's house, and the mother will be thought of as living with her.

The building of the old-style sandstone Hopi house was an event rather than a chore. The end product was almost identical to ancient structures, and done in such a traditional way that one suspects that the approach was quite similar at Chaco, Kayenta, or Mesa Verde. It was carried out according to prescribed rules that controlled the workers from the initial selection of the site to the great feast that opened the house as a dwelling. Most houses were built one room at a time, and if an existing wall was available it was used for one side, so that only three new walls were needed. The second room to be added was usually built behind the first, and the third room was built on top of the second room, so that it used the roof of the first house as its terrace. Buildings showed little regard for overall planning, except that front orientation, as far as possible, was toward the east.

Once the site of a house had been determined, its dimensions were roughly marked out, either on the ground or on top of the lower house where it was to be placed. Next came the gathering of the building materials. In this task the communal spirit of the Hopi was strongly in evidence, as the builder, with the aid of the town crier, called upon the assistance of all the relatives who belonged to his own clan. The helpers received no compensation except their food. And, as is the case with all communal labor, the work was carried to its completion with a spirit that is often lacking in the non-Indian world. George Wharton James says the Hopi made a party of it, and he once saw twenty-three women engaged in the building of a house.[91]

The accumulation of building materials was no easy matter. The stone could be quarried from the top and sides of the mesa on which the village

Hopi architectural details. Method of building transoms over openings to provide for air circulation. A Crow Mother Katcina stands in the lower left corner.

stood, although, with work being done only as time permitted, it might take up to a year to cut and shape it. Unless timbers from an abandoned house were available, the tree-beams were hauled from great distances. Cedar and cottonwood trees could be obtained in the immediate area, but if the room was especially large, the main beams had to be of pine and brought from the tops of mountains sixty miles away. As we found to be the case at Chaco Canyon, all such beams were hand-carried, and at the end of the journey back to Hopi,

Architectural details redrawn from V. Mindeleff. *a*, notched doorway. *b*, doorway with double transom. *c*, sealed doorway and small transom. *d*, stone steps. *e*, doorway with one notched jamb. *f*, notched ladders carved from logs.

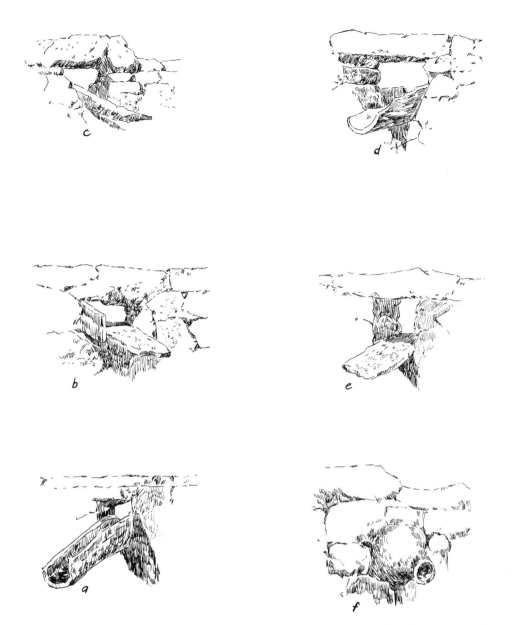

Architectural details redrawn from V. Mindeleff. Roof drains: *a*, wooden. *b*, stone trough. *c*, single stone. *d*, curved stone. *e*, single stone consisting of discarded metate. *f*, gourd.

they still had to be lifted for as much as six hundred feet up narrow and precipitous trails. Most main beams used for the average-sized roof structures were smaller pine or cottonwood, but timber was so hard to obtain that every tree indigenous to the country was employed in one way or another in house construction.

Once the building materials were gathered, the builder went to the chief of the pueblo and obtained from him four small eagle feathers to which short cotton strings had been tied. The feathers were sprinkled with sacred cornmeal, and one was placed at each corner of the house, where it was covered with a cornerstone. The Hopi call these feathers *Nakwa Kwoci*, meaning breath prayer, and the ceremony of placing them is addressed to Dewa, the Sun.[92]

The next step was the location of the doorway, which was marked out by placing food on each side of where it was to be. Also, particles of food, mixed with salt, were sprinkled along lines where the walls were to be raised. Then the construction itself was begun. Among the Hopi, the masons were generally men and the plasterers women (but visitors often found that the women did the entire work of house construction, the materials being brought by the men, who sometimes assisted in the heavy work of lifting the long beams for the roof). While the men were preparing the stones, the women brought water from the springs. Clay and earth were then dug adjacent to the site and mixed to form the mortar, which was applied sparingly between the layers of stones. Most walls were spalled as completely as possible, and instances are known where no mortar at all was applied until the rains came and made it easier to mix the mud. Hopi walls were irregular in thickness, varying from 8 to 18 inches (20 to 45 cm), and were raised to a height of 7 or 8 feet (2.1 or 2.4 m). The masonry was crude compared to that of classic Chaco and Mesa Verde, a fact that bothered the Hopi very little. Even then it sometimes took weeks to get the walls up.

The roof beams were placed on top of the walls and were spaced from 2 to 3 feet (61 to 90 cm) apart. Above these were laid smaller poles running at right angles and 4 to 12 inches (10 to 30 cm) apart. Across the poles were laid willows or reeds as closely together as possible, and then came a dense layer of green rabbit brush and bee plant and a final six-inch coating of mud. When the mud was dry it was covered with 3 inches (7.5 cm) of dry "clay well" that was thoroughly stamped down.[93] The roof was finished flat and usually a foot lower than the tops of the walls, so that the earth covering would not be washed or blown away. Drains of various kinds were then inserted in the copings to carry off storm water and to prevent leaks. When this was done, the women plastered the exterior of the house, and in this task the children often made a messy but enthusiastic game of helping.[94]

Construction ceased at this point while the owner prepared four more eagle feathers, tied them to little sticks of willow to make pahos, and inserted these between one of the central roof beams and the ceiling. No Hopi home was considered complete without this, for it was the soul of the house and the sign of its dedication. These feathers were renewed each year at the feast of Soyaluña, celebrated in December, when the sun is called back and begins to return northward. Also an offering was made to Masau'u in the form of food particles placed among the roof poles, with prayers for good luck and prosperity in the new home.

These ceremonies completed, the interior of the house was plastered by the women, who spread on the plaster smoothly with their hands. The surface left thereby was slightly textured and pleasing. The hand strokes remained on the walls and sharp corners were eliminated, leaving only soft irregular curves. Ruth D. Simpson states that one small wall patch was left unplastered in the belief that a Katcina would come and cover the spot with invisible plaster.[95] I assume this served as an invitation to the Katcina to come and share in the building of the house.

After the plastering, a coat of whitewash, or white gypsum, was applied to the interior walls to brighten the room. Some women left borders of the darker clay plaster exposed for decoration. Others painted simple designs on the walls, and still others left the walls plain. Simpson says that the whitewash was applied with a rabbit-skin mitten with the fur left on, and that it was renewed frequently.[96]

In one corner of the room the women built a fireplace and chimney. The firepit was a foot or so deep and lined with clay. The chimney hood was plastered. Most houses had an opening in the roof for the smoke to escape through. In others the hood was extended through the ceiling to a chimney of

Architectural details redrawn from V. Mindeleff. *a*, piki stone and andiron. *b*, piki stone and chimney hood. *c*, ground cooking pit covered with a chimney.

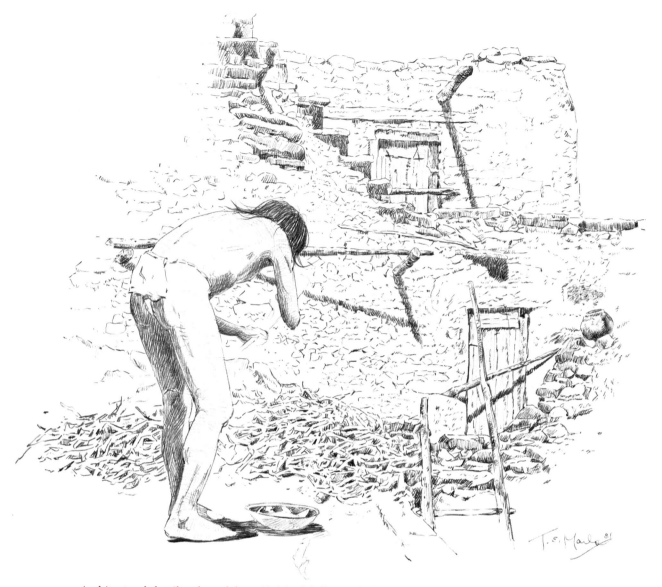

Architectural details adapted from V. Mindeleff: paneled wooden doors and stone steps.

bottomless clay jars set on top of one another. Finally, the floor was laid, a coating of earth packed down with water that was generally mixed with plaster.

In pre-American days a roof hatchway and ladder system provided the only entrance for a first story or for a one-story house. There were no windows, and openings left in the wall while work was in progress were sealed up as soon as they were no longer needed.

When the house was completely finished the owners gave a feast for all who assisted with the building, and each of these in turn brought a small gift to help the family begin their housekeeping.

John G. Bourke stayed at a Hopi home in Sichimovi in 1881, and the room he occupied as a bedroom was 30 feet (9 m) long, 18 feet (5.5 m) wide, and 6 feet 6 inches (1.95 m) high, a sizable room by any standards. But when he had an opportunity to investigate the various villages on the mesas, he determined that the average room was 12 feet (3.6 m) long, 10 feet (3 m) wide, and 7 feet (2.1m) high. The masonry was "slouchy," and in the few instances where windows occurred, glass was already being obtained from the whites. "Neither mica nor selenite was to be seen."[97]

Whenever a second or higher story was added, the roof of the house below would serve as its floor. In such instances the fireplaces of the upper rooms were built with raised walls, instead of being recessed into the floor. Rectangular and T-shaped doorways and windows were fashioned in the upper-room walls, some of which may still be seen in the older structures. The earliest doorways were closed with mats or blankets, but later on plank doors were installed. Some of these were set in pivot sockets so that they swung, being secured with wooden bars. Here and there a transomlike opening was left above the door for ventilation.

Each room in a building was regarded as a complete house, even though an extended family might occupy several rooms. There were no bedrooms as such. All dwellings had one room that included a masonry bench extending along one wall and about 2 feet (.6 m) high, a floor-level storage bin, and a partition that divided one side of the room in half. In one of these halves would be the mealing bins, with three metates of different coarseness set side by side and far enough out from the wall to permit the women to kneel behind them and face into the room. If the partition was omitted, the bins were placed close to a room corner.

Long poles that hung by thongs from the ceiling, or short pegs protruding from the walls, served as clothes hangers. By tradition, in an upstairs room the fireplace was situated to the right of the doorway, and water ollas and canteens were placed on the left. Sometimes small openings made interroom communication possible. Until they were "Americanized," the Hopi had no furniture. Food was served in a pot that was placed on the floor, and everyone ate with fingers from the same pot. Blankets and animal pelts served as beds, and during the day they were folded or rolled to be used as seats.

On especially cold nights a family whose house included more than one story would work, visit, and sleep in a first-floor room, since it was the easiest to heat. In good weather the first-floor rooms were more often used for storage. Roof terraces also served as storage places for firewood and as drying places for crops and meat. Another use for the terraces was as passageways from house to house. Serving as such, they became places for social gatherings and work parties. People also stood on the terraces to watch the public dances connected with ceremonies.

Women living in upstairs homes often cooked in fireplaces and ovens that were built on the terraces and rooftops, since the thick coat of adobe provided good protection against fire and the open air dispersed the smoke.

Access to Hopi dwellings was gained by ladders that could be drawn up in case of attack or when privacy was desired. Most ladders were of the two-pole type to which rungs were lashed, but some were a single V-notched log. Later, the use of rungs that slid into holes burned in the poles became popular. A hatchway-ladder combination provided access to ground-floor rooms, and

Architectural details redrawn from V. Mindeleff. *a*, chimneys made of stones and broken pots. *b*, second-story fireplace. *c*, fireplace and mantel. *d*, terrace cooking-pit and chimney. *e*, chimney hood. *f*, terrace fireplace and chimney.

the upper rooms were reached either by ladders to the roof or by stone stairways.

It must again be emphasized that architectural features varied, and that the foregoing is only a general view of building procedure.

The need for compactness as a security measure is gone now, and a number of separate houses, some of them considerable distances apart, have been built. Hopi men with training in carpentry and masonry fashion sharp corners and dress the stones as well as professional masons. All the common building tools are employed. Most new houses have several rooms and are a single story in height, although a few are of two stories. Third-story additions are seldom built. Some roofs, as at New Oraibi, are gabled and covered with tin, and some walls are of cinder or concrete block. Regular glass is used for the windows. Factory-made doors are present in all ground-floor rooms of newly built sandstone houses, and doorways have been constructed in many of the older dwellings. Metal hinges, doorknobs, and padlocks are common. Since the practice of reusing building materials from abandoned houses continues,

Architectural details redrawn from V. Mindeleff. *a,* house interior. *b,* stone grain bin. *c,* metate. *d,* mealing stones.

a

b

c

d

A kiva hatchway at Hano, on First Mesa.

the evidences of ancient Hopi architecture become fewer with every passing year. Coal-burning iron stoves and stovepipes, beds with springs, metal kitchenware, buckets, dishes, cutlery, washtubs, tin cans, tables, chairs, dressers, kerosene lamps, gasoline stoves, store-bought foods, toys, and bedding are regular parts of the Hopi scene today, as are automobiles and trucks. Electric appliances are few, being limited to those villages that have electricity available. Chimneys are still made of masonry and capped with bottomless jars.

KIVAS

Extensive consideration has already been given to Hopi-like kivas found at Antelope Mesa, and there is little need to consider kiva construction and layout in great detail here. To maintain a subterranean aspect, Hopi kivas were usually built in mesa-edge clefts, and one or more walls were above grade and

exposed. The roof hatchway was only slightly above the surface of the ground. Kivas built on top of the mesa were placed in natural depressions and are only semisubterranean, since they extend aboveground. To reach the roof hatchways, stone steps were built, and these are the only instances of permanent steps that lead directly into a ground-level structure in ancient Hopi architecture.

Mindeleff provides a detailed description of the building of a Hopi kiva in the 1800s,[98] and Dorsey and Voth give the subject some consideration also.[99] Kiva building began with virtually the same ceremonial acts as those employed for house construction. The chamber was rectangular, and the roof sloped noticeably from the center to the ends. A central hatchway served as an entryway and as a smoke vent. A long-poled ladder, whose ends projected 10 or 12 feet (3 or 3.6 m) in the air, extended through the hatchway and rested on the kiva floor with the butts held in place by the edge of a platform 10 or 12 inches (25 or 30 cm) high that occupied about a third of the south end of the kiva. Im-

Sectional view showing interior and construction details of a subterranean kiva.

mediately in front of the ladder was the square firepit, and beyond it, the sipapu, which was in a cavity covered usually with a 10-inch-wide cottonwood plank in which there was a small opening with a wooden plug to close it. At the far end of the kiva was a ledge 2 feet (61 cm) high on which ceremonial objects were placed during ceremonies. A small niche in this ledge was called the *kihu*, or Katcina house, and served as a repository of secret paraphernalia. Other niches were made in the side walls. Benches on which participants could sit were sometimes built along the sides of the kiva. Loom fittings were arranged along the side walls, and the kiva floor was paved with closely laid flagstones.

Bourke entered several kivas. One was 25 feet (7.5 m) long and 15 feet (4.5 m) wide, and the ceiling was 10 feet (3 m) high. The walls were so completely hidden by ceremonial dance paraphernalia that he couldn't tell whether they were decorated or plastered.[100] Another kiva was larger still, being 35 feet (10.5 m) long, 25 feet (7.5 m) wide, and 7 feet (2.1 m) high. Since it was built against the mesa side, the outer wall had three small windows to assist in ventilation—something Bourke appreciated, for he found the "stench" of the filled kivas to be almost unbearable during ceremonies, and he welcomed the chance to "run up the ladder into the pure air."[101]

Interesting secondary features connected with the kiva entrance included a reed mat made of yucca fiber and grass, with string used to close the hatchway, and bunches of green brush suspended around the hatchway to dry before it was burned as fuel. Men did the rough work for the kivas, but plastering, whitewashing, and the like were done by the women. Besides meeting in the kivas, society members often gather for ceremonial purposes in the homes of the clan heads, using a room somewhat as they do the kiva.

New kivas are seldom built today. The only need for one is when a group becomes exceptionally large or is divided by dissension. Since clans do at times become extinct, amalgamation of two or more clans is permitted. Some kivas are abandoned, and then taken over by new owners. More is said about this further on.

Lesser forms of Hopi architecture are shrines, outdoor ovens, corrals, garden walls, chicken houses, and field shelters. Sheep corrals vary in size, but most of them are quite small and consist of enclosures formed of thin, rude stone walls.

Mindeleff noted that as early as the 1880s farm shelters were playing important roles in the resettlement of the Hopi. Some shelters a long way from the pueblo village were so well built they became true summer homes. Then, as families tired of the long trips to and from the pueblo, the summer home became a permanent residence and a small village would be created.

SHRINES

In earlier chapters, mention was made of shrines found by archaeologists at various ruins. So too, in walking about the Hopi villages one can recognize many things connected with religious life, especially shrines. Some are extremely significant and interesting. Beneath the mesa cliffs and among the rocks is the Walpi shrine marking the center of the world. Other shrines abound near every pueblo and are likely to be happened upon in out-of-the-way places among the rocks where the offerings are scattered about; some are new, with fresh paint and feathers, and some are much weather-worn. Near the Sun Spring at Walpi there is a place where many rounded blocks of wood are scattered on the ground. This is the Eagle Shrine mentioned earlier in the hunting material.

It is not by any means good policy to pry around these sacred places today, for the Hopi do not appreciate it, and they are always watching. But the early visitors made casual visits to some of the more interesting shrines and wrote about them.

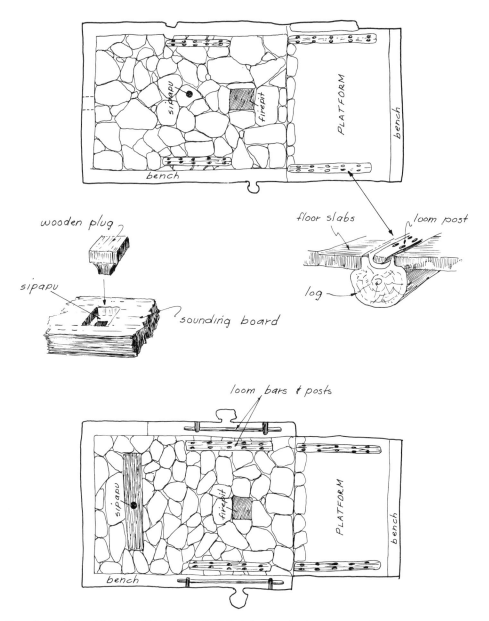

Top, floor plan of kiva at Shipaulovi. *Middle left,* detail of an unusual square sipapu opening in a Mishongnovi kiva. Sipapu plugs are often used. *Middle right,* method of installing loom posts in kivas. *Bottom,* floor plan of Chief Kiva at Shipaulovi. After Mindeleff, 1891.

At the point of the Walpi Mesa, where the original town stood several centuries before, were several shrines, to one of which the Katcinas went after their ceremonies to deposit their evergreen boughs and to make offerings of paint and meal. Here also they made offerings of food to the dead. At another spot the bushes were hung with little disks of painted gourd, each with a feather representing the squash flower. A heap of small stones was a Masau'u shrine, and a stone was added by every Hopi who passed it as an offering to this terrible god of the earth, death, and fire. No traditional Hopi would fail to toss a stone accompanied with a prayer to Masau'u, of whom all spoke in fear and with bated breath. For a good reason, then, many shrines to this god could be seen in Tusayan. Everyone who went to Walpi saw the great shrine in the gap which was called the "shrine of the end of the trail." Its base and sides were large slabs of stone, forming a box, and within it were various odd-shaped stones surrounding a coiled fossil believed by the Hopi to be a stone serpent. During the winter Sun Ceremony, this entire box abounded with feathered prayer sticks that almost hid the shrine, converting it into a thing of beauty.[102]

Other holy places, many of them ancient ruins of abandoned villages, are visited at times by the Hopi, who cheerfully make long journeys to mountains, lakes, and running streams for sacred water, spruce boughs, or herbs. They carry prayer sticks and sacred meal to be left as offerings to the spirits of the places. One of the streams from which sacred water is brought is Clear Creek, near the town of Winslow, seventy-five miles south of Walpi. Each field has its own shrine, and pahos are regularly placed there. Until recently, in the center of the main plaza of each pueblo could be seen a stone box with a slab of stone for a door, which opened to the east. (One or two have been moved or redone so as to be less noticeable.) The box is called the *pahoki*, or "house of the pahos." The central shrine of the village, it is carefully sealed up when not in use.

The caves and rock recesses of the Hopi mesas are used as depositories for certain of the sacred belongings of the societies. These places, while not properly shrines, are kept inviolably sacred, and few white visitors have peered into them, even those highest in the good graces of the priests. Hough informs us, "Once by chance two explorers came upon such a treasure house and with some trepidation took a photograph of it." In a dark cleft under the rocks were the jars in which the "snake medicine" was carried. These were arranged in disorderly fashion near a most remarkable carved stone figure of Talatumsi, the Dawn Goddess, painted and arrayed in the costume of that deity.[103]

FARMING

As I have noted in previous chapters, Anasazi men became extremely proficient dry farmers. The Hopi carried on this venerable tradition, and early visitors were amazed to see corn and other crops grown in desert land where the average annual rainfall seldom exceeded seven inches. Eastern and midwestern corn would have been burned out by the blazing sun of Hopi country, but the strains of corn passed down from Basketmaker times were developed for their task. From five to eight stalks grew on a hill, and at maturity they were three or four feet high. The broad blades were long and bent over almost to the ground, shading the roots from the sun. The ears were smaller than in midwestern varieties, and only a little water was required to raise a crop. A single covering by a flash flood in the rainy season could accomplish it. One visitor from the east took some of the corn back home and planted it in an area where there was plenty of rain. To his astonishment it grew over six feet tall.

Left, farmer with typical corn plant. *Right*, wooden farming implements: pitchfork, digging stick, hoe, beater.

In the early 1920s, the Hopi had fifteen hundred acres of land planted with corn and squash, and a thousand acres in peaches. The average corn crop was twenty-five thousand bushels annually. After the harvest, the corn was dried on the housetops and stored for winter. Each year a third of the crop was laid away to guard against the time when a drought might cause the crop to fail.

Each Hopi family was assigned an equal share of the tribal land, but fences were unknown, and fields being planted were marked out either with strings fastened to stakes or with lines of small rocks. Planting consisted mainly of digging a small hole with the same kind of rude digging stick used by the ancient Anasazi, and then dropping from ten to twenty seeds into the hole. The owner might do a little hoeing to clear away a few weeds or blown-in brush, but, for the most part, nature did the rest. Actually, few weeds grew on the desert, for the hard soil crust held down the growth of all vegetation. After the planting the farmer erected a brush shelter under which he lay watching his crop grow and guarding it from crows, burros, sheep, and a dozen other hazards. Burros were a Hopi beast of burden, and as such were greatly appreciated. But when one was caught raiding a cornfield its ears were cropped to warn other farmers of its thieving nature. Most of the burros in Hopi country had short ears. Wind was a special factor to contend with, since wind and the sand it carried could easily rip the plant leaves to shreds. So as the stalks grew the farmer piled sand, boards, cans, and whatever else he could find around the stalks as windbreaks. If birds were especially pesky, he made scarecrows to frighten them away.

The planting procedure has changed surprisingly little in the past seventy years, although trucks are often used for transportation and hauling. Land is cleared and weeded in February. Planting begins in April and continues at intervals for the next three months. Sweet corn is planted during the first phases of the May moon. During the waning of the May moon and the period of the June moon all the other seeds are planted—muskmelons at half moon in June, corn and beans during the early June moon, squashes and water-melons as it wanes—and the most distant fields are always planted first.

Cornfield near Oraibi Pueblo, 1924.

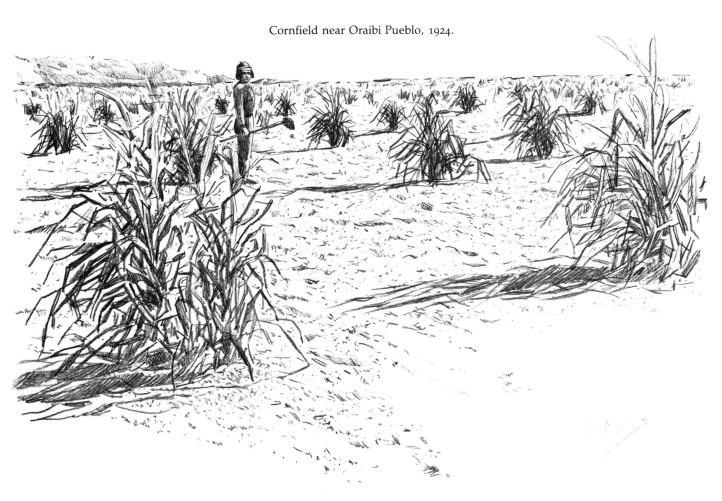

According to Simpson, the modern Hopi farmer usually plants several cornfields, the average size being about an acre. Each clan controls more land than its members need, and a member can have several plots. He tries to select these so that each will have a somewhat different kind of soil and a different source of water, marking their outlines either with lines of stones or with corner pillars of stone to advise others that they are in use. Sand-dune acreage is always in demand, because the dunes retain water and require little irrigation. Also, the dunes serve as natural windbreaks.[104] Each man's main field is located on the floodplain of a wash where the farmer can usually count on summer floods to irrigate his crops. To make the best use of this flooding, control dams are built in the washes, and ditches are dug to shunt water to as many other fields as possible. However, if the floods are especially heavy they can easily destroy some or all of the plants. If, on the other hand, they do not come at all most of the crops will die, which helps explain why the Snake Dance and other special rain-producing ceremonies are held during the summer.

Small cornfields below the mesas are irrigated, if necessary, with water from springs. The harvests from these are at least more dependable and, to-

Oraibi woman sorting the harvest. White ears are placed to her left, red and blue ears to the rear, and the best of each is saved for seed. From photograph by O. C. Havens, 1924.

gether with the emergency supply kept on hand by each family, they will see the Hopi through a minor drought. Long experience has taught the farmers that springs occur where the tops of impervious strata are exposed, because underground water that has been carried for miles along an impervious stratum will surface at an exposed place. They also know that wherever such a stratum extends into the valley at a shallow depth, it will be covered by only a thin layer of sand sufficient to retain water which elsewhere would be lost. At First Mesa, spring runoffs are frequently dammed, and the water is diverted into small irrigation channels.

Hopi corn has twelve rows of kernels, which may be white, yellow, red, blue, black, or variegated in color. The kernels are even, and not indented. In September, when the sweet corn is fit for roasting, tall columns of smoke will be seen rising from the roasting pits in the fields. Large pits are dug in the sand, heated with burning brush, filled with roasting ears, and closed up tightly for a day. The opening of a pit is an occasion for feasting, and laughter and song prevail. Some of the corn is used at once in making puddings and other dishes, and what remains is dried on the cob and stacked or hung in bunches in the houses. The other corn is gathered and stored away, the ears being piled up like cordwood in symmetrical walls, and separate from the past emergency supply, which may now be used. In good weather the women bring out the corn, spread it on the roof to sun, and carefully brush off each ear before returning it to the granary, for in this dry country insect pests are numerous. Hough says that among the superstitions connected with corn is the Hopi belief that the cobs of the seed corn must not be burned until rain has fallen on the crop, for fear of keeping away or "drying up" the rains.[105]

There have been disputes over which Hopi villages own certain lands in the washes between the mesas. It is generally accepted, however, that First Mesa farmers are to use the land on both sides of the mesa, with the Tewa of Hano Pueblo being confined to lands upstream. Second Mesa farmers are to plant the adjacent lowlands and Polacca Wash. The boundary line between Second and Third Mesa lands is drawn on the Second Mesa side of Mañyao'vi Peak in Oraibi Wash.[106]

Most gardens are planted near springs and are irrigated by hand, while a lesser number of garden crops are raised in the cornfields. A few small corn and garden crops are grown on the mesa tops. Men and boys tend the corn and cottonfields, and women and girls tend the gardens.

Ruth Underhill says that besides corn, the Pueblos raise two kinds of squash (properly called pumpkin). These are the large green *Curcurbita moschacha* and smaller, striped *Curcurbita pepo.* When a pumpkin is brought in from the fields the rind is hacked off with a knife, and the fruit is cut in half and hung up in the sun for a few days. When the thready part of the center of the fruit has dried out and the meat is soft, each half is cut in a long spiral strip. This is dried thoroughly and then wadded up in a bundle to be kept. When soaked in water, its delicious pumpkin taste returns, just as that of commercially dried and processed products.[107]

The large kidney bean *(Phaseolus acutifolius,* var. *latifolius)* grew only in Mexico and the Southwest, and the Indians of those regions were the first to cultivate it. The Pueblos have it today in many shades of red, white, and spotted varieties, and it is a good source of protein. The different colors are planted separately to keep the strains pure. When they are harvested, men thresh them with sticks to break open the pods. Then women winnow them in a flat tray of coarse basketry, which they shake gently until the light pods and chaff come to the top. A quick tilt lets the breeze carry the chaff away, while the heavier beans remain in the tray. Beans and squash have their place in ceremonial, though not as great a one as corn. Artificial, man-made, squash blossoms are placed on some of the altars as prayers for growth, and at the February Powamû Ceremony small bean plants are planted in boxes and cultivated in the warm underground kivas.

Another crop raised by the Hopi is sunflowers. These are a special variety the Anasazi domesticated long ago, for their seeds are found in the ruins. Sunflower decorations have a place in many ceremonies. For example, at one point in the Snake Dance, ceremonial runners return to the village at dawn, bringing sunflowers and fresh cornstalks for the maidens. Each girl who gets one of them will have good luck for the year. Sunflower seeds also are a good source of oil. They are roasted, too, and eaten like peanuts. Wild seeds are gathered and planted in the Hopi gardens, where they grow very well. Some are used as food, some in other aspects of Hopi life. Saltbrush, mint, wild potatoes, ironwood, cottonwood, yucca, juniper, cattail, and other plants play at least minor roles in Hopi economy. A number of Caucasian crops have been adopted. Among those introduced by the Spaniards are onions, chile peppers, watermelons, tomatoes, wheat, beets, lettuce, peanuts, coxcomb, peas, sorghum, radishes, cabbage, cauliflower, artichokes, fennel, carrots, cucumbers, coriander, turnips, and grapes.[108] But the most important addition is in fruits. Currants, prickly pears, and other berries and cactus fruits were the only local native fruits available until the Spaniards introduced peaches. Then came apples, apricots, cherries, and pears, all of which are planted today in sheltered coves on the mesa tops and in seepage areas around the bases of the mesas.

More than 800 acres of fruit and almond orchards are tended by the men today. In 1936, Stephen gave as an average planting for the three mesas 3,600 acres in corn, 2,000 acres in other edible plants, and 1,000 acres in orchards. He estimated a corn yield of 2,500,000 pounds, of which 1,500,000 pounds would be consumed and the remainder sold to traders, used in general barter, traded to the Navajo, and stored for future emergencies.[109]

As in the past, wild plants are gathered for food. These include yucca fruits, spring greens, nuts, seeds, cactus, and various fruits. Sumac and mistletoe berries and thelesperma are collected for use in beverages. Some plants and herbs are collected for medicines, religious observances, and dyes. Thus, while the Hopi are predominantly farmers, they are also gatherers in the ancient tradition.

Outdoor horno, or baking oven, adopted from the Spanish.

According to Simpson, the Hopi classify their foodstuffs in several different ways. For example: edible or not; edible by some people, not by others; staple or rare; garden or field; and by flavors, which are nonstaples. "People learn to like staple foods and often make themselves learn to dislike those that are rare."[110] Cooking methods include stewing, boiling, roasting, grilling, baking. Meat may be stewed, grilled, roasted, or boiled. Roasting is accomplished in hot ashes. Meat often is dried, later shredded by pounding, and frequently eaten raw. In the division of labor, the planting, care of the corn in the fields, and the harvesting may belong to the men, but once the colorful ears are garnered, the women's work begins.

No other feature of the Hopi household is so interesting as the row of three or more metate slabs placed slantwise in stone-lined troughs sunk a few inches into the floor; these are their mills. They are of graded fineness, and that is also true of the oblong handstones, or manos, which are rubbed upon them with an up-and-down motion, as in using a washboard. Sometimes three women work side by side at the mills; the first woman grinds the corn into coarse meal on the coarse stone and passes her product over to the second, who grinds it still finer, and the third finishes it on the last stone; sometimes one woman alone carries the meal through the successive stages, but most homes can furnish at least two grinders. The skill with which the woman spreads the meal over the grinding slab by a deft move of the hand as the

Maiden using mano and metate to grind corn.

mano is brought up for the return stroke is truly remarkable, and the rhythmic precision of all the motions suggests a machine operation. The song sung by the grinders and the rumble of the mill are characteristic sounds of the Hopi pueblos, but grinding is backbreaking work, and as the women grinders powder their perspiring faces with meal while they work, they soon begin to look the part of millers. Girls are taught to grind at an early age, and quickly become accomplished in the work. The finely ground meal is piled and patted into conical heaps on the flat basket trays, making in the end a display of which the Hopi women can be justifiably proud, since it indicates diligence as well as a bountiful supply of the staff of life.

While cornmeal enters into all Hopi cooking as the chief ingredient, most of it is made into "paper bread," called piki. This bread is made from batter, colored gray with wood ashes, and dexterously spread very thinly with the hand over a heated slab of stone. Piki bakes quickly, coming immediately free from the slab and then being rolled up in a form so crisp that it crackles like paper. Sometimes it is tinted with attractive colors for use in the Katcina ceremonies. Before a public dance the women busily prepare food and the girls go about speechless, with mouths full of meal, "chewing yeast" for the corn pudding. This and other little-known facts of the kitchen can make a knowing traveler somewhat shy of the otherwise attractive-looking Hopi food.

Some of the villages now have communal piki houses where women cook this delicious corn bread, which is prepared for all feast days. These are small masonry rooms built near the houses. Each has a corner fireplace covered by a smooth, flat, rectangular stone on which the piki is fashioned.

Since corn is so vital to the Hopi, all the powers of earth and sky are invoked to grant a good crop by giving rain and fertility. It constitutes the central motive of the numerous ceremonies of the villagers of Tusayan, and as Hough says, if the prayers of the Hopi could be formulated it would probably be in the words "Grant us corn!" Nor are the villagers ungrateful for the blessing of corn. A man will stand looking over his thriving cornfield and say, *"Kwa kwi,*

Top, cooking corn in an outdoor ground oven. *Middle left,* section showing construction of ground oven and smaller flue. *Middle right,* rolled piki bread. *Bottom,* making piki bread; *left,* spreading the batter on a hot stone; *right,* peeling the bread off the stone.

Kwa kwi,' "Thanks, thanks," and it is evident that the utterance is made with true thankfulness and devotion.[111]

Someone has pointed out that a constant diet of corn produces disagreeable physiological effects, and hence it is wise to mix it with chile and other condiments, meat, and vegetable substances. The Hopi came by some means, perhaps just hard experience, to recognize this, and learned to prepare a number of corn dishes. In consequence, the vocabulary of corn in the Hopi language is extensive and contains words descriptive even of the parts of the plant. The importance of corn is also reflected in the many words describing the kinds of meal, the dishes made from corn or into which corn enters, and the ways in which it is prepared. Hough found that by 1896 there were, for example, fifteen kinds of piki or paper bread; three kinds of mush; five of shortcake; eleven of boiled corn; four of corn baked or roasted in the coals; two cooked by frying; four stewed; and eight of cooked shelled corn—making fifty-two varieties.[112] After the paper bread, perhaps the most popular food is pigame, or sweet corn mush, wrapped in corn husk and baked in an underground oven. Another favorite is shelled corn soaked and boiled until each grain swells to several times the normal size. The Hopi like their food well cooked and know the art of making each starch grain expand to the limit. They know how to make plain food appetizing without milk or eggs, and aren't afraid to try new and strange combinations. There are cakes made from dried fruits, chopped meat, and straw, put on the roof to dry, dumplings formed around old hammerstones, corn dodgers, pats of cornmeal mush wrapped in corn husk and boiled or baked, and many other styles of food that would seem strange to other than a Hopi epicure. The seeds of grasses and other plants are ground up and added to cornmeal to improve the flavor of bread, or, perhaps, a prized bread is made entirely of the ground seed of some desert plant. Oily seeds, such as those of the piñon, pumpkin, and melons, are ground to form shortening in various cakes and to add richness to stews. Some foods are colored with harmless vegetable dyes.

The Hopi no longer eat with their fingers from a single pot. They sit at tables, use silverware, and eat just as everyone else does.

Long journeys have been made to obtain essential items. For centuries, the Hopi have undertaken the long trip to salt deposits near the junction of the Colorado and Little Colorado rivers, and excursions are still made to the San Francisco Mountains for tobacco, pinenuts, various woods, and game. The berry patches scattered over the open country are still visited regularly by Hopi women.

Corn remains today the Hopi staff of life, but distinct and progressive changes have occurred in the Hopi food economy since the white man first arrived. The animals brought by the Spanish eased the problems facing the family providers. Sheep and cattle provided meat, while horses, and to a greater extent burros, served as beasts of burden. Cotton has been replaced by sheep's wool to such an extent that the production of this prehistoric staple has almost ceased.

Hopi animals are owned and cared for by the men. Since few individuals have time to tend their flocks continually, the task is handled on a community basis. Herds are grouped together and the men take turns watching them. Boys also aid in this work. When lambs are born, or when shearing time arrives, all the owners work with the herds. Since it is usually necessary now to take the flocks far from the mesas to graze, some herders and their charges are away from home for considerable periods of time. When it was possible to do so, the herders and sheep used to return to the mesa tops each evening, the flocks being bedded down in stone-fenced corrals just outside the village or just below the mesa rim. But the Bureau of Indian Affairs has lately required the Hopi to pasture and corral their sheep so far from the village that large flocks are no longer feasible. Those stockowners who are forced to take their charges far from home occasionally hire Navajo men or boys to tend the animals.

Through government action that began in the 1950s standards of animal husbandry were gradually raised, the range water supply was improved, and stock cooperatives were formed. Unfortunately, the condition of the rangeland has always presented a serious problem, and consistent overgrazing has led to a depletion of the food supply and to erosion of the soil. To combat this, the government long ago ordered sharp reductions in the size of individual herds and flocks, and by so doing brought hardship to many a Hopi family. The government sought then to help the Hopi by obtaining loans and off-the-reservation grazing privileges for them. One partial solution attempted was the use by the Hopi of lands on the Colorado River Reservation, and several Hopi families went there. This meant, however, the transplanting of families and estrangement from Hopi ways and environment. It was doubted by many that such experiments would succeed, since historically the Hopi have preferred a vigorous way of life with their own kind in their homeland to easier living amid foreign surroundings.

Twentieth-century Caucasian agricultural influences have been predominantly technical, such as school training in new methods, the use of machinery and steel tools, and the use of horses, burros, wagons, automobiles, and trucks. Tools, seeds, and machinery are available at the trading posts. Canned goods, flour, sugar, salt, meat, potatoes, and more may be obtained in trade for corn and other crops, blankets, silver jewelry, Katcina dolls, and other arts and crafts. The traders on the reservation and in the nearest towns who will advance credit and supply food in time of emergency have become in fact an important and mostly welcome aspect of the modern economy. Most of the traders working on the reservation are Hopi. Their trading posts remain small, but still important in the daily lives of the people. Cities that are frequented by Hopi for general services include Tuba City, Flagstaff, Winslow, Gallup, and Holbrook, and Keams Canyon has some public facilities.

The Hopi are expected to survive as a biologically distinct ethnic group because they remain culturally conservative, and because most of them are reluctant to marry outside the tribe. Still, they have adopted health standards as far as possible, hygiene is better, and contagious diseases are almost elimi-nated. Resistance to the use of the Public Health Service fades year by year, and what was once an abnormally high infant-mortality rate has been reduced appreciably.

Some Hopi have also intermarried with non-Hopi, including to a large extent Indians of other tribes. There are also far more Hopi progressives than there were. Hopi have moved away to live in other Indian communities, and in ethnically mixed towns, thus abandoning the female descent principle. This migration-and-readjustment pattern will assuredly continue. Therefore, those who wish to see some of the Hopi living and functioning much as they always did will need to make the trip soon.

HUNTING

Meat obtained from markets and domestic animals have all but replaced wild game on the Hopi menu, but until a few decades ago men were hunters as well as farmers, and it was their responsibility to keep the family supplied with meat. Before overgrazing by sheep became general, small animals, antelope, and deer frequented the Hopi mesas in small numbers. The deer were partic-ularly valuable, since they supplied meat, hides, sinew, bone antlers, and hoofs. Communal animal hunts were common and had religious and social as well as economic significance. Rituals were observed first to bring success to the hunters and then to "thank" the animals they pursued and killed. Game was trapped, stoned, flooded out of hiding, run down, and killed with arrows, clubs, and throwing sticks. Animals hunted included deer, wolves, mountain sheep, mountain lions, rabbits, foxes, coyotes, turtles, and smaller game. Ea-gles were sacred birds to be trapped by hand and carried to the villages alive. There they were catered to and then ritually killed for their feathers. Hawks and other birds also supplied feathers. Turkeys were domesticated, and in par-ticular provided feathers for prayer sticks. The turkey and the dog were the only domesticated animals kept by prehistoric Hopi.

Hough's references to the often plucked and ragged Hopi turkey are quite amusing. He says the Hopi believe the markings on turkey tail feathers were caused by the foam and slime of an ancient deluge, and so, because of their mythical association with water, turkey feathers are prescribed for all pahos. The Spanish of the sixteenth century spoke of "cocks with great hanging chins" at the pueblos. The Hopi village turkeys were roaming about freely in Hough's time, and sometimes, he says, "they dispute the entrance of a village by a stranger and put him to a great deal of annoyance by their attacks, which are usually in the nature of a surprise from the rear."[113]

The primary means of capturing larger game was the "surround," which consisted of a large group of men surrounding a group of animals and then driving them to where they could be killed by a fall or with bows and arrows.

Since surrounds required the help of all the men and boys in a village, there were hunt chiefs and hunt societies that organized and carried out the communal ventures. The leaders were, of course, experienced and skilled in their profession. They knew the best seasons and territories, and they knew the medicine that guaranteed success.

Prescribed ceremonies always preceded a hunt, whether it was communal or being carried out by an individual. Songs were sung, prayers were offered, prayer sticks were placed at shrines, tiny stone fetishes were made to be placed on the trails to point to and to "draw" the game. When the hunt was successful, ceremonies were performed to thank the animals that were killed, so their spirits could transmit this message to their "brothers and sisters," who, being pleased, would have a good attitude toward the Hopi hunters and thus be available another year.

James was told of a certain "beautiful scarlet gilia" that grew on the talus of the great mesa on which Awatovi stood. This was the only locality where the plant had been collected in the Hopi region, although it grew in profusion in the White Mountains. His informant explained that it was the *pala katchi*, or red male flower, and that it was very good for catching antelope. Before a hunt, the hunters rubbed up the flowers and leaves of the plant and mixed them with the meal they offered during their prayer to the deities of the chase. This was done because the antelope was very fond of the plant and ate it greedily when he could find it.[114]

To capture deer, the Hopi simply formed a circle of men around a place where the animals were feeding. Then two men entered the circle and drove the deer toward the other Hopi, where they could be shot with bows and arrows.

Antelope traveled in herds, and so they were stampeded and driven to where a group of hunters was stationed. To accomplish this, the Hopi selected a place that was closed in by hills and trees. There they built a corral that consisted of a fence of tree trunks with a single opening. Wings of brush formed a funnel leading to the opening, and then individual piles of brush extended this funnel, or pathway, for as much as ten miles. Men would be stationed at each pile to keep the antelope inside the pathway once they had been chased into it.

As soon as a herd was discovered near the mouth of the pathway, boys were sent to round them up. Their first step was to build a fire that started the antelope moving. Then they closed in, making as much noise as possible and running them toward the pathway. Once the antelope entered it the boys closed in behind them and in concert with the men hiding behind the brush piles kept them running until they entered the corral and were shot.[115]

Mountain sheep were still present in Hopi country as late as the 1880s. These too were "surrounded," but whenever possible they were driven off a precipice and killed by the fall. Those who got stranded on rock points as they sought to escape were lassoed and hauled in to be killed. Underhill says that a male and female pair were always left alive to provide sheep for later years.[116]

It is said that on rare occasions the Hopi went east to hunt buffalo.[117] In such instances they would have again resorted to the surround method of hunting, wherein the buffalo would be driven over a small cliff into a prepared place where those not killed by the fall could be finished off with bows and arrows.

Cottontails and jackrabbits were the only game that continued to exist in strength around the Hopi mesas, and rabbit-hunting parties were common in the early 1900s. Hough was fortunate enough to see such a hunt in action, and he describes it as "a novel experience." Dogs were barking, and a hundred men were screaming in concert and running in every direction; Hough feared he had "met the Peaceful People on the warpath." The hunters were smeared with clay and presented "a strange appearance." They carried bows and ar-

Hopi rabbit hunter with throwing stick. From a photograph by O. C. Havens, 1924.

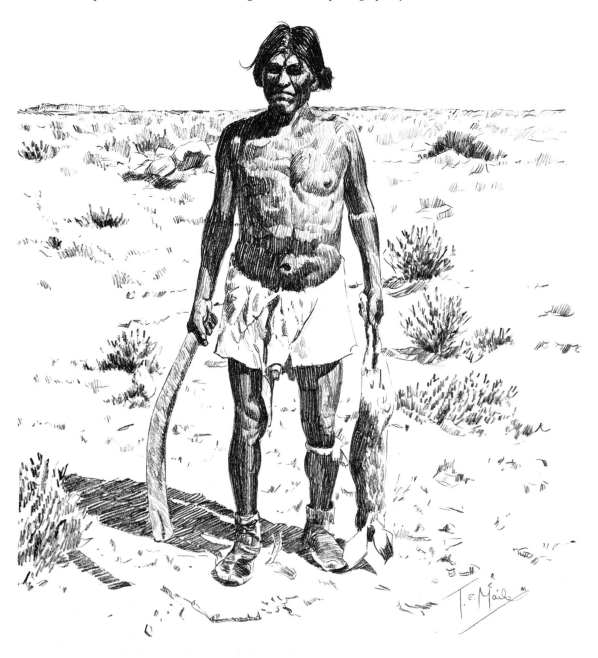

rows, curved throwing sticks of oak, and various clubs and sticks. One of the party was delegated to carry the rabbits, and rode a burro. In and out of the rocks of the mesa sides the men and boys skirmished "like coyotes, and with quite as fiendish a noise." The rabbits had little chance unless they plunged into a hole. Even then the men would stop and dig most of them out. The hunt was demanding, requiring sixty or seventy miles of running before it was over.[118]

Hough describes these as ceremonial hunts which, if unsuccessful, left the Hopi dejected and quiet. If on the other hand the hunt turned out well, there was a triumphal entry into the village "with much shouting and song."[119]

Hunting was not only a communal venture. Men often went out alone or in pairs according to individual family needs. Since a pair of hunters could in no wise surround the animals, they either used traps or simply ran the game until it was exhausted. Having trained for this since boyhood, the Hopi male could run all day and night if necessary. Grazing animals on the other hand would weaken without a chance to feed, and ultimately the hunter caught them, sometimes simply throwing a captive to the ground and smothering it.[120]

Any man or boy leaving the village to gather wood or to do any other task carried his curved throwing stick along, and often he brought back a rabbit, rat, ground squirrel, or bird. Traps built by the Hopi were the deadfall type, of which several kinds were made, although they all worked in the same fashion. A good-sized stone slab was held up at an angle by an upright stick. Bait was fastened to the stick so that when the animal attempted to take it he would dislodge the stick and be killed by the falling stone.

Neither nets nor snares such as those used by the Basketmakers were employed by the Hopi. Even prairie dogs were captured by turning rainwater into their holes to drown them out.[121]

EAGLES

Eagles were, and still are, an item of extreme importance to the Hopi. Their feathers are absolutely essential for ceremonial purposes, and to achieve the necessary religious goals the eagles must be taken in a prescribed way—not obtained by petition from a warehouse as government law now requires. Accordingly the law gives the Hopi no recourse but to violate it, and the Hopi do just that. After all, the Hopi Way preceded the law by untold centuries, and during all that time the eagle did not become an endangered species.

All eagle nests in the Hopi area are considered to be the property of clans. According to Hough, the Snake Clan claims the eagle nests near their old village of Tokonabi to the north of Walpi; the Horn Clan those to the northeast; the Firewood Clan those at the upper end of Keams Canyon; the Bear Clan those at the mouth of the same canyon; the Tobacco Clan those on the crags of Awatovi; the Rain Cloud Clan the nests in the Moki Buttes; the Reed Clan those in the region of their old town forty miles north of Navajo Springs on

Top left, the most frequently made type of paho, or prayer stick. According to Stephen, 1936, page 164, the deity being addressed sees the sticks and the attached items, and reads what is in the maker's heart. *Right,* a captive eagle. *Bottom left,* ritual burial of the eagle carcass as a prayer of thanks to the eagle and to the deities for more eagles in years to come. From Dorsey, 1901.

the Santa Fe railroad; the Lizard Clan the nests on Bitahuchi or Red Rocks, about forty miles south of Walpi; and the eagle nests west of the pueblos along the Little Colorado and Great Colorado belong to the Oraibi and Middle Mesa villagers. One cannot meddle with eagles within forty or fifty miles of the Hopi towns without trespassing on property rights.[122]

The eagle preserves are near the places occupied by the ancient clans, and thus show the lines of migration by which the several clans traveled to the villages where they now live.[123] The self-sustaining eagle rights are jealously guarded by the Hopi, and they have been sore spots in relations with the Navajo. Hopi leaders have often, but to no avail, asked the government to define their eagle reservations by survey and to establish boundaries around them.

Sacred hunts for eagles are still carried out every spring. In former times, eagle-catching places were built. These consisted of small, circular stone towers about 4 feet (1.2 m) in height. Poles were laid loosely across the top of the tower, and a dead rabbit was tied to the poles as bait. The hunter underwent a ritual head-washing, placed prayer offerings at a shrine, and then hid in the tower. Once an eagle attacked the bait and settled down, the hunter reached between the poles, grasped the eagle's legs, pulled him struggling down into the tower, and tied his legs together. The system was quite similar to that employed by Plains Indians, except that there a pit was used instead of a tower.

As time passed, the Hopi took upon themselves an even more difficult and hazardous method of obtaining eagles. Today, several men go to a place where there are eagles still too young to fly. According to Underhill, they take along offerings of several kinds and leave them at a mountain shrine dedicated to eagles. A small man or a boy is lowered by rope down the cliff face to where the nest is. He extracts one or two eaglets from the nest with one hand and uses the other hand to fight off the adult eagles if they attack him. The job does not sound like an enviable one. Observers say that eaglets are always left to continue the species and that, when mature birds are hunted, at least one is always freed by the hunter with a prayer stick tied to one leg to carry good thoughts to his fellow birds and associated spirits.[124] The number of eagles taken varies from year to year, but thirty-five is an average number. Hawks are also taken, and a certain large kind called *palakwahu*, or red eagle, is especially desired. Its feathers are extensively used for prayer offerings, masks, and other paraphernalia.[125]

In his notes on the Eagle Cult among the Hopi, Voth states that, after the young eagles are captured, they are tied to a wood rack and carried to the village. There they are kept as captives on the rooftops, tied to a beam, rock, or peg by one leg. They are fed rabbits, field mice, and other small animals until about July, when they have grown to full size.

In virtually all the principal ceremonies the eagle is remembered by prayer offerings, which consist usually of small eagle or hawk feathers tied to a twisted cotton string about four inches in length. The offerings are given to clanspeople who are part owners in an eagle preserve and who deposit them along with sacred meal in shrines that are devoted to eagles.[126]

During the open Katcina season the Eagle Katcina is represented by impersonators. His mask has an artificial eagle beak, and sometimes an eagle-feather costume is worn on the arms and back. The Katcinas receive prayer offerings at the dances and deposit them at Katcina shrines as a prayer "that eagles may not fail to lay eggs and hatch them again the next year."[127] Hough informs us that among the rocks below Walpi one may stumble upon a collection of oval wooden objects, some weathered and some bearing traces of spots of white paint and feathers. "This is an eagle shrine," he says, and the "wooden eggs are prayers for the increase of eagles prepared during the Soy-aluña Ceremony . . . At present, figurines of the domestic animals are also offered for the same purpose."[128]

About eight or nine o'clock on the morning after the July Niman Ceremony concludes, all the eagles in the village, except those not fully grown, are killed. Voth says that while one person holds the rope, another throws a blanket over the eagle and carries him down from the roof, choking him while he descends.[129] Underhill claims the eagles are killed by squeezing them to death.[130] Voth goes on to say, however, that "no eagle is killed by any other method" than the one he gives.

When the eagle is dead, the larger feathers are plucked and sorted. The eagle is then flayed and the skin is carefully dried to preserve the feathers still remaining on it. Prayer offerings are then tied to the wings and legs of the carcass, "that the eagles not be angry but hatch young eagles again the next year." During this time a small tray, a small flat doll, and a few small rolls of piki are prepared.

When all preparations are completed, the carcass, the prayer offerings, and a pointed stick are taken to one of the graveyards especially devoted to eagles. There a grave is dug with the stick, and the carcass and offerings are placed in the hole. Eagle graveyards are situated fairly close to all the villages.[131]

The larger eagle feathers are used on masks, standards, altars, and arrowshafts and for many other purposes. The typical Hopi sun symbol is profusely decorated with eagle tail feathers which, in this case, represent the rays of the sun. In the extremely beautiful Flute Ceremony every Flute player wears such a sun symbol on his back as a part of his ceremonial costume. He also wears on his head a ring of corn husks, into which are thrust eagle breath feathers (down feathers), while other participants in this, as in most Hopi ceremonies, have a smaller eagle feather fastened to their hair.

In all ceremonies of any importance whistles are blown that are often made of eagle wing bones, and the chief priest uses an eagle (or buzzard) wing feather when he discharms the participants in the ceremony from the whip (the ailment for which the society has the power to cure) peculiar to that order of ceremony. To the "tassels" on the corners of the bridal costume, eagle prayer feathers are tied, and an eagle feather *pühu* (road) is placed to the west of the grave of departed Hopi to show them the way to the Underworld. Also, certain prayer offerings placed on graves are made of an eagle feather. Other eagle feather roads, with a longer string, are placed by Hopi doctors on the paths that lead away from the village to show the evil spirits of disease the road on which they are to depart from those whom the medicine man has discharmed. The *natsi* or society emblem of the Lagon and of the Oaqöl fraternities contains two eagle tail feathers, and certain standards and other ceremonial objects of other societies are decorated with the same feather. The whips that Snake priests take on their Snake hunts and use in the Snake Dance consist of a handle with two large eagle wing feathers fastened to it; to the point is fastened a small fuzzy eagle feather that is painted red. A number of similar, small red feathers fastened to short, twisted cotton strings form the prayer offerings which the Snake hunter also takes with him and throws with sacred meal to a reptile he intends to capture for the ceremony.[132]

WARFARE

The Kokop Clan, mentioned earlier in connection with Sikyatki, is also associated with Old Oraibi, where they were by far the order most closely concerned with warfare. An extensive myth describes their settlement at the pueblo.[133] They brought with them, as their cultus heroes, Masau'u and the Little War Twins, and according to Titiev's informant, who was reputed to be the last surviving member of the order, they introduced into the pueblo the *real* Warrior Society. Since the Little War Twins are the grandsons of Spider Woman, the Kokop developed a partnership with the Spider Clan and joined in directing the Warrior Society known as the Momcit or Mutcwimi.

In the days when active fighting still went on, there was a clear distinction between a warrior, who was any member of the Momcit even if he had never been in a battle, and the *real* warrior. The latter was one who openly acknowledged the killing and scalping of an enemy, had subsequently gone through a demanding four-day-and-night initiation ritual in the kiva, and then "escaped" his victim—who sometimes came after him in the guise of a real Masau'u. Titiev's informant tells the full story of the initiation and the enemy's revenge visit.[134]

The Momcit Ceremony was performed every fall, soon after the Marau Ritual. Every normal male joined and the membership was large. Members were divided into two groups, the regular Momcit and the Stick-swallowers Society. Both groups met in the same kiva, but sat in different areas while the ritual was conducted. A complicated altar and war medicine were made, and then the men painted and dressed and held a practice dance outside the kiva. While the Momcit danced, the Stick-swallowers by some clever means swallowed their eagle sticks, which were about a foot long. During the next day's dance they swallowed a lightning stick of similar length. This interchange of performances was continued until the final day, when the entire membership appeared as a body, and all the men swallowed their sticks in unison. To conclude the ceremony, the sticks that had been used were deposited at night at the Spider Woman's shrine.[135]

The principal enemies of the Hopi were the Apache, Ute, and Chimwava. Navajo scalps were considered worthless.[136] Warriors wore regular clothing, with hide caps fashioned from mountain lion and wildcat skins to which eagle feathers were attached. Weapons included the bow and arrow, stone war clubs, throwing-sticks, and lances. Whether the warriors carried shields for protection is not known for certain, but the mural paintings at Awatovi and

Kawaika-a include illustrations of shields, suggesting that they were part of the equipment.

Before departing from the village, warriors would pray to the spirits of deceased warriors, and to Masau'u, asking for their help. Songs associated with death-dealing were rehearsed just before an attack was mounted. Some songs were designed to gird-up the warriors, and others to cause the enemy to sleep while the Hopi approached. There were also direction songs to keep the men oriented, so as not to get lost, during the fighting.

The village war chief led the men into battle dressed to impersonate Pukonghoya, one of the two Little War gods, and he carried only a stone club. It is assumed that the *real* warriors came next, and then the regular Momcit. If an enemy was killed, the player sang a scalping song while he scalped the victim, and cut a piece of buckskin from the man's apparel. This was later tied to the special plumed sticks worn in the hair by the Momcit member.

When the warriors returned home, the scalps were hung on poles, washed in yucca-root suds, and ritually fed from time to time. According to Titiev's informant, a scalp was considered to be the "son" of its taker. It was kept in his house, and a prayer stick was made for it at Soyaluña as if it were a living thing. When the Hopi warrior died, the scalp was buried with him. Any booty taken by the war parties was divided equally on their return, and then thrown to the villagers, who anxiously awaited the warriors' coming.

Momcit members were not allowed to take credit for killing anyone, but the *real* warriors were expected to boast, and sometimes they drew marks on the ground to show how many enemies they had killed. Victory dances were held in which the scalps were displayed, and in the fall the Howina'aiya, or Warrior, Dance was performed. Rehearsals took place in the kivas, and girls would come there to choose their partners for the public dance, wherein the couples danced together in traditional costumes. After the dance, the men climbed to a designated rooftop overlooking the plaza and threw gifts that had been collected by their relatives to the waiting crowd below; hence the name, Market Dance.[137]

WEAVING AND APPAREL

As we know, the Anasazi ancestors of the Hopi used yucca fibers, feathers, fur, and cotton to fashion their woven garments. As early as A.D. 1581, Spanish explorers reported that Hopi wove white cotton dresses. The first sheep were brought to Hopi country by the Spanish sometime in the sixteenth century. Some researchers believe that sheep were used for food for a while before the potential of their wool was recognized, but during the seventeenth century the Hopi were weaving with it, and by the eighteenth century wool was playing a major role in the Hopi weaving complex and economy.

As commercial cloth became available in the 1880s, Pueblo other than the Hopi took advantage of it, and their weaving industry began to decline. The

Hopi chose not to succumb to this, and their traditional weaving continued. In consequence, they became the suppliers for the other Pueblos. This is not to say that the Hopi themselves have not been affected by modern times. In 1931, it was estimated there were two hundred Hopi weavers at work. By 1975, this number had dwindled to a score or so, most of whom devoted their energies exclusively to the production of ceremonial garments.

When Hough visited the Hopi just before the turn of the century, he observed that the weavers seemed to have appreciated the value of wool "at once," and the ancient garments of feathers and skins had virtually disappeared. Cotton remained in use only for ceremonial costumes or for cord employed in the religious ceremonies, and the rabbit-fur robes of yesterday were largely displaced by blankets that were "gorgeously dyed and cunningly woven." Hough also notes that before the introduction of trade dyes the Hopi had been satisfied with somber colors—dark blues and browns derived from

Making a rabbit-skin robe. From an E. H. Allcutt photograph, 1899.

The Hopi spinner pulling the lumps out of the yarn. *Upper left,* typical wooden spindles, one with corncob stuck on the end. From Frederick Monsen photographs.

plants—and that even in 1896 the Hopi weavers were keeping to those colors for blankets and dresses and were refusing to employ the zigzag designs of the Navajo.[138]

In fact, the women of all the pueblos of the Southwest were dressing in black, dark blue, and brown. The dress cloth itself was very durable, and more than one generation enjoyed the service of a given piece. For instance, when an older woman no longer used one of her blanket dresses, garments were fashioned from it for her children. Those who examined the early Hopi blankets were invariably surprised at the skillful weaving. The body of the blanket dress was often woven in black, and the two ends were bordered in blue with a damask or basket weave. Sometimes an entire blanket was of damask, giving it a surface with an especially pleasing effect. The body of the women's cotton ceremonial blankets was white, with broad blue and red borders, sometimes showing three kinds of weaving and several varieties of cording. The women's belts also incorporated a broad range of patterns. Hough thought that the Hopi were more adept at weaving than their rivals, the Navajo.[139]

The carding and weaving were done thoroughly, and the resulting yarn was strong, even, and twisted tightly with a simple spindle. Sometimes a spinner dressed and finished his yarn by means of a corncob smoothed by long use. Women usually did the dying, and the dye they concocted from sunflower seeds or blue beans was a fast blue. In former times the cotton had been prepared for spinning by whipping it with slender switches on a bed of sand, and this custom was still employed in 1896 to fashion sacred sashes from the material. But by now nearly every family also had wire cards that were purchased from traders.[140]

The spindle was a cylindrical wooden rod about twenty inches long, with one of its ends sharply pointed. The whorl, which was a circular disk made of stone, bone, gourd, or wood, was slipped over the rod and fastened on about seven inches down from the unsharpened, or butt, end. The disk acted as a flywheel and also served to hold the yarn on the rod.

The weaver took one end of the roll of carded wool or cotton in his left hand and held it against the point of the spindle, which he rolled rapidly across his thigh and leg until the material caught and twisted spirally down the rod, the butt of which rested on the floor. As the loose roll twisted around the spindle it was reduced rapidly in size, a process that was assisted by drawing the thread away from the spindle in forceful jerks. Once a section was slim enough, it was allowed to roll up on the spindle shaft, after which a new arm's length was drawn out for spinning. When the spindle held all it could, the yarn was removed and rolled into a ball. Yarn had to be respun a number of times before it was ready for weaving.[141]

Whenever a kiva was not being used for a ceremony it was common to find there one or more weavers busily working at rude vertical looms. The upper yarn pole of the loom was fastened to the main beams of the roof, and the lower yarn pole was secured to pegs or loops driven or mortared into holes that were drilled either into the stone floor slabs or into logs that were recessed in the kiva floor. The warp was tightly stretched between these yarn beams.

The weaver squatted on the floor in front of the loom, and by his side were placed the few simple implements of his craft. Those consisted of a highly polished wooden knife, or batten, that was used for beating down the yarn; a wooden comb for pressing down the woof; and bobbins, which were merely sticks with the yarn wrapped forward and backward spirally upon them. The weaver picked out a certain number of warp threads with the batten, passed it through the bobbin, beat the yarn home with infinite patience, and so continued, making slow headway.[142]

There were several reasons that the kiva was favored by the weavers. First of all, they would not be bothered by active wives and children. Second, the subterranean rooms were cool in the summer and warm in the winter, and the light streaming down through the hatchway passed across the surface of the web, allowing the stitches to be seen to good advantage. Third, the kiva ceiling was high enough to allow the stretching of the warp to the full length of a blanket, which could not be done in the low living rooms of most houses. As stated earlier, the ceiling heights of dwellings averaged only 7 feet (2.1 m), while those of the kivas averaged 8 feet (2.4 m). Nevertheless, men did set up looms in their houses also, and they could often be found working at these looms in the evenings. Besides, present-day vertical looms often are portable, and in the summer some are set up outdoors under or alongside the cool, shady rock ledges close to the villages. Such areas always become well known, and they are thought of as sacred locations set aside for the weaving of ceremonial garments.

Belts, garters, and hair tapes were woven on a second type of loom. This one was quite small and provided with a reed or heddle frame. Usually, these

Hopi man weaving a woman's dress on an upright loom.

were employed by women weavers. The belt loom was actually a kind of harness, for the warp was stretched out either between the weaver's feet or between a wall hook and a yoke that extended across her back. The wool yarn
used for belts was obtained from traders. Hough thought the old belts were
"marvels of design" and among the most pleasing of the art works of the
Hopi.[143]

A third type of loom is an upright version of the waist loom just described.
According to Nancy Fox it is used to manufacture tubular strips that, when the
warp is cut, are twice as long as the height of the loom.[144]

Braided sashes are plaited on a specialized type of horizontal loom.[145]

Hopi weaving is still done by the men. A few women make woolen blankets and weave belts, garters, and sashes. The men card and spin the cotton
and wool, and the women usually prepare and apply the dyes. Ruth Simpson
says that in former times indigo was obtained by trade from Mexico, while
other dyes were made from minerals and plants.[146] These were replaced in
historic times by synthetic indigo, bayeta cloth, inferior aniline, and other
chemical dyes introduced by white traders. The brilliant colors seen on embroidered pieces are rarely applied to blankets and other items of regular use.
For these, somber aniline or native colors are still preferred, as they have been
through the centuries.

Whether the Hopi works with native cotton, sheep's wool, or commercial
yarn, the technical procedures are the same today as they were yesterday.

Textiles may be fashioned by a simple straight weave, by a diagonal twill,
by the diamond twill, or by braiding. The techniques of twill weaving are very
old, and the Hopi men are masters in their use, employing subtle variations of
style to give the textiles the distinctive, decorative quality of damask. Many of
the twilled patterns are woven into the textiles without changes in woof color,
but other textiles are decorated with woven patterns in divers colors. Blankets
receive stripes and panels in blue, black, and brown. Some ceremonial textiles
are decorated with bands of red and black woof in symbolic elements woven
into end panels. When embroidered decorations are applied, the native stitching is done with needles made from the points of yucca leaves or cactus spines,
or from pieces of wood or bone. Some of the finest examples of embroidery
are done on the women's bridal robes after they have been used for their primary purpose. Brocading is practiced by the Hopi in the decorating of ceremonial sashes with conventionalized Katcina designs. Further reference to the
brocaded men's dance sash will be made when the Katcina ceremonial costume
is described. Some articles are made by braiding the cotton or woolen yarn,
and the wedding sash is an excellent illustration of the braiding technique.

The Hopi no longer grow as much cotton as they did, preferring to purchase the long-staple kind produced in southern Arizona, and they can purchase cotton string at the trading posts. Cotton ceremonial garments include
men's sashes and kilts, women's robes and wedding sashes, and maiden's
shawls. Woolen garments are accepted apparel for dress occasions and even
for some ceremonies. Apparel has changed materially during the last quarter
century. The white man's clothing is worn for daily purposes, while the ev-

eryday clothing of other generations has become the ceremonial attire of the Katcina today—with this exception, that the conservative Hopi still wear the traditional garments of their ancestors on special dress occasions and when ceremonies are held in the villages. The present-day adult Hopi costume is identical to that worn by all working people in the United States: cotton shirts, Levi's, and work shoes for the men; cotton house dresses, shawls, shoes and stockings for the women. The boys and girls dress as do all other schoolchildren. Common in all the mesa-top villages are Pendleton blankets and Czechoslovakian shawls. The oldest garments still being made and worn by the Hopi are a few yucca fiber sandals, G-strings, breechclouts, and, for ceremonial use, rabbit-skin robes of the type known to the Southwestern Indians for more than a thousand years. The women still cut the rabbit skins into strips and wrap them around heavy fiber cords, which are then sewn together.

The breechclout is the only traditional undergarment still worn by Hopi men. Made of cotton or wool, it is about eighty inches long, eighteen inches wide, and brown or black. The ends are sometimes dyed dark blue. With the advent of Spanish and Mexican influence, Hopi men began to wear white cotton trousers made with individual legs that were tied to a belt at the waist; the breechclout was worn outside. The trousers, velveteen jackets, leather or woolen leggings, and moccasins constituted the Hopi man's costume when he dressed up in traditional style. However, trousers are seldom worn by modern ceremonial participants. One exception is Natachka, the ogre, who wears dark blue pants. Velveteen jackets worn for dress reflect the influence of the Hopi woolen shirt and Spanish shell jacket. In prehistoric times Hopi men wore cotton shirts made in a simple poncho style. These old-style shirts are seldom woven today, but some that have been cut from cotton robes can still be seen. In historic times the men began to use a three-piece woolen shirt. To make this, they folded the largest piece in half and cut a poncho-style opening in the center of the fold for the head. At first they tied two smaller pieces of woolen cloth, and later sewed them, to the sides of the larger piece to serve as sleeves.

Until recently every Hopi male had a woolen "wearing blanket" to throw over his shoulders, but today such a blanket is seldom used. The men's blanket was finely woven of black and white yarns. The central areas were done in a diagonal twill weave, and the borders in a diamond twill. The boys' blankets were similar in style, but were brown and white, done in a simple straight weave.

The earlier blanket consisted of stripes running the short way of the blanket. Some had a white background with groups of dark stripes, others had blue and black stripes interspersed with an occasional light stripe. Later, the Hopi developed a plaid in black and white.[147] Domestic blankets are prepared today in a tapestry weave and decorated with parallel stripes. Such blankets are common household items and are favored as bedcovers.

Ceremonial garments are worn for both the open and the closed halves of the ceremonial cycle,* but unmasked male dancers, who appear in the closed season, also wear kilts of several types, including the short, ceremonial cotton

*The costume of the masked Katcina impersonators is discussed on page 108.

type decorated with two panels of embroidered and multicolored symbolic designs. The kilts are approximately fifty inches long and twenty inches wide, and they are worn after the manner of wraparound skirts. Nondecorated cotton kilts of this nature are traded or sold to men of other pueblos, who apply their own designs. Kilts less frequently used include those fashioned from horsehair, yucca leaves, wool, and deerskin. Other articles of male apparel include a white cotton sash, woven woolen belts, and ceremonial mantles of cotton cloth decorated with painted designs.

Details of wearing apparel vary with the ceremony and with the village, and they are far too numerous for discussion here, but a few of the most important are worth noting: hair-ties made of cotton cord are wrapped around the gathered hair to make the *chongo;* individual strands of yarn are used as garters or leg bands; anklets of cloth and leather are decorated with evergreen, horsehair, colored yarn, and porcupine quills; yarn or leather armbands are fashioned, into which evergreen boughs may be stuck; pendant fox skins are fastened to the belt at the back, as in the case of the traditional Katcina costume; velvet shirts are worn, bandoliers are hung over the right shoulder; rattles are either carried, tied to the legs, or worn elsewhere on the costume.

The colors most commonly used in Hopi weaving are white, red, blue, green, yellow, black, and brown. Most of the colors are those available in commercially dyed yarns, but some vegetable dyes are still made, and kaolin is obtained from local sources and rubbed into garments to whiten them.

The most characteristic article of Hopi women's clothing in historic times has been the woolen dress, or manta. It is rectangular and includes two types of weave: the black or dark-brown central area is done in a diagonal twill; the broad blue or black borders are executed in a diamond or zigzag weave. The two long edges are brought together and loosely sewn along the right side. A slit is made in the fold for the right arm to pass through, and the left shoulder and arm are completely exposed. The dress hangs from the right shoulder and reaches to the knees. An average dress is about four feet long and three and a half feet wide. The dress is occasionally used as a blanket or mantle, and it is a popular item at all the pueblos of Arizona and New Mexico. Even today, some of the conservative women use these dresses for daily wear and, as has been noted, brides wear them under their wedding robe.* The earlier belts were made of yucca fiber and cotton, but belts now are woven solely of wool. Women's belts are narrow compared to sashes. They are from three to five inches wide, and long enough to wrap twice around the waist and still leave ends to hang down. Most are from five to seven feet in length. Favored colors are red, green, and white, although many colors are actually used to produce a variety. The weave is very tight, and the patterns are geometric. Symbolism is employed, but in a limited way.

Maidens wear beautiful white wool or cotton shawl blankets woven in a diagonal twill. Most are about thirty-six by forty-four inches. The ends are decorated with bands of bright red and blue, usually done in a diamond twill. The blanket may be worn over both shoulders, but the traditional manner is

---

*The Hopi woman's wedding robe and braided sash have already been discussed on page 32.

Left, woman in native woven dress and belt sash. *Top right*, men's brocaded dance kilt. *Middle right*, anklet (or ankle band) rawhide, canvas cover, and thread design. *Bottom right*, pair of men's dance armbands, double thickness of rawhide painted turquoise blue.

to wear it over the right shoulder and under the left arm, and it is always worn in this manner while the wearer is sharing as an observer in religious ceremonies. Some Katcina impersonators also wear the shawl. The only native footgear most Hopi women possess is the pair of white moccasins made for their wedding.

Hopi men still wear moccasins, and in 1896, Hough discovered that, without them, the men could not run well over the yielding sand. Since there was no village shoemaker, every man had either to make his own or to go barefoot. Frequently in the villages one met a Hopi chewing at the rawhide and busily plying his awl and sinew while he went gadding about. Just before the Snake Dance, when every Snake performer had to provide a pair of new moccasins for himself, this art was very much in evidence.

The moccasin-making Hopi took pride in hiding his stitches, and his sewing was exceptionally good in spite of the crude tools of his craft. He prepared

Moccasin styles and patterns. *1*, men's and boys'. *2*, pair of boys' moccasins. *3*, women's wraparound. Until modern times, for daily situations women and children usually went barefooted. From Underhill, 1946.

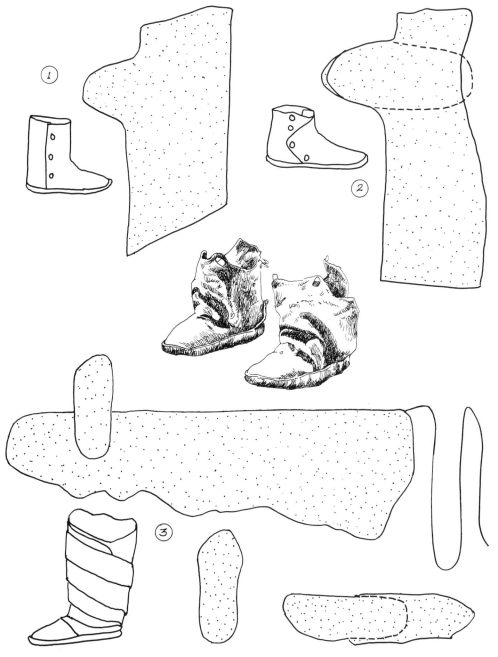

the leather with the same skill he displayed in other crafts. The simplest way of giving color to the leather was to rub red ocher or other clay into the soft-tanned skin, as was seen in the red moccasins of the Snake dancers. A warm brown might be given to the leather, with an infusion of the bark of the water birch, and a black dye was made by burning piñon resin with crude native alum. Sometimes moccasins were dyed with aniline red or blue. To manufacture a pair of moccasins, a piece of well-curried cowhide, preferably from the back of the animal, was obtained. The outline of the foot was marked out on it and a margin was left by the cutter for the turning up of the sole. This is all the moccasin maker seemed to require, and although his formula for the height of the instep was not divulged, it was effective, because moccasins were made to fit with greater art than was displayed by many Caucasian shoemakers. The soles were buried in damp sand to make them pliable, and the front section of the top was sewn around the edge, reaching about to the ankle bones. The moccasin was then turned inside out and the ankle section sewn on. Tie strings were added, or if special style was desired, silver buttons made by Navajo from dimes or quarters took the place of the ties.[148] Cowhide was used for the moccasins because, as I have mentioned earlier, overgrazing by domestic animals had caused the deer to move. By 1896, the Hopi already lived a very long way from the range of the deer, but hunting parties went in search of them. Deerskin and buffalo hides were obtained also through trade with the Navajo, Havasupai, and other neighbors, such as the Rio Grande Pueblos. Deerskin remained in demand, in particular for brides' white wedding moccasins—the long wraparound type that reached to the knee.

Moccasins in all pueblos except Taos and Picuris have a hard upturned sole, formerly of buffalo hide, now of cowhide. The hide is cut an inch or so larger than the wearer's foot. It is then moistened and turned up around the edges, and it hardens in this position. Around the toe it must be crimped into shape. The upper is sewed to it with invisible stitches of sinew, which do not go all the way through the leather of either piece. The upper is of buckskin, dyed a brownish red with mountain mahogany and sumac, or made white with clay. It always reaches above the ankle, and sometimes halfway up the calf. It may be fastened by buckskin thongs passed through slits in the upper, or by silver buttons or by dimes or quarters used as such in the Navajo manner. Although each man used to make his own moccasins, he may now trade for them with specialists.[149]

In a second male style, the moccasin upper is all in one piece. The curved part forms the toe and is sewed to the toe of the sole. The edge is then sewed to the sole along the outer side and around the heel until it joins the toepiece. This leaves a projection standing up as a tongue. In the completed moccasin, the point of the longer extension buttons over on the outside. The upper is not sewed together but only to the sole.[150]

A third male style is made by cutting the previous model closer to the toe, making a moccasin that comes halfway up the calf or more and buttons in a straight line, like a gaiter. Or it can be tied at three or more points with leather thongs.[151]

The Tewa at Hano fashion an upper that is in two pieces. The toepiece is sewed around the toe of the sole. The narrower, less regularly cut part of the toepiece stands up loose as a tongue. A large piece is then sewed around the heel of the sole, so that one point on its shorter side overlaps another point on the sole. Yet another point then folds over on the outside of the foot, where it may be buttoned or tied.[152]

The woman's moccasin worn in the majority of the pueblos has an upper that is in two pieces, the larger of which is not shaped but is wound around the leg like a puttee. The toepiece is sewed to the upturned sole. The rest of the toepiece stands up loose, as a tongue. The upper is a strip three or four feet long, made of half a buckskin. It is cut straight on one side but may be irregular on the other, growing slightly wider toward one end. Toward the narrow end, a niche is cut in to fit around the heel and is sewed so that one of its points overlaps a point of the toepiece, already sewed to the sole, and another of its points overlaps a second point of the toepiece. This is all the sewing that is done. When the wearer puts the boot on, the loose point is folded over the tongue, and the long strip is wound round and round the leg toward the inside, finally being tied at the knee with a long string.[153]

CERAMICS

Pottery, baskets, and plaques compose most of the household and ceremonial utensils used by the Hopi. Mention was made earlier of the potter Nampeyo and her husband, Lesou, in connection with Sikyatki. Walter Hough had the rare opportunity of getting to know Nampeyo and her family, and he watched one day as she brought into being some of her splendid ware.

He says that everyone who visited Tusayan would bring away as a souvenir some of the pottery of Nampeyo, who lived with Lesou in her parents' house at Hano, the little Tewa village on the great Walpi mesa near the gap. The house belonged to Nampeyo's mother according to Pueblo property right, and in it she and her husband, both aged and ruddy Tewa, lived amicably with their children and grandchildren, as was usual among the Peaceful People. The house below the mesa topped with a glowing red iron "government" roof was Nampeyo's, who thus had two houses, but she spent most of her time in the parental dwelling.

Hough found Nampeyo to be a remarkable woman, "barefoot, bonnetless, and clad in her traditional costume." She was the sole survivor in Hano of the generations of women artists who had deposited the products of their handicraft in the care of the dead. Yet, in the household her aged father and mother remained the final authorities on the interpretation of ancient symbolic or cult representations in art. Nampeyo carefully copied on paper the decorations of all available ancient pottery for future use. Her archaeological methods were further shown by her quest for the clays used by the excellent potters of old Sikyatki, and by her emulation of their technique.

Left, Nampeyo at work, from a Southwest Museum photograph. *Middle*, Nampeyo jar. *Top right*, Sikyatki polychrome. *Lower right*, modern Hopi jar by Priscilla Namingha Nampeyo.

One noon under the burning August sun, Doctor Fewkes and Hough climbed the East Mesa, the former to attend the Flute Ceremony at Walpi and the latter with an appointment to "pry" into the pottery secrets of Nampeyo. In the house, pleasantly cool and shaded, sat the old couple and Lesou. The baby was secured to its board for its afternoon nap, while Lesou spun. Nampeyo was there, prepared to display her talent. Samples of various clays were at hand, and Hough was initiated into the qualities of the *hisat chuoka*, or ancient clay, white, unctuous, and fragrant, to which the ancient Sikyatki potters owed the perfection of their ware; the reddish clay, *siwu chuoka*, also from Sikyatki; the hard, iron-stained clay, *choku chuoka*, a white clay with which vessels were coated for finishing and decoration and which came from about twelve miles southeast of Walpi. In contrast with Nampeyo's four clays, the Hopi women used only two, a gray body clay, *chaka-butska*, and a white slip clay, *kutsatsuka*.

Nampeyo transferred a handful of well-soaked ancient clay from a bowl on the floor by her side to a smooth, flat stone, like those found in the ruined pueblos. The clay was thrust forward by the base of the right hand and brought back by the hooked fingers, the stones, sticks, and hairs being carefully removed. After sufficient working, the clay was daubed on a board, which was carried out and slanted against the house to dry. In a short time the clay was transferred from the board to a slab of stone, perhaps because the clay after drying to a certain degree adhered better to stone than to wood. Shortly the clay was ready to work, and the plastic mass was ductile under the fingers of the potter.

Nampeyo set out first to show the process of coiling a vessel. The even "ropes" of clay were rolled out from her smooth palms in a marvelous way. The concave dish called *tabipi,* in which she began the coiled vessel and which turned easily on its curved bottom, seemed to be the nearest approach of the Pueblos to the potter's wheel. As the vessel was a small one, the coiling proceeded to the finish and the interims of drying, as in the manufacture of large jars, were not necessary. Then gourd smoothers, *tuhupbi,* were employed to close up the coiling grooves, and were always backed from the outside or inside by the fingers. Finally the smooth "green" vessel was set aside to dry.

A toy canteen was begun by taking a lump of clay which, by modeling, soon assumed the shape of a low vase. With a small stick, a hole was punched through each side, a roll of clay was doubled for the handles, and the ends were thrust through the holes and smoothed down inside the vase, through the opening. The neck of the canteen was inserted in a similar way. To close the opening in this soft vessel from the outside, Nampeyo threw a coil around the edge of the opening, pressing the layers together, gradually drawing in, making the orifice smaller until it presented a funnel shape. Then the funnel was pressed toward the body of the canteen, the edges closed together, soldered, and smoothed, and just like that it was done and all traces of handling were hidden. Anyone knowing the difficulties appreciated this surprisingly dexterous piece of manipulation. Afterward, Nampeyo made a small vase-shaped vessel, by modeling alone, without the addition of coiling as in the shaping of the canteen.

The ware, when it became sufficiently dry, had to receive a wash of the white clay called *hopi chuoka* or *kutsatsuka,* which burned white. Thereupon it was carefully polished with a smooth pebble, shining from long use, and was ready for decoration. The use of the glaring-white slip clay as a ground for decoration was probably brought from the Rio Grande by the Tewa, since ancient Hopi ware was much more artistic, being polished on the body or paste, which usually blended in harmony with the decoration.

Nampeyo exhibited samples of her paints, which consisted only of red and dark brown. The red paint was yellow ocher, called *sikyatho,* and it turned red on firing. It was mixed on a concave stone with water. The dark brown paint was made from *toho,* an iron stone brought from a distant mesa. It was ground on a slab with a medium made from the seed of the tansy mustard *(Sisymbrium canescens).* Each of the brushes was a single strip of *mohu (yucca glauca),* and one brush was used for each color. With these slender means and without measurement, Nampeyo rapidly covered the vessels with designs, either geometrical or conventionalized, human or cult, figures or symbols. The narrow brush, held like a painter's striper, was effective for fine lines. In broad lines or wide portions of the decoration, the outlines were sharply defined and the spaces were filled in. No mistakes were made, for emendation and correction were impossible.

Quite opportunely the next day, an invitation to see the burning of pottery came to Hough from an aged potter who resided at the Sun Spring. "When the great Hopi clock reached the appointed place in the heavens," the bowed yet active woman was found getting ready for the important work of firing the ware. In the heap of cinders, ashes, and bits of rock left from former firings, she scooped out a concave ring. Nearby was a heap of slabs of dry sheep's droppings, brought down in the indispensable blanket. In the center of the concave kiln floor a heap of this fuel was ignited with the aid of some frayed cedar bark and a borrowed match from the "people of the far water," the name by which white men were known. When the fire was well established, it was gradually spread over the floor close to the margin of the ring, and decorated bowls brought from the house were set up around it, with the concave sides toward the fire. Meanwhile, the potter brought, in her blanket, a back load of friable sandstone from a neighboring hillock.

Under the first heat, the vessels turned from white to purple gray or lavender, gradually assuming a lead color. They were soon heated enough and were ready for the kiln. Guarding her hand by the interposition of a fold of the blanket, the potter set the vessels, now quite unattractive, aside, raked the fire flat, and laid thereon fragments of stone at intervals as rests or stilts for the ware. Larger vessels were piled on top of smaller vessels, and all were arranged as compactly as possible. Piece by piece, dexterously as a mason, the potter built around the vessels a wall of fuel, narrowing at the top, till a few slabs completed the dome of the structure, itself kiln and fuel.

Care was taken not to allow the fuel to touch the vessels, for a discoloration of the ware would result. Gradually the fire from below crept up the walls till the interior was aglow and the ware became red-hot. Little attention was now needed except for closing burned-out apertures with new pieces of fuel; the potter, who before, during the careful and exact dispositions, had been giving little ejaculations as though talking to a small child, visited the kiln intermittently from the house nearby. She sought refuge there from the penetrating, unaromatic smoke and the blazing sun.

Hough concludes by saying that the Hopi had an odd superstition that if anyone spoke above a whisper during the burning of pottery the spirit inhabiting the vessel would cause it to break. He thought the potter had this in mind while she whispered, using all her blandishments to induce the small spirits to be good. "She remarked that when the sun should hang over the brow of the mesa at the height indicated by her laborious fingers, the ware would be baked, the kiln a heap of ashes, the yellow decoration a lively red and the black a dark brown on a rich cream-color ground. Next day, with true foresight, she brought her quaint wares to the camp and made a good bargain for them, incidentally asking, 'Matches all gone?' "[154]

The rarity of Hough's experience with Nampeyo and the aged potter can be appreciated only in the light of Fewkes's remarks concerning the state of the ceramic art in 1891. He says that the decoration of pottery among the living Hopi had practically been abandoned, and that help in decoration could only be had by copying the pottery found in ancient ruins. But only one or two women were imitating ancient patterns in pottery, and their products were distinctly inferior to the ancient wares.[155]

Fewkes mentions in the same discussion a certain man, known to Americans as "Morphy," who lived in Walpi and made decorated tiles. "Although a man, he wore woman's clothes throughout life and performed a woman's duties." This is the only reference I've come across to a Hopi method of dealing with transsexuals, who, apparently, were rarely found in Tusayan.

We know that pottery-making has been practiced by the Anasazi for about fifteen centuries. Yet, in most of the pueblos, the ceramic craft became for a time almost a lost art, and even among the Hopi, the heritage is strong today only on First Mesa, where the Tewa are its leading exponents. Pottery is made at Hano, Sichomovi, and Walpi, and in the village of Polacca.

Hopi women still use the ancestral quarries, where they break out lumps of clay and carry them back to the villages to pulverize, sift, and knead. Metates and manos are used to pulverize the clay, and the vessels are made from long coils, beginning with a base built in a form—usually the bottom of another vessel. Surfaces are smoothed with a piece of glass or metal and, when they are dry, the vessels are given a slip and polished with a tiny pebble. Most vessels are decorated. The finished products are fired in an oxidizing atmosphere, beneath heaped-up fuel cakes of impacted sheep-droppings. Simpson states that evidence indicates Hopi women have fired their pottery in an oxidizing atmosphere for about seven hundred years. Prior to that time, a reducing atmosphere predominated.[156]

The oldest Hopi pottery types recovered are black-on-white and red-and-black-on-orange wares dated prior to A.D. 1300. Later strata yielded, in order, black-on-red pottery of the fourteenth century; Jeddito yellow wares of the fourteenth, fifteenth, and sixteenth centuries; Sikyatki orange and yellow pottery of the fifteenth, sixteenth, and seventeenth centuries; and the later "Mission" and "Early Modern" pottery. The contemporary ceramic period has been adapted from pottery of Sikyatki style.[157] The pottery types that are peculiar to the Hopi postdate A.D. 1300. Jeddito yellow consists of a series of wares with a yellow background and geometric decoration in black and brown. Realistic decorative motives were exceedingly rare, but the quality of the pottery was excellent, and the designs were distinctive. The Jeddito wares suggest an early southern culture influence, followed by a later eastern influence; together they evolved into the Sikyatki style, where Hopi ceramic artistry reached its height at Sikyatki, the type site, and in the other villages where this ware was produced until the middle of the seventeenth century. The yellow-orange background and conventionalized bird, insect, and animal designs are so distinctive and so closely associated in the public mind with the Hopi that this pottery is a prime culture trait.[158]

During the Mission Period, an era of ceramic decadence began. Finished

84

pieces became scarce, the paste was soft, the vessels' walls were thick, and the designs were crude. A Zuñi influence is plainly reflected in many vessels of this period. From late in the seventeenth century until late in the nineteenth, the Hopi pottery craft continued to deteriorate, until the art of making fine wares was almost lost. Then, at the close of the nineteenth century, a new era began with Nampeyo, who copied the technique, the colors, and the designs, and thus inaugurated the renaissance of the Sikyatki ceramic period. Nampeyo died in July 1942, but she left her legacy (with her children and other women) of beautiful pottery in the villages of First Mesa. Elsewhere a cruder pottery continued to be made. Today, Sikyatki-style ware is still manufactured, though in smaller quantity. The women no longer copy the ancient patterns, but create new ones in the ancient style. Thus the contemporary movement is described as a "reversion to" rather than a "duplication of" Sikyatki pottery-making.[159]

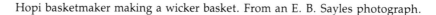

Hopi basketmaker making a wicker basket. From an E. B. Sayles photograph.

The modern smooth ware made on Second and Third mesas is characterized by a white or yellow slip and by comparatively crude decoration in black and red. Throughout the Hopi villages, potters fashion utility wares—cooking pots and other nondecorated vessels. Hopi pottery distinguished by a yellow or orange background has not been slipped. Slipped vessels have a red or white background that is derived as follows: fine-quality white or red clay is thinned with water until it has the consistency of cream, then it is applied to the surface of the vessel in several coats. Firing changes the color of the slipped surfaces and tends to accentuate the red element. The beautiful mottled quality of the unslipped ware results from varying the intensity of the heat that reaches different parts of the surface. Yellow, brown, ocher, and red are obtained in the decoration by firing ocherous paint. Black is derived from a mixture of black clay, ground hematite, and the boiled juice of tansy mustard. The slip is applied with tufts of rabbit fur, and decoration is executed with brushes of yucca leaf. These are split to size, and then the end is shredded with the teeth.

The most characteristic forms in modern Hopi ceramics are broad, shallow bowls with incurving rims and interior decoration; jars with broad, flat shoulders, small openings, and exterior decoration; canteens with one flattish side and one convex side in the form of a human breast; and bowls with outcurving rims and interior decoration. Also included are: flat, decorated tiles; utilitarian dippers; ceremonial bowls with terraced rims; ceremonial dippers; pipes; rattles; paintpots; children's toy replicas of vessels; miscellaneous pieces; and wares for tourist consumption. There are also undecorated cooking pots and very large storage jars; some of the pots and jars are coated with piñon gum to make them waterproof. Whenever such utility jars are made, ground white sandstone is added to the clay as temper.[160]

BASKETRY

Basketmaking assumed a lesser role in the Pueblo I through III periods, and then there was a minor renaissance in a few pueblos that began about A.D. 1200 or 1300. According to Gene Weltfish, Fewkes found fragments of coiled basketry at Chavez Pass and at Chevelon Ruin.[161] In 1896, basketmaking at Hopi was being apportioned to those who had the skill to do it. The women of the three towns on First Mesa did not make baskets at all, those of the Second Mesa fashioned only coiled baskets, and the women of Oraibi wove wicker baskets exclusively. Thus, there was no difficulty in saying just where a Hopi basket came from, and there was also no excuse for not recognizing the Hopi specimens at first glance, for they had a strong individuality that separated them from all other baskets made by Indians.

The most skillful basketmaker of the Second Mesa, Kuchyeampsi, taught Hough a great deal about the construction of coiled baskets. It took some time and patience for him to discover that the grass whose stems she gathered for the body of the coil was named *takashu*, which botanists knew as *Hilaria*

Elderly Hopi woman shelling corn in a large tray-type yucca basket.

jamesii, and that the strips that she sewed over and joined to the coil were from the leaves of the useful *mohu (yucca glauca).* The yucca leaves were stripped, and split with the thumbnail to uniform size; some were dyed various colors, for which anilines were principally used. One had to have an eye for the colors of the natural leaves of the yucca to select the yellow or yellowish green of the old leaves, the vivid green of the young leaves, and the white of the heart leaves, for the basket weaver used all these in her work.

The strips were buried in moist sand, and the grass was moistened. To make a plaque, the slender coil at the center was built up of waste bits from the leaf stripping and wrapped with yucca strips; then a few first stitches were taken with the encircling coil, since the bone awl was too clumsy for continuous stitching at the outset. After the third round the bone awl was plied, continuously piercing through under the coil and taking in the stitches beneath strips. As a hole was made, the yucca strip was threaded through and drawn tight on the grass coil, and this patient work continued until the plaque was complete. The patterns that appeared on the baskets were stored up in the maker's brain and unfolded as the coil progressed with the same accuracy as was evinced by the pottery decorator. The finish of the end of the coil gave an interesting commentary on Hopi beliefs. It was said that the woman who left the coil end unfinished did not complete it because doing so would close her life and no more children would bless her.

At Oraibi one could watch the women as they made tray baskets. Three or four slender sumac twigs were wickered together side by side at the middle and a similar bundle was laid across the first at right angles. Then dyed branches of a desert plant known as "rabbit brush" were woven in and out between the twigs, and as the basket progressed other radial rods were added until the basket was large enough. The basketmaker finished the edge by bending over the sumac ribs, forming a core around which she wrapped strips of yucca. One could only admire the accuracy with which the designs were kept in mind and woven into the structure of the basket with splints of various colors or strips of tough yucca. The translation of a design into the radiating sewing of the coiled basket or the horizontal filling of the wicker basket illustrated the necessity of different treatments, contrasting with the freedom of the potter in decorating the smooth surface of her ware. So far as was known, the Hopi women never failed to apply their traditional designs, however intricate. Frequently these represented mythical birds, butterflies, and clouds.

Certain of the Hopi villages were noted for their local manufactures. Thus Walpi, Sichomovi, and Hano were practically the only towns where pottery was made, Second Mesa towns were headquarters for coiled baskets, and Oraibi furnished wicker baskets. Hough thought the meaning of this might be that these arts belonged to clans, who had preserved them and knew the secrets, and that with the dying out of the workers or migration of the clans the arts either disappeared or were transformed. Another factor that suggested itself was the local abundance and quality of the required materials in the surrounding plains and mountains.

Basketry had at least as many uses as pottery among the Hopi, and a number of kinds besides the familiar plaques with symbolical decoration were already being sought by collectors. Field crops were borne to the mesa houses in carrying baskets, resembling panniers, which were worked from wicker over a frame of two bent sticks crossed at right angles. In the house the coiled and wicker trays were heaped high with cornmeal, and baskets for parched corn and for sifting were always found near the corn-grinding stones. In the bread-baking room was the coarse, though effective, piki tray, and occasionally one could still see a neatly made floor mat. The thin checker mat of ancient days had long since disappeared, but, as we know, formerly the dead were wrapped in such mats before they were placed in the earth. Over the fireplace was a hood of basketry plastered to prevent burning. The wicker cradles to which infants were bound must not be forgotten. Several small globular wicker baskets for various purposes were also displayed among the household belongings. The mat of grass stems in which the wedding blanket was folded was also a kind of basketry, as were the twined mats for covering the hatchway of the kiva and the wickerwork fence around the fields.[162]

The Hopi also were great collectors of baskets from other tribes. One often saw in Hopi houses the water bottles coated with pitch and the well-made basket bowls from the Havasupai of Cataract Canyon, the Pimas of southern Arizona, and other tribes touched by Hopi commerce. Parts of old masks used in the ceremonies were of basketry, generally a section cut from a Ute basket bowl, which showed one of the most interesting employments of baskets among the Hopi. The highly decorated trays might also be said to have a sacred character from their frequent appearance in the ceremonies, where they were used to contain prayer sticks, meal, and paraphernalia. Appropriately, the women's ceremonies displayed many baskets on the altars, and in the public dances each woman carried a bright plaque. On this account these ceremonies were commonly called Basket dances. A frequent sight in a Hopi village was a woman carrying a heaped-up plaque of meal of her own grinding as a present to some friend. This usually happened on the eve of a ceremony, and an equivalent present was religiously brought in return. The Hopi valued their baskets, and they fully appreciated their beauty, often using them for wall decoration.[163]

Basketry is one of the most ancient arts still practiced by the Hopi. Women are encouraged to continue this work by government schools, traders, and tourist demand. The weavers follow both the coiled and the woven methods of basketmaking. They have evolved many subtypes of these techniques and have learned to make baskets of many kinds. Distinctive characteristics are apparent in the products from the various Hopi mesas. For example, women from Oraibi are famous for their wickerwork basketry, while the basketmakers of Second Mesa fashion a unique kind of thick-coiled basket.

Among the less distinctive types of Hopi basketry are wicker "peach baskets" and other twined containers made for use in the home; coiled and twilled-twined gathering baskets; coiled, watertight jars made of willow splints; twined, twilled, and coiled utility baskets made in various forms; headstraps, headrings, and breast bands; rough twilled baskets and mats; and coarse-wicker trays.[164]

The most important and characteristic Hopi basketry wares are the yucca-fiber checker baskets and trays. The yucca basket is a utility basket produced in many forms and for many uses: as sifters; winnowing trays; and containers for shelled corn, beans, seeds, yarn, and small utensils. To make these, the leaves are plaited, and the rim is produced by turning the ends of the leaves down over a sumac frame, binding them in place with strands of yucca, and trimming them. Wire frames are often used in place of sumac, and twilled plaiting is the accepted technique. Designs are achieved by this twilling and by the use of green, white, and yellow elements. Both Basketmaker and early Pueblo influences are reflected in modern Hopi yucca-fiber baskets, which are made in all the mesa-top villages.

The coiled ware of Second Mesa consists of containers, trays, and plaques. These have a bundle foundation of grass or shredded narrow-leaf yucca, and the foundation coils are wrapped with split-yucca elements. They are ornamented with carefully woven designs that are geometric, pictographic, and symbolic—in most instances less elaborate than those on the wicker baskets. Katcina figures constitute so typical and distinctive a decorative element that they are quickly recognized as a mark of Hopi artistry. The decoration is, of course, intimately related to Hopi religion.

The natural color of the yucca is retained as a background for all designs. Native colors used for the figures are black, yellow, red-brown, orange, and green. Black dye comes from sunflower seeds, navy beans, soot, coal, resin, and alum. Yellow dye is obtained from ocher, sunflowers, and the flowers of rabbit brush; occasionally yellowed yucca is employed. Red-brown dyes come from many sources, including *se-e-ta,* alder bark, sumac berries, cockscomb flowers, and hematite (iron ocher). Orange dye comes from saffron flowers. Green yucca fiber is used without dye. Dyes are applied by boiling the fibers in the dye and then hanging them in the smoke of burning wood, which "sets" the colors.[165] Aniline dyes added, for a time, blues and brighter greens to the available native colors, but they were a fad that did not survive, and the artists of Second Mesa returned to their natural colors, which are softer in tone and much more attractive. Earth colors of clay or rock are ground on a flat stone and then mixed with an oil made by chewing squash seeds. The paint is applied with a piece of fur or a rabbit's foot, either before or after the twigs are woven into a basket.[166]

In prehistoric times, coiled baskets were made only in the form of plaques and trays. Today, small, coiled, covered containers are made for storage of small articles, including seeds, and containers of varying sizes are manufactured to supply the demands of traders and tourists. Third Mesa wicker baskets date as far back as A.D. 1200 and are usually made of sumac and rabbit brush, with the twigs of the latter being worked over a foundation of the former, although occasionally wild currant or willow will be utilized in place of the sumac twigs. At the central crossing, the warp elements are wrapped or woven in position; the warp stems radiate out to form a framework. Edges are finished by winding yucca over the bent ends of the sumac stems. Usually it is necessary to introduce additional warp elements about halfway between the center and the rim.

There are two classes of wicker baskets: one that is crudely made, often of undyed materials; and one that is exquisitely woven for plaques and ceremonial meal trays. Designs on the latter are more complex and varied than those used for the coiled baskets. The most popular forms are birds, butterflies, snakes, antelope, whirlwinds, rainbows, clouds, stars, the sun, and Katcinas. Birds are common, but Katcinas are not. As on the coiled wares, designs may be conventionalized, geometric, or pictorial.

Dye colors used on wicker baskets include those listed for the coiled wares, plus blue, brown, white, pink, cerise, purple, carmine, and violet. Blue dye is derived from indigo, navy beans, larkspur flowers, sunflower seeds, shells. Brown dyes are made from *se-e-ta* blossoms, navy beans, and iron ocher. White comes from kaolin or limestone. Pink, cerise, purple, carmine, and violet dyes are derived from cockscomb flowers. The yucca elements are dyed before the work begins, being boiled in the color and then smoked over a fire of burning wool. Backgrounds are often whitened with kaolin. Aniline dyes as well as the native colors are used, although a willingness on the part of traders and tourists to pay more for baskets colored with vegetal dyes has kept the native decorative art flourishing.[167]

WOOD CARVING

The Hopi practice wood carving on such a large scale that it is a major craft. The stone knives and abraders of yesterday have been replaced by metal knives, chisels, and other tools of the white man, and woodworkers can create broad flat surfaces with comparative ease. Although cottonwood is no longer easy to find in the proper sizes, it is the favored raw material, because it is the best for Hopi needs. The inner pulp decays rapidly, and the outer shell is well suited to the making of drums and containers. Ladles, bowls, and other domestic articles are carved, but such vessels are seldom made today. Cottonwood roots are made into gaming cups, feather boxes, and domestic articles, including weaving tools, parching rods, firemaking sticks, throwing sticks, dig-

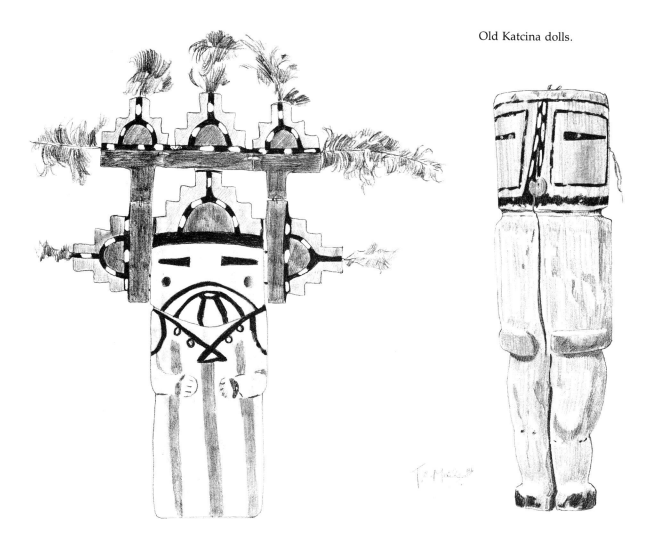

Old Katcina dolls.

ging sticks, and traps. Ceremonial articles include chief's emblems, lightning sticks, swallowing sticks, altar frames and figurines, wands, prayer sticks, mask parts, dolls, storage boxes, paddles, and other dance equipment such as the water serpents for *palulokong*.

An item that almost everyone is familiar with is the *tihu*, or Katcina doll. Katcina dolls are carved wooden figures that in earlier years were painted, and in later years have been painted and dressed to represent the Katcina impersonators who dance in the annual ceremonies. They are carved by men and according to tradition are given to infants and girls at the conclusion of dances, to be hung in their homes. Since the dolls have no spirit power, it is assumed that their principal purpose is as teaching instruments. A secondary purpose is economic, for the dolls have become extremely attractive to tourists, and many are considered as prime collector's items. The newer models sell today for anywhere from a hundred to more than a thousand dollars, and extremely old ones fetch phenomenal prices.

Although cottonwood root is becoming hard to obtain, the traditional doll is carved from this material. It carves easily and dries without splitting, although it is easily broken, and most dolls end up being glued here or there. The root is thought to have some association with the Katcina Cult, and while dolls are without power, the carvers will usually not paint one in front of children. The best Hopi dolls of former days were carved in one piece from a single large root, but as the action and size have increased, arms or legs are often glued on before the doll is painted. The Zuñi carve dolls to a lesser extent than the Hopi, but they frown upon their production for commercial gain. The Zuñi doll can sometimes be distinguished from the Hopi doll by its movable arms.

It is believed that the first Hopi dolls were made prior to 1870, and examples show that their design has evolved through several stages since then. The earliest are known as *puchtihus*. They are hardly more than flat boards with little carving, painted to represent the various Katcina masks. The *puchtihus* are still made, but they are not the dominant doll form.

About 1870, visitors from the outside began to show interest in the dolls as learning tools. With these in hand they could consider more carefully the costuming and paint variations of the actual Katcinas. The Hopi carvers were quick to take advantage and they started to add details by elaborating upon the carving. At first the masks were emphasized more, and the arms and legs were roughly shaped. A few models even depicted some action in a mild fashion, and as time passed, bits of costume in the form of fur, cloth, corn husks, hair, and feathers were added.

Shortly after the turn of the century, natural paints gave way to commercial tempera paints, and from this time on the Katcina doll was progressively given more detail in costuming and action. Most dolls produced until 1965 were sumptuously adorned and extremely expressive. Within the last years, though, an overemphasis upon the commercial market has led to a serious decline in quality. The government's ban on eagle feathers has also robbed the Katcina doll of much of its value to collectors, who always prized the Hopi carver's careful attention to detail and faithful representation. Fewer than half of the dolls appearing on the market in the last decade have been worth having.

Museums commonly include Katcina dolls in their collections, placing special emphasis upon the older dolls. One of the finest collections of old models is at the Southwest Museum in Los Angeles, California. Another excellent collection is at the Heard Museum in Phoenix, Arizona. Books on Katcina dolls are numerous. I have eight in my library, and there are several more available.

The Hopi have a museum of their own, the Tribal Museum and Cultural Center, built a few years ago at Second Mesa. It is a striking complex in Hopi architectural style, and it includes the museum, shops, a restaurant, and a motel. There are also picnic grounds nearby. Thanks in part to the efforts of anthropologists from the Museum of Northern Arizona in Flagstaff, particularly Harold S. Colton, the Hopi have steadily broadened their economic base since the 1930s through the production of excellent arts and crafts, featuring in particular silver jewelry, Katcina dolls, pottery, and baskets. Several individually owned shops are clustered around Second and Third mesas, and there is a flourishing Hopi Tribal Arts and Crafts Guild.

Some of the living Hopi artists have achieved renown in America and Europe. Among these are the painter Fred Kabotie and the silversmiths Preston Monongye and Charles Loloma.

SILVERWORK

It is thought that the Zuñi were the first Pueblos to become silversmiths, learning the craft either from Mexican traders or from Navajo. The early silver was quite heavy, and if turquoise was inset, only a few large stones were used in a given piece.

Until sometime after 1890, the Hopi obtained their silver jewelry from the Zuñi and the Navajo.[168] By 1905, men from all three mesas were engaged in silverwork. According to Margaret Wright, the style of that time was similar to that of all Indians practicing the trade in the Southwest, and it continued for the next thirty years.[169] Items included bow guards, conchas for belts, rings, pins, bracelets, and necklaces. Cast and hammered techniques were employed. Casting called for melting silver ingots and then casting the silver in sandstone molds. Hammering called for sets of iron-stamp designs, or dies, which could be hammered into silver plate made from melted coins. After 1935, the Hopi were producing silver overlay. This was accomplished by cutting design holes in a silver plate and then soldering that plate over another, so that the design became a kind of relief. Somewhere along the way, the Hopi silversmiths began to combine silver and turquoise to fashion magnificent jewelry creations. Nowadays, other kinds of stone also are set in silver, and a few artists have produced gold items that are stunning.

STONEWORK AND BONEWORK

By A.D. 1700, metal and metal tools were finding their way into Hopi country. Until that time, they used the stone tools that we know were common to all the Anasazi regions. When early Hopi men made a trip outside the village, they were always on the lookout for choice pieces of stone from which to make tools. Glasslike chert and jasper were needed for arrowheads, slivers of quartz for knives, heavy diorite for hammers, and slabs of sandstone for smoothing wood. A man either gathered his own supply of unworked stones or had a relative who did it for him. Desirable stones were kept in a storage room, awaiting the winter days when there would be time for toolmaking.

The toolmaker worked out of doors, where he could get a tough, flat stone to pound on and sand for rubbing. He had a jar of water at his side, a round, smooth stone to hammer with, a strip of buckskin to protect his hand while working, and a piece of deer-antler bone to pry flakes from stone edges. It was a pueblo rule that people made the articles they used. Women made their stone-grinding slabs and their piki ovens, and men made the hammers, knives, and arrows they would use in cutting hides, working wood, and hunting.[170]

There were two main kinds of stone tools: those for hammering and those for cutting.

Hammerstones, including axes, were lumps of heavy stone that did not split easily, like granite or diorite. These were roughly chipped into shape by hammering them with another stone. Underhill watched a Hopi craftsman as he made a hammerstone. A flat stone was first sprinkled with sand, then dipped in water and rubbed patiently over the hammering stone until it was well shaped and smooth. Finally he ground it to a fairly sharp edge, much as a knife blade is ground with water and whetstone. Anasazi hammering tools were all shaped in this way, and shallow grooves were ground above the mid-point of the stone where wooden handles could be wrapped and tied on. The handle was usually a willow branch bent on while the willow was green. Sometimes a stick of hard, green wood was split and forked at the far end, so that the two parts of the split section could be fitted along the groove at either side of the axhead and then lashed together with a leather thong or strips of yucca. With such axes Hopi men cut or pounded down small trees to serve as beams for their dwelling roofs. An Anasazi hammering tool can always be identified by the "full" groove that goes all the way around the head. Indians farther south made their grooves only three quarters of the way around. Thus, when archaeologists find a three-quarter-grooved tool in the north, they assume it got there by trade.

Cutting tools were made of stone that split easily, such as chert, jasper, quartz, chalcedony, volcanic glass, and obsidian. These brittle stones always break with a sharp, jagged edge, and the worker sharpened the edge still further by pressing an antler point or a bone sliver against the stone, near the edge, tapping it lightly until a tiny flake flew off. When these flakes were forced off in a continuous row, an edge was produced that was faintly scalloped and sharp enough to be used for a knife. Usually the men made it in a triangular shape, like an arrowhead about three inches long. They also chipped small notches at the base of the triangle, so that a wooden handle could be tied on about as an arrow shaft is tied. With this knife a man could skin an animal or remove an enemy's scalp. It would also cut hair and cut out a moccasin pattern, but one could not tailor cotton or wool garments with it. Arrow points were also used for cutting tools. A stone awl that had a long and slender point and was triangular in cross section was used to make holes in buckskin so that items could be tied together with leather thongs. A heavy stone point about a foot long was broken off to make a jagged edge and sharpened very roughly to make the pick used in breaking pieces of stones loose from rock surfaces.[171]

Deer bones also made excellent tools with very little shaping. Splinters of bone made perfect awls. They were used in basketry and for punching holes in buckskin. Also eyes were pierced in them, so that they could be used as needles. Sections of deerhorn eight or ten inches long were sharpened for use as chisels. The tip of a long, curved section was sharpened into a point so that it could be used as a pick, the favored implement for hacking out stone in the early turquoise mines. Deerhorn tools were smoothed and polished on slabs of fine sandstone, which worked as sandpaper does. Wood was sanded too, and men kept a selection of sandstone slabs of different sizes in their storerooms.[172]

Stone implements, so plentiful in the ancient villages, play a lesser role in Hopi material culture today. Arrowheads, axes, mauls, hammers, and knives seen at the mesas are found objects, retrieved from ancient sites and kept as charms or religious objects. Some of the finely wrought old axes and other artifacts are reused for pecking wall stones and for other domestic purposes, and their beauty is soon destroyed. Fetishes are still made from soft stones that have natural shapes suggesting the desired forms. Usually these need little alteration, but their meaning is accentuated with a few features, some incised lines, and paints. Such paints are derived from mineral substances, including ocher, hematite, malachite, and galena. Stone artifacts still in use include abrading and polishing stones, baking slabs, oven covers, potters' slabs, paint mortars and slabs, mortars and pestles for food pounding, hand hammers, metates, and manos. The methods used in making stone articles today are the same as those employed by the ancient Anasazi: flaking, chipping, abrading, pecking, grinding, and polishing. Stone arrowheads were replaced by metal arrowheads early in historic times, the latter reaching Tusayan through warfare and trade.

PICTOGRAPHS AND PETROGLYPHS

Fewkes believed that Tusayan pictographs and petroglyphs offered a "particularly advantageous field for research." He found hardly a trail leading to the mesas where they were not found. Most of the subject matter dealt with mythological personages or the representations of masks similar to those that

Fewkes still saw in the 1890s in religious ceremonies. The same symbolism was appearing on modern articles of Hopi manufacture, such as pottery, baskets, and clay tiles. He also found it instructive to compare his Katcina dolls with the pictographic inscriptions.

The priests of Fewkes's time were helpful sources for interpreting the pictographs and symbols in general, and Fewkes wished fervently that someone would go among the Hopi and gather all the information the priests could give. Much had already been lost, and the time when anything but a fanciful explanation could be obtained was limited. "In a short interval," he said, "the opportunity will be lost forever."[173] Some of the pictographs delineated by Fewkes in his article had already survived those who were competent to tell what they signified.[174]

The Hopi pictographs were in some respects identical with those found near Anasazi ruins, and Fewkes thought they told similar stories of Katcina dances.

SAND PAINTING AND WATERCOLOR PAINTING

Sand paintings are part of the altars of most ceremonies, and they require skilled artisans who know the traditions to obtain and prepare the earth colors. Each symbol has its prescribed color, form, position, and meaning. My altar illustrations include some of these.

Watercolor painting was introduced to the Hopi in the early twentieth century, and a number of talented artists have emerged, the most famous of whom is Fred Kabotie, who is noted for, among other things, his mural paintings in a tower at the Grand Canyon.

THE CLAN

Reference has been made in this and in earlier chapters to the Anasazi clans, and to their migration myths, or legends. It was noted that Frank H. H. Roberts placed little stock in the historicity of Anasazi myths. Parsons also thinks they have "little or no historic validity," but finds them "notable as indicating the ceremonial associations of maternal families and their clans—contemporaneous associations."[175] Assertions from such eminently qualified people can hardly be ignored, but they are at the same time troubling. Clans do exist. They did come from somewhere sometime, and as yet the sciences have deciphered remarkably few of the answers. The Pueblos have not seen fit to explain how they interpret their mythology. It may well be that the Anasazi themselves never actually thought of their legends as literal history, or even as more than embellished history, yet one is hard pressed to explain why they center their very lives so fiercely in myths if that is the case. Not many intelligent people are willing to stake their present and future existence on full-blown self-delusions. One who knows the Pueblos well does not question their intelligence, even though it is intensely infused with religion and expressed in ways often alien to those of non-Indians.

Somewhere along the way there ought to be a reconciliation of views, rather than a nourished dichotomy. Anthropology, particularly the archaeological branch, always thinks of religious and secular views and practices as evolving, from a primitive form through various stages as time passes. One of the joys of archaeology is seeking through found things to trace and measure this evolution. It is, in fact, *the* pursuit whose underlying anticipation carries the explorer through the labor and tedium that prevail between discoveries. Religious and secular views are lumped together, no distinction being made by the anthropologist: as man adapts to his environment he invents out of his own limited facilities what he needs for survival. So too, his religious life is not "given," he makes it up as he is confronted with life's exigencies.

But Indians do not as a rule think of religious views and practices as evolving. They recognize that certain minor additions to ceremonies have been made from time to time, but the essences and the greater parts are accepted as *given* by living supernatural powers at specific times and places in history. Myth to them is vibrantly real. For example, Calf Pipe Woman, the Lakota Culture heroine, is not, in their minds, an illusion that explains how they came to have the Sacred Pipe and certain of their religious views and rites. She came and she bestowed at a point in history. In the same way the Pueblos accept a historical Emergence from the Underworld, the existence of the chief Katcinas, the inception of the clans, and more. The fact that ceremonial chambers came into being at a later date would hardly be a problem for them, since they would answer that protokivas and kivas were built for ritual practice when time and place made it possible to indulge themselves in comparative economic security, and they were instructed by the spirit powers to do so.

How else does one explain why amazingly complex rituals are performed, not just because they work, but because they have *always* worked, so long as they were done without deviation? Of course, it is known that at various times one pueblo has adapted certain of its performances from another pueblo. But such adaptations, never adoptions, are seldom, if ever, looked upon in the same light as those ceremonies considered intrinsic to the pueblo. I speak now of ceremonies known to have been practiced for at least six hundred years. That may not circumscribe the entire life-span of the Anasazi, but it is an impressively long time to maintain a practice. Moreover, if a practice was in vogue at Awatovi in A.D. 1350, then a priori it had been in effect for some time before that. It seems reasonable to assume that a ritual and its paraphernalia were not recorded in sophisticated form the day it came into being.

To quote Fewkes as he describes the Walpi Flute observance: "It is demonstrable that in a complicated ceremoniology there is much mythological lore intimately connected with the ritual. This lore is known to the thinking or devout members of the priesthoods, and it is referred to by them as explanatory of ceremonials. The ritual is not to them a series of meaningless acts performed haphazard and without unity, varying in successive performances, but is fixed by immutable, prescribed laws which allow only limited variations. Modifications are due to the death of celebrants, or other circumstances equally beyond the control of the priests; and as the ritual of peoples changes very slowly, that of the Tusayan Indians is one of the least modified of their customs. Throughout the Flute ceremony there is the same rigid adherence to prescribed usages which exists in other rites, and there is the same precision year after year in the sequence of the various episodes."[176]

In another article, "Fire Worship of the Hopi Indians," Fewkes has more to say on the subject. He learned that living priests often did not know why they performed certain rites, "for they are not antiquarians and no sacred books exist among them; explanations that have survived have been transmitted by memory and have lost or have been modified much in transmitting." Individual priests had certain definite functions to perform in a great ceremony, but while they might know the meaning of these they were densely ignorant of other rites, and they often confessed that the rites are meaningless to those who perform them. "We sing our songs, say our prayers, because they have been transmitted to us by our ancestors, and they knew more than we what is good." Fewkes concludes that rites practiced for a long time are looked upon as efficacious, and that that, to the Hopi, is sufficient evidence that they are best for the purpose.[177]

Fewkes was concerned about lost meanings. He wanted to know *why* each ritual was done, and the meaning of its parts. Freely confessing a personal interest in the same thing, I must also admit that the passion for understanding is a trait of the whites, not of the Indians, where ritual is concerned. The Indians do not presume to interrogate the spirits as to why they instruct the created world to perform as it must. It is accepted that the spirits always know what is best, and if man wishes to receive their blessings he will do what is required. He will not distress his benefactors by impeding the process with questions about things his finite nature cannot fully understand anyway. He accepts that many things are simply beyond human comprehension, and that human joy is found in knowing that greater powers than one's own are doing for him what must be done. The Indian finds no shame or diminishment in admitting that he is dependent upon higher powers. It is the Way, and he does not allow pride or preoccupation to cut him off from a cornucopia of blessings. In his mind, only the foolish do that. Perforce the silly and bawdy ceremonial clown serves in some instances as a constant reminder of what man will be if he forgets or ignores who he is and what his responsibilities are.

Such a circumstance may distress our inquisitive nature, but the Indians have for good reason ceased to be concerned about what we think. They do not ask us to investigate them, they do not perform for us, and it would trouble them little if we all agreed to keep our questions to ourselves.

Of course, it must be pointed out that Indians are not entirely bereft of understanding where ritual practices are concerned. Centuries of use have brought comprehension. Certain things done make certain things happen, and the two are tied together. But even these enlightenments are given reluctantly to researchers, for one reason above all others: most scientists dispense with any possibility that a prehistoric people could possess a true relationship with a real and living God who, by various means, be they monotheistic or pantheistic, has imparted truth and tangible blessings to those who entrusted themselves wholly to Him. Virtually every missionary has adopted the same view as the scientists.

Since the traditional Indians know full well the opinions of scientists and missionaries in this regard, why then, they wonder, do we still expect them to be utterly open in revealing and explaining, insofar as they are able, their religious life? It is of utmost importance for professionals to recognize that, so long as any of them treat the Indian religions as false, in that they have relation to no true and living God, the Indians will remain silent. Consequently, as books and articles are written, Indians will continue to be projected to the reading audience as less in intelligence and quality than the so-called civilized peoples, hence never to be listened to, always to be pitied, and certainly to be converted. It is a condition untenable on the basis of Scripture itself, disastrous for Indian and white relationships, and counterproductive; it cuts the non-Indian world off from information about life and survival that it sorely needs. The time is long past for the condition to be corrected, and the accounts of Hopi and other Pueblo religions in the following pages should substantiate the argument.

It cannot be overstressed that life to the traditional Hopi, to other Pueblo families, and undoubtedly to the Anasazi in the distant past, has constituted a single unit, in which all aspects are one. Economic, social, and religious categories simply do not exist. The religious and the secular form an interrelated and inseparable unit, for all creation is looked upon as a unified system that functions according to divinely prescribed rules that were in effect while the people still lived in the Underworld before Emergence.[178]

Not surprisingly, then, government in its historic form is truly democratic. That is not to say that it has been perfect, for it has never been able to deal effectively with factionalism. There is a Hopi governmental council consisting of a village chief, a kiva chief, a war chief, a crier chief, and the heads of the clans who are also chiefs of the societies. Village laws are traditional and unwritten. In 1896 Walter Hough found infractions of the laws to be so few that it would be difficult to say what the penalties were—probably ridicule and ostracism. Theft was almost unheard of, and the taking of a villager's life by force or under the law was considered abhorrent.[179]

The government situation has been affected to an appreciable degree by the election, at the urging of the Bureau of Indian Affairs, of a Hopi Tribal Council, which met for the first time in 1937. Most of its early members were progressive, and some villages refused to recognize them, preferring to continue the historic autonomy of each Hopi village. Consequently, progress has been slow for the council, and to this day it does not truly represent all Hopi. A law-and-order code adopted in 1940 is enforced by a Tribal Court and a few policemen.

The Hopi's kinship system exemplifies their view of the ancient unified system in action. Emphasis is on kin related by blood through the mother's line only, with grouping according to clans. Each clan consists of one or more matrilineal lineages that descend from a common ancestress. The core of the lineage is a closely knit group of females consisting of a senior member, who is usually the oldest and is thought of as the "head," and her sisters, plus all their female descendants. The brothers of the female head, one of whom fills the role of the male "head," and all the male descendants of the females in the lineage are also members of the lineage. Relatives by marriage of those just mentioned do not belong to the lineage.[180]

The females of the lineage, together with their husbands and their unmarried male descendants, occupy two or more households that are, especially in the older Hopi villages, usually built adjacent to one another. When the men of the lineage marry, they go to live in the households of their wives, yet they continue to look upon the households of their mothers and sisters as their real homes. They return to these when participating in the ceremonial life of their clans and secret societies, and they return there to live in cases of divorce or the death of a wife.[181]

Hopi households are virtually independent economic units, the members of which work together for the welfare of all. The women do those tasks traditionally assigned to them: gathering, preparing, cooking, and storing the food; carrying water; cultivating gardens; making pottery and baskets; caring for children; building, cleaning, and repairing houses. Men do their traditional work: farming, hunting, weaving, working hides, gathering fuel and timber, herding, and sometimes assisting in house construction. Besides this, men and women alike are involved regularly in the ceremonial activities connected with their clans and ceremonial associations.[182]

In the Hopi kinship system, ownership is usually synonymous with use. Hence the women own their houses and virtually everything in them, together with the family springs and gardens. The children also belong to the woman, and in the event of a divorce they remain with the mother. Men own the farms, livestock, and fruit trees, but their produce belongs to the women. Men also own their personal effects, their working tools, and their personal ceremonial regalia.

One household in each clan is considered as its traditional ancestral house, and the two heads of this household are its clan leaders: the woman being the Clan Mother and real clan head, her brother being the ceremonial clan head. The focus of the clan is here. Meetings and certain of the clan rituals are held in the house, and it is here that the clan mask, certain other sacred paraphernalia, and the clan corn fetish, or tiponi, are kept and ritually cared for.

According to Parsons, when the maternal heads move their households, taking their mask and tiponi with them, the clan is thought of as moving, although not all the clan members need literally do so. In this regard, Hopi tradition dictates that members of clans with masks and tiponi, hence with ceremonies, must obtain permission to build homes away from the clan house cluster, while members of clans without ceremonies—and there are some of these—can build wherever they wish to.[183]

Each clan is closely related to a nonhuman partner, called *wuye*, which is an animal, plant, or a natural or supernatural phenomenon that gives the clan its name, its "whip" or curing power, and its protection in return for certain related services. This association is very old, dating back to migration days. While the people were traveling about in units of one or two clans each, they had adventures with certain nonhuman objects with which they formed partnerships based on totemic relationship.[184] The members of the clan refer to their nonhuman partners by kinship terms such as mother, father, or mother's brother. Each clan also considers itself to be related to a number of other nonhuman partners, thought of as secondary *wuye*, although they belong to another clan. Any group of clans sharing a *wuye*, either through primary or secondary ownership, are considered to be related, and marriage between these is forbidden. *Wuye* relatives also share clan names and have an ongoing interest and responsibility in one another's ceremonies. Such related-clan groups form exogamous units, called phratries, and function chiefly to regulate marriage; the phratry is the largest group in Hopi society that is based directly upon kinship. While all the phratry groups would, in the kinship system, ideally be found in each village or on each mesa, this is not the actual case. For instance, at Walpi-Sichomovi there are ten phratries, but the number of living clans in them is not clear, while at Third Mesa's Oraibi there are nine phratries that include twenty-nine clans.[185] A full list of these phratries and their associated clans is given by Titiev.[186]

The possession of a stock of clan names that can be given by women to their clansmen's offspring is a clan character. Also, clan land is subject to redistribution only within the clan.[187]

The names listed by Titiev for clans associated with major ceremonies for Old Oraibi are as follows: Chicken Hawk, Parrot, Bow, Kwan, Bear, Badger, Spider, Patki, Snake, Lizard, Sand, and Kokop, or Fire.[188] More properly these are called Chicken Hawk People, Parrot People, and so forth.

Clan names given by Parsons for Sichomovi are Mustard, Badger, Rabbit, Tobacco, Patki, Corn, Sage, Coyote, Reed, Bear, Millet, Horn, Snake, Katcina, and Cottonwood.[189]

Migration legends describe a long period of wandering before the people arrived at Hopi country, coming at different times and from different directions. One clan unit arrived first at each of the original pueblo sites. Later, other clans arrived, and after a period of probation, or after having demonstrated some valuable ability such as the power to produce rain, were admitted to those pueblos they petitioned. In this manner the Hopi villages came into being.[190] (After half a century of attempting to record and clarify the migration myths, anthropologists have now abandoned the quest as futile.)

Having learned that nonhuman *wuye* are referred to as mother, father, etc., the non-Hopi finds it confusing that a son should classify his clan relatives, and thus pattern his behavior toward them, according to a system not translatable into English. The term "mother" is applied to his own mother, to all her sisters and their female cousins related through his maternal grandmother, and to any woman of his own clan. The term "mother's brother" is applied to his mother's brothers, his mother's mother's brothers, and any elderly clansman of his mother's generation. "Sisters" are his sisters and female parallel cousins. "Brothers" are his brothers and his male parallel cousins, yet he distinguishes between those who are older or younger than himself.

On the other hand, a father belonging to a different clan has his own unique classifications. A full rendering of kinship terms is not, however, pertinent here, since reference will seldom be made to them. It is sufficient to emphasize the core position that the kinship system gives to the woman in the Hopi household in contrast to the peripheral position of the man—although that role is reversed in the kiva—and to acknowledge the consanguinity of mother and daughter which remains the cornerstone of Hopi society. In its fuller sense, the kinship system stands as an all-encompassing governor. First of all, it establishes the standard for Hopi attitudes and correlative behavior within the clan and the tribe. Second, it controls interaction with non-Hopi. Third, since each Hopi is related through kinship or an extension of it to everyone else in the pueblo, behavior in every instance is compliant. And fourth, because certain natural and supernatural entities are thought of and addressed in kinship terms, behavior pertinent to this sphere is regulated too.

Taken as a whole, then, kinship is the integrating mechanism in Hopi life, a factor that becomes increasingly significant as the religious and secular aspects of the unified life-Way are considered, and one sees the worthwhile fruit borne of it.[191] This is not to say that the kinship system does not foster problems, but what system doesn't?

THE KATCINA CULT

The most splendid, enchanting, and characteristic of the Pueblo ceremonies are those involving Katcinas. Hopi stories involving the origin of Katcinas vary somewhat, but it is generally accepted that when the Hopi emerged from the Underworld they brought with them a large number of living spiritual beings known as Katcinas, whose songs and dances constantly obtained good things from the higher powers for the Hopi. According to a mythical account told to Titiev, the Katcinas accompanied the Hopi in their early wanderings until they settled at Casa Grande. There they were attacked by Mexicans, all the Katcinas were killed, and their spirits returned to their homes in the Underworld. To maintain contact with them, the surviving Hopi kept the masks and costumes of the Katcinas and developed the custom of impersonating them in rituals. By this means, Katcina-obtained blessings continue to be bestowed,[192] principally in the form of rain, but also in well-being. Both these are related to curing and fertility, which assure the reproduction and perpetuation of all created things.

In another version of the loss of the original Katcinas, the people began to take for granted the blessings bestowed by the supernaturals, and even had the audacity to argue with them. So the Katcinas decided to leave. But first they taught a few faithful young men how to perform some of their ceremonies and how to make the necessary paraphernalia, assuring them that as long as the ritual details were followed to the letter and were performed with good and pure hearts, the real Katcinas would come and take possession of those who wore the masks. Rain and well-being would follow.[193] Conversely, if rain did not fall and other serious problems occurred, it would be proof that something was done wrong or someone was not pure in action or heart.

After citing the two stories just given, I have learned that Frederick J. Dockstader, in his book *The Kachina and the White Man*, offers the same versions of the Katcina origin myth. We agree, apparently, that the two versions cover in general terms the ideas most prevalent among the modern Hopi concerning the subject.[194]

In addition to the original Katcinas, the Hopi dead are believed to return to the Underworld through the sipapu whence the people first climbed to the earth's surface. Here, in communion with the original Katcinas, they carry on a ritual and secular existence that is a replica of Hopi life on earth. Each of the main Katcina ceremonies is held twice yearly at the villages, once in a major and once in a minor form. At the same time that the major form is being performed on earth, the corresponding minor ritual is being performed by the spirits in the Underworld, and vice versa. It follows also that the seasons are reversed. When it is midwinter in the Underworld, it is midsummer on earth. The one exception in living pattern is that the spirits eat only the soul of food; thus, weighing nothing, some can be transformed into Katcina Clouds that bring rain and other benefits to the living. The dead are also invited to come back to the village on the fourth night of the Tribal Initiation Ceremony. (Reference to that auspicious rite will be made shortly.)

Two hundred and fifty or more Katcinas are personified in ceremonies, although a certain few are the most popular and most frequently represented. Katcina types include animals and birds, Katcinas identified by a peculiar physical aspect or a special costume feature, Katcinas associated with certain sounds, Katcinas related to fixed seasons, melon Katcinas, rodent Katcinas, and so on. In effect, everything is represented that is necessary to a full and fruitful life on earth and in the Underworld. Only men, and specifically those who have been properly qualified by passage through the required tribal rites, can put on masks and costumes and impersonate Katcinas.

Katcina impersonations most often take the form of group dances, performed from daybreak to sunset with intervals for rest. The society members secretly rehearse the songs and dances for several days prior to a public performance, and then are carefully painted and elaborately dressed in refreshed masks and costumes. In many cases the costume and paint are distinctive, but it is the mask that holds the power to transform a living man into the Katcina he impersonates.[195] In a sense, the mask is invested with the transmittable spirit of the actual Katcina. The result is that, when in association with the prescribed ritual the society member dons the mask, he is transformed, he becomes that Katcina for the time he wears it. He has all the Katcina's powers and attributes.

Usually, although not always, the Katcina impersonators are masked, and they appear in proper season at all the eastern and western Pueblo villages, although in the Rio Grande area non-Pueblos are not permitted to see them. In fact, non-Pueblos, including other Indians, are not even allowed in a Rio Grande village when a Katcina dance is being performed. Consequently, there is a dearth of eyewitness descriptions, although informants have revealed something of them. At Hopi and Zuñi the masks, with the exception of clan masks, have been more openly displayed, and there is a mass of published material on their Katcinas.[196]

The Cloud Katcina masks are manufactured by their owners. They are refurbished each time they are used, and redecorated if a different style of Katcina is to be represented. In addition, there is a periodic introduction of new Katcinas to deal with new situations, and some of the old ones periodically become obsolete. The efficacy of the Katcina is usually the controlling factor in this, and a Katcina is called upon only so long as it brings benefits to the people.

There is almost no limit to the number of variations and innovations that are permitted. The exceptions are the few special types known as *Mon*, or Chief Katcinas, whose masks are permanent and never duplicated. In most instances these belong to a specific clan, are regarded as the *wuye*, or clan ancestors, and may be impersonated only on particular occasions. Parsons informs us that some of the clan masks are never exposed in dances or copied for dances, but in the more esoteric ceremonials they may be brought out and worn, with the admonition to all witnesses that they must not describe the mask to anyone.[197] The clan mask is in the keeping of the clan head or chief (Dutton says "the respective clan mothers"[198]), who is required to feed the mask ritually each day and to know the prayers and the songs connected with it.[199]

The entire Hopi tribe is admitted at a prescribed time in life to what ethnologists call the Katcina Cult. Little children are taught to believe that the Katcinas they see performing are actually supernatural visitors with awesome powers. Since this pretense can only be kept up so long, sometime before the age of ten the child is initiated into the Katcina Cult and thereby taught, as they see the masks removed, that men are actually impersonating Katcinas in ritual practices that have preserved the Anasazi for centuries. Adults accept the human dimension, but continue to believe that the impersonator becomes the actual Katcina. However, being accepted in all respects for who he is, the Katcina impersonator is called a "friend" rather than a god.

There is an annual open season and an annual closed season for Katcina activities. The open season runs approximately from the winter to the summer solstice, and all Katcina rituals, with a single exception, must be held during this time. Only the Masau'u Katcina, representing the god of death, may appear in the closed season. During the open season the Katcinas are present in the villages whenever rituals are being performed. Otherwise, they dwell in Underworld homes in the mountains, lakes, and springs, more specifically on the splendid San Francisco Mountain peaks just north of Flagstaff, Arizona. During the "closed," or other, half of the year, the Katcinas remain and perform in their Underworld homes, and dances that do not require their presence on earth are held.[200]

In theory, all Katcina appearances are "owned by" (under the control of) the village chief, but in practice the Badger and Katcina clans cooperate in conducting the annual cycle. The former clan is in charge from late summer when the preceding season ends until the Powamû ritual is held in February. The latter takes over at that point and retains control until the open season ends, when the Niman, or Homecoming, Dance is performed soon after the summer solstice.[201]

In treating the open and closed seasons for the Katcina ceremonies, Stephen gives a summary of the moons and seasons, and the months and ceremonials, as follows.

MOONS AND SEASONS

November   sparrow hawk, novice, initiate. In this moon the fields for the following year's planting are cleared of brush, etc.

December   most-worthy, sacred; undesirable; afraid; no work is done in this moon.

January   Moisture moon; also called katcina coming, the return of the katcina, and katcina come up (through the sipapu).

February   the purification with ashes on buzzard feather. During the ceremony of this moon, plants growing in the kiva are purified by the Wü'wiyomo katcina.

March   to whistle low, half under the breath as a Hopi does, the first faint whistling of moderating cold; winds which contain or convey the first faint whistle of warm breath. This moon is called by some cactus moon, because in early times food was often scarce at this season and the cactus was almost the only vegetal food the Hopi could then obtain.

April   wind-breaks, stems of the shrub *Bigelovia graveolens* are set close together along the lines of the planted seeds to protect the young plants, except corn, from being torn and bruised with sand during the strong gales that prevail during the spring and early summer.

May   Waiting moon. The sweet katcina corn is planted this moon.

June   Planting moon, go to plant; also called plant moon; also novice moon, as plants are now weak and young, like novices.

July   hoe; they are now hoeing among their plants.

August Moisture moon, the summer rain moon. Names are in-
differently applied to August and September in reference to beans and watermelons ripening in these moons.
September to eat to repletion, referring to abundance of fruits.
October carrying the burden basket, also called cornhusking
moon.[202]

MONTHS AND CEREMONIALS

November Wü'wüchimti

December Winter solstice ceremony; Warrior ceremonial

January Snake-Antelope or Flute ceremonial
Katcina Return

February Powamû

March Horned water serpent dance
Wet-running katcina including Shalako

April Katcina dances

May Katcina dances

June Katcina dances

July Niman

August Snake-Antelope ceremony or Flute ceremony
Somakoli ceremonial

September Lalakon ceremony

October Manzrau ceremony
Owa'kültü ceremony
Masauwüh ceremonial[203]

In his treatise on Hopi Katcinas, Fewkes sets forth the lists of elaborate
and abbreviated festivals,[204] and then describes in greater detail than Stephen
the tabular view of the ceremonies in a given year:

TABULAR VIEW OF FESTIVALS IN A HOPI YEAR

The following ceremonies, celebrated annually at the East mesa of Tusayan,
are mentioned with the months in which they occur, beginning with the New-
fire or November festival.

November, Kelemuryawu (Novices' Moon)
Wüwütcimti (New-fire ceremony)
Naacnaiya (with initiation of novices).

November is generally considered the opening month of the Hopi year,
and on the character of the New-fire ceremony, whether elaborate (Naacnaiya)
or abbreviated (Wüwütcimti), depends that of the following festivals, for if the

former is celebrated the winter ceremonies, which follow, are always more complicated.

December, Kyamuryawu

1. Soyaluña (All-assembly, Winter-solstice).

Synchronous meeting of all clans in their respective kivas with altars and prayers to Muyingwu, the germ god. An elaborate sun drama occurs in certain kivas during the festival.

2. Momtcita (war dance of the Kalektaka or warrior priesthood of the Pakab clans).

Stone images of the Hano warrior gods, corresponding to the Hopi Püükoñ hoya, Paluña hoya, and their grandmother Kokyan wüqti (Spider woman), are displayed at the Winter-solstice ceremony (called Tañtai by the Tewa). At Hano the rites of these gods are combined with those of the germ gods, but at Walpi they are distinct, following Soyaluña.

In this festival there is an altar and prayer-stick making. The Hano warrior altars are erected in the same rooms and at the same time as those of the Winter-solstice ceremony.

January, Pamuryawu

1. Pamürti.

A dance celebrated at Sichomovi by the Asa and Honani clans, dramatizing the return of the sun, followed by their clan-ancients or katcinas, called by Zuñi names.

2. Leñya or Tcüa paholawû (Flute or Snake prayer-stick-making).

Winter or lesser Flute or Snake prayer-stick-making. The Flute or Snake fraternity of the underworld is supposed to meet at this time, and there is a sympathetic gathering of Flute priests in even years and Snake priests in odd years. In the odd years certain rites occur in the kivas during the Soyaluña ceremony to harmonize with the preeminence of the Snake chief in those years.

3. Mucaiasti (Buffalo dance).

4. Tawa paholawû (Sun prayer-stick-making).

Winter or lesser assemblage of the Sun priests.

February, Powamuryawu

1. Powamû (bean-planting).

A ceremonial purification festival celebrating the return of the clan-ancients of the Katcina clan, in which several other clan-ancients likewise appear.

2. Lakone Paholawû (Lakone prayer-stick-making).

Winter or lesser sympathetic meeting of the Lakone priesthood, who make offerings and deposit them in distant shrines.

March, Ucumuryawu

1. Palülükoñti, or Añkwañti.

Theatrical performance or mystery play, illustrating the growth of corn; its purpose is the production of rain.

2. Marau paholawû (Marau prayer-stick-making).

Spring meeting of the Marau fraternity, who make offerings and deposit them in distant shrines.

3. Sumaikoli.

Spring meeting of the Sumaikoli and Yaya fraternities. A festival of short duration in which new fire is kindled by frictional methods.

May, Kyamuryawu

Abbreviated Katcina dances.

Masked personations of different clan-ancients or katcinas, in public dances of a single day's duration, sometimes accompanied with secret rites.

July, Pamuryauu

Niman Katcina (Departure of the Katcinas).
Elaborate celebration of the departure of the katcinas.

August, Powamuryauu

1. Snake dance (Tcüapaki).

In odd years at Walpi, alternating with the Flute festival in even years.

2. Flute dance (Leñpaki).

3. Tawa paholawû (Sun prayer-stick-making).

Prayer-stick-making by the Sun priests.

4. Sumaikoli.

Meeting of the Sumaikoli fraternity.

September

Lalakoñti.

Basket dance of the Patki (Rain-cloud) clans. Meeting of the Lakone fraternity, in which an elaborate altar is erected and a public basket dance is celebrated.

October

1. Owakülti.

Basket dance of the Buli and Pakab clans. Meeting of the Owakültû society, when an elaborate altar is erected and a basket dance is celebrated.

2. Mamzrauti.

Hand-tablet dance. Meeting of the Marau society, when an elaborate altar is erected and a hand-tablet dance is celebrated.

Each of the above-mentioned ceremonial festivals is performed by a society of priests and is simple or complex according to the relative strength and social influence of its priesthood.[205]

It should be emphasized that while the Hano Tewa have embraced the Katcina Cult and many of the Hopi rituals, they have not adopted the major Hopi ceremonies or the men's fraternities. Kiva groups do hold Katcina dances and other observances, such as games and races, including carry-overs from the Rio Grande Region. They have their own Tewa clown, they emphasize curing, and Dutton thinks it "probable" that kiva membership is associated either with Katcina initiations or with winter solstice ceremonies.[206] The village chief, assisted by officers, controls all religious matters, while a war chief settles internal quarrels and "guards" the village against enemies and witches.

KATCINA COSTUMES

When ceremonies are being performed in the kivas it is customary for the members who are taking part to divest themselves of all clothing except the breechclout, and to allow their long hair to hang down the back.[207] However, at those times when the Katcina spirits return, the appropriate Katcina costumes are worn by those who impersonate them.

There is a standard Katcina costume worn by a substantial number of those who are impersonating male Katcinas. In addition to these basic garments there are embellishments that vary greatly and often help to identify the Katcina and his associations.

The essential costume piece is a woven white cotton kilt that is rectangular and embroidered with wool designs on both narrow ends. The first kilt a boy receives when he starts to participate in ceremonies is plain black, of cotton, and it has two painted circles on it. When he comes of age his ceremonial father gives him the white kilt as a replacement, and thereafter the "son" wears it in Katcina dances. Voth says the kilt is worn by most Katcinas, also by priests and in social dances, and sometimes by women in ceremonies.[208] If a young man dies while he is wearing it, he is buried in it.[209]

Taken together, the embroidered designs on the kilt are a prayer for rain. Pyramid figures represent clouds; zigzag lines, lightning; a series of straight vertical lines below the clouds, rain. Wright says that alternating red and white stripes portray the sun shining red through morning rain, and black and white stripes represent the rainbow.[210] Some kilts have colored yarn tassels on the lower corners.

The kilt is wrapped around the waist in such a way that the bottom edge is above the knee and the design panels fall on the Katcina dancer's right side. The kilt has tie strings on the upper edge, but depending upon the Katcina portrayed, it is firmly secured by a woven "woman's" belt, a broad brocaded sash, or a combination of the two. Depending on the dance, spruce boughs may be inserted under the sash and at intervals around the kilt.

The Katcina sash is a part of nearly every Katcina costume. Most are brocaded on both ends. They are wrapped around the waist over the kilt and tied in such a way that the ends hang on the right side with both brocaded panels facing out. A few Katcinas wear the sash looped around the neck with the ends lapped over.

The brocaded sash consists of two long, narrow panels of cotton joined together at the unadorned end, and brocaded with woolen panels of symbolic designs at the other, extreme ends. Terminating the panels is a strip of red ribbon cloth longer than the sash is wide, and also some white fringing.

There is an unembroidered white sash that varies in breadth. This sash is also quite long, and at each end the yarn is formed into a number of yarn balls that are wrapped around a corn husk ring, from which long fringes hang. It is commonly called a "rain sash," but all sashes are properly such, in that when used they are a prayer for rain.

Footless stockings are worn by some performers. These are knitted in a technique that replaced the early Anasazi finger weaving. James mentions that in several cases he found blind men making themselves useful by knitting stockings with needles of wood. One "poor old man, stone blind, was winding yarn into a ball." He squatted upon the ground, with the yarn wrapped around his feet and knees.[211]

Most male dancers wear high-topped buckskin moccasins. At Hopi, the majority of these are painted either a dull red or a blue green. Some of the

Men's ceremonial dance moccasins. From the Heard Museum collection.

blue-green moccasins have colored and edge-cut buckskin tabs (most of which are perforated) attached to a red buckskin band that encircles the moccasin at the top, then runs down the side and turns across the instep. The sole is a separate piece of rawhide, left white, which turns up slightly around the edges to protect the foot. Dance moccasins are an absolutely elegant product.

Over the moccasin, the performer often wears an elaborately woven wool anklet that varies in width from two to three and a half inches. Some anklets are tied onto the moccasins with thongs; others, especially the narrower ones, may be sewn directly onto the moccasin. Sometimes the Katcina mana impersonators wear the anklets on otherwise bare feet.

Roediger describes anklets wherein the base for the wool consists of an oblong piece of hide slit internally in narrow, lengthwise strips, with the ends left uncut. These strips are then wound with colored wools in geometric patterns.[212] I have, however, two pairs of anklets whose internal base is cloth. The cloth is slit like the hide she mentions, and then wrapped tightly with wool. The entire outer edge is bound with plain cloth to fix the colored wool in place. Thongs are passed through the binding to tie the anklet onto the moccasin. In former days dyed porcupine quills were employed rather than wool to make the decorative patterns. These old and valuable items are seldom seen today.

A fox skin with the hair left on hangs at the performer's back and extends from the tops of the kilt to within a few inches of the ground. This is the Katcina emblem, and it completes the standard Katcina outfit. The tip of the fox head is either tucked under a roll of the kilt or tied to the kilt, and the body and tail hangs straight down. Usually, the skin is not decorated, but I have seen a few specimens that had the animal's four paws wrapped and decorated with yarn and special appendages.

Armbands are often worn by the Katcina impersonators. They vary in design, but a typical band is made of a four-inch-wide strip of heavy rawhide that is painted (commonly in a turquoise blue). The band has holes in each of its rounded ends, and a buckskin thong is run through these to secure the band on the inner side of the arm. Pendant feathers of various kinds dangle from the ends of the thong.

Katcina impersonators usually carry a gourd rattle in their right hand and Douglas fir or spruce branches in their left hand, although, among the great pantheon of Katcinas, one will see a tremendous variety of items being carried, such as staffs, dolls, melons, cornstalks, corncobs, knives, scissors, feathers, throwing-sticks, whips, hoops, lightning-sticks, wands, woven plaques, bows and arrows, baskets, and more. Dancers have other rattles, as described on pages 112–14.

Jewelry is often worn to complete the costume. Turquoise and coral necklaces are common, as are leather wristbands with crafted silver plates attached, and belts with silver conchas.

Beyond the basic mask, standard kilt, sash, fox skin, and moccasins that are worn for a large percentage of Katcina impersonations, the variety of costuming is such that it would require thousands of words to describe it. At this point the picture is truly worth many words, and the Katcina books that depict the regalia in full color become invaluable.

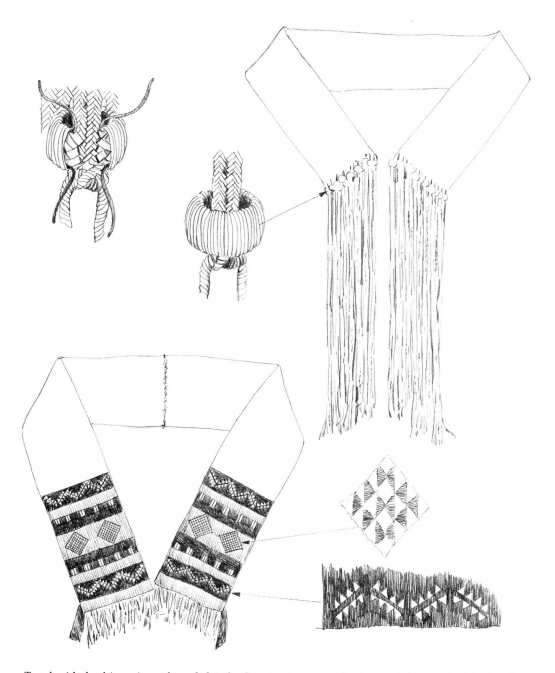

Top, braided white rain sash and details showing how corn-husk cored rings and plaited and twisted fringes are appended. *Bottom,* brocaded men's ceremonial sash. The width of all sashes varies according to the desires of the weaver.

A single example that will illustrate my point is the Masau'u Katcina costume. Since Masau'u is the deity of death and fire, and because he is associated with darkness and the Underworld, his mask and costume are designed to portray these things with utmost clarity. The mask has great staring eye openings and a large round mouth with grotesque teeth. Folded over his shoulders like a shawl is an embroidered kilt that has actually been removed from a grave. Prayer feathers tied to the back of the mask in a large cluster are taken from shrines. The colored splotches on the mask represent clouds com-

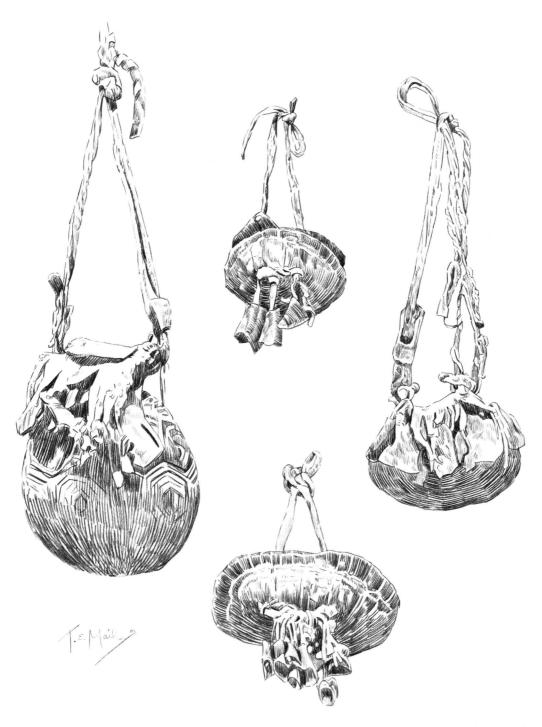

Musical instruments. Turtle-shell leg rattles with animal hooves attached. From the Heard Museum collection.

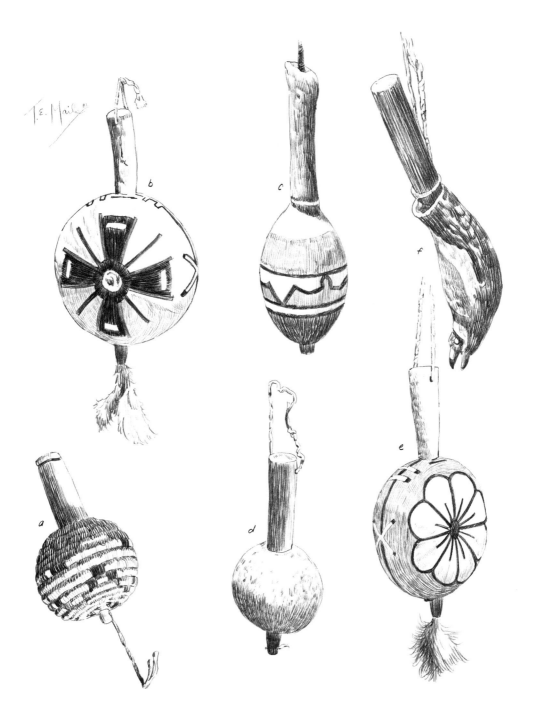

Musical instruments. Rattles: *a*, quilled gourd. *b*, painted gourd. *c*, painted gourd. *d*, un-painted gourd. *e*, painted gourd. *f*, carved wooden bird. From the Heard Museum collection.

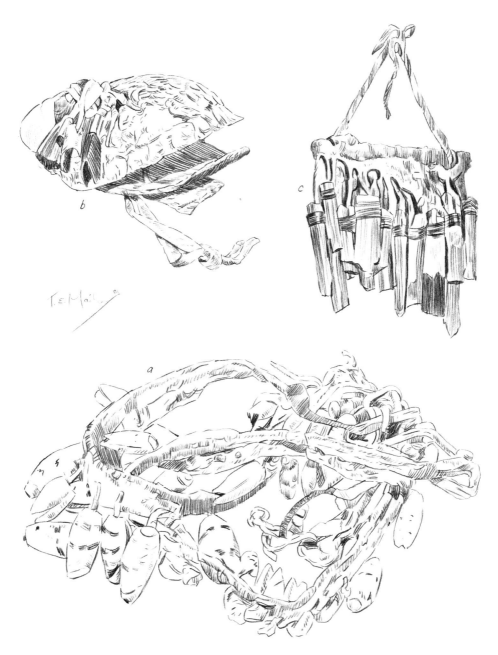

Musical instruments. Dance rattles: *a*, canvas bandolier band worn over right shoulder with seashells attached. *b*, turtle-shell leg rattle. *c*, wooden sticks attached to hide. From the Heard Museum collection.

ing from all directions. The Katcina impersonator carries a gourd rattle in his right hand, and a spruce branch in his left. When he comes as a warrior he carries a whip. When he accompanies the Ogre Katcinas he holds a willow switch.[213] Masau'u wears the ancient rabbit-skin robe reaching to the knees. It is tied on with a belt to which are attached hoofs and animal bones, including sheep and cow skulls. He dances in a crouch, and he is *impressive*.

Some impersonators have capes of fur, hide, or cloth draped over their shoulders, and others wear poncho-type shirts. The cloth capes may be plain or embroidered. For some of the costumes, dancers fold their kilts and wear them like a breechclout. Others wear an actual breechclout, either with painted symbols or with a few lines of yarn attached to the front and back panels to make a simple design. Once again, the manner depends upon which Katcina is being impersonated.

In Katcina mana portrayals, where female Katcinas are being impersonated by men, the performers usually don the traditional women's dress, moccasins of the wraparound type, and most often a robe that wraps around the shoulders, ties in front at the chest, and hangs to the knees. Typical of this is the magnificent Palhik Mana or Butterfly Maiden, the Hemis Mana, and the Kokopelli Maiden. The Shalako Mana Katcina is an exception. Its long wraparound robe is entirely covered with eagle feathers, and it is a stunning item to behold. Finally, some impersonators wear only the dress and omit the robe.

Katcina Manas using rasping sets, and gourd and drum resonators to provide musical accompaniment for the He-Hea Dance. Adapted from a Jo Mora photograph.

Left, Masau'u, wearing his rabbit-skin robe, a kilt over his shoulders, a fox skin, a woven belt sash, and a belt of animal hooves, bones, and shells. *Top*, wooden ceremonial hoes with cloud and rain symbols. *Lower right*, bear paw worn by certain society members and used in healing. Artifacts in the Southwest Museum.

Costumes. *Left,* the Hemis Katcina Mana. She wears a red-and-black-bordered maiden's blanket over her shoulders, a loomed black dress, a white rain sash, and wraparound moccasins. She generally appears at Niman, the last masked dance of the year. *Right,* the Crow Mother Katcina. She wears a fur collar (or spruce), a large white rain sash tied at the left side (as do all female Katcinas), an embroidered bride's robe over her shoulders, a loomed black dress, and white wraparound moccasins. She carries a woven plaque with corn and bean plants that have been grown in the kiva. Her mask is blue with black designs and has crow wing feathers at the sides.

KATCINA BODY PAINT AND MASKS

Virtually every Katcina impersonator and every non-Katcina dancer—male or female—employs body paint as part of the traditional costume. Women sometimes limit the paint to some brownish-black corn smut or a red spot on each cheek. But male dancers cover significant areas, if not the entire body, with marvelous combinations of paint. Here again, though, the subject of body painting is far too involved to be treated fully. In conjunction with my descriptions of certain ceremonies I outline the relevant costume and paint, and the reader is referred to the Flute and Snake ceremonies for sample information on body painting during rituals held in the closed, or non-Katcina, season. I also include illustrations of numerous Hopi Katcinas, plus the full detailing of present-day Hopi costumes for three recent Katcina dances I have seen, and the subject receives additional treatment in the present-day Rio Grande material.

According to Colton, the base used for the paints is clay, colored by pulverized minerals. Hematite is used for red, limonite for yellow, malachite for blue-green, and kaolin for white. Soot is applied for black, corn smut for a brownish black, and a certain spring mud for blue.[214] Bourke says that a mixture of carbonate of copper and piñon pitch produces green and an oil for mixing comes from pumpkin seeds.[215] Fewkes states that the use of brownish-black corn smut is a prayer that O'-mow-uh, Clouds, will send his rain to wash it off.[216]

There are, essentially, two types of masks used by the Hopi: the helmet, which covers the entire head, and the maskette, which covers only the face. All masks are refurbished for each dance, but there is a difference. The clan masks are repainted but never stripped of their appendages. Other masks are scraped, repainted, and if possible equipped with new appendages. Paint removed from any mask is saved and placed at a shrine.[217]

Since masks are symbolic, the depictions upon them are not realistic, although one can often recognize frogs or other animate objects. The ordinary mask owned by an individual is usually passed down to a son or other relative who is entitled to impersonate Katcinas. It can be stored for safekeeping in the kiva, at a shrine, or at home.[218]

There are circular masks that are made from yucca sifter baskets, and there are non-Katcina masks. The Mudhead clown wears a sack mask. The oldest sack masks were of hide, but later models were fashioned from commercial cotton or hemp sacks. They are described together with the clown costume.

Seldom treated in the literature is the fact that masks are a fine-art form, in which the helmet itself and the appendages combine to make a balanced, multicolored sculpture. Sensitivity and artistic quality are apparent. The mask and its features are carefully and cleverly assembled. Some of the methods devised for attaching parts, so that they will either remain firmly in place or move about while the performer is dancing, inspire utmost admiration.

As an example I illustrate a Velvet Katcina mask and its manner of design and construction. This Katcina is of fairly recent introduction and may represent advanced methods of assembly.

Masks could never be comfortable to wear. The helmet variety is tight-fitting and constricting. The hide is thick, it does not "breathe," and the holes by no means provide adequate air or vision. At the bottom of the mask there is usually a ruff or collar of some kind that hides the neck. It is tied by thongs that are attached to the mask. Spruce branches, Douglas fir branches, juniper branches (all scratchy), cloth rolls, and sometimes rags are used for this purpose. Dancing under a blazing sun with the mask on must demand the utmost endurance from the impersonator. Perhaps this is intentional. It may be that the Hopi want their impersonators to be extremely cognizant of their role, but it is certain that the rest periods when masks are removed are profoundly appreciated.

The Hopi are relatively small in stature, and the helmet masks are much too limited in size for an average white man to put on.

The most familiar maskettes are those worn by the Anga Katcinas, and there are several minor variations in style. The Anga Katcina is more commonly known as the Loose Hair or Long Hair, since the impersonator lets his long black hair hang down his back. His hair seems, in fact, almost to be part of the maskette itself, so beautifully do the two balance each other. The Katcina is associated with gentle rains. He is extremely popular with villagers and tourists alike; he dances in a graceful, splendid manner, and he is perhaps the best-known performer outside the Snake dancer.

The Anga maskette reaches from ear to ear and from forehead to mid-chin. Its larger base piece is fashioned from stiff, heavy leather, and it is rectangular. It has two rectangular eyeholes. At the top a narrow red or black fringe of human hair, yucca fibers, or horsehair is sewn on so that it looks like a trimmed hair bang. The base piece is painted, according to the Katcina represented, in a flat color, and triangular designs are placed around the eyeholes. Over the lower fourth of the basic piece is added, sandwich fashion, a second and narrower strip of leather that is painted in different ways to represent teeth. Between the two layers or at the lower edge a long beard of red or blue horsehair is attached. It is as wide as the mask, and it hangs down to mid-chest. Some Anga maskettes also have string and breath-feather appendages that dangle from the top of the "tooth" strip and in front of the beard. Maskettes are secured with thongs that are attached to the side of the mask and tied together at the back of the head.

A second example of spectacular art form is the face mask with a tablita attached to it. Of these, the best known are those of the Hemis Katcina, the Sio Hemis Katcina, the Shalako Taka Katcina, the Shalako Mana Katcina, and the Palhik Mana Katcina. The first two are helmet masks with tablitas, and the last three are maskettes with tablitas. My drawings will illustrate them more quickly than words can, but they are stunning creations in size, form, and color. The tablita portion of the Hopi mask, for most Katcinas, is huge com-

four strips of
⅛" wide buckskin

white string

method of attaching
eagle breath feathers
to crown of mask

two upright
feathers
overlapped

7" long ties

to obtain its oval shape,
the mask case is cut halfway
up the sides at five places
and then stitched together
so as to draw the sides in
at those places.

quills of eagle
feathers tied to
blue denim
strips in
pairs

roll of denim

roll of buckskin

two upright
golden eagle
feathers loosely
inserted

mask hide

method of attaching
eagle feathers to
back of mask

Construction details of the Velvet Katcina mask to show how "helmet" or "case type" masks in general are constructed.

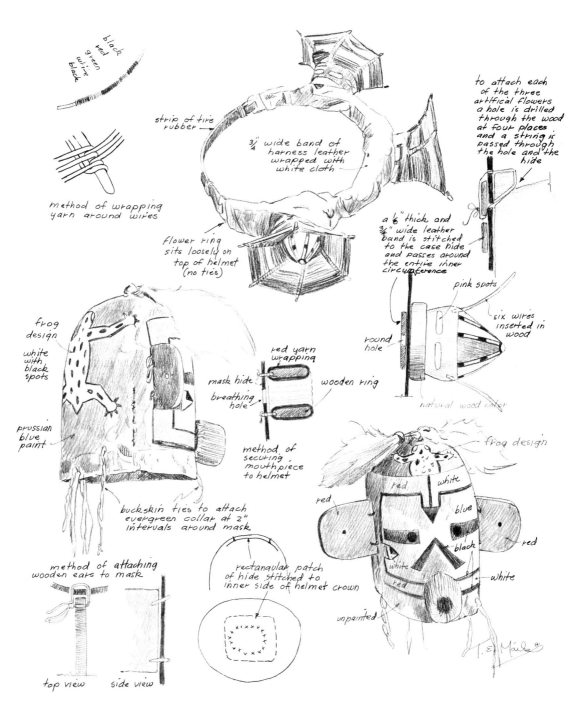

black
red
green
wire
black

method of wrapping
yarn around wires

strip of tire
rubber

¾" wide band of
harness leather
wrapped with
white cloth

flower ring
sits loosely on
top of helmet
(no ties)

to attach each
of the three
artificial flowers
a hole is drilled
through the wood
at four places
and a string is
passed through
the hole and the
hide

a ⅛" thick and
¾" wide leather
band is stitched
to the case hide
and passes around
the entire inner
circumference

pink spots

six wires
inserted in
wood

round
hole

natural wood color

frog
design

white
with
black
spots

prussian
blue
paint

red yarn
wrapping

mask hide

breathing
hole

wooden ring

method of
securing
mouthpiece
to helmet

buckskin ties to attach
evergreen collar at 2"
intervals around mask

method of attaching
wooden ears to mask

top view   side view

rectangular patch
of hide stitched to
inner side of helmet crown

frog design

red   white

red

blue

black

red

white
red

white

unpainted

Construction details of the Velvet Katcina mask to show how "helmet" or "case type" masks in general are fashioned.

Navan, or Velvet Katcina, front view unmasked, and side view masked. Adapted from Museum of New Mexico photographs.

Anga, or Long Hair Katcina dancers at Shongopovi, June 25, 1977. The mask of the Anga or Long Hair Katcina was turquoise blue with a band of blue and black squares at the lower edge. The beard was of red horsehair and had three turkey feathers on twisted cotton string and an eagle down feather as pendants in front of it. The feathers on the crown of the mask were yellow, with a single upright orange macaw feather in the center. Four downy eagle feathers attached to a string with a tiny plaque at the end as a weight hung down the back of the head (some used tiny clay pots, small ears of corn, or small clay ladles as weights). The body paint was reddish brown over the upper torso, arms, and lower legs. The upper legs and hands were white. The rest of the costume consisted of an embroidered kilt, a rain sash with evergreen tucked in front and back, a fox skin, blue moccasins (some wore decorated ankle bands), a turtle-shell rattle on the right leg, black yarn around the left knee, right wrist, and the neck, a gourd rattle, and a bough of evergreen. The dancing positions were as shown.

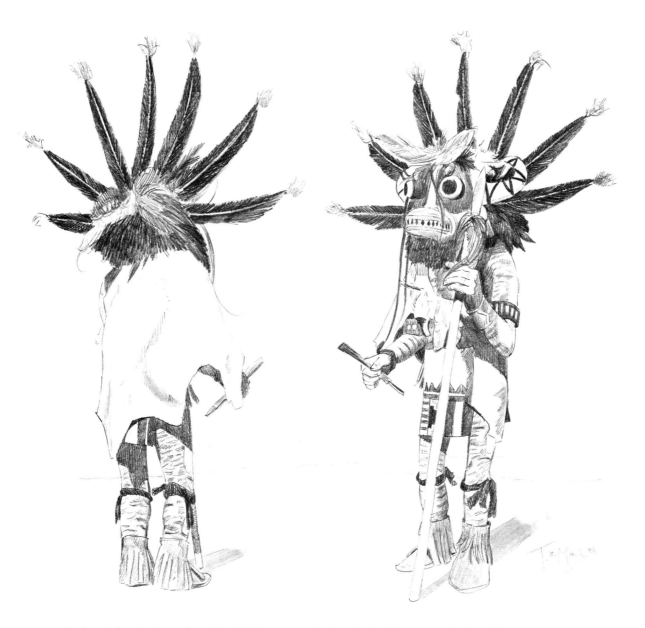

Back and front views of an Ogre Katcina, one of whose tasks is to appear in the village once a year and threaten children who need discipline. By prearrangement with the parents the awesome Ogre comes to the home and threatens to take the offending child away to the Underworld. After the child is properly cowed, the parents "ransom" the child with gifts of food and candy, and the Ogre goes away—promising to return if the child's behavior doesn't improve. It follows that the relieved child grows closer to the parents out of gratitude for their "intercession."

pared to those of the Rio Grande Pueblos. In all instances, though, tablitas are thin flat wooden panels that parallel the shoulders and extend to the sides and top of the mask. In former times they were made from yucca strips lashed together with thongs, and they were extremely light. Nowadays they are fashioned from plywood. Symbols painted on the tablita boards depict clouds, corn, flowers, rain, rainbows, butterflies, and other images associated with rain.

Small River Katcina. From an H. F. Robinson photograph, Museum of New Mexico.

While it seems to be a well-settled matter among the Hopi, the origin and antiquity of Pueblo masks is still being debated by anthropologists and ethnologists. For a surprisingly long time some of them maintained that masks were introduced either by the Spanish or more indirectly from Mesoamerica after the conquest.[219] Recent evidence, however, makes it certain that masks in one form or another were in use prior to European intrusion. Evidences summed up by Watson Smith include pictographs of what appear to be masked persons; the finding of a wooden Katcina doll of the thirteenth or fourteenth century in Double Butte Cave, Arizona; wooden mask fragments found in Canyon de Chelly and Chaco Canyon, and of course the presence of Katcina masks in the Jeddito Valley and Kuaua murals.[220]

I see no reason that masked Katcinas should not be considered indigenous and as functioning shortly after the true kiva came into being. If this is not the case, one might well ask what different manner of ritual life was being practiced then? The general absence of mask finds is easily understandable. For one thing, most parts of masks are perishable. For another, sacred as they are, and being extremely light, they would surely be taken along when any group moved from one place to another. The guardian of the mask of the Tewa Bear Clan informed Parsons that if anyone told him to leave the mesa he would go, but he would take his Bear Clan mask with him.[221] Also, it is common custom to retire a mask to a secret sacred place when it becomes so fragile it can no longer be repaired and used. Masks retain power, and they are not to be profaned. In the rare instance when one is sold without authorization to a non-Indian, the Pueblos do everything they can to get it back, and they object to public displays of masks and other sacred items. The Zuñi are seeking at the present time to recover all the wooden War Gods of theirs that can be tracked down, for they believe the War God holds its force until it deteriorates entirely.[222]

Most of my illustrations depict Hopi Katcinas as single figures, and at prescribed times they do appear alone or in small groups in the villages. But as a rule, they come as a dance group that can number from fifteen to forty of some of the most impressively costumed individuals to be seen anywhere in the world. Usually they are all dressed alike, with masks that are shaped the same even though the painted symbols may vary from mask to mask. My Katcinas are shown singly to emphasize costume details.

A Katcina dancer is distinguished primarily by his costume, but there are also differences in the songs and dances that are appropriate to each Katcina. Most Katcinas dance with a dignity that is unforgettable. The leader stands in the center of the line, and the novices at the ends. To begin, the leader shakes his rattle sharply and offers the first note of the song. Muffled by the mask, it might be only a deep and resonant "whoo," but as the other dancers take up the beat and the volume increases, chills run up and down the spines of spectators.

The leader raises his right foot and stomps it on the ground, accompanied now by a booming double-headed drum played by a Mudhead. The line begins to move forward slowly as the rest of the dancers stomp in unison. The movement is accompanied by graceful gestures of arms and head. Quickly now there will be a pause, followed by several rapid steps. At another time the entire line will turn—either as one man or as a flowing movement that runs down the line and back.

Sometimes there is a male chorus for accompaniment instead of the drum, or the chorus will do all the singing while the drum is silent as the dancers exert themselves for a particularly energetic performance. But usually the Katcinas do their own singing and accompany themselves with their rattles. The number of songs determines the number of times the Katcinas will come to the

Right, the Hopi Shalako Mana or female Shalako Katcina doll. There is also a male called Shalako Taka. The male stands about eight feet tall, the mana is a little shorter. He has a pink face, pendant eagle breath-feather earrings, and wears male moccasins. The female has a white face, square turquoise earrings, and white wrapped-on women's moccasins. The Shalako wears a face mask attached to a large tablita. At the *left* are three views of a Zuñi hide face-mask to show how the mask is constructed. It is not, however, a Shalako mask.

128

plaza for public performances. Twenty is common. All the songs express the same idea. They are prayers for rain, abundant crops, fertility, and growth. Certain songs become popular, and the Hopi working at home or in the fields hum and sing them just as the outside world does those of its culture heroes.

Although the basic concern of the dances is religious, the ceremonies also provide the only social outlet for the Hopi. At no other time do they forsake work simply for recreation or entertainment. They have no Sundays, no holidays, and not even the feast days celebrated at the Rio Grande pueblos. This fact encourages wholehearted immersion in the ritual life, for not only would the universe cease to function as it should if the dances ceased, their world on the lonely mesas of Tusayan would be plain and monotonous indeed.

MUSICAL INSTRUMENTS

The Hopi use only a limited number of musical instruments for their rituals, and ceremonies are virtually the only places music is heard in the conservative villages. They employ a drum, a flute, a whistle, rattles, a rasp, and a rhombus.

According to Clara Lee Tanner, the two-headed wooden drum currently in service in the pueblos was introduced by the Spanish.[223] Yet it seems certain that drums of some nature were in use in prehistoric times, even though specimens have not been found in excavations—other than foot drums.

The two-headed drum is made from a fallen cottonwood or aspen log. The piece is cut to whatever length the drum maker wishes and hollowed out. Tanner says a knife is used for this purpose, but I have seen a professional drum maker at Cochiti using a hammer and chisel, and it was hard going for him at that. When the log has been scraped to an ideal thickness, both ends are covered with animal skin. Underhill says that drums were once covered with antelope, deer, mountain sheep, or even buffalo hide,[224] but horsehide and goat skin are acceptable substitutes today. The skins are cut in the shape of a circle four inches larger in diameter than the log. Then scallops are cut in the edges, and the skins are soaked overnight. To attach them to the log, the points of the scallops are pierced, and a skin is stretched over each end of the log. Rawhide thongs are threaded through the holes and the two hides are laced tightly together. A rawhide loop is attached to the thongs on one end to provide a handle for the drum while it is being played.

The thongs angle from one scallop to the next and create an interesting texture pattern on the side of the drum. Sometimes the V-shaped areas of the log are painted with bright colors, with pleasing effects. Usually the drum heads are not painted.

Drum beaters are long straight sticks with pads of stuffed buckskin on the end. In former times a stick with a loop formed in one end was used, and this is still the type preferred by the Apache. Some authorities also say that the Hopi once made pottery drums whose sound was tempered by the addition of water before the skin head was placed over the opening.[225] This too is done by the Apache.[226]

Hopi flutes are fashioned from a piece of cottonwood or some other soft-wood with a soft core. In prehistoric times the pulp was pushed out by some unknown method, but burned out with a hot wire in the historic period.[227] Flutes are from two and a half to three feet long and have four holes cut in the far end. At the near end a slanting piece of wood is inserted as a reed. The flute is held vertically and is blown from the mouth end rather than from the side. Some flutes are painted blue and further decorated with feathers and hide fringes. The flutist does not play tunes, and some say he does not accompany singers or performers. Voth, however, in describing the winter ceremony of the Blue Flute Society dated January 20, 1898, which he witnessed, says there were seven flute players, three of whom were boys, who accompanied the songs that were sung.[228] Fewkes cites several instances in which flutists accompany singers. At Hopi, flutes are most commonly associated with the Blue and Gray Flute societies.

Whistles are used to call the spirits, birds, and animals. In the Oraibi Po-walawu Ceremony the war chief ascends the kiva ladder and blows yellow oriole feathers and corn pollen from a yellow reed tube toward the north. Then he blows a few short, sharp notes on a whistle fashioned from an eagle wing-bone. Returning to the kiva, he repeats the ritual at the other three cardinal directions, from three sides of the altar. Parsons says he is "summoning or imitating one of the birds of warm weather."[229] When the Powamû chief blows his whistle into the altar medicine bowl, he is calling to the birds of the six directions—the oriole, bluebird, parrot, magpie, asya, and roadrunner—who in turn will ask the deities of the Zenith for rain clouds. The Antelope Society messenger to the sacred water-spring blows four times on his bone whistle to announce his arrival and to call the water spirits.[230]

Most of the Katcina impersonators accompany themselves with rattles fashioned from large pear-shaped or oval gourds that grow wild in the South-west and Mexico, although Pueblo people do sometimes raise them for food and for musical instruments. To make a rattle, the tip of the neck and the rough stem at the other end are cut off. This leaves a small hole at each end. The gourd is put out to dry until the meat and seeds inside became shrunken and loose; the currents of air passing through the two holes keep it from rot-ting. Then small, sharp pebbles are dropped inside and the gourd is shaken roughly. The pebbles break the meat and seeds loose and the contents are dumped out. To dry the gourd interior, one hole is plugged and the gourd is filled with sand to help it maintain its shape. It is placed in the sun, and the walls become as hard as wood. The sand is poured out and a handful of peb-bles are inserted to make the rattling sound. These must be smooth and round, and so they are gathered from black-ant hills where round stones are plentiful.

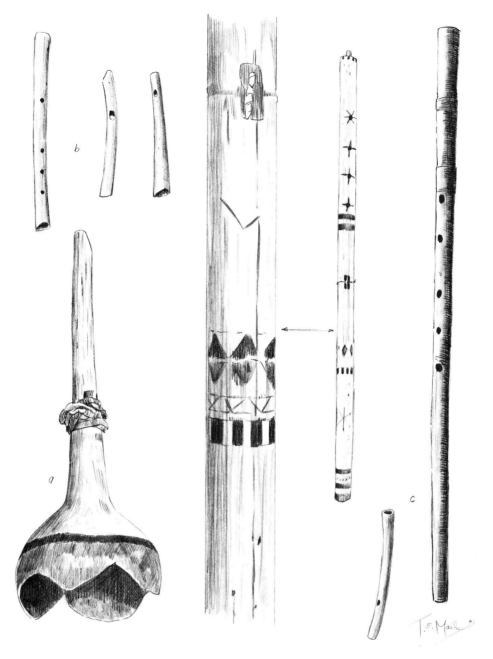

Musical instruments. Flutes: *a,* gourd type used in the Flute Ceremony. *b,* bone flutes. *c,* wooden flute and bone flutes showing comparative size. From the Heard Museum collection.

The Hopi prefer pebbles of white quartz or crystal. A short, round stick is run through the holes in the gourd, so that it protrudes at both ends. The bottom end extends only an inch or so, and either it is fastened with piñon gum or a wooden cotter pin is inserted to keep it in place. The top end extends five or six inches to provide a handle. Some gourds are left plain, others are painted according to individual views.

Other rattles are made from small tortoiseshells. The tortoise is allowed to die and dry inside its shell, and the remains are removed with sharp pebbles as with the gourd. Round pebbles are placed inside the shell, which is then plugged and equipped with thongs so that it can be strapped on the back of the leg just below the dancer's knee. A row of dancers wearing these will raise their knees in unison and stamp their feet, so that the rhythmical accompaniment comes automatically. Dancers also tie bunches of antelope hoofs to their knees or belts, and sometimes to the tortoiseshell rattle itself. Leg straps with metal sleigh bells have recently become popular as dance rattles,[231] and the Snake-Antelope dancers often have deer or antelope hoofs, or metal cones, attached to the lower edge of their kilts to serve as sound makers.

The rasp consists of three pieces. The first is a slender stick about eighteen inches long that is carved on one side in a series of toothlike ridges. Some such sticks are painted red on one side. The second is either a shorter stick or a deer or sheep shoulder blade (scapula). The third is either an overturned basket or a hollow round gourd with a round or square hole cut in one end; the edge of the cut is padded with white cloth. This cut provides a flat surface for the gourd to rest on.

The rasp is most often played in ceremonies by men who are impersonating female Katcinas and are accompanying impersonators of male Katcinas, and at least some of the gourds are painted white or black or with cloud symbols. One that I saw at the Shongopovi Niman in 1977 had alternating white and blue-green stripes.

The players kneel on quilts or pads facing the male Katcinas. The gourd is placed on the ground in front of them, resting on the cut side. The notched stick is held in the right hand at an angle, with one end resting on the gourd. The scapula is scraped downward over the notches in quick strokes. The gourd acts as a resonator and produces hollow, rasping sounds in time with the dancing. At certain points in the performance the stroke slows or accelerates, as appropriate. When the gourd is not in use the notched stick and scapula are placed inside it.

According to Parsons, the rhombus (also called a bull-roarer or whizzer) is swung to simulate wind, since wind "calls" or brings storm clouds. The rhombus makes a sound like thunder.[232] It consists of a long, thin, and sometimes pointed stick tied near its center on the end of a cord, and the stick is swung like a propeller to make the noise.

The Hopi use the rhombus in pilgrimages to springs and in other processions. It is carried and swung by a warrior who serves as guard. Hopi Koyemshi use it, as does the Hopi Cloud Katcina in the Palulokong, or Water Serpent drama. In the Flute and Snake-Antelope ceremonies it is swung in the kiva, at the kiva hatch, on the trail, and at the spring. The Hano place it on altars, and the Hopi anoint it with honey. Each Hopi rhombus is painted in a color associated with one of the cardinal directions. Sometimes one end is carved to represent a cloud terrace with a lightning design issuing forth from it.

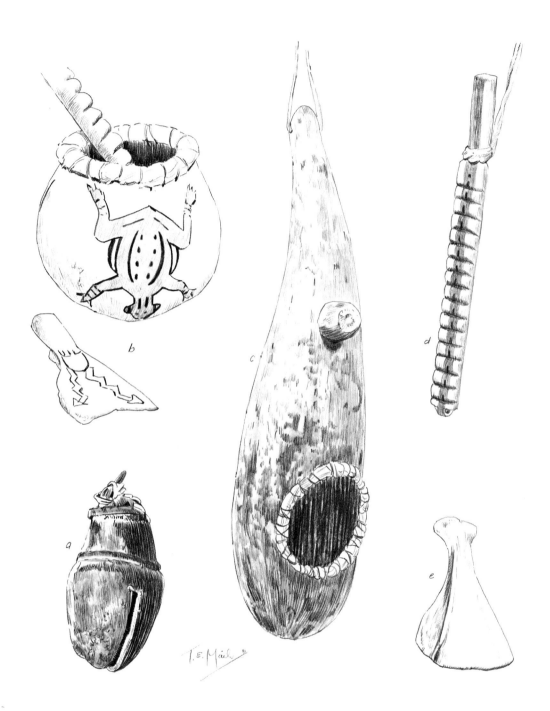

Musical instruments. *a*, hide rattle. *b*, painted pot resonator and bone scraper. *c*, gourd resonator. *d*, painted wooden rasp. *e*, bone scraper. From the Heard Museum collection.

Musical instruments. *a*, leather leg straps with hawkbells. *b*, rattle consisting of wooden stick with animal hooves attached. *c*, wooden rasp stick. *d*, wooden rasp stick, bone scapula scraper, and gourd resonator.

THE CEREMONIAL CYCLE

The enthralling and instructive ritual life of the Hopi has been least affected by intrusive foreigners. Accordingly, it can be described in the present tense. But this will not for long be the case, since the outside world is managing to take its inexorable toll. When the head of the Mamzrau on First Mesa became a Christian in 1903, the ceremony he led passed into limbo. No one from within the lineage structure was prepared to take over his role. In the same way the Oraibi Horn Society ceased to exist when Mennonites persuaded the society head to burn its ritual paraphernalia.[233] These are literal instances that only touch the surface. The broader and deeper picture presents a circumstance that ought to make any just person shudder.

Frederick J. Dockstader, in his book *The Kachina and the White Man*, describes in detail precisely what has been done to the Pueblos in regard to their religious life. Beginning with the earliest Spanish, i.e., Roman Catholic, contacts in 1540, he spells out the influences brought to bear on the Indians and the disastrous consequences. In particular, there has been from the beginning a determined effort on the part of the government and missionaries acting in concert to stamp out the Indian culture. So successfully has this been accomplished in some instances that losses have been suffered that can never be regained. "The older men died off, and the younger were diverted by schooling and outside economic and social forces from learning the traditional rites." Each year it becomes increasingly difficult to obtain recruits for Katcina dances, for ceremonial offices, and for passing on the traditions. Some ceremonies have already ceased to exist for lack of continuants, and others are threatened. The lineage system makes its own contribution to this, since without a proper ritual transfer, any order will soon become extinct.[234]

The attempt to suppress ceremonies in which the sexual aspects of fertility are emphasized has led to the replacement of formerly natural ideas about sexual activity with an increasingly unhealthy emphasis upon sex, a conscious attempt to strike back by shocking visitors during public dances, and the withdrawal of the more phallic personations to the kiva sanctuary.

Dockstader makes a particularly frightening observation. As the tribal elders react to younger Hopi who have been confused and deterred by white schooling and other influences, he thinks they may eventually consider it unwise to entrust the youth with the essential ritual knowledge, limiting it instead to a small ceremonial group. This process would greatly increase the probability that ceremonies will lapse with the deaths of their practitioners.[235]

Over and against this, there has come in recent years an extremely determined effort on the part of the Hopi and other Pueblos to undergird and preserve the old ways. No one can guess how successful such efforts will be. Intrusionists could help by leaving the Pueblos alone in this effort and by making changes in a public educational system that has attempted until recently to shame the Indian into repudiating his heritage. One wonders why human cultures in danger of extinction are not thought of in the same terms as wildlife.

It is against the law today to kill an eagle, but there are no laws to protect the human mind, heart, and soul of one who is considered an "uncivilized," hence a priori unsaved, man.

Albert Yava sees in the area of religious beliefs a steady drift away from the traditional Pueblo attitude toward nature and the universe. He does not expect the drift to end until all Indians are assimilated. "In one or two hundred years you won't find a full-blooded Indian anywhere."[236] At the same time he is convinced from experience that the Pueblo ways are essentially good, and that correct religious knowledge is supposed to produce good behavior. He knows it is necessary for the youth to learn what they must to achieve and compete in the modern white world, but he wonders openly why outsiders find it right and fair to call the Pueblo religion false, when the Pueblos cherish their beliefs and are constantly aware that the Great Spirit exists "and that without it we would not be here."[237]

In addressing a missionary, Yava asks, "How can you just assume that we are barbaric? Have you ever taken the trouble to study our ways and find out what our religious beliefs are?"[238] Yava seems to think that if everyone did, it is entirely possible that the knowledge gained thereby would cause a fair examiner to decide that in religious matters, outside influences neither were nor are needed, right, or good.

Fortunately for us, while the Rio Grande Pueblos have, with possibly one or two exceptions, always closed their kiva rituals to outsiders, the Hopi and the Zuñi have allowed certain non-Indians to witness and record in writings and photographs portions of the ceremonial rites. A number of these accounts and pictures have been published, and can be drawn upon for enlightenment.

Whenever reference is made to Hopi ceremonial life, it should be borne in mind that, while views and practices from village to village agree in essentials, there are differences in how things are done. For instance, the religious thoughts and ritual ways of Old Oraibi are not precisely like those of Walpi. Also, as Fewkes writes, it by no means follows that the rites performed during each moon of one year are the same as those performed during the same moon the next, and it is well known that some ceremonies recur after long lapses of time.[239] The following material does not as a rule account for differences, but the reader who desires such information can find it in the extensive works of Elsie Clews Parsons, Mischa Titiev, Alexander M. Stephen, Jesse Walter Fewkes, the Reverend H. R. Voth, George A. Dorsey, Alfonso Ortiz, Edward P. Dozier, and several others.

Differences between villages have not, at least in the past, kept them from honoring one another's ceremonies and revealing a mutual acceptance and dependence. Fewkes describes a Niman dance at Walpi during which five runners from Oraibi and five from Mishongnovi entered the plaza and stood in line watching the dancers. They had run all the way from their homes to see the dance, and they later ran back to report what they had witnessed. They all wore ceremonial kilts, sashes, and jewelry. A cluster of brightly colored, variegated feathers was on their heads, and they carried bows with arrows tied to them. Five runners were painted blue, and five yellow. The Mishongnovi representatives had longitudinal lines on breast, arms, and legs, and those from Oraibi had longitudinal bars similarly placed. The faces of the ten runners were also painted.[240]

In every Hopi pueblo the populace is organized into a number of secret societies, each of which is responsible for a single ceremony.[241] A particular clan has charge of each society and of its associated ritual and paraphernalia. In historic times, members, including those who become minor officials, have been selected from any clan in a village, without distinction.

The head man of a clan is usually the chief of his group's society, and he is the keeper of the most important object related to the performance of his society rite. This is the tiponi, or fetish, that is made up of an ear of corn, feathers, corn and vegetable seeds, piñon seeds, and a variety of outer string wrappings. Fewkes thinks the tiponi was originally an ear of seed corn kept in reserve in case all other seed failed.[242] The Hopi call it the "mother" or "heart" of a ceremony. It is highly venerated, and when not in use it is kept in a secret place in the clan house of the clan's head woman. To judge from Fewkes's description of the careful refurbishing of the Flute societies' tiponi at Walpi, it may be that all tiponis are redone by the head man during each annual performance of a rite. In particular, the old ear of corn is replaced with a new one, as are the feathers and the paint.[243] Other paraphernalia are sometimes entrusted to the keeping of secondary officials.[244] Parsons says she was told that each chief had a tiponi in the Underworld prior to emergence.[245]

There is a fixed time of the year during which a society is expected to perform the observance in its care. The time to begin some of the rituals is determined by the sun's position along the horizon at daybreak. Some are begun when a certain moon appears, some when a given number of days have elapsed after the completion of the preceding ritual. Leaders whose ceremonies are inaugurated by solar observation are notified at the proper times by the village sun watcher. Other society chiefs must determine their own starting dates. Ordinarily, the society members assemble in their kiva for the ceremonies, but lesser rites are sometimes conducted in the main houses of the clans in charge.

Kivas are owned by the clans whose members built them, and there are as many kivas as there are clans in each village. If one is abandoned, its ownership may be transferred to the clan that buys it and/or undertakes to repair it.[246] Its identifying name is related to the controlling clan, and the head man of the clan is commonly both the leader of his group's ceremony and chief of his kiva. His office requires of him certain ritual duties, including his acting as father of the Katcinas on specific occasions, meeting and smoking formally with messengers who come to announce impending ceremonies, sponsoring the Niman Dance in the years when that obligation, which rotates annually, falls to his kiva, and caring for the shrines associated with his kiva. In addition, he serves as the leader of many secular tasks that are performed by kiva groups, including communal hunts and spinning bees. He must also keep the kiva in good repair and stock it with firewood during the winter months. He will choose and train a successor, and this man will assist the kiva chief in his special duties.[247]

The office of the clan chief is filled by inheritance and apprenticeship. A chief chooses his successor from within the maternal family long before death approaches, for the educational program is involved and difficult. The apprentice goes with the chief as secular tasks are performed, and he is instructed as they walk and work together. But the successor must not be taught indoors or near the village where others can overhear. When the chief knows he is close to death he announces his successor. There may be protests, but the chief's choice is absolute and must be accepted.[248]

As I have mentioned, not every ritual act is performed in a kiva. For example, certain of the Flute Society rites are held in surface rooms, or houses, and some of these rooms are in upper stories. In such instances the *na'atsi*, or society standard, is set up on the kiva.[249] Fewkes entered several such rooms while Flute rituals were in progress and reports that within each of the houses there was an altar, similar in most respects to kiva altars, but lacking a sand painting. The altars are described in the material pertinent to the Flute Ceremony (page 175).

Females are barred from kivas except on special occasions, as when certain Katcina dances are performed or when women's ceremonies are going on. But boys are expected to visit the kivas as soon as they have passed their Katcina initiations. Usually a boy associates himself with the kiva to which his ceremonial Katcina father belongs, but in later life he transfers to the kiva that houses his particular branch of the Tribal Initiation rites.[250]

Members of both sexes begin their actual participation in ceremonial life when, before reaching the age of ten, they are initiated into the tribe's Katcina Cult. A few years later they take the next step by joining one or more of the secret societies. The girl seeks admission to the Marau, Lakon, or Oaqöl societies, all of which are controlled by women. Ordinarily, this marks the extent to which women may participate directly in Hopi ceremonial life, but certain women with desirable qualifications are sometimes asked to fill special offices in the men's rituals, and men may do the same for the women. The second step for a boy is to join one or more of the non-Katcina Blue Flute, Gray Flute, Snake, or Antelope societies. To enter a society, a male or female candidate must choose a ceremonial father or mother from among the members of the group. The novice is called *kelehoya*, or little chicken hawk. He or she receives an ear of corn and sometimes a wooden head scratcher. When a society performance begins, the novice enters the kiva with the sponsor and observes the rites. About the fourth day the novice undergoes purification when the head is washed in yucca suds and the ceremonial parent gives him or her a new name.

The boy's selection of a society is usually influenced by the affiliations of the ceremonial father who put him into the Katcina cycle and to whom he is a "son." But there is no compulsion. A young man can refuse to enter an additional ceremony, or he can select another ceremonial father whose group he does wish to join.

No limit is placed on the number of societies a boy can choose, but soon after adolescence and usually before he marries he is expected to join another order by going through the Tribal Initiation, after which he may automatically reach the apex of his ceremonial life by being admitted to Soyal observances.[251]

The Tribal Initiation marks the transition from boyhood to adulthood, and virtually the entire male population at age fifteen or over undergoes it. The rite is known collectively as the Wuwutcim, but it is divided into four branches, of which Wuwutcim is one and the others are Singers (Tao), Horns (Al), and Agaves (Kwan).[252]

While adult status can be achieved by joining any one of the divisions, membership in the Wuwutcim is by far the most common selection. On Third Mesa it is controlled by the Kele, or Chicken Hawk, Clan, whose head man is considered Tribal Initiation chief. Candidates are called "little chicken hawks," and the November moon during which annual observances are held is called *kel-muya*. Yearly rituals do not always include the induction of new members, since a sufficient number of novices must be available to warrant the lengthened and full tribal Initiation rites.

Those who have witnessed the Tribal Initiations agree that they are the most complicated and vital of all Hopi ceremonies, and that their significance must be understood before one can hope to grasp the essential meaning of Hopi religion.[253]

Mischa Titiev draws upon his own firsthand accounts and those of Fewkes, Voth, Stephen, Parsons, and Steward to present an engrossing chronological summary of the main events of the Tribal Initiation.[254] At Oraibi it begins when the Al chief, in his office as Sun Watcher, announces that the sun has risen at a point on the horizon known as Dingapi. The heads of the four divisions smoke and make prayer offerings that are given to the crier chief. Before sunrise the next morning, he places these in specified locations and proclaims the coming celebration. Shortly after dawn on the fourth day following, the four chiefs enter their kivas, the *na'atsi* are placed, and the rites begin. Altars are built and special offerings of cotton strings to which pine needles are tied are prepared.[255]

Fewkes states that on the day when the New Fire is kindled all the other fires in the village are extinguished. The streets are dark and deserted. The men are in the kivas, and the women and children are secreted in their houses. All the trails leading to the village are symbolically closed; no living thing is permitted to enter the place. To close the trails, a sacred-meal mark is drawn at right angles to the path. To open the path again, a prayer-meal mark is drawn lengthwise on it.[256]

In late afternoon, the members of the three assisting groups enter the central kiva, which is that of the fourth group, to hold joint observances. After prayer and singing, the Al and Kwan men light two fires with rotating drills. When the fire blazes, the pine-needle offerings are prayed over and thrown one by one into the flames as sacrifices to Masau'u, and an Al man, wearing

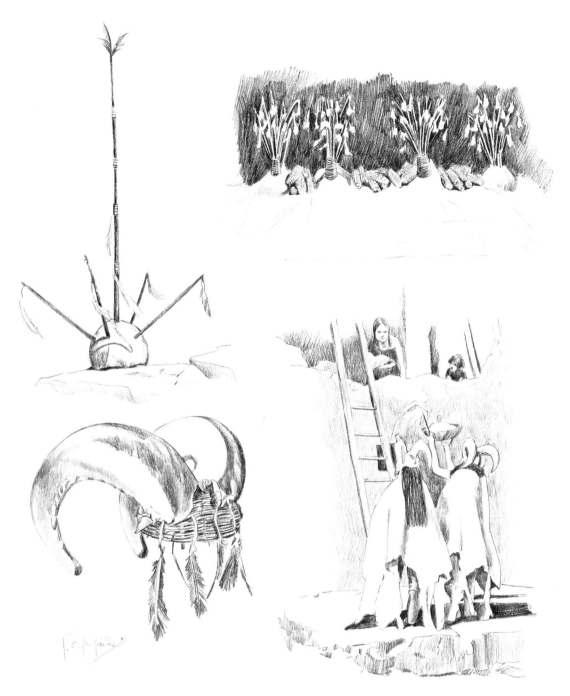

New Fire Rite. *Top left, natsi* of the Kwan Society. From Voth, 1912. *Top right,* altar of the horned priests. *Bottom left,* helmet worn by a Hopi priest impersonating mountain sheep. *Bottom right,* Horn priests begging for cornmeal with which to make trails on the ground to certain shrines, so as to "open the trails." From Fewkes, 1920.

the two-horned headdress of his order, lights a cedar-bark torch from the fire and hurries out of the kiva to kindle fires at all the other participating kivas. At the same time, another Al man goes to a shrine from which he brings back the image of Dawn Woman, an important deity whose image is displayed on kiva hatches until the fifth day of the observances. All fires are kept going for the full nine days of the ceremony.

The entire group proceeds then to the shrine of Sand-altar Woman, the female counterpart of Masau'u. A brief ceremony is conducted to honor her, and the group is led by an Al officer to a space below the mesa said to be one great sipapu where the wise old men live, who are now Katcinas in the Underworld. These are prayed to for rain, health, and abundant harvests. (At Walpi they go first to the sipapu area, and then to the shrine of Earth Altar Woman.)[257]

Prayer offerings are deposited, the sacred area is circled four times, and the men return to their individual kivas. Fewkes believes that at this time the spirits of the dead are invited to visit the village.[258] The day's rites completed, the candidates go to sleep wrapped in the same blankets as their "fathers." But other society members carry out night patrols throughout the village, and the Tao group performs a dance the next morning. There are rituals throughout this second day, and patrols again this night.

On the third day there is another morning dance, and in the afternoon the Wuwutcim give a public performance in which some of their men appear disguised as women, some pregnant, and some married, with phallic symbols painted on their garments. This begins two energetic days of very bawdy encounters between society members and the women of the village. When properly understood, these are important fertility rites made vividly instructive through the graphic displays.

On the fourth day of the ceremony, visitors are again barred from the village and all the trails are closed, save one. "This night," says Titiev, "is a night of mystery and terror," and no white man has ever witnessed it.[259] The villagers remain indoors and are forbidden to look outside, for on this awesome night the dead are invited to return along the one open trail to the pueblo. Food has been prepared for the expected guests and set out at sundown on one side of the village. Everyone who lives on that side goes to stay with a relative on the other side.

All night long, patrols of Kwan and Horn men rush madly about the village, constantly challenging one another and keeping up a frightful noise as they look anxiously for deceased spirits and for living intruders who, if discovered, will supposedly be beaten or killed. While all this is going on, an even more awe-inspiring event is taking place in the kivas. It is said that each spirit returning from the Underworld is supposed to enter the kiva with which the person was associated while alive on earth. To dramatize this, four Kwan men, wearing well-known and foul-smelling garments removed from recently buried Hopi, appear suddenly before the novices. In their astonishment and terror, boyish lives are resoundingly terminated as the novices are reborn as men.

On the fifth day the fathers who sponsor the novices and their fellow members wash their own hair with yucca root. Then sponsors wash the hair of their sons and give them a new man's name. The boyhood name is either discarded or retained as a nickname.

On the sixth day a few dances are given, but fuel-gathering and hunting are featured by the four society groups. The seventh day is quiet, except for mild teasing between the members and women as the members dance in public. On the eighth day the dances become quite serious, and germination motives are emphasized by the costumes worn and by clay, loaf-of-bread-shaped molds studded with ears of corn that the Singers carry and then distribute to the women spectators at the conclusion of the dance.

Long before dawn on the ninth and closing day the Kwan men dress and practice in their kiva an unusual dance step. Then they chant their secret songs, in such a subdued manner that no one else can hear them. After this, they leave the kiva and proceed to the plaza, where four Horn Society men, their horned headdresses reversed, have built great bonfires and are mimicking the antics of frolicking mountain sheep. When all four societies have assembled, the Kwan chief conducts some preliminary rites and sprinkles a broad path of cornmeal, starting at the west end of the line, as the Kwan men sing. The song ended, the chief breaks the path by sweeping across it. The Kwan men return to their kiva, remove their costumes, and are permitted to return to their homes. Later in the day the Tribal Initiation rites are completed with the performance of public dances by the Wuwutcim and the Singers.

In attempting an interpretation of the Tribal Initiation, Titiev emphasizes that the candidates are required to sit on the kiva platform and to adopt for several days the supposed fetal posture of unborn birds. Each novice is also given a wooden head scratcher that he uses as a bird does its claws. On the fourth day each ceremonial father gives his son a traditional-style ceremonial poncho he has woven for the occasion. Its design is such that when worn it gives the novice the shape of a hawk, with feathers, wings, and tail. In all this the novice is represented as undergoing a new birth, or rebirth, and the concept is given literal expression in many ways during the course of the rites. At First Mesa, the initiates are first carried into the Chief Kiva like babes in the fathers' arms. Later, they are carried about like children, wrapped in blankets, on the backs of Singer's men, and finally they are allowed to walk like children, each holding the blanket of the one preceding him.[260]

Dawn Woman is regarded as the mother of the novices, and the return of her image to its shrine on the fifth day indicates that she has been safely delivered of her children. Also, a blanket is stretched over the kiva hatchway to keep the sunlight from striking the candidates, in duplication of the Hopi practice of preventing the sun from shining on newly born infants and their mothers.

Taken as a whole, the Tribal Initiation appears to be a reenactment of the Emergence story, which centers in gestation, birth, communion with the dead, and death itself. In this instance the sipapu plays its well-known role as the avenue through which these happenings are carried out. In particular, then, the Kwan society fulfills its special and singular role in the Initiation Ceremony. It is intimately associated with Masau'u, God of Death, and it is the keeper of the home of the dead. Normally, the chief of the Kwan is the head of the Masau'u Clan, and he impersonates Masau'u throughout the rites. When the fires are kindled on the first day, he is present in the kiva but hidden behind a blanket, for it is Masau'u who first taught the Hopi how to use fire. Also, Masau'u is one of the main war gods, and the Kwan Society is a warrior group. They paint their bodies with warrior markings and carry lances as part of their paraphernalia. The Kwan are the key, in fact, to whether a Tribal Initiation will even be held, for they refuse to perform their part of the ceremony unless there is at least one candidate for their order.

Fewkes connects the New Fire Ritual with the idea of New Birth. In his view, the relationship of Masau'u to the rite becomes understandable when we recognize that physical death in the Hopi mind is only the prelude to a new birth and life in the Underworld.

When the Tribal Initiation Ceremony is reduced to its essentials, it is readily seen that the four societies fall into two divisions. The Kwan and the Al represent and venerate the powers of germination and the organs of reproduction. Taken together, the four groups dramatize in their ceremonies the principal elements of the Emergence myth. Since the earth is a mother rather than a creator, the Kwan worship Masau'u, who owns all the crops; the Al revere Tuwapontumsi, who owns all the animals; the Tao petition Talautumsi, goddess of childbirth; and the Wuwutcim concern themselves with crop increase and general fertility.[261]

Deriving maximum effect from the masterful use of theatrical devices, including the transformation of the subterranean kiva into a dark replica of the Underworld, the four societies unfold, step by step, the Emergence story for the novices. When at last the youngsters have experienced fully the details of their origins and destiny, they are no longer regarded as little chicken hawks. Their lives as children are terminated, they are reborn as men, and they are prepared to fulfill the responsibilities of life and death. As Titiev sums it up, each initiate receives spiritual status and a specific station in the after life. This helps explain also why the Kwan leader must baptize village chiefs, and other high officers, before their positions as rulers are assured both in this world and the next. And, it explains why only those who have been initiated may go on the salt-gathering journey which "takes men to the very brink of the home of the dead."[262]

Titiev emphasizes that a belief in life after death is the most widely spread of the basic concepts of Hopi religion.[263] This truth is manifested again and again in ceremonies. In keeping with this belief, Fewkes adds: "The modern Hopi recognize in man a double nature, corresponding to body and soul, and to the latter they give the expressive name breath-body . . . It is the breath-body or shade of man which passes at death through the sipapu, or gateway, to the underworld."[264] With this faith firmly in hand, death is considered as being little more than an important change in status. There is no real loss to society, for the dead are reborn to go on living in the Underworld much as they have on earth; as Cloud People, or rain-bearers, they continue to serve the living in a vital way. Likewise, the living serve the dead, in that their *nakwakwosis*, or prayer offerings, encourage and even compel the spirit people to join in all that is done.

Fewkes explains that, accordingly, the object of the winter ceremony of the Flute Society is to announce to those believed to be engaged in simultaneous rites in the Underworld that the priests in the upper world are occupied with their devotions.[265] As to the use of the words "simultaneous rites," it should be remembered that when the minor or winter rite is being held in the upper world, or on earth, the major or summer rite is being held in the Underworld.

The induction of novices in any given year causes several changes in the ceremonial calendar. The Soyal is held in an extended form, and some of the newborn men take part in it for the first time. Powamû is lengthened by the inclusion of Patcava rites. In May, the Nevenwehe, or spinach-gathering, celebration takes place, during which the former novices fill their Tribal Initiation ponchos with the freshly plucked blossoms of edible plants. Then, before the spring ceremonies occur, a fertility rite known as Maswik Katcina is held on the sixth night of Soyal to announce the coming observances. Masau'u is featured in the performance, and the Katcinas are called Maswik, which means Masau'u-following-at-the-heel, because they enter a kiva first and are soon followed by the Masau'u impersonators. Men who have gone through the Tribal Initiation the previous month join with more experienced society members in serving as the Katcinas.

In performing the ritual, the kiva chief, after a smoke, announces that in the spring, during bean-planting time, Nevenwehe will take place. After this the dancers are costumed, some as males and others as females. While they sing and dance, the Masau'u actors come, put their hands on the shoulders of the male and female leaders, make the howling cry of Masau'u, receive *na-kwakwosi* and meal from the kiva chief, and then exit to the shrine where they deposit their offerings. The Katcinas finish their dance, and the entire performance is repeated in the other kivas. In this way the announcement of Nevenwehe is made.

In the month of May, at the proper time, the Sun Watcher advises the people to plant their bean crops. At the same time the older members of the officiating kiva begin to practice for an involved Maswik Katcina performance in which dances are given, and the former novices and girls, dressed in traditional costumes and wearing the ancient hairstyles, exchange gifts of specified food. In this manner Nevenwehe fulfills and completes the Tribal Initiation observances. The November rituals promised fertility and bountiful crops. Now, the generous bestowal of edible plants by the newborn men on the village maidens illustrates that the promise is bestowed in its fullest aspects.[266]

All major rituals of the Hopi that take place in kivas are of nine days' duration, and every ritual has its origin legend that is repeated in its songs and acts. When, however, new members are admitted to the Tribal Initiation Ceremony, the duration is extended to seventeen days. Ordinarily, the Initiation begins with a brief preliminary meeting known as Prayer-stick-making, eight days before the main rites occur. This first gathering can take place either in the controlling clan's house or in the kiva. Once the prayer objects are made, some of them are placed at designated shrines by messengers, and others are given to the town's crier chief. He deposits these at daybreak in a shrine located on the roof of the house from which he makes the announcement that the ritual observance is about to occur.[267]

The most common form of prayer offering is the paho. This prayer stick or plume is inseparably connected with all religious ceremonies and prayers. It is a prayer in itself, and it makes the spoken prayer associated with it effective. Pahos are manufactured in several forms. One consists of two sticks, which often are painted green with black points and tied together with cotton string cut to a prescribed length. One of the sticks is male, the other female. According to Stephen, only the female, as a rule, is given a face, consisting of two dots for eyes and one for a mouth.[268] A small corn husk shaped like a funnel and holding a little cornmeal and honey, it is attached to the pair of sticks where they are joined together by the tie string. Added to the husk is a short, four-strand cotton string, on the end of which are tied two small feathers. Above the butt end of the sticks are tied a turkey-wing feather and a sprig of two specified herbs.

Other pahos are made of flat pieces of board ranging from 1 to 3 feet (30 to 91 cm) in length and 2 inches or more (5 cm +) in width, to which feathers and herbs are attached. Painted on the boards are symbolic figures of Katcinas, natural objects, animals, and reptiles.

Pahos used on altars are numerous, and they vary considerably in design. Some are long, thin sticks with cotton strings and feathers attached near the ends. Others are thicker, with a profusion of feathers tied on at their center. Some are bent over in a cane or "crook" shape. Others are just straight rods. Some are long willow switches to which feathers of the eagle, hawk, turkey, flicker, and other birds are tied.

All pahos have meanings that are understood by the society members, and they are employed accordingly. A cane shape is usually a prayer to a very old person who has died and gone to the Underworld, but who, by the stick's presence, is now called back to share in the ceremony and to assist in the fulfillment of its purpose.

All pahos are made with care and solemnity, and they are prayed over each time they are used. It will be noted that there are ceremonies for making pahos. The kiva leaders meet to fashion them, and they always perform prescribed acts before the actual construction of the pahos begins.

Stephen explains the theory behind the prayer stick and prayer feather. He says that a man makes a prayer stick because he wants something good, some benefit from Cloud, the Cardinal chiefs, the Ice chief, or Planting one. From these and other chiefs all benefits proceed. A man makes a prayer stick as prescribed because the thinking old men of the old time knew and said that it should be made thus or thus. Feathers are used in prayer sticks and prayer feathers, *nakwakwoshi*, because they are *kapü'tü*, not heavy, but light, and Cloud and all the other chiefs desire them to make ka'lamoñwû, the prayer feathers hanging in front of the forehead.

The Hopi barters his prayer sticks and prayer feathers with the chiefs for material or other benefits, and he places on his prayer stick the prescribed feather and grass emblems in accordance with the kind of benefits he may desire. The birds whose feathers are used are the yellow bird, warbler, bluebird, turkey, eagle, hawk, duck, and owl. If a Hopi desires rain, he ties on a yellow bird or duck feather, and a turkey feather is tied to every prayer stick. For the hot weather needed to make a good peach harvest, owl and yellow bird feathers are used. For game, the feathers of the turkey and yellow bird are used; also sü'hü, the grass that deer and antelope prefer. The feather of the bluebird is for snow and ice.

The father of a young boy makes him a pü'htabi *nakwakwoshi*, to which is tied the primary wing feather of the hummingbird. This is a long pü'htabi (road marker) prayer feather of the ordinary form. He places the free end of the string of this prayer feather against the base of the shrine, the feather toward the sunrise, and prays for swiftness and endurance, that his movements may be like those of the hummingbird, as swift and tireless.

As Sun journeys across the sky, he sees the prayer sticks and prayer feathers and comes to them, inhales their essence, and takes them with him—not the actual sticks and string and feathers, but their breath body, or likeness. He places them in his belt and carries them with him as he goes in at the west to the Underworld. There he gives all that he has collected, through each day's journey, to Mûyingwu, who knows all prayer sticks and prayer feathers. As Mûyingwu takes them up one by one and looks at each, he says to the other chiefs, "This is for you, or you," according to the way the prayer sticks are designed. Those that are poorly made, or made by thoughtless men or men of evil hearts, he casts away, saying, "This is from an evil man, or a foolish one." The chiefs thank Mûyingwu and the makers of the emblems. They decorate their foreheads with the feathers and send the benefits that the prayer-maker desires.[269]

While she could not feel a relationship to the paho because of her education in non-Indian schools, Elizabeth White's father gave her a beautiful explanation of a certain two-stick paho. The blue-green chipped-off place at the top was the "face" of the prayer stick. It represented a mossy place, moisture. Below that was the "body." Its red color, like sand, represented the earth that received the moisture. The corn-husk bundle tied to the sticks held grass seeds, cornmeal, pollen, and honey. When all these things were present in a paho bundle, it was a prayer for a plentiful harvest. The feathers represented the spirits that were "in" the prayer. No paho was to be touched for four days after it was placed. To do so would bring terrible harm to the offender. Even after that it was to be touched only with the left hand, for the left hand was on the heart side of the body, and it did not grab as the right hand did. Also, it was cleaner, it did not touch the mouth during the eating of food, and it did not clean the body after waste was released. In healing, the medicine man always used the left hand.[270]

The town crier chief is an important religious officer, known as the "mouth

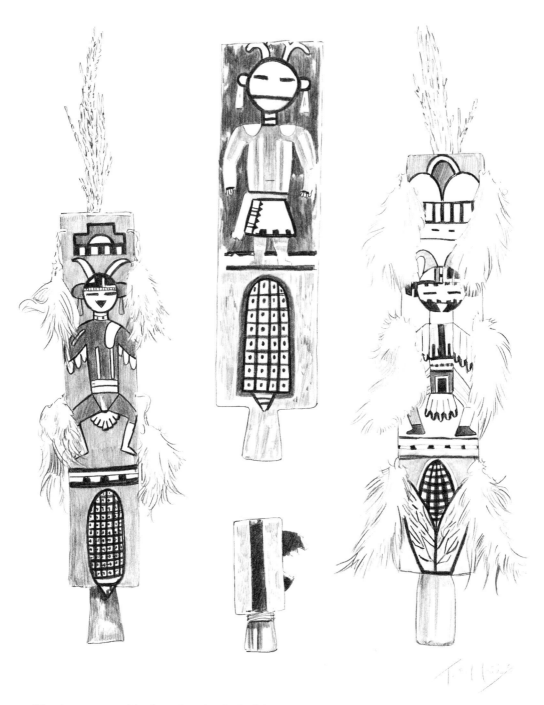

Wooden prayer sticks featuring the God of Germination. From the Heard Museum collection.

of the village chief," who announces the major ceremonies such as Soyal, Tribal Initiation, Niman, Snake, Flute, Marau, Oaqöl, and Lakon, as well as communal enterprises and planting parties. Titiev adds that at Oraibi the town crier chief calls out from the Kele Clan house, sometimes speaking in a low voice to show he is addressing the Cloud People rather than the villagers.[271]

Once the eight intervening days have gone by, the leaders proceed to their kiva and erect a *na'atsi,* or standard. This is placed where everyone can see it, either on the south side of the entrance hatch or suspended from a rung of the

Typical Soyal and Powamû pahos. Left to right, two bent or crook types; one large stick type; two standard types; two willow-stick types with eagle, turkey, hawk, flicker, and other feathers tied on. Bottom, the Powamû altar and sand mosaic.

kiva ladder. It gives notice to one and all that the society is in secret session. From this time on, none but members may enter the kiva, and all participants must refrain from salt, fat, and sexual indulgence. Any nonmember who breaks this rule is forced to join the society.[272]

The first day of a nine-day ceremony is called *Yungya'a,* or Entering. It is important only in the sense that it is the beginning, and the full membership is rarely present. The next four days are numbered from one to four, and the last and more significant four days have descriptive names: Once-not-anything, Piki-providing, Food-providing, and Dance day.[273] Ordinarily, the first seven days are given over to ritual, the eighth day sometimes combines public activities with private, and the ninth day usually features a public dance by the society. Titiev says that despite the zeal with which the various societies guard their rites from one another, there is little difference in procedure. They all tend to conform to a regular pattern, although the order in which particular acts are performed may vary widely.[274]

Most of the secret ritual in the kiva is devoted to smoking, singing, and praying and is accompanied by shell or gourd-rattle music and by the manufacture of prayer offerings. The offerings are placed at specified shrines, and one or two members are sent to make four circuits (of progressively decreasing size) around the village on four successive days. During each circuit, prayer offerings are placed at a number of sacred places. At different times, society members impersonate figures to which the cult is devoted. In addition, altars are erected, sand paintings are made, and medicine water is prepared.

The Hopi altar is set up at the north end of the kiva, and it has two parts. The first is a reredos or back screen, and the second consists of a group of ritual objects set on the floor in front of the screen. Each ritual has its own altar or differing design and objects, and in his articles on Hopi ceremonies Fewkes has illustrated a number of these.[275] The usual reredos is made up of a row of vertical wooden slats, together with clay tiles or flat stones, that are all affixed to an upright wood frame. On these are painted symbolic or realistic representations of natural and supernatural things related to the ceremony in progress. Typical are corn, rain clouds, lightning, heavenly bodies, sacred animals, and cultus heroes.[276] The base of the altar reredos rests directly on the

The town crier.

kiva floor, and in front of it are placed tiponis, the effigies of sky and earth gods and of cult patrons. Also a medicine bowl sits on a low pile of sand. Six radiating lines of sacred meal are drawn out from the bowl to represent the six cardinal directions. On top of each line is placed an ear of corn whose color corresponds to the direction with which it is associated. The north ear is yellow, the west is blue or green, the south is red, the east is white, above is black, and below is speckled. Appropriate bird feathers, aspergilli, crystals, stone animal effigies, varicolored pebbles, and other objects are also placed along the lines.

When they make their medicine, the officers of the society mix the ingredients while the other members sing sacred songs, shake their rattles, and beat on the floor of the kiva to let the people in the Underworld know what is happening. Obviously, either those in the Underworld do not always know, by their supernatural powers, what is occurring on earth, or the living members are expected to acknowledge by sounds that they know the Underworld persons are listening and sharing. They must be notified, even though, it is said, at the same time that a ceremony is being enacted on earth its counterpart is taking place in the spirit world. Therefore, for the period when medicine is being made the sipapu is uncovered, that is, the wooden plug is removed from the hole in the board cover.

Water in which the ingredients are mixed is brought from a special spring in a netted gourd. As the water is being poured into the medicine bowl, various objects from the radiating lines of sacred meal already mentioned are dropped into it at intervals while specified songs are sung. Sometimes a crystal is used to reflect light into the bowl. Stephen states that this may be interpreted as a prayer for fertility, since there are several myths that describe how women became impregnated when a sun ray fell on the vulva.[277] Sometimes smoke is blown into the bowl as a direct appeal to the home of the Clouds.[278] Nearly always, a member kneels and blows an eagle or turkey wing-bone whistle into the bowl. This, says Titiev, is a means of summoning the deities.[279]

Nearly every secret society is able to control a particular illness. This illness is called its *wuvata*, or whip, and the ability to control it is inherent in the sacred paraphernalia of the society. Titiev gives a list of the Old Oraibi societies, controlling clans, home kivas, and their associated ailments, which include twisting sickness, lightning shock, weight loss, earache, rheumatism, snakebite and abdominal swellings, epilepsy, facial sores, head eruptions, running sores, and sore throat.[280]

The whip, or illness, strikes all who trespass on ceremonial secrets, but it may also afflict persons and things that come into contact with religious objects even in legitimate ways. To prevent this, the members of a society purify themselves by a rite called Navotciwa. They take a pinch of ashes in their left hand and wave it counterclockwise over a person or object while singing a discharming song. In particular, the Navotciwa Rite is performed at the conclusion of a ceremony so that the members can mix once again with the people without danger to themselves or others.[281]

Parsons makes reference to several Hopi methods of purification in addition to the use of ashes. Prayer meal is also used, and self-induced vomiting is common. On unmasking, the Hopi Katcina impersonator waves his mask around his head four times, and after that a pinch of ashes.[282]

The Hopi believe that whatever causes a disease may cure it. Accordingly, those who suffer from an illness controlled by a given society will call upon that group to heal it. The cure is generally accomplished by waving ashes over the patient while the society's discharming song is being sung. Titiev states that, as a rule, the cured person usually joins the society that cured him, "either permanently or for a period of years."[283]

During the nine-day ceremony, one of the society chiefs directs the fashioning of a sand painting. Usually it is laid out freehand, but sometimes mechanical aids are employed. Portrayals are similar to those painted on the altar reredos. The colored sands are controlled, Navajo-style, by letting them trickle in a fine stream between the thumb and forefinger.

The kiva rites usually terminate on the eighth day, at which time the altar is dismantled and the sand painting is destroyed. The next day, virtually the full membership appears in public in spectacular costume to perform what is popularly called a dance, although as Titiev points out the term is not always an apt description. When this dance ends, all participating society members are expected to refrain from salt, fat, and sexual indulgence for four more days and retire to the kiva and remain there to avoid temptation. After this they emerge and resume their secular activities.[284]

THE OPEN KATCINA SEASON

According to Titiev, the annual and cyclical Katcina calendar of the Old Oraibi Hopi is as follows:[285]

In late November, on the day following the end of the Wuwutcim rites and sixteen days before the start of Soyal, the Winter Solstice ceremony, the Soyal Katcina (one of the Chief Katcinas) opens the Katcina season. Since the Katcinas have been resting and sleeping for six months, the Soyal Katcina comes alone to the village, supposedly from the shrine of the village's founder, in the guise of an aged, weary, sluggish man wearing shabby garments. He first performs a brief dance in the plaza. Then he deposits prayer sticks at the Chief kiva, sings and dances awkwardly, and makes paths of sacred meal in the four cardinal directions. This opens the kiva to Katcinas arriving from any direction. The village chief then arrives at the kiva, and the two exchange offerings. The chief makes a cornmeal path toward the shrine whence the Soyal Katcina came, and the latter follows it back out of the village.

Then in December, at the time of the winter solstice, Soyaluña, or Soyal, is held to begin the new year.

The next Katcinas to appear are two Mastops, who come on the afternoon of the eighth day of the Soyal. They run into the village and by various and

Hopi Sio Hemis Katcina

Hopi Land's Walpi Pueblo

Snake Gatherers Leaving the Kiva at Old Oraibi

Hopi Priest at the Shrine

Hopi Hemis Katcina and Katcina Mana

Hopi Snake Dancers

San Juan Sun Basket Dancer, 1920

Santa Clara Male Comanche Dancers

Santa Clara Butterfly Dancers at Puye Cliffs

San Juan Male Deer Dancer (*original egg tempera*)

Santa Clara Female Rain Dancer

San Juan Winter Buffalo Dancers

Zuñi Shalako

Santa Clara Corn Dancers

Comanche Dancers on the Kiva Roof at San Ildefonso

Lazy Day at Laguna Pueblo

Intermission at Acoma Pueblo

Santa Clara Rainbow Dancers

Laguna Bow and Arrow (or Comanche) Dancers

Zuñi Pueblo, 1885

The Rio Grande Sacred Clown (*original egg tempera*)

Apache Clowns for the San Juan Deer Dance *(original pastel)*

Santa Clara Male Basket Dancers

Santa Clara Male and Female Harvest Dancers

San Juan Deer Dancer

Soyal: In mid-December, Ahulani and his two sisters, Blue Corn Girl and Yellow Corn Girl, appear beside the Chief *(Mong)* Kiva at Walpi. They come to bless the corn crop for the coming year. The sisters carry distinctive corn bundles as they sing and slowly process through the village. Pictured here is the Yellow Corn Girl sister. From a Jo Mora photograph.

excited gestures indicate they are consumed with sexual desire. Arriving at the Chief kiva, where the Soyal rites are under way, they stop to discuss their desire, pretend to notice nearby women for the first time, run to them, place their hands on the women's shoulders, and by making little jumps simulate copulation. They continue to do this until all the women present have been seduced. The purpose is obvious. A fertility rite is being performed in which it is shown that during the Katcina cycle the village will be blessed by the perpetuation of all things needed for well-being. Accordingly, the women submit willingly to the Mastop performances, and females of all ages, infants to grandmothers, are included. When the Mastop finish, four Soyal celebrants, bearing sacred offerings, emerge from the Chief kiva, circle the kiva four times, and then deposit their offerings at Flute spring.

On the ninth and final day of Soyal, the Qöqöqlom Katcinas perform the first group Katcina dances of the season. Although masked, they wear a mixed costume of native and white garments and inject comedy into their routine. Their primary purpose is to supplement the Soyal Katcina by opening the various kivas. They do this by having two of their number sprinkle meal at the kivas while the rest dance. The exception is when most of the Qöqöqlom pause

Soyal: The Mastop Katcina. The nine foot-shaped marks at the top of the mask are said to represent the nine days of the ceremony, the dots over the eyes the Pleiades, those on the cheeks the Dipper. On top of the mask are feathers and red horse hair. At the sides are corn-husk ears. At the base is a wreath of dry grass. On the back are frog designs.

to share in the opening of the Powamû kiva. Kiva sponsorship for the Qöqöqlom rotates annually in a fixed sequence, and the kiva in charge of the opening group dance in December is also in charge of the concluding Katcina performance the following summer. Moreover, the head of the Qöqöqlom Katcinas is the chief of the Powamû Society and the head of the Badger Clan, who manages the first half of the open Katcina season.

Because a whole new year is opening, the Soyaluña Rite promotes a festive attitude among the Hopi. The people exchange greetings and make offering presents consisting of prayer feathers and of pine needles tied to cotton strings called "breath lines." Leaders for the ceremony itself are the Soyal priests, a war chief, a hawk or thunderbird man, and other personages. All societies of the village cooperate in preparing prayer sticks and ritual paraphernalia.

Soyal: The Qöoqöqlöm Katcina. The mask painting probably represents, in a conventionalized form, a growing cornstalk. The feathers of many birds are worn on top of the mask. *Bottom left*, items used for consecrating pahos: grass fuse, three pipes with reed stems, reed cigarette.

In the Chief kiva an elaborate ritual is conducted for nine days. Only the highlights will be touched on here, but with misgivings, since the entire ceremony is extraordinary. The main altar is decorated with bunches of grass and hundreds of brightly painted artificial flowers. On its top are rainbow symbols covered with cotton that represent snow-bearing clouds. In front of the altar is a pile of corn stacked like a row of cordwood. The corn has been collected from the village residents, and it is returned to them filled with "fertility power" when the ceremony ends. Beside the corn are tiponis. In front of the corn is a mound of sand on which are placed corn fetishes made of stone and wood. Also in front of the reredos are the medicine bowl, a number of pipes, prayer sticks, and other items peculiar to the Soyal ceremony. Besides this altar, one other is built as the ritual progresses, plus a screen representing Mûyingwu, the god of germination.[286]

The secret performances held on the fourth and fifth days are particularly dramatic. Members first sing the traditional songs, accompanied by rattles, flutes, whistles, and bull-roarers. The songs are interspersed with prayers, and when they are all finished an initiation ceremony for novices is held. Then the first and splendidly costumed birdman enters the kiva, followed by the second birdman and the Soyaluña maiden, who perform an esoteric dance together. After this, Eototo, the principal chief of the real Katcinas, enters bearing corn, and a pretense battle breaks out between the Thunderbird men, leading members from other kivas, and the Soyal sun-shield bearer, who represents the War God. With overt and dramatic action, the Thunderbirds and other members lash out and strike their shields against the sun shield, as if locked in deadly combat. For a time it appears they might defeat the sun, but just at the critical moment the sun-shield bearer forces them back and drives them from the kiva.

On the ninth and final evening, a man enters the Chief kiva dressed in magnificent ceremonial garments, on his forehead a large four-pointed star. In one hand he holds a shaft with a large sun symbol attached to the end. While the priests are seated around the altar and sing, this performer dances rapidly and spins the sun symbol as he does so. His dance concludes the Soyal Ceremony, which celebrates with maximum joy the arrival of the Winter Solstice, and has as its primary object the driving of the sun into his northward path, so that he returns and brings life back to the Hopi.[287]

When the Qöqöqlom ends, the Katcina season is opened, and society dance groups may impersonate any of the ordinary Katcina types they choose. Before the first public dance takes place, though, the kiva that is to perform the Niman, or Homegoing, Dance at midsummer must present a preview of that performance. This takes place on the third night after Soyal, and it includes the composition and learning of one of the songs that will be sung at Niman. When the song has been mastered, the men dress in their Katcina costumes but do not mask. After a short rehearsal they visit each kiva, where they perform the new song, and the leader announces that he will sponsor the Homegoing Dance that year.[288]

Soyal: The Star priest in the act of twirling the sun symbol at the climax of the ceremony. During his performance the leader of the War ceremonies, representing the War God, sprinkles him with sacred water from a medicine bowl. Behind them is the large Soyal altar. To the left is the small Soyal altar, and the screen representing Mûyingwu, God of Germination.

Once the introductory Katcina rites are concluded, which is by early January, the cycle of dances is in full swing, and the entire month is one of happy activity. Because of uncertain weather, Katcina dances are held at night in the kivas, with each group making its rounds of all the kivas in the village.[289]

Night Katcina dances are informally organized, and they are performed whenever the village chief gives the sponsors his permission for them to do so. As word of this spreads, the head of each kiva chooses the type of Katcina that will be impersonated by his group. Songs, masks, and costumes are prepared, and practices are held. Uninitiated youngsters are not permitted to attend these, and so performers are sometimes careless about concealing their identities. Dance days are inspiring and exciting ones for the entire village as each kiva group seeks to outdo its rivals. By late afternoon the men are holding rehearsals in the various kivas, and the muffled sounds of singing and dancing fill the pueblo.

The men go home for supper, and then return to their kivas and dress. With masks in hand they withdraw to a private house and hold a final rehearsal. Titiev mentions how, on one occasion during his stay in Oraibi, he was honored when his house was used as a dressing room. "Never," he says, was he "more impressed with the dramatic quality of these performances. The atmosphere was exactly like that which prevails back-stage just prior to the curtain's rising."[290] Meanwhile, the rest of the village, along with visitors that include whites and Navajos, file into the kivas where their nearest kin belong, although visitors are welcome in any kiva. Married women and infants sit on the south platform, unmarried girls sit on the west wall banquette, boys on the east and north banquettes. The father of the Katcinas sits just in front of the ladder, and west of the firepit crouches a fire-tender who is responsible for providing adequate light and heat. Before long the sound of bells, rattles, and sometimes a drum announces the approach of the Katcinas. As they approach the kiva they shout and hoot, while the father and the spectators call out for them to enter.

After the Katcina leader announces that he has just come to the village from the shrine where his Katcinas dwell, he responds to good-natured persuasion from the father, and the Katcinas enter the kiva. The father now stands and thanks them for coming, sprinkles them with sacred cornmeal, and exhorts them to dance with happy hearts. The sprinkling and exhortations continue while the Katcinas perform. When the dance ends, the Katcina usually distribute gifts to the spectators and begin to file out of the kiva. If the dance has been pleasing, and it most often is, encores are called for simply by preventing the Katcinas from leaving.

On dance nights, each Katcina group makes two complete rounds of all the kivas, singing and dancing to one song the first time, and to another the second. When the last dance has ended, the spectators hurry to their homes and the dancers return to their kivas to remove their costumes and to wash. For the next four days the dancers must refrain from sexual indulgence, but otherwise they live regular lives. Most families hold a feast on the morning after a dance, but there is not as much emphasis on this as there is after the Katcina dances that are held in the spring and summer. At frequent intervals throughout January, night Katcina dances are performed. The Hopi also have gambling games for men and women, and Buffalo dances, since these are not connected with the ritual calendar.

Parsons describes a Buffalo Dance she saw at Sichomovi on November 20–21, 1920.[291] The Lizard-Snake clansman in charge assembled the dancers and the dance paraphernalia. A choir and a drummer provided accompaniment. There were two male dancers and two female dancers. The men held wooden lightning sticks and rattles, and each of the women held two notched sticks.

The women wore traditional attire, but no calico underslip. Neck and arms were bare. A man's dance kilt was draped over the shoulder as a bodice, and on top of this was an abundance of necklaces, "borrowed as usual from all the family connection." Each woman wore the fringed wedding sash, and on her

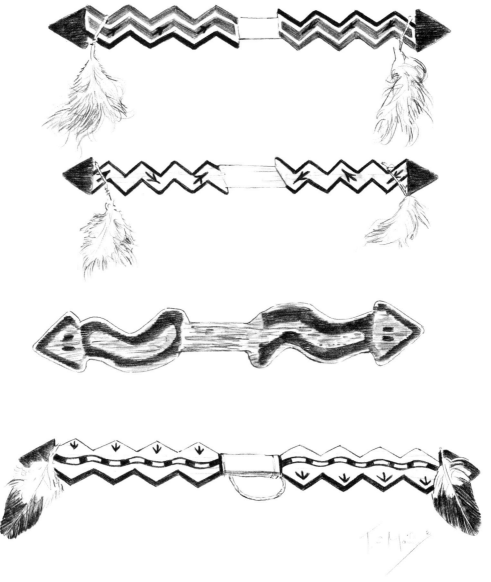

Wooden lightning prayer sticks carried as dance wands in the Buffalo Dance. From the Heard Museum collection.

back was a circular sun tablet. This was painted with a design representing the face of the sun. Around the perimeter of the circle was a border of red horse-hair, and a larger circle of radiating golden eagle tail feathers. The woman's hair was left flowing in the back, and over the forehead and eyes was a fall of artificial black hair that extended to the tip of the nose. On top of each woman's head was a large bunch of downy eagle feathers. On the right side of the head was the conventionalized cotton or wool squash-blossom common to Hopi masks, with a pendant of red yarn. On the left side of the head, at right angles, were some eagle-wing feathers. Slanted across each cheek were two parallel black stripes. The rest of the face and the hands were whitened. There were hanks of yarn around the wrists, and silver bracelets.

The male performers were barefooted. Their feet were whitened, and their legs were blotched with white. They wore fringed buckskin anklets. For a kilt they employed the maiden's white woolen blanket bordered with red and blue, and fastened it on with a broad rain-sash. Their "buffalo" horn headdress was actually a sheep pelt with small horns attached, and a headband of porcupine quills. Downy eagle feathers were secured to it at the top, and a small feather was tied to the tip of each horn. From six to eight eagle wing feathers were

Below, sun shield worn as bustle by female Buffalo dancers. From the Heard Museum collection. *Above*, wooden racks used to carry captured eagles.

attached to the back of the headdress. These were joined at the quills, and the tips fanned out. The face paint was black, with a touch of white on the chin and white smeared across the lips.[292]

In general, these costumes are identical to those I have seen in recent years, except that the male headdress is sometimes fashioned from an actual buffalo hide.

Below, feather bustle worn by Buffalo dancers. From the Heard Museum collection. *Above*, traps used to capture small birds needed for feathers. The weights are pieces of sheep bone carved to represent animals. Horsehair or human hair loops entangled the bird's feet as it walked into them to get the bait. From the Southwest Museum collection.

CLOWNS

A personage of some magnitude in the ceremonial cycle is the ritual clown. Hopi clowns are usually referred to as Mudheads because of their favorite mud-colored attire, but, depending upon what they seek to portray, clowns dress themselves in a number of ways, and not all should be called true Mudheads. Even the clan chiefs play true Mudhead roles, and the Mudheads are considered Katcinas, while most other clowns are not.

Each Pueblo group has its own name or names for its clowns. At Hopi it is Tachukti or, alternatively, Koyemshi. A Mudhead figure occurs at Zuñi, and it is known there by the identical name Koyemshi. In fact, it is believed that the Hopi obtained their Mudhead clowns from Zuñi. If, however, the Mudheads did come from Zuñi, especially after 1850, as some say, then it is also certain that the Hopi had other clown forms long before that. The clowns are

Mudhead drummer providing music for ceremonial dance on a very large double-headed drum.

too much a part of the Hopi religious Way to not have originated earlier. They probably occurred as soon as any original Katcina, since the Pueblos associate clowns with the act of Emergence itself. In fact, legends say that clowns were with the people when they came out of the sipapu and onto the earth.[293]

Most often, the clowns are referred to as those who entertain the people. This they do, performing during the rest periods that occur between dances and sometimes even when dances are going on. They put on humorous acts, play childish games, play tricks on people, and sometimes indulge in obscene acts, gestures, and talk. The Hopi take all this in good humor and laugh wholeheartedly, because they understand what is going on. In the midst of the solemnity and power invoked by the dances, and the consequent possibility that the Hopi might begin to think too highly of themselves, the clowns bring the people "down to earth" again and keep them ever conscious of who they are as compared to the deities.

To emphasize the fact that they are, however, more than just ordinary clowns, the clown impersonators sometimes dance seriously along with the Katcina impersonators, and they often play the musical accompaniment on the drum. During major kiva rituals, Mudheads fill key roles. They appear to bless initiates who are joining the Katcina Cult, and as actors they perform in the Water Serpent drama at Palulokong.

The standard costume for the true Mudhead consists of a mask and no other costume save a G-string, a black breechclout, and red moccasins, although the performers are at liberty to work variations on this theme. Formerly, the mask (most often called a "sack mask") was made of thick hide, and I have seen several such. Somewhere along the way these were replaced by cloth, and commercial sacks from the trading post became a popular item from which to fashion Mudhead masks. Many of the sack type still bear the manufacturers' printed trademarks and propaganda.

The cloth sack is saturated with a dull-red clay, and tube-shaped rawhide eyes are sewn on, along with a roll of cloth shaped to form a mouth. Holes are torn in the mask where the eyes and mouth are located, for vision and breathing. Four large cloth knobs are then fashioned. These are filled with raw cotton, seeds, and, Virginia Roediger says, "earth from the footprints made by the inhabitants in the streets around the pueblo."[294] Supposedly, this last act gives the Mudheads a magic power over the people that permits the clowns to demand their respect and reverence.[295] The knobs are also covered with red clay and are sewn onto the mask with string, one at the top, one on the back, and one on each side. A canvas band about five eighths of an inch wide is interwoven around the mask so that it can be drawn in around the neck to make the mask smooth and secure. On occasion, simple designs are added to the front of the mask with black paint. Some masks have cotton strings attached to the outer surface of the knobs, and to the strings white breath feathers are attached. Sometimes a black cloth scarf is tied over the mask around the neck and hung in front. According to Roediger, a small bag of seeds from native crops is concealed under this.[296]

Mudhead mask made of canvas, daubed with pink paint and with black design on front.

The same clay as that used for the mask is employed to paint the entire body of the true Mudhead. Ordinarily the regular Mudhead wears a black breechclout or a black kilt over this paint, but the leader of a Mudhead group may wear a short black dress that passes over only one shoulder. The Mudheads may wear moccasins or go barefooted.

When they are to perform, clowns arrive at random intervals in the plaza attired in makeshift costumes of every imaginable kind and carrying any manner of accouterment they need to carry out the acts they have in mind. They come as whites in mixed-up attire, hippies, animals, Navajos, as shoddy depictions of certain Katcina impersonators, or whatever, usually mocking in their attire and actions whomever they are depicting. The clowns are extremely popular and appear to have a ritual importance that has escaped most observers.

Albert Yava, in referring to the clowns at his village, Hano, agrees that the clowns play a significant ceremonial role. He says that clowns once had their own fraternity and still observe the same kiva responsibilities and tabus as other Katcinas. They are involved in the portrayal of Emergence stories, and they rehearse for their public performances. Their obscene behavior, he says,

Clowns. *Left*, the Hano clown called Paiyakyamu, with body striped in black and white—derived from the Rio Grande Pueblos. *Right*, Hopi Mudhead clowns (Koyemshi or Tachukti) attempting to sweep up water with a broom and yucca basket. The reverse, or backward, behavior reminds viewers of the Underworld, where life is always opposite to what is going on on earth. As such the clowns represent the dead and can comfort the bereaved. They also can do the forbidden and bring humor to ease tension.

is really intended to tell people how *not* to behave, and in so doing they remind everyone how important it is to be decent, respectful, and harmonious in their way of life.[297]

Hopi clowns often mistaken for Mudheads are the Tsuku. They look something like Mudheads, but they wear no mask. Instead, the face is painted with black quarter moons under the eyes and lower lip. They wear a cloth skullcap with corn husks attached in the shape of horns worn backward, and their hair sticks out. The body is painted with brownish clay. They wear a white rag around the loins, a black breechclout, a black neckerchief, and black arm and knee bands. A bandolier passes over the right shoulder and under the left arm. They wear high-topped red moccasins. In a special ritual performance they walk to the plaza over the rooftops and descend, behaving as though they don't know what Katcinas are all about. So disruptive are they that before the dance is over they are whipped and otherwise abused by Katcina warriors. This is done to teach them, and the Hopi parents in the audience, a lesson as to what will happen if they neglect the education of their children in Katcina lore.

At Hano, the Tewa village, one may see the Rio Grande version of the ritual clown. Here he is called a Koshari, and his attire is quite different from that of the Mudhead. His body is painted with horizontal black-and-white stripes. His face is white, and black semicircles are drawn around his eyes and under his mouth. On his head is a black-and-white skullcap with two tall horns appended, topped by corn husks. He wears a black breechclout, a woven sash, arm and leg ties of hide, and high-topped red moccasins. On a thong around his neck is a small medicine pouch. His counterpart receives further treatment in the Rio Grande chapters (page 428).

POWAMÛ

As soon as the February moon is seen, all other dance performances are suspended, and the Powamû ritual begins.

After a preliminary rite called Powalawu, during which prayer offerings are made, the Powamû chief makes the rounds of the kivas, smokes with each kiva chief, presents him with prayer offerings, and tells him he can now begin to plant beans. When the Powamû chief departs, members of each kiva gather soil, water, containers, and seed beans for planting, making every effort to hide these activities from uninitiated children. In each kiva, the containers are planted with from fifty to one hundred beans and watered. From this moment until Powamû is concluded a hot fire is kept going in the kiva, and members tend the bean crop while they learn new songs composed for the coming bean dance.[298] Although each man will actually share in the yield, the plants are said to be grown for the Eototo and Aholi Katcinas. Eototo is the spiritual counterpart of the village chief who has charge of the Eototo mask. Only the village chief can impersonate this Katcina. Second in importance at Old Oraibi

Soyal: Eototo, the Katcina chief, and Aholi, the Katcina chief's lieutenant going through the village and rubbing meal lines on various houses. *Top left*, a *mongkoho*, the badge of office, or membership, of different societies and priests. This one is used by the Ahl (Horn) Society.

is the Aholi Katcina. He is impersonated by the Pikyas chief, who is first assistant to the Bear Clan leader in the Soyal performance.

The Eototo and Aholi representatives plant small crops of corn either in the kivas or in homes. These are carefully watched while they mature, for their success assures a productive farming season, and a bountiful crop is a sign that a person has a good heart. In the eight-day interval between Powalawu and Powamû, the village hums with activity as kivas are refurbished and children receive special short haircuts. Women weave basketry plaques, and men carve Katcina dolls, little bows and arrows, shinny sticks and balls, and rattles—all to be given as gifts at Powamû. Men meet in the kivas every night to rehearse Bean Dance songs, and they hold unmasked, uncostumed, and informal Katcina dances at which they use old songs to help the beans grow. Reciprocal kiva visits are made to see one another's performances and to compare bean crops, at which time good-natured rivalry is expressed.[299]

When the eight-day interval comes to an end, the Powamû chief raises his standard at the Powamû kiva, and the observance of secret rites gets under way. Little of note occurs until the fifth day, when the altar is built and sacred songs are sung. Also, in those years when youngsters are to be initiated into the society, the inductions take place on this day. The ritual for the initiation is more elaborate, and it includes a sand painting and the impersonation of the Tcowilawu Katcina, one of the *wüye* of the Badger Clan that controls the Powamû Ceremony. Membership in the Katcina Society is open to children of either sex, and the form of induction follows the customary pattern of Hopi initiations. After initiation, the males are entitled to be present at ceremonies to learn all the secrets of the order and to act as Katcinas; even as Katcina fathers. The females may sprinkle Katcinas with sacred cornmeal and participate in Powamû ceremonies whenever the presence of women is required.[300]

Other children in the village who are initiated only into the Katcina Cult are not allowed to participate in the Powamü Ceremony, and they cannot serve as Katcina fathers. For these there is a separate initiation on the sixth day of Powamû. This is conducted in another kiva, where two important sand paintings are made. When the village chief and the officers assisting him in Soyal have taken their places in the initiation kiva, thirty or more novices are brought to the kiva by their ceremonial parents. The Powamû novices also come to watch the proceedings. After some preliminary acts, including one in which every initiate steps into a hoop and has it lifted and lowered over his body four times,[301] the Powamû chief, in the mask and costume of Mûyingwa, the God of Germination, lectures the initiates about the tribe's sacred lore concerning Katcinas. Four times while he speaks, Mudhead Katcinas come out from behind a blanket in the corner, carrying an ear of corn in one hand and feathers in the other. Holding their hands together, they wave them in a prescribed way toward each novice and return to their hiding place.[302]

When Mûyingwa departs, two Hu Katcinas and one Hahai'i Katcina arrive with great fanfare, circling the kiva hatchway four times and beating on it with long yucca-leaf whips. When the initiates are properly cowed, the three fierce-looking Katcinas enter the kiva. One by one the terrified candidates are placed on the sand painting by their ceremonial parents to receive four severe lashes with the whips. If a ceremonial father wishes, he can pull his "son" away, put out his own leg, and take one or two of the four lashes.[303] When the whips grow limp from use, they are replaced with new ones. Whippers take turns, and it all goes very fast. When all the initiates have received their lashes, the Katcinas whip one another, and the Katcina chief dismisses them with gifts of prayer feathers and cornmeal. The children are sternly warned never to betray the secrets they have learned on pain of dreadful punishment at the hands of infuriated Katcinas, and the ceremonial parents take the children to their respective homes for a grand feast.[304] Three days later, Katcinas come to the homes and give presents to the initiates.

On the eighth day of Powamû, a messenger returns from Kisiwu, one of the most important mountain shrines, and tells in detail about his trip. The concluding rites are performed, and the altar is dismantled. Masks and other paraphernalia are readied now for the ninth day, and dress rehearsals are held.

Long before the following daybreak the men harvest their bean crops, and twenty-four hours of crowded observances begin. The sprouts are brought secretly into each home in the village that has uninitiated children, so that the children can be convinced the sprouts were brought in their developed state by the Katcinas. Also, each society member ties bean shoots to the ceremonial gifts he has prepared either for his uninitiated ceremonial children or for favorite relatives. One or two costumed men from each kiva, choosing whatever Katcina impersonation they wish, take the gifts and receive instructions as to who is to receive them.

At dawn the village chief, preceded by the Soyal war chief and followed by the Soyal crier chief, leaves the kiva to pray to the sun. Shortly thereafter the Katcina mother, Hahai'i, comes slowly into the village and proceeds to the Powamû kiva, where she is blessed. She symbolizes a recently married girl's return to her home after her nuptial rites. Next, the Eototo and Aholi Katcinas emerge from the Chief kiva and approach the Powamû kiva, indicating by various acts as they do so that the pueblo belongs to them. They then perform a water rite that signifies the coming of ample rain. Next they return to the village, go to the homes of important persons, make ritual drawings, and give the owners some of the recently sprouted bean plants. The rest of the afternoon is given over to feasting in the Chief kiva and in households.[305]

Late in the afternoon men dress in a great variety of Katcina costumes and roam the village streets entertaining the people and handing out more gifts. Returning to their kivas, the men disrobe and prepare for the night showing of the Powamû Katcinas in the popular Bean Dance. According to Voth, the So'yoko is performed at this time, when a group of threateningly costumed and armed Ogre Katcinas tour the village threatening to take disobedient children away from their parents but are bought off with gifts of food instead. At Old Oraibi the Ogre Katcinas appear also at times other than Powamû.

Late in the evening, final preparations are made for the Bean Dance, in which the performers wear all the strange secular apparel they can borrow from family and friends, that of women and men alike. About midnight the Powamû chief announces that everyone should dress, the bizarrely garbed men vacate their kivas, the spectators come in, and in due time the unmasked Powamû Katcina performers return. As the men enter the kiva, one of their fellow members calls down jests at the expense of each Katcina impersonator. The men announce, though, that they are real Katcinas. Adding it all together, the initiates in the audience soon realize that the Katcina impersonators are their relatives and fellow villagers. "In such dramatic fashion is the most important of all Katcina secrets revealed to Hopi children."[306]

A fast dance is performed, and the Katcinas then file past the west bench where the unmarried girls in ancient dress and whorl hairdo are seated. Gifts are exchanged, and a young woman can, if she wishes, use the occasion to offer a loaf of *qömi* to her lover as a marriage proposal. It is almost daybreak when the dancing ends, and the performers gather at their kivas to feast on gifts made to them. At the same time the newly initiated boys and girls are taken to the homes of their ceremonial mothers, where their heads are washed and they are given new names.[307]

In years when there has been a full Tribal Initiation during the preceding November, the Powamû is extended to include the Patcava performance. This begins at twilight on the day following the Katcina initiations. On two successive evenings, He'e'e, one of the mothers of all the Katcinas, leads processions of various Katcinas about the village. On the morning of the ninth day of Powamû she goes to each village shrine, collects Katcinas, and brings them into the village. This is an enactment of the Katcina myth told at the Initiation Ceremony. The following day the legendary admission of the Badger Clan to Old Oraibi is dramatized, and in this play the clan leader illustrates how his promises to raise corn and bean crops through the agency of the Powamû Ceremony are fulfilled annually.[308] Three days after the conclusion of Powamû, a racing season with definite religious connotations is begun.

The Powamû terminates the period of Badger control. It is the midpoint of the open Katcina season, and authority is transferred at this point to the head of the Katcina Clan. Night dances in the kivas, known as Anktioni, or Repeat dances, are resumed. In some of these the Koyemshi, or clowns, are featured. At Old Oraibi in recent times it was customary to include in the first series of Repeat dances the Palulokong, or Water Serpent, drama which was similar in some respects to the Powamû.[309] In this performance, puppets that represent the mythical serpents are manipulated from behind a screen. It is a single act in a night series of Katcina dances, and it moves from kiva to kiva. Titiev finds it strange and difficult to pin down, in that it lacks the familiar tiponi, altar, and other features, yet it requires detailed preparation, employs many religious properties, "and it carries a deeper significance and embodies a more elaborate set of rites than any other Katcina performances except the Powamû and the Niman."[310] Once again beans are planted in all the kivas, and beans and corn are cultured in the officiating kiva. Kivas may also be cleaned and replastered. When the leaves of the corn plants begin to open, the sponsor announces the fifth day following as the date for the performance of the Water Serpent Dance.

Titiev states that at Old Oraibi four serpent effigies were generally used: a large male with a red belly, black head, and black stripes on the back and sides; a big female with a white belly; and two children with white bellies like the mother's.[311]

In the preliminaries, He'e'e Katcina appears at night and leads her "children" around the kivas in an involved series of visits. Almost immediately afterward the corn plants are harvested in the kivas. They are attached to small conical mounds of mud that will be used in the performance, and they are distributed equally among all the kivas, to be secreted until the performance begins. Toward evening that day the images are carried to Oraibi's main spring by the four men who will manipulate them, several Katcina impersonators, four Chief Katcinas from the Powamû kiva, and four members of the Blue Flute Society in full regalia. At the spring, guards keep spectators away while a ritual is performed. There are songs, prayer offerings are deposited, the participants smoke, flutes are blown on the surface of the water, and the heads and tails of the serpent images are dipped in the spring.[312]

While the ritual is being enacted at the spring, the spectators file into the empty kivas and await the return of the Katcinas. Walter Hough is one of the few white men who have seen the Palulokong, or Water Serpent drama, and a paraphrase of his vivid description follows.

In the middle of the kiva two old chiefs sit close to the fire, which they feed with small twigs of greasewood to produce an uncertain flickering light. Strange cries outside the kiva and a ball of cornmeal thrown down the hatchway are answered by invitations to enter. The fire is darkened by a blanket held over it, and the actors climb down the ladder and arrange their properties.

The serpent screen at Walpi. From Fewkes, 1918.

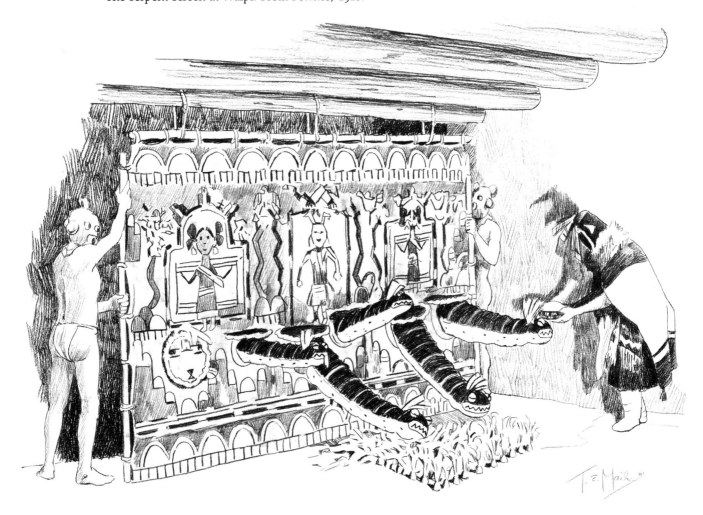

The fire-tenders drop the blankets, and as if by magic there appears a miniature field of corn on the floor made by inserting sprouted corn in clay pedes-
tals. Behind this field of corn is a screen, decorated with figures of human
beings, corn, clouds, and lightning, and along the screen there are six openings covered by flaps. On each side of the screen stand several masked men.
One is dressed as a woman and holds a basket tray of meal and an ear of corn.

A song begins and the actors dance to the music. The hoarse roar of a
gourd horn resounds through the kiva, and instantly the flaps in the screen
are drawn up and the heads of six grotesque serpents with goggle eyes, feather
crests, horns, fierce teeth, and red tongues appear in the openings. Farther
and farther they extend themselves out, until four feet of the painted body can
be seen. As the song grows louder the plumed serpents sway in time to the
music, biting at each other and darting toward the actors. Suddenly they bend
down, sweep the imitation cornfield into confused heaps, and raise their wag-
gling heads as before. Now it is seen that the central serpent has udders, and
she suckles the others. Amid the roars of the horn and great excitement, offerings of meal and prayers are made to the plumed serpents. Quickly then the
props are dismantled and the actors file out. But this act constitutes merely the
first of a series of which the sixth is even more remarkable. Back of the field of
corn on the floor there are two large pottery vases with lids. As if by magic,
the lids fly back, and from the vases two undulating serpents emerge. They
swoop down and scatter the cornhills, after which they struggle with each
other and then withdraw into the vases. In the dim light of the kiva fire, the
cords by which the serpents are manipulated cannot be seen, and the realism
of the act is wonderful. In some years the acts are even more startling, for
masked men wrestle with serpents, who try to coil about their victims. To
accomplish this, the actor thrusts one of his arms in the body of the snake, a
false arm having been tied to his shoulder.[313]

Titiev explains that the corn plants are knocked over to signify that the
Serpents are harvesting crops they produce and own. Then, while the performers are on their way to the next kiva, the father of the kiva where the
ritual has just been enacted gathers up the scattered corn plants and distributes
them among the spectators. Other kiva units then visit the kiva at intervals
and dance for the audience.[314]

At Old Oraibi, two large puppet dolls representing Shalako Katcina maidens who grind corn have become associated with the Water Serpent Rite, and
in recent years they have been shown in place of the Water Serpents at one of
the night dances. Their performance resembles in many ways that of the Water
Serpent Rite, and it is followed by Katcina dances.[315]

The magnificent Shalako Katcina is impersonated at various times during
the Anktioni season, sometimes as part of the Water Serpent drama, sometimes separately. The Shalako Katcina is always escorted by other Katcinas,
most of which, at Old Oraibi, are supposed to belong to the Bow Clan. She is
preceded into the kiva by male Katcinas who wear cloud headdresses and by
several rain-bearing girls. These provide the music, consisting of rattles and
rasps, while Shalako dances. With this group there are four impressively costumed guardian Katcinas.

Left, Katcina mana costume worn at Long Hair Katcina Dance at Lower Moenkopi, June 25, 1977. The mask of the mana was ocher with turquoise squares at the lower edge. Her hair was worn in a *chongo* with a red fringe going around the forehead. The mask beard was black with three pendant turkey feathers tied to twisted cotton strings. She wore a yellow shirt and black knitted stockings. *Right,* masks of Mountain Lion (or Wildcat) Katcina and dance leader seen at Second Mesa. One informant at this dance said it was a ''Hawk Dance,'' another said it was a ''Mountain Lion Dance.'' The upper area of the Katcina's mask was blue with black eye markings. The lower face and beak was white with blue spots. A white string and attached plume hung from the beak. On the back of the head was a fan of six orange hawk feathers. The feathers on the crown were peacock, parrot, and macaw. The entire upper torso was painted red with a wide stripe of yellow paint running like a band over both shoulders. On each arm were two blue stripes enclosing a yellow band. The dance leader's mask *(bottom)* was red with black on white for the mouth and yellow crescents over the eyes. On his cheek was a white star. A narrow beard contained a small beak, and a red-ribbon tongue protruded from the mouth. A white plume hung by a twisted string from the chin. The head covering was black velvet with a band of white wool wrapped around a piece of string. The body was rubbed loosely with black paint.

Titiev believes that the Old Oraibi Palhik, or Corn-grinding Maiden Ceremony, differs somewhat from the Palhik at other villages. Men impersonate both male and female Katcinas, with the latter wearing the costume of women whose white masks and terraced tablitas are virtually identical with those of the Shalako Katcina. Those who impersonate male Katcinas are dressed in the usual kilts and sashes, and they carry gourd rattles in their right hands. But their bodies are painted like those of Powamû Katcinas in the Bean Dance. On their heads are blossom symbols like those worn by flute players in the Flute Ceremony, and they hold flutes in their left hands, indicating a tie between Palhik and Flute ceremonies. The men wear blue masks, and on their backs they carry rainwater shields similar to those worn by the instrumentalists of the Blue Flute Dance. Koyemshi provide the singing and drumming for the Palhik Dance. Several men in Paiyatamu clown costume also dance, but they do not perform comic acts.[316]

The Anktioni season at Old Oraibi also includes the Huyan, or Barter, Katcina Dance. The male participants prepare a number of dolls with which they run about in the kivas while women attempt to grab the dolls. Women who are successful must then provide food for the Katcinas. In addition, any woman who wants a doll but does not get one can put on a feast for the kiva members, after which the men are required to give her a doll as soon as possible. Parsons explains that on First Mesa the Huyan Katcinas trade dolls with women who desire to bear children. Huyan Katcinas carry long yucca whips with which they lash one another before a dance. They also enter a kiva by climbing headfirst down the ladder, and those able to do so leave feet first. If one of them falls, the others promptly whip him.[317]

By the time the Anktioni season ends in late March or early April, the weather is pleasant and Katcina dances can be held outdoors. These continue on a sporadic basis until the Niman dance is performed in midsummer. Every dance day is a holiday, with open houses, guests freely welcomed, and much feasting.

Anyone whose heart and community standing are good can sponsor a Katcina Dance in this period by obtaining permission from the village chief. The sponsor selects the type of Katcina to be impersonated and makes the necessary arrangements. Individuals prepare their own masks and costumes, and rehearsals are held in the officiating kiva. An all-night session devoted to smoking, praying, rehearsing, and prayer-feather-making precedes the day of the dance. About dawn the men paint and dress themselves, and with masks in hand they proceed to a shrine. The masks are placed on the ground in a line, and the men form a line parallel to the masks. The first song to be sung is rehearsed, and as the sun begins to rise the masks are put on.

The men proceed single file to the village. Where the houses begin, the father of the Katcinas meets his "children," and by sprinkling cornmeal as he goes he makes a path for them all the way to the village plaza. From then to sunset the Katcinas dance and sing. There are breaks for rest and food, and masks are removed only when the Katcinas are away from public view. On several occasions the Katcinas bring gifts to the plaza, and these are placed on

Hemis Katcina Dance, Shongopovi, July 30, 1977. On this particular day thirty-four Hemis Katcina dancers, eight Katcina manas, one Hoho mana, and three medicine men participated in the dance. Each Katcina mana wore a yellow mask with red-brown fringe and a beard of bunches of bluebird tail feathers, pendant earrings of turquoise, a white woven shawl with a red and black strip, white leg wrappings, and either white or brown moccasins. Each carried a gourd resonator and evergreen. The Hoho mana wore the same clothing as the Katcina manas, but with an evergreen collar. Her mask was black with white designs and had red ears. Turkey feathers were appended to the crown of the mask. Each Hemis Katcina wore an embroidered kilt wrapped to close on the right. Two sashes, one over the other, were worn around the waist. One was a traditional brocaded Hopi sash, the other was red and green. Evergreen boughs were tucked under the brocaded sash, with each bough extending down below the knees. A fox skin hung down the back from the waist. The body paint was black. The masks were blue/green with white circles, ocher trim bands, and with a rainbow of stripes on the visor at the top. The tablitas were various colors and designs topped with parrot, turkey, and eagle feathers, a macaw feather, and yellow wheat. The mask collar was evergreen. The positions of the dancers in each of the first three sets is as shown.

the ground while they dance. When the dance ends the gifts are distributed to the audience. About sundown, the father of the Katcinas gives each of the performers a prayer offering and cornmeal. They return to the kiva to undress, then deposit their offerings at Katcina shrines or in their fields. They must then observe four days of continence.[318]

Clowns often appear in the dance plaza in the afternoons. Some belong to organized clown groups, but others are merely volunteers who give impromptu performances for the amusement of the audience. They may mimic the Katcina dancers, or they may act independently, often performing burlesques and gluttonous and obscene pranks. They focus upon excess and upon the base nature of man. Some are exceedingly skilled at this, and the Hopi spectators respond with enthusiasm.

NIMAN CEREMONY

As the sun draws near the summer solstice, the open season comes to a close, and preparations are made for sending the Katcinas back to their homes to rest and sleep. Four days after the summer solstice, the sixteen-day ceremony begins that is called Niman, or Homegoing. The masks worn in the ceremony by the Hemis Katcina are among the finest and most impressive, and when the long line of dancers is assembled the spectacle is absolutely breathtaking. However, other Katcinas may be used as the Niman Ceremony Katcina, including the Sio Hemis, Ma'alo, Tasap, Kuwan Heheya, and Angak'.[319] When the Niman Katcinas come to the plaza they bring with them great bunches of cornstalks from the first corn harvest of the year. Tied to these or tucked also in their arms are carved Katcina dolls, bows and arrows, cattails for pollen, and other gifts that are to be given away to the audience at specified times during the dance.

The Katcina Clan chief, assisted by the head of the Powamû Society, leads the Homegoing Ceremony, seeing that all the necessary paraphernalia are gathered and rehearsals are held. The dance procedure follows the customary routine, but when the dance ends, the village chiefs bless the dancers with smoke and medicine water and give them prayer offerings and sacred cornmeal. Their father offers an extended speech in which the Katcinas are thanked for past favors. Then he prays devoutly for their continued help and that of their Cloud relatives. After this the dancers are led to a special covered hollow shrine not far from the village. The cover is removed, and each Hemis impersonator drops his offerings into the shrine. When the lid is replaced, it symbolizes the unofficial closing of the open cycle. The performers unmask, remove their costumes, and return to the village as regular people.

Early the next morning the Eototo Katcina, the Katcina and Badger leaders, and other officials perform additional rites that terminate at the hollow shrine, where the cover is again removed, more offerings are deposited, and the cover is replaced. On this occasion Eototo wears over his head a simple white bag with small ear-like appendages and a sprig of evergreen on top.

Round holes are cut in the bag for the eyes and mouth. He wears a white cotton shirt and white knitted leggings. A fox skin hangs at his back, and he carries a digging stick, a small water jar, a special black paho, and a bush with four colored disks appended to it: a yellow disk for the North, a green disk for the West, a red disk for the South, and a white disk for the East.[320]

The Katcina season is now officially closed, and no further impersonations can be performed until the Soyal Katcina arrives to launch a new season. The one exception is Masau'u, the God of Death. He can come in any season because death comes when it pleases. Three days later the above-named chiefs meet again for a smoke, and the retiring sponsor of the Niman Dance names his successor. This man then carries a Katcina mask to his home kiva to indicate his acceptance.[321]

THE CLOSED SEASON

Flute Ceremony

The duty of the Gray Flute chief, to whom the village chief entrusts the sun watcher's job, is to observe the sun's path from the close of Soyal until the summer solstice is reached. During his time of watching, both the Gray and the Blue Flute societies hold specified ceremonies. When at last the Gray Flute chief is certain the sun is at its summer home, rituals are held during which prayer offerings are made to be placed at the summer solstice shrine and elsewhere.

Voth states that the sun plays an especially significant part in Hopi religion. There was, as far as he knew, no secret or altar ceremony where some prayer offerings for the sun were *not* prepared and deposited. But in no other societies' ceremonial did the Sun Cult "occupy such a large part as in that of the two Flute orders."[322] Fewkes wrote an extensive article about the "sun worship" of the Hopi, but then, paradoxically, he states in it that the Hopi *do not* worship the sun. "The sun itself is not worshiped, but in their minds became a symbol, a representative of powers back of the sun controlling meteorological phenomena."[323]

In addition to their solar observances, the two Flute societies conduct elaborate ceremonies biennially in August. Although prayers to the sun are prominent in these, petitions for rain and germination are dominant. Contrary to the practice in other Hopi ceremonies, the altar building and other acts are carried out in the main homes of the controlling clans. Usually, the two societies meet separately, but their main public performances are held jointly.

In their nine-day Le-len-ti Ceremony, the first four days are given over to the customary procedures already outlined for other rituals. On the fifth day their tiponi is reverently unwrapped and then covered again. Before dawn on the ninth day a kisi, or cottonwood shelter, is erected in the dance plaza, and a Masau'u impersonator sits within it. At sunrise, men race from the plain below up to the village, and that afternoon the culminating rites of the Flute

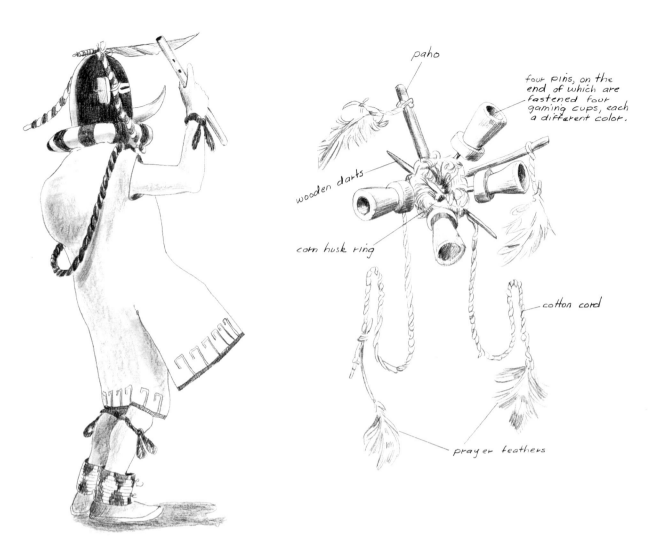

Right, headdress worn by the Flute priest at Oraibi. From the Field Columbian Museum, Chicago. *Left*, Kokopelli, the Humpbacked Flute Player, perhaps the best-known Katcina figure next to the Hemis Katcina. Kokopelli is an ancient personage, common to all the major tribes of the Southwest and Mesoamerica. His main association is with fertility, and he is openly phallic in nature.

Dance are held. First, the two societies assemble at the main spring of the village. The men engage in a ritual smoke, after which they dress and paint, with the experienced performers assisting the others. What evolves is one of the most splendidly costumed groups to be seen on the mesas, for their attire is as sensitive and graceful as their flute music.

In the Walpi Ceremony, the two warriors, one from each house, wear an embroidered kilt and red moccasins. Daubs of white paint are placed on each breast, under each breast, and on the abdomen. White bands are drawn on the outside of the arm, thigh, and calf. The hair above the forehead is plastered with white paint or clay, and two chevron-shaped designs impregnated with metallic hematite are drawn on the cheeks. A feathered hair ornament is worn on the back of the head, and a skin quiver is slung on the back. Over one shoulder is a buckskin bandolier with arrowheads, shells, and other items attached to it. Each warrior carries a bow and arrows in one hand, a bull-roarer in the other.[324]

A mana from each house wears the traditional bordered white blanket over her shoulders, tied in front with green threads. A tassel at each corner of the blanket has a feather attached, and feathers are also tied on the back of the blanket at the shoulder blades. A white rain sash is worn, hanging on the left side. The hair is let down and tied back with a string. A small white feather is attached to the crown of the head. The chin and lower jaw are painted black with corn smut, and a narrow white line extends from ear to ear just above the black paint. According to Fewkes, this line is made by dipping a string in

Flute Society. *Left*, member dressing for the ninth-day rite at the spring. *Right*, society priest.

white paint and laying it across the face.[325] The top of the foot and the back of each hand are painted black, and a black zigzag line is made on the outer side of each leg and forearm. The maidens wear huge, square turquoise earrings and many necklaces.

Two boys wear the white embroidered kilt. The face, feet, and hands are painted like those of the manas, and zigzag lines of white are painted on the breast, one on each side, and on the outside of the upper and lower arms and legs.[326]

Four young boys, not more than ten years old, carry the Flute standards. Their bodies are painted red, with parallel yellow stripes on the breast, legs, and arms. On their heads is a large cluster of red, yellow, green, and white feathers. They wear plain white kilts, with an ear of corn thrust under the belt. They are barefooted and wear bandoliers with shells attached.[327]

Four Flute members carry stalks of corn, and Fewkes gives them the name "corn-bearers." These are the flutists. They wear white kilts that are secured with brocaded sashes. In their hair is a cluster of white, yellow, and red feathers. The left breast and shoulder, right leg, and left forearm are painted green. The legs are painted with green and yellow bands, and green and yellow stripes extend from the breast down along the side of the abdomen. They also wear the traditional fox skin hanging from the waist at the back.[328]

One or more members wear sun symbols on their backs, consisting of a disk with a sun-face symbol painted on it, surrounded by red horsehair fringes and radiating eagle feathers. Other members wear rectangular moisture tablets that symbolize the fact that the earth has been fertilized.

When a runner returns from depositing prayer offerings at a distant shrine, the two groups take their places at the spring, the Gray Flute Society standing on one side, the Blue Flute Society on the other. Several elderly men sitting close to the water's edge sing and shake their rattles. Meanwhile, the two costumed warriors keep watch on the banks above and twirl their bullroarers from time to time.

One man, naked except for a breechclout, wades into the spring, and after removing surface debris, he takes a lighted pipe and blows four puffs of smoke toward the water. He then hands the pipe to another man, wades into deeper water, and partially immerses himself three times before dipping entirely under the surface. At the very moment he rises to break the surface the songs end with dramatic suddenness, for he holds in his hands sacred rods to which netted gourds are attached. All who are present thank him enthusiastically, since his prize symbolizes the way in which the spring continues to supply the people with precious water.

The two societies proceed to the village. With their chief in the lead, the Blue Flutes go first, followed by two young girls and a boy who takes a position between them. Next come the members, the boys carrying their intriguing standards, the men shaking rattles or blowing flutes, and all singing. Behind them the Gray Flutes are arranged in similar fashion. The groups advance in stages, stopping at intervals while the Blue Flute chief draws three rain and cloud symbols on the ground with sprinkled cornmeal. Then the children, in rotation, attempt to throw into the designs looped rings and a cylinder that they carry on the tips of shafts. Wherever they land, the leader picks them up and places one in the center of each symbol. Then the groups advance again, and in this wise the long procession makes its way slowly to the village dance plaza and kisi. Songs are sung there, and some of the water gourds brought from the spring are placed by each Flute chief within the kisi, after which the societies disperse and go to the house of their controlling clan.

The Flute ritual is a rewarding moment for the Hopi people, for the performance at the spring has demonstrated their confidence that the Cloud People will bring rain. The spirits in the Underworld also rejoice at receiving this assurance, for it is a reminder that the newly Emergent Hopi created the sun by throwing into the air a sun symbol like that painted on the sun shield worn on the backs of Flute members. The flute music itself represents the sound of locusts whose arrival is always an indication of summer. Thus, as Titiev states, the Flute rites complement the Soyal in that they send the sun on its return trip to its winter home.[329]

Snake-Antelope Ceremony

The most widely publicized ceremony of the Hopi is the Snake-Antelope Rite, which alternates years with the Flute Ceremony. Actually, the two are closely related, and their ritual patterns are much the same. At present the Snake-Antelope Rite is held in August in years ending in even numbers at Hotevilla, Shongopovi, and Shipaulovi. In odd years it is held at Walpi and Mishongnovi. Each village uses somewhat different paraphernalia and procedures, although dance costumes are virtually alike.

So mesmerized and horror-stricken are white visitors at the sight of Hopi Snake Society members holding live, lethal rattlesnakes in their mouths and hands, and so often have whites speculated on how the performers survive bites without the slightest hint of distress or aftereffect, that the ritual holds in their minds a place entirely out of proportion with its actual significance. And it has been described so many times in publications that I choose not to give it more than its due.

Functionally, the Snake and Antelope are independent societies that join together only when their biennial rite is to be celebrated. Six months before the scheduled date the two groups make winter offerings. In August, the actual rite gets under way, following for the most part the customary pattern of ceremonial preparations. Prayer sticks are made, paints are ground, the medicine with which the snakes will be washed is mixed, and prayers are offered. Only the society leaders are so involved, the rest of the members continuing to work at their farms.

On the second day the Antelope chief goes to a shrine and offers prayer sticks and sacred meal to the ancestor spirits, asking that the answer to the prayers return in the clouds. The next day he captures a large rattlesnake, ceremonially washes it, and ties a breath feather to its neck. He carries the snake to the west end of the village, where he places it within a circle of meal drawn on the ground. When the snake crawls away and breaks the circle he "opens the gate" for rain to come and marks the direction of its approach. While the Antelope chief is occupied with the snake, the Snake chief prepares a vegetal liquid which the Snake dancers must drink every day before they dance.

Beginning on the fourth day, Snake men go out with pouches and digging sticks for four successive days to hunt snakes, first to the north, then west, south, and east. They capture from eighty to one hundred and fifty snakes, of which more than half are rattlesnakes. These are kept in the Snake kiva, where

Walpi Snake priest, 1897. From a photograph by George H. Pepper.

two elderly men confine them to the north end by the gentle use of feathered snake-whips. On the eighth night the snakes are driven across the altar and to the south end of the kiva.

On each morning that the snakes are being gathered, the Snake chief visits the Antelope chief in his kiva. They have a formal smoke, and sand paintings are made in the two kivas. On the fifth day the original standards are replaced by a bow decorated with eagle feathers, and that evening the entire Snake Society goes to the Antelope kiva, where the two societies hold a joint ceremony. An altar is built, medicine is made, they sing and pray, and a costumed man and woman who represent the cultus hero and heroine of the Snake legend appear in the kiva. This performance is repeated on the sixth night. The seventh day is noteworthy only for the building of the altar in the Snake kiva, and for sending a courier to the spring to fill a netted gourd in preparation for a foot race from the valley to the mesa top that will occur on the eighth day to attract rain clouds. The race is run at daybreak by the young men of the village, and the entire population watches. The winner receives the netted gourd and carries it to the Antelope kiva, where sacred rites were begun the moment the race started. The other runners plant prayer sticks and sprinkle sacred meal at the north end of the village.

In late afternoon of the eighth day the Antelope men, followed by the Snake men, appear in the plaza and dance four times around a cottonwood kisi that was built earlier by the Snake men. In front of this is a foot drum consisting of a board placed over a shallow hole in the ground. As each man passes the board he sprinkles it with sacred cornmeal and stamps on it with his right foot. When the four circuits are completed, the Snakes and Antelopes line up facing each other. After a few songs, the Snake chief and an Antelope officer leave their groups and assume the positions the dancers will take the next day, with the Snake chief standing behind the Antelope man and resting his left hand on the Antelope man's left shoulder. The two then dance to the kisi, where the Antelope officer receives a bunch of vines and other vegetation from a man seated inside. He lets this dangle from his mouth just as the snakes will dangle from the dancers' mouths the next day. The dance ended, the vines are placed on the ground, a Snake member retrieves them, and the societies make four more circuits of the kisi and return to their kivas.

Another foot race is held very early on the ninth day. Then a Badger Clan member from the Snake Society goes to obtain certain herbs that are used to prepare an emetic that will be drunk at the close of the Snake Dance. In the morning, initiations into the society may be held in the Snake kiva. During the day the snakes, consisting of rattlesnakes and various nonpoisonous kinds such as bull snakes and red racers, are ritually washed with yucca suds. Fewkes describes this ritual as "the wildest of all the aboriginal rites of these strange people." The song, he says, grows louder and wilder, until it bursts into a fierce, blood-curdling yell. It was a sight that haunted him for weeks.[330] In midafternoon the snakes are taken in a sack to the kisi, where they are deposited. After this the men paint and dress.

182

The Antelope men are painted solid white from foot to knee and from wrist to elbow. A white zigzag, or lightning, line is made on the upper legs and on the outside of the arms. White cloud shapes may be placed on the shoulders, and a lightning line runs over each shoulder and down the body, front and back. A thin white line is made across the mouth and cheeks. The hair is disheveled and hangs loose. A white cotton kilt is worn, its embroidery

Snake Dance. *Top,* consecrating the pahos with a ''cloud blower'' pipe. *Bottom,* Antelope priest placing the pahos in the shrine of the Spider Woman.

Snake Dance. Herding the snakes in the kiva after the ritual snake washing.

showing at the right side, and it is tied on with a broad white sash embroidered with rain symbols on its ends. A fox skin hangs at the back. Moccasins are stained a dull red and topped with a fringed buckskin anklet of the same color.

The Snake man's face at some villages is rubbed with red paint, and at others the lower half, including the chin, is painted black with a vivid white streak smeared across the mouth. A thick smear of white clay is daubed in the hair at a point above the right eye. The torso is given a wash of black paint, and some dancers place white oval designs on that and on other parts of the body. To do this they dip the palm of the hand in thin white clay and lay a smear on the outside of the calf, mid-thigh, forearm, and upper arm, on each breast, and on the stomach.

The dull-red dance kilt of cotton or canvas (in former times buckskin) bears a bold snake or serpent design painted in black and white, and it is secured with a long, fringed buckskin belt. A tortoiseshell rattle attached to a deerskin strip is tied on the right leg behind the knee, and a deerskin band is tied on the left leg. Fringed anklets are tied on over the moccasin tops, and both are stained red. A bandolier with numerous appendages, such as animal teeth,

Snake Dance. The chief Antelope priest in front of the Antelope kiva hatch. The Bow *natsi* is in place on the kiva ladder, and the priest holds in his left hand one of the Antelope tiponis. In his right hand is the distinctive rattle used by the Antelope and Snake dancers.

claws, and hoofs, is hung over the right shoulder and diagonally across the body. Feather-fringed or plain wooden arm bands are worn on the upper arm. Necklaces consist of a hodgepodge of fur, feathers, shell, turquoise, and coral. The usual gray fox skin hangs at the back of the kilt. A fringed, sacred meal pouch is held in the left hand, and a snake whip in the right hand. On top of the head is a bunch of red-stained eagle-breast, bluebird, and owl feathers.

Just before sundown everyone proceeds to the plaza, Antelopes going first and Snakes following. They shake the ground as they march with warlike de-

Snake Dance. In the foreground is a Snake dancer in typical paint and costume, although the paint and costume details vary from village to village. In the background the kisi is being built. The boy with the broom wears a novice's kilt made of cotton and dyed blue-black. The circles are black. From Voth and Dorsey photographs, 1901.

termination. The dance is performed in much the same manner as on the day before, except that the Antelopes at one point remain in line, singing and shaking their rattles, while most of the Snake men, including novices, pair up as the Snake chief and Antelope officer did the day before. The rest of the Snake men stand ready to gather up released snakes. The pairs then dance in turn to the kisi, where each Snake man kneels and takes a snake from a man stationed inside. He places it in his mouth and holds it there as he rises and dances on. After making several circuits around the plaza, a dancer places his snake on

Snake Dance. *Top left,* one of the shrines where pahos are deposited on the eighth day of the ceremony. *Bottom left,* it is difficult to show with clarity the actual positions of a group of Snake dancers. These dolls from the Heard Museum illustrate the actions of the dancer and the hugger, with one of the line of Antelope priests to the left. *Top right,* returning the snakes to the desert. *Bottom right,* shrine where the snake jars are placed after the ceremony. The image of Spider Woman leans against the box in the middle.

the ground and goes to the kisi for another. This continues until all the snakes have been danced with and released. If a rattlesnake gets loose, the closely crowded spectators scatter madly in all directions to escape it. The dancers resent this expression of fear, but pretend to ignore it.

When the last snake has been collected, the Snake chief goes to the end of the plaza, where he draws on the ground a circle of cornmeal and divides it into quadrants. The snakes are then thrown into this circle, and the women and girls of the Snake Clan toss cornmeal on them. Seconds later the youngest Snake Society members scoop up handfuls of the writhing snakes and run off, separating into four groups to carry the snakes to shrines in each of the four cardinal directions. Once deposited, the snakes go into their holes in the ground, carrying the songs and petitions of the living Hopi to the spirits in the Underworld. When the youths return, all the Snake men wash off their paint, drink the emetic, vomit as a ritual purification, and bathe, and the ceremony concludes. If the ceremony has been done properly, and if all goes as planned, rain will shortly begin to fall. Even though the sky was clear when the dance got under way, clouds will have gathered by now, and the Cloud People will have come. Most often it happens just that way, and many a white visitor, soaked to the skin, has recorded his astonishment at the "miracle" of it!

Fewkes believed that the Snake Dance has two main purposes—the making of rain and the growth of corn.[331] Titiev adds to this a mortuary aspect in that the spirits of the deceased Snake and Antelope men, represented by the crook-shaped prayer sticks placed before the altar, are thought to be present and sharing in the dance.[332] Parsons links the Snake Ceremony to ancient warriors who wore paint similar to that of the Snake performers into battle.[333] Titiev also finds a solar aspect and sees in the dance a concern with sun worship.[334]

Snake dancers returning to their kiva with their dance costumes after the closing ceremony on the ninth day.

Marau Ceremony

As I have mentioned earlier, the annual cycle of rituals is carried out primarily by men. But women are initiated into either the Katcina Cult or the Powamû Society, they impersonate cultus heroines in the Soyal, Flute, and Snake-Antelope ceremonies, they take part in the public features of the war rituals, and they play reciprocal roles in gift-giving and other exchange situations symbolic of fertility. Besides, they have three societies of their own, the Marau, the Lakon, and the Oaqöl, wherein a few men, usually relatives of the female leaders, serve in minor capacities. The three societies and their rites are highly regarded by all villagers, even if, surprisingly, some participants are menstruating at ritual time. As Titiev notes, the Hopi are among the few Indian peoples who have no tabus about menstrual blood.[335]

Generally speaking, the women's nine-day rituals follow the same pattern as those of the men. They are conducted by secret societies, and fetishes are used that are owned by particular clans. The ceremonies consist partly of secret kiva rites, and they end in a public dance that is held on the last day. Although women are ordinarily restricted in their use of kivas, certain kivas are made available to them for conducting their secret rituals; at Old Oraibi the Marau Society once had its own kiva.[336]

The women's groups hold their major rituals in September and October, and the Lakon and Marau also hold meetings in January. According to Voth, it was customary at Old Oraibi for the Oaqöl to be performed in odd-numbered years and the Marau and the Lakon in even years.[337] Writers often call their performances "Basket dances," but the title by no means gives them the significance they deserve. Initiation into the women's societies follows the same scheme as those of the men, and women are permitted to join as many of the female societies as they wish. Since by legend they originated as the sons and daughters of the same sun deity, the Wuwutcim men and the Mamzrau Society women regard each other as ceremonial brothers and sisters, and there are many similarities in their observances.

The Marau Winter Ceremony lasts for nine days, in January or February. The Marau Society standard consists of clusters of small hawk feathers, and members tie hawk breath feathers in their hair. The altar is made on the first day, and it includes a number of sticks that represent the deceased members of the order. Also, the floor of the kiva is struck to announce to the spirit members that the ceremony is in progress. On the fourth day prayer offerings are made for departed family members and relatives and are placed on a tray filled with cornmeal. The women form a semicircle around the tray, singing as they will during their public performance on the ninth day. The offerings are later distributed to the four cardinal directions, and it is believed that the deceased tie them to a string around their head so that the feather hangs down in front of the face.[338]

On the fifth day the altar is dismantled, and the women wash their heads in ritual purification. About sundown, the altar having been taken away, they dress in mixed-up male and female costumes, and then appear in public to taunt the men with bawdy songs of a phallic and obscene nature. The men retaliate by dousing the women with water or urine, and by seeking to smear them with filth. Once again, those readers who are perplexed by such acts must remember their basic intent and the perceptiveness revealed thereby. They are concerned primarily with fertility and harvest, and reveal that the supernaturals bless the created world, in this case humans, with reproduction even though man has a base nature and the initiatory sex act has its ungainly and humorous aspects. In the Hopi view, man must in honesty see himself as he is, and recognize his dependence upon the Creator if the Creator is to bless him. The bawdy acts of the Hopi are graphic reminders of this, and through their annual repetition the lessons are neither ignored nor forgotten. Everyone laughs, but everyone knows underneath what is going on.

The lewd performances continue on the sixth and seventh days, and at times the women put on burlesque Katcina dances.

Stephen describes a Buffalo Dance that was put on by the women. Between 4 and 5 P.M. most of the women gathered in the kiva. Only one man was present. They began decorating for the dance and made some excellent disguises. At about sunset, the leader, wrapped in a scarlet blanket, took her feathered rod and led the assemblage out of the kiva. A tall woman, her hair dressed like a Navajo woman's, followed her, carrying the drum, then eight other women partly disguised as Navajo women. As the tall woman stood on the hatchway roof beating the drum, the others gathered around her, singing and calling the Buffalo performers to hurry. When these had joined them, the whole assemblage went in an irregular procession, singing to the drumbeat, to the dance court at Antelope mound. The leader, the drummer, and the eight other women halted at the east side of the court and remained there to serve as the chorus, constantly singing to the vigorous drumming.

The performers were eight married women who gave a tolerably effective rendition of the Buffalo Dance as it is performed by the men. Two were disguised as male buffalo. On their heads was the greater part of a dark sheepskin, to which the short curving horns of a young sheep, goat, or steer were affixed. Their faces were blackened with soot, and the edge of the sheepskin next to where the horns were fastened was drawn close over the forehead, the skin covering the head and falling over the shoulders. The women wore a close-fitting dark print shirt and a pair of dark cloth trousers held up by a big belt. They carried a rattle and a dingy wooden prayer stick.

With each male buffalo was a female buffalo, wearing a smaller headdress of sheepskin and horns, the wool shorter and the horns smaller, so as to depict a cow buffalo devoid of its mane. Their faces were covered with vermilion, and they wore a blue tunic gown that was fantastically looped up with strings. In their hands were a rattle and two long eagle feathers. All were barefooted. These Buffalo danced in pairs, male and female, with the female following and imitating the motions of the male. Behind each pair of buffalo were two women excellently disguised as warriors. Their hair was worn in two long queues wrapped with bright ribbon or yarn, and with silver ornaments and eagle tail feathers appended. Their faces were decorated with red and vermilion. They wore velvet shirts or jackets, and trousers of scarlet flannel with broad margins flapping down the outside leg. They carried shields of cloth, rattles, and pistols. All were barefooted; in fact, all the performers and chorus were barefooted, no moccasins being worn during the whole nine-day ceremony. They performed with considerable gesturing and posturing, keeping time to the song of the chorus and the drumbeat. The eight Buffalo dancers did not sing. The dance continued for a little more than twenty minutes, and then all the performers gathered in a group and walked toward the kiva.

When they were alongside the house nearest to the kiva, some of the men, who had been lying in wait for them on the house terraces, poured down upon them the contents of several large vessels of urine. The women, instead of trying to avoid it, seemed to court it, redoubling the shrieking volume of their song and taunting the men to throw more. Arriving at the kiva, they removed their disguises and rubbed the face decoration off with a little water. In the early night there was singing for about an hour.[339]

On the eighth day of the Marau winter ritual the altar is built again, and the observances duplicate those of the first day. That evening, Katcina dances are held in all the kivas, and on the ninth day the ritual is concluded by a day-long Katcina Dance in which the women play little or no part, although the portrayals by the men are usually those featuring the cultus hero and heroine of the Marau Society, Palahik-tiyo and Palahik-mana.[340]

The fall observances of the Marau are a carbon copy of the winter rites, except for those of the fourth, eighth, and ninth days. On the fourth day a member is sent as a messenger to a shrine, where she invites the departed spirits of Marau women to come and join in the rites.[341] On the eighth day a load of farm produce is brought into the kiva and some of it is tied into a bundle. A Bow clansman fashions two sets of reed arrows, with four arrows in each set. A moisture shield like that worn in the Flute Ceremony is made, but with Mûyingwu, God of Germination, depicted on it, and the women fashion the unique prayer sticks they will carry as they dance on the ninth day. In the evening the members, carrying ears of corn instead of their prayer sticks, give a public performance in the plaza, after which the altar is dismantled and there is a ritual head-washing.

Very early the next morning, loads of cornstalks with young ears on them are brought to the village and the women dress for a day-long series of public dances. All but five wear mantas, traditional dresses, and striped ceremonial blankets. They are barefooted, their faces are smeared with sacred cornmeal, and they carry bunches of cornstalks. The other five dress in the Blue Flute kiva in men's costumes. Two carry bows and arrows and bundles of farm produce. Two carry netted wheels and lance-like poles. One carries a wand decorated with horsehair, and has a fox skin attached to her left wrist. All five wear elaborate headdresses.

When everyone is dressed, the Marau Society head leads the women in single file into the plaza, where they form a semicircle. As they sing, they wave the cornstalks up and down and from side to side, and the entire line moves slowly sideways. At the proper moment the archers arrive, throwing the bundles of produce ahead of them and shooting their arrows at these. Then come the lance bearers, rolling their wheels and throwing their lances at the wheels. The archers and lancers then fashion, from cornmeal and water, balls of qömi, or dumplings, which they toss to the spectators. The archers and lancers return to the Blue Flute kiva, the Marau end their performance with a song, and the dancers return single file to their kiva. The cornstalks are placed on the ground, and the male spectators scramble for them. Once the women have removed certain portions of their costumes they are discharmed with ashes and cedar smoke, after which they return to their homes for breakfast. The dance is repeated several times during the day, and on each occasion a new group of women enacts the five special roles related to the Blue Flute kiva. Some dances include obscene songs directed at the Wuwutcim men, but the last dance is solemnly performed, and the society leaders offer special prayers before the dancers retire to the kiva.

According to Parsons, the Marau Ceremony is performed for reproduction or fertility, for favorable weather, for war, and for cure.[342] The whip of the society is the power to control twisting sickness (facial spasms) and venereal disease.

Lakon Ceremony

The women leaders of the Lalakonta Society are assisted in their Lakon Ceremony by a few of their male relatives, but as their whip is running sores, men who are so afflicted might also seek a cure by joining in on occasion. Titiev states that the major emphasis of the ceremony is probably germination, since the worship of Mûyingwu plays a prominent part in the rites, and that other elements such as war may be found.[343] Parsons believes that the Lakon may in addition have had the cure for venereal disease.[344] Fewkes finds a strict parallelism in the Lalakonta and Mamzrau Society purposes.[345]

The first seven days of the Lakon Ceremony closely parallel those of the Marau. On the eighth day the society enacts a ritual at one of the village springs, and then the women race back to the village. One member runs with the society's standard, and when she is overtaken by another she passes it on to that person. The final one to bear the standard is dressed early on the morning of the ninth day to impersonate the Lakon Maiden, the cult's heroine. So attired and carrying a tray, she proceeds to a place some distance from the pueblo where a group of young men await her. Arriving there she breaks into a run and the men chase her. As with the standard, the tray is passed on until there is an ultimate winner. While this is going on the Lakon women, carrying empty woven trays, proceed single file to the dance plaza. There they perform much like the Marau women, except that they wave the trays instead of cornstalks, and the line does not move sideways. When the race winner arrives, he forces his way through the dance line and proceeds to the Hawiovi kiva. The women then go to the kiva for a rest and breakfast.

During the day they return several times to the plaza and dance as before. But on each occasion two Lakon Maidens, dressed to represent the Lakon heroine, come toward them bearing on their backs large bundles of gifts, and in their hands two varicolored corn ears with feathers attached. A male officer walks in front of them carrying a basket of cornmeal or pollen with which he advances by stages, drawing colored cloud symbols on the ground. The girls seek to throw their ears of corn into the designs in their proper ritual order, North, West, South, and East. When the dance line is reached the man returns to the kiva, while the Lakon Maidens move within the open circle, face each other, and then bow once in each of the four cardinal directions as the male spectators crowd closely around the dancers in anticipation. The Lakon Maidens place their gift bundles on the ground, and taking handfuls from them whirl suddenly and throw the gifts in all directions as the men scramble wildly for them and seek to wrest them from one another. All this is done in good humor, although by the time it is over many men have their clothing torn to shreds.[346]

When the packs are empty, the Lakon Maidens return to the kiva, and the dancers follow shortly. The performance is repeated throughout the day, and different women impersonate the Lakon Maidens each time. To end the day, a male chief comes to sprinkle the dancers with cornmeal, and from a tray he deposits prayer offerings and cornmeal in the plaza shrine. He then throws the tray as far as he can, and the male spectators race to obtain it. The women finish their last song, and the ceremony concludes.

Oaqöl Ceremony

The Oaqöl is a comparatively recent addition to the ceremonial cycles at Walpi and Old Oraibi, dating to some time after A.D. 1700. Its whip is eruptions that occur on top of the head. Although its songs were reputedly stolen from other ceremonies by a witch named Kelwuhti,[347] it is a popular society, and villagers welcome its ceremony in the ritual calendar. It is thought by observers that both winter and fall rites are performed, and that their association is with germination and fertility. Mûyingwa is represented on their altar, and he is impersonated by some of the male officers.

The initiation of candidates is like that of the Marau, in that the novices jump into a ring made from yucca stems and the ring is then lifted over them four times.[348] The novices also grind corn for their ceremonial mothers for the first four days of the Oaqöl rite, in exchange for which the mothers give their "daughters" basket trays to be used in the public dance on the ninth day.

A footrace at dawn begins the final rites, which culminate in a public performance in the plaza. The Oaqöl costume is identical to that of the Lakon, the performers carry similar basketry trays, and they assume the same formation for dancing. In this instance, though, the two Oaqöl Maidens, wearing a splendid headdress of parrot feathers, attempt to hit their netted wheels with a feathered corncob dart. Gifts are thrown to the crowd in Lakon fashion, and after this the ceremony is ended.

Left, the Oaqöl maiden. She holds in her right hand a netted wheel and one of the feathered arrows, in her left hand the other arrow. *Middle,* two-handed paho carried by Marau members. *Top right, natsi* of the Blue Flute Society at Mishongnovi, and of the Oaqöl Society. *Bottom right,* altar of one of the Oraibi Flute societies. The objects in front of the altar are Flute birds. From Voth, 1903, and Fewkes, 1896.

Top, some of the objects used in the Oraibi Oaqöl Ceremony: left to right, aspergill, bone whistle, netted gourd, self-scratcher used by novices, prayer feather taken from an eagle, "road" feather placed in a path as a road marker. *Bottom*, repainting some of the figures used on the Oaqöl altar. From Voth and Dorsey, 1903.

Chapter 2

ZUÑI, ACOMA, LAGUNA

ZUÑI HISTORY AND LIFE

Hopi and Zuñi were once considered the "Western Pueblos," as opposed to the "Eastern Pueblos" of Acoma, Laguna, and the Rio Grande. This was for more than geographic reasons. As Parsons put it, the Hopi and Zuñi calendrical systems correspond more closely than at first sight appears.[1] More recently, opportunities to analyze the situation carefully has led some specialists to classify all four as the Western Pueblos, because of shared characteristics—Hopi, Zuñi, Acoma, and Laguna.[2]

In their origin, Zuñi seem to have been a blend or hybrid, composed of physical and material influences from the major Anasazi regions that surrounded them on the west, north, and east, and from the Mogollon on the southwest and south. The greater Zuñi area became in time a sprawling community unto itself, with an impressive number of small villages that were peripheral to major village-building sites. Fewkes composed at one time a map of the area, on which more than forty individual villages are sited. The Zuñi are isolated linguistically, and indications are that the Zuñi-speaking people have been in their present location for eight hundred years or more. They call themselves the A'shiwi, the "people," as distinct from everyone else.

When Cortés conquered the Aztecs in 1520 and 1521, the legend of the fabled "Seven Golden Cities of Cíbola" was already a part of Spanish mythology. The story had been told and retold that seven bishops of Mérida had escaped Moorish invaders in A.D. 1150, and with their followers had sailed across the ocean. After months of travel and searching, they had built seven golden cities that became the object of every Spanish explorer who heard the tale.

The known history of the Zuñi begins sometime after A.D. 1528, when four Spaniards survived a shipwreck off the west coast of Florida. They were afterward taken captive by Indians, escaped, and made their way back to Mexico, arriving there in 1536. Somewhere during their arduous journey their leader, Alvar Núñez Cabeza de Vaca, heard from other Indians reports of seven fabulously rich cities to the north, whose streets were paved with gold.

As witnessed by Spain's overt actions in Mesoamerica, nothing stirred the Spanish king and his viceroys into action faster than reports of opulent places to seize, and the tie to Cíbola was too much to ignore. Fray Marcos de Niza,

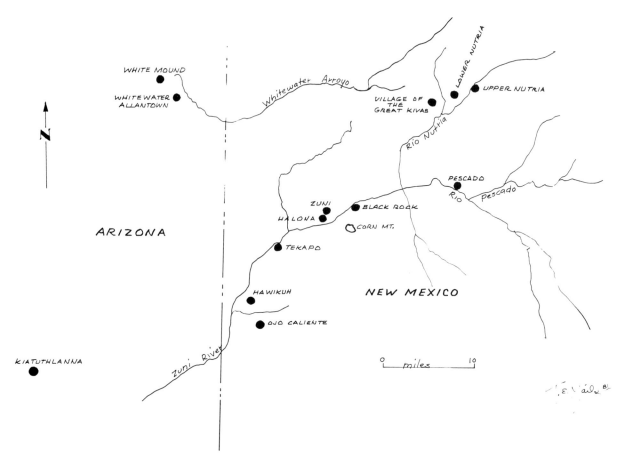

Map showing the locations of past and present villages of the Zuñi Region.

who had with his group one of the Núñez party, a certain Estevan (Stephen), a freed black slave, was dispatched to explore the fabled north country. When in 1539 Fray Marcos reached what is now southern Arizona, he sent Estevan and some Sonoran Indians from Mexico on ahead to prepare the Indians of the great cities for his arrival.

Accordingly, Estevan became the first European to arrive at the Zuñi town of Hawikuh. It was an impressive town, but its streets were not gold. It is said that Estevan had sent a messenger on ahead to tell the Indians he was coming, and that the Zuñi sped the messenger back with instructions to warn Estevan to stay away. He came on anyway, and it proved to be a serious and final mistake. Perhaps Estevan was disgusted with what he found, or arrogant, and made this plain. No one really knows. In any event, he was not allowed to enter the town, and the next day he and several of his companions were killed.[3] Frightened survivors carried word of this to Fray Marcos, who was prudent, going just far enough to view Hawikuh from a distance and then turning back to Mexico. For some incredible reason he reported that in the north there were in truth seven great cities comprising a rich and prosperous province, undoubtedly the Cities of Cíbola. Some authorities, such as F. W. Hodge, claim there were only six Zuñi pueblos at the time, and it would follow that six, not seven, would be reported. Whichever, the news was sufficient to sponsor a new and better-outfitted expedition under the command of Francisco Vásquez Coronado. In 1540, he ventured forth with an army of horsemen and footmen to conquer the rich cities and to explore and settle the rest of the territory. With him were three hundred foot soldiers, eight hundred Indians, five hundred war horses, a thousand work horses and mules, hundreds of sheep and cattle, provisions, and munitions. As he entered Zuñi country, anticipation began to build with every step. Yet even before he marched with his men into the Zuñi villages he knew he had been duped. From a distance he could see that the villages were stone masonry and adobe; the streets were pure dirt. One brief battle at Hawikuh, and the contest was over. Shortly thereafter Coronado went on, marching first to Tiguex, visiting Tusayan and the Grand Canyon, and then returning to spend the winter at his headquarters on the Rio Grande. Everywhere he went he made trouble. In his disgust he exacted tribute from each of the pueblos, and pushed the Indians around whenever they were uncooperative. With fewer than a hundred members of the expedition remaining, the disillusioned explorer returned to Mexico in 1542, convinced there was little in the north worth staying for. He did leave behind some of the agricultural products and domestic animals mentioned in the Hopi section, and these would ultimately alter the economic base of the Zuñi and other pueblos.

The rest of the Spanish entrada story proper is told in the Rio Grande section beginning on page 330. It is not a pretty story, for the Pueblos were to suffer considerably. After Coronado's visit their lives would never again be the same. Zuñi took its lumps with the rest. When the Pueblo Revolt erupted in 1680, the Zuñi were already reduced to living in three villages: Halona, Kiakima, and Matsakya. The last-named was the largest and finest of these; its

A portion of the Hawikuh Ruin. From Fewkes, 1896.

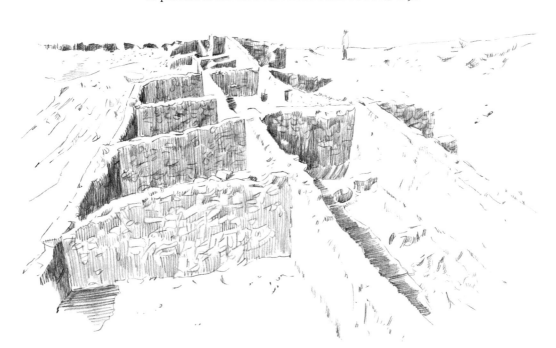

higher buildings having walls and loopholes on the top stories for defending the lower roofs.[4] A weakened Hawikuh had fallen to the Navajo and Apache, including its Roman Catholic priest and his mission, which had been built sometime after 1629.[5] The Zuñi residents were scattered and demoralized, and they never saw fit to reestablish the town. Relationships with the Spanish and the church vacillated. In 1632, the Zuñi killed two friars, and in 1680 one more.

By the time Diego de Vargas returned to accomplish the Reconquest of the Pueblo area in 1692 and 1693, the Zuñi had contracted still further. Although he found them ensconced on Corn Mountain, they had been living together in the single village of Halona. This is the place known today as the town of Zuñi, New Mexico. It is situated about thirty-five miles south of Gallup, on the north bank of the Zuñi River in a relatively flat, desertlike valley.

The average altitude of the Zuñi valley is approximately 6,500 feet above sea level. The country is fairly rugged, and covered with sagebrush, cacti, and lesser growths, together with some juniper and piñon trees. In the highest places there are pines and deciduous trees. An occasional oasis, spring, or shallow stream together with a good-sized reservoir fed by the Zuñi River make limited agriculture possible. Frequent rains occur during the day in the summer, but the moisture is so soon dissipated by the dry sand and soil and the hot sun that both man and beast find existence difficult.

But Zuñi has its scenic attraction. Just east of the village is Towayalane, Corn Mountain, the great sacred mesa to which the Zuñi fled often to escape the Spaniards and other Indians. Its tints are always changing with the light. In winter it is a deep brick red, salted with snow. In summer it is pink, or purple, a pale yellow, or touched with green. Eroded pillars on its face represent, to the Zuñi, beasts and people associated with its mythology. The pueblo itself sits nestled in a kind of amphitheater surrounded by mesas at various distances, and from this point of view it does seem to be a "middle place."

A Roman Catholic church was begun at Zuñi Pueblo in 1660, but the Zuñi paid scant attention to it. The edifice was damaged during the Revolt, and repairs were not completed until sometime between 1699 and 1705, when Our Lady of Guadalupe became patroness. The Franciscans stayed resolutely with the mission throughout the 1700s, but by 1821, troubles with the Navajo and Apache, plus a lack of support from Mexico, caused them to leave. The mission buildings began to deteriorate and in time they became ruins.

The Zuñi were experiencing the same problems. Attacking Spanish, Apache, or Navajo sometimes forced them to abandon the entire town and move to the top of the sacred mountain. It was a harassment that continued for years, and it left such a stain that even today Mexicans are not welcome at Zuñi.

On March 2, 1883, Adolph F. Bandelier went with Frank H. Cushing to inspect the top of six-hundred-foot-high Corn Mountain.[6] He found the scenery there to be the grandest of all he saw in New Mexico. At the edge of the mesa, stones had been piled up as barricades. The masonry ruins on the mesa top were scattered into six groups, usually enclosing courts. The mesa was full

Towa Yal'lanne, Corn Mountain. Sacred place of the Zuñi.

of caves in which there were statues and prayer offerings. All water had to be carried up from the foot of the mesa, and living conditions there were at least difficult.

The Franciscans returned to Zuñi in 1921 and built the present-day St. Anthony mission in the northwest part of the village. In 1966, restoration of the old church was undertaken, and by 1968 it was sufficiently complete to hold Mass on Christmas Eve and Zuñi dances. The formal dedication of the church took place on May 29, 1972. The restored edifice is most inspiring, and every visitor to Zuñi should see it. Of extreme interest are its superb murals done by Zuñi artist Alex Seowtewa, depicting figures in full costume from the summer and winter ceremonies, and in particular the personages of the well-known Shalako ritual.[7]

In 1776, Zuñi had a population of 1,617. Today it numbers about 7,000, including several hundred non-Indians. To its farming and hunting economy it has added excellent jewelry of the inlay and turquoise types, cattle raising, and wage work. The town boasts a modern tribal headquarters building that accommodates also the police and visitor quarters and a tribal craft shop. Zuñi has public schools, grocery stores, gas stations, and a cafe. The old homes of stone and adobe are giving way steadily to cinder-block and frame structures, some of which are products of the Department of Housing and Urban Development. Zuñi has had its own high school since 1956, and more than 80 percent of the Zuñi graduates have gone on to receive training in vocational schools and colleges. Most Zuñi are bilingual, speaking Zuñi and English. The Roman Catholic mission has two Franciscan priests and about thirty employ-

Grinding the family's daily ration of cornmeal. From a photograph by Charles Martin, 1920.

ees. Nearly four hundred children attend the mission school. Other missions at Zuñi include the Baptist Church, Christian Reformed Church, and Church of Jesus Christ of Latter-day Saints.

Greater Zuñi includes four permanent farming villages, Pescado, Nutria, Ojo Caliente, and Tekapo.

The Tribal Council includes a governor, lieutenant governor, and tenientes. Former officials do not become permanent council members. Aberle says that sheep and cattle officers attend meetings that include business pertaining to livestock. He also says that a serious weakness exists because of the absence of principals, "whose duty it is to maintain the continuity of the business of the pueblo from year to year, to help the new officers learn their work, and to form a consultant group wise in the ways of government."[8] An addition of recent vintage has been that of Zuñi's own resident archaeologist, at present a white.

Not long ago, the alert Zuñi became cognizant of a federal law of 1834 that lay unused, but permitted Indians to rule their own reservations with the approval of the Secretary of the Interior. The Tribal Council held a public election that approved a new constitution, and in 1970 a comprehensive development plan the council had worked out was accepted by the federal government, allowing the Zuñi to become the first Indian tribe to assume control of their own affairs. Either signing party can cancel the agreement by giving 180 days' written notice, but so far the arrangement is working well.

It was formerly believed that some houses in Zuñi were as much as seven stories high, which if true would make it the highest pueblo extant at the time. But early photographs show buildings reaching only five stories from the ground level. Since the old part of the village sits on the crown of a hill, the idea of seven stories may be the result of an optical illusion.

When the architecture of Zuñi is examined carefully, it appears that the original pueblo on the north bank of the river was built of adobe bricks and enclosed a small courtyard. As new rooms were added the overall complex assumed a rectangular shape with tiered and terraced rooms in the pueblo style we are already familiar with. The Roman Catholic church stood on the edge of the house blocks. Eventually the buildings formed around it enclosed it entirely. Victor Mindeleff furnishes us with exhaustive architectural details in his Bureau of American Ethnology Report of 1891, and it is easier to redraw some of these (as in the illustrations on this page) than to describe them in words. Room sizes, with an exception to be mentioned, were about the same as at Hopi, although ceilings were a little higher. Room furnishings were similar also.

Mindeleff spent parts of 1880, 1881, and 1882 in Zuñi, obtaining details and measurements with which to construct a model of the town that was to be exhibited at the Columbian Exposition in Chicago. His stay there was espe-

Corral in Pescado. Adapted from V. Mindeleff.

cially fortunate, for with the arrival of the transcontinental railroad that passed through Gallup, Zuñi was introduced to modern outside life and building materials. Within fifty years the multistoried dwellings had practically disappeared.

As at Hopi, the women of Zuñi have performed the major role in house-building. Before concrete block came into vogue, the men usually laid the stones and heavy beams, and the women did the rest. Nowadays, the men are professionally trained masons, carpenters, plumbers, and electricians and often construct the entire building. There are also a number of mobile homes on the south and east sides of Zuñi Pueblo.

The Zuñi pueblo of Matilda Coxe Stevenson's time, starting in 1879, resembled to her a great beehive, with its houses built one upon another in a succession of terraces, the roof of one forming the floor or yard of the one next above, and so on until in some cases five tiers of dwellings were successively erected. Only a few houses, however, were over two stories in height. Among the Zuñi, as among other peoples, wealth and official position conferred importance upon the possessor. The wealthy class lived in the lower houses; those of more modest means, next above; while the poorer families, as a rule, contented themselves with the uppermost stories. The houses, which were built of stone and sun-dried adobe bricks composed of earth and straw molded in wooden forms, were clustered about three plazas, or squares, and there was a fourth plaza on the west side of the village. There were also three covered passageways and several streets.

The women delighted in house-building, Stevenson says, especially in plastering the houses. They considered the plastering to be their special prerogative and would feel that their rights were infringed upon were men to do

A portion of the village of Pescado. After V. Mindeleff, 1891.

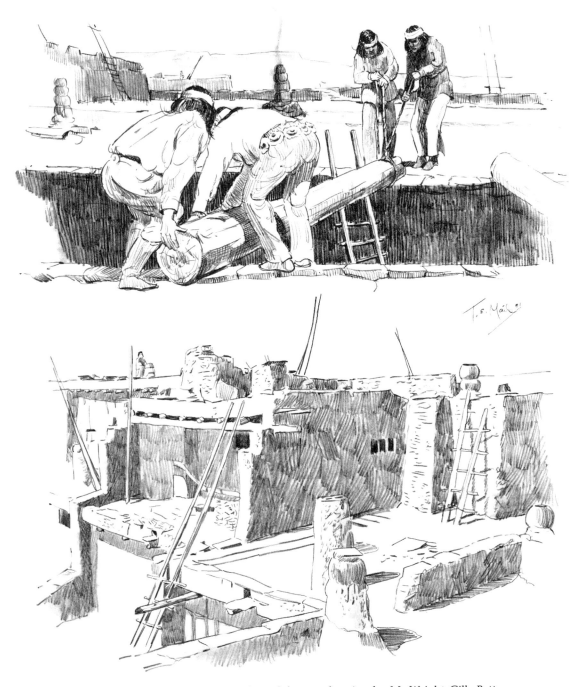

Top, placing the main roof beams. Adapted from a drawing by M. Wright Gill. *Bottom*, perspective view of typical roofs, walls, copings, and chimneys. After V. Mindeleff, 1891.

it. Men laid the stone foundations, built the walls, and placed the huge logs which served as beams to support the roof. These logs were brought from a long distance and were dressed by the Zuñi carpenter. After they were placed, carefully selected willow boughs were laid crosswise upon rafters, brush was spread over these, and the whole was covered with earth, "forming a roof substantial enough for this climate." Little girls assisted in bringing the water used to mix the mortar, trudging constantly back and forth from the river with their diminutive water vases on their heads.

The lower houses and those above had exterior doors, plus hatchways in the roof, through which ladders passed. The doorways were so small that in many instances it was difficult to squeeze through, yet they were an improvement on the more ancient entrances, "which were in some cases circular openings in round stone slabs of considerable thickness, just large enough for one to pass through by assuming a horizontal position. These doorways were closed with round stone slabs held in place by props of strong poles." The houses were so well provided with interior doors that inhabitants of almost the

Architectural details redrawn from V. Mindeleff. *Bottom,* house interior. *Top left,* wooden stools. *Top right,* wooden chair.

entire older portion of the village could communicate without passing outside the communal structure. Small window openings made in the walls to admit light were filled with irregular pieces of selenite, a crystalized gypsum. The chimneys were composed of clay cooking pots with the bases removed, placed one on top of the other and cemented together. When a cooking pot could no longer serve its original purpose, it was stored away for future use in a chimney. After the house walls were constructed, the exterior and interior walls were covered with a reddish-brown plaster made of earth and water. It was

Architectural details redrawn from V. Mindeleff. Roof openings: *a*, with ladders in place. *b*, with raised coping. *c*, with one elevated end. *d*, with stone cover. *e*, sloping selenite window resting on wooden sticks at base of wall on upper terrace. *f*, window glazed with selenite.

applied with the hand, which was swept over the wall in semicircles. In working the plaster, the woman kept her mouth filled with water, which she skillfully applied to the wall to keep it moist. The inner walls were whitened with a white clay dissolved in boiling water and applied with a rabbit-skin glove. The gloved hand was dipped into the liquid and rapidly passed over the wall. The outer walls were usually finished in a dark color.[9]

It has been customary at Zuñi to have in each house that wishes to sponsor a Shalako one extremely large room. The Shalakos dance in this room to, among other things, bless the dwelling. The room might be subdivided after

Architectural details redrawn from V. Mindeleff. *a,* wooden roof drain. *b,* roof drain with splash stones on roof below. *c,* roof construction method. *d,* stone trough drain.

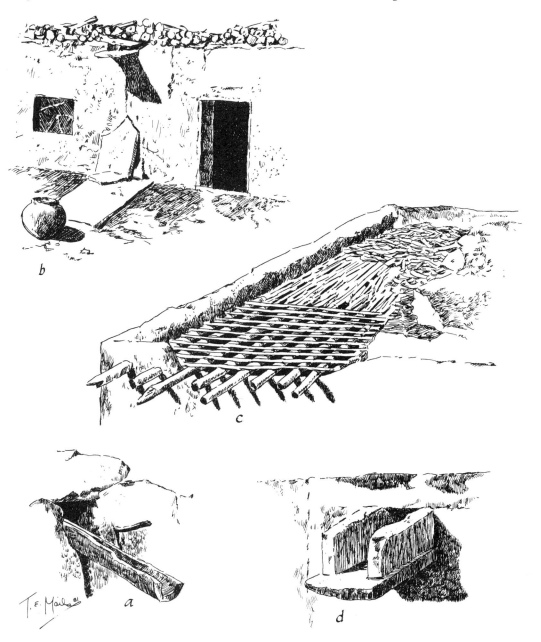

Building the horno, or adobe, oven. As Mindeleff learned *(top)*, the outdoor oven, adopted from the Spanish by the Pueblos, was begun by laying a row of foundation stones, and then completed by installing successive rows of adobe and stones. The oven was finished with a smooth plaster coat, sometimes embedded with straw and pieces of pottery to help it withstand the rain. A vent hole was provided at the top and a large stone was used to close the doorway.

that, but some residents leave the room as it is. One reason is that specially designated rooms in the pueblo are used for various ceremonial observances. The rooms must be oriented on an east-west axis, since alters built in them should face the east and be struck by the first rays of sunlight entering through an east window.

Whenever rituals are held, the family vacates the premises. The room is meticulously cleaned and then refurbished with whitewash, and the required paintings and items pertinent to the clans or fraternities involved are installed. When the rites are completed, all but a shrine hanging from a beam is re-

Top, Zuñi polychrome jar from the 1880–1900 period. Denver Art Museum collection. *Bottom,* baking bread in a roof horno, or oven. Adapted from drawing by M. Wright Gill, who made all of her studies from photographs taken about 1902.

moved, and the family returns. The shrine remains until it is replaced by one used for another ceremony.

A common sight at Zuñi and other pueblos is the *horno,* an oven shaped like the top half of an egg or a beehive. Some think it was introduced by the Spanish, and it may be so, although the Pueblos practiced baking or roasting in ovens of various sorts long before the Spanish came. *Hornos* are made of stone and adobe, with an opening at the top to release smoke and a side doorway to facilitate the placement of bread loaves. The manner of construction is illustrated on page 207.

Cedar wood is widely used for the fire, which burns for several hours to heat the walls properly. The ashes are then raked out, and the loaves are inserted in the *horno* on long-handled wooden spatulas. Many loaves are baked simultaneously, and a single firing can accommodate two or more bakings.

The Zuñi have faces that are combined Eskimo and Mongol. The people are stout, compact, and of medium height, and their eyes are shiny black. They have a friendly appearance, and their bodies look as if they were carved from a mahogony tree. When Henry Craig Fleming, M.D., examined several hundred of them in 1921, he was astounded to find that, despite poorly ventilated houses, primitive sanitary conditions, and "subjection" to medicine men, the people were in remarkably good condition. Their muscles were extremely resilient and often very powerful, thus affording great agility and endurance. It was a common sight to see a man run fifteen miles without stopping to rest. Examination of men after a grueling stick race revealed comparatively little evidence of fatigue. Blood pressure was remarkably low. Many men of approximately seventy were leading lives of extreme physical activity and registering systolic blood pressure between 110 and 125 and diastolic pressure between 60 and 75. Tuberculosis and syphilis were not common. The most serious disease, and one that still plagues the Pueblo, was trachoma. It was rampant at Zuñi, yet so easily treated that Fleming thought its existence was a disgrace to the Indian Medical Service.[10]

APPAREL

For everyday dress the Zuñi men of 1880 wore white cotton or calico shirts hanging outside loose cotton trousers, which were formed of two straight pieces joined at the top, leaving the breechclout to complete the covering. The calico shirt was a folded slip with two cuts midway, one crosswise, the other lengthwise from the center of the crosscut, through which the head passed. Only the upper portion of the sleeve was attached to the shirt, the under side being left free or open. The shirt was fashioned after the native woven garment, the difference being that the calico sleeve was sewed from the hand to the top while the woven sleeve was fastened only for a short distance from the hand upward and so was open most of the way. The woven shirt was now used exclusively for ceremonial occasions. The shirt frequently was belted in with a leather strap, on which silver medallions were mounted. The moccasins were of tanned deerskin, reddish brown or occasionally black. They had rawhide soles and were fastened Navajo style on the outer side with silver buttons. For additional warmth, the foot often was wrapped in a piece of cloth before the moccasin was drawn on. In wet weather the moccasins were usually not worn, and when there was snow or it was very cold, pieces of goatskin or sheepskin were tied over the feet, the wool inside. Deerskin leggings, which extended from below the knee to the ankle, were usually of the same color as the moccasin. They had a line of silver buttons down the side, were wrapped around the leg, and were held in place by woven red garters. A footless knit stocking of blue yarn was worn under them. A silk kerchief or a bandanna, wrapped around the head, was worn by men who could afford the extravagance; others wore a cotton band. A leather bow guard, ornamented with silver, was commonly seen on the left wrist. Necklaces of white shell, turquoise, and coral beads, whose elaborateness varied according to the wealth of the wearer, were the principal adornments. Turquoise bead earrings, tipped with

Zuñi man using a stone hammer to pound a wedge into his ax. From a photograph by O. C. Havens, 1923.

bits of coral or a certain red stone precious to the Zuñi, were attached to the necklaces, unless they were removed for ceremonial occasions and worn in the ears. The well-dressed Zuñi seldom appeared without his blanket unless it was unusually hot, and every man who could secure one possessed a Navajo blanket, which he wore in preference to the coarser and less ornamental weave of home manufacture. Rabbit-skin blankets, woven of strips of the skins, though much used in the past, were now very rare.[11]

Female dress was first donned when a girl was about four. Until this time the children of both sexes wore little or no clothing in warm weather. The dress was of black cloth, woven diagonally in one piece, embroidered at top and bottom in dark blue. The cloth was folded vertically once and sewed to within a short distance of the top, and again the top edges were caught together for a few inches, draping gracefully over the right shoulder. The right arm passed through the opening, while the dress was carried around under the left arm. A long woven belt of Zuñi or Hopi manufacture was wrapped several times around the waist. It was generally drawn tightly by the younger women and tucked under, the ends falling a few inches and one end of the belt having a long fringe. A cotton undergarment, similar in shape to the dress, was worn, and a high-necked and long-sleeved garment was also worn under the dress and next to it; this was left off for ceremonials. The neck and wrists of this garment were finished with bands, which were fastened with silver buttons. A piece of white cotton or of calico, tied in the front at the neck and falling over the back, was an indispensable article of dress. Over this might be worn on dress occasions a shawl of foreign manufacture from Santa Fe or Albuquerque. The cotton one was never removed except for ceremonials. Every Zuñi woman wore a silver necklace and earrings. Necklaces were made of coin-silver beads with pendant crescents; occasionally a number of crosses or other forms were added. Silver rings were also worn by the women. Turquoise earrings, which were worn only in ceremonials, were the same as the men's, and the women borrowed the men's bead necklaces to wear at such times.

Knit stocking legs and moccasins completed the woman's dress. The elaborateness of the moccasins varied according to the wealth of the wearer; the more deerskin used, the handsomer the moccasins. After the white moccasin with polished black sole was put on the foot, the deerskin was wrapped around the leg, giving it a bulky look, but causing the foot to appear much smaller than it really was. In summer the women and girls usually had their feet and legs bare. All moccasins were made by the men, who also did the sewing for the female members of the family as well as themselves. They sewed away from instead of toward themselves. The men knit the stocking legs and also knit foot coverings of bright colors for women and little girls, who wore them in moderate weather.[12]

The woolen garments of home manufacture were washed occasionally in the river in suds of the root of the *Yucca glauca*, "the Indians appreciating the necessity of sometimes cleansing them in order to preserve them," but cotton clothing was worn until it fell apart from use. Once a garment was replaced by

Method of forming the hair to make the *chongo (upper right),* and the *que (lower right).*

fresh ones for ceremonial occasions, it was put on again and worn until full service had been rendered.

No one dressed his own hair. Women combed the men's hair and one another's, unless a lover or a bridegroom greatly enamored of his bride played the part of hairdresser. The man's hair was parted from ear to ear over the crown of the head, a fine straw being used to make the part perfectly clear. The front of the hair was allowed to fall in heavy bangs over the forehead, while the back hair was carefully brushed. A bunch of broom corn tied about four inches from its cut ends served a double purpose, the longer portion being the broom, the shorter portion the hairbrush. When every hair was in place, a long string was wrapped once around the hair and tightly drawn at the nape of the neck. The man whose hair was being dressed held each end of the string while the hair was brushed again; and the hair was frequently spat upon as it was folded over and over. The hairdresser, taking first the right-hand string, wrapped it tightly around the hair, which was formed into a bow. The other end of the string was also wrapped around the hair, and the string was firmly tied. The tongue was used frequently in smoothing every hair into its place. The bow was now wrapped with a red woven garter or with red yarn. When the hairdresser had finished, the man separated the bangs, which fell to the eyebrows, and, brushing both sides back with the hands, tied a kerchief or a silk band around his head.

The woman's hair was done up in a similar manner in the back. Instead of a bow she wore a queue, so wrapped with a garter or yarn as almost to obscure the hair, except in certain ceremonies when the hair, which had previously been braided to render it wavy, fell down the back. After the hair was dressed, the woman or girl, "by a peculiar manipulation of the fingers, separated her bangs, which fell to the lower lip, on one side and caught up the hair behind the ear." In dancing, grinding, and all other ceremonies the bangs fell over the face. Bangs were worn for the same reason that Turkish women veil their faces. The Zuñi say, "It is not well for a woman's face to be exposed to the gaze of men."[13]

In Fewkes's time, one often noticed little Zuñi children with their hair closely shaved, with the exception of a single lock on the forehead or back of the neck. It was not unusual to see a child with the crown of the head shaved, and with a growth of hair over the head about the forehead and ears. This custom is no longer followed. Fewkes also says that if a man's hair was cut off without a certain ceremony he feared he would die within a year, and he must preserve a lock of it to guard against harm.[14]

Among the Pueblos long hair is a sign that the bearer has been initiated into one or more of the religious societies. Because it is a badge of honor and commands respect among the conservative Pueblo people, the U.S. Government found the cutting of long hair in the early days a ready means of humiliating the men. To shame them into doing what the government wished, desperately needed commodities were distributed only to those with short hair. Not incidentally, whoever submitted gave the impression he was cooperating with, and thus approving of, government wishes and views. The overall consequences are plain.

In general, the material culture of Zuñi is similar to that of Hopi. Those who would like detailed information concerning that of Zuñi, and its variations from Hopi, can find it in the works of Stevenson, Cushing, Bunzel, Leighton and Adair, Eggan, John M. Roberts, and the writings of the Zuñi themselves. All these are listed in the bibliography. There is a fair-sized amount of literature regarding Zuñi games. Since illustrations help to clarify these, they are explained in the captions that accompany the drawings. Matilda Coxe Stevenson gives a report in *American Anthropologist*, n.s. 5, 1903, pp. 468–97, in which she describes a number of games played by Zuñi adults that have ceremonial import. Many of these belong to the gods of war, "who were great gamesters," and four belong to the Koyemshi. Some are included in my illustrations.

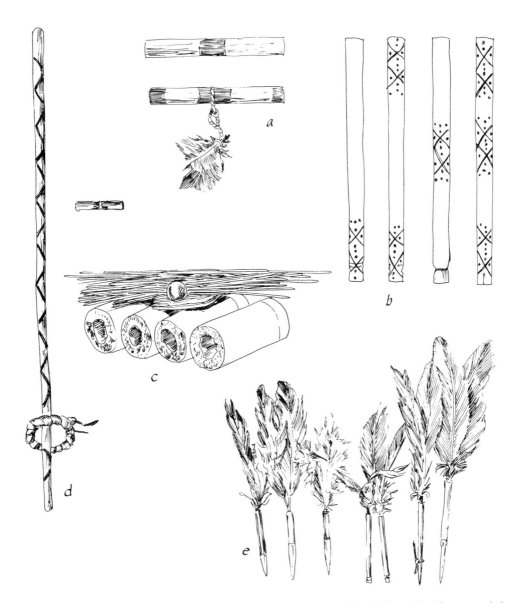

Games. The war gods of the Zuñi and other Pueblos invented and first played many of the games. Some are ceremonial; they bring rain and keep the sun moving. Others foretell the future. Gaming pieces are often the most important items placed on altars and they are regularly depicted in symbolic paintings. Deep meaning underlies all Zuñi games. The game items shown here are essentially for adult contests, but some may be played by youngsters. *a, tikwane,* a footrace by young men who represent on the one side the elder God of War, and on the other the younger God of War. The sticks shown are offerings to the gods, and are kicked ahead of the runner as he runs. *b,* Sholiwe, arrow reeds, a gambling game played for rain. *c,* Lankolowe, a hidden ball game with four cups to hide the ball in and straws for counters. Each group of players represents one of the Gods of War. *d,* Sikonyamune Tikwane, a footrace game for rain run by the Great Father Koyemshi. Women play against men, tossing the yucca ring with their sticks. The men use the small kick stick. *e,* Lapochiwe, a Gods of War game played indoors in which the sticks are thrown and the next player tries to hit the opponent's sticks. From Stevenson, 1903.

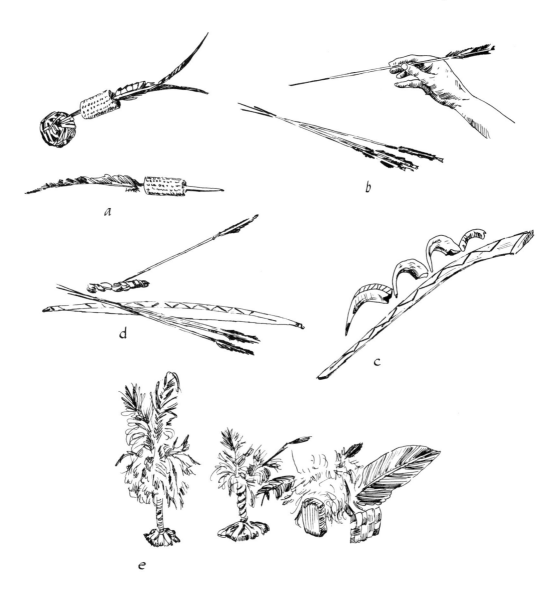

Games. *a,* Hokamonne, a Gods of War game played for rain, particularly at the winter solstice. The corncob darts are thrown at a yucca ball. The one who hits it the greatest number of times wins the game. *b,* Showialtowe, an arrow-tossing game in which each contestant seeks to have some part of his arrow land on his opponents' arrows. *c,* Saiahlatawe, Horns Kill, played with goat horns. The horns are thrown at the rabbit stick, and a player keeps throwing as long as he is successful. *d,* Hapoanne Pihlkwanawe, bow and arrows. Arrows are shot at a roll of husks that is hidden under a mound of dirt. *e,* Pokiannawe, Jackrabbits Hit. A game in which shuttlecocks are tossed into the air with one hand only. From Stevenson, 1903.

SOCIAL ORGANIZATION

Although in recent years some Zuñi have moved to farming villages closer to their fields, the villages have little independent existence. The main village remains a unit, whose physical compactness is reflected in an intricate and closely knit social organization.

Eggan explains that Zuñi is divided into perhaps "13 (although there may be 15) matrilineal, totemically named, and exogamous (a man should marry outside his own and his father's clan) clans, each of which is composed of one or more unnamed lineages." Clans, he says, were formerly grouped on a ceremonial basis into phratries (major groups including a number of clans) associated with the six directions, and there is some mythological sanction for a dual division. Dutton says that traces of a dichotomous organization have been detected at Zuñi, "with recognition of a north people and a south people, or a summer and winter people."[15] Eggan adds that certain of the larger clans are composed of named subclans, which have some resemblances to the Hopi system.[16] "The economic unit is the household, which normally is composed of an extended family based upon matrilocal residence. The central core of the household is a maternal lineage, 'a woman or group of women and their descendants through females,' to which are added husbands and miscellaneous male relatives."[17]

Zuñi also has an elaborate complex of ritual organizations: the Katcina Cult centers in six kiva groups, the priesthoods, and the Medicine societies, all of which cut across clan and household groupings. This complicated structure is held together, in large part, by the bonds of kinship, so that an analysis of the kinship system serves as a convenient basis for studying the structure, functions, and interrelations of Zuñi social organization.

Fewkes was told that there were six caciques, religious leaders, at Zuñi, of whom one or perhaps two were said to be women. Two of the caciques were members of the Bow priesthood. The head cacique was the cacique of the sun, and one of the doors of his house opened into the kiva in which the first of the Rain dances was held.[18] The house of a head-man friend of mine at Zuñi also opens into his kiva. In addition to duties connected with major rituals, the cacique must fast, recite prayers, and make and deposit prayer sticks. The making and depositing of prayer sticks are daily responsibilities, and in the evening caciques are often seen applying themselves to these tasks at the river and elsewhere. They do not govern the tribe, but they are respected and influential advisers.

Thanks to the dedicated efforts of Frank Hamilton Cushing, Matilda Coxe Stevenson, and Elsie Clews Parsons, who spent considerable time at Zuñi, the secular, social, and religious life of the Zuñi are fairly well understood.

Cushing was a member of an expedition sent to Zuñi in 1879 by Major J. W. Powell, Director of the Bureau of Ethnology. He was enthralled with the Zuñi and remained with them for several years. He learned to speak the Zuñi language, lived as much as he possibly could as a Zuñi, and wrote detailed accounts of their culture. While some of his intrusive habits distressed the

Zuñi, he was nevertheless accepted, given the Zuñi name that meant "Medicine Flower," and initiated into the Bow priesthood as a war chief.

William Webb and Robert A. Weinstein have succinctly pointed out that Cushing and Stevenson (who also lived among the Zuñi for several years) "were outrageously arrogant and condescending busybodies who felt no reservations about prying into the most secret and private parts of Zuñi life."[19] They find Mrs. Stevenson's accounts particularly embarrassing to read today, "as much for their unabashed confessions about how she obtained her information as for the perverse lengths to which the pursuit of objective science can carry one . . . We read these papers only to discover uncomfortably that we end up knowing more than we want to know, having learned more than we want to learn."[20]

One can only sympathize with the authors' view. And, they need not limit their criticism to Cushing and Stevenson. They could add Bourke, the Mindeleffs, Hodge, Fewkes, Voth, Kidder, Hewett, and Parsons, since every one of them pushed his way in on occasion. No doubt the Indians were at first gullible as to the ways of writers and photographers. They did not know what would come from the investigations. Yet they were plainly open and friendly to many of the people who came to learn. How else can one explain the reams

A grandmother giving a lesson in pottery decoration. From a photograph by Charles Martin, 1920.

of detailed material that resulted? As one reads, it becomes clear that the western Pueblos could shut out white people when they felt it necessary. Hence certain things at Hopi have never been seen. Of some of the Zuñi rituals, Cushing witnessed only fragments, and when a fair assessment is made, an interpretation through white people's eyes is never the real thing anyway.

I suppose that a conference on the ethics of anthropological investigation should have been held long ago and a code established, yet if that had been done we would be without much of the information of great value that we possess. All of us who are in the field, including Webb and Weinstein, read it avidly, and from it we gain a profound respect for the Indian peoples and useful guidance for ourselves.

References to Zuñi mythology have already been made in Chapter IV dealing with the archaeological work of Frank H. H. Roberts. To summarize, the Zuñi tell about their ancestors coming up from the Underworld and emerging onto the earth at a point some distance from present-day Zuñi. Following instructions from the gods to find the "middle place," or center of the earth, and there to establish their home, the Zuñi migrated for years in search of it. At last they found the Place, and they have lived there ever since. Either along the way, or soon after their arrival at the Middle Place, their cults came into being: the beast gods, the Bow priesthood, the Corn Maidens, the animal fetishes, and the others. Stevenson gives a full account of Zuñi mythology and origins in *The Zuñi Indians*, pages 20 to 60. Because the Zuñi followed directions, the gods have continued to bless them, and the Zuñi express their gratitude in an annual cycle of prayer and ritual.

The Roman Catholic Church has exerted less influence on the Zuñi than it has on the villages of the Rio Grande. The Zuñi do bury their dead in the churchyard and, until the 1920s, they hanged their witches from the church rafters.[21] But they have not been truly Christianized. Four hundred years of missionary effort have proved that their devotion to their ancient faith is deep-seated. They have succeeded in keeping their ritual and their ceremonies untouched by outside influences.

Some authorities believe that, at Zuñi, ceremonialism has reached its highest development in Indian life; in any discussion regarding them, ceremonies are the main topic. As I have said, the Zuñi social system is divided into household, kinship groups, clans, subclans, phratries, secret societies, and cult groups. A man may belong to several of these and be constantly occupied with their several observances. The Zuñi live in a world of symbolism. To them every object has a spiritual life of its own. The hierarchy of their "gods" is complicated, "gods" being an incorrect substitution used here only for convenience. "Higher powers" or "Spirit powers" would more accurately express their understanding of their supernatural beings. The souls of the dead go first to Kothluwalawa, Katcina Village, where the Council of the Gods dwells, and frequently return to Zuñi to dance. The dead are the Uwannami, or rainmakers, with the exception of the dead of the Bow priesthood, and the Ashiwanni, who become the lightning-makers. The Zuñi are among the few Indians who

Cloud symbol and fetishes of the Rain priest of the Nadir previous to the placing of the fruit and grain offerings.

do not fear lightning, "because it never destroys the good in heart." The greatest of the spirit powers is Kianilona, Owner of Springs, who sits in state at Katcina Village and receives messages from the Council of the Gods. The Zuñi have a cult of rain controllers which is made up of twelve priesthoods, the Ashiwanni. Membership in these is usually hereditary in the matrilineal family residing in the house in which the fetish of the group is kept. These fetishes are the most sacred objects in Zuñi. The public does not see them, since the Rain priesthoods meet where the fetishes are.[22] The rainmakers are directed by the Council of the Gods. They work behind the clouds, and ceremonial smoking is the means employed to make "cloud masks."

There is but one universal power. He is the supreme life-giver, Awoniwilona, and under Him in importance are a great number of lesser powers, celestial, terrestrial, Underworld, and combinations of these. Among the combinations is found the plumed serpent, and among the celestial spirits is a being who has knife blades for wing and tail feathers, is cloud-capped, and is often seen in the shrine hanging over the altars at Shalako time. The Sun Father is anthropomorphic, and carries the sun as a shield. In the Zuñi view the sun is the source of life, and he is recognized as such at the solstice observances. The most holy man is the Sun priest, who has charge of the solstice ceremonies and keeps the calendar. He also builds the altars for ceremonies and installs new priests, including the Bow priests.[23]

The Zuñi ceremonial organization includes many religious societies, each of which venerates certain supernaturals or groups of spirit powers. Each society has a priesthood, a meeting place, a body of secret ritual, possession or "control" of fetish-derived power, and a calendrical cycle of ceremonies that are associated with lunar observations.[24]

Twelve curing societies control a cult of beast gods at Zuñi, and men and women are allowed to join these. The cult centers upon animals of prey, especially the bear, who live in the east, control the length of life, and are the givers of medicine and magical power. Each group practices general medicine, and also specializes in treating specific diseases, as do the kiva fraternities at Hopi.[25]

There is a cult of war gods that is controlled by the Bow priesthood, whose members formerly were those who had slain an enemy. Its leaders are an elder and a younger Bow priest, who represent the Twin War Gods and obtain power from them. The Bow priesthood serves as the executive arm of the religious hierarchy.[26] Dutton says that in recent years this society has deteriorated and that opinions vary as to whether the priesthood even exists.[27] In 1970, the last of the old Zuñi war chiefs died. Since "he believed in God, and not in the old way," none of the war chiefs visited him after he was ill, and some of the priesthood secrets died with him. Thus the new war chiefs must function without this information, and their role is significantly changed from war relationships to the enforcement of religious law, to guarding religious secrets, and to seeking out witches.

The Zuñi, as do other Pueblos, believe that their ancestors passed through three underworlds, and that when the A'shiwi first emerged onto this world they had tails, long ears, and webbed feet and fingers. The War God Twins, sons of the Sun Father, had guided the Zuñi from the Underworld to earth, cut the webs apart with a stone knife. The Zuñi believe that the Hopi and the Navajo emerged after them. This mythology finds its counterpart in the priesthoods and fraternities, and myths are acted out during the dances. As at Hopi, the Zuñi year is divided into two parts, or halves, both of which are marked by the solstices. When the time of either solstice approaches, the cacique of the sun takes his place near a certain petrified stump east of the town and each day watches the sunrise. When the sun reaches its appointed place the cacique has the town crier announce that the time for the pertinent ceremonies and dances has arrived.

Leighton says that the body of religious knowledge at Zuñi is "so tremendous" that it can be compassed only by the concerted efforts and cooperative endeavors of an entire corps of priests and curers who devote their lives to religious duty. Understudies of the older priests begin to learn the prayers and rituals at an early age, persevering until they can perform every prayer and act to the letter. When the elders die and go to join the Katcinas, the novices take their place, inheriting through clan lines the sacred corn bundles, called *et-towe*.[28]

In ritual performance, limited freedom is allowed only in the choice of songs, costume, and dance patterns. Beyond this the spirit powers must be compelled to perform what is needed by precise adherence to tradition. "The organization of the priests and the part each plays in the working whole are as precisely defined as the prayers they utter for the public good. Each of the priests is trained to carry on his own duties, which interlock with those of other priests like the gears of a delicate machine."[29] Thus, as I learned at Hopi, any failure to attain the desired goal is due to man's failure to be and to perform what he ought.

FETISHISM

All Pueblo Indians use fetishes, but none to the extent that the Zuñi do. Citing the Encyclopedia Americana, Ruth F. Kirk states that "fetishism is the worship of material things as abodes of spirits, or more strictly, the belief that the possession and worship of an article can procure the services of a spirit lodged within it."[30] It is important to note that the power resides in the indwelling spirit, not in the fetish itself. In the Zuñi mind the power is always there, always potent, and when properly employed it will perform whatever it is capable of.

Every society and ceremonial group at Zuñi practices some form of fetishism. Kirk says that masks worn by Katcina dancing groups are considered fetishes, as are all other religious paraphernalia.[31] Every male, when he is initiated into his Katcina society, is given a personal fetish, made with a perfect ear of corn as its foundation. Concretion fetishes are strangely shaped rocks that are believed to be relics of organs of deities. Large animal fetishes are used as altar items. Small animal fetishes are carried by individuals to bring good fortune. Cushing gives extensive treatment to hunting fetishes, calling them "Prey Gods of the Hunt."[32]

Depending upon its origin and purpose, a fetish may be owned by an individual, clan, society, or entire tribe. It is regarded as alive and must be cared for and ceremonially fed, usually with cornmeal by whoever owns it. Most fetishes are kept in special fetish jars, taken out only when being cared for or used for a ritual. Fetishes are said to "live" inside their jars. They usually lie on a bed of down, into which powdered turquoise and shell has been sprinkled, with their heads turned toward the feeding hole "so they may breathe and eat."[33] The top of a fetish jar is usually covered with deerskin, and a flat rock is laid on top of the skin to help seal it and keep the dust out.

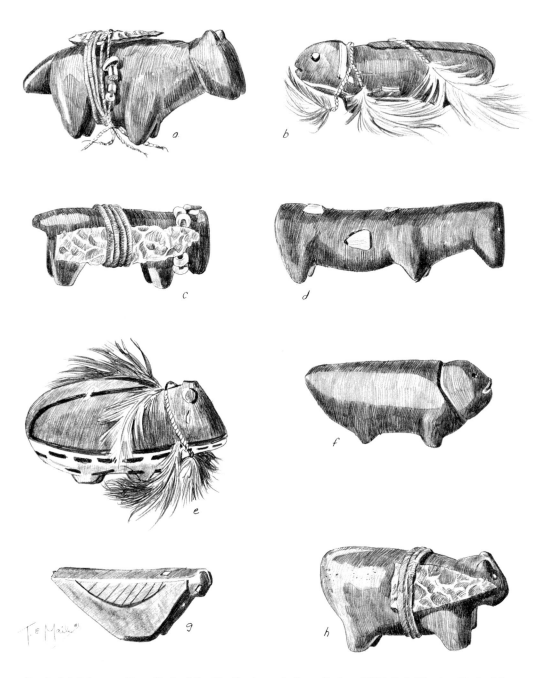

Typical fetishes: *a*, Prey God of the Six Regions. *b*, Prey God. *c*, Wild Cat, Hunter God of the South. *d*, Wolf, Hunter God of the East. *e*, Prey God of the Hunt. *f*, Coyote, Hunter God of the West. *g*, Eagle, Hunter God of the Upper Regions. *h*, Mountain Lion, Hunter God of the North. From Cushing, 1880–81 report, printed in 1883.

Fetish Pot, ten and a half inches in diameter, nine inches high. Mudhead figures are carved from animal antlers. Hole for ritually feeding contents of pot can be seen to the right of the highest figure.

SHRINES

As do the other pueblos, Zuñi has its shrines where offerings are regularly made. During his stay at Zuñi, Fewkes visited twenty-one different shrines and saw evidences of long use.[34] Some were rock shrines out on the plains around the village, some were at the base of Corn Mountain, and others were on top of the mountain. Prayer sticks in varying stages of decay were found at all the shrines, and the skulls and other bones of animals such as mountain lions, bears, and wolves.

Eagle Cage. Redrawn from V. Mindeleff, 1891.

Of special note was the shrine called He'patina, the symbolic Middle Place, which lay on the open plain a few hundred yards south of the old ruins of Halona. Fewkes describes it as a stone structure three feet high, facing east. It has two chambers, one larger than the other, both partly closed by a flat slab of stone. The top is covered by a flat stone, upon which are placed rounded cobbles.[35] Ickes says that under the symbolic shrine is a subterranean room about six feet square that is carefully sealed off, being opened only by certain of the priests for special purposes.[36]

At what Fewkes refers to as a dance of "unusual character," the Ham-po-ney, which he saw near mid-August in 1890, the participants, including four children, marched on the concluding day three times around He'patina, praying while the priests of the Bow whirled their bull-roarers. The flat stone that closed the shrine was removed, and the children deposited within the shrine small jars of sacred water and beautiful new prayer plumes.[37]

The most elaborate shrines were two on top of Corn Mountain, said to be devoted to the Twin War Gods, an elder known as U'yuyewi and a younger named Ma'sai'lema. Each was represented by a small log on which was "a rudely carved face." Around it were strewn many other pieces of wood carved in the same way, "which had evidently once stood in its place." The upright

Sun priest at He' patina, shrine symbolizing the center of the world. Front stone slab has been removed so that the interior is exposed. On top of the shrine is a conical "corn goddess" stone exactly like those found at Mesa Verde.

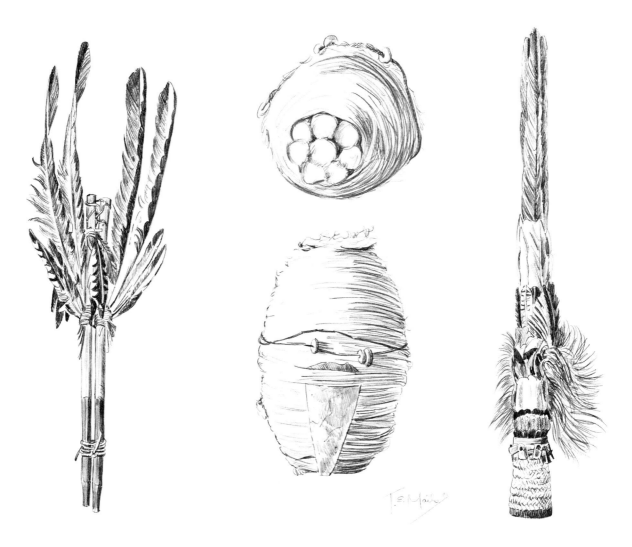

Left, plume offering made at shrine of Pai' yet' yamo, God of Music. Middle, top, and end view of fetish of the Rain priest. *Right*, ear of corn covered with plumes–insignia of the Order of Life Givers.

figure had tied to it a string to which were appended feather offerings, strings of shell beads, and an offering placed there by the Bow priests. This offering was a miniature shield made of a hoop over which a string mesh was stretched, with a miniature bow and arrows, seashells, and a carved wooden stick to which the tiny items and some larger prayer plumes were fastened.[38]

These logs, Fewkes discovered, were actually wood sculptures of the war god known to the Zuñi as Ahayuida. The twins are carved every year, painted, adorned with prayer feathers, prayer sticks, cotton cords, flint points, shells, pollen, and sacred cornmeal. They are treated ritually and placed in open shrines to protect the Zuñi (in fact, everyone in the world) from war and evil. The god representatives are tribal property. The usual carved figure is about 4 inches (10.16 cm) in diameter and 2 feet 6 inches (76.2 cm) in length, the elder god being slightly longer than the younger god. An imposing symbolic head is carved at one end, and a small carved peg is inserted into the front of the

Shrine on Twin Mountains. The most recently made figures of the elder God of War are in place, and piled behind them are the displaced gods of former years.

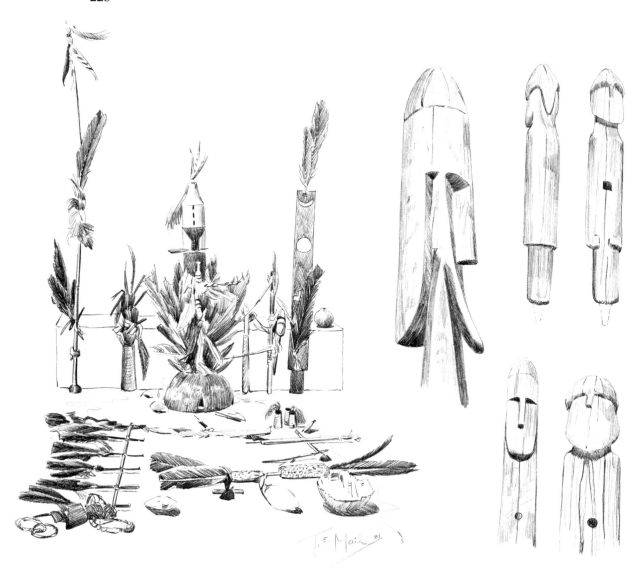

Left, altar of the War God, from a reproduction in the United States National Museum. *Right*, front, side, and back views of old War God figures. The portion at the bottom, pointed so that the figure can be driven into the ground, has decayed and is indicated by the dotted lines.

body as a phallic symbol. Further information about war gods is given in the Acoma material on pages 265–67.

Along a trail leading upward from the base of Corn Mountain, Fewkes was shown a cave strewn with hundreds of petroglyphs, some of "monstrous" size, some very small. A little to the west, the rock was honeycombed with small holes in which offerings had been placed, possibly by parents desiring a child.[39]

Cave shrine of Pa' Ya Tämu.

KATCINAS

The diversity of the Zuñi Katcinas is considerable, but their total number is not equal to that of the Hopi. In 1929, Ruth Bunzel published her monograph on the subject, *Zuñi Katcinas*, listing one hundred and fifteen figures that differed considerably in costume, mask, and role. Undoubtedly there are more, but these were as many as she and other observers had seen.

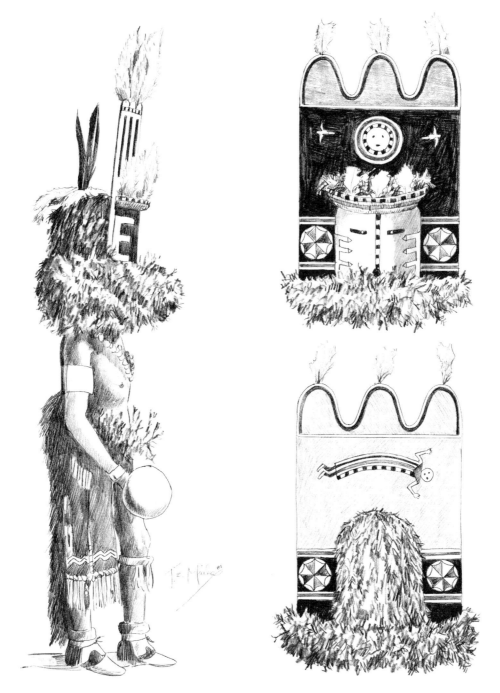

The Zuñi Hemis Katcina, written Heyamasheque by Fewkes, and Hémishiikwe by Stevenson. Figure at left from Fewkes, 1891. Masks at right from Stevenson, 1902.

According to Zuñi mythology, the Katcinas originated during the Migration.[40] The people were in the midst of searching for the Middle Place when they lost some of their children as they forded a lake. The children were squirming in their mothers' arms and were dropped into the water, where they were thought to be drowned. Later, when the Middle Place had been discovered and the people were still mourning their loss, the children, in the form of Katcinas, visited them and explained that they were still alive as souls, living

Katcina masks. *Left*, front, and rear views of the mask of the Owner of Springs. *Right*, mask of the Shumai' koli of the Zenith.

at the bottom of the lake. They had a village of their own there, where they were very happy and danced all day. At intervals after that, the Katcina came and danced for the Zuñi.

This made the people on earth happy too, except that whenever a Katcina Dance ended and the performers returned to the lake a Zuñi died. It was the Katcinas' custom to take a soul with them. Finally, the Zuñi and the Katcinas had a meeting to discuss this, and the Katcinas agreed to change their proce-

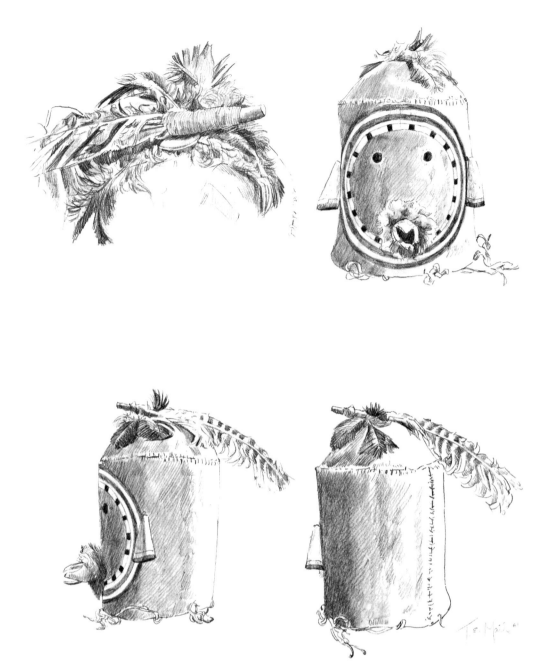

Warrior Katcina mask. Front, side, and back views, with detail showing how turkey feathers are secured to a wooden stick and attached to the crown. Mask is painted a dull red, and the colors of the design on the front, reading from outer band in, are dark blue, yellow, red, light blue, and white with black squares. Each ear is a carved white wooden cone tipped with a red and blue band.

dure. From that time on the Zuñi would make copies of the Katcina masks and give them "life." Whenever the Zuñi danced with the masks on, the real Katcinas would come and stand before the people.[41]

The entire pantheon of Zuñi Katcinas continues to make its home at the bottom of the sacred lake, which is situated about eighty miles from the town of Zuñi, at the conjunction of the Zuñi and Little Colorado rivers. This sacred place is known as Katcina Village, and when Zuñi of a certain religious status die, their souls swell the ranks of the Katcinas.

According to Parsons, impersonation remains within the lineage in charge of the mask; "there is no cult group." Certain masks are kept permanently in certain houses chosen by the Katcinas themselves on the day they first visited Zuñi.[42]

Bunzel considers the Katcina priests, who perform only priestly functions, to be a cult within the Katcina Cult, even though there are close associations between the two groups, because the primary concern of the priests is "human rather than crop fertility"; they play a central part in the annual Shalako Ceremony. She adds that the masks of the priests are ancient and permanent. They are tribally owned rather than individually owned and, like the *ettowe*, they are carefully guarded and ritually fed.[43] There are at least fifty-two masks, and they are second only in sanctity and power to the rainmaking fetishes.

Left, old Katcina doll, twenty inches tall. *Right,* old Long Hair Katcina doll, sixteen inches tall.

All adult males belong to the Katcina organization; women belong only to fulfill special duties. This tribal cult is organized into six divisions, each of which is identified with one of the four cardinal points, plus the zenith or the nadir. Every society has its own kiva and officers, who set the dates for the society performances. Membership is determined shortly after birth, when the male child's ceremonial father is chosen from the household of the natural father's sister. The ceremonial father sponsors the boy at the time he is formally initiated into the tribal cult.[44]

At Zuñi, the kivas are square rooms enclosed within the house blocks. Entrance is via a hatchway in the roof, although, as I have said, when a head man's home is adjacent to the kiva there may be a doorway leading from a room of his house directly into the kiva. Small ventilation openings are provided in the kiva's exterior walls. The kivas are basically plain, with wall benches to provide for seating. They also have central fireplaces, but no sipapu.[45] Murals or symbols are painted on the walls as they are needed for ceremonies.

Characteristic garments worn by Zuñi Katcinas are much like those employed by the Hopi: kilts, sashes, belts, moccasins, and fox skins. Fewkes thought the fox skin might be a survival of the time when skins were put on for animal impersonations. Bunzel says, "It is considered as a relic of the earliest days of man, for the katcinas were transformed while mankind was still

Men's ceremonial dance moccasins. Museum of New Mexico collection.

tailed and horned."[46] Body painting is elaborate and considered sacred. "No one must touch a man when he has on his body paint."[47] Those who impersonate females at Zuñi wear ordinary woman's costume.

KOYEMSHI

According to Zuñi mythology, the Zuñi clowns, known as Koyemshi and Mudheads, originated when the rain priest sent two of his children, a young male and a female, to find a good place for the people to build a village. While the maiden rested on a mountaintop, her brother scouted the country. Returning and finding her asleep, he desired her and took her. The sister was enraged, but the union resulted in the birth of ten children that very night. The first was normal in all respects, but the others did not have their seeds of generation within them, and accordingly were not fertile. Their seeds were "outside," contained within great wartlike knobs that began to grow on their heads. They also had puckered mouths that garbled their speech, and so they spoke unintelligibly and became silly, even though they were as wise as the gods and the high priests.

The rain priest's errant son and the nine infertile children became the ten Koyemshi, the son serving as the father. He decided they should not appear in public without their masks. Later, one of the religious fraternities copied these masks, with the head man representing the father and nine others the sons.[48] The masks are like those of the Hopi Koyemshi, but most of them have several small knobs in addition to four major ones. The costumes are also similar, although the Zuñi Koyemshi all differ slightly in appearance and deportment.

SHALAKO

Because it has always been open to the public, the Shalako Ceremony is Zuñi's best-known ritual. Every year, in late November or early December, crowds of interested viewers, whose size is determined only by the weather, flock to Zuñi to see this beautiful and dramatic ritual, which combines theater and worship. Anyone who goes, however, should be forewarned. It can snow and be unbelievably cold, and so that is actually the best time, because the crowd of outsiders is small, the houses are less crowded, and the dancers can at least be seen. But it can also be mild, which means that several hundred outsiders will come; viewers may be more comfortable, but unable to see much of anything.

The Shalakos are messengers of the gods, and they dance all night long in newly completed homes to bless them and the Zuñi people. They do so in one or more of the large rooms previously mentioned, and since the Shalakos can be as tall as twelve feet, counting the mask feathers, the floor is excavated to provide a ditch along one side for them to dance in. The Zuñi sit or stand in the same room, as do the singers, but the white spectator, unless he is an invited friend of a Zuñi, stands either in a peripheral room or outside the house, peering through windows while the dance goes on. And even though the Shalakos may be dancing in six houses simultaneously, everyone is jammed in, compounding the problem by wearing or carrying bulky coats. Usually the coat is needed, since it will be at least frosty outside. The pot-bellied stoves inside and the body heat, however, combine to keep the rooms like the interior of a furnace.

The Shalako Ceremony is often referred to as a house-blessing rite, but it is vastly more than that. It lasts forty-nine days and is a reenactment of the Zuñi Emergence and Migration myths. It is also a compound prayer for rain, for the health and general well-being of the people, and for the fertility and increase of plant and animal life.

As with Hopi rituals, the spirits of the dead return by invitation to be honored and fed, and in the last hour of the ceremony a long hunting rite is performed in the Council of the Gods House.

Those who are to impersonate the Shalakos, and the sponsors for their performances, are chosen during the previous winter solstice ceremony. All the past impersonators of the central figures form a cult group that alone knows the secret of the particular ritual performance, and it is they who select the next impersonators.[49] The complex preparations for the event commence immediately thereafter, occupying much of the participants' time for ten months. There are long, complicated songs to be learned, prayer sticks must be fashioned and placed every month at specific shrines associated with the migrations of the Zuñi, and there are monthly rituals to be carried out.

In addition to the ritual aspects, the dwellings that will honor and in turn be blessed by the Shalakos must be either constructed or extensively remodeled. Under ideal circumstances, six will be available for the Shalakos to dance in, one more for the "Long Horn house," and one more still for the "Koyemshi house." Sometimes there are not enough new houses available, and the Shalakos "double up" in performing. The Zuñi accept this today, since houses are so expensive to build, and those who offer a house must also provide food for the participants, Zuñi spectators, and all outsiders who come to visit. A family sacrifices virtually everything to do this, save the house itself, and it can take several years to recover from the expenditure.

Six major figures are impersonated for the ceremony, plus a certain number of Koyemshi: Shalako, Sayatasha, Hututu, Shulawitsi, Yamuhakto, and Salamobia. Their persons and costumes are briefly described here and shown in the illustrations.

There are six Shalakos, one to represent each of the six Zuñi kivas. Every Shalako has two impersonators, who take turns dancing in the mask and costume as the night passes. The Shalako mask is of the helmet type and the body is conical, being held up on a long center pole by the impersonator.

The mask is painted turquoise blue, and it has bulging eyes, a beak, and two horns. The eyes are like half of a white ball with a movable black dot in the center. The beak is long and cylindrical, split in half so that it can be

Shalako participants. *Top left*, Koyemshi (Mudhead) mask. *Top right*, Shalako mask. *Middle*, side view of the Salamobia (Warrior) of the Nadir or "below" mask. *Bottom*, front and side views of the mask of the Warrior of the Zenith, or "many hues of the sky."

opened and closed from the inside by drawstrings. Its sharp clacking sound is amplified by the hollowed-out lower half of the cylinder. The beak is painted the same blue as the mask, but black bands are placed at the tip and at intervals along the lower half of the beak. The horns are shaped like steer horns and painted blue. A white breath feather is attached to one tip, a red-dyed breath feather to the other.

A great black horsehair wig covers the top of the mask. It is cut to make bangs in the front, and it hangs down the back for about five feet. Yellow breath feathers are attached to the crown of the wig, just in front of a fan of golden eagle tail feathers (twenty-four in one I saw) that crosses the mask transversely. Just behind the fan is a group of three long, vertical, orange macaw tail feathers, and around the base of these is a cluster of shorter blue feathers. On the back of the head is still another assembly of feathers, formed in a fan shape and mostly bright blue with an admixture of orange and yellow. At equal intervals in the hair hanging down the back are tied four white down feathers, and at the end of the hair is suspended a very large and perfect turquoise. A thick collar or ruff of black raven plumes completes the mask.

The Shalako's body consists of a cone-shaped hoop frame wrapped in layers of embroidered robes. It is approximately four feet in diameter at the bottom. At the impersonator's eye level a small V-shaped opening is formed to provide vision through the robes. This opening is barely visible to spectators. An eagle tail feather hangs tip down just below it. Just under the mask ruff at the throat there is a great seashell, and around the Shalako's shoulders is a fox skin worn as a cape.

The two impersonators wear similar costumes. The most distinctive part is a white cloth skullcap (sometimes buckskin) with pendant sides or flaps, and scalloped along the back. One impersonator's cap in 1977 had no side flaps, and the other had diamond-shaped perforations along the back edge of the cap and the flaps. At the crown of the cap is a small upright tuft of cloth or buckskin. Along the front of the cap is a trim of three ribbons, red, yellow, and black, with four or five large silver buttons appended. Different colors may be seen, and brass buttons. The impersonator's hair is cut to form bangs, trimmed at the sides, and left long in the back, where it is pulled together like a ponytail and wrapped with red and yellow yarns. The rest of the costume consists of a short black kilt, tied in place with a brocaded white sash and a woven belt, and a long-sleeved shirt, of velvet or cloth, with cuffs. Some observers have seen impersonators in black shirts. I have seen them in blue, red, and orange shirts. Red, yellow, and white, and other color combinations of ribbons pass over each shoulder. In the front the ribbons hang loose with the ends cut in a V-shape. In the back they are gracefully looped like a three-strand necklace. Over the shoulders proper the ribbons are fluted to form a kind of ruffle. Beautiful, high-topped, painted moccasins are worn.

The face has a black line drawn horizontally under the eyes, and there is a red spot on each cheek. One observer says the leg paint she saw was yellow. If so, the color has something to do with the kiva represented, for some of those I watched used a light coat of white. Jewelry consists of turquoise and coral necklaces, and a silver bowguard on the left wrist. A stone-headed axe with a black horsetail pendant on the end of the handle is thrust under the belt at the left side. When the impersonator dances to accompany a performing Shalako, according to my experiences, he carries in the right hand a yucca

The Hututu Katcina.

wand and in the left hand a long prayer wand with eagle feathers and others appended to the tip. Again, I have read that the impersonators carry two yucca wands. In any event, the wands are tied together at four equally spaced points with string or buckskin, and the portion held in the hand is painted white.

Sayatasha (alternatively spelled Saiyatasha) is the Rain God of the North. He represents the north kiva, and oversees all preparatory activities for the Shalako appearance. His white mask is decorated with black lines, and has on its right side a long blue horn. The horn is said to be symbolic of long life for the Zuñi people. On top of the mask is a white down feather that indicates he is a priest. His costume includes a white shirt, a white dance kilt embroidered in blue bandoliers, fringed white leggings, a fox skin, and colored moccasins. He carries painted deer scapulae, a bow and arrows, a mountain lion skin quiver, and prayer plumes. Around his neck are beautiful arrangements of turquoise necklaces.

Hututu is the Rain God of the South. He is the deputy of Sayatasha, and a warrior of the kiva of the south. His costume is similar to that of Sayatasha, as is his mask, except that his mask has slightly different markings and two "ears" instead of one ear and a horn. He is named in accordance with the "Hu" sound he makes when performing.

Shulawitsi, the Fire God, represents the sun. He is impersonated by a young boy of the Badger Clan. This is the fire-making clan, and Shulawitsi is known by the firebrand he carries. His entire body and mask are painted with a base coat of black, over which are daubed dots of yellow, red, blue, green, and white. His costume consists of a black breechclout, red high-topped moccasins, a fawn skin filled with seeds and worn diagonally over his right shoulder and under his left arm, two cottontail rabbits hanging on his back, and turquoise necklaces. He carries the firebrand in his right hand, and a fire drill and board in his left. His mask is topped with a turkey feather, from which hang two heavy, twisted cotton strings.

Whenever Shulawitsi performs, he is preceded by his ceremonial father, who usually dresses in white buckskin, including a hide he wears as a cape. A horizontal black line crosses his face just below the eyes. His hands are whitened, and he carries a sacred cornmeal bowl or basket, from which he sprinkles the meal onto planted prayer sticks.

There are two Yamuhaktos. They represent the warriors of the west and the east. The helmet part of their mask is blue, and the collar is black and white. A white cottonwood stick with feathers and yarn hanging from each end sits horizontally on top of the helmet, and at its center is a tuft of orange feathers. The stick symbolizes their authority over the forests. The body above the waist is usually bare and rubbed with earth-colored paint, but on extremely cold days they may wear white buckskin shirts. They wear an untrimmed deer hide for a kilt, secured with a brocaded sash whose ends hang at the right side; colored moccasins that are basically blue, bead bandoliers, and turquoise necklaces and bracelets. They carry deer horns and tiers of prayer sticks.

The Salamobias represent all six kivas, although only two are included in the Council of the Gods at Shalako time. They are warriors, and their principal

The Little Fire God Katcina.

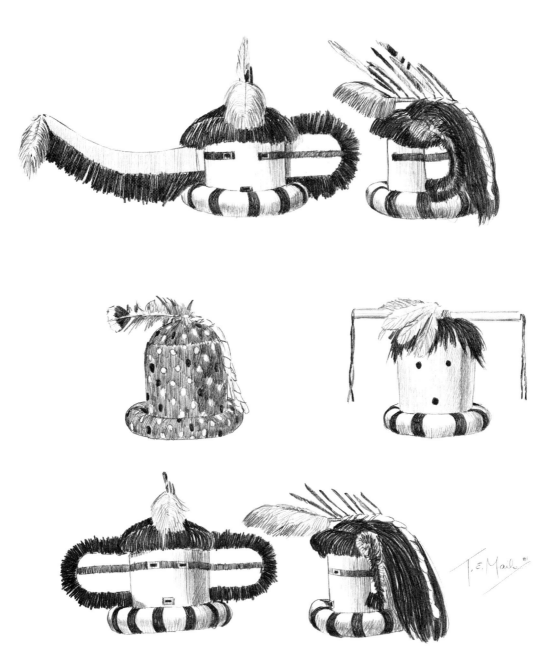

Shalako participants. *Top,* front and side views of Saiyatasha (Longhorn) mask. *Middle left,* Shulawitsi (Fire God) mask. *Middle right,* Yamuhakto mask. *Bottom,* front and side views of Hututu mask.

task is to keep spectators away from the performers. For this purpose they carry long yucca whips. The helmet portions of their masks are painted in colors associated with the kivas they represent. Characteristic is a thick collar of black crow feathers at the base of the helmet, and a long beak. They usually run while they are performing, and they make a unique call to announce their presence as a warning to spectators to keep away from the impersonators.

The ten Koyemshi participate in Shalako. They are led by the one known as Awan Tachu, meaning "Great Father." The other nine have names that represent aspects of Zuñi life, such as Water Drinker and Game Maker. The leader is appointed in January at the close of the winter solstice rite, and he selects the nine others who will assist him for the coming year. All ten are closely associated with Shalako, and as such must forego gainful employment for the year while they engage in religious and home-building activities. Since the sponsoring households must provide for them, that burden is added to other expenses involved. In particular, eight days before Shalako they appear in the village to exhort the people to complete their preparations for the coming of the gods, and then they go into retreat, requiring full care at this time. For six days after the Shalakos leave, the Koyemshi and their twenty or so attendants must again be provided for. If for some reason there is a delay in getting one or more houses ready, it is permissible to postpone the date of Shalako for ten days.

Four days after the Koyemshi arrive, Shulawitsi, Saiyatasha, and their attendants, having "retraced" the Migration of the Zuñi from their ancestral home, arrive from the west after dark. With Shulawitsi lighting fires along the way to guide them, they proceed to the Council of the Gods House to spend the night. Sometime the next morning they leave the village secretly and prepare for their return later in the day. When all is ready, the group assembles at Hepatina, the symbolic shrine of the Middle Place.

By midafternoon on Shalako Day (it was 3 P.M. in 1977), Shulawitsi, preceded by his ceremonial father, enters the village on a dirt footbridge that has been specially built across the river for Shalako. A drainpipe has been inserted through the bridge, even though the riverbed may be dry. (In 1976, Shulawitsi was a boy of thirteen or fourteen, in 1977 no more than ten.)

Shulawitsi and his father make a tour of six shrines at various places around the village. Each shrine consists of a small, shallow hole and a stone slab set upright at one edge. They deposit several prayer sticks in the hole, and Shulawitsi spits in it as a ritual cleansing gesture. Prayers for the rainmakers of the various directions are said at every shrine as the sticks are deposited.

When they have finished, Shulawitsi and his ceremonial father return to meet the Council of the Gods at Hepatina, and the entire group enters the village. In most dramatic fashion this magnificently costumed group makes a circuit of the six shrines, depositing prayer sticks and performing centuries-old rituals as they do so. It is a profoundly moving experience to see them in action. As the party goes from shrine to shrine, Zuñi come from their houses and sprinkle the gods with cornmeal. The little Fire God, following his father, comes first and spits in a shrine hole. Then Sayatasha and Hututu come and dance at the shrine. They place several prayer sticks in the hole and then meet face to face four times, stamping their feet and bowing toward one another, crying, "Hu-tu-tu, Hu-tu-tu." When they leave a shrine the stone slab is removed, the hole is filled in and the ground is smoothed over, and a small rock is placed in the center of the place where the hole was. A tourist coming along later would never know it was there.

After the shrines are visited, the group proceeds to the Council of the Gods House. Sometimes the members will climb a ladder and enter by a roof hatch. On one bitterly cold occasion when I was there, a few entered via the roof, the rest by way of the door. On December 3, 1977, the council occupied a room about 25 by 50 feet (7.5 by 15 m), oriented on a north-south axis. An altar was built at the north end, and from above hung a cross-shaped shrine decorated with five carved birds. At about the middle of the room was another ceiling shrine, the "House of Clouds," this one bearing carvings of Sayatasha and Hututu. To the left of the altar was a basket filled with prayer sticks, two boxes of native cigarettes, a water bucket and dipper, and a large turtle.

Directly in front of the altar a T-shaped mound of sacred white pollen or cornmeal had been sprinkled on the floor. On the bar of the T were three glass balls about the size of Christmas ornaments. On the stem of the T, three bowls holding cornmeal were placed in a row. South of the bowls was the gracefully placed body of a deer, tail toward the altar. (Later that evening I saw the same deer lying on a box in the back of a pickup truck, its head and nose sprinkled with pollen.) A few feet south of the deer was a board 14 inches (35.5 cm) square covering a hole that contained prayer offerings. Nine singers sat in the northeast corner. At the south end of the room sat Zuñi spectators. On a bench along the west wall sat the Council of the Gods, and in front of them and facing them sat nine medicine men or priests. From left to right in order on the council bench were three high priests, the two Salimobias, a Yamuhakto, Hututu, a Yamuhakto, Sayatasha, Shulawitsi, and the Ceremonial Father.

Before the council was seated there had been an elaborate blessing ritual for the house. Then masks were removed, in the sense that they rested on top of the head, the council was seated, blankets were wrapped around their shoulders, the attendants were seated, and from then on until midnight the time was spent in singing ancient chants and smoking cigarettes. In essence, the chants recounted the history of the Zuñi and included prayers for everything needed for a blessed future. At intervals a fraternity priest stood at the altar and twirled a bull-roarer.*

About 7:30 P.M. the six Shalakos and their attendants crossed the specially prepared bridge, placed their masks on the riverbank, and entered the village. Once they reached the streets, trucks and crowds led each marching to his sponsor's house with auto lights and police car lights piercing the mist and the familiar Hu-hu-hu sound echoing about. An hour and a half later each Shalako had returned for his mask and was again escorted to his sponsor's house.

When each Shalako reached his house, he set the mask and costume down outside the doorway. The impersonators smeared cornmeal on the house wall, knocked, and entered the house to conduct a blessing ritual. The house had been prepared for Shalako's arrival, and the room he would dance in was magnificently decorated. It is always a large room, at least 20 feet (6 m) wide and 40 feet (12 m) long. At one end is a reredos-type altar, in front of which is a bowl on the floor filled with sacred meal, a basket to hold the prayer sticks that will be carried by each impersonator when he dances to accompany Shalako, a water bucket and dipper, and some sugar. Directly above the altar hangs a ceiling shrine, and in the middle of the room hangs a second shrine. A ditch 20 inches (50 cm) deep has been dug along one side of the room for

*Kathleen Whitaker gives a full account of the blessing ceremony and the entire Shalako in the Southwest Museum Masterkey issues of July and October 1974.

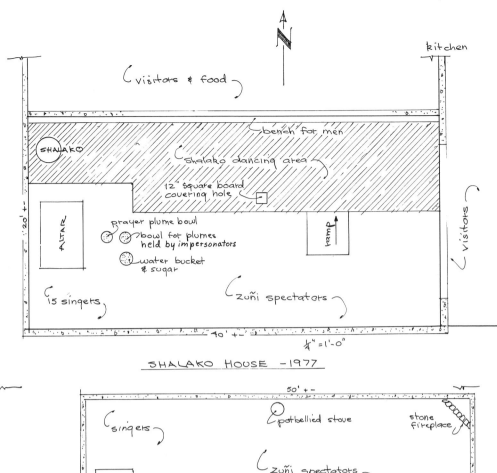

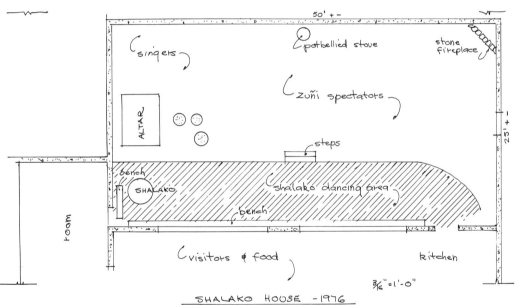

Shalako field sketch No. 1. *Top,* plan of Shalako house in 1977. *Bottom,* plan of Shalako house in 1976.

Shalako to dance in, and at the edge of the ditch is a board 12 inches (30 cm) square covering a sipapu hole in which special offerings have been deposited. Along the wall edge of the ditch is a long bench for fraternity members to sit on while the dancing is in progress. A group of fifteen or so singers will sit in a circle alongside the altar, and they accompany Shalako with rattles, drum, and song while he dances. Beautiful shawls folded to form triangles make a

Shalako field sketch No. 2. *Top left*, typical decorated deer head mounted on a wall. *Top right*, typical ceiling shrine (most are more profusely decorated with Shalako and Council of the Gods figures). *Bottom left*, interior of a painted ceremonial bowl. *Bottom right*, type of structure used for Shalako house altars (details vary).

resplendent border around the top of the walls, and other colored cloths are hung like banners below these, so that virtually the entire wall surface is covered. On the wall of one house I counted nineteen mounted deer heads and one duck, all of which had bunches of turquoise necklaces strung on them. In the Council of the Gods House that same year the wall mounts consisted of seventeen deer heads and one bear.

Once the house was blessed and prepared to receive Shalako, the Shalako figure was carried into the house and placed upright in front of the altar, facing into the room. The two impersonators sat on a bench, facing a priest who rested on another bench with his back to the wall. The three participants carried on a lengthy dialogue in song, recounting the Emergence and Migration myths in their entirety. When this ended, women brought food in bowls and placed them on the floor. The impersonators wrapped some of the food in blue paper bread and carried it to the river. There they deposited it as offerings to the ancestor spirits living in the Underworld. When they returned, the bowls of food were taken to the impersonators' homes, where a feast was held. Meanwhile, visitors were invited to dine at the Shalako houses.

As the night wore on, visitors began to pack the spectator areas of the Shalako houses, as did the Zuñi, who wisely brought chairs. Entire Zuñi families were there. Everyone shared in Shalako, even though some slept or drowsed at intervals. The impersonators sat with eyes closed on a bench at the end of the pit, seemingly lost in a trance.

The Council of the Gods were in their house, where performances took place, and the Koyemshi were in their house, which they had blessed and dedicated.[50] They sat in a row on a bench along one wall, wrapped in blankets with their masks pushed to the tops of their heads, while they carried on intermittently a sacred litany.

Visitors are told that Shalako dancing will begin about midnight, but it may start as late as 1:30 A.M. When it did, everything came suddenly alive. By some mysterious signal, since no one had come to make an announcement (even though people knew this was happening in every Shalako house simultaneously), from two to four men rose and held a large blanket like a curtain in front of the Shalako figure. An impersonator entered the Shalako, and lifted it up so that its mask emerged above the blanket. As it did so, the lead singer shook his orange gourd rattle sharply, and the dry sound called everyone to attention. The blanket was removed, the singers began as the drum boomed, and Shalako, gliding like a giant, graceful bird, started his swooping dance, searching, ever searching for the Middle Place, his great beak clacking like dull firecrackers at intervals, while alongside him the other impersonator danced in an enthralling half crouch, his feet drumming constantly to accompany the music, and the bells on his legs jingling all the while. He jutted his chin out in a style peculiar to the impersonator, and his eyes were mere slits as he concentrated grimly on his task. It was a grueling one, for the dance would not cease for a moment until the sun rose.

The impersonators changed off at intervals of forty-five minutes or so, although there seemed to be no rule for this. Each time they did so, the transfer took place behind the blanket. At various times groups of performers came to the house to dance with the Shalako. These included the Salamobias, Yebetchis to honor visiting Navajo friends, Koyemshi, and others. When the Koyemshi arrived, the Shalako played with them, chasing any Koyemshi who dared to step into the ditch and bearing down like an avenging bird as the

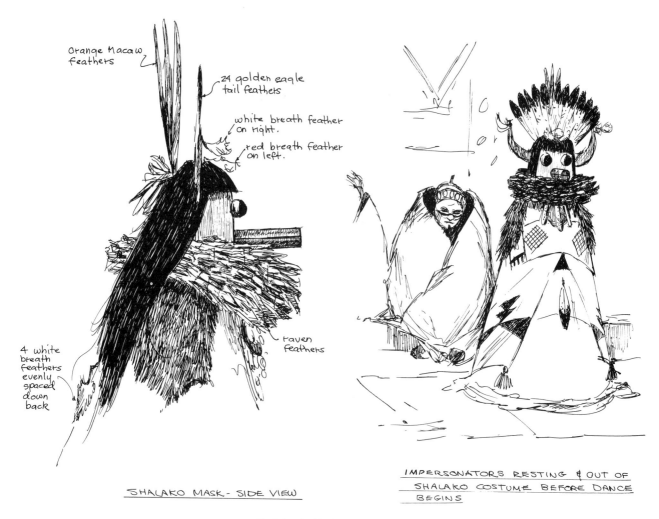

Orange Macaw feathers

24 golden eagle tail feathers

white breath feather on right.

red breath feather on left.

4 white breath feathers evenly spaced down back

raven feathers

SHALAKO MASK - SIDE VIEW

IMPERSONATORS RESTING & OUT OF SHALAKO COSTUME BEFORE DANCE BEGINS

Shalako field sketch No. 3.

clown ran away in mock terror. At times the Shalako played with the audience, sitting as if to rest on the edge of the pit.

Finally it was dawn. At 7:20 A.M., the singers gathered around the Shalako and sprinkled him with pollen. The head man prayed, a large black blanket was held in front of the Shalako, the impersonator stepped out of the costume, and the ceremony of the night was ended. The participants were fed, and a rest period followed.

At the Long Horn House the night-long ceremony ended differently. Just at dawn, Sayatasha climbed a ladder to the roof of the house, faced the east, and recited a long prayer. He climbed back into the house and thanked the choir for its assistance. The heads of all the participants at that house were then washed in a purification rite. Everyone had breakfast, and they rested.

Before noon, all the Shalakos and the Council of the Gods were stirring again and preparing for the next event, an afternoon race. As the Zuñi waited patiently, and the non-Indians impatiently in the bitter cold, the Shalakos arrived one by one with their attendants at the specially built bridge and with many pauses crossed it. They went to a cleared field on the far, or south, side, where they sat in a row and awaited the coming of the Council of the Gods.

Endurance was an ally as one waited for the Shalakos to arrive. The first came from the west at 12:30 P.M., the next came at 1:05, the third at 1:20, the fourth at 1:30, the fifth at 1:37, the sixth at 1:45, and the council did not arrive until 2:30 P.M.

Once everyone was assembled, the council danced as it did at the shrines when the prayer sticks were deposited, and then the Shalakos ran back and forth in an east-west direction, the race ending at 3:30 P.M. After this the entire party filed off to the south, and the spectators left for home.

Shalako field sketch No. 4.

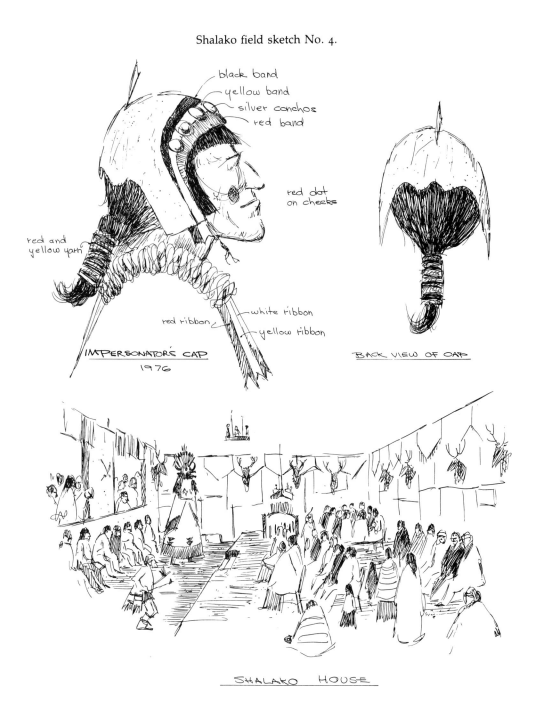

250

Although spectators were much too far away to see them, shrine holes had been cut into the earth on the racecourse to receive prayer sticks, and these were visited by the council at the same time they visited the other shrines. Every Shalako ran in a traditional pattern to every hole, standing over it while he deposited prayer sticks and sacred meal offerings. There are varying views as to why the race is run, but the Zuñi say it is simply a test to see how faithful the Shalako impersonators have been to their vows and assignments during the year of preparations. Those who weren't will fall, and all will see it and remember.

There is more to it than that. Shortly after Halona was built, Kian'astepi, a deity who came from the south, revealed to the Zuñi their correct choice of a Middle Place by spreading his legs at a point (where the He'patina shrine is now) directly beneath his heart and saying that that was the Middle Place. The Shalakos reenact this when they stand directly over the shrine holes with legs apart to place their offerings.

1976 impersonator wore blue velvet shirt. 1977 impersonator wore red velvet shirt with blue, orange & green ribbons - black fringe on right wrist, silver & turquoise bowguard on left wrist.

Shalako field sketch No. 5.

white cloth cap

small cloth tab

blue velvet shirt

black stripe across face

prayer stick with upright & pendant feathers

bells on legs tied on with black yarn

IMPERSONATOR COSTUME - SIDE VIEW - 1976

ribbons over shoulders applied in butterfly shape

3 ribbons evenly spaced on back

stone ax with horsetail pendant, inserted under sash

light coat of white paint on legs

loosely tied broad white sash

rain sash

narrow red belt sash

IMPERSONATOR COSTUME - BACK VIEW

SHALAKO CHASING MUDHEAD

SHALAKO CLOWNING

Shalako field sketch No. 6.

There are all kinds of stories regarding the rare incidents where Shalakos have fallen down. One observer reports that in 1954 two fell and consternation reigned.

A non-Pueblo Indian friend of mine who attended the 1975 Shalako told me that two Shalakos went down—slowly, like toppling towers—and that the Salamobias went instantly to work with their whips getting the Shalakos upright again. Meanwhile the Zuñi spectators seemed frantic, turning their backs instantly on the racecourse and hurrying to their homes. The six Shalakos came back across the footbridge, their attendants singing a death song.

The same friend was told a year later that the stricken Zuñi did not leave their homes for four months, that the two impersonators and six of their relatives had died within the year, and that the Zuñi jewelry industry had gone sour. The night of the Shalakos' fall, my friend heard outside his motel the sound of a wolf, "just like the death chant, with the same pitch." As he drove through Hopi country the next day, he heard the sound of the wolf again. This time the cry changed in the middle to a chant, to drums, and then back to the wolf call again.

Imaginations can be vivid, and such stories do abound. But when I questioned a head man friend at Zuñi about the falls and their reputed consequences, he confirmed the falls but had no recollection of any impersonator or relative dying as a result. The only real death lay in the impersonators' humiliation. But even then, everyone knew that the giant costumes were difficult to handle in the wind. They believed, but they were also realists. As for Zuñi's jewelry business, it was in a recession, but that was because an outside investor had withdrawn his support. It had little to do with Zuñi's religious life, and it was probably only a temporary setback.

My illustrations will help to visualize some aspects of the wondrous Shalako Ceremony. However, they are memory sketches, and must be accepted as such, since on-the-spot photography, drawing, and note-taking are strictly forbidden. In any event, they would be next to impossible in the dark and in the crush of the crowds—even if one were foolish enough to attempt them. Moreover, the consequences if one were apprehended would be justifiably severe. No pictures are here that cannot be seen by any visitor at Shalako time, and as I have said, the Council of the Gods' costumes are prominently displayed in the Roman Catholic church murals. At one time, photographs of the Shalako were even permitted, and several can be found in publications, along with many photographs of the village.

The Zuñi have for a long time fretted about the depictions of Shalako by white writers and artists, and they have prepared a paper for visitors. The text was written by Andrew Napetcha, the Zuñi Tribal Historian, Tribal Division of Education, for the Shalako held on November 27 and 28, 1976, and distributed to all who sought information at the Visitor Center. The Zuñi prefer to speak for themselves, and I include the paper in an appendix so that they can do so. It will serve as a guideline for those making their first visit to Shalako in the future.

After the Shalakos depart, there is a week of Katcina dancing in which the Zuñi experience fully the happiness Shalako brings. The dances are held in the houses that were blessed, and the feasting continues each night. Katcina performances at this time have great variety, and their purpose is mainly entertainment.

The dramatic and aesthetic effect of the dances is splendid. A dance lasts about twenty minutes, and every team performs one night at each blessed house; if an observer stays in one place he sees them all. Though dances may be repeated, the repertoire is different. The same dance may be done twice on successive nights, but by different groups of men. The music for the dances is highly developed; every chant is sung over and over, but every dance has its own chant. As I have said before, some melodies are such they can be remembered and hummed as are popular songs.

Ogres in menacing masks, paint, and bear-like fur boots and mittens appear often at these post-Shalako night dances, and they will be seen prowling about in the daytime "searching" for the errant children of the village.

The Katcina dancers may be masked or unmasked, and the costumes they wear are stunning. Some don bright velvet cloaks of purple, blue, and red, with silk ribbons falling from the shoulders. There are embroidered kilts and brocaded sashes, painted masks with collars of spruce boughs, and other boughs stuck in armbands and waistbands. There are headdresses festooned with flowers, and feathers of every color. The dancers carry decorated bows and arrows, yucca wands, prayer plumes, and rattles. Body paint may include lines to indicate rain, huge butterflies for fertility, and colored spots or stripes to call in the universe. So grandly do they dance thus attired that the audiences are as if mesmerized. Not a sound is heard save that of the swaying dancers and the throbbing music. Taken as a whole the pulsating drama depicts what Shalako has brought and assured, and it removes every doubt in the Zuñi mind as to the power of their gods; the need of their renewed awareness is vividly stressed by what follows immediately.

With the conclusion of Shalako and the week of rejoicing, an ardent bilateral act has been set into motion. I have mentioned earlier that a period comes each winter when the Hopi "fear" they will lose the retreating sun forever. The Zuñi pass through an identical experience, and in a fervent way. The Zuñi sun priest expresses the anxiety of the moment by working out the winter solstice date and then standing all day long for ten days by that certain petrified stump outside the village, where he watches for the sun to rise at a specific point on Corn Mountain. This is an interval of uncertainty and danger, the time when the sun must by traditional means be "called back." The Zuñi people participate in it fully, remaining in devout prayer at home. No outside fires are made, no cars are driven, no ashes are thrown out of doors. For periods of various lengths the people do not indulge in sexual intercourse, eat meat, or engage in trade. When the ten days have passed and it is announced that Sun has risen in its appointed place and will return, a new fire is kindled, and the yearly cycle begins all over.

A few weeks after the winter solstice ceremonial, and over a period of five or six weeks, each of the six Zuñi kivas presents a Katcina Dance. When a kiva society does not wish to participate fully, it can send a single figure to dance with another kiva group. Parsons says that the dances given in the winter are repeated in the summer in the same order, "at least theoretically."[51]

During his stay at Zuñi in 1883, Bandelier saw with Cushing a Mountain Sheep Dance, in which four men impersonating the sheep were led by a "high priest." A second priest, painted yellow and carrying a bow, followed the sheep and danced toward and away from them. Around him danced boys and girls in elaborate costumes. Cushing had not seen the dance before, but he thought it was an incantation to subdue the mountain sheep before starting on a great hunt.[52]

Fewkes states that the sacred dances for rain are among the most important and striking of the summer ceremonials.[53] The dance that peculiarly belongs to the summertime is called the Kor-kok-shi, or "Good Dance," of which eight are held. Their object is to obtain rain for the growing crops. They begin about the time of the summer solstice, and the first is followed in rapid succession by others similar in character. The preparations are similar to those of the Hopi, including the rehearsals of songs. In winter, the ceremonies are even more numerous and follow each other more rapidly than in summer.

According to Parsons, the Zuñi calendar for 1919 was as follows, in summary form. (The complete, involved calendar appears at the conclusion of her report.)[54]

January	ceremony of Wood society and Big Firebrand society. Katcina dance, all kivas represented. Saint's dance.
January/March	Katcina winter dance series by kivas in rotation (but other kivas may participate).
February	Ritual (retreat, etc.) by rain priesthoods. Ceremony of Wood society. Ceremony of Shi'wannakwe.
March	ceremony by Snake-medicine society.
March 26/April 15	Spring Katcina dances by kiva.
April/May	War society ritual, and races by kiva, by clan, at large.
June	Summer solstice ceremony.
June/August	Ritual (retreat, etc.) by rain priests.
September/October	Katcina dance (including visit to Ojo Caliente).
October	Count of forty-nine days till Shalako begins. Preceded by monthly prayer-stick planting by Shalako impersonators and chiefs of clown groups. All Souls' day.
November	Shalako (Katcina advent) ceremony. Katcinas go. Molawia (Ne'wekwe ceremony).
December	Winter solstice ceremony.

While Zuñi does not appear to have an open and closed Katcina season, as Hopi does, the winter and early spring series of Katcina dances are more elaborate. Games with ceremonial overtones are played in winter, and Zuñi kick-stick races are run in the spring. Women's ceremonies are harvest rituals, and as such are held in the autumn.[55]

Parsons also notes the marked difference between Hopi and Zuñi prayer sticks. They are different in design and color, those of the Zuñi being more elaborate, and the rite of offering at Zuñi is more frequent. For example, every Zuñi society member makes a monthly offering of prayer sticks, and the Zuñi make prayer sticks for their fetishes.[56]

Racing to draw down rain and snow is practiced at Zuñi as it is at Hopi, but the Zuñi races are more competitive and at some races there is considerable gambling on the outcome. In their preparation, Zuñi runners observe an over-

Craftsman using a pump drill to make holes in turquoise. From a William M. Pennington photograph. The drill consists of a round wooden stick to which a metal point has been attached, a wooden crossbar linked to the stick by buckskin thongs, and a spindle. The thongs are wound around the stick, and when the crossbar is pressed down the stick rotates. A skillful user can keep the pump going by applying the right pressure.

night retreat and seek omens for the outcome of the race. Whereas at Hopi a ball is used, the Zuñi use a stick. There are two competing teams of four or more runners each. A team has a cylindrical stick about five inches in length and half an inch in diameter with red paint marks to distinguish it. The race is run on the open plain over a prescribed course of fifteen to twenty miles. Both teams start at the same line, on signal, and run the entire distance without letting up. They kick the sticks as they go, at no time being permitted to touch them with their hands. Even if the stick falls into cacti or a prairie-dog hole, it must be recovered by foot only, under penalty of disqualification. Obviously, the race is demanding, and the Zuñi say they could not do it if it weren't for the "power" that comes from the stick. It is, therefore, common for men and boys who are traveling considerable distances on foot to kick a stick before them for practice.

It appears that the Zuñi hold initiations for children only when there are enough available to warrant it. The rite includes the whipping of the children by the Katcina Society, and it is held in February or March. The Zuñi have no equivalent for the Hopi Flute and Snake-Antelope ceremonies.[57]

The Zuñi remain today a devout, quiet, agricultural people, and they raise cattle, sheep, and pigs. Mutton is their everyday meat, and the number of sheep slaughtered for the Shalako feasting is amazing. Muskmelons and watermelons, squashes and gourds are raised, and the women plant onions and chili in little gardens near the river. Peaches are grown in the foothills and brought in to be dried on the housetops. But wheat and corn are their main crops. Baking is still done in the beehive-shaped outside ovens, and meal is ground on stone metates.

The Zuñi vie with the Navajo in the quality of their silver work, but the types are quite distinct. Zuñi pottery has always been excellently made and decorated. The most frequently recurring designs are a large squash blossom and the figure of a deer with a "breath line" drawn from heart to lips. The plumed serpent appears on ancient ceremonial bowls. Some ceremonial fetish bowls have been covered with a crust of clay taken from the sacred spring and mixed with deer's blood and bits of powdered jet and turquoise. The terraced bowl, symbol of rain clouds, is made for altars, and figures of frogs, tadpoles, water snakes, and dragonflies emphasize the importance that water holds in their life. The Shalako figure appears on old pottery.

ACOMA HISTORY AND LIFE

When Coronado sent a detachment to explore Acoma, known in those days as Acuco, about seventy-five miles from Zuñi, the Spaniards were met by the Acoma below the mesa bearing presents of turkeys, piñon nuts, corn, flour, much bread, and tanned deerskins. The trail up to the mesa top with its handholds and footholds and piles of rocks at the top to roll down on invaders was described by Captain Alvarado, who apparently led his men up across the

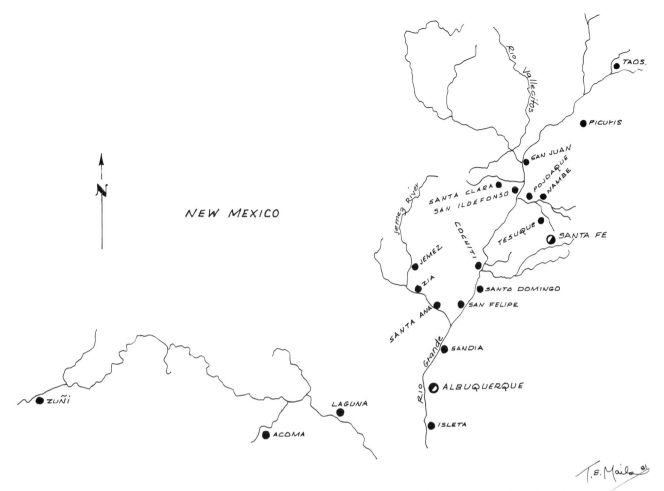

Map showing location of Zuñi, and of the eighteen eastern, or Rio Grande, pueblos in existence today.

formerly closed trail. There was no fighting at this time, but Juan de Oñate's field officer and nephew, Juan de Zaldívar, was killed in 1598 within the pueblo as he requisitioned supplies, and a punitive party in 1599 captured the pueblo in a fierce battle, burning and slaughtering the residents. Only one of the seventy attacking Spaniards was killed. Acoma casualties are estimated at eight hundred men, women, and children. Seventy or eighty warriors and five hundred women and children were taken prisoner.

To avenge further the death of Zaldívar, about seventy of the Indian prisoners were cut to pieces and thrown over the cliff. The rest of the prisoners were taken to the Rio Grande pueblo of Santo Domingo, where they stood trial in February 1599, on the charge that they failed to submit peacefully when Oñate's troops came to punish them. Oñate condemned all males over twenty-five years of age to have one foot cut off and to serve the Spaniards thereafter for twenty-five years. All males between twelve and twenty-five and all females over twelve years were sentenced to twenty years of servitude. Girls under twelve were to be distributed by Fray Alonso Martínez wherever he wished; boys under twelve were given to Vincente de Zaldívar, leader of the punitive expedition, and were soon sold into slavery despite the fact that such was illegal in New Spain.[58]

The Acoma Pueblo Mesa.

About 1629, the Franciscan friar Fray Juan Ramírez went to Acoma and ingratiated himself by acting like a medicine man, reviving a child by casting on it the holy water of baptism. Ramírez succeeded in getting his church built and, as he lived in Acoma for many years, he was successful in indoctrinating the townspeople. However, Acoma joined in the Great Revolt of 1680, killing its missionaries and ravaging the church. In 1696, the town made its final show of resistance by keeping Don Diego de Vargas, the reconqueror, off the mesa. All Vargas could do was to shoot four captives and burn the cornfields.[59]

The Acoma did not submit again to Spanish rule until 1699. About fourteen years later the church was restored, and the Acoma received horses, sheep, and cattle. Before long the Spanish and the Acoma joined in an alliance against the warlike Navajo. With the American conquest of the Southwest came title to the Acoma lands, and the Acoma have lived peacefully since that time.

Considering their history, one may wonder that most of the Acoma are devout Roman Catholics today, celebrating several feast days to which visitors are welcomed.

Acoma is taken from the native name "Akóme," meaning "people of the white rock." It is about sixty miles west of Albuquerque and about ten miles south of the San Jose River. Its linguistic group is Keresan, and it is the westernmost pueblo of this group. Sherds found at Acoma indicate that the site has been occupied for at least one thousand years. Its population in 1948 was 1,477. Today it is 3,000.

The pueblo, called "Sky City," contends with Oraibi for the title of oldest continuously occupied town in the United States, and it is easily one of the most spectacular of the pueblos. Situated on a 357-foot-high, isolated 70-acre sandstone mesa, it is an outstanding example of a defensive location. Nearby is the fabled "Enchanted Mesa," Katzimo. The majority of the population now live in secondary villages, McCartys and Acomita, which are near the farmlands along the San Jose River. They return to the old town only when the various dances are held, and every family maintains a house there. Part of the town was burned by the Spanish in 1559, but it is believed that the present stone-and-adobe buildings follow the aboriginal pattern of terraced house blocks in parallel lines. There are three main blocks, two and three stories high. The great stone-and-adobe mission church, built prior to 1644, has undergone burnings and numerous repairs. Since there is no loose soil on the rocky surface of the mesa, all the earth used to build the pueblo and the church and to fill and level the deep courtyard in front of the church had to be carried in hide bags from the valley below. The six kivas (possibly only five today) at Acoma are rectangular and enclosed within the house blocks.

For countless generations, Acoma has produced fine, thin pottery, very well fired, distinctive with its white slip and designs in dark brown or black, reds, yellows, and tans or orange. The designs range from geometric to involved curvilinear patterns, often featuring the parrot. Nowadays, most of the pieces made are relatively small and serve no utilitarian purpose other than tourist sales.

Katzimo, the Enchanted Mesa, is steeped in tradition. According to legend, long before the Spanish came in 1540, the Acoma lived on top of that 450-foot-high mesa. An easy trail made the top accessible, and the Acoma built a pueblo there quite like the present town. One day, when nearly all the people were away working in the fields, a great rainstorm undermined the natural rock ladder leading to the pueblo. It fell to earth and stranded two old women and a male caretaker named A-chi-to. When the Acoma returned there was no way up or down, and the desperate women and caretaker cried out for rescue until at last they died. After this the mourning people moved three miles west and built the present village. It is said that the Acoma never pass by the foot of the Enchanted Mesa in daylight without hearing the trio's tragic cries.

For a long time, archaeologists debated the legend of Katzimo, questioning whether anyone actually lived there. In September 1897, F. W. Hodge led a well-equipped expedition that made its way via a great cleft to the top. He found there arrow points, bead remnants, and pottery flakes—evidence that the mesa had indeed been inhabited at some time.[60]

When Hewett visited Acoma in the 1930s, he thought that, for situation, Acoma was one of the most remarkable of the Indian towns. No other pueblo gave one such a clear sense of living in ancestral times; no other so vividly illustrated the title of the book *Ancient Life in the American Southwest*. "Watching the people passing up and down those dizzy rock trails, the girls carrying water jars on their heads, the life and times of the cliff dwellers are reconstructed before our eyes. Acoma is the culmination of the idea of contemporary ancestry. One realizes how little guesswork is necessary on the part of the archaeologist of the Southwest in restoring the picture of ancient life in its essential aspects."

Acoma was already noted for its excellent pottery. Many small ramadas had been erected along the highway, and at each "a movement of colorful shawls on graceful figures" attracted passing motorists. Those who stopped found a pleasing array of pottery from which to select pieces. Some weaving of such articles as belts and headbands was carried on, and a few baskets were produced. As at Laguna Pueblo, lack of opportunities had forced the younger

Top, women at the Acoma mesa-top well, after Curtis. *Bottom,* the Acoma Roman Catholic mission as of 1930. From a T. Harmon Parkhurst photograph.

people to seek employment away from their native village. Many of the men were employed by the Santa Fe Railway, some by the government, and others had found miscellaneous means of making a living.

An Indian Day School was maintained at Santa Maria de Acoma, and one at Acomita, where the Acoma children were given an elementary education. There were Catholic churches at Santa Maria de Acoma and at Acoma proper.

Top, Katzimo, the Enchanted Mesa, as seen from the south. *Bottom,* the Enchanted Mesa in relationship to the Acoma mesa top. From Bolton photographs, 1927.

The ceremonial organization was under the direction of the head war chief and four assistants—elected annually—and of the several caciques. The caciques inherited their position matrilineally as members of the Antelope Clan. Acoma had a council of about ten principal men. The Medicine societies were comparable with those at Laguna Pueblo.[61]

At Acoma today the council is made up of the governor and his staff. The staff consists of two lieutenant governors, interpreter, secretary, and usually ten principal men chosen by the cacique. Mayordomos, cattle and sheep officers, fiscales, and sheriffs are not members of the council, but they have a

Top, the Fortress House. After a photograph by Father O'Sullivan, 1925. *Bottom,* the middle row of Acoma's houses. After a photograph by Bolton, 1927.

Left, Acoma man in typical attire of 1925. *Right*, Acoma man in ceremonial attire for the Corn Dance, 1925. After photographs by Father O'Sullivan.

voice in the meetings, as does anyone in the village who wishes to attend. It is also permissible for the council to hold private formal meetings.[62]

The cacique appoints all the officers with the exception of his own successor and the medicine men.[63] Four mayordomos are nominated and elected by the people using the ditches for farming purposes. The villages of Acomita and McCartys have two mayordomos each. The cattle and sheep men elect their own officers.

Acoma's position about midway between the Keresan villages of the Rio Grande and Zuñi is reflected in its cultural circumstance. It belongs definitely to the Keresan pattern, but its conformity is somewhat diluted because of its distance. Being close to Zuñi, it shows marked evidence of western influence, and Acoma and its neighbor, Laguna Pueblo, appear to have their closest affiliations with western pueblos.[64]

The geographical environment of Acoma is generally similar to that of Zuñi and Laguna, with the exception of the water supply. Old Acoma has no constant source of water other than small springs at the foot of the mesa and three large natural reservoirs on the mesa top. The modern economic situation is like that of Zuñi. Corn and mutton are the staples; wheat, beans, alfalfa, and other crops are grown in irrigated fields. The women once had corn-grinding associations, but these no longer exist. In theory all land is communally owned, but farms "belong" to particular families as long as they are cultivated. The cacique has authority to allot unused land.[65]

Eggan gives the population of Acoma as 200 men in 1540; total population was 700 in 1910, and 1,254 in 1941, equally divided between the sexes and representing some 212 families. He says that Acoma and Laguna represent the western dialect of Keresan and are understood with difficulty by their eastern kinsmen, and he classifies the pueblo as an independent social, political, and ceremonial unit. "The village is divided into several matrilineal and exogamous clans; there are no phratry groupings, nor are there moieties or dual divisions. The economic unit is the household—apparently of the same general type as among the Zuñi and Hopi." The movement out to the summer farming villages has, however, brought about changes in social organization that may be seen in many institutions; psychological disintegration is taking place, and the pueblo is tending to break up into family groups.[66]

White says there were four clans at Acoma that were custodians of ceremonies or that had ceremonial prerogatives. The Corn Clan had the Curatca Ceremony, the Pumpkin and Parrot clans jointly shared the salt-gathering ritual, and the Antelope Clan provided the cacique and was the head of the Katcinas. These clans were the only ones to have clan houses where meetings were held and ceremonial paraphernalia were kept. "The other clans had nothing to meet about."[67]

The ceremonial organization of Acoma centers on the Katcina Cult and the Medicine societies; there are also Warrior, "Clown," and Hunting societies. But Acoma does not have the Rain priesthoods, which play such a central role at Zuñi. White describes the Acoma social organization as consisting of two strata: "the kinship (and clan) level and the socioceremonial level." He sees kinship as the substratum upon which the ceremonial structure is reared; the two are not sharply divided but cofunction at many points. It is this interrelationship that gives to Acoma its strong social integration.[68]

Leslie A. White, who has written the most comprehensive material available on the Acoma, says that the government as of 1930 was theocratic: The officers were priests and the authority they exercised was religious. The officers and secret societies were the chief custodians of sacred lore, paraphernalia, and ritual. Pueblo administration was concerned chiefly with ceremonies, which could be divided into two classes: those that promoted the growth of crops by influencing the weather and the heavenly bodies and those that cured disease and exorcised evil spirits from the pueblo (the Medicine Cult). Secular duties of government were delegated to the governor and his aides, who had come into existence for this purpose and for screening the sacred officers from the eyes of the whites.

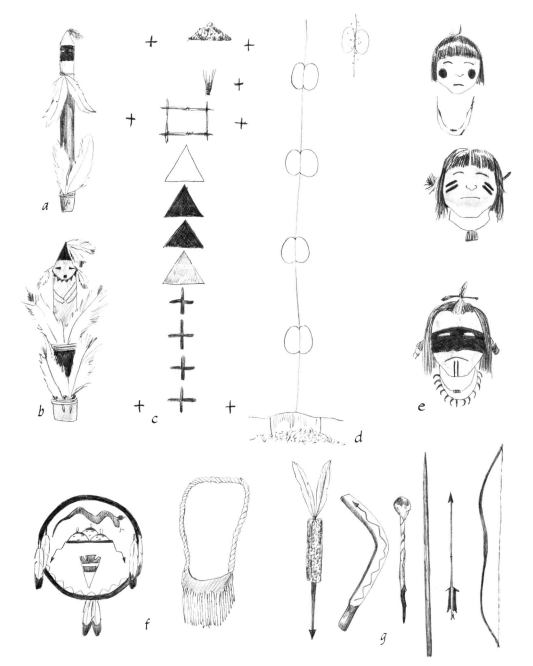

Acoma: *a*, Katcina prayer stick, or paho. *b*, Fire Society paho. *c*, sand painting and paraphernalia for exorcism. *d*, groove in rock for rite of forgetting the dead. *e*, face paintings of the dead. *f*, shield and pouch of the Twins. *g*, weapons given by Sun to the Twins. From Stirling, 1942.

Ceremonialism at Acoma was a conspicuous part of the life. Functionally, one could view ceremonies as serving religious, social, and aesthetic ends. Most ceremonies incorporated these three factors in varying degrees. The most conspicuous cults at Acoma were the Katcina Cult, the Medicine Cult, and the War Cult. The Warriors' Society and the Koshare once functioned in a war capacity, but with the end of warfare this phase of ceremonialism had largely disappeared, as had the Hunters' Society.

The Acoma pantheon was as follows: The Sun, Ocatc, was a great spirit, perhaps the most important of all supernaturals. He was called Father. People prayed to him and made offerings to him. In myths he is seen as the father of twin boys, sometimes of the Twin War Gods, Masewi and Oyoyewi. He was the chief object of the solstice ceremonies. He was pictured in petroglyphs on the face of rock mesas. He was represented in myths only in symbolic form; pictures of him show a face with lines like rays radiating from the outer edge. Masewi and Oyoyewi were the patron gods of the Warriors' Society and of the war chiefs, but anyone could pray to them for strength. They were represented with masks in dances and were depicted on altars of curing societies. On the eastern edge of the mesa of old Acoma there were two rock pillars that were said to mark the place where the spirits of these two gods lived after they had left the Acoma people. They symbolized courage, strength, and virtue. They were also represented in mythology as great rainmakers. Masewi and Oyoyewi were the champions of the Acoma people in the early days when the Acoma lived in the north and were on their long migration to the south.[69]

A Pueblo friend of mine was kind enough to write an account of the Laguna-Acoma War God:

"Know that we are the twain to hold the high place in the worlds."

They are called "Mah-se-wi" and "O-yo-yo-wi," the twin warrior sons of the Sun Father. One or the other appears at Acoma every four years not as a Katsi-nah [Katcina] but rather more as a deity.

"Mah-se-wi," the elder twin, is painted yellow, his face the color of pollen, fertility and new life. His face is also marked with warrior marks, red the color of life, white the color of the morning star.

"O-yo-yo-wi," the younger twin, is painted white, the color of the morning star. Tall lighted wonderful warrior, champion of the "Opi," warrior society.

The twin warriors come to Acoma every four years to settle the quarrels of the people who have found many bad words to use against each other and also to settle the feuds and fights that have arisen. They come at this time with the Katsinah Chief (head man) to teach the people how to be good in the supernatural manner of the "Katsinah" and to drive away the "Kah-nah-dyai-yah," the witch people.

The wood figure of the War God is renewed and painted every four years. It is carved from a tree that has been struck by lightning by the Warrior Society directed by the "war chief" "Tsah-dyah Ho-cha-nee," his name means "going before," "holding the people together, leading, marking four sacred trails—four sacred trails reaching from the earth to the sky, holding the earth and sky in place, because earths and skies were made to last—forever."

The War God is then "dressed" with prayer sticks made by the "Chi-yani," the flint and fire people who are the medicine societies at Laguna and Acoma.

"You have seen the fathers
You have seen how the life-bearing willow is painted
And how the mist people, the rain people
are clothed—with white shell and sunrise.

You will do things in the same way
And this you are to carry into the future.
In this right way
For as long as there is Life."

Also at this time the masks are brought to life. The Chaiyani again have prepared the altars in the kivas during these four days when the War Gods appear. When all is ready and the songs are finished, the men who have made the masks to be brought alive are waiting in the kivas. Again the ceremonies are conducted by the Chaiyani and life is given to the masks, just as it is done for the fetishes and Corn Mothers on the altars. The masks are then named for the Katsinah they represent. In this way they now become the "friend" of the one who is bringing (dancing) the mask. The Chaiyani then "blow" the new life of the mask to the owner and give it to him saying: "This is now real and it has the same power as given to the warrior twins. If you do not treat this in a sacred manner it will have the power to destroy you."

Also at this time every four years the children, all the boys ten, twelve, fifteen years old, are initiated and must know about these things and even the little girls, just as they know about Santa Claus.

> "Even as I a common human
> In this right way, representing you
> The power of your body
> The power of your mind
> Into my mind, my body, entering.
> Help me to represent you as you would have it.
> Goodly
> Help me to represent you 'really'
> You that are real
> make me real."
> I was lost.
> The wind blew hard across a flowerless plain.
> To the place of the four winds it took me.
> Thus did I seize up and make into a bundle
> Those things which were my enemies'
> and thus did my enemies' good
> fill my being.

And thus was it told to me.

The k'obictaiya were spirits who lived in the east where the sun rose. They also lived at a crater-like place southeast of Acoma. The k'obictaiya were regarded as very powerful and beneficent spirits, but they did not reveal themselves as clearly and as definitely as did the Katcina, hence information concerning the k'obictaiya was meager and vague. So far as White could learn, they were not assigned to any particular function except during the winter solstice ceremony, when they promoted fertility and strengthened weak and sick people. Prayer sticks were deposited for the k'obictaiya, and masked men impersonated them at the winter solstice.

Iatiku was very sacred and of the greatest importance. She was called the mother of all the Indians. Her home was Shipap, the place of Emergence, in the north. After death a person returned to his mother, to Shipap. A short prayer and a bit of food were offered to Iatiku before each meal. Prayer sticks were deposited to her. She seemed to watch over human beings, not at any special time but in relation to the well-being and continuance of life itself. In certain rituals one spoke of getting the breath of life from Shipap.

The moon was said to be a female spirit. Prayers were offered to her, but she seemed to be relatively unimportant.

Stars were considered supernaturals, but White was not able to ascertain which ones. They were not important, and they were mentioned only in prayers.

The earth was mentioned in prayers.

The clouds were very important, especially storm clouds. They were prayed to, feathers on the tops of masks were said to symbolize clouds, and clouds were often depicted on medicine bowls and altars. Men in curing ceremonies blew bubbles to symbolize clouds. The clouds were called henati, but shiwanna was used to refer to the Cloud People, or rainmakers. In paintings on the walls of ceremonial chambers, clouds were represented as having eyes and mouth.

Lightning was sacred and associated with rain and hunting. Hunters prayed to lightning when they started out on a hunt. Flints were called lightning stones. Since lightning sometimes struck and killed, it was allied to hunting. Lightning represented power, and flint was thought of as a capsule capable of containing this power, which could be drawn upon. Some people wore a flint arrowhead tied on a thong around the neck and thus gained the power of lightning. Medicine men had large flints, which they used to secure "power." There were two kinds of lightning, zigzag and sheet. There was a little plant that sometimes was placed on top of a house to keep the lightning from striking it.

The four rainmakers of the cardinal points were supernaturals merely mentioned in prayers.

Hunting gods included the sun, which was called upon at rabbit hunts, but the main hunting deity was the cougar, or mountain lion, and they possessed a little stone figure of this animal. Formerly there was a Hunters' Society called the Caivaik, whose business it was to supply hunting medicines to hunters and to assist in communal hunts.

Medicine gods possessed the power to cure disease.

San Estevan was the patron saint of Acoma. His fiesta day, September 2, was observed at Acoma with services in the old Spanish church and with a Corn Dance in the plaza. The saint is regarded as having some power and is inclined to help the Acoma people.

Yoshthi (Dios, God), the Christian god, was also regarded as a supernatural and hence had some power, but he did not have as large a following as San Estevan, who had a peculiar obligation to Acoma. Dios was not well disposed toward the people. It was said that he punished some people after death; none of the native deities did this. Sometimes prayer sticks were offered to God, but they were always accompanied by sticks for Iatiku.

Cristo (Christ) was also regarded as a supernatural, but not primarily as one for the Indians. He had very little following.

White furnishes the following list of annual ceremonial observances for Acoma, with the approximate dates for each:

December 24	Christmas Eve, ceremony in church.
December 25, 26, 27	Miscellaneous dances.
December 28	Elections announced.
January (?)	Installation of war chief.
January (?)	Scalp dance, k'atseta, for the incoming officers.
June 20–21	Summer solstice.
June 24	San Juan's Day, rooster pull.
June 29	San Pedro's Day, rooster pull.
July 12–14	Natyati, the summer masked dance.
July 24	Rooster pull.
July 25	San Diego's Day, Corn dance.
August 10	San Lorenzo's Day, Corn dance at Acomita.
September 2	San Estevan's Day, fiesta at old Acoma.
September 20 (cir)	Fall masked dance.
December 21	Winter solstice.

Additional ceremonies were:

G'aiyabai'tsani, the fight with the katcinas. This came every five years, usually in the early spring.

The masked dance of the Corn clan came every five years, usually in the middle of the summer, about the last of July.

Scalp dances were formerly held after a kill, or at the direction of the Warriors' Society.

Rabbit hunts.

Miscellaneous dances.

Depositing prayer sticks.

The dates of some ceremonies, such as saint's days, were fixed, but the dates of other ceremonies could be fixed only approximately, since they varied somewhat. The big summer masked dance, for example, might begin on July 11 or 12. The cacique set the date for this as well as for other ceremonies that might vary chronologically. White did not know how the cacique arrived at the date for the summer Katcina Dance; the time for the solstice ceremonies he determined by watching the sun rise.

Rabbit hunts accompanied almost all important occasions.

Rooster pulls (see page 355) and miscellaneous dances were of minor importance and optional. Miscellaneous dances included among others the Eagle, Comanche, Buffalo, and Corn dances, and they were merely recreational in character. Anyone who wished to dance could join in. They were not sacred and could be witnessed by whites or Mexicans. Dances of these kinds always followed Christmas Eve, and a Comanche Dance was nearly always held at Acomita on San Lorenzo's Day, but these dances could be held at other times. During the winter at old Acoma, people frequently got together for dancing, and even during the summer they sometimes had a Corn Dance in one of the houses.

Acoma held kick-stick races similar to those performed at Zuñi. They were competitive, and wagers were made on the outcome. Kiva groups furnished the two teams, and the races were run at the foot of the mesa. Courses varied in length from two to ten miles. The purpose, as at Zuñi, was to bring rain in spurts, "the way a kick-stick was propelled."

All important dances were preceded or accompanied by the making and depositing of prayer sticks. These were fashioned for all important ceremonial occasions concerned with the supernatural world and were the most formal and satisfactory means of establishing rapport with the spirits.

The Katcina Cult comprised spirit rainmakers, in appearance exactly like the masked dancers. In the old days, when the Acoma people were still living in the north, the Katcinas came to the village when the people were lonesome or sad and danced for them; this cheered them greatly. The Katcinas used to bring gifts, too, and they taught the people arts and crafts and hunting. After the people began to grow their own food, the Katcinas would come to the village when the fields were dry and dance. Rain always followed. The Indians owed almost everything to the Katcinas.

But after a great fight erupted between the Katcinas and the people, the spirits refused to come to the village anymore. However, they told the Indians that they could wear masks and costumes to represent the Katcinas, and could act as if they were real Katcinas. If they did this the Katcinas would come and enter the persons of the masked dancers and all would be well—rain would come. That is why the Acoma people had masked dances, and why the Katcinas were revered.

The Katcinas lived at a place called Wenimats, "somewhere out west, perhaps near the Zuñi Mountains." There they lived very much as the Indians at Acoma did. They had a chief, or *hotceni*, named k'imaco. They had fields, and they hunted, gambled, and danced much as the Acoma people did. There were some Katcina women, too. They were usually called *k'otcininak'o*, or yellow woman. But some of them had faces of other colors (the face alone has the distinguishing color), such as the white-faced *g'acinako*. According to some myths, these women were virgins; they never lived with the male Katcinas.

Not all the Katcinas, however, lived at Wenimats. A fair number lived near Acoma. White thinks this belief was due to the long occupancy of the mesa of old Acoma; every inch of ground near there was very familiar to the people, and some of the sites had become associated with myths and legends.

As to the belief in Katcinas, the people of Acoma were divided, as at Hopi, into two groups: the children, who believed that the masked dancers were really gods, and the adults, who knew full well they were the men and boys of the village wearing masks. Children were told that the dancers were great gods from Wenimats and were taught to regard them with awe.

The day of awakening came when they were initiated into the secrets and mysteries of the Katcinas and the dancers. Boys and girls alike were initiated, but the role played by women in the Katcina organization was negligible. The women prepared food for the dancers and assisted them in their distributions of gifts, but no woman ever wore a mask in a dance, even though a *k'otcininak'o* (a Katcina woman) was being impersonated by a woman. The people who had been initiated into the secrets of the Katcinas were called *G'uiraina tcaiani*. Children were affiliated with the kiva of the father.

Left, the Kuapichani Katcina in typical Katcina costume. *Right,* some of the Acoma Katcina masks as painted by an Acoma Indian for Matthew W. Stirling, 1942.

There was a head man for each kiva. He was appointed by the cacique and served for life. His duties were in general the administration of the unit of the Katcina organization belonging to his kiva; specifically, he was the custodian of the masks, keeping them safely secured between ceremonies; he took them out and painted them for dances, fed them, and offered them cigarettes; he summoned his men for ceremonies and instructed them in matters of preparation.

The war chief kept track of the children to be initiated, and initiations were held at intervals of five or six years. In the old days initiations were held at the winter solstice; nowadays* they are held during the summer. Formerly, children were initiated at ages ranging from nine to twelve. Now, however, the initiation is usually postponed until the children come back from the schools to stay in the village. When the war chief thinks the time has come for another initiation, he confers with the cacique, who sets a date. Then the war chief goes through the streets four days before the initiation is to take place and announces the forthcoming event.

The Initiation Ceremony is quite similar to that of the Hopi, including the whipping and the retelling of the Emergence and Migration myth. The conclusion, however, is different. The cacique takes the child to the head Katcina, who holds prayer sticks in his hands. The child's hands are placed under those of the Katcina, and the cacique places his hands under the child's. The cacique prays at great length. He blesses the child, asks that he might have a long life, that he might be successful in farming and in hunting, that his parents might live long. Then the cacique formally presents the child to the head Katcina, stating that he is now a member of *G'uiraina tcaiani*, Katcina Society.

White states that the people of Acoma continue to throw sun offerings into crevices at the eastern edge of the mesa. They also bury a miniature suit of clothing at their Sun House, which is at a point thought to be beneath the southern end of the sun's course.[70] Florence H. Ellis explains that miniature offerings of any kind are believed to become enlarged to full size for the use of the supernatural power who receives them.[71]

BIRTH

According to what White observed in the 1920s, during pregnancy a woman modified her ordinary conduct somewhat. She should not stand in a doorway; this would retard delivery. She should not go out walking very much. She is not supposed to eat fruit. She must not work too much. One should never "talk bad" in her presence. A midwife assisted at childbirth.

When the child was born the father made a wabani, which he took to a medicine man, and offered a long prayer; after that he asked him to come to his house to take the baby out to see the sun and to give him a name. About 2 A.M. on the fourth day after the child was born, the medicine man solicited by the father came with his wife to the house of the child. The parents had cleared a space in a room for him, and there he made a four-direction sand painting and laid out his paraphernalia. The design of the sand included a horned toad or a turtle. Two or three personal fetishes were placed on the turtle if a turtle was chosen (on the toad if that was chosen). A medicine bowl was placed on the turtle's head, and medicine was mixed in it. Flints, miscellaneous fetishes, and perhaps a bear paw were placed on the sand painting on either side of the turtle's head, and a basket of prayer sticks near the head.

---

*Since no later published material on Acoma is available, I am assuming that, except for ceremonies or offices that may have terminated, the religious life at Acoma is the same today as White found it to be in 1929 and 1930. Accordingly I describe it in the present tense.

While the medicine man was making his sand painting and arranging his paraphernalia, his wife was bathing the mother and baby. When all was ready, the medicine man sat near the turtle's head and began to sing, keeping time with a gourd rattle. He sang for some time. His wife sat on the floor near the head of the turtle, with the baby in her lap. The mother sat near by. As the medicine man sang, he dipped eagle plumes into the medicine bowl from time to time and sprinkled the baby.

Shortly before sunrise the medicine man asked the parents if they had prepared feather bunches for prayers. The mother and father brought these and, standing on either side of the turtle's head, prayed. When they finished they laid their wabani in the basket of prayer sticks. Then the medicine man asked the parents if they had selected a name for their child. If they had not done so, the medicine man selected one himself.

Just before sunrise they all rose and went outdoors. The wife of the medicine man carried the baby, following her husband to the east edge of the mesa. The parents stopped a few paces outside their door. The medicine man carried with him the basket of prayer sticks, a fetish, a flint, his eagle feathers, and the bear's paw. The medicine man sat on the edge of the cliff and prayed to the sun. As the sun rose the wife of the medicine man held the baby out toward it. The medicine man prayed. When he finished, he threw the basket of prayer sticks over the edge. Then he rose and approached the baby. He gathered in his arms all the air he could hold and blew it toward the baby; he gathered air from the four directions, north, west, south, and east. As he blew the air toward the child, he spoke its name, for he was giving the child the breath of life. He also painted lines or bird or animal tracks under the eyes and on the cheekbones if it was a boy or smeared the face with corn pollen and meal if it was a girl.[72]

The medicine man and his wife returned to the house with the baby. As they approached the door, he called out "K'aiya!" (Hello!). The father answered "Haiyeh!" the mother "Heh O!" Then the medicine man said, "Baby [mentioning the child's name], this is his home; here he comes; he is going to live here. May he have long life and all kinds of crops, fruits, game, beads, with him. He is coming in." The parents replied, "Let him come in!" Then the medicine man stepped aside and allowed his wife, carrying the child, to enter first. The mother stood just inside the door to receive the baby in her arms. The family gathered around. The medicine man took up the bowl of medicine and poured a little into the baby's mouth. Then he gave some to the mother and father and to the relative. Finally he gave some to his wife and took some himself. Hot food was now brought in for the medicine man and his wife and put down in front of the turtle's head. The medicine man wafted steam from the food over the altar four times with his eagle plumes. He might also take a morsel of food and deposit it near the bowl of medicine. Then everyone sat down a short distance from the sand painting and ate. After breakfast, the medicine man swept up his painting, gathered up his paraphernalia, and went home with his wife. Before departing he prayed over the baby's cradle and sprinkled it with medicine. The mother had selected an ear of corn which she would tie on the cradleboard at the left side of the baby. The corn was also prayed over and sprinkled.

When the medicine man was gone, the father or mother shelled some of the corn, put it in a little buckskin bag, and tied it on the left side of the baby board. The remainder of the ear was kept until planting time, when it was planted. A small flint was tied to the cradleboard near the bag of corn. When the child left the cradle, the flint often was hung from a string around his neck. In former times a father often took a young son to one of the Warrior society

Top, typical Acoma pottery. *Bottom*, Acoma woman in daily attire of 1925. After Father O'Sullivan photographs.

members, who made a small leather bowguard for the left wrist. This was to protect the wrist from the recoil of the bowstring and to give the child "power." If the child was slow in learning to talk, his parents would put some shelled corn in a mockingbird's nest and leave it there for a few days. Then they took it out, ground it, and put it into the child's mouth, slightly moistened. Cradleboards were made of wood taken, preferably, from trees that have been struck by lightning. During the winter solstices these boards were frequently taken to the medicine men who were curing in their chambers, to have them "cured" and charged with "power."[73]

MARRIAGE

Monogamy was the rule at Acoma. The Catholic faith being professed, divorce was theoretically impossible. Many couples were married in the old mission church at old Acoma by the Franciscan priest. Marriages usually took place on September 2, the feast of San Estevan, Acoma's patron saint. But frequently a man and woman lived together as man and wife without any formal ceremony. Although divorce was not recognized, there were several cases of "separation," after which one or both parties might live with someone else. Very few adults slept alone. Domestic violence was extremely rare.

There were many illegitimate children. Many girls became mothers before they married (or lived with a man); sometimes they had two children before marriage. Some never married but reared large families. Quite often, after a girl became a mother she married; frequently, but not always, she married the father of the child. Among the unmarried there was a great deal of sexual intercourse. But, it was said, a woman usually remained faithful to her husband after marriage.

Neither illegitimacy nor extraconjugal sexual relationships were considered sinful or immoral. That boys and girls would exercise sexual functions before marriage was taken for granted. The "unmarried mother" was not looked upon with pity or with condemnation. Her status was practically equivalent to that of a widow with a child. Marrying a girl with an illegitimate child involved an economic consideration sometimes, but not a moral one; some men did not wish to support the child of another man. But this did not figure strongly in the pueblo, where the husbands frequently went to live in the houses of their wives, and where the women contributed so much to the support of the families. A woman with children who never married did not become destitute. She continued to live with her mother or sister and contributed much to the support of her children through her labors in the garden and in pottery making.

Men and women usually selected their own mates. Parents sometimes expressed their wishes, but the young were free to disregard them. At Acoma, after a couple had become sexually intimate the girl was as likely to urge marriage as the boy.

Regarding marriage with non-Acoma persons, White received the impression that marriage outside the pueblo was not to be encouraged, even with other Pueblos, and marriage with whites or Mexicans was disapproved of.

There was no fixed custom regulating the residence of wife and husband after marriage. The husband might go to live at the house of his wife, or vice versa. Or a new house might be built.

Nearly every family had at least one child. Practically all adults seemed to be fond of children, especially very small children. Very often men, particularly old men, took care of children when they were about the house or village.[74]

DEATH

When death came, the face of the deceased was painted a reddish brown by medicine men. The designs used for boys and men were the same as those painted on their faces on the day they were first presented to the sun as infants. Pollen was put on female faces. The father made four prayer sticks, painted black, which he put in the right hand of the deceased. Then he made four more, which he placed in a pottery bowl, together with four made by the mother. The hair of the deceased was cut, and a breath feather was tied to the crown of a married woman's head. Shortly after death the body was interred in the compound in front of the old Spanish church at old Acoma; this was consecrated ground. A burnt stick was laid where the body of the deceased had been in the house. The body was buried in the best clothes owned by the deceased. No tools or weapons were buried with the body. After the grave had been filled in, pottery bowls of water were broken over it by a relative to give the deceased "his last drink." Sometimes a few flowers were planted on the grave, but they soon died.

The soul of the deceased went back to Shipap, then to Wenima, and became a Katcina.[75] (There is a little hole in the floor of Mauharots, the head kiva, where, it is said, the soul goes after death.) Nothing specific was known of the existence of an individual after death; he simply returned to the place of Emergence, to Iatiku, the mother of them all.

Four days after the death, a medicine man, solicited with a gift of cornmeal by the father of the deceased, took the burnt stick that had been placed where the deceased lay, the prayer sticks made by the father and the mother, and a "lunch" and went to the grave, where he prayed. Then he went down the sand trail to the foot of the mesa, and then to the north. He went out to some mesa or canyon, where he deposited his burden. The sticks were for Iatiku.[76]

On the night of All Saints' Day, November 1, the souls of the dead returned from Shipap to visit their relatives, spending one night and then returning to Shipap. In preparation for this the women placed food in the church compound and put a lighted candle by it. "Boys and the old people come and get the food," eating it there or taking it home.[77]

The chapel at Laguna.

LAGUNA HISTORY AND LIFE

Laguna is Spanish for "lake," and the name is associated with a large pond that once existed to the west of the pueblo. The Pueblo name is Ka-waik. It was founded in 1697 or 1698 by Keresan-speaking peoples from the Rio Grande, primarily from Santo Domingo, Cochiti, and Zia. In 1699, Governor Cubero gave it the name San Jose de la Laguna. It is on the north bank of the San Jose River, about forty-five miles west of Albuquerque and fifteen miles northeast of Acoma. Its population in 1800 was 800, in 1910 it was 1,441, in 1948 it was 2,894, and today it is more than 5,500.

Fred Eggan is convinced that, despite its eastern origins, Laguna "has close cultural affiliations with Acoma, and its social structure belongs with the western Pueblos." He emphasizes that the geographical conditions of Laguna are similar to those of Acoma and Zuñi. Also, the dialect is similar to that spoken at Acoma, "the two apparently forming the western dialect of Keresan, which is understood with difficulty in the Rio Grande villages."[78]

Although it is listed as the largest of all the pueblos, the original Laguna village is actually small; it and nine suburbs make up the total population. Old Laguna sits like a flock of birds on a rounded, rocky knoll above the river. Photographs taken in 1887 show stone masonry and adobe three-story houses enclosing a main plaza. The oldest part is that immediately around the plaza and a section just to the south. The gleaming white church, built about 1700 and plainly seen from the broad state highway that sweeps past the village today, is just outside the main area.

Greater Laguna includes the old central village and the farming suburbs of Paraje, Paguate, Encinal, Casa Blanca, Mesita Negra, and Seama, the last-named itself having three satellites: New York, Philadelphia, and Harrisburg. All the suburbs are situated at varying and considerable distances from old Laguna.

Movement to the outlying areas began about 1850, when the threat of raids by marauding Indians was diminished and irrigation projects had become possible. In the 1870s a schism over new customs led to a migration of conservative families to Isleta Pueblo in New Mexico. On ceremonial occasions, the conservative Lagunans from the suburbs return to the old village, which remains the center of ceremonial life.

Parsons gives one view of the schism just mentioned, and Hewett gives another. Hewett claims that the Lagunans of 1935 were organized into two social groups, the Conservatives and the Progressives. Thirty or so years before, about 1900, this grouping had something of a political element in it, but by now it had become almost purely social in nature. The Conservatives were made up of seven medicine orders which, excepting one order that performed independently, worked in groups of two in performing their medicine dances and healing ceremonies. An individual could obtain healing from any order he wished.

The Progressives were the followers of a certain Quimu, a Lagunan who had been educated in Durango, Mexico, and who, prior to 1871, had returned to the pueblo bringing a law book, perhaps a Bible. Through this book he sought to expose what he said was the fraudulence of the medicine men's practices of exorcism, jugglery, sword-swallowing, witching, and so on. His followers also condemned these practices until Laguna was split into two factions in the 1870s. "It was at this time that Mesita Negra was founded."[79]

Parsons says that through some interchange with Tusayan there had come to be at least one Hopi lineage in the Sun Clan of Laguna; also that there were Zuñi, Acoma, and Navajo lineages or intermarriages at Laguna. Because of this, she is not surprised that Laguna was the first of the pueblos to Americanize through intermarriage. About 1870, George H. Pradt, a surveyor, and the two Marmon brothers, one a trader, the other a surveyor, married Laguna townswomen and raised large families. Walter G. Marmon, appointed a government teacher in 1871, married the daughter of Kwime, chief of the Kurena-Shikani medicine men and father of Giwire, who was supposed to take his father's position. This group led what became the Americanization faction, which was opposed by most of the hierarchy, the other Clown Society (the Koshare), the town chief, the war chief or head of the Scalp-takers, and the Flint, Fire, and Shahaiye societies or their chiefs. According to José or Tsiwema, who was a Shahaiye shaman, the withdrawing ceremonialists first took their altars and sacred properties up a mountain to hide and protect them, and later brought them down to Mesita Negra, three miles east of Laguna. Meanwhile, during Robert G. Marmon's term as governor, the two kivas of Laguna were torn down by the progressives. This resulted in a meeting during which the old women in charge of what was left of sacrosanct things brought them out and gave them up. The Koshare and the town chief continued to live at Mesita Negra, but about 1880, the Flint, Fire, and Shahaiye chiefs moved on to Isleta and became affiliated there with the two medicine societies known today as the Town Fathers and the Laguna Fathers. After the Great Split and the laying of the railroad through or on the edge of town, no Katcina dances were held at Laguna for some time; "then in some obscure way a demand arose for their revival."[80]

Hewett found the Lagunans of the 1930s to be a people of exceptionally high class, industrious and thrifty. There had been a steady growth in their population, and it numbered 2,288, with the result that they were faced with inadequacy of land. There were 269,879 acres in their reservation, but only 1,500 acres were tillable. Formerly, the Lagunans were able to run their stock on land adjoining the reservation, but this was fenced off now, and the Lagunans were restricted to the use of their own lands. This had necessitated great reductions of sheep and cattle. The sheep flock had already been cut from 45,000 to 25,000, and they would soon have to reduce the size again. In addition to sheep, they ran about 1,000 head of cattle. The government figured that 15,000 sheep were all that could adequately run on the reservation. Yet, to make a fair living, each family herd should have 500 sheep. The proposed reduction would cut the number to 175, and they could not live on that. So they were faced with a grave problem.

Consequently, the younger people of Laguna were forced to seek work away from home. The Santa Fe Railway was a helpful solution to their problem. It found that the Indians made steady, reliable laborers, and it was presently employing about two hundred Laguna men. Besides, the Soil Conservation Service and other governmental agencies had provided employment for approximately a hundred Lagunans.

Grazing and agriculture remained, however, the leading pursuit of the settlements. Villages along the railway and the state highway made a good grade of pottery and had a good market for their products. Other suburban villages, which had no direct outlet for sales, did little or nothing with pottery making. Some basketry was produced, consisting mainly of the wicker baskets made from small willow twigs. Weaving output consisted only of women's belts and small bands. No Lagunans had as yet achieved prominence as artists.

There was an Indian Day School in each of the villages, except for Paraje and Casa Blanca, which shared a common school located midway between the two settlements. At one time, the Baptists had maintained a mission school at Laguna. Then the school passed into the hands of the Presbyterians. In 1872, the government took control of it, and after that a public school was maintained in the village. In 1934, a young Laguna woman graduated from the University of New Mexico, the first Pueblo Indian graduated from that institution. In recent years, the Presbyterians had been losing their hold in Laguna settlements, and many of the residents had reverted to the Roman Catholic religion. Only one Protestant church, that of the Presbyterians at Casa Blanca, was still maintained. But there were Catholic churches in all the other villages, and new structures had been erected at Encinal and Mesita Negra within the last few years.[81]

Hewett informs us that although American funerary practices had come to be adopted to an extent by some Lagunans, the older people still adhered to their ancient customs in burying the dead. For sanitary reasons, burial followed death as quickly as possible. When a child was born, the father's people washed his body, and later, when he died, the same group washed the body and prepared it for burial. The face of the deceased was painted with different earth colors. Horizontal streaks placed under the eyes represented the colors of corn, or life, which were to prepare him for the next world. Cotton was placed in tiers on top of the head, symbolizing rain clouds. It was believed that the deceased would return to earth as a sort of spirit, bringing rain to bless the earth. Pollen was placed in the dead person's hands. Dressed in his best Pueblo costume, he was wrapped in a blanket, carried to the cemetery some distance from the village, and buried. A jar filled with water was placed at the head of the grave. In many cases the jar was broken. The grave was watched the first night, and generally for the following night, "in the belief that some prowler might disturb it." On the second day after the burial, food was prepared in the home of the deceased, and some of it was taken to the grave. The home where the death occurred was then thoroughly cleaned and whitewashed.[82]

According to Eggan, the central position of Laguna is challenged today by certain of the farming villages, notably Paguate and Mesita Negra. Laguna itself is divided into matrilineal, exogamous clans, which have totemic names and ceremonial, juridical, and economic functions. There is some slight clan linkage, and a dual organization of clans in connection with ceremonial organization, but there are no exogamous phratries or moieties. The basic economic unit remains the extended maternal household. The movement out to the suburban farming villages has brought about some instances of clan localization and changes in social structure that may parallel those taking place at Acoma and other pueblos. The ceremonial organization is composed of the Medicine societies, the Katcina Cult, the kiva groups, and the "Clown" organizations. For certain dances there is an east-west division by clans according to their location in regard to the plaza. At one time, Eggan says, there were presumably the War and Hunting societies associated with the other Keresan pueblos.[83]

Nearby Mount Taylor is the tallest peak in the region, and it holds a special place in Laguna legend and ritual. A cave serving as its sipapu is located in its foothills at a point northwest of Encinal.

Ellis says that the conservative segment of Lagunans living at Mesita Negra still uses the Snake Pit, "a deep cavelike depression with top opening, once a hot spring, near Correo," as its major sun shrine. According to legend, a two-headed water serpent who lived in the former lake made a final swim eastward, and in so doing cut the channel for the San Jose River. It then descended into the earth through the Snake Pit. Excavations in this pit in 1949 turned up ancient curved fending sticks and atlatls, indicating its prolonged use as a shrine. Prayer and other offerings are still deposited here and solstice ceremonies observed, at which time the priests receive advance information as to the success of the crops during the coming year. A sun shrine about four miles east of Laguna sometimes substitutes for the cave shrine.[84]

The present Laguna Council is made up of the governor and his staff. The staff comprises two lieutenant governors, a head fiscal and two assistant fiscales, interpreter, and secretary. The treasurer is a non-member. All Pueblo residents are invited to the meetings, and Aberle found there was a keen interest in civil affairs.[85]

Laguna's six villages each nominate a man for governor, and the people cast their votes at general meetings, voting for only one man of the six. Officers are then installed according to the number of votes received; the governor is the one who receives the most votes, the lieutenant governors the next higher totals, and so on.[86]

Chapter 3

RIO GRANDE REGION

HISTORY

A survey of site developments in southern Arizona and New Mexico indicates that the majority of present-day Pueblos are the cultural descendants of an amalgam of the Anasazi and Mogollon. Since in the final phases of development in Pueblo III the Anasazi tended to overwhelm the traditions adjacent to them, it can be reasonably assumed that in the Hopi and Rio Grande areas the Anasazi Culture became predominant, although the extent to which this is true can no longer be known.

Whether this amalgam should be spoken of in terms of persons or customs is also a matter for debate. Obviously, it would be helpful to know the percentages of each. For example, were there more Anasazi who adopted or adapted Mogollon customs, or vice versa? From architectural, agricultural, and ceramic evidence, it appears the former was the case. The overall cultural development pattern is more like that of the Four Corners area than it is of their southern neighbors. In any event, all authorities agree today that the Pueblos of Arizona and New Mexico are the cultural, and to some unposited extent physical, descendants of the Anasazi, and as such are properly called by that name, or Anasazi-Pueblo. Compounding the evolution configuration is the fact that the present-day Rio Grande people speak two unrelated language stocks that derive from two different prehistoric traditions, whose origins are assumed but not pinpointed. The first language is Keresan, and the second is Tanoan, which is further subdivided into the Tiwa, Towa, and Tewa.

In attempting to analyze the prehistoric development pattern of the Rio Grande Region, it is helpful to divide what is now the state of New Mexico into five districts, each of which in early times was distinguishable according to its archaeological patterns. Occupying at least the northern third of the western edge was the Chaco Canyon Region. In the southwestern corner were the Mogollon, who after centuries of development in close proximity with Anasazi forebears left in cave shrines artifact deposits so Pueblo-like that modern Pueblo men recognize them and know their purposes. In the middle Rio Grande area there emerged the first villages of consequence. In north and northeastern New Mexico there are the remains of a Pueblo-like people known as the Large-Gallina, and in northwestern New Mexico recent excavations have permitted archaeologists to trace a line of habitation and development from

Paleo-Indian occupation, pre-8000 B.C., through village sites related to the late Basketmaker III and Pueblo I periods of A.D. 600 to 850. Chaco has been described, and the following sample sites from each of the other districts will provide a better feel for the early development pattern of the Rio Grande Region. Every pueblo excavation seems to provide one or more bits of information either not found or not emphasized by the excavators of other ruins. Once these accounts are assembled, like pieces in a puzzle, a fairly comprehensive picture is formed. Each makes its general statements, but one will emphasize how surface dwelling walls were built, another will stress kiva details, a third will examine shrines, a fourth pithouses, and a fifth cave sites. Most of the information for this portion of my account has been compiled from the writings of A. V. Kidder, C. B. Cosgrove, J. A. Jeancon, Stanley A. Stubbs, Alfonso Ortiz, Laurance C. Herold, and Edward P. Dozier, and from the recent summaries of Emil Haury, Jesse D. Jennings, and Gordon R. Willey.

New Mexico skies are often patterned with stunning clouds, yet the climate is relatively arid, with an average rainfall of perhaps fifteen inches in the east, and considerably less in the west. Not counting the mountain ranges, elevations vary from 5,000 to 7,000 feet. Along the southern portion of the Rio Grande the country is fairly flat, but as one moves northward it changes to low mesas and shallow canyons before Santa Fe is reached. Halfway from there to Taos an ascent begins into what become rugged mountains in the northern end of the state. Away from the Rio Grande there are mountain ranges, higher mesas, and canyons, whose vegetation is of the desert type: grasses, cacti, and some piñons and junipers. In the higher mountain elevations are forests consisting of spruce, fir, pine, and aspen. At one time, deer, bear, antelope, mountain goats, and fox were abundant here.

By 500 B.C., those who inhabited the greater Rio Grande area were beginning to frequent caves to the extent that they left pre-Ceramic artifacts of both secular and ceremonial natures behind. This cavity-type occupation would continue until perhaps A.D. 1000, even though by A.D. 100 pithouses were in evidence. By A.D. 600, small surface settlements with ceramics began to appear, and they progressively developed over the centuries into villages consisting either of assemblages of unit clusters or of large house blocks.

D. Bruce Dickson notes that the Developmental Period of A.D. 600 to 1200 begins with the introduction of agriculture. There is a marked paucity of sites in the early phase, and a noticeable increase in the size and number of sites in the late phase.[1] Wendorf states that during this period the Northern Rio Grande remained peripheral to the main developments of the Anasazi culture to the west.[2]

Dozier believes that farming was a "precarious occupation" for the prehistoric and historic Pueblos because of the "limitations" of the mountain desert areas.[3] As we will see, though, Kidder found the Pecos area of the middle Rio Grande to be very fertile and productive. Dozier does seem to agree by pointing out that in spite of the limitations, the late Mogollon and Anasazi farmers "increased in population and developed more complex societies" than the hunters and gatherers that preceded them.[4] He thinks that shortly after A.D. 1000, new peoples began to flow into the Rio Grande Region, and that the legends of the Pueblos support the belief that most of these came from Anasazi regions to the west and northwest. Yet, while there is evidence of Anasazi settlement in small communities along the Rio Grande long before A.D. 1340, it was not until this date that major villages began to develop,[5] followed by a contraction and consolidation from about A.D. 1400, as typified by the history of the Pecos pueblo and the founding of the Taos pueblo.

Dickson makes an interesting division of the northern Rio Grande area into primary natural districts, secondary natural districts, and tertiary natural districts, according to their agricultural capabilities. By careful analysis of statistical data he determines that periods of population growth were not always the result of influxes of new peoples. For example, as agricultural technology and the introduction of a new strain of maize led to increased crops between A.D. 900 and 1100, the population expanded from within until it reached the carrying capacity of its environment. Once the primary natural district was accommodating all it could handle, the secondary and tertiary districts came into play. Conversely, when the greater influx of migrating Anasazi did begin after A.D. 1200, the newcomers moved into the peripheral districts, overburdening areas already limited in capability. As the resources of these districts became depleted, a contraction began about A.D. 1400 into the few primary natural districts that remain, for the most part, as the pueblos of today—a process abetted in time by the pressures of the Spanish entradas.[6]

As to which of the larger migrating Anasazi groups arrived first, Dozier thinks it probable that the Tanoans preceded the Keresans "by several hundred years." He supports this by observing that linguistic diversity is generally the result of long residence in a region and of the isolation of population units. As I have said, the Tanoans speak Tiwa, Towa, and Tewa. Also, the Tanoans surround the Keresans on three sides, so that the latter assumes the appearance of a "wedge" driven into the former.[7]

Laurance Herold, perhaps following Wendorf, lists five periods, or stages, for cultural development in the Rio Grande Region.

Pre-ceramic	14,000 B.C.–A.D. 600
Developmental	A.D. 600–1200
Coalition	A.D. 1200–1275 or 1325
Classic	A.D. 1325–1600
Historic	A.D. 1600–present[8]

Since the Spanish colonization of the Rio Grande area did not begin until A.D. 1598, and the records of Pueblo life remained scarce until then, the separation date between the prehistoric and historic time periods is usually set at A.D. 1600.

SOUTHERN RIO GRANDE: HUECO BASKETMAKERS

While the prehistory of the Anasazi of the Rio Grande Region parallels to some extent that of the Little Colorado Region, one of the Rio Grande's most exciting additions to what we already know has to do with findings made in the dry caves along the border dividing southern New Mexico and northern Texas. Here some of the first tangible evidences of specific religious practices are spelled out in terms of individual paraphernalia used in ancient ceremonies.

During a five-year period, from 1926 to 1930, C. B. Cosgrove and his wife were able to secure from caves in extreme southwestern New Mexico and in adjoining parts of Texas an impressive collection of excellently preserved materials. These represented at least two stages of Basketmaker development in areas previously unexplored, and also objects relating to the later Pueblo periods. As I have said in previous chapters, the dry caves of the San Juan were the preservers of our only knowledge of Basketmaker life. The great stretch of land situated between the San Juan and the country examined by the Cos-

Maps showing locations of sites discussed in the first part of Chapter III, the Rio Grande Region. *Left*, location of important villages and areas. *Right*, location of caves of the Upper Gila and Hueco areas.

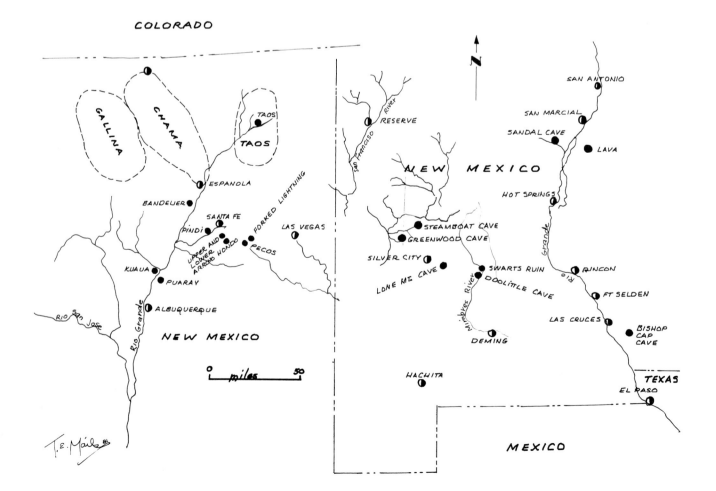

Top left, entrance to Ceremonial Cave, Hueco Mountains, New Mexico. *Top right,* plan and section of corner storage bin in S A Canyon. The wall stones are coated with adobe. *Bottom left,* plan of Steamboat Cave, Steamboat Canyon, New Mexico. *Bottom right,* bird's-eye view of some of the cists in Steamboat Canyon. After C. B. Cosgrove, 1947.

groves contains few such shelters. Only along the Mexican border do there occur numerous habitable caves with remains similar to those of the San Juan Basketmakers. These are the sites examined by the Cosgroves, in the Hueco Mountains on the Texas–New Mexico border and in the Upper Gila country north of Silver City, New Mexico. For simplification, Cosgrove uses a single title, the Hueco Basketmakers, to designate the inhabitants of both areas as he gives the general descriptions of artifact finds.[9]

In his extremely valuable report on the cave sites of the Hueco Basketmakers, Cosgrove states that evidences of a clearly defined development, or progression, are absent from the area. Instead there was a lag in development similar to that of the other peripheral Anasazi areas, and Basketmaker II and III times seem to have merged into a single period ranging from A.D. 1 to 700.

While certain other investigators use the term "Cave Dwellers" to describe the Hueco and Big Bend, Texas, area residents, Cosgrove and Martin are convinced that the early peoples of the Upper Gila and Hueco were affiliated, though perhaps remotely, with the San Juan Basketmakers; that as one moves northwest from the Pecos and Big Bend areas into the Hueco area proper, "similarity to the San Juan Culture becomes more marked."[10]

Caves in the Hueco and Big Bend areas contained grass-lined sleeping and storage pits and fiber-chinked slab cists. Upper Gila sites included grass-and-slab-lined storage pits and grass-and-leaf-lined sleeping pits. Some of the latter had stones piled around them to provide windbreaks. Some Gila cists were partially lined with stone slabs. Nothing in the Upper Gila and Hueco areas indicated to Cosgrove that houses developed from the cists, but in the Big Bend region a rough semicircular dwelling in Bee Cave "faintly suggested" such an evolution.[11]

He thought it was probable that some of the rock shelters in the Upper Gila were used only as summer camps by people living in villages, but that those close to tillable land could have served as permanent dwelling sites. Many masonry-walled granaries in rock crevasses typified the Anasazi method of protecting harvests for continuous use. Numerous caves in the Hueco area were large and ideally located, but none seems to have served as a permanent dwelling site.

The early-developed variety of flint corn, dating to about A.D. 100, was found in all parts of the Hueco Basketmaker Region. Squash parts, agave quids, nuts, and seeds were also found, but they could not be dated because they were not associated with Basketmaker artifacts.

With few exceptions, implements employed for hunting and warfare were the same as those used by all Basketmakers. Atlatls, darts, and grooved fending sticks were common, although sinew-wrapped sticks of an aberrant form were discovered. Miniature duplications of wooden dart bunts, one of them inserted in a reed arrow shaft, suggested to Cosgrove that the bow and arrow made its appearance before the end of the Basketmaker Period. The hinged-stick snare and the noose-cord snare were found in all parts of the Hueco and Gila areas.

Hueco coiled basketry was non-Basketmaker in style, but the fact that two-rod-and-bundle uninterlocked specimens made up about 20 percent of the total found argued in favor of the existence of a relationship between the Hueco and San Juan areas. Hueco sandals were not comparable in form to the fiber-and-cloth square-toed sandals of the San Juan Basketmakers. The difference was less pronounced in the full-length crushed yucca-leaf footwear. In fact, one form from the Upper Gila area was similar in weave to sandals found in Marsh Pass.

Absent from the Hueco area was the unfired pottery of late Basketmaker II common to the San Juan. Where pottery was found in the Hueco area, it was always a surface find best associated with Pueblo periods.

Fur-cloth blankets made in the same way as those of the northern area were discovered in the Hueco region, but feather-cloth robes were absent.

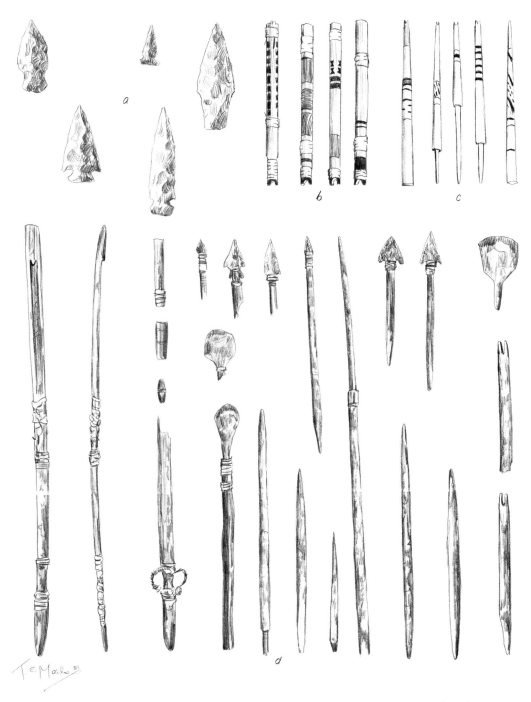

Top: a, stone projectile points. *b,* typical painted owner marks on nock ends of reed arrows. *c,* typical carved, incised, and painted owner marks on arrow foreshafts. *d,* Upper Gila and Hueco atlatls and dart foreshafts. The blunt stone points are called "dart bunts." At right are the types of nocks carved to receive the stone points. From C. B. Cosgrove, 1947.

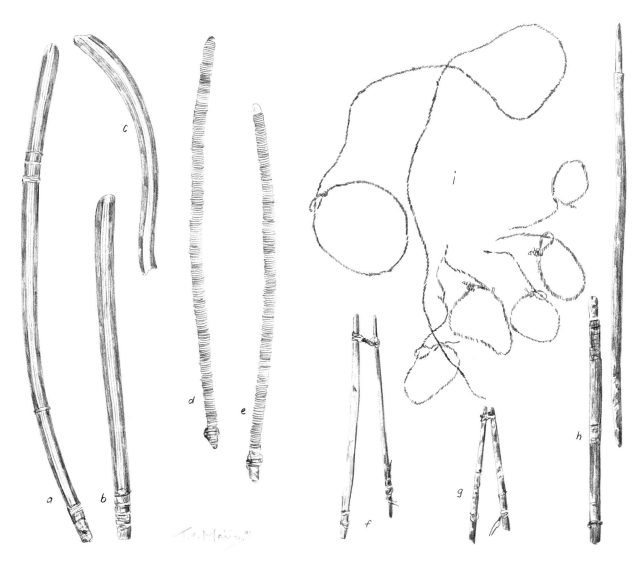

Upper Gila and Hueco areas: *a–c*, grooved fending and throwing sticks. *d–e*, sinew-wrapped and round throwing sticks. *f–h*, hinged-stick snares. *i*, string snares. From C. B. Cosgrove, 1947.

Yucca-string aprons corresponded in style to northern products, but no coarse-bark loincloths or woven human-hair aprons were found. Using colored yucca cords as their only material, the Hueco Basketmakers closely duplicated the twined and intricate weaving of the north. They were equally competent in producing coiled netting. The coiled-netted technique was in general use to manufacture coarse carrying nets of stripped and loosely twisted yucca leaves, knotted-cord netting for bags, and game and fish nets. Human and animal hair was rarely used for cordage; yucca furnished the principal fiber. Tie twining was used to bind together bundles of crushed material, but twined sewing was not employed. Crude, flexible, and semi-rigid cradleboards were used in the Hueco area, and infants were wrapped in fur-string robes.

Personal ornaments discovered in the caves included seed necklaces, large stone beads, beads fashioned from reeds, and abalone shell pendants, all similar in style to ornaments from northern regions. Along with these were hair decorations consisting of a single wooden pin to which feathers were attached.

a–b, craniums of skeletons showing both deformed and undeformed characteristics. *c*, bone gaming pieces. *d*, single die. *e*, pair of bone dice bound together. *f*, wooden fire drill and hearth. *g*, cedar-bark torch. *h*, wooden planting stick. *i*, woman's apron consisting of yucca-fiber strands. *j*, braided yucca tumpline. *k*, stone disk bead necklace. *l*, glycymeris shell brace-let. *m*, olivella shell used for bandolier rattles and for necklaces. *n*, shell pendant. *o*, yucca checkerweave basket. *p*, yucca rod and bundle basket. From C. B. Cosgrove, 1947. Typical artifacts discovered in the Upper Gila and Hueco caves show remarkable similarities to those found in the Basketmaker and Pueblo caves and ruins to the north and west.

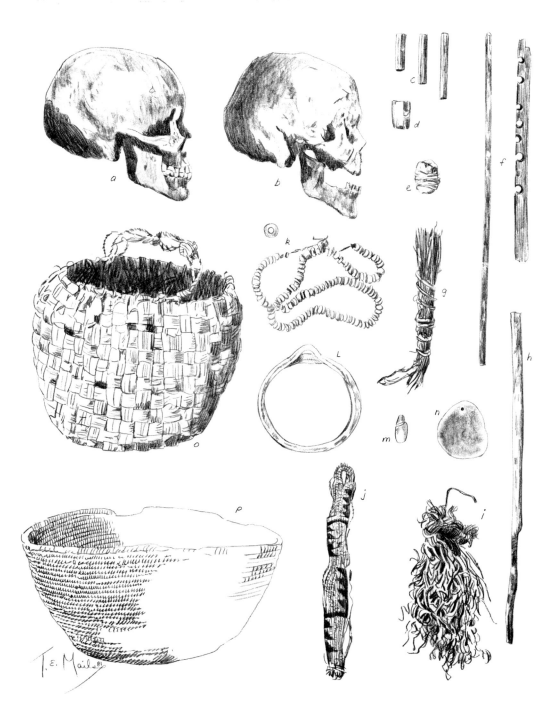

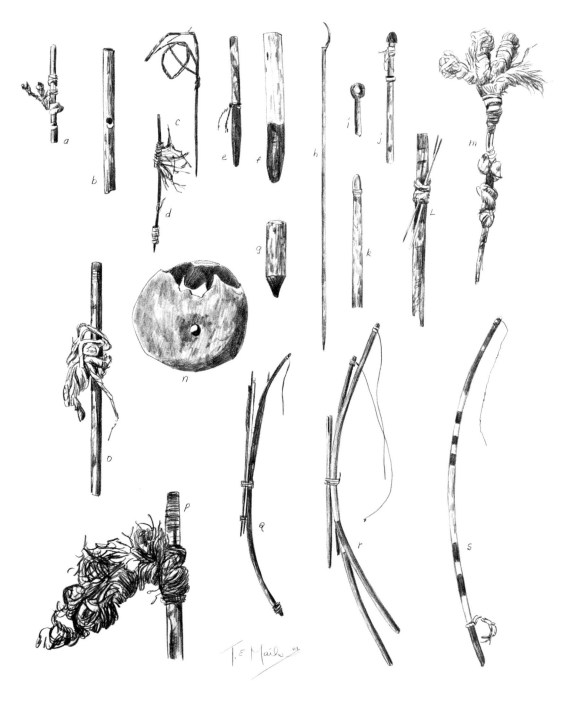

Typical religious objects from the Upper Gila and Hueco areas. *a,* reed cigarette. The bindings hold feathers, beads, and small pendants. *b,* reed whistle. *c–d,* unpeeled twig pahos. *e–g,* painted stub pahos. *h–k,* pahos, some of which are painted and have cord wrappings that held feathers. *l–m,* pahos of sotol stalks and atlatl darts with fiber bolls and miniature arrows attached. *n,* fragment of a gourd rattle (a turtle-shell rattle fragment was also found). *o–p,* arrow pahos with cotton cord attached. *q–s,* miniature ceremonial bows. From C. B. Cosgrove, 1947. It is important to note that religious items in particular reveal the forms of sacred objects as they developed into those still used in modern pueblos. Portrayed here is much of what is employed in secret today. Accordingly, this and the following drawings are devoted to religious finds.

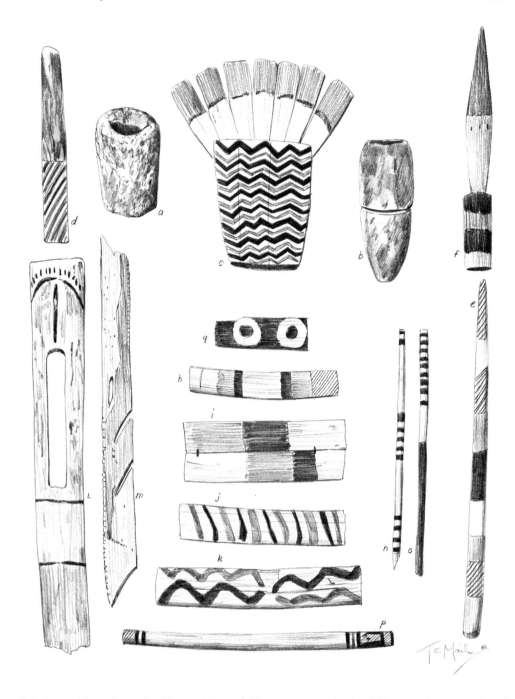

Religious objects from the Upper Gila and Hueco areas. *a–b,* cloud-blower pipes. *c,* painted wooden tablita. *d–e,* painted stub pahos. *f–k,* fragments of wooden tablitas. *l–m,* painted split-stick wands. *n–p,* painted sticks. From C. B. Cosgrove, 1947.

Other wooden objects found were the tree-shell trowel and wooden dart-straightening wrenches, some of the latter being made from broken fending sticks. One large wooden pipe was discovered. All other pipes were stone, of the short, tubular shape common to the Basketmakers of all regions. Bone objects included an antler dart wrench, flakers, punches, and a short, stubby awl with either a fiber or leather paddle-handle. Hide items from the Hueco area consisted of pouches fashioned from whole rodent skins, unsplit animal necklaces, and small medicine pouches filled with pollen or sacred meal.

Several unfired clay fetishes were found at Bee Cave in the Big Bend area. These were plummet-shaped and painted, and they did not resemble clay objects found in the northern Basketmaker regions. In the Upper Gila numerous caves were utilized as shrines by the Anasazi of the Pueblo periods. Whether or not they were so used by the Basketmakers was not clearly indicated to Cosgrove by the character of Basketmaker artifacts found in association with them. But the quantity of religious offerings left in such places as Greenwood Cave, Mule Creek Cave, and Cave I, Goat Basin, revealed that these were sacred retreats visited regularly by the Anasazi of the Pueblo periods. The same was true of Hueco Ceremonial Cave, which had previously been long used as a Basketmaker shrine. Although Pueblo village ruins are present in the vicinity, few utilitarian objects were found in the Hueco area caves, causing Cosgrove to assume that superstitious people refrained from going there for anything other than special reasons.[12] This was not true, however, in the Upper Gila, where some sites containing Basketmaker ceremonial objects were occasionally lived in by the Pueblo.

Comparisons left no doubt in Cosgrove's mind that dart and stalk pahos and the miniature fending sticks peculiar to the Hueco Ceremonial Cave were of Basketmaker origin. His certainty was only slightly less in regard to twig pahos, split-stick wands, wooden tablitas, and reed cigarettes. The last-named were widely distributed in the southern Anasazi regions and definitely pertained to its pre-pottery culture. The great accumulation of sandals found at Ceremonial Cave reveals that it was common practice to leave behind the footwear worn out in making the pilgrimage to the shrine.

Burials in the Hueco and Big Bend areas were markedly similar to those of the San Juan area. Inhumation in cave trash piles or in grass-lined pits was common. A principal difference is that cremation was practiced east of the Huecos in the Guadalupe Mountains, and near the mouth of the Pecos River, in Texas. These burials of calcined bones were accompanied by Basketmaker artifacts of the San Juan types and by such unique items as plaited matting, manos, and metates. With the exception of the Upper Gila area, where at the time of Cosgrove's excavations only Pueblo burials had been found, cremations and flexed bodies alike were accompanied by fur-cloth robes, colored twined-woven bags, and coiled baskets. Objects more rarely found included an atlatl, a dart, and a hide pouch containing meal. Mortuary offering placements were generally made like those of other Anasazi areas. Skulls found in burial sites were generally undeformed.

Pictographs from the Upper Gila and Hueco areas. Notable in particular are the figure at the *upper right,* so similar to altar figures at Hopi; the buffalo; the tablitas; the figure at the *bottom left* that seems to be formed by painted altar slabs; and the plumed serpents at *lower right* that relate to modern Pueblo ceremonies and to Mesoamerica. From C. B. Cosgrove, 1947.

In summarizing his views regarding the Upper Gila, Hueco, and Big Bend areas, Cosgrove states there were no impassable barriers to prevent nomadic Basketmakers from spreading south from the San Juan to southern New Mexico and northern Texas. The finding of Basketmaker material at numerous sites such as Jemez Cave, north of Albuquerque; Laguna Shrine; Sandal Cave, south of San Marcial; the cave near Lava, farther south; and caves near Las Cruces, Chavez, and Bishop's Cap tends, in his view, to confirm the migration. He concludes that "the Hueco Basketmakers were an offshoot of the San Juan Basketmaker, that they concentrated for a time in the Hueco area, then to some extent spread southeast along the Rio Grande into western Texas and perhaps into Coahuila, Mexico, and that they finally either degenerated or else amalgamated with the succeeding Plains Indians or the more sedentary agricultural races."[13]

More recent authorities would argue that the Basketmakers of Hueco merged with the Anasazi of the Rio Grande Region. It is generally agreed today that the Hueco area was essentially Mogollon country, and that by A.D. 1100 the Jornada branch of the Mogollon had extended farther northward into the southeastern part of New Mexico, where their closest neighbors were Anasazi of the Arroyo Seco focus. After A.D. 1200 the two cultures began a progressive combining of cultures that was not completed until after the Spanish had begun to colonize the area and constant pressures from raiding Apache and Comanche forced the last of the Mogollon to join their relatives among the southern Tewa of Isleta and Sandia. Isleta legends support this by telling of groups that moved up from the south and eventually joined their own people.[14]

SOUTH CENTRAL RIO GRANDE: ARROW GROTTO

One of the most fascinating articles encountered while I was doing my research was "The Inner Sanctum of Feather Cave, a Mogollon Sun and Earth Shrine Linking Mexico and the Southwest," by Florence Hawley Ellis and Laurens Hammack, published in *American Antiquity*, in 1968.

In this article, the authors describe a cave called Arrow Grotto, an inner cavity deep within a mountain in south-central New Mexico, and reached only by a crawlway from Feather Cave, one of the Rio Bonito sites. The site is six miles east of Capitan, in Lincoln County. According to the authors, ceramic types place the ruins of the Rio Bonito in the Northern Jornada Branch of the Mogollon.

Feather Cave had first been excavated by students from the University of New Mexico, under the direction of Paul Reiter, in 1950–52. Not much was found then, only masses of reeds and one hundred and fourteen sandals of a type worn only for running. This was, however, a good indication that the cave had been used for religious purposes. It will be recalled that Cosgrove also found an accumulation of sandals at Ceremonial Cave in the Hueco area and explains that it was the custom to leave worn pilgrimage footwear behind when returning home.

Perhaps awareness of this custom is what led to further investigation in 1964 by members of the National Speleological Society. After they wriggled through a passageway that was thirty-six feet (12 m) long and terribly constricted that began at the back of Feather Cave, they discovered Arrow Grotto. When archaeologists entered the grotto shortly after, it was found to contain "one of the most complete ceremonial deposits yet known to Southwestern archaeologists,"[15] all of which had lain untouched for six centuries or more. The date range for cave use is believed to be from about A.D. 1100 to 1350.

Some of the elders of the Acoma, Laguna, Santa Ana, Zia, and Cochiti pueblos were asked to examine artifacts and photographs. Their conclusions led to the certification of the grotto as "a shrine for Earth Mother and Sun Father, visited at the period of biannual solar ceremonies."[16]

Ellis and Hammack state that parallels among Arrow Grotto, other prehistoric ceremonial caves, and even the Anasazi sipapu reveal a pattern of use "surprisingly similar" to that of a number of Pueblo ceremonial caves in use either today or in the recent past. They also find in the grotto strong evidence

Feather Cave, offerings from the outer room: *a–b*, crook pahos. *c–d*, pahos. *e*, base of bird quill pierced for making a feather paho. *f*, reed arrow paho. *g*, fragment of a paho. *h*, fragments of painted wooden bird figures. *Top right*, handprint symbol of Koshare clown on rock in upper room of Arrow Grotto. *Bottom right*, plan of Arrow Grotto and passageway connecting it to Feather Cave. From Ellis and Hammack, 1968.

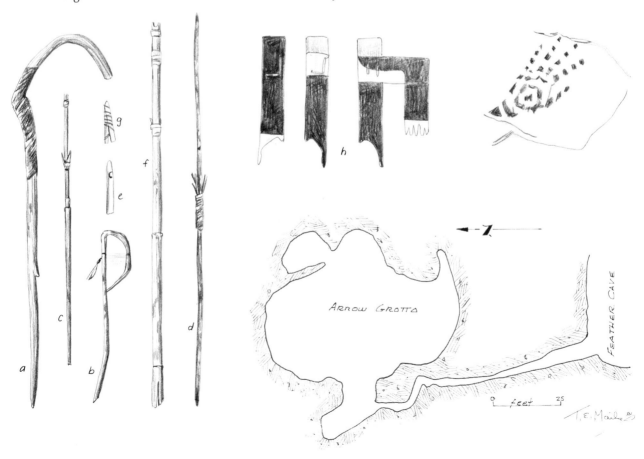

for a series of rapid northward diffusions of religious ideas from Mesoamerica. They cite the original owners of the cave and grotto as probably Piro, or Tompiro, a Tanoan-speaking group who left the Rio Bonito Valley to become mingled, eventually, with southern Tiwa relatives.[17]

The most common artifacts discovered in the grotto consisted of decorated ceremonial bows and arrows, both miniature and full-sized; crook pahos made of twigs; and corncobs. Also found were a miniature throwing stick; a zigzag piece of wood; a wooden ball; small worked stones; various sticks, some with burned ends; sunflower-stalk remains; and various other items associated with present-day Pueblo ceremonies.

The authors are convinced that the artifacts of Arrow Grotto indicate an overall picture of offerings ritually deposited as petitions to the sun, earth, fire, and perhaps cloud beings and that the times of deposit coincided with the two solar solstice ceremonies. This is further substantiated by pictographs on the cave walls that are related to the sun and by lines drawn on the wall to "seal" the cave ceremonially against intruders not qualified to enter.

The authors believe it is clear that most of the Gila caves and possibly some in the Big Bend area of Texas are related to Feather Cave in content and use, although no others are so obviously sipapu representations. They also think it is clear that all or most of the caves are prehistoric prototypes of caves that today represent the home of Earth Mother and Sun Father, where offerings are placed during the semiannual solar ceremonies.[18]

Ellis and Hammack conclude their engrossing article with a lengthy and persuasive argument favoring the diffusion northward of Mesoamerican religious concepts via the Mogollon and perhaps the Hohokam.[19] It is a section well worth reading, although one wishes one could sit in on some of the pro-and-con discussions among authorities regarding it. I recall that Paul S. Martin describes himself as being once an avid diffusionist who since has opted for, in most respects, independent invention.

WESTERN MIDDLE RIO GRANDE: JEMEZ CAVE

Excavations at Jemez Cave, located directly above Soda Dam, have produced valuable finds. Toward the end of 1934, individuals who were pot-hunting in the cave found the body of a child attended by corncobs and wrapped in a feather-cloth robe, two hides, and, as an outermost wrapping, another feather-cloth robe. They brought it to the Field School of the University of New Mexico School Museum, whereupon excited members of the school, H. G. Alexander and Paul Reiter, undertook a survey of the site. Mortuary offerings in the grave allowed them to date it at about A.D. 1250.[20] Further work in 1965 by R. I. Ford and Marjorie Lambert disclosed remains indicating that the cave had been occupied seasonally from about 500 B.C. to A.D. 400.[21]

It appears that the cave was used only for temporary shelter and lodging. The mineral waters of the Soda Dam area have been sought for generations for their medicinal and purgative value, and the region is considered a sacred shrine by the Jemez people, who have regularly held ceremonies there.

Alexander did not find walls of adobe or stone in Jemez Cave, although he discovered the remains of a wattle-and-daub structure 3 to 4 feet (91 cm to 1 m) below the surface of the fill. Since Jemez legends say the cave contains a shrine, it is possible that the structure was part of it.

The bones of deer, sheep, goats, rabbits, birds, fish, dogs, cats, bears, and buffalo were present in the deep cave fill, and some were charred or whitened by fire. Corn and squash remains were also found. The pottery finds consisted of indented utility ware and of a decorated black-on-white, about half of which was the typical Jemez variety. The rest was akin to Wiyo and Santa Fe black-on-white.[22]

Stone items included arrowheads, spearheads, knives, drill points, rubbing stones, pounders, and metates. Bone awls and deer-antler tools were also uncovered. Of particular interest was the abundance of woven work, which included yucca sandals of several types, coiled basketry, string, rope, netting, bags, feather-cloth robes, and a tumpline strap.

Wooden objects consisted of digging sticks, prayer sticks, arrow shafts, and parts of fire-making equipment. Several pieces of tanned skin were found, including a small pouch and the two hides wrapped around the child's body.[23] Some sandals had hide soles.

NORTHERN NEW MEXICO: LOS PIÑOS PITHOUSES

In the Los Piños phase sites of the Pine River Valley of northern New Mexico, portions of two early villages, dating from A.D. 100 to 400, were excavated in 1960 by Frank W. Eddy for the Museum of New Mexico. These are designated as the Valentine and Power Pole sites. Of the fifteen dwellings examined, most were round or oval, and some had antechambers on either the south or the east side that gave the overall structure a dumbbell shape. All the dwellings were situated on a bench overlooking the river, and all were randomly placed.

Architectural features of these early dwellings included firepits and storage pits; a special feature caused Eddy to divide the structures into two types: ring and non-ring. The ring type had a ring of cobblestones laid as a paving around the perimeter of a shallow, basin-shaped floor area. The non-ring type lacked the stone ring. The largest dwellings measured about seventy square feet for the dwelling space and thirty square feet for the storage antechamber.[24]

Jesse D. Jennings suggests that the cobblestone rings are actually nothing more than the remains of toppled walls and represent early experimentation with mud and stone masonry.[25] Paul S. Martin agrees with the suggestion.[26]

Implements discovered at Los Piños phase sites included choppers, scrapers, bifacial blades, stone mortars, hammerstones, metates, manos, and projectile points. The same kinds of tools were found both inside and outside dwellings. Pottery sherds included a brown ware similar to ceramics encountered at the Hay Hollow site, and an unfired gray. Corn is the only vegetal matter referred to in Eddy's report, but it is assumed that wild foods were also eaten by the Los Piños people.

UPPER RIO GRANDE VALLEY: TAOS AREA

No pueblo in the upper Rio Grande Valley is better known than Taos. Its splendid location attracted hunting Indians as early as 14,000 B.C., although little is known about those who dwelt there before A.D. 900, when pithouse communities began to appear. After this time the settlement pattern became widespread. According to Herold, who has excavated in the area under the auspices of the Fort Burgwin Research Center, the Developmental villages of the Taos area were definitely Rio Grande Pueblo in type, yet they included several nontypical traits.[27]

The pithouses actually outnumbered the surface structures in many areas. The adobe pueblos were small, and kivas did not accompany every one of them. While some pithouses were square, most were circular, and they possessed characteristics found in kivas elsewhere in the Rio Grande area. They had circular clay-lined firepits, ventilators, and occasional sipapus. But they lacked benches, pilasters, conventional deflectors, antechambers, and recesses. Their adobe wall finish coats were sometimes reinforced with vertical rods, and the traditional four-post-and-beam system supported the roof.[28]

Herold describes the pottery found in the pithouses as a utility ware of thick gray paste, either neck-banded or corrugated, and as having Chaco-derived patterns on Taos Black-on-white. Other lesser material-culture artifacts included stone notched axes; fully grooved mauls; manos and metates; projectile points; stone pipes; clay pipes; and bone awls. Burials were flexed and made in the trash mounds.

The Developmental Period ended about A.D. 1200, and it was followed by what Herold calls the Rio Grande Coalition Period, which lasted from A.D. 1200 to 1325. He sees a closer tie at this point between the Taos-area people and the rest of the Rio Grande Pueblos. Pithouses were still built, but the majority of the Taos-area population was living in larger, although still medium-sized surface structures. Building walls were coursed adobe. Dwelling rooms were small and entered by roof hatchways. Interior openings between rooms indicate that families lived apartment-style, just as Kidder believes the Pecos pueblo residents did.[29]

Kivas were circular and subterranean. One that was excavated by Jeancon at the Llano Ruin was 7 feet (2.1 m) deep, with adobe floors and walls. There was a central, circular fireplace, an ashpit, a ventilator on the east, and an entryway on the west. There were no banquette, pilasters, recess, or sipapu. Four posts set in from the walls gave additional bracing to the roof beams.[30]

Lesser material-culture artifacts remained the same as those fashioned and employed in the Developmental Period.

After A.D. 1250, the area's population contracted to the Pot Creek Pueblo, about eight miles south of present-day Taos, in the mountainous southeastern part of the greater Taos area. This became the largest prehistoric dwelling to exist near Taos. It consisted of an assemblage of multiple units that totaled several hundred rooms enclosing central plazas. Building walls were adobe. Surface kivas of D or rectangular shapes were not built. There were, however, a very large kiva and another clan-sized kiva that were subterranean.

Beginning around A.D. 1275, the greater Taos area seems to have been abandoned for about fifty years, and sites indicating a merger of Rio Grande and Mesa Verde styles, such as that which took place farther south at this time, are absent. Herold thinks it possible that the residents of Pot Creek Pueblo and other contemporary sites moved to the Taos or Picuris pueblos, since these became the major settlements occupied after Coalition times.[31]

NORTHEASTERN RIO GRANDE: LARGO-GALLINA

East of Aztec, in the Largo drainage of northeastern New Mexico, are the extremely interesting remains of a Pueblo-like people. Chronologically, these fit into the Pueblo III Period, but they are not entirely Anasazi in culture. The name Largo has been given to this cultural phase and area. Tree-ring dates place the period of occupation from A.D. 1100 to 1250.

Largo inhabitants lived in pit and surface houses of considerable size. The latter had massive walls up to 4 feet (1.2 m) thick. All the dwellings contained low-walled storage bins. Apparently, the development sequence proceeded from pithouses to surface houses of uncoursed masonry, and then to houses with coursed masonry walls. Structures thought to be later may be described as "small pueblo," but this decision is still held in abeyance by the investigators.

Black-on-white pottery that was Puebloan in character was made, but most of the utility vessels were unlike anything created elsewhere by the Anasazi. They had round-pointed bottoms, were tall and slender, with wide mouths, and were decorated with narrow bands at or just below the rim. Also, they were made by the paddle-and-anvil technique, foreign to the Anasazi in general. In fact, the vessels most resemble Navajo cooking pots and Woodland pottery from more eastern areas.

Largo-Gallina: *a*, the distinctive Gallina-type stone ax head. *b–c*, stone knives from Cerrito. *d*, mural painting on a bench in the corner of a house at Cerrito. *e*, elbow pipe with projecting "feet." *f*, arrow-straightener stone with ridge on crest. *Bottom*, reconstruction of Rattlesnake Point tower and unit house. After Hibben, 1938.

Other distinctive artifacts included triple-notched axes that required a T-shaped hafting, stone arrow-shaft smoothers, and elbow-shaped pipes. On the bowls of the pipes were two little legs that provided a base to rest on when they were not in use. There was also an extensive use of elk and deer antlers for implements.

In north-central New Mexico east of Largo country and on the other side of the continental divide are sites similar to those of the Largo inhabitants. This area is called the Gallina, and when considered together the two areas make up what is known to archaeologists as the Largo-Gallina Region. Gallina dwellings consisted also of pithouses and surface structures. Most of the sites were in what seem to be good defensive positions. Isolated dwellings were found, but sites were usually made up of three or four house units grouped together. Most dwellings were towerlike structures that were square, with rounded corners. They ranged from 18 to 20 feet (5.4 to 6 m) on a side, and at the time of the first excavation they had walls as high as 17 feet (5.1 m) still standing. Some walls were as much as 6 feet (1.8 m) thick.

Tower-house features included flagstone floors and storage bins with sandstone-slab covers set up, usually, on the south side of the room. On the north side was an adobe bench, and murals were sometimes painted on the wall above the bench. The roof consisted of poles overlaid with adobe and finished off with thin flagstones laid like shingles. It is thought that a roof hatch and ladder were used for entry, even though the walls were very high. Of some interest is the fact that pithouses were often found in conjunction with the tower-houses.

Lesser material-culture items that were Anasazi in nature included black-on-white pottery and pointed-bottom utility pots similar to those of the Largo area, twilled yucca sandals, coiled basketry, feather cloth, twined bags, stone axes, stone arrow smoothers, antler objects, and unusual stone knives. The knives were leaf-shaped blades with notches in the sides close to the center. The pointed end was hafted, and the more blunted end was used for cutting.

In general, the Largo-Gallina Region is thought of as a Pueblo phase, probably derived from the Rosa phase of the Governador area, New Mexico. The Rosa phase was a marginal Anasazi development that existed in Basketmaker III and Pueblo I times, and it is thought to have been subjected to influences from the north.[32]

WESTERN MIDDLE RIO GRANDE: TYUÓNYI

Seventeen miles west of Santa Fe is an area known today as Bandelier National Monument, in El Rito de los Frijoles. It is a region of spectacular cliffs and canyons that are honeycombed with cliff dwellings and covered with surface ruins. One of the principal ruins is Tyuónyi, a large D-shaped stone structure that encloses a large plaza. Its encircling rows of rooms were as much as eight deep, and the plaza held three circular, subterranean kivas. This pueblo, as well as the several small villages that were constructed along the base of the north cliff, were built of blocks of volcanic tuff. Many small caves in the cliff walls were also utilized as dwellings. Some were entirely manmade, others were enlarged natural cavities. Petroglyphs decorate the canyon walls, some incised, some painted.

It is believed that the monument region was built and inhabited by emi-

Bandelier National Monument, New Mexico, which contains the famous cliff dwellings of Frijoles Canyon, the ruins of Tyuonyi, Long House, and Ceremonial Cave. Radiocarbon dates indicate occupation as early as 1750 B.C. *Top left*, pictograph from Painted Cave of a sacred clown whose appearance is the same as that of Rio Grande Pueblo clowns today. *Top right*, ceremonial cave. *Bottom*, a small segment of the Frijoles Canyon surface and cave ruins.

grants from the Four Corners area during the 1200s and 1300s. By the time the Spaniards arrived in A.D. 1540 the El Rito de los Frijoles Region was already abandoned. It is assumed that the Anasazi had joined the other Pueblos living along the Rio Grande. The residents of Cochiti Pueblo, as well as some other Keresans, claim that the Rito Region was the home of their forebears.

Farther up in the canyon and one hundred and sixty feet up on a cliff face is a large cave that contains the remains of dwelling walls and a well-preserved kiva. Keresans believe it was a ceremonial cave. Down the canyon from Tyuónyi is a small ruin named Rainbow House, which reached its occupation peak between A.D. 1400 and 1500.

MIDDLE RIO GRANDE: FORKED LIGHTNING, DICK'S, ARROWHEAD

In his report on the Pecos Pueblo, Kidder refers also to several nearby and related Upper Pecos Valley sites, briefly describing three of these: Forked Lightning Ruin, Dick's Ruin, and Arrowhead Ruin. They were the early villages in the valley, perhaps pre-Pecos in inception. Arrowhead was the last of the three to be abandoned, about A.D. 1400.

Stanley A. Stubbs estimates that Forked Lightning Pueblo, about a mile and a half south of Pecos, was occupied from about A.D. 1225 to 1300, and Kidder concurs in this assumption.[33] The village walls were essentially of adobe, although a few rooms of masonry were erected later. Kidder thought charcoal was added as temper when the adobe was mixed, but straw, such as that used by the Mexicans for their dwellings later, was absent. There were no foundations. The walls were built directly on the smoothed surface of the ground. The walls were laid up so wet that courses or lumps, such as those discovered by Judd at Paragonah, Utah, were not discernible. Walls averaged 11 inches (27.5 cm) in thickness, and when dry they cracked badly. A finish coat of adobe was applied to cover these, but it also cracked in time.

Rooms considered by Kidder to be kivas were of two kinds: five were surface, and two were subsurface. The surface kivas consisted of two that were almost square and three that had one curved wall. Kidder called these "corner kivas." The subsurface, or subterranean, kivas were circular and without masonry-lined walls. They had firepits and ventilators, but no sipapu. They also lacked benches and pilasters. The surface kivas possessed about the same architectural features. Most of them had adobe walls, and one had masonry walls.[34]

While Forked Lightning did not come to a violent end, it nevertheless was abandoned because of pressures from the Plains tribes. At its peak the pueblo consisted of two large structures, each containing about seventy rooms. They were separated by a plaza, which together they enclosed on three sides.

Dick's pueblo was an L-shaped structure a quarter of a mile southeast of Forked Lightning and architecturally similar.

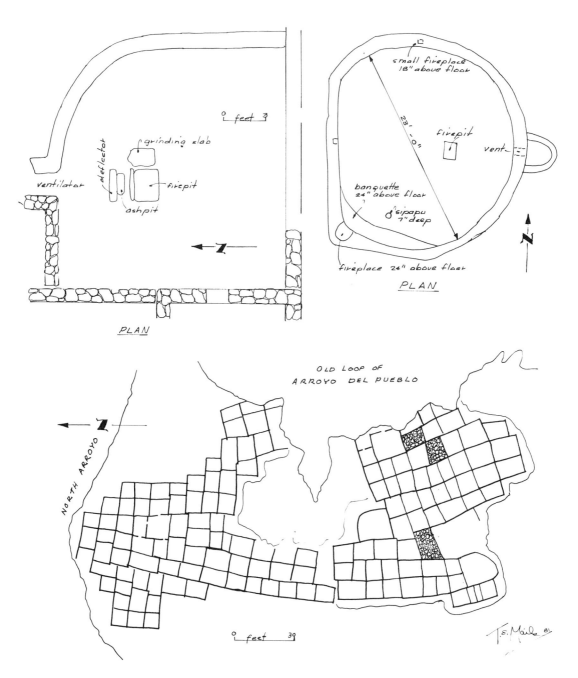

Top left, corner kiva, Dick's Ruin. *Top right,* kiva at Arrowhead Ruin. *Bottom,* plot plan of Forked Lightning Ruin, East Pueblo. After Kidder, 1958.

The Arrowhead pueblo, about two miles east of Pecos, is noted mainly for its unique D-shaped kiva that had a sipapu on its southwest corner and what is thought to be a banquette. Various authorities give the pueblo a date range of from A.D. 1340 to 1393.[35]

MIDDLE RIO GRANDE: PECOS

From 1915 to 1925, Alfred V. Kidder, under the auspices of the Robert S. Peabody Foundation for Archaeology, Phillips Academy, Andover, Massachusetts, excavated the ruined pueblo of Pecos in San Miguel County, New Mexico.

According to Kidder, Pecos proved to be a frontier community almost from the beginning. "It lay on the extreme eastern edge of the Pueblo area, yet it became the largest village of its time, and it was continuously occupied longer than any other Southwestern site of which we have knowledge."[36]

Some of this was due to the fine resources of the Pecos Valley. The Pecos River, a perennial stream, was less than a mile to the east. Along its course were plots of land that could be irrigated. An arroyo ran close by the village, and there were springs at many places along its banks. Near the pueblo was unlimited upland acreage, and rainfall was ample for dry farming. Kidder thinks that crops planted in the mountain valleys would never have failed. Early frosts at those altitudes would usually have prevented the corn from achieving full maturity, but it could have been gathered green and preserved by cooking in a subterranean oven, as is done by the Zuñi. Assuredly, also, the Pecos people kept stores of corn on hand to provide for emergencies. The nearby mountains were populated with deer, elk, and wild turkeys. Rabbits were all around. Antelope ranged the open country, and buffalo could be obtained only a few days' journey to the east. Wood for beams and fuel was close by. In sum, the Pecos Valley was an ideal spot for the Anasazi to flourish.

Guesses are that the settlement of the Pecos Region took place between A.D. 1000 and 1100, during Pueblo III. Until that time, the area had been untenanted by sedentary, agricultural Indians. As of 1932, no trace had yet been found of Basketmaker or early Pueblo stages of development. But sometime during Pueblo III a number of small villages came into being, not only in the Pecos country, but as far east as Las Vegas, New Mexico, and as far south as Anton Chico. How long they lasted is not known, but some of them did grow to considerable size and underwent several rebuildings.

Ultimately, either subsistence adjustments and/or pressures from nomadic and warlike peoples coming from the east and southeast caused the abandonment of the outlying villages. The entire populace gathered first in two or three towns in the upper valley, and finally in the single large Pecos Pueblo, on the summit of a defensible flat-topped ridge of sandstone about a mile west of the Pecos River. Kidder believes this last concentration took place about A.D. 1250, and it is known that Pecos Pueblo was not abandoned until A.D. 1838, after an occupancy of nearly six centuries.

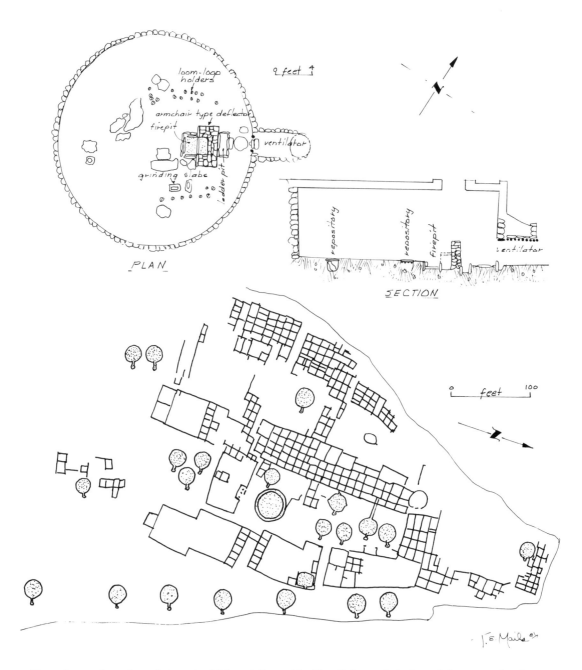

Top, plan and section of clan-sized kiva at Pecos Pueblo. *Bottom,* plot plan of Pecos north of the South Pueblo. Parts of the central portion rose to a height of five stories. The shaded areas represent one Great Kiva and twenty-one clan-sized kivas. After Kidder, 1958.

The duration of Pecos Pueblo gives it particular archaeological value, since its remains were in excellent stratigraphic order, not only permitting the excavators to work out the entire development of the local culture, but also providing a basis for a confident chronological arrangement of the material found in the more transitory villages nearby.[37]

During the work at Pecos, eight chronologically sequent groups of pottery were recognized: Black-on-white, Glaze I Red, Glaze I Yellow, Glaze II, Glaze III, Glaze IV, Glaze V, Glaze VI, and Modern Painted. There were also two so-called Biscuit wares, one found with Glazes I and II, and the other with Glazes III and IV.

The history of Pecos prior to A.D. 1540 could be reconstructed only by archaeological methods, and using these methods Kidder learned that the earliest structures were low and straggling, enclosing large rectangular courts. Ceramics for this first stage spanned Black-on-white through Glaze II. At the end of Glaze I the last outlying settlement was abandoned, and in Glaze III compact three- and four-story pueblos were developed and the first defense walls were built. Since a general contraction continued, pressure from nomadic enemies is apparent. Pecos presumably experienced raids on its fields, but evidence suggests that entrance to the pueblo itself was not gained. Evidences of intermittent trade with tribes of the Plains indicate in addition that warfare was not unceasing. Kidder feels that enemy pressure may in fact have welded the Pecos inhabitants more solidly together. The Glaze III, IV, and V eras mark the periods of greatest growth and prosperity for the pueblo. By the time the Coronado expedition entered New Mexico in A.D. 1540, Pecos had become the largest and richest of the Anasazi towns.[38]

Coronado assigned a lay brother to Pecos and left a flock of sheep with him. Kidder believes that the lay brother was promptly killed and the sheep were eaten, for no mention is made of them by subsequent explorers. Other Spanish parties visited Pecos during the latter part of the sixteenth century, and De Sosa had an altercation with the residents in 1590. But no permanent Spanish influence was exerted until New Mexico was colonized in 1597. Soon thereafter a priest established residence, and a very large adobe church was completed before 1620.

An abundance of sandstone at the Pecos site made it possible for the residents to construct a masonry pueblo. The earliest walls were the best, yet even those were none too good. The completed North Pueblo was a vast quadrangular structure, enclosing entirely a large, rectangular plaza. Some of its rooms were as high as three stories, and a few were four and five stories aboveground. Bandelier's estimate in 1881 was that the North Pueblo contained 585 rooms, and the nearby South Pueblo 517 rooms, making a total of 1,102. Kidder thinks there may have been 80 or so fewer rooms, and that related families occupied "apartments," or groups of rooms, as opposed to the family-to-each-room arrangement of early Tusayan. This allows a possible population range for Pecos of from 1,000 to 1,400.[39]

Twenty-two circular and subterranean kivas were found in the Pecos Ruin. Seventeen were excavated, along with four almost-square aboveground structures, which Kidder calls "guardhouse kivas." Common features associated with the circular kivas included a slab-lined rectangular firepit with an adjacent "legless armchair" type of ashpit/deflector combination, a wall-type ventilator, a ladder pit, potrest holes, niches, and loom holes. Most of the kivas had crude masonry-lined walls, and fewer than half contained sipapus. Two kivas had cists containing stone idols. With one exception the circular kivas averaged 20 feet (6 m) in diameter. The other was of Great Kiva size, its diameter above an encircling banquette being 44 feet (13 m). The floor was not finished, no firepit was installed, no roof had covered it, and Kidder concluded that it was never completed.[40]

Guardhouse kivas were so named because each of them was located at one of the entrances to the quadrangle. The actual function of these surface chambers was not determined, but they contained the same type of firepit and ashpit/deflector as the kivas. Two of them had rounded corners quite like those found in certain surface rooms at Mesa Verde's Cliff Palace.[41] The average wall length of a guardhouse kiva was 20 feet (6 m).

Kidder's summary of the artifacts of Pecos Pueblo was published in 1932, and his archaeological notes were issued in 1958—reversing the usual order for such reports. He had his reasons for this, and they need not trouble us. What is important is that his later treatise allowed him to update the earlier volume and to correct what he admits were mistakes and oversights. Some of these he feels were due to inexperience, and others to his "preponderance" of interest in pottery and other sorts of artifacts "rather than in their makers." Not really trying to excuse this, he nevertheless observes that in the "teens and twenties" archaeology and ethnology were almost entirely unrelated, and that at that time the archaeological "ceramic tail was beginning to wag the archaeological dog." "But," he goes on to say, "pottery was never more than a minor art. It can tell far less of the social and religious life of a preliterate people than can their dwellings, their ceremonial structures and paraphernalia, or the products of the higher arts."[42]

So extensive is the Pecos Ruin that in six field-seasons only 12 to 15 percent of the total area was cleared. Even this much work revealed, however, that during the entire period of occupation the residents kept shifting about in typical Anasazi fashion, abandoning, razing, rebuilding, and building. "Almost every part of the mesa top," Kidder says, "was occupied at one time or another, and at several places the ruins lie three and four deep."[43]

Although great quantities of rubbish accumulated around every successive structure, the bulk of it was thrown over the eastern edge of the mesa, where it formed in time an enormous sloping midden nearly a quarter of a mile long and twenty feet deep. Excavations were made in all parts of this fill, dwelling spaces were cleared, subterranean kivas were excavated, and nearly two thousand graves were opened. Millions of sherds were removed and categorized. Yet Pecos did not prove to be rich in sumptuous specimens.

There are several reasons for that. Pecos is an exposed site, and it lies in a region of relatively heavy rainfall, and so almost everything of a perishable nature has long since disappeared through decay. Also, since it was neither destroyed nor abandoned, what was produced was used up. Besides, Kidder thinks, the final abandonment was so gradual that little needed to be left, or whatever did remain was probably soon carted away or destroyed by Mexicans living in the valley. Even the graves were poor in offerings. The Pecos people were never lavish with mortuary gifts, and during the final periods practically nothing was interred with the dead.

Interestingly enough, Kidder concluded that the lack of spectacular lesser

Clay items of a religious nature found at Pecos Pueblo and Forked Lightning Pueblo. *a–b*, front and side views of typical flat-bodied human effigies. *c–d*, heads from flat-bodied effigies. *e–f*, human effigies. *g–h*, fragments of round-bodied human effigies. *i*, horse effigy. *j*, bird effigy. *k–l*, incised pipes with polished black surface. *m–n*, pipes of unusual shape with lizard and frog decoration. From Kidder, 1932.

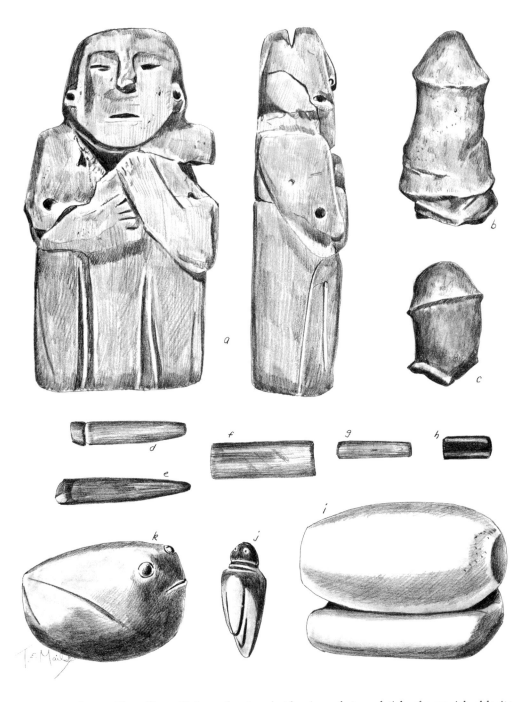

Religious objects. From Pecos Ruin: *a*, front and side view of stone fetish of greenish chlorite schist from repository in the main plaza, height, 11¼ inches; *b–c*, two of nine fertility stones found with the fetish; *d–h*, stone medicine cylinders, fine-grained and highly polished; length of e, 2⅝ inches. From Forked Lightning Ruin: *i*, lightning set—rubbing stone and hearth of white quartz; friction produces a glow symbolic of lightning; *j–k*, fetish stones. After Kidder, 1932.

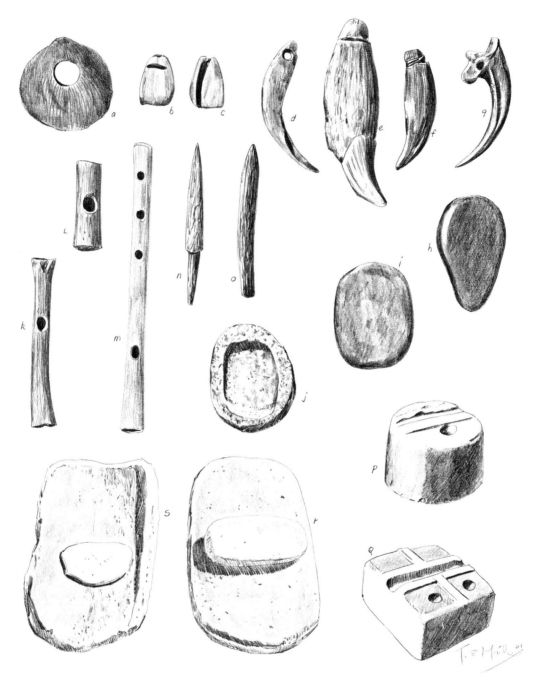

Lesser material culture objects from Pecos and Forked Lightning pueblos. *a,* glycymeris shell pendant. *b–c,* shell tinklers of type attached to dance bandolier. *d–g,* teeth perforated for use as pendants: d and f, wolf; e, grizzly bear; g, coyote. *h,* floor polishing stone. *i,* rubbing stone. *j,* paint-grinding stone. *k–l,* bone whistles. *m,* whistle made from ulnae of golden eagle. *n,* antler bone foreshaft for reed dart or arrow. *o,* antler flaking tool. *p–q,* arrow shaft smoothing stones. *r,* plain-surfaced metate from Pecos Ruin. *s,* one of two trough metates found at Forked Lightning Ruin. From Kidder, 1932.

material-culture finds at Pecos became a factor in his team's favor, since it concentrated on all the discoveries rather than upon the "spectacularity" of the collections. By this means the team gained data of a valuable kind that is often overlooked in the quest for the handsomest articles.[44]

Most of the stone implements and weapons found at Pecos were in fact similar to those discovered in the Little Colorado Region. But while Kidder has spoken of his finds as unspectacular, many of them having to do with ceremonial practices merit special attention.

For example, considering how infrequently stone idols have been found elsewhere, it is noteworthy that four were uncovered at Pecos. The finest was discovered two feet below the surface in a stone boxlike cist at the south end of the plaza, in ground overlying a kiva. With it was a smaller, badly battered image and several oddly shaped stones, some of which appear to be phallic. A third idol was discovered in a cist in a plaza-fronting room, and the fourth image was found in a sealed recess in the west wall of a kiva.[45]

Also uncovered were a few fetish stones, some polished stone medicine cylinders, a pair of white quartz lightning stones, several slate-gray phyllite slabs, two painted sandstone slabs that may be altar slabs, and some perforated slabs that could have been associated either with sipapu enclosures or with ventilator-shaft openings.[46]

In several kivas there were waterworn stones that may have served as fetishes. Little concretion stones formed what appeared to be parts of small medicine bundles that occasionally were found in graves.[47]

Among the objects most frequently found in the upper levels of the refuse deposits were small effigy figurines of burned clay. These were in human, animal, and bird forms, crudely done, but with "artistic" charm. None was polished, slipped, or painted, although some were incised to emphasize details.

An abundance of elaborate ceremonial pipes was unearthed at Pecos. Like the pottery, they show changes in style from the early to the late stages. Almost all are of burned clay, tubular, and one piece in construction. As in the more western Anasazi pipes, the smoke passage was formed by molding the moist clay around a small reed or grass stem, which was then either pulled or burned out.[48]

Also noteworthy among the Pecos artifacts are the bone flageolets, the majority of which were made from the ulna of the golden eagle, although some were fashioned from the wing bones of whooping cranes, hawks, and turkeys. Sounding rasps were fashioned from the ribs, leg bones, and scapulae of large animals.

Among the wooden objects still existing at the Pecos site were the traditional digging sticks, arrows, balls, weaving tools, and ceremonial paraphernalia. The last-named include lightning sticks, parts of tablitas, wands, bullroarers, and a tiny ceremonial bow. Cloth finds were rare, but they included feather and cotton. Evidence also indicated that buffalo hides were used, for robes and for apparel.[49]

I have said earlier that nearly two thousand burials were examined, a far greater number than encountered elsewhere, and it would be logical to assume that much would be revealed thereby. On the contrary, very little was learned, other than the fact that most bodies were flexed to some degree at time of inhumation.

Of particular interest, however, is the evidence regarding cranial deformation. As we know, this was an identifying feature of the Anasazi from Pueblo I on, and its presence at Pecos would offer a clear tie to the Anasazi peoples of the Four Corners area. It does occur at the Pecos and Pindi pueblos,[50] yet in a far less pronounced form than might be expected. In many instances deformation is entirely absent. This circumstance might indicate a Mogollon admixture, or it might mean that as the great migrations ran their course the deformation custom was phased out. Indeed, at a number of the later-date Rio Grande sites there was no cranial deformation at all. What overall significance this has is open to conjecture, but it warrants further consideration as the ethnic makeup of the early Rio Grande villages is assessed.

Kidder believes it was probably 1620 or 1630 before the remains of domestic animals, china dishes, and metal implements became common enough in the Pecos refuse heaps to allow the excavator to posit the beginning of European influence. Accordingly, he establishes the historic period as opening about 1630. He notes also that the Pueblo Revolt of 1680–92 failed to result, as it did in the case of so many other villages, in the destruction of the town or in its removal to another site. About the middle of the eighteenth century, however, a combination of Comanche raids and sickness caused a serious decline. There was a progressive decrease in population, and by 1838 Pecos was wholly abandoned. A tiny handful of survivors joined their linguistic kindred at Jemez Pueblo, where their descendants live on today.[51]

SOUTH CENTRAL RIO GRANDE: KUAUA

When Awatovi Pueblo was being described (Vol. I), reference was made to murals that were discovered at a ruin in New Mexico named Kuaua, just north of Bernalillo. Historians once thought that Kuaua might have been the place where Coronado made his headquarters in the winter of 1540–41. With this in mind, the Museum of New Mexico, School of American Research, began excavations in 1934 to see what evidence could be found. After five years of searching, they concluded that the guesses about Coronado were wrong. In the meantime they did uncover something of even greater value to Pueblo students.

Kuaua—pronounced Koo-wah-wah—was begun toward the end of the thirteenth century when a small adobe unit pueblo was built. Sometime around A.D. 1350 the original structure burned. Remaining buildings enclosed two large plazas, and a third and smaller plaza on the east end. Within the bigger plazas were five large, circular, subterranean kivas. In the smaller plaza was a single rectangular kiva. In addition to these six ceremonial structures, certain of the rooms within the dwelling block contained architectural details common to kivas, such as firepits, ashpit/deflectors, and loom-anchor holes.

A small, circular kiva in the southwest part of Kuaua yielded up the earliest cultural artifacts. After it was abandoned it had become a trash receptacle, and from its contents, archaeologists were able to date it to the early fourteenth century.

But it was the square, subterranean kiva, designated as Kiva III, that contained the truly exciting find. Once its sixteenth-century fill was removed, it was discovered that the four walls were decorated with magnificent true fresco murals.[52] Each wall measured 18 feet (5.5 m) in length, and there were paint-

Bottom, Kuaua Ruin, now designated as Coronado State Monument, New Mexico. The northernmost village in the Tiguex Province, Kuaua contained more than twelve hundred rooms and housed several hundred residents. *Top,* examples of kiva mural art in Kuaua. At left is Kupishtaya, chief of the lightning makers. In the center is an eagle dropping seeds in a fertility rite. At right is a black clown with lightning and rainstorm symbols.

Mural figures from Pottery Mound, New Mexico. *Top left,* Basket dancer who bears a close resemblance to a Hopi Mamzrau member. *Top right,* figure holding macaws. *Bottom,* costumed figures holding pahos and netted gourds or jars. After Frank C. Hibben, 1975.

ings on many of the layers of plaster still remaining on the walls. In the east plaza, Kiva VI had also been painted, although only a few fragments could be recovered. Kiva III has been carefully restored to its original state, and replicas of the murals have been painted on its walls and altar.[53] Descriptions of these are given by Bertha P. Dutton in her book *Sun Father's Way.*

A museum with walls of sun-dried bricks has been built at Kuaua. It contains artifacts recovered from the pueblo and neighboring sites, and reproductions of the now-famous murals. It also has an excellent topographical map of the old Tiguex (Tewa) Region.

NORTHEASTERN RIO GRANDE: PO-SHU-OUINGE

In 1919, an expedition led by J. A. Jeancon excavated a ruin named Po-shu-ouinge, meaning "Calabash at the end of the ridge village." It is in Tewa country near Abiquiu, on the south side of the Chama River and perhaps twenty miles northwest of Española. At the time of excavation it was one of ten or more ruins in the immediate vicinity of which virtually nothing was known. Both San Juan Pueblo and Santa Clara Pueblo claim the ruin as the site of a former occupation of their ancestors.

Po-shu's location was ideal. The land was beautiful and splendid for farming, and nearby were all the materials needed for buildings, supplementary foods, and crafts.

The pueblo was built of adobe, and its rooms enclosed two plazas. None of the walls was standing aboveground at the time of Jeancon's excavation, and he had difficulty establishing boundaries, but he was able to determine that one plaza was oblong, with a rectangular indentation at its northeast corner, while the other was square and smaller. The longest row of rooms measured 690 feet (207.65 m) in length, the shortest row 109 feet (32.3 m). In some places the rows of rooms were three and four deep. The main buildings were originally two and three stories high, a fact determined by the amount of fallen adobe and by the location of charred remains. Along the west side of the largest plaza the rooms were probably one story high and two rooms deep. Covered porches lined the front walls of rooms bordering the plaza, a feature commonly found in modern pueblos.[54]

Dwelling rooms were unusually large for structures on the Jemez Plateau, a fact that indicated a late pre-Spanish date to Jeancon. Dendrochronology techniques were not yet in vogue, and so architectural styles and ceramics were still the only gauges of antiquity. Rooms averaged more than 9 feet 8 inches (3 m) long and more than 6 feet 9 inches (2 m) wide. Ceiling heights may have been as much as 5 feet 9 inches (1.78 m). On the basis of objects found in them, Jeancon guessed that four of the rooms were ceremonial. Each one was in the same relative location in a building row on the north, east, south, and west sides of the plaza, although not all were on the same floor level. None, however, had a bench or other distinguishing feature such as occurs in a kiva or kihu.[55]

At the northeast corner of the smaller plaza was a round surface room built on top of an oblong one. It consisted almost entirely of boulders taken from the river bottom, laid in mortar, and plastered over. Whether it was a watchtower or a kiva, Jeancon was not prepared to say, although Bandelier called it, without hesitation, a watchtower.[56]

The walls at Po-shu had foundation stones consisting of rows of large cobbles. The interstices were filled in with nodules of adobe, and the adobe wall was built on top. Jeancon was able to watch a Santa Clara woman as she built a similar wall, and he believes she followed the method used at Po-shu.[57] Accordingly, his account gives us our best description of pre-Spanish adobe con-

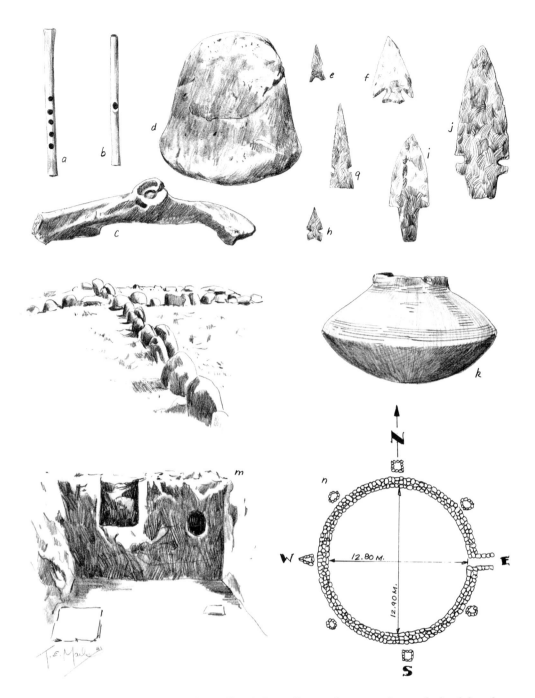

Po-Shu Pueblo Ruin: *a*, bone turkey-caller. *b*, bone flute. *c*, bone tanning tool. *d*, adobe plug. *e–h*, stone projectile points. *i*, spear points. *j*, ceremonial spearhead. *k*, incised jar—the jar form was a favorite one at Po-Shu. *l*, foundation stones for house walls. *m*, room with doorway, vent hole, and some floor slabs still in place. *n*, plan of the World Shrine. From J. A. Jeancon, 1923.

struction as it was practiced in the prehistoric and early historic Rio Grande villages.

The only change in Rio Grande building techniques after the Spanish began to colonize in 1598 was that of forming adobe bricks in wooden forms, rather than molding them by hand. Bainbridge Bunting states that modern adobe bricks measure 10 x 14 x 4 inches (25.4 x 35.56 x 10.16 cm) and weigh about thirty-five pounds. Also, he says, northern Rio Grande builders add straw to the adobe because it aids in drying them, and in the Albuquerque area they use sod with fairly deep roots.[58]

In Jeancon's experience there was none of the ceremony that attended the building of an early Hopi dwelling. The Santa Clara woman selected and laid out the line where the wall was to be built. She mixed her clay or adobe thoroughly and, taking pieces about the size of a large apple, laid them along the line, patting and molding each one as she placed it. When she had obtained the desired height, she left the wall to dry. Jeancon was surprised to discover the next day that the shrinkage from drying was not following the line and form of the nodules. It was "more or less" forming quare and oblong masses of various sizes and making what appeared to be fairly regular courses. He observed the same type of shrinkage in the newly erected church at Santa Clara. The cracks caused by the shrinkage were afterward filled with wet clay and allowed to dry before the final wash was put on.[59] Jeancon, his assistants, and his Tewa work crew tore apart sections of the Po-shu walls and found the same kind of nodule, shrinkage into square or oblong masses, plus cracks filled in with adobe. One difference was that the whole wall surface in the cracks was smoke-filled. A laborer who had been born at Hano explained that whenever the Hopi wanted a wall to dry quickly they built a fire along the base, thus accounting for the smoke. No foreign matter was mixed with the adobe of the Po-shu walls, yet they were exceedingly durable and hard, especially after they were plastered. The average wall thickness was 12 inches (30 cm).

A plaster wash was put on the dried wall, and in one instance Jeancon found twenty-three coats. The average number was seventeen, and if washes were renewed annually, indications were that the pueblo was inhabited for perhaps twenty-five years. In some places there were evidences of painted plaster, with red, black, and yellow being used.

Small wall openings are common in Anasazi ruins. But an interesting wall feature employed at Po-shu was that of small, round openings, which probably served as vents or air holes and were often filled with adobe plugs. Usually these holes were near corners or doorways, and they were the only wall openings.[60] There was no evidence of windows. Also there were no exterior doorways. Openings did occur, however, in the inner walls between rooms. Jeancon assumes there were doorways leading out onto terraces. It appeared that door lintels were formed of parallel poles, as at Chaco Canyon, and that stone slabs were used for sills. No traces of recessed jambs, such as those found at Mesa Verde and elsewhere, were evident. Jeancon thinks that closure slabs were simply leaned against the jambs to close the doors. "Nothing suggesting wooden slab doors or hangings of hide, cotton, or other fabrics" used as door closers was found.[61] A typical doorway measured 1 foot 2¼ inches (36 cm) in height, and 1 foot 1½ inches (34 cm) in width.

Room floors were composed of a mixture of ash, grease, very fine charcoal, water, and adobe. This unusual mixture was applied in a semiliquid condition. When it was partly dry, it was beaten down to form a solid mass, then polished with a flat stone, many of which Jeancon's party found. He assumes that additional washes of the same mixture were applied as needed, for different-colored layers were superimposed upon one another. The average thickness of a polished black surfacing was 1½ inches (3.81 cm). In only one room did he find evidence of stone-slab paving.[62]

Storage pits of various shapes and sizes were randomly situated in the room floors. Fireplaces occurred in many rooms. These varied in makeup from simple groups of boulders to "well-plastered and arranged fireplaces that would do credit to a more modern pueblo." The sides of one, for example, were built of stones set on end and plastered. The plastered room wall formed the back. Most fireplaces were against the middle of the wall, although a few were found in corners. There was no evidence of chimneys, even though fireplaces often occurred in interior rooms, and Jeancon finds the question of how they disposed of smoke to be a perplexing one.[63]

Most mealing bins were in or near corners. They were oblong or square, and well plastered.

Careful analysis of the remains indicated that the roofs of Po-shu dwellings were constructed in the same manner as in most prehistoric ruins in the Southwest.

The four ceremonial rooms previously mentioned were examined by Jeancon, but he found only one kiva. Even then the difficulties of excavation were such that his party abandoned attempts to clear it. They did learn that it was unusually large, being 41 feet 3 inches (12.3 m) in diameter. It was only semi-subterranean, and at least two interior posts had given added support to the main beams. The wall construction was the same as that of the dwellings, and seven coats of plaster had been applied.[64]

Lesser material-culture objects found at Po-shu included the usual range of ceramics, stone, bone, and wood. Jeancon thought it interesting that in direct conjunction with the crudest type of stone artifacts were some of the finest specimens that could be desired. He thinks this fact indicates they were made by both experienced and inexperienced workmen and that some trading in the pieces had taken place.

Stone implements included axes, mauls and hoes, cutting edges or flakes, pointed stones that may have been fitted with handles, knives, spear points, arrowheads, spheroids of unknown purpose, pottery polishing stones, manos and metates, mortars and pestles, arrow smoothers and straighteners, lids, and baking stones. Of special value were two large spearheads, whose probable use was ceremonial. When the first of these was found, the Tewa workers gathered around and examined it "very carefully with exclamations of pleasure, and with a sort of reverence."[65]

Upon being questioned as to its special value, the oldest man in the party, Aniceto Swazo, put it inside his shirt against his naked left breast, pressed and patted it, and repeated this act on each of his cheeks and forehead. Then he held the spearhead about an inch from his mouth and inhaled deeply several times. He explained that the piece was ceremonial and would bring the owner strength and courage in the chase and in battle. This information was later verified by other Tewa. The manner of actually using the spearhead was to bind it to the naked left breast over the heart, which Swazo located at the nipple of the left breast.[66]

Bone implements were abundant at Po-shu. They included flakers, scrapers, daggers, beads, turkey callers, flutes, awls, needles, pins, spatulas, knife blades, fleshers, and weaving tools. Especially noteworthy were a breastplate of some antiquity, made of rib bones, and the remains of what was probably a deer-horn dance headdress, such as that still worn by Rio Grande men in the Buffalo Dance.[67]

All but one of the Po-shu pipes were tubular, and similar to others found in the Rio Grande Region. The exception was L-shaped, a type used in modern rituals but rare in prehistoric pueblos. Some Po-shu pipes were stone, others clay. Jewelry pendants were made of selenite and clay, the former constituting the "handsomest" examples Jeancon had ever seen.[68] Shell finds were abundant, indicating trade with, and journeys to, the ocean peoples. Jeancon says there are well-defined traditions among the Pueblos of "pilgrimages" to the "sky-blue water," during which the party made a "journey of death" over a great desert. His informants also told him enough to confirm that they knew what the oceans looked like from firsthand experience.[69]

The pottery found at Po-shu proved to be one of the most perplexing problems of the entire excavation. "Almost every type of pottery known and attributed to the pre-Spanish period of the Jemez Plateau is represented in the collection." The native wares of Po-shu itself were evenly divided among a black-coiled ware, biscuit ware, and incised ware. There were also some queer, seemingly transitional, pieces showing influences from other regions, plus wares brought in by barter or as gifts. Jeancon gives a most detailed description of the Po-shu ceramics in pages 34 to 65 of his *Excavations in the Chama Valley.*

The fetishes found at Po-shu merit special attention. Jeancon states that it was the custom in 1919, and still is, for conservatives to carry small pouches containing copper ore, agates, polished stones, concretions, and the like. These bring good luck and protection to the bearer. Many of them were found in the ruin. A Santa Clara informant told Jeancon that small highly polished and beautiful stones were "good luck," and that in former times men carried them in buckskin bags to make magic. When they went to war they put one in their mouth to make them brave. When one was running, such a stone in the mouth made one strong.

In addition to the good-luck stones there were two beautiful specimens of fluorite, stained a delicate purple, of a type used as bases for prayer plumes, plus some unusually well-made fetishes of animals and birds. One made of clay represented a bird, and one made of stone was perhaps a bear. Jeancon observes that the "bear fetish is the most popular animal fetish in use today on the Rio Grande." Ceremonial paint sticks are rarely found, but one such was uncovered at Po-shu. It was made of polished burnt sienna, with some kind of grease serving as a binder. Two of the most interesting fetishes turned up were made of black earth and grease. The winter cacique at Santa Clara told Jeancon that they were used in some of the ceremonies of the Koshare, and that there ought to be four in a set. He added that the material they were made of was the "maposhune" (meaning unknown), or black ceremonial paint, used by the male dancers. The fetishes had holes in the top, which were receptacles for prayer feathers. When Jeancon showed them to a few men in Santa Clara Pueblo they caused "much talk," and he assumes they are very sacred.[70]

What he thought was the most interesting fetish was a clay maternity figurine, used by the wife of one of the workmen who bore a child while they were still in camp. The woman explained that she wore it in her belt over the abdomen and that "it helped her wonderfully." A groove ran the full length of the image's back. Special liquid medicines were poured into this, the figurine was tipped up, and the medicine was allowed to run into her mouth. Jeancon says that similar images were found in Porto (Puerto) Rico and are described at length by Fewkes in the Twenty-fifth Annual Report of the BAE.[71]

A curious object made of lava was said by the Tewa to be a symbol of the Koshare fraternity. Its horns represented the horns worn by the Koshare head man.[72]

Beautifully shaped, large white-quartz pebbles are used in the rain ceremonies of the Tewa. They have been found in all the ruins, including Po-shu. During the rain ceremonies a drum is beaten to represent the thunder and the quartz pieces are rubbed together to produce an incandescent glow that resembles lightning.[73]

Bits of finished turquoise indicate that turquoise inlay was practiced at Po-shu, but to what extent could not be determined. A few turquoise beads also turned up, as did shells drilled for stringing as beads and pendants. Only a few wooden objects still existed: some kicking or gaming pieces and a miniature arrow.[74]

From general indications, Jeancon believes that basketry was "fairly plentiful" in the village. Types included twilled weave and the two-rod-and-bundle weave.[75]

Only two pictographs were found in the vicinity of Po-shu. One was of a turkey cock, the other of a snake, both of which were inscribed on the top of the same rock. Also on the top and side of the rock were cupping stones and manmade cupped places, which Swazo said were used at certain times during the year and during specific ceremonies. "Women go to these at daybreak and pound on the cups to attract the attention of sun." The constant pounding accounted for the holes.[76]

Shrines were everywhere present near Po-shu. Paths formed by double rows of stones led in all directions away from the ruin and always ended at what appeared to be shrines, usually consisting of a square or circle of stones, of which, Jeancon says, there were thousands. He designated one in particular as the combined world (middle) and cardinal-point shrines. This composite is about three fourths of a mile southeast of Po-shu, and its main portion is a large circle of stones, whose inner diameter is 41 feet 6 inches (12.85 m), with an entry passage on the east side. Jeancon thinks the wall was originally higher than when he saw it and that it might even have been topped with a low adobe

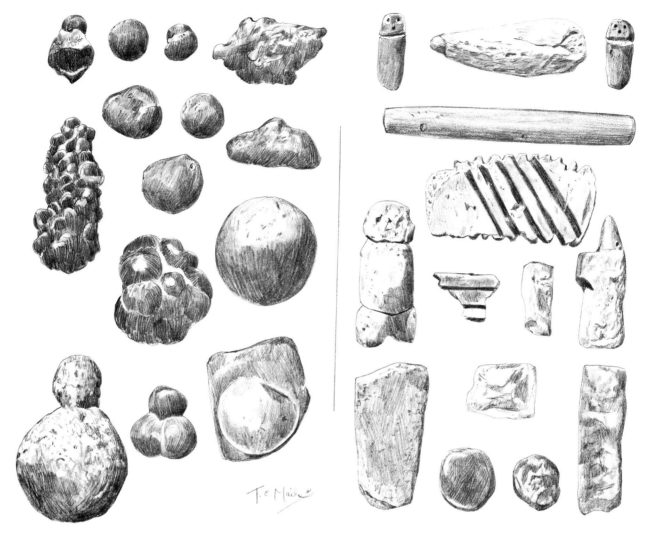

Po-Shu Pueblo: Lesser material culture religious objects. *Left*, concretion stone fetishes. *Right*, an assortment of ceremonial pieces. From J. A. Jeancon, 1923.

wall. Outside the wall and surrounding it, like markings on a clock, are seven smaller stone-walled shrines. Those at the north and south cardinal points are square. At the east and west is a triangle, and at midpoints between the cardinal points are circles. Leading from the east entryway is a path lined on both sides with stones. Some 890 feet (228 m) northeast of the entryway are three stone tanks surrounded with interesting designs: squares, circles, triangles, and other figures. Triangles outside the base line point toward the village. Leading in a straight line from the northwest corner of the tanks is a stone-lined path that leads directly to the village.

Swazo explains that when there was a long dry spell the caciques, with some other men, would spend four nights and days at the world shrine in prayer and in making medicine. On the fifth day before sunrise they would follow the path to the tanks, making medicine as they went. They would reach the tanks just as the sun rose, and rain would fall directly into the tanks. Not a drop would fall anywhere else. A runner was then sent to the village to tell people to come with ceremonial cups. No human hand was allowed to touch the water. Some was drunk, and medicine was made with the rest. In a short while it rained everywhere and the drought was broken. Swazo said the same ceremony was still being performed (in 1919), but that only a few men knew how to do it.[77]

Few burials were unearthed at Po-shu, and these revealed little of consequence. There seemed to be no pattern in positioning, although most bodies were flexed. One adult had a cloth over his face. Mortuary offerings were either simple or absent.

Po-Shu Pueblo: Typical lesser material culture objects. *a–b,* selenite ceremonial items. *c–j,* tiponi or prayer plume bases. *k,* lightning or "firestones." *l,* Koshare fetish. *m,* wooden ball. *n,* mineral stone probably used as fetish. *o–p,* stone pipes. From J. A. Jeancon, 1923.

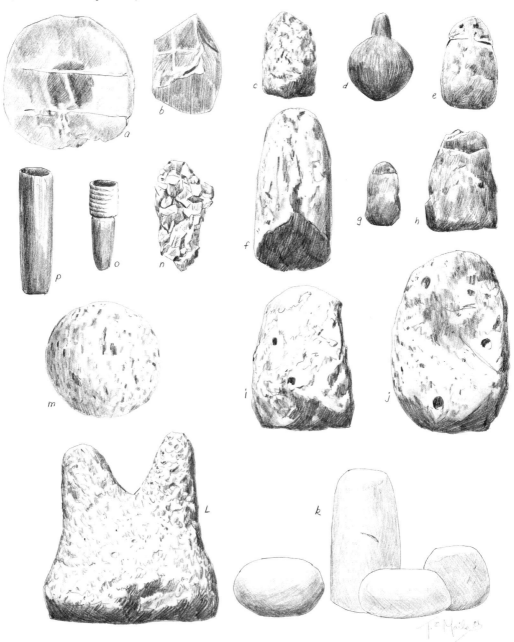

Jeancon's conclusion is that Po-shu was abandoned suddenly, but he was not able to determine why. The structure was not destroyed, yet almost no large pieces of pottery were left behind. The residents were farmers, as was shown by the seeds of squash, pumpkin, and gourd that were found. But corn was not discovered in any great quantity. It is reasonable to assume that meat supplemented the Anasazi diet. The Tewa say that Po-shu was a place where great fairs were held. Jeancon thinks the village may have marked one of the "steps" in connecting the Rio Grande area with regions farther west.[78] It does seem evident that the pueblo achieved a place of real significance during the peak period of its longevity.

MIDDLE RIO GRANDE: PINDI

From December 1, 1932, to June 1, 1933, the ruins of Pindi (Turkey) Pueblo were excavated by a party led by Stanley A. Stubbs, under the auspices of the Laboratory of Anthropology, Santa Fe, and the Civil Works Administration. The ruin is on the north bank of the Santa Fe River, about six miles southwest of Santa Fe, and directly opposite the village of Agua Fria. Stream cutting had already washed away half of the site at the time of excavation, and since then so much of the exposed portions have been used for the manufacture of adobe houses that today the site no longer exists in a recognizable form. A combination of tree-ring and ceramic analysis gives an approximate outside dating for Pindi ranging from A.D. 1217 to 1348.

By careful examination, Stubbs learned that Pindi was a typical site "of the late Black-on-white period in the area, ca. A.D. 1300."[79] It, together with Forked Lightning, constituted the two largest sites of the well-populated region. Other smaller pueblos of the same kind seemed to have been occupied for a time and then completely abandoned. The residents of Pindi stayed on, but in usual Anasazi fashion they continually shifted about within the pueblo, repairing, remodeling, or building anew as was demanded by the ever-eroding adobe walls. Some parts of the pueblo eventually reached three stories in height, but two-story units were more common.

Stubbs found that he could roughly divide the occupation into four parts.[80] During late Pueblo II there was a small settlement consisting of crude pit-houses and jacal surface structures. After a time gap of unknown duration, part two began with an elongated irregular block of rooms erected along the crest of the hill. East of this was a second block of rooms. In the court between the blocks were three subsurface kivas and many clay pits. All these recesses were gradually abandoned and then filled with debris. Part three of the construction phases is indicated by an addition of rooms that encircled the original units, so as to form a large block enclosing a central plaza with an open passageway leading toward the river. A small block of rooms was also built one hundred feet west of the main pueblo. The north end of the main pueblo was eventually deserted, and over it the fourth phase of construction developed a

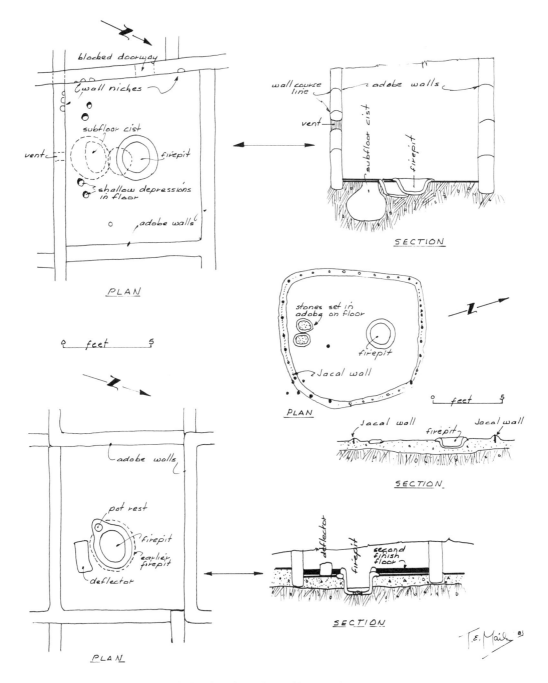

Top and bottom, architectural details of Pindi Pueblo dwelling rooms. *Middle,* pre-Pindi jacal structure later overbuilt by Pindi rooms. From Stubbs, 1953.

T-shaped unit. Two other detached buildings were erected at this time. Refuse deposits were scattered everywhere. They were on all sides of the building blocks, in abandoned dwelling rooms, in kivas, and in the clay pits.

The jacal dwellings seem to have been nothing more than temporary structures. The pithouse was about 8 feet (2.4 m) in diameter and was excavated to a depth of 3 feet (91.4 cm). The roof was braced by a single center post, and smaller poles were in some way laid against this to form a conical wall structure.[81]

The adobe walls of the pueblo itself were the "puddled" type. That is, they were shaped entirely by hand without the aid of forms. Stubbs finds the designation to be inadequate and suggests that "puddled" be replaced with "coursed adobe."[82] The method was similar to that employed at Po-shu, and reported by Jeancon. The adobe contained no binding material, being mixed only with water. Findings by Stubbs that supplement those of Jeancon are troughs, about 6 feet by 3 feet (1.8 m by 91.4 cm) by 1 foot (30.5 cm) deep, used for the mixing of adobe, mud, and sometimes wall plaster; trenches varying in depth from a few inches to 2 feet (61 cm) to receive foundation stones or adobe courses; and a variety of corner details.

Regarding the above, only twenty of the two hundred room walls excavated were undergirded with cobblestones. The rest of the foundations were adobe. The average wall thickness was 9 inches (22.9 cm), and foundations were either the same size or, on occasion, filled the entire width of the 18-inch (45.7-cm) foundation trench. Wall courses were built up by the handful to an average of 15 to 18 inches (38.1 to 45.7 cm) in height and allowed to dry. Courses were usually as long as the wall, and the top of each course was made convex to form a better bond with the next-higher course. Stubbs thought the lower stories reached heights of 7 feet 6 inches (2.25 m) to 8 feet (2.4 m).[83] Contrary to the Anasazi custom with masonry, the adobe builders of Pindi sometimes bonded abutting walls.

Usually the bonding was done by bending one or two of the courses of one wall at a right angle and then continuing on with this same course to form the other wall. The rest of the courses were simply abutted.

Room sizes averaged 6 feet 6 inches by 9 feet (1.95 by 2.7 m). Floors were finished with an adobe layer about 1½ inches (3.8 cm) thick. Most walls had only a mud finish, no plaster. Five rooms retained fragments of painted wall decoration. Entry seems to have been via a roof hatchway. Many interior walls were perforated with a hole averaging 6 inches (15.2 cm) in diameter, apparently used for communication. Many walls were provided with holes of smaller diameter thought to be receptacles for the ends of poles that served as shelves or hangers. Fragments of decayed wood were found in many of the holes. Doorways occurred, but were relatively rare, decreasing in number from the early to the late stages of occupation. Only twenty-four firepits were found, and five of these were in rooms that may have been ceremonial.[84] The latter were rectangular and contained firepits, ashpits, and ventilators. Some also had floor cists.

Five kivas were found and excavated at Pindi. Three were subterranean, circular, and placed in front of the first-building-period block of rooms. Two were surface types built in the corners of the plaza and belonged to the later building periods.

The kivas had dirt walls. They were not masonry lined. Two of the kivas did have walls that were reinforced with a continuous series of upright poles, and over this ribbing was laid a thin veneer of adobe. An offset was provided at the top of the wall, and when it was reached the adobe veneer was thickened to form a surface wall that rose to a height of 2 or 3 feet (61 or 91.4 cm)

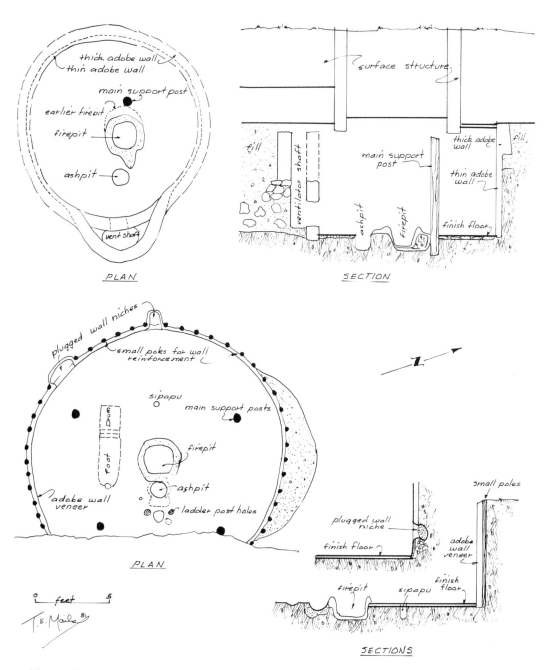

Plan and sections showing construction details of two kivas at Pindi Pueblo. From Stubbs, 1953.

above grade. A mud wash or thin plaster was spread over the veneer to complete the wall finish. The subfloor and finish floor were laid before the wall veneer was put on, but were stopped short so that the veneer passed by them and extended down to the ground. Whenever a new adobe floor was put down, a layer of grass was first spread over the old floor. As a rule, the subsurface kivas of Pindi had clay-lined round firepits, ashpits, and wall niches. But these varied in manner of construction. Two kivas had sipapus, one did not. The surface kivas were roughly D-shaped and contained about the same interior details as the subterranean units.[85]

Meriting special attention was the location of four turkey pens associated with the second and third building stages. When these are added to the occurrence of turkey droppings in some outside rooms, indications are that domesticated turkeys played an important role at Pindi. Stubbs believes that turkeys were used for food as well as for their feathers, for turkey bones were liberally scattered throughout the rubbish heaps.[86]

As to lesser material-ceramic-culture finds, Stubbs explains that Pindi was in a region "clearly defined by the association of certain local black-on-white types." The region occupied roughly a crescent around the southern tip of the Sangre de Cristo Mountains. The crescent stretched from Pecos and Forked Lightning to the vicinity of Santa Fe. The crescent contained many small pueblo sites, the majority of which have yielded up the following ceramic types: Santa Fe Black-on-white, Wiyo Black-on-white, Pindi Black-on-white, Galisteo Black-on-white, and Poge Black-on-white. Beneath all these, and dating roughly in the 1100s, is a generalized black-on-white type quite similar to the widespread Chaco II, from which a local type named Kwahe'e Black-on-white developed. Stubbs believes that Galisteo Black-on-white was the direct result of Mesa Verde Anasazi moving into the Rio Grande Region immediately after A.D. 1300.[87]

Other lesser material-culture finds of stone, clay, bone, and basketry are enough like those of Pecos and Po-shu to require no further comment. Nothing special was turned up.

"Ninety individuals were represented by burials and scattered fragments found during the excavation."[88] As usual, bodies were found in refuse piles, abandoned rooms, and subfloor pits. The majority were flexed to some degree. As I have stated in the Pecos material, cranial deformation was being practiced, but the custom was being phased out.[89]

A.D. *1539 to the Present*

When the first Spanish explorer arrived in Rio Grande country in A.D. 1539, the Anasazi were living on the few sites they now occupy on the banks of the Rio Grande River or its tributaries. In addition, there were dozens of other villages that covered a large area reaching from El Paso in the south to Taos in the north, and penetrating into the eastern foothills of New Mexico. The earliest Mogollon and Anasazi sites had been deserted for some time, but certain of the existing Rio Grande sites were already of considerable antiquity, although none came close to matching in longevity the oldest of the western pueblos. After hundreds of years of progress, if the Rio Grande villages were not in florescence, they were at least close to it, and one can only wonder what might have been achieved had not the Europeans come in search of conquests to add to those already made in once-glittering Mesoamerica, Central America, and Peru.

In A.D. 1540, Coronado led his vast retinue north into the Rio Grande country. Despite the shock of these awesome encounters with white men, the Rio Grande Pueblos were in the beginning friendly, and Coronado established his headquarters at Tiguex Pueblo, near present-day Bernalillo, New Mexico. For two years thereafter he and his party were reluctantly supported by the Tiguex residents and nearby pueblos, while Spanish groups were sent at intervals to explore and "measure" the Rio Grande inhabitants, as well as to investigate and exploit further the more western villages of Acoma, Zuñi, and Tusayan.

In time, the burden of supporting the Spaniards became such that the Pueblos grew deeply resentful and finally the Tiguex rebelled. Coronado's bet-

Pindi Pueblo: *a–b*, cranial types found in burials. *c*, whistles. *d*, full-grooved stone mauls. *e*, stone pot supports. *f*, stone knife. *g–j*, stone projectile points. *k*, stone drill point. *l*, remains of possible eagle or turkey coop along plaza wall. From Stubbs, 1953.

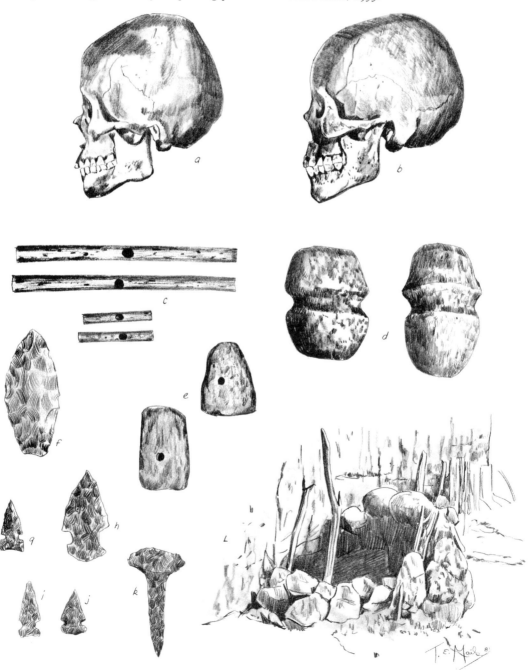

ter-armed men were much too strong for them, however. The revolt was quickly quelled, and to teach the Pueblos a lesson, several hundred Tiguex were executed. Word of this vicious lesson spread rapidly, and a barrier formed that profoundly affected Spanish and Pueblo relations for centuries to come. After Tiguex, there could never be trust and harmony between the two.

Coronado made his way back to Mexico in 1542 and informed the Viceroy that the Pueblo country lacked both the material riches and the cultural resources the Spanish leaders had hoped for. Nevertheless, second thoughts, and perhaps the persuasion of church officials, brought a small party commanded by Francisco Sánchez Chamuscado to the southern Rio Grande area in 1581. When Chamuscado and his soldiers returned to Mexico, they left behind three priests to begin missionary work. Shortly thereafter the still-"smoldering" Pueblos put the priests to death.

When no word was forthcoming from the friars, another expedition, this one led by Antonio de Espejo, came north in 1582 to see what had happened. Espejo brought with him a priest, fourteen soldiers, and a number of Mexican Indian servants. Not finding the priests, he decided to explore the whole Pueblo area to look for mineral resources. He visited Zia, Jemez, Acoma, Zuñi, and Tusayan, came back to the southern Rio Grande, proceeded north to Tanoan country, and went back to Mexico by way of the Pecos River. He had not found his minerals, but he could see there were possibilities and humans to be exploited, and he petitioned the government for a contract to establish settlements in Pueblo country.

Espejo's manner of mind is sufficiently illustrated by his actions at a certain Tiwa village near present-day Bernalillo. Angered by Pueblos he thought were making fun of him when he requested food, Espejo ordered his men to seize some of the Pueblos and put them in an estufa (kiva), after which the village was burned, including screaming residents trapped inside houses. Then he took sixteen Pueblos from the kivas, two at a time, and hanged and shot them.

Considering his volatile temper and his obvious disdain for the Pueblos, it is surprising to find him responsible for our best and most complete account of Pueblo life in 1582.

Adolph F. Bandelier states that after describing the reception accorded him by the Piro, Espejo "tells" the following:

> . . . they gave us a quantity of fowl of the land, and maize, beans, and cakes (tortillas) and another kind of bread they make with more care than the Mexican people, they grind on big stones crushing the grains raw; five or six women grind in one mill and of that flour they make many kinds of bread . . . There are many rooms in one house and in many of their houses they have their ovens for winter-time, and in the squares, in each one of them, they have two estufas, that are underground houses, very well protected and with seats to sit upon. At the door of each estufa they have a ladder to go down and great quantities of firewood of the community, so that strangers may gather there.
>
> . . . in this province some of the natives dress in cotton and cow skins and in tanned deer hides. The mantles they wear after the fashion of the Mexicans except that (follows a description of the breechclout), and some wear shirts and

the women skirts of cotton, many of them embroidered with colored threads, and over it a mantle like that of the Mexican Indians, tied by a handkerchief like unto an embroidered napkin, which they tie to the waist by the fringes. The skirts serve as shirts on the skin, all men and women wear shoes and boots, and soles are of cowhide and the uppers of tanned deerskin. The women keep the hair well combed and arrange it in folds, one on each side, with the hair curiously placed (wound) around it, without anything on the head. Each village has its caciques (chiefs), according to the (number of) people in the pueblo, so the chiefs, and these in turn have their criers that are like constables, and carry out in the villages what the chiefs ordain. When the Spaniards asked the chiefs for anything these call the criers, who proclaim it through the village in loud voices, and forthwith the things are brought quickly. The painting of the houses and whatever they use for dancing, their music, and the rest, they have like the Mexicans. They drink pinole, which is toasted maize diluted in water, and no intoxicating beverage is known to them. In every one of these pueblos they have a house whither they carry food to the demon, and they have idols of stone, small ones, which they worship. Just as the Spaniards have crosses on the highways so they have, from one village to the other in the middle of the path, little heaps like shrines, made of stones, where they place painted sticks and feathers saying: here the demon comes to be powerful and speak to them. They have fields of maize, beans, squashes, and piciete (spruce berries) in great quantity, with irrigation and without, good water channels which they work as the Mexicans do. In every field they have an arbor on four pillars whither they carry the eating at noon and where they rest, because commonly they are in the fields from morning till night as in Spain; in this province there are many pine forests and many salines; on each side of the river, for a distance of a league and a half on both banks, there is good sandy soil, proper for raising maize. Their weapons are bows and arrows, clubs and shields. The arrows are of hard wood, tipped with flint, that easily go through a coat of mail. The shields are like targets, made of cowhide; the clubs are of wood, half an ell long, are very big at one end. With these they defend themselves when inside of their houses. We did not understand they had war with any province; they are quiet and keep their bounds. Here we ascertained from them there was another province farther up the same river and after the same order.[90]

While Espejo's petition was still pending, Castano de Sosa led an unauthorized expedition north in 1590. He established headquarters at the huge Pecos Pueblo and explored the entire Rio Grande Region. But Sosa was arrested by a military group sent after him, and taken as a prisoner to Mexico. In 1592, two other Spaniards sought to found a colony at San Juan Pueblo, but on an exploration trip to the Plains area they were killed.

The contract for colonization was finally awarded to Don Juan de Oñate in 1595. In 1598, he came to the Rio Grande Region with a large group of soldiers, settlers, servants, and friars. He made his headquarters at a pueblo across the river from present-day San Juan. Its name was Yuqueyunque, and he renamed it San Gabriel. In 1610, the seat of the provincial government was established at Santa Fe. Efforts to "civilize" and Christianize the Pueblos got underway immediately after that, and by 1630 Father Alonzo de Benavides was able to report with pride that sixty thousand Pueblos had been converted and ninety chapels had been built (with Indian labor) in as many villages. Of course, the Pueblos had been baptized wholesale, but not really converted in the sense that they understood the new religion. Submission to the Church in this wise was prudent, for those who resisted were dealt with harshly.

In the fall of 1598, the people at Acoma killed one of Oñate's Spanish officers, and Oñate retaliated in early 1599 by ravaging the pueblo, killing hundreds of the residents, and taking hundreds of slaves. Two Hopi who were simply visiting Acoma had their right hands severed and were sent home as examples of what those who defied the Spanish could expect.

Thus did Oñate notify the Pueblos that even an eye for an eye was not sufficient recompense for disobedience. The Spanish believed in debilitating every Indian who had the audacity to raise a hand in defense of his own land, person, or possessions. It was a position that would characterize Spanish rule during the entire seventeenth century. Injustice, abuse, and cruelty were meted out by both church and civil authorities, and for a time the cowed Pueblos, a people who by nature were inclined toward peace, submitted.

The entire Pueblo country was divided into seven missionary districts, with priests assigned to each. Priority was given to the building of churches and chapels and to establishing mission headquarters in the larger villages. The Pueblos were compelled to furnish the labor forces, including the hauling by hand of enormous trees from the mountains to serve as mission-roof beams. Indians not occupied with building were conscripted as servants or were taught trades that could supply the Spanish with goods they needed to spur the growth of their colonies. Some Indians were assigned to herding sheep and cattle, others to farming and tending the orchards. All industries were under strict Spanish control, and every Pueblo farmer was required to give 10 percent of his personal crop yield to the Spaniards.

The Roman Catholic mission church at Santa Ana Pueblo. The mission structures are some of the finest architecture in New Mexico.

Meanwhile, the priests carried out their clerical duties, including the introduction of the Pueblos to the various aspects of a proper Roman Catholic life: baptisms, masses, marriages, and burials. Some Indians were taught to assist the priests and to perform lay teaching. One leader in each pueblo was given the responsibility of enforcing attendance at mass and maintaining the church and its grounds.

In 1620, the King of Spain issued a decree requiring each pueblo to choose annually by popular vote a governor, lieutenant governor, and whatever other officers were needed to conduct pueblo affairs—all of which was done under the close supervision of the Spanish church and civil authorities. Every governor was to receive a silver-headed cane, which would be passed on to his successor as a symbol of office. When Mexico replaced Spain in 1821, new silver-headed canes were given to the governors. In 1863, President Abraham Lincoln continued the custom by presenting each pueblo governor with a silver-crowned, black-ebony cane. Some of the canes have been lost over the years, but the rest are still displayed in the pueblos who preserved theirs.

In the accepted view of the time, a suitable conversion to Catholicism could only be accomplished by first obliterating what were considered to be heathen beliefs and practices and then replacing them with the Roman Catholic faith. Little thought was given to justifications for this, and none to explanations as to why the Pueblos should embrace a faith whose advocates performed so brutally as did the Spanish. Nor did the missionaries seek to understand the Pueblo religion. What could be seen was sufficient. The beliefs and practices were plainly idolatrous and, as Espejo reported, "devil worship."

The major ceremonies were the first to be attacked, and in particular the masked dances were prohibited. Naturally the Pueblo could in no wise give these up, and so they resorted to secret performances. When word of the rituals leaked out, the priests called upon the governor and his military organization to punish the offenders. Religious leaders were whipped, and some were executed. At regular intervals, Pueblo kivas and dwellings were raided to seize and burn Katcina paraphernalia, prayer offerings, and other ritual items. Under such coercion, the Pueblos began to practice the externals of Roman Catholicism, but they in no wise surrendered their beliefs. Concealment became an art, and it has continued to be so through the centuries.

Not every pueblo was inclined, however, to let the Spanish run them over. In 1650, six villages representing peoples along the full length of the Rio Grande—Taos, Jemez, Cochiti, San Felipe, Alameda, and Isleta—attempted to unite with the Apache to drive out the Spaniards. But the plot was discovered. Nine of the Pueblo leaders were hanged, and the others were pressed into slavery.

Compounding the problem for the Pueblos was the conflict that developed at this time between the church and the secular authorities as they began to vie for Indian services and produce. Perhaps out of spite, since it could hardly have been due to sympathy, the civil leaders began to oppose the suppression of the Pueblo rituals. During the 1650s, Governor Lopez announced publicly that the Katcina ceremonies were harmless, and he gave his official permission for them to be held. He also objected to the invasion of Pueblo homes and kivas and to the destruction of ritual paraphernalia. The priests were scandalized and indignant, and as so often happens in a quarrel, both sides vented their frustrations on the middleman, the seemingly helpless Pueblos.

From 1659 to 1669, Governor Mendizabal ruthlessly exploited Pueblo labor, and other civil officials joined him in this. The missionaries complained loudly that Pueblos were being taken away from their mission tasks and that in consequence church progress was being hampered. The secular agents countered by charging that missionaries were living in comfort at the expense of the Pueblos and were meting out excessive punishment to achieve their goals.

Midway through Governor Mendizabal's reign, the Pueblos knew they had to do something. A three-year drought began in 1665, and the Pueblos were certain it had occurred because their ritual cycle had been interfered with and the spirits were displeased; their suffering over this was such that anything would be better, even though they had by no means forgotten the earlier lessons at Tiguex and Acoma. The final straw came in 1675, when forty-seven Pueblo religious leaders were charged with witchcraft. Four were hanged, and the rest were publicly flogged in front of the Palace of the Governors in Santa Fe. Then they were imprisoned—although briefly, for a few days later a group of resolute Tewa warriors confronted Governor Juan Francisco Trevino and demanded their release. The simmering idea of a full-blown revolt came to a boil now, although they knew that failure would bring catastrophic consequences. Only a united effort by all the pueblos would rid them once and for all of the oppressors. It was an entirely new concept to be grasped, since pueblos were autonomous and no means had ever been desired to unite them. They desperately needed a leader, and one emerged in the person of a San Juan Pueblo medicine man named Popé, who made his headquarters at remote Taos.

Using the cover of an interrelated pueblo-wide ceremonial association, Popé was able to obtain the cooperation of villages throughout the eastern and western areas. Only Isleta, closely hemmed in by colonists, declined. August 11, 1680, was established as the target date, and messengers carrying knotted deer-hide cords were sent to all the pueblos to advise them. But when two Tesuque messengers carrying details of the uprising were captured on August 9, Tesuque officials notified Taos. The alarmed Popé sent other messengers out with instructions to the villages to proceed immediately with the execution of every priest and settler, and a Spanish official at Taos was summarily killed to set the stage.

Santa Fe sounded the alarm concerning the planned revolt, and some of the Spanish colonists fled south. It was a good thing, for at dawn on August 10, the Feast of San Lorenzo, Pueblos everywhere began to kill every Spanish priest and settler they could get their hands on. When the Tanoan Pueblos had disposed of their enemies, they converged in force on Santa Fe, where more than a thousand colonists had taken refuge. They laid siege to the city, and men from other pueblos soon joined them. After nine days of furious battle, and when water supplies were cut off, Governor Otermín decided it would be best to abandon the city and join other refugees that he knew were gathering at Isleta. His party set out, and the Pueblos let them go.

In the more central and southern pueblos a similar pattern of killing was followed. Priests and settlers who tarried were quickly put to death. Those who escaped headed for Isleta, and when the rumor reached that pueblo that every colonist north of Santo Domingo Pueblo was dead, even Isleta was abandoned by the Spanish. On August 14, 1680, refugees mounted their long trek south into Texas. The Isletans feared both the Spanish and their brethren now, and they too departed for safer places.

Otermín and his large party reached Isleta on September 3, only to find it empty. He sent word ahead for the earlier group to await his coming, and the two parties joined up on September 13, at Fray Cristobal. Together they proceeded on their way southward into Mexico. The Pueblos let the weakened and slowly moving mass of survivors go. Still, the revolt had been a bloody one. Twenty-one priests were dead, and perhaps three hundred and eighty colonists. Three hundred Tanoans died in the attack on Santa Fe, and forty-seven others that had been captured were executed by the Spanish. The missions, together with their furnishings and papers, were either burned or torn down. Spanish houses suffered the same fate, and some Spanish captives were taken.

The Pueblos who survived were free again, though, and it was a moment to celebrate. Kivas were repaired, and ceremonies and feasting took place. As quickly as possible the Pueblos returned to their old ways, and word went out that anyone who even uttered the name of Jesus would immediately be put to death.

The Pueblos should have known that the Spanish would not give up easily. In the winter of 1681–82, Otermín made an unsuccessful attempt to reconquer the Pueblos. He did learn, however, that the individual pueblos had abandoned their united front and returned to their separate roles. He also gained some understanding of why the revolt had occurred in the first place.

One of his more interesting findings was that warfare of this nature was so contrary to Pueblo views that it affected them internally. They began to bicker among themselves, and, before long, battles between some of the villages erupted. The people had become aware of something alien and disturbing, a taste for war, and they felt an uncommon kind of fear, one of the other.

A second and stranger ally would assist the Spanish in their desire to rule the Pueblos once again—the nomadic tribes. Once they realized that the pueblo villages and fields were no longer guarded by the Spanish, they increased the frequency of their raids into Pueblo country. Most of these raiders were Apache, Navajo, Ute, and Comanche, and before long the pueblos were wondering if it might not be well to have Spanish protectors back with them again.

After two other expeditions had failed in 1688 and1689 respectively, a new

338

governor, Don Diego de Vargas, entered Pueblo country in 1692. He received the formal submission of twenty-three villages, freed their Spanish captives, and returned to Mexico. Much of his success could be credited to the fact that Otermín's earlier punitive expeditions, while only partially successful, had killed several hundred Pueblos and pillaged their villages. In addition, many of the Indians, knowing retaliation was inevitable, had left their pueblos and retreated to more defensible sites in the mountains and mesas. Some of the Tanoans moved north into Tewa country, and other groups migrated northward into southern Colorado or west to Tusayan.

Examples of Rio Grande subterranean kivas. *Top,* Zia. *Middle,* Santo Domingo in 1880. The visible wall is higher now, and most of the vigas are not visible. *Bottom,* San Ildefonso. From Museum of New Mexico archive photographs.

A segment of the Pueblos entrenched themselves in Santa Fe, and when De Vargas came north again in 1693 with more than a thousand soldiers, colonists, and servants, he camped outside the city for two weeks, demanding their surrender. Finally tiring of this, he attacked in force and won the city easily, losing only a single soldier. His victory was partly due to the fact that certain Pueblo leaders outside the city, troubled by inter-pueblo dissension and by the aforementioned enemy Indian raids, wanted the Spanish back, although on new and fairer terms. With this in mind they aided De Vargas at Santa Fe, perhaps even persuading their Pueblo friends inside to capitulate, and then accompanied the governor to various pueblos to accomplish the same purpose.

The shrewd De Vargas seized his golden opportunity, promising forgiveness, amnesty, and joint efforts to end the threat of the raiding Indians. The Pueblos returned to their Rio Grande villages, and before long a relationship of sorts between the two adversaries had resumed.

Actually, De Vargas had no intention of keeping his promises, and he quickly executed seventy of the Pueblo leaders who had resisted him at Santa Fe. Entire Tanoan families were turned over to the soldiers and colonists as slaves, and the remainder of the Tanoans were dispersed among the northern pueblos. It was not long before conditions matched the pre-revolt stage. In 1694, the Tano and Tewa retreated to the top of Black Mesa, near San Ildefonso Pueblo. Sending war parties out from here, they harassed the Spanish settlements until finally De Vargas had no recourse but to lay seige to the mesa. After nine unyielding months a truce was reached, and the Pueblos returned to their villages.

Then, in 1696, a number of northern pueblos mounted a second revolt, this time killing five priests and a score of Spanish colonists and soldiers. They also burned several churches, and then retreated to the mountains. De Vargas' troops pursued the rebellious Pueblos and in time persuaded them to return to their villages. Some, who knew that retribution was certain to follow, fled westward. It was at this time that the Hano went to live with the Hopi.

With the advent of 1697, all the Rio Grande pueblos were adjusting for a second time to Spanish rule. It took longer to bring the more western pueblos to heel, and the Hopi would never again be under Spanish control. Thankfully, the Franciscan priests and the civil authorities began now to exercise more humane treatment of the Pueblo people, so that, year by year, relations became less and less tense. The encomienda, or assignment of Pueblos as servants to the Spanish, was also terminated.

Warfare with the Spanish and nomadic Indians, migrations, forced labor, and periodic smallpox epidemics had, by A.D. 1700, reduced the Pueblo population by about two thirds. Their number now was perhaps fifteen thousand, and many of these bore the scars of battle. There was also a drastic change in settlement pattern. The Piro villages in the south were entirely abandoned, as were the southern Tiwa settlements. Isleta was resettled, and Tiwa returning from Tusayan in 1741 founded Sandia Pueblo. The Tano were dispersed among their northern relatives. Some Keresans moved west in 1697 or 1698 to establish Laguna Pueblo. The Zuñi consolidated their several villages into one large town. The Hopi moved to the mesa tops, and we know what happened to Awatovi and other Jeddito valley sites.

Within their first century and a half of tormented adjustment to Spanish rule the Pueblo Indians had gained new skills, some domestic animals, and new plants. But they were not truly Christianized. Few if any of them understood or believed what the priests attempted by compulsion to teach them, and efforts to eradicate the native faith without the slightest attempt to understand it perplexed the Pueblos and made them all the more determined to maintain a lifeway they believed had proved itself over the centuries to be good. When they compared what they already had to what the Spanish missionaries offered—and to the rude manner of life exhibited by the Spanish—they chose to stay with what they had. Common sense did call for an accommodation. They would accept the externals of the Roman Catholic faith if the Spanish would let them carry on their traditional practices at the same time. The efforts to suppress their ceremonial rites did relax, and by the late 1700s the Pueblos were practicing, primarily in concealment, their native rituals.

This does not mean that church and civil oppression ceased, only that the methods were less brutal and the techniques changed. The church and civil officials continued to extort produce and labor from the Pueblos, and the Indians were once again the rope in the tug-of-war between the two. One of the greatest gains in relations with civil authorities came when the Pueblo and Spanish men were brought into a partnership to control nomadic Indians. For this purpose the Pueblos were supplied with arms and horses, and in time their military force outnumbered that of the Spanish.

Dozier points out that the non-Pueblo population of the Rio Grande area in the late eighteenth century was far from being uniformly Spanish. There were Mexican settlers, captured Indian servants, Indian servants obtained in trade with the Ute and Comanche, and mixed bloods resulting from Pueblos who joined the Hispanicized villages.[91] The additions swelled the New Mexican population considerably. According to O. L. Jones, in 1750 there were 3,779 settlers and 12,142 Pueblos. Fifty years later there were 18,826 settlers and 9,732 Pueblos.[92] New Mexico was on its way to becoming the impressive cultural melting-pot that it is today.

During the nineteenth century, this mixture of non-Pueblos, to which Dozier applies the name "Hispanos,"[93] shared with the Pueblos a considerable number of social and cultural traits, excluding, naturally, those features associated with the core culture of the Pueblos.

In 1812, twenty-six Rio Grande Pueblo villages and one hundred and two settler villages were being served by only twenty-two priests. Spain's power in the New World was steadily weakening, and the provinces were suffering accordingly as services in general declined. A few benefits from this did accrue to the Pueblos, the best of which had to do with the ownership of land.

Since the Anasazi of Tusayan, Zuñi, Acoma, and the middle Rio Grande were sedentary village dwellers as compared to the nomadic Indians, the Spanish described them as "Pueblos." And, because the Pueblos adopted some aspects of the Spanish culture and were baptized as Roman Catholics, land grants were assigned to them by the Spanish that were denied to other Indians. When the present New Mexico area became part of the Republic of Mexico in 1821, the Pueblos were allowed to keep their land grants, to become citizens, and to do with their land as they wished. This was not benevolence. The Mexican Government was simply too busy with its own internal affairs to pay attention to the Pueblos, and thus the priests were soon hampered and ineffective. Accordingly, there was a resurgence of traditional Pueblo religious practices at the same time that church associations deteriorated.

Relationships with the colonists became, on the other hand, friendly and cooperative. The divergent customs were respected, if not approved, and nearby communities of Pueblos and non-Pueblos worked together on projects of mutual consequence, such as water allocations. Retaliatory raids and defense measures became joint enterprises whenever the activities of Indian enemies required them. Faced by the threat of heavy taxes, the two joined in a revolt in 1837 against the Mexican governor. It was successful, but in just six months the Mexican Government was back in control again. With the outbreak of the Mexican War in 1846, the United States gained control of New Mexico. In 1847, Pueblos and Hispanos joined hands again to revolt against American occupation. This outbreak centered in the Taos area, and was very limited in scope.

The first Anglo-Americans to enter Rio Grande country were mountain men, trappers, and fur traders. They arrived in the area in the early 1800s, and by 1820 other Americans were following to take advantage of exciting new business opportunities. What is referred to as "the Santa Fe Trail" was opened, and Santa Fe became a major redistribution center in 1822. Soon thereafter, trade became an important aspect of New Mexican life, and it remained so until the railroads arrived in the last part of the nineteenth century. These were the Atchison, Topeka, and Santa Fe line serving in the southern Rio Grande area, and the Denver and Rio Grande line serving in the north.

The war between Mexico and the United States ended with the Treaty of Guadalupe Hidalgo, signed in 1848. In this, Mexico relinquished all claims to territory east of the Rio Grande, ceding the New Mexico and California territories to the United States of America. Certain articles of the treaty provided for recognition and protection of previously established Indian rights. Confusion about Indian land grants would, however, lead to continual problems, for few of the pueblos could produce the Spanish documents that established their original grants.

Meanwhile, the railroads brought an ever-increasing number of residents and tourists to New Mexico. These changed the land and economic system markedly and rapidly projected the Pueblos into the modern world. The transition was also accompanied by a recurrence of efforts to stamp out the "heathen" customs and practices of the Pueblos. During the first twenty years of the twentieth century, American missionaries and government officials became, in true "Spanish fashion," appalled at the religious views and rituals of the Pueblos. Indian Service personnel were instructed to put an end to the "immoral" and "indecent" acts. Whatever was contrary to accepted Christian standards was to be prohibited, and Indian leaders who encouraged ritual practices were to be "severely punished."

On April 26, 1921, Charles H. Burke, Commissioner of Indian Affairs, issued a directive to his reservation superintendents. It stated that the dances of the Indians tended to be too frequent and too long. They interfered with farming and family responsibilities and often contained "barbaric features." "It is not," he said, "the policy of the Indian Office to denounce all forms of Indian dancing. It is rather its purpose to be somewhat tolerant of pleasure and relaxation sought in this way or of ritualism and traditional sentiment thus expressed. The dance per se is not condemned. It is recognized as a manifestation of something inherent in human nature, widely evidenced by both sacred and profane history, and as a medium through which elevated minds may happily unite art, refinement, and healthful exercise. It is not inconsistent with civilization. The dance, however, under most primitive and pagan conditions is apt to be harmful, and when found to be so among the Indians we should control it by educational processes as far as possible, but if necessary, by punitive measures when its degrading tendencies persist."

Moreover, "the sun-dance (of the Plains Indians) and all other similar dances and so-called religious ceremonies are considered Indian Offenses under existing regulations, and corrective penalties are provided." "Similar dances" were defined by Burke as those involving "acts of self-torture, immoral relations between the sexes, the sacrificial destruction of clothing or other useful articles, the reckless giving away of property, the use of injurious drugs or intoxicants, and frequent or prolonged periods of celebration which bring the Indians together from remote points to the neglect of their crops, livestock, and home interests."

A supplement to this directive was issued on February 14, 1923. It mentions a conference held in October 1922 by missionaries of several denominations. Six recommendations made at the conference were included in the supplement, and some were ridiculous. One was "that the Indian dances be limited to one in each month in the daylight hours of one day in the midweek, and at one center in each district; the months of March and April, June, July and August being excepted." Another was "that none take part in the dances or be present who are under 50 years of age."

In his report to the Secretary of the Interior in June 1923, Burke again refers to the Indian dances, stating this time that "the main purpose, however, was to draw their (the Indians') attention more closely to the industrial necessity of making their own living; of caring for their crops and livestock; and of awakening in them a homemaking interest with higher ideals of family life."

According to this last report the measures outlined by Burke and the missionaries were only suggestions, yet the Pueblos could see their portent, and were alarmed and perplexed. They failed to understand how the whites missed the fact that Pueblo ceremonies have as their very aim and cause for being the propagation of crops and other things needful for sustenance and maintaining the family.

No matter, the punitive measures continued. The government boarding school became a principal tool in the destructive war waged against the traditional culture. Because they were taken great distances from their homes, it became increasingly difficult for children to maintain their cultural pride and ties. At first a few boys were released from schools for short periods to be instructed by tribal elders. Then the Commissioner, calling the Pueblos "half animal," ordered the practice stopped, even though the elders pleaded that as a result the Pueblo religion would die.[94] At the schools, the Indian students were compelled to receive the teachings of the Christian religion without the permission of parents and clans. Parents could not even select the denomination into which the child was being immersed. Little by little a wedge was driven between the child and the parent, between the native culture and the foreign culture. Meanwhile, the citizens of the United States exulted in the free enjoyment of liberty and property, in the free exercise of individually chosen religion, and in the championing of human rights.

At first the Pueblos were optimistic, friendly, and cooperative, for they wanted their children to be educated. They refused to believe that cultures so different as the Spanish and Anglo-American could find such agreement in cultural superiority and religious arrogance. But when more and more children were indoctrinated without parental consent, when they were denied the use of their native languages and customs in the boarding schools, and when the new missionaries invaded the pueblos to harass the people about the error of their ways, they finally got the message. Any thought of ever again opening the kivas to outsiders was dispensed with. The Rio Grande Anasazi retreated into a shell as solid and encompassing as that of the turtle or armadillo. It was the only way the people could remain what they were and adamantly preferred to be. It still is.

There is yet another aspect to the closed kiva whose basis is purely theological. We have already learned that at Hopi certain religious knowledge and secret ritual are not divulged to the uninitiated. All the Pueblos, especially those of the Rio Grande, believe that when religious secrets are imparted to those outside the cult, the "power" of the secrets depreciates, and the life of the informer is endangered.[95] Hence to request secret information from a Pueblo friend is the same as asking him to jeopardize himself seriously for one's own selfish desires.

New Mexico was finally admitted to the Union as a state in January 1912. In 1924, Congress declared that all Indians born in the United States were to be recognized as citizens. Nevertheless, the state of New Mexico excluded the Pueblos, as "Indians not taxed," from this status. Not until 1948 was legislation passed that allowed them to vote in the state as well as in the national elections.

Today, the Pueblo people still reside where the invading Europeans found them. They have experienced a great deal, and profound changes have occurred in their economy and in their relationships with outsiders. Time and foreign intrusion have left their indelible marks, yet the Pueblo have retained a remarkable part of their traditional culture, and they are intact as a people.

It should be emphasized that, as Joe S. Sando points out, while the pueblos are classified on the basis of social and cultural differences by anthropologists, the present-day pueblos continue to share a common traditional native religion, a common life style and philosophy, and a common economy.[96] There are variances in the way these things are treated and expressed, for every village is an entity in its own right. The people think of themselves accordingly. One is a "Santa Claran" or a "Santo Domingan" first, and a Pueblo second. But there is not the slightest question in their minds that they are "Pueblo," as distinct from other Indians, and they all live "as Pueblos do."

Based upon data obtained by the Commission on Indian Affairs of the State of New Mexico in 1972 and 1973, the "Eastern," or Rio Grande, Pueblos of today and their languages and populations are as follows:

VILLAGE	LANGUAGE	TOTAL POPULATION	PERCENT RESIDENT
Cochiti	Keresan	830	60
San Felipe	Keresan	1,820	70
Santa Ana	Keresan	490	80
Santo Domingo	Keresan	2,440	85
Zia	Keresan	560	80
Nambe	Tewa	360	50
Pojoaque	Tewa	120	50
San Ildefonso	Tewa	1,410	70
San Juan	Tewa	1,630	65
Santa Clara	Tewa	1,170	60
Tesuque	Tewa	280	75
Isleta	Tiwa	2,869	65
Picuris	Tiwa	180	55
Sandia	Tiwa	275	75
Taos	Tiwa	1,710	70
Jemez	Towa	1,890	70

Most of the villages enclose from one to four plazas, two being the most common number. The plazas are never paved and are used primarily for the public dance performances. In pueblos with more than one plaza, the dance is frequently repeated in each, so as to make a circuit of the village. Some plazas, such as those of San Felipe and Laguna, are square, others are rectangular areas, and Santo Domingo uses a wide street. This difference affects the way in which some dances are performed. For example, the Tablita dancers form a large circle in the villages with square plazas, and a long narrow oval in some other villages. At Santo Domingo they are able to perform more extensive and complex movements because of the space available.

The area closely surrounding the villages is irrigated for farming, and land plots are privately owned. Charles H. Lange says they can be acquired by inheritance, through trade or purchase, homesteading, or by petition to the governor for an idle plot.[97]

Community-owned structures within the pueblos include the kivas, community centers, ceremonial houses, society houses, and the church. Community ceremonial houses are used for meetings, rites, and dance practices. Society houses serve the same purposes for the secret societies.

As I have said earlier, the Keresan villages had and still have two circular surface kivas. It is generally believed that the Tanoan pueblos have one communal kiva, plus one or more kivas associated with the dual divisions of the society. According to Dozier, the Tewa villages have one large kiva and a smaller one or no second kiva. Nambe and San Juan hold masked performances in the large kiva. Both Tesuque moieties rehearse in the same kiva, but perform in the plaza, and San Juan and Nambe do the same. Factional disputes caused San Ildefonso and Santa Clara to cease intermoiety cooperation about 1900, and Santa Clara now follows a two-kiva pattern. In the Tewa pueblos, either separate surface rooms or the homes of association heads are used as meeting rooms.[98]

The large kiva used for communal purposes is sometimes called the "big kiva." Florence Hawley Ellis has traced the history of these in the Rio Grande area, and she published her findings in 1950. She defines the function of the big kivas as structures where community ceremonies are held, especially those that involve masked dancers of the Katcina Cult. Small kivas and ceremonial houses might also be present in a village, but they are associated with religious societies that have specific duties and restricted membership. Moiety houses are rooms where activities restricted to one moiety take place or where the group's ritual paraphernalia are stored.[99]

The church building is owned and maintained by the Indians, and native decorative motifs such as birds, corn, or cloud symbols adorn some of the edifices. At San Felipe and Santo Domingo the church nave is used to hold native dances after the Christmas Eve Mass.

Individually owned property includes houses, outdoor ovens, barns, sheds, corrals, and some outdoor toilets.

Traditional houses are made of adobe bricks with the walls plastered over. The outside walls are an earth color, but the inside walls are whitewashed. Roofs are flat and supported by wood beams called "vigas." Most homes have a corner fireplace. The floors are either of wood or of hard-packed adobe. Outside the houses and at several locations around the village are numerous horno ovens.

Newer houses are built away from the village center and have yards. Concrete block, wood, or adobe is used in their construction, and most of them are equipped with modern kitchens and bathrooms. All the houses have contemporary furnishings. The walls are adorned with Navajo rugs, Mexican shawls, baskets, family photographs, and pictures of Catholic saints or of Christ. Pueblo crafts are sometimes displayed, especially if the owner is an artist. Many Indian women still prefer a wood-burning stove to others. Indoor plumbing and electricity are available to most families in most, but not all, pueblos. Corn grinding bins are a thing of the past along the Rio Grande.

The outdoor horno, or baking oven, adopted from the Spanish.

As we have learned, the ancient Pueblo Indians grew corn, beans, squash, cotton, and tobacco. To these the Spanish added wheat, alfalfa, chili, and fruit trees. Fortunately, the Rio Grande Pueblos had their rivers and tributaries and were not solely dependent upon rain for the growth of their crops. They developed substantial irrigation systems, and it appears that these were in use long before the Spanish arrived.

At many pueblos there is an annual irrigation ritual that attends the work on the ditches. At the Tiwa village of Isleta, it begins with a ceremony performed to prevent invasions by grasshoppers. The Pueblos in general think that grasshopper plagues are caused by witches, usually those "of another town." They "plant" a Grasshopper chief whom his people will follow. The Isletan town father seeks to capture this chief before he can do any harm. "Witchcraft," says Parsons, "is a momentous and horrendous problem to all Pueblos." They are a danger that the medicine men and War chiefs must face and control. Witches are always lurking around while rituals and dances are being performed, and the War chiefs or captains must always be on the lookout for them.

Once the town chief catches the Grasshopper chief, he puts him in a ceremonial bowl and brings him back to the village, where the town fathers, War chief, and War captains, the chiefs of all the Corn groups and of the Directions, and women members of the Medicine Society hold a ritual designed to take away the Grasshopper chief's power and strength. This done, the irrigation work proceeds.

Townsmen clean and repair ditches as a communal service. In this connection rituals are performed to please the water spirits who control the flow and to appease the Earth and Water People who would otherwise be offended when the earth was "cut."[100] Labor on the ditches continues for three days, and those who refuse to help may be punished by the Kapo, or clowns. Exempted are the chiefs, who remain in retreat, fasting and continent. On the fourth morning the moiety chiefs deposit prayer feathers and other offerings, such as seeds, in the ditch to pay the Water People for the water they will let run through the ditch. After this there is a procession back to the village, where a dance is held using turtle rattles, for turtles are associated with the moieties and with water.[101]

A digging stick, a wooden hoe, and a pitchfork or shovel were once the only agricultural tools used by the Anasazi. After Spanish colonization, the wooden plow was adopted, and it was pulled by oxen, along with Spanish carts, called carretas. Spanish threshing methods were also put into practice for wheat and other grains. To form the threshing area, adobe and water were taken to a "flat and windy" spot where a hard-packed oval floor about 30 feet (9 m) in diameter was laid. A fence was erected around this, and sheaves of grain were piled on the floor to be tramped down by horses or burros. Grain was winnowed simply by using baskets to throw it into the air. The hand sickle was used to cut grain. Lange says that the first threshing machine was purchased by Cochiti in 1916, but acceptance of it came slowly. It was, after all, a white man's tool. It made no allowances for the living ties between man and nature, it had no knowledge of how Mother Earth feels when she is violated and of how to treat and thank her to appease the violation. The conservatives believed that mechanical breakdowns were caused by Earth Mother, who by this means expressed her displeasure. Today most of the pueblos own community tractors and other modern farming equipment.

As in the case of the preplanting rites just mentioned, rites attend the planting itself, the maturation process, the harvest, and the thanksgiving for produce. All these are considered in detail further on.

After the harvest, the Pueblos turn to hunting activities. Game-animal dances are held at the various pueblos throughout the winter months, and the animals impersonated in the dances reveal the animals that are important to the Pueblos religiously and economically. Buffalo, deer, antelope, mountain sheep, and elk most often appear in these dances. At dawn on the morning of the public dance, the animal impersonators in costume make their way down from the hills and into the village as men and boys fire guns into the air and chase the "animals" to simulate a hunt.

Actual hunting continues to involve ritualistic procedures, especially where deer are concerned. Until big game grew scarce, communal hunts were the normal way employed to capture deer, antelope, buffalo, elk, and mountain sheep. Sometimes a bear or a mountain lion was also included in a catch. In late fall, San Juan Pueblo turns from agriculture to hunting after the "sweeping of the deer earth navels." This ritual act is performed under the direction of the hunt chief. It includes a visit to a certain sacred area, where prayer feathers and sacred cornmeal are left at shrines to "encourage the deer" to pass over a transitional zone between their natural habitat and the lowlands. At Cochiti, the eyes of the "stone lions" are sometimes sprinkled with red ocher to increase the hunter's vision and to bring good luck.

Hunting usually continues until February, when the planting season begins again. There are restrictions upon hunting after this time. Ortiz says the restrictions are ecologically important, since they prevent the destruction of female animals with young.[102]

In former times, hunts along the Rio Grande were accompanied by elaborate ritual, but by 1930 very few people were hunting, especially in a communal sense,[103] and the hunting societies no longer existed. Lange draws heav-

Left, opening the ditches at Jemez Pueblo. *Right*, a Rio Grande kisi, used as a drying rack and as a work shelter.

ily upon the reports given by Bandelier in his journal of 1880 to formulate a picture of what remained then of the ancient hunting practices, and the account is well worth reading, although it is much too long even to summarize here.

Present-day hunts are often communal activities involving drives or surrounds. Rabbits, gophers, and ground squirrels can be hunted in this manner within close range of the village. Some communal hunts are specifically designed to procure meat for the village chief. Other hunts permit women to run after the dead animals and claim one, regardless of who shot it. Later the fortunate woman makes a gift of food to the hunter to show her appreciation.[104]

Early weapons were atlatls, clubs, and then bows, arrows, and lances. As the use of firearms became more popular, individual hunting replaced most of the communal efforts. However, community hunts are still held periodically at Santo Domingo and elsewhere, although hunting activities and the associated ceremonies continue to decline.

Buffalo were hunted occasionally in the Pecos drainage and on the plains to the east, and pueblos would join forces. The expeditions also afforded the Pueblos contact with the Plains Indians, and certain of the dances and songs are the only remnants of this contact. Gertrude Kurath thinks the Pueblo Buffalo Dance and some others may have been influenced by the Comanche or other Plains Indians who venerated and mimed the animal. She adds, however, that while the headdresses and costumes for some of the Pueblo Buffalo dances are of Plains materials and inspiration, the actual dance form and style are typically Puebloan.[105]

Some dead animals, such as deer, are ceremonially treated. At Isleta the bones are handled in a prescribed manner, a string with prayer feathers attached is tied between the antlers, and the bodies are sometimes decorated with a woman's manta and turquoise, because the hide is to be given to a woman for her moccasins. Every visitor to the hunter's house will ritually draw breath from the deer and will sprinkle it with cornmeal from a basket. The town chief, hunt chief, and all relatives will receive a piece of venison, which brings good luck and assures more deer in the future.[106] Deer killed for meat to be used in a ceremony must be smothered, so that they die without bloodshed.[107] Every part of an animal is used. Skins and furs are often worn as parts of ceremonial costumes; in particular, there is an ongoing need for fox and skunk skins for dance costumes.

Lange states that while most of his older informants were aware of the methods employed by the Hopi to capture eagles, they seldom followed them. "It was too dangerous." Some did dig eagle pits and use bait, but at Cochiti the usual ways were to kill the eagles with weapons, to catch them in traps, or, infrequently, to capture the young birds in their nests. And, while eagles were cherished for their feathers, the Cochiti informants could not remember a captive eagle in the pueblo.[108] Nevertheless, there are photographs taken in the 1920s of captive eagles in other Rio Grande pueblos. Eagles, like other birds, are caught for their feathers. They are not eaten.

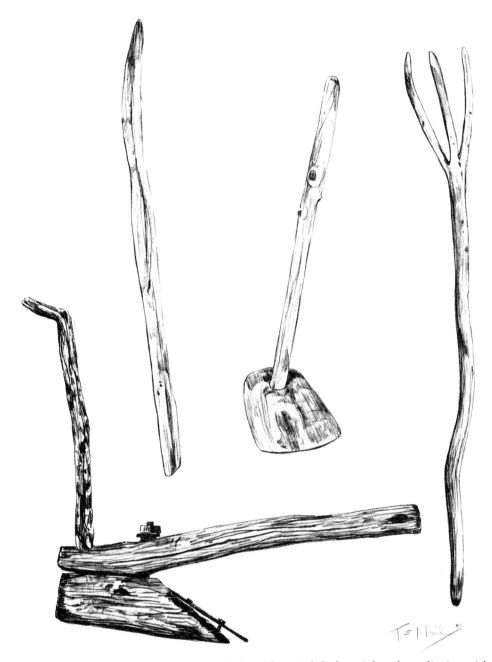

Wooden farming implements from the early Spanish period. Left to right, plow, digging stick, hoe, pitchfork. From the Museum of New Mexico collection.

Trading is still an aspect of pueblo economic activity. Most of this, however, is confined today to the patron saints' day dances. In particular, a great deal of trading occurs during the celebrations at Laguna, Zia, Jemez, and Taos. The Navajo who come to watch the dances bring rugs, jewelry, and sheep. The Apache bring beadwork and dried deer meat. The Spanish bring fruit, chili, and sheep. The Pueblos have food, pottery, and jewelry to trade or sell. Pueblo dancers at San Felipe emphasize the pleasure derived from trading by dressing on occasion as visiting Navajo traders. They hang small objects they

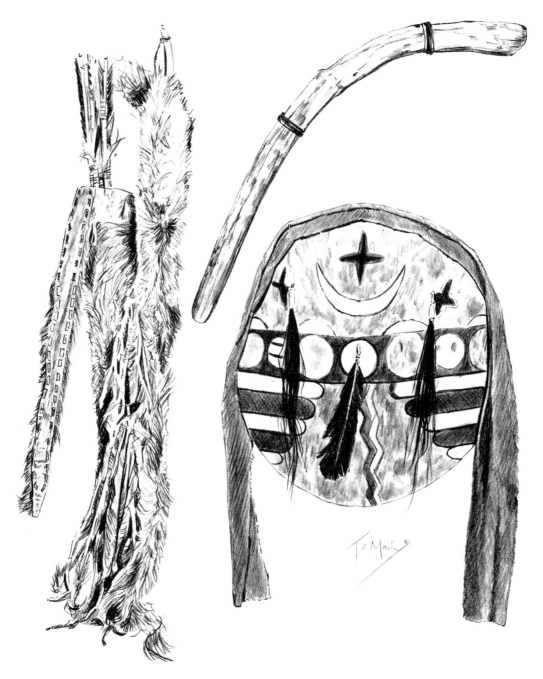

Hunting and warfare items. Left to right, mountain lion bow case and quiver with beaded pendant; wooden fending or throwing stick; bull-hide shield from Middle Rio Grande. From the Museum of New Mexico collection.

would like to trade from their belts, and the spectators offer them money or goods in lively barter.

As a rule, trading became progressively less frequent when the Pueblos began to function on a cash system and when agriculture and hunting were no longer the primary economic activities. Government offices and projects, as well as city jobs, offered new possibilities for wage work, and it became easier to earn cash with which to purchase food and clothing. The advent of the automobile permitted tourists to visit the villages, and Pueblos to visit the

Captive eagles whose feathers are used for ceremonial purposes.

nearby cities. As a result, Pueblo Indians also became more dependent upon the cash system for the sale of crafts, which include pottery, some basketry, textiles, jewelry, carving, and painting.

Most of the household utensils used by the Pueblos are store-bought, but pottery remains a prime source of income for the residents of some villages.

Rio Grande pottery is manufactured in much the same fashion today as it was centuries ago. The potter's wheel is not used, and with few exceptions pottery is made by women.

Clay is dug from special beds and is later pulverized, sifted, and stored. Pottery is usually made during the summer, since in cold months it dries poorly and firing is hazardous. When a potter is ready to begin, the processed clay is mixed with a grit or temper. In some pueblos this is fine sand, in others it is ground sherds. The mixture of clay, temper, and water is then kneaded to whatever consistency is desired. The base is molded in the hand, and the walls are constructed by building up successive layers of rope-like coils of clay. When it is ready, the vessel walls are scraped to a uniform smoothness with gourd-fragment scrapers. Today such modern conveniences as emery sandpaper have been adopted by some potters.

When the pot is smooth and dry, the surface is slipped with a finely ground clay-and-water mixture that has the consistency of thin soup. Smooth river pebbles and pieces of leather or cloth are then used to polish the surface. Before they are fired, ceramics are sometimes heated in the oven of a wood range to reduce the danger of cracking. Firing is hot work, and it is usually done early in the morning. Most pottery is still fired in a homemade oven over a low-burning fire. For this, the potters use grates, sheets of iron, old washtubs, or wire mesh. Cakes of dried animal manure and sometimes corncobs are placed over and around the vessels and lit. However, neither flame nor fire is allowed to touch the pottery during firing, or it will be smudged. As a rule, the firing lasts less than three hours, and an approximate temperature of 1500° Fahrenheit is reached.

One exception to this ancient firing method is found in the use of electric kilns by some young students in school classes. Another exception is the black pottery produced at San Ildefonso and Santa Clara pueblos, which is created by smothering the fire with finely ground manure. The smothering causes a "reducing" atmosphere in which the trapped carbon causes the surface of the pottery to turn black.

Surface treatment is the principal means of identifying the source of any piece of traditional pueblo pottery. Highly polished wares are produced by the Tewa pueblos of San Juan, Santa Clara, and San Ildefonso, where the slip is polished prior to firing. San Juan red ceramics are also noted for their incised-design elements, which are usually geometric and confined to the top third of the vessel. Sometimes, mica flecks are present in the clay. Taos and Picuris are known for the use of mica clays in their nonpolished pottery.

Santa Clara pottery is noted for its surface treatment both in color and design, which includes an unmistakable "bear paw" imprint and a deeply carved serpent design. Santa Clara and San Ildefonso are especially distinctive for their blackware, produced by the "reducing" atmosphere just described. Members of the Tafoya and Naranjo families are among the particularly well-known Santa Clara potters.

The best known of the San Ildefonso potters are Maria Martinez and the other members of her family: Julian, Popovi Da, and Tony Da. Maria is credited with the rediscovery of black pottery. This is classified as a "rediscovery" because blackware had been produced a century earlier in the Tewa villages. Maria was also instrumental in influencing pueblo potters to sign their work. She no longer produces pottery, but her earlier creations included such styles as red-on-black, red-ware, blackware, and polychrome. It is reported that Maria never decorated her pottery, that decoration was first done by her husband, Julian, and later by Popovi Da. Popovi Da is generally credited with popularizing pottery with a sienna or tan color. He and Tony Da are also noted for their use of silver, turquoise, and a stone called heshi as decorative materials on pottery. There are many other well-known San Ildefonso potters, including Blue Corn, Adam, and Santana.

Also distinctive are the white wares from Cochiti, Zia, and Santo Domingo pueblos. Common shapes are the bowl, jar, and olla, and the color and design

Examples of Rio Grande Pueblo pottery of the 1880–1900 period. *a*, Santo Domingo. *b*, San Ildefonso. *c*, Cochiti. *d*, Santa Clara. *e*, San Juan. *f*, Tesuque. *g*, Santa Ana. *h*, Zia.

styles vary to distinguish each pueblo's work. All these pueblos use a white background, on which the design elements are superimposed. In addition to the vessel forms, bird, animal, and human figurines are modeled by potters in the three pueblos. Figures of seated women with children are called "storyteller" dolls. The most famous doll maker is the Cochiti potter Helen Cordero.

Most of the painted decoration of the pottery is done prior to firing. However, at Jemez and Tesuque pottery is often painted after firing, and in some cases even sun-dried, unfired pottery is painted. Moreover, the paint is a water-based poster paint, which smears when rubbed with a moistened cloth.

Only a few people know the art of basketmaking today, and they are seldom active in the craft. Those who are include men and women. All the baskets are wide, shallow, and loosely woven from the long leaves of the amole, or soapweed. A willow rod, bound in the shape of a hoop, serves as the rim foundation of a basket. The leaves are soaked in water to make them pliable, and they are laid on a flat surface. They are then interwoven at right angles to one another to produce a simple twill. The weaver places his feet on the finished portion to hold the leaves in place while he completes the remainder. The hoop is incorporated by bending the yucca leaves upward to form a basin. The leaves are then wrapped and tied around the rim and trimmed off evenly to form a simple fringe on the outside. The baskets receive no decoration. The average diameter is 20 inches (50.8 cm), the average depth 5 inches (12.7 cm).[109]

The principal outlets for Pueblo arts today are individual sales at the pueblos, art shows by the better-known artists and families, shop and gallery sales, and the large group shows. The annual festivals of Santa Fe and the Eight Northern Pueblos are major outlets, as is the State Fair at Albuquerque.

The arts and crafts are creative and social outlets, as well as sources of economic gain. The pueblos have other diversions, although these all fit within the religious sphere. Even games are given to the people by the deities, and they serve dual purposes: they entertain, but at the same time they bring needed blessings when performed in the traditional ways. On the other hand, to play the games incorrectly or out of season can offend the supernaturals and cause them to withhold blessings.

At certain times during the summer, usually on saints' days, the Pueblo men will ride their horses from house to house collecting items to use as prizes for a chicken-pull contest. After the gifts are collected, the men assemble near the church. A live chicken or one of the gifts is given to a horseman, who gallops off while the other horsemen chase after him and try to grab the chicken or gift. The winner is the man holding what is left of the chicken or gift when time is called. The race is then repeated until all the chickens or other prizes are gone.

I witnessed a second variation of the "Chicken Pull" at Santo Domingo on Thursday, July 25, 1974. By 2:30 P.M. about a hundred men and boys were riding around the village and in the open area near the church where the "pull" was later held. They made an exciting display. The horses were regal, the older men wore bright scarves and headbands, the young men either let their long hair fall loose and flowing or bound it in a *chongo.* Some men had blankets wrapped around their waists.

In the first competition, the contestants sought to take a twisted piece of cloth away from one another. This was an elimination procedure to cut down the size of the group. A man standing near the church gave the cloth to a rider who raced away with the others in hot pursuit. He used the cloth for a quirt, while a drummer beat on his drum, another man rang the church bell, and the spectators called out encouragement. This kept up until a pursuer captured the cloth. The men rode as though desperate, the horses running wildly into one another and rearing up as they crowded together. The race appeared to be somewhat distinguished by age groups, into older men, youths, and boys. Everyone whooped and called out as he rode, and the chase continued for at least forty-five minutes.

After the struggle, the men still remaining in the contest lined up by the church, and eight chickens were brought out. Although a chicken was alive when they first received it, two men would wrestle to gain control of it, one holding the head, the other the feet, and the feathers flew. The eight pairs of men who received the chickens were mounted, and they struggled so hard to get it that two men fell off their horses. Winners would take what was left of the chickens and either give it to someone in the crowd or ride with it to someone's house. All in all, horses and men became a bloody mess, which is supposed to bring good luck.

Boys aged about five to twelve, in groups numbering ten to fifteen, were also given chickens. They fought so hard that the chickens were virtually destroyed, but a proud winner always rode off with whatever fragment remained to make a gift of it to someone special.

A third variation of the contest is to hang the chickens, one at a time, on a rope stretched between two poles. When the riders race for the bird it is hoisted up to make it harder to get. This continues until one of the men is able to stretch high enough or is fast enough to get the chicken.

These are festive events, and clowns mounted on horses and donkeys frequently appear to increase the enjoyment of everyone present.

Relay races are another form of recreation, but with distinctly religious overtones. Most of them are run to "keep the sun moving."[110] Young men hold the races at San Juan at the time of the summer solstice and close to the autumnal equinox at Taos and Picuris.[111] September 30, San Geronimo Day, is Taos' favorite day for such races, and many of these have been seen by tourists. On the evening before the race two groups of men wearing breechclouts and carrying cottonwood boughs hold a dance on the straight racetrack. Night-long rituals are held in the kivas, and the next morning the dance is repeated. The race follows. Half of each relay team stands at one end of the track, with managers to choose the runners and start them off. The first two runners run the length of the track and then take their place at the rear of their team line as men from the front of the line take off on the return lap, and so on, until one team laps the other. Runners wear tufts of down feathers "to make them light." When the race ends, the runners dance down the length of the track, and the women throw food to them. The *chiffonetti* are prominent at Taos on race day, and reference is made to their performances further on in the Taos material.

At Isleta, the racing season opens about March 15 with the town chief's relay races "for Sun." According to Parsons' informant, it is said that "the town chief is going to clothe the Sun (give him prayer sticks) and help him run; that is why they run east and west." She adds that the permanent racetrack of Isleta, like those of all the Tanoans, "the road belonging to our Father Sun," lies east and west.[112] Rituals follow in the moiety house, and the unusual practice of planting prayer sticks at night is carried out to "pay Sun for the race next day." Witches are always abroad at night, and any ritual held outdoors after sundown must be carefully guarded. Since "black magic" is sometimes used during a race, a special medicine water is drunk by the runners and sprinkled on them to make them strong and protected.[113] The town chiefs' races for Sun and Moon are followed by a race for Corn groups, but with less ritual and with wagering on the outcome.

Parsons informs us that racing and war are conceptually related by the Pueblos. At Isleta, for example, on the day of a race a War Dance may be performed as well as a scalp ritual in the Round House where scalps are kept and where offerings are made to the Navajo dead. At this time also, the return of the war party is sometimes dramatized.[114] Since this material pertains to 1940, it suggests continuations of the practices well into modern times, but if they are performed today it is probable that vastly altered forms of ritual are being used.

The ancient game of "shinny" is still played in the spring by men, women, and children. The game, similar to hockey, is played with a curved stick and, for religious purposes, a ball made of deerskin that is stuffed full of seeds. Like the foot races, the game is played to make the waters run. Two groups of men, one from each moiety, run across the fields propelling the ball with their sticks. There is no goal. The game ends when the ball finally breaks and the seeds scatter. The spilling of the seeds is considered a portent of good crops. The Tewa and other Tanoans also play shinny just for pleasure, but on such occasion they stuff the ball with deer hair rather than seeds.[115]

Several other forms of spring ball games are reported by Underhill[116] and, in many of these, teams of women play against teams of men. The Tiwa make a ball of new leaves, which the teams attempt to keep in the air. The team that drops it loses. At Isleta, a game fairly reminiscent of baseball is played with a buckskin ball stuffed with feathers.

There are games played with sticks and stones, bows and arrows, darts, dice, wooden reeds, hidden ball, and more. However, tabus and superstitions are extended even to the commonest games and acts. For example, Pueblo children often play marbles or jacks. But these games should only be played during the winter, since they use "cold-producing minerals." All games are associated with the proper season, just as dances are.[117]

SOCIAL ORGANIZATION

The family remains today the basic social unit of the Rio Grande pueblos. The household may include a widowed parent, a married son or daughter, and their children, and sometimes an adopted child. If both parents work, the children are often cared for by the grandmother or older siblings.

THE CLAN

Clan development among the Rio Grande villages ranges from the pronounced system of the Western Keres to nonexistence at the Tiwa pueblos. Between these two extremes, the Eastern Keres maintain a slightly active clan system, and Parsons says that while the Tewa clans exist, they are ceremonially insignificant.[118] Keresan clans are exogamous, but except for Cochiti the rule is not strictly followed. The Tewa say that clans do not affect marriage choice in any way. Lange believes that with the continuing deaths of older traditional people, clan rules of marriage (and clans themselves) will hold increasingly less significance, and that the incest rules of Roman Catholicism will become in time the only determinant for marriage.[119] As at the western pueblos, clans are named after plants, animals, and natural phenomena.[120] As the clans gradually became less important in Tewa and Keresan pueblo villages, the curing rites of clans, clan races, and clan work activities declined also. Goldfrank says there is no direct relation between clan and society membership, but that there is a tendency for members of a family to affiliate with the same society.[121]

THE MOIETY

A dual moiety system is the primary unit of pueblo social and ceremonial organization. Moieties divide the residents of a pueblo into two large groups rather than several clan groups; they do so for ceremonial rather than kinship purposes. The dual, or moiety, divisions of the Rio Grande Tanoan and Keresan pueblos are completely without kinship ties. The Tewa moieties are called "Summer" and "Winter." The Keres refer to their sides as the "Pumpkin" (or "Squash") and the "Turquoise." Summer or Pumpkin moieties are related to the south, femininity, and plant life. The Winter or Turquoise People are related to the north, masculinity, and minerals. This dualism is apparent in the management and conduct of political, social, and ceremonial activities.[122]

A moiety has its associated kiva, and every initiated member of the village belongs to one of the two divisions. An individual usually belongs to his father's moiety. However, a Tewa woman normally changes to her husband's side by undergoing, as she did while a child, three moiety-specific rituals of "water giving, water pouring, and finishing all over again." When the next water-giving ritual is held, her mother-in-law "adopts" her, she acquires a new ceremonial sponsor, and she is given a new name appropriate to the moiety.[123]

Moieties perform differently in the dances held at different Tewa villages. At San Ildefonso every group has its own plaza and kiva, and the two moieties will often perform different dances on the same day. They sometimes execute the dances simultaneously, and although they can be heard the village over, the different songs and drumbeats never seem to confuse the dancers. At San Juan and Tesuque the two moieties dance together and use the same dance kiva and plaza.

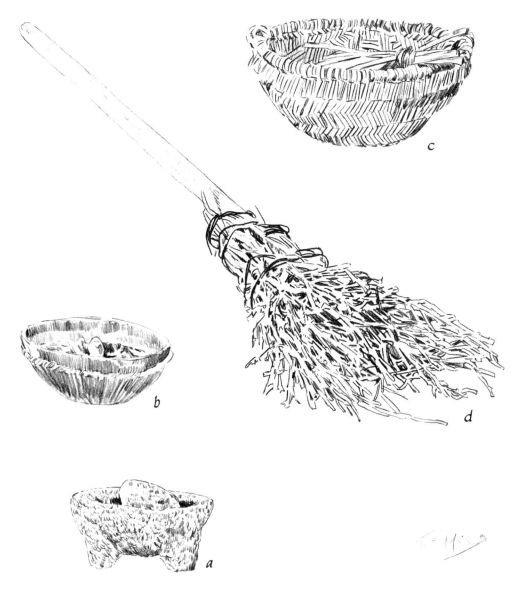

Household items, ca. 1860. *a*, stone grinding bowl. *b*, food dish. *c*, woven basket. *d*, wooden broom consisting of handle with bundle of sticks attached. From the Museum of New Mexico collection.

At the Keresan villages, the moieties usually alternate in dancing the Tablita Dance. The Turquoise People dance first, and it is they who decide when the last dance will be. Each moiety has its own kiva, drummer, and chorus. A healthy rivalry is common, and the dancing groups seek to surpass each other in the perfect execution of the dance patterns. The moieties can always be distinguished in Corn dances, first by the color of the men's body paint, which is commonly yellow or pink for the Pumpkin and blue or gray for the Turquoise moiety, and second by the tablita worn by the women. The Pumpkin tablita often has white breath feathers attached, and the Turquoise tablita has gray feathers. At times only one moiety will hold a dance. The Buffalo Dance at Santo Domingo is an example.

In addition to the family, clan, and moiety bonds, ties are formed between the child and his ceremonial sponsor and godparents. There are also comrade relationships.

GOVERNMENT

The current political organization of the pueblos is a blend of native and Spanish systems, in which sacred and secular leaders play featured roles. In the native system, the head of the village is the cacique. While the Keres have only one cacique, the Tiwa and Tewa villages have two, a cacique who controls ceremonial affairs during the spring and summer, and a cacique who is in charge during the fall and winter. Caciques hold office for life, and except for selecting officers in certain instances deal only with religious functions. They are never asked to involve themselves in secular decisions, since they need to "be at peace" while organizing religious rites and the dances that are performed throughout the year. A cacique who neglects his duties can be punished only by the war captains.

War captains serve as the executive arm in the native system. There are usually two, and they represent the Twin War Gods. War captains are selected by the cacique on an annual basis. Their duties are numerous. They set the dates for some dances, and it is their responsibility to notify, through their assistants, the composers, singers, and dancers. At the proper time, the assistants summon the male dancers to four evenings of practice, after which the females are called to rehearse for four evenings.

War captains must also punish violators of religious regulations during the public dances. The place an outsider is allowed to stand in while viewing a dance depends on the type of dance and when it is performed. At patron saint's day dances visitors can usually stand close. However, during a Koshare Initiation Dance at Santo Domingo, a non-Indian may be asked to watch from the far end of the plaza. In the same way, when Santo Domingo's Buffalo Dance is held at Christmas, tourists may stand near, but during the February performances the public keeps its distance. The War captains check for visitors seeking to use cameras or sketch pads when dances are going on. If cameras are forbidden and one is found, it is taken away, the film is destroyed, and a fine is imposed for the violation.

The secular government structure is given for each village as this is described in the material immediately following, but as a rule the Spanish system provided for a governor, lieutenant governor, sheriff, sacristan, ditch bosses, and fiscales. All these officers serve for one year only, and they are chosen by the cacique and council. Governors were originally chosen for their ability to deal with Spanish and American government officials. According to Dozier, the governor regulates the peddlers who come to sell at the village, and he works with the Indian Service officials and the All-Pueblo Council. The lieutenant governor assists the governor, the sheriff deals with secular offenses, and ditch bosses oversee the communal cleaning of the irrigation ditches each spring. Fiscales are responsible for mission activities and work with the priests. There is a secular council made up of former governors, lieutenant governors, and war captains, which serves as a check on the authority of the secular officers. Also there is a council of ceremonial priests who deal with religious matters.

Ortiz states that the political system handles social control on two levels. The governor and the secular council serve as a court of law for legal crimes and misdemeanors, such as drinking, fighting, or stealing, and the war captains deal with antisocial acts that break with religious customs and responsibilities.

The list of native and Spanish-derived government officials for each pueblo is given in the next chapter.

THE ANASAZI-PUEBLO VILLAGES OF THE RIO GRANDE

KERESAN

Five eastern pueblos speak Keresan. They are San Felipe, Santa Ana, Santo Domingo, Zia, and Cochiti.

The present-day Keresan councils consist of the governor and his staff. The staff includes one lieutenant governor, governor's helpers, a War chief and helpers, fiscale and helpers, and ex-governors (who are all permanent members). Also included as council members are interpreters and a town crier at Santo Domingo, the mayordomos at Santa Ana, and interpreters at Cochiti.[124]

At Cochiti, the governor and lieutenant governor are nominated by the Giant Curing Society.[125] The War captain and first lieutenant are nominated by the Flint Curing Society. The fiscal and his lieutenant are nominated by the Cikame Curing Society. All these are presented by the head men of the societies to the caciques for their approval. The governor, fiscal, three of the head men, and the War captain are always selected from kivas different from those of their first assistants. The six fiscal helpers and the six helpers of the War captain are nominated and elected by the caciques. Half belong to the Squash group, and half to the Turquoise group.[126]

San Felipe Council officers are selected by the cacique, with the assistance of two society heads.[127]

At Santo Domingo, the War chief and his helpers are appointed by the Flint Society, and the other officers by the Cikame Society.[128]

Santa Ana's main officers, including the ditch boss, are chosen by the cacique, but it is not known whether he or the head men select the helpers for each office.[129]

At Zia, the cacique solicits the advice of the Giant and Cikame societies in choosing the council officers. The names are then presented to the principales for their approval. Aberle says that one War chief is chosen from each kiva group.[130]

When Bertha Dutton was studying the Rio Grande Keresans fifty years ago, she learned that dialectical differences were less pronounced than those between the western (Hopi, Zuñi, Laguna, Acoma) and eastern groups (Cochiti, Santo Domingo, San Felipe, Santa Ana, and Zia). Fundamentally, there were many similarities between the two groups, but time, contact with European cultures, and intermixture with other Indian peoples had brought about notable variances. The Spaniards had exerted more influence upon the Eastern Keresans than upon the Western. The Spanish language was found to be used much more in the Rio Grande valley than in the western villages. The utilization of chili, which was used extensively by the Spaniards as a food product, followed a similar concentration. The Eastern Keresans had remained more conservative, had adhered more tenaciously to their old customs; the Western had been more progressive.

Common to both groups was the legend of their emergence from Sipapu, a great underground chamber in the North, where their mother, Nauziti (Beautiful Corn), still dwelt, and with her the hero twins, Masewi and Oyoyowi. From Sipapu the people migrated southward and settled in the localities where they were now found. Both groups had prominent secret orders, or Medicine societies, the organization of which seemed to be fundamentally the same. They appeared to hold relatively uniform ideas as to the cause and cure of diseases.

While the eastern towns were divided into moieties, with an apparent lessening of the importance of clanship, the western villages did not have the dual divisions, and stress was laid on the clans. Probably because of its conservatism, as well as to its being the largest pueblo of the Rio Grande Keresans, Santo Domingo had the greatest number of clans. Aside from the fact that the larger villages had more clans, there appeared to be little difference in clan distribution. The clans were matrilineal and exogamous.

Pueblo endogamy was still strongly favored, despite the tendency to break down the custom, which had resulted chiefly from the young peoples' attendance at government boarding schools. Exogamy did inject some friction into the families concerned.

The Keresan pueblos of the Rio Grande valley each had two kivas, or ceremonial chambers; these were circular and aboveground. (This was changed for a time. An internal division in 1947 led to the burning of one Zia kiva, but it was later replaced.[131])

Dutton says that the native Keresan costume remained far more constant among the women than it did with the men. There was a noticeable similarity in the garb of the women. It consisted of the traditional manta of natural black wool, stitched together (formerly with yucca, in place of the bright-colored wools of today) over the right shoulder, with the left shoulder exposed. It was now woven only by the Hopi Indians. Prior to the latter half of the nineteenth century, no other garment was worn, but the traders then introduced un-bleached muslin, and the wealthier Pueblo women began to fashion night-gown-like undergarments. These led to the blouse-underskirt garments that were first seen about this time. Woven belts, and moccasins of cowhide with deerskin uppers, formerly completed the female attire, while a simply de-signed blanket served as wrap. Since the 1880s jewelry had come to be com-monly worn—silver, coral, and turquoise being the favorite. Colorful scarves, embroidered aprons, and bright shawls had been added to the costume. Man-ufactured shoes and cotton hose frequently took the place of moccasins and leggings. In the main, the men had adopted the commercially manufactured trousers or overalls of their white brothers, with shirt and coat of the same source, although homemade shirts of attractive prints were also seen, and a blanket might take the place of a coat. Many of the older men still wore their hair long, and if so it was usually bound into a *chongo* at the nape of the neck. A colorful kerchief usually served as headband and did away with the neces-sity of a hat. Some of the men wore moccasins, others ordinary shoes or cow-boy boots. After attendance at government schools away from the pueblos, many of the younger generation dressed in the usual American fashion "at least for a while."[132]

San Felipe Pueblo

San Felipe is Spanish for St. Philip. The Pueblo name for the village is Ka-tishya. It is situated on the west bank of the Rio Grande, about thirty miles north of Albuquerque and five miles south of Santo Domingo Pueblo. It is thought that the present village was built sometime during the early part of the eighteenth century.[133]

San Felipe is among the most conservative of the present pueblo groups. The main portion of its adobe village encloses a large central plaza. Of late, there has been considerable building away from the village proper, with new dwellings scattered along the east bank of the river. The central plaza is unu-sual in that it is sunken, the dance area proper being three feet or more below the ground level of the banks and dwellings surrounding it. This bowl-like setting for the splendid and sensitive dances performed by the residents af-fords one of the best spectator facilities of all the pueblos. Some think the dance floor has been worn down by dancers. It is a nice thought, but since that has not happened even slightly in pueblos of far greater longevity, it is probably not so. The plaza may have been excavated to provide for a ball court or something else.

The circular surface kivas of the village are situated outside the main plaza, one north, and one east. A second dance area, not enclosed and not really a plaza, lies southeast of the main plaza.

Parsons states that in A.D. 1540, Katishya was situated at the foot of Black Mesa. (He derived this information from Spanish documents.) After the Revolt of 1680, in which San Felipe took part because the town had been sacked and the kivas burned by the Spanish, the residents moved to the top of Black Mesa and built a pueblo at its very edge. Strangely enough, it was then attacked by the people of Jemez Pueblo, as well as by those of other pueblos, reputedly because it had given refuge at one time to a missionary fleeing from Cochiti. Within a decade or two the harassed mesa village was abandoned, and the people moved back to the Rio Grande valley to settle on the western side of the river. Eventually a bridge was built to make a connection between the western and eastern banks. Today the town is easily closed off when Katcina dances are held by the simple expedient of blocking the bridge.[134]

In the 1930s, Hewett found San Felipe to be a large and well-preserved Keresan town, numbering 603 inhabitants. The people were as conservative in their views as their neighbors at nearby Santo Domingo. They spoke an identical tongue, did little with any of the ancient arts, but were fairly well-to-do, their land being fertile and well watered. Their ceremonies were among the finest to be seen, if, he says, one could be so fortunate as to find out when they occurred. It seems the residents had succeeded in keeping some of their most interesting "public" dance dates quite unknown. Hewett thought that one of the best of all surviving examples of early Franciscan architecture was to be seen in the old church at San Felipe.[135] It is south of the main plaza.

The town population was 784 in 1948, and today it is 1,820. Modern arts and crafts are virtually absent from the pueblo.

Santa Ana Pueblo

Santa Ana is Spanish for St. Anne. The Pueblo name for the village is Tamaya. It is on the north bank of the Jemez River, about eight miles northwest of Bernalillo. It was probably founded about A.D. 1700, and its buildings are constructed of stone masonry and adobe. The population was 228 in 1948, and the pueblo members number about 500 today.

Hewett describes the Tamaya of 1930 as being "set down in the midst of the sand dunes on the north side of Jemez creek, with but little tillable land nearer than the Rio Grande valley, six miles away." He says it numbered 242 people, and that the population was slowly increasing. The town of that time was practically abandoned during the "cropping" season. Except on fiesta days, all the people, with the exception of a few old men who served as guards, were in the camps and lookouts near the fields. Santa Ana sat across the dunes and quicksands some miles from the highway and consequently was left alone, which was exactly what the people wanted. This village, Hewett says, with its neighbor Zia above, "is as fine an example of human adaptation to a barren environment as could be found in searching the world over." Generation after generation of people had lived out their lives upon these desolate hills "in all the contentment of a prairie dog town." Yet not many miles away were opportunities in agriculture and industry that would seem to beckon them to a more abundant life. "But Santa Ana sticks to its sand hills and watches the world tearing by on the east and south without the slightest desire to participate."[136]

The pueblo, like Zia, still occupies its barren location facing the sandy bed of the Jemez River. Since farmland water remains at a minimum, most of the people have moved to reservation land along the Rio Grande (the camp areas Hewett mentions), where the settlements known as the Ranchos de Santa Ana have grown up. The new villages have the same appearance as the small Mexican settlements along the valley, being European in layout, but definitely not the result of an amalgamation of racial groups. The pueblo members return to the old village for ceremonies and dances, and a few people live there year round to watch the village and prevent unwanted intrusions.

There are two main plazas, which are roughly enclosed by buildings laid out in street fashion. A Roman Catholic church stands on the north side of the village. Two circular surface kivas are present, one near the center of the village, and one on the south side. Distinctive pottery was produced for many years in this village, and then the craft terminated. Recently an attempt has been made by a few women to revive the craft. The original brick-red pottery was finished with a thin white slip and then decorated with red and black designs. Unlike the usual practice in most pueblo pottery design, the red areas were often not outlined with black.[137]

According to Dutton, until recently some of the older men wove women's belts and the narrower bands that are used either to tie the hair back in the *chongo* style or to serve as garters to hold up leggings. The younger people did not continue the tradition, and accordingly this craft has also ceased.[138]

Santo Domingo Pueblo

Santo Domingo is Spanish for St. Dominic. The Pueblo name is Kiua. It is situated on the east bank of the Rio Grande, about thirty miles southwest of Santa Fe. According to Stubbs, the major portion of the present adobe pueblo has been built since 1886, at which time a large part of the old village was washed away by severe floods. Photographs taken in 1880 show that the street layout was the same as now. This site is known to have been occupied by Santo Domingans since about 1700, although possibly an earlier site exists at this location.[139] In 1935, the population was 923, in 1948 it was 1,106, and today it is approximately 2,200.

Lummis, in his book *Mesa, Cañon and Pueblo*, refers to this town as "Santo Domingo, stiffest necked of the pueblos in clinging to the ways of the old." Stubbs says, "This statement still holds, and visitors and innovations are not welcome," but I have found the people to be gracious whenever I have gone there. All Santo Domingo house-building is confined to the immediate village area, and there is no dispersion of individual houses as is seen in other pueblos. Each individual lives with the group and is closely controlled by tradition. The layout of the village is in long house blocks on parallel streets, the pattern we have already seen in Acoma and Old Oraibi. The wider central street serves as the principal space where dances are held. There are two circular kivas, one at the east end of the central street, the other farther west between the south house blocks. The church is outside the village proper and has no relationship to the village ground plan. The two are separated by an irrigation ditch.

Santo Domingo potters use a cream-colored slip, with geometric decorations in black or red. The ware is usually thick and heavy, and the designs are relatively simple. Painters are not allowed to depict ceremonial figures or anything else connected with the more intimate life of the pueblo.

The economy is based primarily on farming, but crafts are also depended upon. Men and women fashion traditional styles of jewelry with shell, turquoise, jet, and other materials. Some men also make Pueblo-style moccasins for sale.

In giving the history of Santo Domingo, Parsons says the town was visited by the early conquistadores, but the first entrada of moment was made in 1598 by Oñate, "who held a council of the chiefs in kiva and talked about Philip of Spain, protection from enemies, and baptism." The chiefs "kneeled and kissed the hands" of the governor and of Fray Juan de Escalona. A Franciscan mission was established, and Fray Juan completed a church by 1605. In 1607, the friar died and was buried in the church, which was shortly after destroyed by a flood. Again, in 1886, a flood carried away the church, mission, and many houses. "Of all the Pueblos," says Parsons, "surely the people of Kiua or Santo Domingo, as Oñate named the town, have cause to believe in Water Serpent."

In the Revolt of 1680, Santo Domingo killed some Spanish administrators and three priests, leaving their bodies before the altar. Before Otermín's punitive expedition arrived, the small population of 150 fled to Potrero Viejo above the Canada, where they joined refugees from San Felipe, Cochiti, the Tano pueblo of San Marcos, Taos, and Picuris. Otermín burned eight pueblos, among them Isleta and Sandia, and then sacked Cochiti, San Felipe, and Santo Domingo, burning their kivas. The exiles are said to have returned to their towns by 1683, but in 1692, De Vargas found the houses of Santo Domingo in ruin. Santo Domingo people joined Jemez people and built a town north of Jemez. In the Jemez rebellion of 1696, an important chief of Santo Domingo was captured and shot, and Santo Domingo rebels joined in founding Laguna. But Parsons believes they could not have been more than a handful, since, by 1707, the population of Santo Domingo had increased to 204. At the close of the century Santo Domingo is said to have received immigrants from the Comanche-beset Tano town of Galisteo.[140]

Hewett found the Santo Domingo of the 1930s to be the most populous of all Eastern Keresan towns. It numbered 923 residents, which at that indicated some decrease. It had ample land of great fertility and almost unfailing water for irrigation. He thought it would be difficult for "the most zealous of white friends of the Indian to become emotional over the people of Santo Domingo." They were far better off than any white communities in New Mexico, either Spanish-American or Anglo-Saxon. The old form of government was intact, and ceremonial life went on uninterrupted by the pressure of modern life around them. Santo Domingo was the scene of the widely known Green Corn Ceremonial of August 4, always witnessed by thousands of visitors.

Santo Domingo, Hewett says, asked of the white brother or of Washington only the privilege of being left alone. It wanted no schools, no advice about farming, no white man's medicine. Its extreme conservatism was maintained by an attitude of firm hostility, which could become acute on slight provocation, "such as photographing or sketching the dances, driving automobiles into the plaza when sacred performances are going on." A visitor should accept the misfortune of a smashed camera, windshield, or head with amiable equanimity, knowing that it was well deserved and that if he pressed the matter he might get even worse. A good rule to observe in visiting Santo Domingo or any other Indian pueblo was (and still is) to accept the courtesies that are of-

Santo Domingo Pueblo warrior and enlarged view of Santo Domingo war shield. The shield is constructed of two quarter-inch-thick pieces of leather stitched together. Diameter is 19 inches.

fered, such as entering private houses, and let it go at that; in other words, to "act toward these gentle, courteous people about as you would expect polite neighbors or strangers to act toward you and your home."[141] Although the so-called "public" dances are open to visitors, they are still sacred to the Pueblos, an integral part of the secret ceremonies that have preceded them.

Zia Pueblo

Zia is derived from the Pueblo name Tseja. It is on the north bank of Jemez Creek, about sixteen miles northwest of Bernalillo. The present site, on top of a barren basaltic mound, has been occupied since about A.D. 1300. Built of irregular stone masonry and adobe, Zia is today a small, compact village, retaining to a significant degree the prehistoric two-plaza pattern. Two circular surface kivas are situated at the southern end of the village.

According to Parsons, when the Espejo expedition stopped at Zia in 1582, it found there a prosperous, orderly town boasting more than 1,000 houses, some of them three or four stories high. The Spaniards were given turkeys and so many tortillas they had to return some. No matter: after the revolt of 1680, the Spaniards destroyed the town and slaughtered most of the people.[142] Intertribal feuds also were responsible for a dramatic reduction in population from the 1765 Spanish figure of 508. In 1850, American figures indicated 124 inhabitants for Zia, and in 1889 only 113. But, with more peaceful times, the population rose. By 1900 there were 119, and in the days of Parsons' investigations the figure had risen to 177. In 1935 Hewett determined the population to be 196. Today it is about 580.

Anna Wilmarth Ickes offers us a special view of Zia as it seemed to her in 1930. A little north of Bernalillo, she says, a road branched from the main highway leading to the Jemez range. If you followed it for twenty miles you would pass the pueblo of Santa Ana, and six miles farther you would see across the shimmering flats of the Jemez River valley the tiny pueblo of Zia, "tucked up" on the north bank. It overlooked the wide flat where the Jemez River wandered along, its flow increased but rendered unpalatable by the Salado, which salty stream had joined it just above. The river had already been depleted by Jemez Pueblo, seven miles farther up, and by other towns that also took a portion of the water. Ickes writes:

"A pathetic little pueblo is Zia. Once it boasted two thousand people, but now a mere handful remain. Its tragic history of war, disease, and oppression nearly wiped it out, and Mrs. Stevenson, its sympathetic historian, believes that these have caused the mental deterioration that makes it a sad contrast to other more upstanding pueblos."[143]

Lack of water, she continues, had made agriculture on any satisfactory scale impossible. Only the most meager crops were being culled from its fields, and the Zia were forced to trade with Jemez and Santa Ana for food. Fortunately, Zia's potters made good pots, while neither Jemez nor Santa Ana did. The Zia ware formed a medium of exchange with her more prosperous neighbors.

Despite their trade relationship, Ickes claims that Zia was "despised by both Jemez and Santa Ana."[144] The result was a breakdown of morale. Illegitimate children were numerous, and extramarital relations were "not frowned upon as elsewhere." But isolation had had the happy result of preserving tradition and ceremony, so that Zia offered "a fertile field for study by ethnologists."

Among other things they had learned that Spider Woman, "that important power" among the Pueblos, was a male god at Zia. The Zia also had a Snake Ceremony, interesting because of its resemblances to and its differences from the Tusayan observance, "but undoubtedly with some far-distant connection." Ethnologists thought that both Hopi and Zia probably derived their Snake ceremonies from the same source, and that time had led them along different lines in the development of the ritual. Like the Hopi, the Zia did have a powerful cure for snakebite.

There was a flood myth at Zia, according to which the sacrifice of a youth and a maiden brought a recession of the waters. Zia children were taught that to please the gods they must "speak with one tongue as straight as the line of prayer over which these beings pass to enter the images of themselves." Zia, says Ickes, shared with Zuñi the hostile feeling toward Mexicans, and no Mexican was allowed to witness their Katcina ceremonies.[145]

In 1935, Hewett determined that Zia possessed about the smallest conceivable amount of farming land that such a community could exist on. Yet Zia "sat on her black lava knoll, taking the sandstorms of summer and the occasional blasts of winter from the Jemez mountains with perfect equanimity and with every appearance of contentment." The language was practically identical with that of Santa Ana and the other Keres villages on the banks of the Rio Grande. The people were, in fact, more cordial to white visitors than were the communities described above. Zia was joining in the renaissance of Pueblo arts and industries, and the ceremonies had survived "in good form." "One of the best of the old Franciscan churches"[146] stands at the north end of the village.

Zia pottery is very well made. It has the same color combinations as the ceramics of Santa Ana, but it is more serviceable and has better decoration. It can be distinguished from that of Acoma or Santa Ana by tiny black inclusions—ground-up bits of basalt or lava mixed with the clay.

Dutton points out that Zia has been the birthplace of several noted painters and that the famous sun symbol employed by the state of New Mexico as an official seal and flag emblem came from a Zia water jar.[147]

Cochiti Pueblo

Cochiti Pueblo, or Kotyiti, is situated on the west bank of the Rio Grande, where it emerges from White Rock canyon, about thirty miles southwest of Santa Fe. According to Stubbs, sherds found in the refuse mounds show a continuous period of occupation from at least A.D. 1250 to the present. He thinks that Cochiti clearly illustrates the breakup of the old village system. Its main plaza, roughly enclosed by adobe structures, still serves as the core of communal life, but the newer houses are built some distance from it, and the original compact pattern is being lost.[148]

Two circular surface kivas stand on the north side of the main plaza. Ancient foundation stones and wall construction techniques can be seen in all parts of the village, and prehistoric sherds are abundant in the refuse mounds. A Roman Catholic church stands on the south side of the village. The population in 1948 was 497. Today, it is about 850.

Parsons says that Santo Domingo, San Felipe, and Cochiti, which speak the same Keresan dialect, were supposed to have been at one time "an undivided tribe living in the Rios de los Frijoles and on neighboring potreros, whence, because of Tewa hostility, groups migrated southward." Oñate found the Cochiti group at its present site in A.D. 1598. The mission of San Buenaventura was established there. In the Revolt of 1680, the population of 300 withdrew to found with other pueblos the fortified town of La Cieneguilla on Potrero Viejo, where they remained until routed by De Vargas in 1693.[149]

Hewett states that in 1935, Cochiti numbered 309 residents and that, besides having the forceful conservatism of all Keresan peoples, it had the advantage of remoteness from highways and white settlements to protect its native culture. The Cochiteños, he says, made excellent pottery and were sharing in the revival of the Pueblo arts. Their finest artist was Tonita Peña, a Tewa girl married into a Keres town, who had done a large amount of watercolor painting. Second only in artistic merit were Awa Tsira, Kabotie, and Velino. The ceremonies of Cochiti were well preserved. One performance, the Matachina, which was a composite of an aboriginal drama from Mexico and an old Spanish Miracle play, was unequaled.

After Bandelier had been with the Cochiteños on and off for eight years, living in their homes, studying their daily life, and exploring the surrounding country under their guidance, he said, "They are the best people the sun shines upon."[150]

The current pottery of Cochiti is characterized by fine-line black designs on a cream-colored slip. A brick-red color is employed occasionally. The designs often occur as isolated units rather than in connected bands. Graphic representations of sacred symbols, animals, birds, and plants are more liable to be used at Cochiti than at any other Rio Grande village, although many finished pieces are similar to those of Santo Domingo. Cochiti can boast of many craft workers, but is perhaps most famous for its drum makers.

Of particular interest among shrines is one at Cochiti Pueblo. It consists of two massive, crouching stone lions with their heads toward the east. A hollow at each side of the abdomen is known as the "earth umbilical region." The stone images are called "mountain-lion stone fetishes." Bandelier claimed that the Zuñi held the place sacred as the home of their culture hero and of the beast gods. Further, he said, they believed the entrance to Shi'papolima was on the summit of a mountain about ten miles from Cochiti Pueblo, and the two crouching lions, or cougars, guarded the sacred spot.[151]

Tewa informants told Harrington that the Stone Lions Shrine is used by "some secret religious society of Cochiti Pueblo." They added that the entrance of a shrine always extends toward the pueblo at which the worshipers live. That is true of most Tewa shrines, and the Lion Shrine does extend southwest toward Cochiti Pueblo. The Tewa denied that the Lion Shrine had anything to do with the mythical entrance place of the Zuñi and said they knew of no Zuñi belief concerning it.[152]

TANOAN

The Tiwa

In prehistoric times, Tiwa villages were scattered along the Rio Grande valley from Northern Mexico to present-day Albuquerque. Changes already described reduced the number of existing Tiwa villages to four:

south	Isleta
	Sandia
north	Picuris
	Taos

In addition to these there is Guadalupe Indian Village, near University Park at Las Cruces, New Mexico. It is a considerably Hispanicized colony.[153]

Bertha Dutton thinks that because Sandia and Isleta pueblos are understood by Taos and Picuris pueblos only with difficulty, a division between them took place long ago and that the original Tiwa speech has been maintained by the northern pueblos "to a greater degree."[154]

Isleta Pueblo

Isleta (Spanish for "little island") is the southernmost of the Rio Grande pueblos. It is on the western side of the Rio Grande, about thirteen miles south of Albuquerque, and has a current population of approximately 2,900, including two colonies south of the pueblo; Chicale, on the east side of the river, and a settlement named Oraibi, founded by a conservative group that left Laguna Pueblo about 1880. The date of Isleta's founding is unknown, although early Spanish reports include a village by the name Isletu. Isleta has a number of streets dividing its low adobe buildings, which are haphazardly placed on a generally east-west axis. A large, central plaza fronts the mission church, which was established sometime before A.D. 1629.

Isleta has a "round house" similar to that of Picuris, which Bernard Siegal thinks was utilized for races and games, and in particular for ceremonies that involved the entire village. Parsons refers to this and one other structure as kivas. Kidder believes the round house might best be referred to as the "Big Kiva," while the second kiva is no more than a moiety house. "The head of the other moiety likewise uses his living room as a moiety house."[155]

Parsons thinks it is probable that Isleta stands on or near a site that was occupied in A.D. 1540. There is also a town tradition about a more ancient site or sites below the mountains to the east, where there are many ruins.[156] About A.D. 1675, Isleta's population increased when it received migrants from the Tiwa pueblos of Quarai, Tajique, and others east of the Rio Grande. These villages were abandoned because of Apache raids. It is possible that Isleta settlements on the east bank date back to that period. However, as early as A.D. 1581, settlements on the east and west banks were seen by the Rodríguez expedition. The settlement on the west bank, which the expedition called Taxmulco, was described as having one hundred and twenty-three houses that were two and three stories high, and it was probably Isleta.

It will be recalled that when the Revolt of 1680 erupted, Governor Otermín and other refugees fled south to Isleta and that the rebelling Pueblos let him go. Yet he took with him, when he went on from Isleta, 519 captives, of whom 115 afterward escaped. Some of the captive Isletans were settled at Isleta del Sur, below El Paso, Texas, in 1681. Still others from Isleta abandoned the pueblo entirely and are thought to have gone to Tusayan, not returning from there until 1718.

Isleta is referred to by the Pueblos as Shiaw'iba, and by their Mexican neighbors as San Agostín. In Parsons' time, on the eastern side of the village there was a settlement of about six houses, the residents of which were referred to as Yellow Earth people or White Village people. They were said to be "mean people," who also spoke a slightly different dialect from the Isleta people proper. In folktales these names were associated with two different groups, the Yellow Earth people having lived in a site on the bluff above the White Village. Parsons heard also that it was from this district that captives were taken to El Paso. Before Isleta's bridge was built by the government, the White Village people ferried passengers across the river. Then an awesome flood destroyed all White Village's houses save one, drowned a pregnant woman and a youth, and led to the building of the bridge. Only recently had the people begun to return and rebuild White Village.[157]

Three miles southeast of Isleta were two ranching colonies called Shila and T'aikebede, whose residents were known as T'aikabehun. Several miles farther east were the Manzano Mountains, which included a certain peak that Isletans spoke of as "our mountain, White Eagle, the home of the Katcina."[158] Oraibi sat on the southwest border of the town. At the time of its settlement, there was a fairly large space between it and Isleta, but houses built over the years have narrowed this gap.

In 1890, the population of Isleta was 1,059, and in 1948 it was 1,470. From A.D. 1700 until recently, the Isletans made no decorated pottery, although a plain red cooking ware was crafted for domestic use. Now a little pottery and jewelry are made at Isleta, but what is called Isleta pottery, which is red overall with black and red designs on white, is actually fashioned at the settlement of Oraibi.

At Isleta today, the council is made up of the governor, two lieutenant governors, two sheriffs, and twelve appointed members. Six of the latter are appointed by the Bureau of Indian Affairs and six by the governor. The council elects its president and vice-president.[159]

Sandia Pueblo

Sandia is Spanish for "watermelon," and it is also the name for a beautiful mountain range west of the pueblo that turns red at sunset. The Tiwa name for the village is Nanfiath, meaning "dusty place." Sandia Pueblo is fourteen miles north of Albuquerque, just off U.S. Highway 85 and on the east side of the Rio Grande. Archaeologists believe the village was begun about A.D. 1300 and that during the period of the Revolt of 1680 to 1692 a major portion of its residents moved to Tusayan, whence they returned in 1742. Sandia's population is about 250, no crafts are produced, and the people are either farmers or wage workers. It has a Roman Catholic church, and most of the oldest part of the pueblo is in ruins. The inhabited dwellings consist of one-story adobes. The kivas are rectangular and built into the house blocks. Stubbs shows for Sandia only one rectangular kiva, attached to a small room, but suggests that other kivas may be enclosed within the house blocks.[160]

The present Sandia Council is made up of the governor, lieutenant governor, War chief and his staff, fiscal and his staff, sheriff, former governors, former lieutenant governors, former War chiefs, and former fiscales.[161]

When Edgar Hewett visited Sandia in the 1930s, he was shocked to see how the intrusions of other cultures had reduced numerically and altered culturally what had once been a traditional, strong, and thriving pueblo. He wrote at length about this, and his essay is worth repeating for the portrait it gives. "The breaking down of the culture of this town," he says, "is a good example of what happens when a people of a Stone Age culture are affronted by a more aggressive, though not necessarily superior group, well on in the Machine Age."[162]

Sandia, Hewett says, is one of the two surviving villages of the ancient Tiguex Province, and Sandia, Alameda, and Puaráy have been the subject of more dispute regarding their original locations than any other places in the Southwest. Sandia's history has been one of tragedy since Coronado came to the Tiguex Province and wintered there in 1540. It was on the travel route of nearly every expedition that came from the south. After meeting with constant abuse from Coronado's men, Sandia lived in comparative peace for forty years. Then Chamuscado came in 1581 with a small band of soldiers and two monks, López and Santa María, who, when the expedition left, remained to Christianize the several thousand Sandians then living at the pueblo. One of the friars was killed at San Pablo, twenty-five miles northeast of Albuquerque, and the other was killed at either Sandia or Puaráy. As a result of this "outrage" Espejo was sent to investigate the killing in 1583, and the Sandians were again treated badly. Oñate visited the town in 1595, and it was either here or at Puaráy that the historian Gaspar Pérez de Villagra discovered poorly hidden Pueblo wall paintings that depicted the murder of three monks.[163]

In 1680, Sandia took an active part in the pueblo Revolt, after which the entire community decided to migrate to Hopi country, where they stayed for some sixty years. They built a village near Mishongnovi, and the ruins of that site may still be seen. Homesick for their green, fertile valley, they finally returned to the Rio Grande. About 350 in all came back, sometime between 1742 and 1748. They settled on what is the town's present site. But they were shunned by the Rio Grande communities because they had adopted Hopi religious practices, including the Snake Dance. Left alone, they suffered greatly from Apache and Comanche raids. During the historic period Sandia became a mission center, and the ruined adobe walls of the old Franciscan church in the west of the town can still be seen. It was abandoned about 1890, and the small church to the north of the town was built on top of an ancient mound left from buildings that had housed part of Sandia before 1680.

Records kept by the various early Spanish expeditions reveal that fairly accurate accounts were made of the dress, houses, numbers, and customs of the Pueblo people they saw. They reported there were from twelve to sixteen Tiguex towns, and claimed that Sandia and Isleta were the largest and most powerful of all these. Hewett found it difficult to believe that the crumbling little Nanfiath was once the large town it was said to be, for it numbered only 121 residents in 1935.

Its houses, which once were several stories high, consisted now of one-story adobe structures built around in irregular plaza, with the rooms running in all four directions. Beehive ovens, and ovens showing both Indian and Spanish influence, dotted the plaza. In the summer the village was almost deserted, for many of the families moved away from the main town and occupied little huts nearer the fields. Some Sandia houses were well kept on the outside, but most exteriors were dirty and in need of repair. The plaza and alleyways were especially dirty and odorous in hot weather. On the other hand, the church was well kept, but this, according to the Sandians, was because the visiting priest made them take care of it. There was no plan or beauty about the buildings. The doorways were small, and many of the doors and older windows were sealed up. Most of the dwelling interiors were clean. Nearly all the families had stoves, and many cooked with pots obtained from Santo Domingo, Zia, Cochiti, and San Ildefonso. Beds were used, although many families still preferred to sleep on the floor. Broken chairs and boxes were used for seats. Catholic religious figures hung on some of the walls. As a rule the homes were furnished according to the prevailing Pueblo standard and compared favorably with rural Mexican homes.

Sandia's old culture had broken down. The social structure was entirely altered by Spanish and Mexican influence, by the years in the Hopi country, and by American infringement. The clan system was almost gone, although the people still had the Summer and Winter people, and descent was still traced through the maternal line. There was one male cacique and two female assistants who gained their rank through seniority. There was but one kiva left, a square structure of adobe, entered by a hatchway in the top. There were also two rooms in the houses near the kiva that served as ceremonial spaces. Hewett thought their kiva plan suggested a carry-over from the square room kivas and three square plaza kivas at Kuaua, where the Sandia Indians said they had lived originally. The kiva was dirty inside, when Hewett saw it; the altar and interior were badly in need of repair.

Although Sandia's people belonged to the southern Tiwa group, and their language was like that of Isleta, Taos, and Picuris, they also had a knowledge of many Zuñi, Hopi, and Navajo words, which they used in their conversations. In addition they spoke English to some extent, Spanish well, and some of the Keresan and Tewa dialects. The young people knew little of the lore and traditions, and Hewett feared that when the present generation of old men died, much valuable material would be lost. Some of their myths bore a resemblance to those of the Zuñi and the Hopi, and their ceremonies were greatly corrupted. The most often they ever danced was four times a year, and one of the four dances might go unperformed. The most important ceremony was that held on June 13, in honor of St. Anthony. It was a combination of Catholic ritual crudely performed and the Corn Dance. Many participants in 1935 were intoxicated during a dance. Burial customs were a mixture of Indian and Christian rites, and the people exhibited a superstitious fear of the dead. Bodies were generally placed in the ground without benefit of casket. Some were flexed, as of old, and covered with the usual wearing apparel. Superstitions generally were based on old beliefs as well as those passed on to them by Mexicans. They still talked in terms of what would bring "good" and "bad" luck.

The government had degenerated—elections were allowed to slip by, and since there were only about thirty families the choice of governor was, in any event, small. In addition to the governor, there were a war captain, a council of past governors, and a cacique. The government was not taken seriously, but it seemed adequate for Sandia. The people scorned and resented U.S. Government aid, sometimes foolishly. For example, they disliked the idea of putting in an irrigation system, but came to like it very much when it was in place. Education consisted of a new day school, where the children were taught what was required to fit their future needs. Older children were sent to boarding schools if they wished to go. Hewett thought the adults were poor economists, since they failed to conserve a third of what they could have done with such fertile and well-watered land. Yet actual want was unknown, for their needs were simple. They raised corn, peas, melons, tobacco, some cotton, wheat, oats, barley, chili, peaches, and apples. They had horses, cows, goats, sheep, cats, dogs, chickens, and turkeys.

Hewett concluded that the women were bad homemakers in many ways; the arts were lost; married couples quarreled, although they did not divorce. Their greatest vice was drinking, even on the part of the smaller children. There were no means of making a living outside of farming. The men could provide manual labor, and some of the women domestic work, but nothing else. Continued inbreeding had weakened the town, and until recently, when marriages with Mexicans and other Indians were permitted, the town was more than stagnant, it was actually dying out. Only in the last eleven years or so had births begun to exceed deaths. The most serious diseases were syphilis, tuberculosis, and trachoma.

The clothing of the Sandians was similar to that of the other Rio Grande Pueblo Indians. The men wore their hair straight back, and did not as a rule wear bangs. They wore either store shoes or moccasins, overalls, shirts of white or bright colors, and bright bandannas around their heads. The women wore, in ceremonies, the typical black woven Pueblo dress, fastened over one shoulder, but in everyday life they wore bright prints, went barefooted, wore moccasins or cheap store shoes, and heavy store stockings. They wore their hair in typical Pueblo style. They were seldom without their bright store shawls. Jewelry was of a cheap sort, and they wore little of the better silver work made by their neighbors and the Navajos.[164]

Picuris Pueblo

Picuris, like Taos, was a northeastern frontier town, and by the 1950s it already seemed to be a dying pueblo. Parsons obtained in 1925 some information about the pueblo from a Picuris youth, who talked with her away from the town. She learned there were six subterranean kivas, of which four were active. There was also a "round house," which was used in connection with races and games and was only partly below grade. Kidder was told by Florence Ellis that the natives of Picuris considered the round house more sacred than the kivas, and that they went there to pray for rain.[165]

Hewett, in 1937, described Picuris as "a pathetic little place," poor in resources, retaining little of its ancient art and ceremonial life, reduced in population to 115, and that considerably Hispanicized.[166]

But by 1938, the population was up to 130,[167] and by 1972 it was 180. Picuris did not die after all, and as of today it has been occupied for seven hundred and eighty years.

Picuris is situated on the north bank of the Rio Pueblo, about twenty miles south of Taos. It rests on the slopes of beautiful, pine-covered mountains, and it dates back to A.D. 1200, which brings it very close to the longevity of Acoma

Ruins of old Picuris Pueblo. The kiva is left of the main entrance.

and Old Oraibi. Stubbs says the village is also called San Lorenzo, that according to Harrington the name is derived from the Spanish "Picuris," and that Hodge says it comes from the Keresan name Pikuria, meaning "those who paint."[168] Oñate visited the town in A.D. 1598.

Picuris consists today of a combination of ancient and modern structures. In the most recent part of town, west of the gleaming white Roman Catholic church built sometime around 1770, is a new development, complete with central plaza. To the northwest is a group of dwellings built around a small plaza that contains a circular kiva. This portion represents what has survived intact from earlier times. Farther north still the ancient pueblo has been reduced to mounds, only portions of walls remaining.

In 1961, the residents of Picuris allowed archaeologists to excavate its ruins. Several kivas and ceremonial rooms were cleared and restored, including a kiva in which murals were discovered. In the Picuris museum one may now see a cross section of a kiva, replicas of the murals, and some of the artifacts recovered.

Picuris' Feast Day is August 10, and at this time a Corn Dance is given. Social dances are held whenever desired, Corn dances are performed during the summer months, and Animal dances during the winter.

Since the pueblo was subjected to considerable contact with the Ute and other Plains Indians, much of its dress and ceremony was adapted from them. Some of the men wore buckskin clothing that was Ute in style, although the village architecture remained Pueblo. Picuris did not adopt the tipi.

Today, a few residents weave cotton belts, and some women fashion pottery. According to Stubbs, they ceased making decorated pottery around A.D. 1680, but they make a cooking ware with a large amount of yellow mica in the clay, which gives the finished piece a bronzed look and somehow a surface that is excellent for cooking beans.[169]

The Picuris Council comprises the governor, War chief and his staff, fiscal, sheriff, head men, past officers, and all men twenty-one and over.[170]

Taos Pueblo

Laurance Herold thinks that if Taos Pueblo was not founded by local inhabitants, it might have resulted from a northward shift to Tiwa-speaking groups after the beginning of the Rio Grande Classic Period, A.D. 1325–1600. He adds that few details of the Classic Period at Taos are actually known, since the conservatives have banned archaeological investigation there except for limited trenching. Pottery sherds discovered in the trenches suggest that the pueblo's ancestral ruin near the existing site was occupied about A.D. 1325, and that the present pueblo was begun around A.D. 1400.[171]

Taos Pueblo, the northernmost of the Rio Grande villages, is about sixty-five miles north of Santa Fe, near the intersection of state highways 3 and 64. Its population was 700 in 1707, 505 in 1765, 763 in 1935, 907 in 1948, and today about 1,725. When tourists speak of Taos, they usually mean both the town and the pueblo, but these are really separate entities.

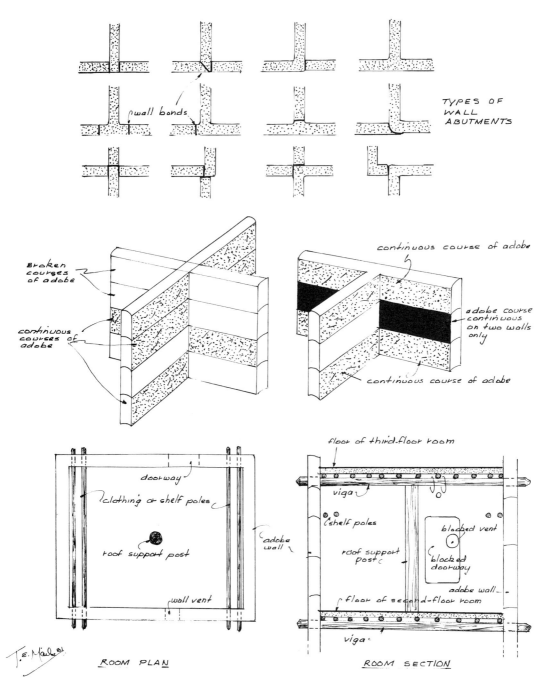

Architectural details, old Picuris Pueblo. *Top,* methods of forming wall abutments. *Middle,* methods of bonding walls. *Bottom,* typical room construction details. Pindi Pueblo was constructed in the same fashion as Picuris. From Stubbs and Stallings, 1953.

The pueblo is the only one on the Rio Grande that is surrounded with a wall. Taos Creek separates the town into a North House that today is five stories at its highest level, and a South House that is four stories. Taos is the only Rio Grande pueblo with covered passageways. The roadway near the river is used for ceremonial races. The original church was destroyed in 1847, and the one that replaced it is situated within the western portion of the walled area.

Ickes points out that Taos was the nearest pueblo to the Plains tribes, and she thinks intermarriage with Comanche and Ute might in some measure account for the different physical characteristics observable.[172] I think they look so much like Jicarilla Apache that early intermarriage with them should be considered a possibility also.

Taos men still wear their hair in braids, wrapped in the manner of the Southern Plains Indians. They are seldom without a white blanket, sometimes covering all the body and head save the face, and at other times simply knotted about the waist. Taos women still wear white buckskin boots, the tops of which are not wrapped as elsewhere. They are wide and flapping, requiring a gait that is different yet graceful. Photographs taken through the 1920s show Taos men and women wearing Plains Indian apparel, sometimes mixed with whites' clothing.

Hewett thought the characteristic Taos costume, a white cotton mantle which shrouds the entire figure, was curiously Moorish in appearance. The origin of this dress was unknown, however, "though it certainly was not aboriginal." One authority says he was informed that it was brought to Taos from the Cheyenne in 1897. The prehistoric dress of buckskin, no doubt "closely resembled that of plains tribes with whom they mingled freely and with whom (the Kiowa) they were linguistically related."

Taos has six kivas in active use. A seventh kiva is the place of at least one ceremonial observance, but plays no part in the formal kiva organization. The active kivas are divided into two groups of equal size. The three in the North Pueblo are all inside the town's wall. Two of the South Pueblo kivas and the seventh kiva are outside the wall, and one South kiva is inside. The Kivas, says Hewett, are "more archaic in type than any other aboriginal sanctuaries in the Rio Grande valley."

All the kivas are circular and subterranean. M. L. Miller, who was at Taos in 1896, describes the hatchways as protruding about a foot above grade, banked with dirt to give the impression of being completely subterranean. Twenty-five years later, Parsons described them as standing higher above the ground and needing a few steps to reach the hatchway. Kidder thinks the dirt banks had washed away, making the difference.[173] Miller was able to enter one kiva. The ceiling was just high enough to allow him to stand erect, and it was covered with soot. A firepit was in the center of the floor. He mentions a small hole for a ventilator, but does not give its position. On the floor were two untanned ox hides and a large drum.[174]

According to Parsons, the unactive kiva mentioned earlier fell into disuse when the days of warfare ended. Its only function thereafter has been in connection with the annual relay race between the men of the North and South pueblos. Early on the day of the race the runners go individually to the kiva to pray to P'achale (Blue Water), evidently a stone image, leaving offerings of sacred cornmeal, pollen, and turkey feathers. The image stands between a terraced deflector, made of adobe brick plastered over, and a hole covered with buffalo hide, into which each runner deposits cornmeal. Parsons once saw spruce boughs lying by the hatchway, suggesting that some kind of ceremony

The South Town of the Tiwa Pueblo of Taos in 1900.

had been carried on there. She was also told by a visitor from Isleta Pueblo that it was a place of retreat for boy initiates. Yet another informant said that enemy scalps were once kept in the kiva.[175]

A place of great religious significance is the sacred Blue Lake, said to be the most important shrine of the Taos people. They speak of it as "part of their life, their Indian church." It rests high in the Sangre de Cristo mountain area back of the pueblo.

In 1906, with accustomed disdain for Indian possessions and religious needs, Blue Lake and its surrounding woodlands were incorporated into the United States National Forests, throwing the lake open to whoever wished to go there for recreational purposes and thus making it impossible for Taos to continue its use as a shrine. Government promises that the lake area would be protected from commercial exploitation were unconvincing, and Taos began an

epic legal struggle to win back the land and lake. A few temporary victories were won, but all the while the Forest Service went steadily ahead, preparing the area for recreation and for use by commercial interests. Taos representatives went nationwide, enlisting the help of white friends wherever possible. Finally, in 1971, the House and Senate passed a bill, and the President signed it, returning the land and lake to Taos.

The Taos Council consists today of the governor and his staff. The staff includes a lieutenant governor, War captain and his staff, fiscal and staff, sheriff, secretaries, and certain persons who have served on the council in previous years in those capacities.[176]

Taos officers are nominated by the cacique and two or more high priests and voted on by the council.[177]

Hewett, like everyone else, fell in love with Taos. He described it as being

Entrance to a kiva at Taos Pueblo.

some miles east of the river, at the foot of the Taos mountains, a spur of the Sangre de Cristo range. For beauty of situation it could hardly be surpassed, and of this the Taos Indians, he says, were keenly aware. Back of the town lay their sacred mountain. In front was their world, "stretching westward to the Jemez range beyond the Rio Grande; a complete horizon of mesas, mountains, and hills encompassing a fertile valley—to the Indians an ideal world." He thought it was a mistake to say that the Indian had no appreciation of beautiful scenes. "Walk with a native of Taos along the little mountain stream that bears the name of the village up to the Glorieta. There is, I think, no more beautiful sacred grove in the world. Stand in that noble circle of cottonwoods and be not afraid to be silent for half an hour at a time. Talk of the grove and the flowers, birds, insects, vines, clouds, getting their names and what is thought about each one, and you will soon know that the Indian is not only a nature worshipper but a beauty worshipper."[178]

The people of Taos, Hewett wrote, were among the most prosperous and virile of all the Indians of the Southwest. They had an abundance of fertile agricultural land, amply watered by the mountain stream that flowed through the town. Crops were all but certain. Fish and game were plentiful. Wild fruits abounded in the valleys. It was not, in Hewett's opinion, to be wondered at that these were among the most independent of all Pueblo people.

Taos was visited for the first time by white men in 1540. A detachment of soldiers from Coronado's army, under Hernando Alvarado, stopped there and probably overestimated the population, at 15,000.[179] Fifty years later Castano de Sosa reported that it contained five plazas and sixteen estufas (kivas) that were well plastered and warm. Access to the houses was by means of ladders, which could be drawn through trapdoors in the roof. Considerable pottery was seen, some black, some painted, and some glazed. The people wore mantas of cotton, and buffalo skins. Juan de Oñate visited Taos in 1598 and may have been the first to use its present name, the meaning of which remains obscure. As I have previously stated, the pueblo rebellion of 1680 was planned at Taos by Popé. When De Vargas reconquered the Pueblos, he punished Taos by removing its food supplies.

According to Stubbs, the 1540 village is not the same as the present one. He says the original structures were on both sides of the stream, as now, but to the north and east of the present location. Traditional stories, he adds, tell of the burning of the old town, probably in 1693 or 1694, the time of the Reconquest.[180]

Parsons reports that, curiously enough, there is no tradition at Taos regarding the Revolt of 1680, "although Popé planned or directed it from the village, and all but two of the seventy Spaniards near Taos were massacred. She claims that twice during the pacification period after the Reconquest the town was abandoned in favor of a fortified canyon.[181]

Parsons also says that during the eighteenth-century fighting with the Apache, Ute, and Comanche, most of the Mexicans abandoned the region. They returned, however, and, by 1815, 190 Mexican families were living on Taos lands, basing their claims in part "on support they had given against Comanche." By 1896, Mexicans were occupying half the Taos grant of twenty-seven and a half square miles. After the Treaty of Guadalupe, Mexican insurrectionists involved Taos in a fight with the newly instituted American authorities. Several Taos men went to the American sheriff to ask for the release of two prisoners. When he refused, they killed the sheriff and prefect, went to the house of Governor Bent, and killed and scalped him and two other men. American troops arrived, killed 150 Pueblos who sought to escape, and executed 15 prisoners.[182]

By 1830, Hewett continues, Taos was headquarters for the trapping industry of the Southwest. Its history from that period was as picturesque as its location. It has, says Hewett, "during the past twenty years attracted artists from far and near, some of whom have painted the place and its people with rare understanding, some with no understanding at all, but their canvases have carried the fame and beauty of this remote little Indian town to the ends of the earth."

Hewett states that in 1935 the village was in two parts, separated by the little stream. Each part consisted of a large community structure, portions of which were six stories high, "a perfect survival of the terraced architecture of the Ancient house builders." By 1935, though, numerous small houses for in-

Training session at Taos.

dividual families had been built close to the old pyramidal structures. Each half, one North and one South, was well furnished with kivas, almost entirely subterranean, "more archaic in type than any other aboriginal sanctuaries in the Rio Grande valley."

In 1935, the ancient social structure was still well preserved, and the old religion and ceremonials fervently adhered to, although the best-known fiesta, San Geronimo Day, held on September 30, had become "so degenerated as to be not worth seeing." The native arts had been allowed to die out, partly because of economic prosperity. The Taos people were of an extraordinarily fine physical type, "but rendered somewhat self-conscious by much posing as artist's models." Hewett thought the Taos Indians were reticent, and many of them a bit insolent. It had not been so forty years before when he first knew them. At that time they were most friendly and hospitable. He was welcomed in their homes and freely taken into their kivas.

The altitude of Taos, being 7,000 feet, was too high to raise cotton. Supplies of this fiber for their mantas "must have been obtained from the Rio Grande valley below Cochiti." Corn, wheat, and alfalfa were now their main crops, with melons, squashes, beans, and fairly plentiful fruits. There was still abundant game in the nearby mountains, and so Taos was quite well-to-do. The people made some undecorated pottery and did a little beadwork, and a few of the men painted pictures to sell to tourists.

They had "their governor, lieutenant governor, war captain, two alguaciles (constables), fiscal (treasurer), and a full quota of principales or head men, or council, made up mainly of former officials (elder statesmen)." These officers were elected annually by vote of heads of families. This was a formality; actually, the two caciques controlled the election. "These sacerdotes"—cacique of the north (winter) and cacique of the south (summer)—had the civil government, as well as all religious matters, pretty well under their thumbs. Hewett thought the ceremonies that could now be seen by the public were comparatively uninteresting. But the fine old rituals of the ancients were by no means extinct. It was a good place to see the clowns, called *chiffonetti*, in action, though there was little that was archaic in their performances. The medicine man was still in high favor, and the Peyote Cult flourished. Hewett is quick to add that this was not to the serious detriment of the people, however. The peyote drunk "did not beat up his wife, nor make the highway gory with his automobile, nor show homicidal tendencies." He just sat in silent ecstasy. "As between the peyote that perennially stirs the emotions of the friends of the Indian, and the rot-gut that inebriates a large fraction of the white population of New Mexico, give me the peyote."[183]

Taos was secretive and lived a deep, undercover, esoteric life into which the anthropologist never got "a look-in." Efforts by scientists and government agents to learn something about these secret practices had, in fact, "induced much high blood pressure." Reliable informants on these subjects could not be had, and since the occasional talkative Indian dearly loved to "put something over" on the white man, the material the investigators received was valueless.

Taos man in ancient attire ca. 1900.

Taos farmer with hoe.

For forty years Hewett had been hearing and reading about the sacrifice of children, blood rituals, murder for revealing tribal secrets, etc., at Taos, San Ildefonso, Santo Domingo, Jemez, "and it can be said categorically that of not one episode of this character has evidence been presented that would have any standing whatever in a court of law. These gentle people have long been the victims of malicious yarn spinners in their own communities, and of gullible white inquisitors."

Hewett says further, "As to clans at Taos, some say they do not exist. Others record sizable lists of both living and extinct orders. Take them all cum grano salis. You can get no general agreement among Pueblo informants as to what clans exist and what are extinct. The people themselves do not know."[184]

THE TOWA

The only remaining Towa-speaking pueblo is Jemez.

Jemez Pueblo

Jemez is derived from the word "Hemis," meaning "Jemez people." Citing Harrington, Stubbs says the Pueblo name for the village is Walatowa, "the pueblo in the canyon," to distinguish it from the earlier villages farther north.[185] The Towa village of Jemez is on the east bank of the Jemez River, about twenty miles northwest of Bernalillo. It dates to the latter part of the sixteenth century. Its population in 1948 was 883. Currently, it numbers about 1,800 residents.

The Jemez Pueblo of today centers upon two long plazas, roughly enclosed by one- and two-story adobe structures. In essence, the village buildings are scattered at random. No planning is evident. A large Roman Catholic church is situated south of the main part of the town.

Jemez is being modernized at a regular pace. There is a community center and a library, and arts and crafts are flourishing. Women make yucca wicker-work baskets and twilled baskets, weave embroidered dresses and dance kilts and even cotton and wool belts, hair ties, and garters. Utility pots are fashioned, and some wares are produced purely for the tourist trade. Nevertheless, only a few women are making a sincere attempt to produce ceramics that match the high standards of pueblos like San Ildefonso, Santa Clara, and Acoma.

Jemez is governed by the same council members as the Keresan pueblos, plus the sheriff and the town crier.[186] According to Parsons, the latter's position is for life.[187] The other officers are chosen by the chiefs of all the societies.

In relating the history of the Jemez people, Parsons says that early Spanish chroniclers who entered the Jemez River valley reported as many as eleven towns. But by A.D. 1662, famine or Navajo raids had depopulated most of these. In 1627, their Franciscan friars persuaded the people to concentrate in the two towns where there were chapels, one dedicated to San José, one to San Diego.

During the second half of the seventeenth century the Jemez often joined with other pueblos in combatting the Spaniards. By 1692, Jemez and Santo Domingo refugees shared a mesa-built town, whence they raided the pro-Spanish towns Zia and Santa Ana. In retaliation, they were attacked and badly beaten by the Spaniards, 84 Pueblos were killed, and 361 were taken prisoner and sent to Santa Fe. The mesa site was abandoned. But two years later Jemez

Jemez mother with child in cradleboard, 1915.

people living in the valley killed their Catholic priest and again fled to the mesa top, where they were helped in a battle against the Spaniards by warriors from Acoma and Zuñi. The Jemez people went then to live among Navajo or Hopi, being among the first of those refugees to the West. Of all Pueblos, Parsons says, the Jemez and the Keresans of Santo Domingo, independently or together, put up the most determined opposition to the Spanish conquistadores, and to this day they have stubbornly resisted penetration by Anglos.

Most of the Jemez returned to the Rio Grande within ten years, building near or at the site of their present town, where by 1704 their population was 500. Sixteen families stayed behind at Walpi and remained there until 1716, when 113 of their descendants were escorted home by two War chiefs and twenty young men. A number of Hopi ways were acquired during the stay at First Mesa, and, since not every Jemez sojourner returned, contacts were probably maintained with Hopi for some time.

The people of Jemez speak a highly differentiated dialect of Tanoan, similar to that spoken at Pecos, which was eighty miles distant. In 1840, the nineteen or twenty survivors of Pecos, whose population had been decimated by repeated Comanche attacks, and various epidemics, migrated to Jemez, escorted by Jemez townsmen, and were given houses and lands. To the ceremonial life of Jemez the Pecos contributed their St. Porcingula, that is, her image and her birthday celebration, including a "sacrosanct" bull impersonation, and the Eagle-watchers or Flute Society, including "three Mothers or fetishes" and, Parsons was told, the society mask.[188]

So far as is known, all the kivas of the several late prehistoric towns of the Jemez area were freestanding, round, and subterranean. At some unknown time a change was made to rectangular kivas built within the room blocks; there are, as Miller states, two kivas at modern Jemez.

Simpson stopped at Jemez on his way to Chaco Canyon and Navajo country in 1850 and was allowed to enter both kivas. One was 20 by 27 feet (6 m by 8.2 m), and the ceiling was 7 feet 6 inches (2.25 m) high. There were elaborate ceremonial paintings on the walls, and Bourke saw different murals on the same walls in 1881. Regan observed other murals there in the early 1900s, and Parsons' informant drew pictures of Jemez kiva murals for her in 1923.[189]

Hewett found Jemez to be a "well-to-do" town in 1930. It had ample land and water, and its residents were noticeably independent. They had lost most of their arts but had preserved their old government and ceremonies. Since then, with the aid of teachers, they have resumed work in textiles with marked success.

Hewett quotes extensively from "recent studies" by Dr. Mamie Tanquist Miller concerning the Jemez Province, although he provides no bibliography, and does not cite the writing. Miller's statements offer a superb picture of a prosperous village of the 1930s and provide an instructive comparison with villages like Pojoaque and Nambe, two pueblos that changed drastically because of intrusive influences (see pages 397 and 399).

Miller informs us that the Jemez Pueblo of the time consisted of one- and two-story houses showing a marked tendency toward scattering. However, they were grouped most compactly on both sides of the south plaza and enclosed another plaza-like court to the north. To the south, on the edge of the town, stood the church, and on one side of the road was a convent, which also housed the government school taught by the sisters. Miller says that Parsons, in 1935, enumerated 143 houses, including two kivas. The houses consisted of two to four rooms. The building material was adobe bricks; pine logs were used for roofing; the walls were plastered; floors were of adobe; the two-story buildings on the plaza or near it were evidently the older houses; the newer dwellings on the outskirts were all single-story. The two kivas were surface rooms enclosed within the regular buildings, not distinguishable from the dwellings, except that there were no windows or doors. Entrance was by a ladder and a hatchway, as was usual in kivas, and the kiva firepit was walled with adobe. The men's societies met in the kivas, but other ceremonial organizations met in the house of the chief, the house of a member of a particular society, or the house where the society fetish was kept. According to Miller, Parsons lists nineteen such houses in all.

The people of Jemez raised farm and garden produce: the field products were corn, wheat, alfalfa, melons; the garden products were grapes, gourds, and chili, and some cotton was grown for ceremonial uses. They had also do-

Jemez Pueblo women washing winnowed wheat.

mesticated animals, consisting of horses, donkeys, cats, dogs, chickens, turkeys, and goats.

Harvesting machinery and plows had been introduced at Jemez, but the
conservatives still opposed the use of the cultivator and harrow. Only hoeing
by hand was allowed. The corn was stacked in the back room, where wheat
was also stored in a walled-off bin.

The Jemez Indians traded with other Indians for articles they desired, bart-
ering their agricultural and garden products for turquoise, dress cloth, deerskin, meat, feathers, silver belts, necklaces, and pottery. Local handicraft was
very meager then. In one family black polished Santa Clara ware was made,
but by a woman of Santa Clara descent. In a few families large undecorated
jars were still made for storage purposes. For storage, and for washing wheat,
baskets of yucca blades were woven, similar to those made in all Rio Grande
towns. There was no weaving. The tablitas worn in the dances were good
examples of wood carving and painting. Mask-making and prayer-stick-making
were also arts of the pueblo.

The women wore the characteristic Pueblo dress of woven black native
cloth over the right shoulder and under the left, belted with a sash woven of
green and red yarn. Over the shoulders and back hung a square of silk or
cotton cloth. Moccasins with their usual leggings of deerskin were still worn
more commonly than shoes and stockings. Women also wore colored commercial shawls. Men and women both wore the belted braid of hair, or *chongo*,
with bangs and sidelocks hanging loose, the bangs reaching to the eyebrows.

The younger men wore ordinary store clothes, and shoes rather than moccasins. Several of the older men wore close-fitting cotton trousers, and shirts
of the same material with the tails hanging outside. Tight-fitting fringed deerskin trousers might be worn on ceremonial occasions, and the older men wore
white cotton trousers slit up the side as at Hopi, and a white shirt.[190]

Hewett also obtained the following cultural information from Mrs. Blanche
Wurdack Harper, who lived several years at the pueblo of Jemez, and who had
prepared a thesis on the Jemez of the 1930s for the University of New Mexico.

Harper states that the populace of the pueblo was divided into two moieties, erroneously called clans. One was known as the Corn Stalk Clan, and
represented the winter group, formerly known as the Turquoise People. The
other was known as the Pumpkin Clan. It represented the summer group,
known formerly as the Calabash People. The actual clans were matrilineal, but
they had come to have little tribal importance. Those recorded were Fire, Corn,
Cloud, Bird, Owl, Watermelon, Turquoise, and Fox.

There were two main Medicine societies, the Little Eagle and the Arrow.
These were subdivided into several smaller groups. There were two groups to
which the women belonged. The formerly important group known as Koshare
had degenerated to a purely clown organization.

With regard to marriage relations at Jemez, if a boy wanted to marry and
had no girl in mind, his father picked one for him. The girl might not know
the boy at all. The boy's father then went to the girl's home in the evening
when her whole family was home, and asked for her for his son. If the girl's

Clothing. Women's wraparound leggings, front and side views. From the Museum of New Mexico collection.

family favored the match it would take place in spite of the girl's feelings in the matter. But if her family did not wish the match, it did not take place. No matter how fond a couple might be of each other, marriage would not take place if the girl's family opposed it.

If the suit was accepted by the girl's parents, the marriage, in the eyes of the Indians, was completed, and the boy went every night to the girl's home. But, before the Catholic church ceremony, the boy had to gather together the girl's wedding costume. His mother made the girl's dresses, and the boy had to furnish the rest of the bride's equipment, including Navajo jewelry, and usually a new Turkish towel for her head.

The names of the pair were read in the church for four weeks preceding the wedding. Then the regular Catholic wedding took place. After the church wedding, the boy lived with the girl's family until he had prepared a home for her. When he was ready to take the bride to her new home, he had to kneel before her and make a cross on the top of her head, thus symbolizing that he was now taking her away from her home and parents forever.

Regarding death, as soon as it occurred lighted candles were placed

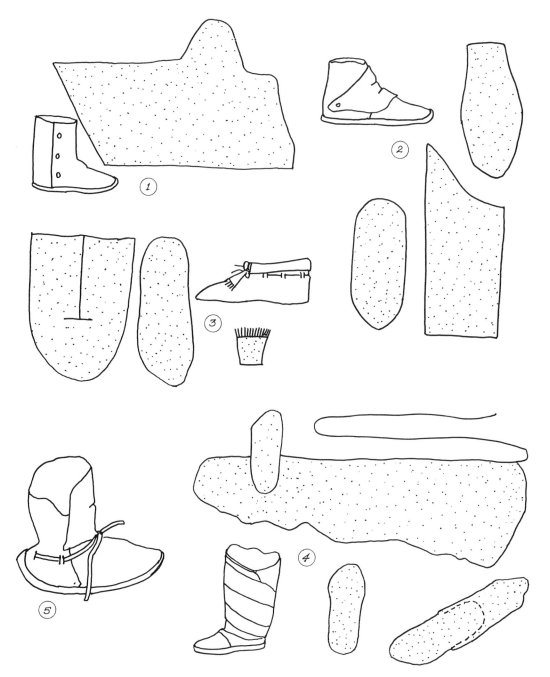

Moccasin styles. *1*, Navajo, worn by men and women. *2*, men at Cochiti, Santo Domingo, Tewa. *3*, men, Taos and Picuris. *4*, women at all pueblos with Taos having its own special style described in the text. *5*, men at San Felipe. From Underhill, 1946.

around the corpse. The body lay just as it was at death for some hours—the time being determined by the time of day the death occurred.

The relatives then went to the house, taking with them a little basket of cornmeal and six medicine bundles consisting of turkey feathers, three blue-bird wings, and a little cotton bound together. All the buttons were cut off the dead person's clothing, and a tiny sample was taken from each garment. The clothing was then removed from the corpse. The body was bathed and the hair was washed with soap bark, after which a bit of it was cut off. The head of the family then covered the corpse with cornmeal, put two medicine bundles under its back, and two in each hand—the hands being placed upon the breast. Then the corpse was raised, and all its clothing, with offerings of new cloth, was placed under it. Shoes and stockings were placed by the feet, and moccasins for dancing in the next world.

The corpse was then bundled up in a blanket that, assuming the mother was still living, was tied with the mother's woven belt, which she had removed from her person. The body was laid in the middle of the room, an ear of corn and a bowl of water being placed where the corpse had lain. Pollen was put into the water. The corn represented the dead and was left there four days. The bowl and corn were covered whenever a person of a different race entered the house. At mealtimes, the head of the family dipped four fingers in the water four times, touched the corn, then put pollen on the corn. This was symbolic of feeding the dead.

At this point the head of the family notified the gravediggers, who were regular town officers, to come get the body. They dug the grave, then took the

A Tesuque Pueblo boy in the plaza in front of the mission.

corpse away on a stepladder litter after each member of the family had either lifted or touched it. The body was taken to the Catholic church, where it was anointed with holy water and prayed for. None of the relatives accompanied it. After burial, the officers "smoked their shovels" by passing burning medicines over them. For two or three weeks thereafter the mother and father had to wear their shawls all the time. They could be worn over the shoulders or around the hips. The mother must not do any visiting. The third day after death, the family had to cook for the Medicine Clan. The third night the medicine men were called in as before, and the next day they planted feathers for the dead.[191]

THE TEWA

The six existing Tewa villages are, reading from south to north along the Rio Grande River: Tesuque, Pojoaque, Nambe, San Ildefonso, San Juan, and Santa Clara.

Tesuque Pueblo

Tesuque, or Tathunge, is ten miles north of Santa Fe. Its population was 124 in 1935 and 160 in 1948, and it is now 270. It is the pueblo closest to the state capital, but in spite of its constant exposure to acculturation, it has preserved much of its ancient charm. Hewett believed, in 1935, that this was accomplished by an attitude of mild hostility toward white visitors,[192] but I have not found this to be so in the 1970s.

Tesuque was for years one of the poorest of the Pueblo communities, owing largely to a scarcity of water for irrigation. Then, in the 1930s, conditions were improved somewhat by the construction of a dam on Tesuque Creek at a point above the village and by an adjustment of land titles through the Pueblo Lands Board. But Tesuque remains a quiet community.

The village is one of the finest remaining examples of the ancient plaza layout in pueblo building, a pattern so often seen in ancient ruins. Sherds found at the site indicate that it has been continuously occupied since about A.D. 1200.[193] The present small Roman Catholic mission church, erected about 1915 and having a cemetery, is in the same location as an earlier mission. Rectangular rooms within the Tesuque house blocks serve as its kivas, although an abandoned square kiva stands just to the northwest of the mission building. The adobe walls of many dwellings surrounding the plaza in the older part of town are deteriorating badly, and because the structural system is exposed it is an excellent place to study.

In 1965, the residents of Tesuque, in cooperation with the U.S. Department of Housing and Urban Development, initiated the building of twenty-five new houses situated apart from each other and some distance from the plaza. These are of both adobe and concrete blocks, and they look very little like typical pueblo structures.

The Tesuque Council includes the governor, two lieutenant governors, sheriff, fiscal, and principal men, who are ex-governors. At times, the War captains are called in to assist with difficult matters.[194]

The council officers are chosen by the heads of the Summer and Winter People and by the Samaiyo.[195]

Pojoaque Pueblo

Hewett describes Pojoaque, or Posunwage, as being situated four miles up the valley to the east of San Ildefonso, on a prominent hill south of the creek. "It is now," he says, "in the realm of archaeology."[196]

For a quarter of a century he witnessed the dwindling "of this little doomed community" from a population of about 20, when he first encountered it in 1897, to what he thought was its literal extinction in 1922. "Finally the last man, Antonio Tapia, with the usual imperturbably Indian attitude, watched on a lonely hilltop the steadily dying flame of community existence. No one ever heard from him a word of lamentation or regret." During the final year of his life, Antonio, a rain priest, brought to Hewett, for the Museum of New Mexico, his set of sacred water vials and explained their use as part of the rain altar, stating that he had used them for the last time.

Hewett miscalculated. Pueblos began to take up residence in Pojoaque, and its population has climbed now to 125. It has often been said that no native ceremonies are performed at the village and that it is essentially part of the Hispanicized community. But I saw there on December 12, 1976, a Buffalo Dance and a Comanche Dance (described on pages 445 and 455).

At Pojoaque, all persons of voting age, which is twenty-one and over, are consulted regarding questions having to do with progress and change in the community. Aberle states that the people decide each year whom they want in office, and the procedure for installing them is informal.[197]

Nambe Pueblo

Sixteen miles north of Santa Fe and five miles west of Pojoaque, on the same stream, is the tiny village of Nambe, which by 1935 was largely Hispanicized. The pueblo was increasing slightly in population at the time, but by amalgamation with a Mexican village. Hewett thought that, as an Indian community, Nambe was "probably destined to disappear in the course of a generation or two,"[198] or by 1955.

The 1935 census showed the population to be 127, and only a little crude pottery was being fashioned there. By 1948, however, the resident count had increased to 155, and it is now about 365. Hewett had miscalculated again. Farming and wage work off the reservation provide income for the village members, some of whom have responsible jobs at Los Alamos.

Nambe is quite old, dating back to about A.D. 1300. At ground level it looks like any one of the clusters of Mexican houses that range up and down the Nambe Valley. Only the circular kiva and the crumbled walls of ancient

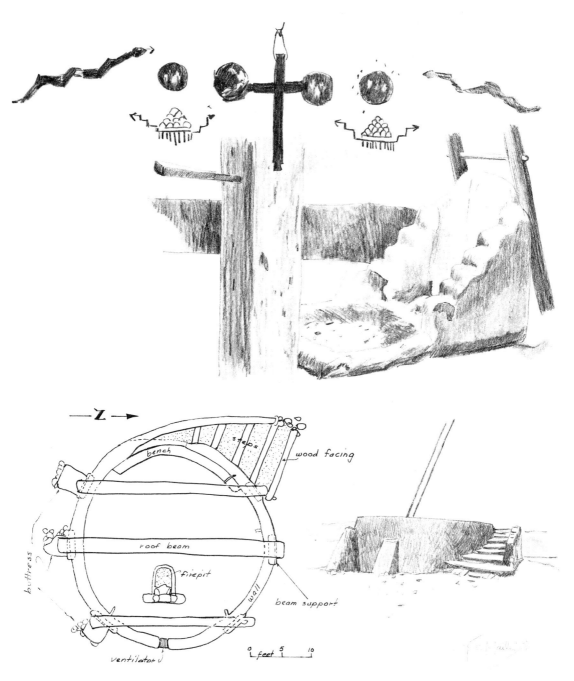

Top, kiva wall mural with hanging wooden cross, and armchair-type firepit. The pueblo where the firepit is located will not be named. When T. Harmon Parkhurst photographed it and died shortly thereafter, the Indians said his "violation" killed him. *Bottom*, plan and perspective of the kiva at Nambe with armchair-type firepit. From Kidder, 1958.

dwellings indicate the Pueblo nature of the village. But Stubbs discovered that from the air the old pueblo pattern is still evident. The largest house block indicates growth by accretion. The sherds found in Nambe refuse suggest a long period of occupation. After surveying the site in 1948, Stubbs agreed with Hewett that the pueblo would ultimately lose its distinguishing characteristics.

Few Pueblo arts and crafts are practiced at Nambe today, although there is a noticeable revival of interest in the ancient arts and ceremonial dances. One indication of this has to do with the original Roman Catholic mission, which collapsed some years ago. To raise funds to replace it, the residents initiated in 1960 an annual July 4 celebration at Nambe Falls, where in a splendid setting special events and dances are held. In the meantime, Catholic masses are still performed at the community center building, which also provides for educational services and social events.

The only active kiva that Kidder ever entered was one at Nambe, in 1922. The local residents saw him taking photographs and made no objection when he and his wife climbed down the ladder. Entirely undisturbed, he took notes and made measurements. He found the interior to be unkempt and the plaster flaking off the walls. When he returned in 1927, the village seemed more alive, and he was politely invited to enter the kiva again, only to find it was completely done over.

The circular kiva was slightly subsurface, and its roof was reached by a broad stairway. It was approximately 22 feet (6.6 m) in diameter and had a ceiling 9 feet (2.7 m) high. The walls were adobe, 2 feet (61 cm) thick, and supported by adobe buttresses. On the west side was a bench 1 foot (30 cm) high and 1 foot wide. Interior details included a wall ventilator shaft; a terraced, armchair-type adobe ashpit/deflector 4 feet (1.2 m) high and 16 inches (40.6 cm) thick with arms extending 2 feet 6 inches (76.2 cm); a firepit with adobe coping; four wall pegs; no sipapu. The interior wall had a brown dado 3 feet 6 inches (1.05 m) high, and the area above it was white. The roof structure consisted of three main pine beams about 2 feet (61 cm) in diameter, topped with 3- to 6-inch (7.5 to 15- cm) peeled poles laid at a right angle to the beams, a layer of brush and straw, and adobe. The central and longest beam was further braced by two rectangular posts set about 4 feet (1.2 m) in from the wall. These were painted with black rings and face symbols. A feature worth noting is that short beams were laid horizontally in the adobe walls for the main beams to rest on. Also, the kiva wall was about 1 foot (30.5 cm) higher than the finished roof.

The Nambe Council consists of a governor, lieutenant governor, War chief, fiscales, and the sheriff. Council positions are for life, and new members are admitted only when a council member dies.[199] The officers are selected by the Winter chief and the town chiefs,[200] although the people may vote for officials if they wish.

San Ildefonso Pueblo

San Ildefonso Pueblo, or Pohwage, is situated eighteen miles northwest of Santa Fe and east of the Rio Grande near the confluence of the stream that comes down from the east and bears the name of the village. In 1935, the pueblo was reduced to 127 inhabitants. By 1948 the count had risen to 170, and today it has soared to 1,450. For a long time, San Ildefonso has been an art center, and it is through the revival of ceramics, painting, and other arts that the entire community has been restored to prosperity. Many residents boast

San Ildefonso horseman.

substantial incomes, and several are world famous. It is here that Maria Martinez developed the black-on-black style for which the pueblo became known.

The village took an active part in the Revolt of 1680, and when the Spaniards returned in force in 1693, the residents took refuge on top of Black Mesa,
that sharp-sided butte that rises not far from the village. It is scalable in very
few places and easily defended, and so the people remained there for eight
months, yielding only when they ran short of water. Many legends exist concerning the mesa and its shrines, which are still used by the religious leaders
of the pueblo.[201]

The history of San Ildefonso's decline and revival is extremely interesting.
The village was begun sometime around A.D. 1300. Prior to the Pueblo Revolt
of 1680, the plaza on which the village centered was on the north side of the
town. The original dwelling units were two and three stories high, and the
town was large and prosperous. But as a result of what some leaders thought
was ''evil counsel,'' the pueblo was extended north, and a new north plaza
was built against the advice of the caciques, who knew that, traditionally, village extensions must be to the south. After considerable argument the move
was finally decided by a game, which the caciques said was won by witchcraft,
and the plaza was built in the north. Then real trouble began, as epidemics,

famines, and persecutions combined to decimate the population, and it continued until nearly everyone admitted the pueblo faced extinction.

Then a new cacique, Ignacio Aguilar, supported by a competent governor, Juan Gonzalez, came into office. The plaza problem was straightforwardly faced, and Hewett was invited to counsel with them. The leaders said their youth were dying faster than they could be replaced and that in twenty years San Ildefonso would "be likely dead Pojoaque." They believed, however, that the course of events could be altered and reversed by abandoning the ill-chosen north plaza and moving the residents back to the south. Hewett concurred.

Accordingly, new homes were built to the south, forming a new plaza around the ancient circular kiva, which they then restored. A second large kiva was constructed to replace the one in the north plaza that was being abandoned. Then, over a period of time most of the community shifted to the new south plaza and all ceremonial enactments were transferred there.

The results of the move met their most fervent expectations. Before long the cacique and his supporters could point with pride to children virtually free from epidemics and tuberculosis. Hewett says that his personal hopes were based largely upon the improvement of morale and sanitation, while those of

Juan Roybal, San Ildefonso potter.

Present-day San Ildefonso Pueblo girls on their way to a feast-day Game Animal Dance. From a photograph by John Running.

the Pueblos were rooted in the efficacy of tradition. "Between us we struck the remedy. Perhaps the visiting nurse deserves part of the credit."[202]

As the shift of dwellings to the south was taking place, many of the rooms that made up the central house block that divided the two plazas were converted to storage rooms. Then they were abandoned, and only recently removed entirely. Another recent change is the addition of a two-story rectangular kiva a short distance southwest of the circular one. A rectangular ceremonial room in a two-story structure in the northwest corner of the old north plaza still serves as the ritual room for that portion of the village.[203] The Roman Catholic church, erected about 1905, occupies the site of an earlier mission, slightly west of the village proper.

San Ildefonso's old circular kiva has adobe walls, and it is freestanding. As I have mentioned, it is in the south plaza of the village, and its roof is reached by a stairway. Since it has a fairly large opening at ground level, Kidder took advantage of this and peeked in one day. He saw that a bench about 2 feet (61 cm) high and 1 foot (30.5 cm) wide encircled the chamber. Above it was a ventilator hole. The terraced ashpit/deflector was similar to that he had inspected at Nambe. Three of six or seven main roof beams were braced by support posts about 6 feet (1.8 m) long.[204]

The council at San Ildefonso is made up of the governor; two lieutenant governors, one for the north and one for the south; and two additional representatives for each side.[205] The governor and lieutenant governor are selected in alternate years, and the four representatives. The head men of the north side choose the governor, and the head men of the south side the lieutenant governor.[206]

A San Ildefonso potter applying the design with a flexible brush.

San Juan Pueblo

San Juan is Spanish for St. John. The Pueblo name for the village is Oke'onwi. It is on the east bank of the Rio Grande about thirty miles north of Santa Fe and five miles north of Espanola. It too may date back to A.D. 1300. Its population was 768 in 1948, and today it numbers about 1,650.

In 1598, Oñate established his provincial headquarters across the Rio Grande from San Juan's present location, and because the Pueblos were kind enough to vacate the site and move east, he gave their new village the name San Juan de los Caballeros. The capital was moved to Santa Fe in A.D. 1609, and today only a few ruined houses and a hillside shrine mark the place where Oñate once dwelt. The resettled pueblo continued on, although in both blood and culture the general area is considerably Hispanicized.

Parsons says that Popé was a native of San Juan but that his "agitation" was not welcome, and "he had to go to Taos" to plan the famous rebellion of 1680. She also says that a certain Father Morfi reported that during the Reconquest by Spain the San Juan people aided him greatly by their "fidelity and valor."[207] San Juan numbered seventy families in 1744 and only fifty families in 1765, when the population was reduced to 316 Pueblos and 175 neighboring whites. Other area dwellings were occupied by Mexicans, and, says Parsons, "there appears to be more intermarriage in San Juan than in any pueblo except Nambe."[208]

San Juan is currently bordered on two sides by the settlement of Chamita, with only a highway separating the Tewa- and Spanish-speaking groups. Actually, two roads that form a kind of cross divide San Juan from Chamita. The south half of Chamita is typical of the American system of individual family dwellings.

The main portion of San Juan is made up of three long and irregular single-story adobe house groups that roughly parallel one another. The kivas are rectangular surface units that are enclosed in the house blocks. San Juan also has a permanent farming suburb named, with some humor, New York.

Today, the village has two excellent craft shops where native arts are both manufactured and sold. Besides pottery, superb embroidery and basketry are done. Wood carving and painting are also featured, as is silver and turquoise jewelry. Various members of the pueblo take turns working in the official village shop. At propitious times, almost any item of Pueblo ceremonial and secular apparel can be purchased at the shops, including wedding dresses.

Polished pottery, both plain red and plain black, along with brown and red ware, was the standard product until about 1930. Then a revival of an old style of decoration began. Geometric lines, often elaborated into intaglio patterns, were incised in the clay before firing. Polychrome decorations on polished red have also been crafted.

In 1969, a large multipurpose educational facility for youth and adults was built at San Juan. Many pueblo residents have found wage work in the cities of Albuquerque, Santa Fe, and Espanola, but most of them either live on the

Woman winnowing wheat at San Juan Pueblo.

pueblo or else return home to participate in the ceremonial life. Irrespective of what has been said about San Juan's cooperation with the Spanish, a strong traditional element exists in the village, and some of the finest ceremonial dances may be seen there.

The San Juan Council includes the governor, two lieutenant governors, two caciques, six society heads, the War chief, fiscal, sheriff, and all former governors. Aberle says that in former times each council member spoke in turn and that since 1943 a majority of the council constitutes a quorum.[209]

The old chiefs form a council to appoint the secular officers, who are then installed by the town chiefs. The office of town crier is for life.[210]

Santa Clara Pueblo

Santa Clara Pueblo, or Kápo, had a population of 417 in 1935 and 573 in 1948, and it numbers about 1,200 today. It sits on the west bank of the Rio Grande, just south of Espanola. It is near the mouth of Santa Clara Creek, one of the few small western tributaries that carry water to the Rio Grande. The village is well supplied with irrigable land, and it possesses a valuable land grant lying west of the town and extending to the top of the Jemex mountain range, where there is abundant timber and grazing land.

According to Hewett, the village suffered an unfortunate schism about

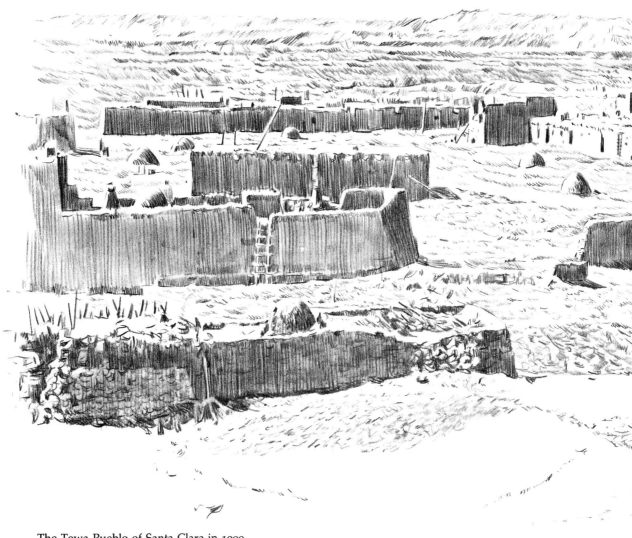

The Tewa Pueblo of Santa Clara in 1900.

1900. As a result, it was for years divided into two nearly equal factions, each with its own organization. One of these, the conservatives, was recognized by the U.S. Government authorities as the de facto government. The other group described itself as "progressive," and it tended to shun the ancient traditions. Because of this sometimes bitter antagonism between factions, Santa Clara has not always enjoyed a tranquil life, and disputes over various matters still erupt today.[211]

Despite the problem, Santa Clara has many things in its favor. One of its sources of distinction was the conservative, Santiago Naranjo, four times governor of the pueblo, one of the best known of all Pueblos, who served also as guide, philosopher, and friend of countless archaeologists, artists, and tourists. In addition, the village has produced some of the finest Pueblo artists.

According to Stubbs, the sherds collected at Santa Clara indicate that the

Santa Clara man in nineteenth-century attire.

Santiago Naranjo of Santa Clara Pueblo.

pueblo was in existence for some time prior to the Spanish entrada and probably dates back to the fourteenth century.[212] A two-plaza arrangement noted by Bandelier in the 1880s still exists, but sections of the older adobe houses are constantly crumbling, and most of the newer homes are built away from the plazas. A number of widely-spaced and modern homes stand west of the village proper.

The rectangular west plaza of the old village has adobe dwellings loosely placed on all four sides and a wide opening toward the northeast. Within this plaza is a large, rectangular, free-standing kiva. To the east is another plaza, circumscribed by houses on its north and south sides, but mostly open to the east. A second large, almost square, kiva sits alone in the extreme southwest corner of the village. A good-sized Roman Catholic church is on the north side of the pueblo. Near it is a day school that accepts children through the 6th grade. Also in this location is a new community center that houses, among other things, the administrative offices of the town.

Since it is close to the atomic center, Los Alamos, Santa Clara has supplied a number of employees for the project, and this source of income has considerably influenced the economy, as have the arts and crafts.

The early pottery made at the village was almost entirely polished black, somewhat like that of San Juan, but not so highly polished as that of San Ildefonso. By 1940, a polychrome style, somewhat resembling the pottery of San Juan, was being produced.

There are far too many outstanding potters to name, but they certainly include the Tafoya family of Camilio Tafoya, his daughter, Grace Medicine Flower, his son, the brilliant potter and metalsmith Joseph Lonewolf, and Joseph's daughters, Rosemary Appleblossom Speckled Rock, and Susan Romero. Joseph's son-in-law, Paul Speckled Rock, is a superb painter and sculptor, and his son-in-law Mike Romero is a fine painter. Other well-known painters from Santa Clara are the eminent Pablita Velarde and her daughter, Helen Hardin.

Santa Clara is a place where visitors may see ceremonial dances beautifully performed, and it is one of the few pueblos where photographs may be taken by permission. In this connection, the Pueblos of Santa Clara trace their ancestry back to cliff dwellers who lived at Puye, a mesa-top and cliff site on the nearby Pajarito Plateau. Puye was built between A.D. 1450 and 1475 and abandoned about A.D. 1590. The cliff ruins are considered the finest existing examples of Pajaritan culture. They are also the largest, extending for two miles. The main structure of the community was Top House Ruin, which contained about two thousand rooms. According to Dutton, some of the older residents of Santa Clara lived temporarily at Puye within relatively recent times.[213] Late in July of each year the northern pueblos join forces to present a spectacular series of dances at Puye, all of which are open to the public and can be photographed. Arts and crafts are also displayed and sold.

The Santa Clara Council consists of a governor; lieutenant governor; eight representatives, two of whom represent each of four parties; secretary, treasurer, interpreter, and sheriff.[214] All officers are chosen by the people.

IMMERSION INTO THE CORE OF LIFE

In considering the Hopi and other Pueblos treated thus far, it has been noted that the religious life of the Anasazi has, from some point early in their existence, continued to be the core of their lifeway. Every aspect of their social structure flows in orderly fashion out of what they believe. In its essence this belief is that Nature and God are one, which does not mean they view Nature and God as one in being, as if God consists of nothing more than the sum of the powers or life residing within each created thing (including space, time, and substance). God has an individual being. He is eternal and all powerful, while gods are lesser beings with limited and specific powers that have been delegated to them by God to use in maintaining balance and harmony in the universe. While every god is essential, gods vary in status. Some have been given more divine power than others, and there is even stratification within god-derived cults. For example, there are original Katcinas who are higher in status than the "made" Katcinas who join them after death.

The Pueblos have arrived at their religious concepts through ages of communion with God and the gods; through intercourse with a vast pantheon of supernaturals. By means of reflection, experience, and participation, the Pueblos have been brought to comprehension. They have been instructed and enlightened, and what they possess today is the culmination of ages of devotion. It benefits nothing here to compare other religions with the Pueblo view. To do so suggests that the Pueblo position may be insufficient, that it is valid only if it compares favorably with others. On the contrary, Pueblo religion rests solidly on its own foundation, and its virtues are intrinsic. Extraneous influences must be acknowledged insofar as is possible, but beyond this the religion stands and can be recommended on its own worth.

The Hano Tewa, Albert Yava, claims that Fewkes was able, through his sensitivity, to understand the Hopi. The same can be said of Hewett in regard to the Rio Grande Pueblos. Personal information confirms his assertion that Pueblo religion rests on two basic ideas: the belief that the unity of life is manifested in all things, and in a dual principle in all existence which is fundamentally male and female.[215] This religion finds expression in every act of life, especially in the "drama dance." Taken in its totality, the ritual and its dance are an intense prayer, either for something to come or in thanksgiving for something that has already arrived.

To effect these things, the individual pueblos are subdivided into moieties and ceremonial associations, but the method and fulfillment are communal in nature. The parts have their independent and vital existence, but only in the sense that what is needed for the entire body is so involved that it must be appropriated by the assignment tasks. No one part does everything, nor could it survive by itself. All parts must mesh and work together if the universe and man are to function. The agency for this intertwining is the tribal ceremonial. By means of ancient and dramatic rites practiced in unvarying traditional form, in which all members of the pueblo must participate for maximum effect, the

Pueblos keep time with the seasons and the supernaturals. The "power" comes, and with it harmony with nonhuman creations, the control of weather and crops, hunting game, curing, witchcraft, and to a certain extent village unity.

Birth

Immersion into the core of life follows the pattern of a swimmer who wades into a lake, every step taking him deeper until at last he begins to swim alongside others who are already in the lake. Childbirth is the first step into the lake.

As White outlines the native childbirth procedures for Santo Domingo and Zia, they are not nearly so complex as those carried out by the Hopi. A midwife cuts the umbilical cord and bathes the child. A male child's legs and feet are put into a black bowl to give him "a heavy voice." A girl's feet are put into a grinding bin. When the sun rises on the fourth day the baby is named. A godmother takes the child out to meet the rising sun and names it as the sun rises. The child is given an ear of corn and a bow and arrow and placed in a "baby board." The godmother receives a basket of corn flour for her services.[216]

Today, most women go to the Indian hospital in Santa Fe or Albuquerque for deliveries. Four days after the baby is brought home from the hospital, it is named. The naming ritual varies from village to village, but the presentation of the infant to the rising sun on the fourth day is a pan-Pueblo act, as is the custom of the godparents' giving an Indian name. Sacred stones and/or perfect ears of corn are sometimes used in the naming rite. The stones, actually small fetishes, are afterward placed in a small pottery bowl that has been used in the birth ritual. A boy is given a new name each time he participates in a ceremony.[217] The child owns the bowl, and it is never again used for a similar purpose. When a Pueblo friend of mine was married recently, his grandmother gave him his birth bowl and fetish, which sat on a bed of cornmeal, and alongside his fetish she had placed another one for the bride. The original Pueblo names are frequently derived from something unusual that happens at the time of the naming, or they may be given the name of an ancestor.[218]

Catholic baptism follows the native naming rite, and often the godparents will give the child a Christian name at this time to use when dealing with outsiders. The Indian name is kept secret. If a child is given the name of a celebrated saint, first his parents, and then he, will be obliged to hold a feast each year on the day of the saint for whom he was named. The Anglo birthday custom has only recently been adopted, complete with decorations, cakes, and presents.

Puberty Rites

Pueblo children undergo three complex native rites between birth and marriage. A splendidly detailed description of these rites at San Juan is given by

Ortiz, and it should be read by everyone who wishes to feel the wonder of Pueblo life as it continues today.

The first rite, called "water giving," is performed sometime during the first year of life. This is a beautiful ceremony in which the mothers wear their traditional costumes, and all the participants are in full regalia. The rite is conducted by the moiety chief, or cacique, in whose season the ceremony is taking place, and while the rites are the same for both seasons, they differ markedly in symbolism. Altars and sand paintings attend the rites, and there are references to the Emergence myth. In this rite the dual organization comes in dramatic form to the forefront, for while name giving is a rite of incorporation into the whole society, water giving is a rite of incorporation into the moiety. Among other things, the child receives a ceremonial sponsor, is given sacred water to drink, and receives another name.

Between the ages of six and ten the child passes through the "water-pouring" rite, which is symbolically associated with the migrations that followed Emergence. He is ceremonially bathed by having water poured over him, and masked Katcinas come into the kiva and dance. From this time on, the children are considered Dry Food People, common Tewa, and they are distinguished sexually for instruction.

The last of these rites is called "finishing," and it completes the process begun with the water-giving ceremony. Girls and boys ten years of age or older are separated in the kiva. The head Katcina god of the moiety comes first to the girls and administers a light blow with yucca whips. The girls leave the room, but the boys remain to receive more painful whippings. Then the Katcina mask is removed, and the secret of the impersonations is revealed. The boys must vow not to tell any children or women that it is men of the village who impersonate the gods. They are also now eligible to assist and participate in the coming of the Katcina gods. Finishing, then, is a deepening of incorporation into the ritual of one's own moiety, the last of three stages of absorption that will form the mold for an individual's entire life.

Most Pueblo children are also confirmed and receive their first Holy Communion in the Roman Catholic Church before age twelve. Sometimes the native immersion rites are postponed because children are away in boarding schools, at other times they are postponed until a sufficient number of children are ready to undergo the ceremonies.

Marriage

The native and Roman Catholic practices are today completely syncretized, and there is no clear correlation between marriage and moiety membership. Ortiz does say that couples who desire to marry must have undergone the Finishing Rite. And, if the bride belongs to the moiety opposite that of her husband she must convert to his by undergoing the rites already mentioned in relation to moieties.[219]

The boy's father, or another male go-between, presents the formal marriage proposal to the girl's father. When he accepts, the boy's family sends gifts to the bride's family. The bride's family must then provide a feast for all the relatives. At this time, long speeches are made to the couple by the elder males present. Ortiz says that at San Juan, although the speeches are in Tewa and they are derived from the native Wedding Rite, reference is often made to the saints, Christ, and the Virgin Mary, along with the Tewa supernaturals. The Catholic Wedding Ceremony is held either before or after the native feast.[220]

Death

Death rites at virtually every pueblo involve both native and Catholic practices. Those of Jemez have been described. At Cochiti, the native rites include washing the hair and dressing the body in the individual's best clothes, which may be daily wear or ceremonial garments. The medicine man then sprinkles herbs on the face of the deceased, and cornmeal or pollen is placed in the mouth. The moccasins are reversed, and a little food may be wrapped in cotton and placed in his left armpit.[221] He then massages the body and ritually "takes out" the soul. The body is sewn into a blanket and sometimes placed in a crude wooden box. If death occurs at night, burial takes place the next morning; if it happens during the day, it takes place the same day. At Cochiti, the sacristan and his assistants dig the grave and place a cross of large pebbles on the bottom. They then come to the home of the deceased, offer a prayer, and carry the body on a ladder to the church, where more prayers are offered. The body, still on the ladder, is placed on a wagon and transported to the burial grounds.[222] In a personal communication I learned that at one time kiva ladders were used to transport the deceased, sometimes being buried with him. But because the kiva is "a living being," all ladders are returned today. When in use, the ends of the ladder poles rest on the shoulders of the two male bearers.

At San Juan a package of food is placed with the body, and the amount of food depends upon the life led by the individual. If the person has led a good life, he will not need a great amount of food because his path to the Underworld will be short and straight. If he was not good, the path will be long and hard, and extra food and an extra pair of moccasins may be included. All souls eventually reach the spirit world, for there is no native concept of eternal damnation.[223]

For the first four days after death, the Tewa soul is believed to wander about in the company of its ancestors. On the fourth evening all the relatives gather to hold an involved rite of separation. If this is not done the soul remains to haunt the people. The Releasing Rite is repeated exactly one year after death, "because it is traditional."

According to Ortiz, after the body is prepared there is a shift to Spanish observances with feasting, singing of Spanish funeral songs, and prayers at the home of the deceased. At dawn the grave is dug by the sacristan and the fiscales. When it is ready, three of the fiscales go to get the body, and one remains to make certain that witches do not enter the grave or place evil objects in it. Once the body is placed in the grave, the Catholic priest conducts a blessing at the burial site. As soon as he leaves, Tewa ideas and practices take over again. Foremost among these is a lecture given by the fiscal to the family and relatives in which he admonishes the family not to let the loss divide the home or alter the traditional way of life.[224]

Lange reports that at Cochiti the medicine man returns to the home after four days and brushes the walls with pollen to remove whatever evil effects "might still be lingering."[225]

Ortiz also states that the general similarities between the (child) Naming and Death rituals give rise to what he believes is "the most important point" made in his entire book. It is that when it matters most, at the beginning and the end of life, "the Tewa emphasize the solidarity of the whole society rather than the dual organization."[226] To affirm this he points out that the rites of Birth and Death have much in common, thus expressing continuity and a sense of community. Despite the moiety system, all Tewa are born, intertwined, and die within the one religious context.

The generalized ancestors are honored at most villages on November 1, All Saints' Day, and November 2, All Souls' Day, with a commemorative mass and a Releasing Rite.[227] White reports that at Santo Domingo a masked dance was sometimes held on the morning of November 1. After the dance, individuals took small bundles of food and buried them outside the village as prayers were said. In the evening, bonfires were lit by the church. Men and boys gathered by these and sang all night.[228]

It can be seen that Pueblo social organization is structured to build a bond among the people of a village. But the lifeway bonds extend beyond this to tie the individual in with all of nature, and with those who create, impower, preserve, and perpetuate it. The Pueblos' is a universal view, in which everything that exists is alive, intertwined, and dual in the sense that by having male and female aspects or beings, it procreates so that at all times in all generations everything needful for life and harmony is present and can be drawn on by proper hearts and ritual.

COSMOGRAPHY

Vincent Scully's book *Pueblo Mountain, Village, Dance,* published in 1975 by the Viking Press, is a beautiful, mainly photographic essay that seeks to point up the strong esoteric relationship between the Pueblo dancer, his village, and the surrounding landscape. It suggests that none of this relationship is accidental and that one can appreciate the Pueblos as one should only when this is borne in mind.

Scully's point is well taken, and one can hardly witness, perhaps better said "experience," a dance without feeling that it is an inseparable part of the village and land in which it is taking place. A marvelous kind of oneness is exuded, an energy flowing deep within the dancers that brings to them an extraordinary peace and strength, and whose overflow encompasses the audience. This is never so when the people dance outside their village, as at Puye or at Santa Fe. Here one sees the beauty of the costumes and the expertise of the performers, but there is no energy, and there is no religious "feel." The function is changed, and so is the meaning. The Pueblos know this, and they do it only to please the viewers and thus to show a community spirit.

The Pueblos define their center, or world, by designating lakes, mountains, and shrines at each of the cardinal directions. The Tiwa Pueblos recognize the four sacred directions of north, west, south, and east. The Tewa Pueblos include the Zenith and Nadir to make six directions. Each direction has its own color, mammal, bird, and mountain that is associated with it. Certain mountains are regarded as the homes of supernaturals, and these are named in Pueblo mythology. Pilgrimages to shrines are often part of rituals and retreats held prior to a public dance, and when shrines are visited by medicine men, guards are stationed to watch for intruders.

Ellis and Hammack, in their previously mentioned report on Feather Cave, stress the significance of caves in the Pueblo system of cosmology and related rituals, a pattern that has been "little recognized by anthropologists because Pueblos are so secretive about the subject." They go on to say that Pueblos feel that persons more closely approach the Underworld "when they meet, store paraphernalia, or deposit offerings in caves." The caves and crevices penetrate the Below where the majority of the Pueblo spirit powers reside. Earth Mother is also there, having remained underground when the people emerged onto the earth.[229] The authors go on to describe several of the caves in current use by the Rio Grande religious leaders, as well as those of Acoma, Laguna, and Zuñi.

Despite his opening reference to the secrecy of the Tewa in regard to religious matters, John Peabody Harrington, in his voluminous, 636-page BAE Report of 1907–8, *The Ethnogeography of the Tewa Indians*, seems to have obtained an extraordinary amount of information regarding their cosmography, which includes the world, the cardinal directions and their symbolism, the sky (which includes sun and moon, sun-dog, stars, and constellations), the underworld, the earth, and water; meteorology, which includes snow, wind, lightning, and thunder; periods of time; geographical terms; place-names; names of tribes and peoples; and names of minerals.

With the exception of Elsie Clews Parsons, there is probably no better authority on Tewa cosmography than Harrington, and those in need of carefully organized and exhaustive detail are referred to his report. Space limitations will permit no more than a summary of it here. Once again, while there are significant differences between Tewa practices and those of the other language groups of the Rio Grande, the aim is to provide only a "feel" for the lifeway, hence the Tewa serve mainly as the example in the material that follows.

Harrington says the Tewa world is synonymous with the universe. It includes everything that is, and it is represented in Pueblo art in various ways. It is thought of as being alive, and it is worshipped as "Universe Man," "world," "man in prime." The Milky Way is said to be its backbone.[230]

The Tewa distinguish six cardinal directions: north, west, south, east, above, and below—usually named in the order given. Cardinal directions are also given a number of series: six colors, six Corn Maidens, six animals, six plants, six birds, six reptiles, and six inanimate objects such as trees, mountains, and lakes.

Divinities in some instances are also multiplied so that one might be associated with each direction, but these identifications are regarded as a portion of secret ritual, and it is difficult to gather information about them. Harrington obtained terms for the cardinal directions in the neighboring languages also. The Taos and Jemez have somewhat complicated systems; even the position of a listener who is higher or lower than the speaker requires different forms of discourse. Each pueblo distinguishes six directions. The Keresan Cochiti recognize six directions, which they name in the same order as do the Tewa.[231]

Color symbolism is the same at all Tewa villages, but it differs from that of some of the other Pueblo and non-Pueblo tribes of the Southwest. The Tewa colors are north, blue/green; west, yellow; south, red; east, white; above, all-colored; below, black. The Zuñi and Hopi assign blue to the north and yellow to the west, but otherwise their designations are not the same as those of the Tewa. The Tewa summer sun is green, the winter sun is yellow, the summer rainbow is tricolored, the winter rainbow is white.[232]

Cardinal mammals of the Tewa are: north, mountain lion; west, bear; south, badger; east, wolf; above, eagle; below, gopher (literally earth mountain lion). All these are considered to be powerful medicine animals, and sacred cornmeal is thrown as a sacrifice to them and to other divinities.[233]

The sky is distinguished from the heavens (the above). The sky is considered a male deity, called Sky Old Man, and he is the husband of the earth, personified as Earth Old Woman. The sun, moon, stars, and the Christian God are said to live in the sky.

The sun is called T'han and the moon is called Po. The divinities resident in them are called Sun Old Man and Moon Old Man. Both are male, but the sun is never called "Father" or the moon "Mother," as among the people of Taos, Isleta, Jemez, and Zuñi.

The sun and moon pass daily from east to west over trails that run above "the great waters of the sky." They see and know as do the Tewa here on earth. When they set they pass through a lake and down to the underworld. They travel all night to the east, where they emerge through a lake and start out on their trails again. When there is an eclipse, the sun or the moon is said to die, but the divinities resident in them cannot die. The Tewa say, "Our Lords cannot die."[234] The sun is said to walk through the sky clothed in white deerskin and ornamented with fine beads. The sun has a beautiful face, which is hidden by a mask. An extracted tooth is thrown to the sun.

Harrington says the Tewa have no designation for the equinoxes. But the winter solstice is called "the sun stands still," and it marks the beginning of the year, which is then described as "new year." The summer solstice is called "the sun lives." The calendar is determined by marking the point at which the sun rises. This is done by sighting along racecourses, hills, or places along the mountain ridges. The Tewa believe the sun has a house in the east and has a wife. But the father of the War Gods is "red cloud," who lives on top of Sandia Mountain, and not the sun.[235] The terms applied to the rising and setting of the sun are also applied to the moon.

The morning star is a male divinity, the evening star is a female divinity. Constellations are recognized and named, but are not considered divinities.[236]

The Tewa Underworld is called "the Below." They believe in a single Underworld, where the sun shines palely at night, like the moon. It was there that the human race and the lower animals lived until they climbed up a great Douglas fir tree, found their way out through a lake called Siṗop 'e, and entered this world. The Underworld is dark and dank, and this world rests on top of it. The Underworld is never personified; it is the base of the universe. In the Underworld is situated the place where the spirits of the people go after death. It is described as a kiva-like place of the spirits of the dead.[237]

When people die, their spirits go to Siṗop 'e, through which they pass into the Underworld. There are many spirits in the waters of Siṗop 'e, which for the Tewa is a brackish lake situated in the sand dunes north of Alamosa, Colorado. Its exact location is generally and definitely known to the Tewa. "Their ancestors," they say, "came out upon the surface of the earth at a place called Ci-bo-be, now a lagune [lagoon] in southern Colorado."

The name Siṗop 'e occurs in varying forms in other Pueblo languages. The Taos form has not been published. Isleta calls it Shi-pa-pu. The Jemez are said to have originated at a lagoon called Ua-buna-tota, and the souls of the dead go to rest there. According to Harrington's San Juan informants, the Cochiti and other Keresan people entered this world not at Siṗop 'e, but at La Cueva in Taos County. The Zuñi form is Shi-papu-lima, said to mean "The Mist-enveloped City." As I have already reported, the Hopi form is Sipapu,[238] and this form is in general use by writers.

The earth is personified as "Earth Old Woman," wife of the sky. She is a female deity. Harrington claims that the Tewa never speak of the earth as Earth Mother, but other and more recent authorities do not support this.

The Tewa name 'Ok'uwa is applied to any kind of cloud. It is distinguished from 'ōk'uwa, "spirit," "Katcina," by having its first syllable short, but the two are connected. Mythological serpents, and Katcinas, are said to come in the clouds and to be seen now and then by people looking upward. The Katcinas, or deified spirits, are supposed to be constantly present among the clouds, and there is a close resemblance between the clouds and the spirits. The Tewa also speak of six mythic persons, youths and maidens, who are known as Cloud People, each with an appropriate color for one of the six directions. "Red Cloud" figures in the War God myth. There also is a "Cloud House," which is a pueblo in the sky above the clouds. In Tewa art, the terrace represents clouds. Tobacco smoke, soap plant seeds, feathers, and other items symbolize clouds in ceremonies.

Rain is of supreme importance to the Tewa farmers, and most rains come from the southwest. Religious rites are replete with practices and prayers

The six masks, or shields, of the Sumaikoli, a Katcina curing society at the Hopi village of Hano, a Tewa community. The "whip" of the society is a cure for sore eyes. From Fewkes, 1920.

whose aim is to bring the rain so necessary for crop growth. The Tewa also hold special dances designed to produce rain. They are variously called Rain Dance, Rainmaking Dance, and Rain Power Dance. Rain is given descriptive names to portray its location, whether it is absent, coming, present, light, heavy.[239]

The divinity of the rainbow is called "Rainbow Old Man." Wind is produced by "Wind Old Woman," who lives on Sandia Mountain. Lightning is produced by Katcina spirits, who throw it from the clouds. Flaking stone, wherever found, is considered to be the result of lightning striking the earth. The arrows of the War Gods were of lightning; they had stolen the arrows. Thunder is caused by "Thunder Old Woman," but there is no Tewa name for thunderstorm.[240]

The aforementioned represent only a few of the supernaturals. Others include a Mean Woman and Mean Man of the North, a Spider Woman, a Salt Woman. All supernaturals can use their power positively or negatively.[241]

The Tewa distinguish only summer and winter. Summer begins in the spring and lasts until fall. It comprises the months of April, May, June, July, August, and September. Winter comprises the other six months. Planting and harvest time are spoken of, but these are not considered to be seasons. Unlike the Tewa, the Jemez distinguish four seasons: spring, summer, autumn, and winter.

All the people of the Tewa villages belong to either the Summer or the Winter moiety. Harrington says the Summer moiety is called "summer people" or "squash (or pumpkin) people." The Winter moiety is called "winter people" or "turquoise people." The Summer People are presided over by a cacique, known as "ceremony-presiding chief." The Winter cacique is known as "hard ice chief."[242]

The native Tewa year contained twelve months known by descriptive names that in Harrington's time were passing out of use and being replaced by the names of Christian saints. They were said to have begun at the time of the new moon, and were divided into summer and winter months.

As has been seen, shrines have played since earliest times an important role in the lifeway of the Anasazi, and they continue to do so in the lives of Pueblo people today.

Just north of Picuris Pueblo is a ruin on a mound called the "Old Castle." It is said to have once been five stories high, but it has decayed to where only three stories are left. There still were, as of 1908, two perfect rooms, which were sealed up and which contained some sacred meal. There is also a shrine on the mound, and on it are a fetish of clay representing an animal, a fragment of an old tubular pipe, and four small stones—one of them a piece of obsidian.[243] Jicarilla (or Jicarita) peak, whose altitude is 12,944 feet, is a sacred mountain of the Picuris Indians. They are said to have a shrine on its summit, and members of certain fraternities frequently visit the shrine in a body.[244]

High Hill is the sacred place of San Juan Pueblo. Unidentified medicine plants were found growing on High Hill. On the summit of the northern peak is a shrine of stones arranged in a U-shape, about a yard in length, with the opening toward San Juan Pueblo. On the summit of the southern peak is a large V-shaped stone shrine with its opening toward the pueblo. At the point of the V is a large slab of yellowish stone.[245]

On top of the hills west of Santa Clara and on the high land just west of the hills are numerous shrines made by arranging stones of various kinds on the ground. Prayer sticks and sacred meal are deposited at these shrines. Christian custom has caused candles to be burned at some of the shrines on particular occasions.[246]

Black Mesa is the most conspicuous geographical feature in Tewa country. It is about midway between the San Ildefonso and Santa Clara pueblos. The formerly volcanic mesa has been used as a place of refuge and defense in time of war since the earliest period. In historic times the San Ildefonso Tewa were besieged on the mesa by the Spaniards at the close of the Pueblo Revolt. Not surprisingly, Black Mesa has much to do with the mythology and religion of the Tewa. Legends tell of a "giant" who formerly lived with his wife and daughter within the mesa. He was so large he could reach San Ildefonso village in four steps, making daily trips to catch children and taking them home for his family to eat. He drank from the Rio Grande. Finally, the giant and his family were killed by the Twin War Gods, and the giant's heart is said to be a certain white stone that still rests on top of the mesa. An ancient altar on its top is perfectly preserved, and offerings are still placed there. The Tewa say that until recent times sacred dances were performed on particular occasions on the mesa top.[247]

The "Very High Hill" is a symmetrical, high, round hill that serves as the shrine of San Ildefonso. A well-worn trail leads from the southeast corner of the pueblo to a group of stones on the summit of the hill.[248]

The shrine of Nambe Pueblo is situated on top of Fire Medicine Mountain.[249]

Another "Very High Hill" serves as a sacred place for Tesuque Pueblo. A stone shrine stands on its top, and an ancient pathway leads from the pueblo to the summit.[250]

Considering the dearth of firsthand reports by whites concerning Rio Grande ritual, certain of Fewkes's observations at Tewan Hano assume prime importance. He describes, for example, the time in August when he was invited by Ka-la-cai, the chief, to attend the ceremony of making *su-my-ko-li bahos*. "This was said to be a Tewan and not a Hopi ceremonial," and Fewkes verifies this by finding no evidence of its taking place in either Walpi or Sichomovi.[251]

Fewkes translates *su-my-ko-li* as "wizards or gnomes," and the ceremony referred to was one of making prayer sticks for wizards or gnomes. We can, without violating the Rio Grande rule of a closed kiva, enter one and see about how the Rio Grande type of ceremonies proceeded.

> In the early morning, as is customary, those who were to take part in this ceremony had their heads carefully washed, and at about ten o'clock ate breakfast, some of those who were to celebrate the ceremony eating with Kā'-lā-cai at his home. After breakfast, Kā'-lā-cai went to the ceremonial room, which is on the second story, facing the south, just to the left of his house, and spread down on the floor, along the side of the west wall, a blanket, over which was thrown a white buckskin, said to be a favorite garment of the *Su-mý-ko-li*. He then brought his feather-box, a pot of honey, and a stone upon which paint is ground. Soon there came in a woman, who brought a small basket of sacred meal, and laid it on the floor in front of the buckskin. At the word from Kā'-lā-cai, she again took the meal, and, going to a dark room under that in which the ceremony was to be performed, made a line of sacred meal from the dark chamber to the room above, through a doorway which is on the eastern side, opposite the buckskin, along the floor, to the middle of the pelt. This is the path along which Kā'-lā-cai brought the shield-shaped *Su-mý-ko-li*, which are kept hanging on the western wall of the dark chamber which she visited.
>
> After the woman had made this line, Kā'-lā-cai took a handful of sacred meal, and, followed by the writer, climbed down into the above-mentioned chamber. Standing in front of the row of *Su-mý-ko-li* hanging on the west wall, he sprinkled them with meal, repeating, as he did so, certain unintelligible words in a low voice. He then took down the *Su-mý-ko-li* shields, one by one, placed them in the blanket which he carried, and, mounting to the ceremonial chamber, arranged them in a row on the buckskin, leaning them against the wall. He then drew on the floor a line of meal corresponding with that made by the woman, and placed on it, at a few feet from the edge of the buckskin, his square *nā'-kwi-pi, sáy-ĕ-wĕ* (Tewan), a bowl with terraced rims, which was to contain the liquid used in painting the *bā'-hos* [pahos]. From this vessel he laid a string, to the end of which were attached the two feathers, as has been recorded in other ceremonies. This was then sprinkled with meal, as were also the *Su-mý-ko-li*, after they had been placed in position.

Top, shrine near Picuris Pueblo. The fetish stone at the upper left is a type common to all past and present Anasazi. *Middle*, the Stone Lions shrine of Cochiti Pueblo. *Bottom*, shrine near Cochiti Pueblo. From Museum of New Mexico archive photographs.

Kā'-lā-cai then took an ancient, spherical gourd bottle, and poured a liquid into the terraced bowl, from the sides corresponding to the four cardinal points, beginning with the east. The order which he then followed was east, north, west, and south. He then took a powder from his wallet and placed a little in the liquid, throwing a pinch to each of the cardinal points in the same order as indicated above, namely, east, north, west, south. He seated himself at the right of the line of *Su-mý-ko-li*, and smoked to the four quarters of the earth, and upon the *bā'-hos*. While he was doing this, another priest came in, took his stand in front of the *Su-mý-ko-li*, filled his hand with sacred meal, and, after scattering it upon each of the *Su-mý-ko-li*, threw a little along the line to the door, and into the air outside.

There were seven of these *Su-mý-ko-li* shields made of skin tightly stretched over a framework. The front side of each was variously colored and ornamented with symbolic designs, while the back on each side was covered with many sticks, to which were bound a large mass of *nā-kwā'-ko-ci*, or wish-feathers. In the middle of the reverse side of each shield was a wooden handle.

Beginning with the left or north end of the line of *Su-mý-ko-li*, the first had a green upper and lower black part. The latter was decorated with concentric half circles, which reminded me of the chin of *Sá-li-ko-mā-nā*, four rainbow-like concentric curves of different colors, in the following order: green, red, yellow, and a center of red. The curves were separated by black lines. The portion of the shield painted black was separated from the green upper portion by a series of indentations which were fringed with a white line. The two eyes of this and all the other *Su-mý-ko-li* were black, elongated, oval marks, surrounded by a white zone inclosed in a black ellipse.

Number two of the series was identical in colors with number one, except that there was one less rainbow line of color on the lower part.

Number three had also a green color; but instead of a black lower half, that portion was occupied by a reddish rectangle fringed with black, the upper side being indented with terraces. This symbol, which occurred in three of the remaining shields, was colored green in number five, red in number six, and green in number seven. The face of number five was red, that of six yellow, and of seven white. All had the same rainbow marks on the lower half, although the sequence of the colors varied somewhat in order, but always being green, red, yellow, or white, the colors corresponding to the four cardinal points, separated by black lines.

The central *Su-mý-ko-li* differed in symbolism from any of the others, and was more elaborate. Its whole face was divided, like a coat of arms, into three regions, the lower of which was like that on number one, but of black color. Above it there was a right and left zone; the former, green, the latter, yellow. In the former, on the lower edge, there were painted three square figures edged with red; in the latter a crook-shaped figure in green with a black border, alternating with white squares. Both of these arose from the upper margin of the lower black zone. The order of colors in the concentric curves on the black lower part of the figure was red, green, yellow, red, all separated by black lines. In size and general shape this shield does not differ from the others.

The ceremony of making the *bā'-hos* [pahos] began at two o'clock in the afternoon, and lasted until about six. Ten men took part in the afternoon ceremony, and sixteen *bā'-hos* [pahos] were made.

Kā'-lā-cai furnished a number of sticks, each two feet or more in length. Every man took one of these sticks, and first tasting a little honey, moistened his hand and rubbed the honey upon the sticks and upon the lower part of his breast. The sticks were then cut into shorter sections, the diameter of an ordinary pencil. They were sharpened and painted black, except the blunt ends, which were painted green, the liquid for mixing the paint being taken from the *nā'-kwi-pi*. Breath-feathers were then fastened to a little string, and four of these strings with attached feathers were tied at equal intervals to each stick. After preparing the *bā'-hos* [pahos], a set of seven cotton strings with attached feathers were also made. A short, many-stranded string, to one end of which was tied two feathers, one a white, the other a small yellow feather, was prepared, and each priest in turn stepped to the row of *Su-mý-ko-li* shields, and one by one tied a single *nā-kwā'-ko-ci* to one of the many sticks already crowded with similar offerings, which were attached to the back of the shields. As each priest did this, he sprinkled all the shields with sacred meal and cast a little along the line of the floor and out of the doorway. This was done carelessly by some, faithfully by the more devout; but it must, however, be noted that several of those present seemed to me to make their offerings in a perfunctory manner.

After all the priests present had tied the feathers to the shields of the *Su-mý-ko-li*, Kā'-lā-cai placed a flat basket tray in front of them and laid the four *bā'-hos* [pahos] which he had made upon it, placing one at each cardinal point. He then threw a pinch of meal in each of the four cardinal directions. The other priests then placed their *bā'-hos* [pahos] near those deposited by Kā'-lā-cai. This was

Ceremonial items. *Left,* a votive bowl with plumed serpent. *Right,* a sacred corn fetish. From the Museum of New Mexico collection.

followed by a ceremonial smoke, during which each man in turn puffed the smoke upon the collection of *bā'-hos* [pahos], raising the tray to his mouth as he did so. At the conclusion of this ceremony Kā'-lā-cai said a prayer, to which the others responded, and one by one followed him with prayers. The four bundles of *bā'-hos* [pahos] were then gathered up, and Kā'-lā-cai, having appointed two of those present as bearers of the offerings, placed them in their hands to deposit in different shrines.

It will be noticed that the ceremonial circuit of the cardinal points adopted by Kā'-lā-cai is not the Hopi ceremonial circuit from the north to the west, but from the east to the north. Possibly this may have been accidental; but it is not certain that such was the case. I have also detected a slight variation between the Hopi and the Tewans in the colors which they assign to the cardinal points. Yellow corresponds to the north, blue to the west in Hopi; but in Hā'-no it is exactly the reverse, blue (green) is north, and yellow, west with the priests of the last-mentioned pueblo.[252]

Ellis and Hammack state that modern crook pahos "differ according to the religious society depositing them, and also as to whether they are made for summer or winter ceremonies." At Santa Ana, for example, color and decoration vary to indicate "the donor society, the season, and the specific recipient."[253] The illustrations show some of the important features described by Ellis and Hammack in their article on Feather Cave.

KATCINA CULT

The Rio Grande Katcina Cult is referred to as Katcina, Oxuhwa (Tewa), or Shiwana (Keresan). As at the western pueblos, Katcina spirits are impersonated in dances by the members of the cult. The main associations of the cult are with rain, fertility, and general well-being. Katcinas are referred to as the spirits of the dead, but there are actually two categories, the original Katcinas and those who die and become Katcinas. Ortiz says that only people who have devoted their lives to religious activities will join the Katcinas after death. The Katcinas represent male or female deities, animals, insects, and vegetation. When the masks are donned, the impersonators take on the spirit of the Katcina.[254] They are named by the call they make, their origin, or by the way they look or walk. One may be recognized by his limp, another by his fast steps, and a third for favoring his left foot and hand. There are many Katcinas recorded in the literature. Since information regarding these is derived entirely from "informants," the degree of accuracy regarding the masks and costumes is not known. But many of them are redrawn herein, at least to give a rough comparison with the Katcinas of Hopi and Zuñi.

Leslie White records the mythical origin of the Katcina dances as it was related to him by Santo Domingo informants. In it, the Keresan term "shiwana" is used in place of Katcina, but all pueblos recognize the term Katcina.[255]

"The shiwana lived in Wenima. They used to come to Santo Domingo to dance. Every time they came you could hear the ducks and geese hollering at night. The shiwana came riding on their backs. After the dance was over the shiwana would turn into ducks and geese and fly away again. After a while the shiwana gave the people their masks and costumes. They didn't want to come any more. They told the people that they could dress up like the shiwana and dance, and it would be just like the real shiwana dancing. It brings the rain."[256]

The complexity of the Katcina Cult varies with the pueblos. Dozier says the cult is less important among the Tewa and that, except at Isleta, the Katcina supernaturals are not impersonated in the Tiwa pueblos. The cult maintains its importance among the Zia, where White received information about thirty masks, and at Cochiti, where more than fifty masks were recorded by Lange.[257] No one really knows what the actual situation is. Rio Grande Pueblos deny out of hand the existence of the cult as a continuing reaction to the policies of the early missionaries.

In all the Keresan pueblos, control and management of the Katcina Cult is in the hands of the Medicine associations and the clown organizations, although the cacique and his assistants play a prominent leadership role. As I have previously stated, the War captains are related to the Twin War Gods, Masewi and Oyoyewi, already familiar to us from Hopi, Zuñi, Acoma, and Laguna.

RELIGIOUS ASSOCIATIONS

After joining the Katcina Cult, an individual may also join an esoteric association, although membership in such is not considered a privilege or an obligation to the community. As at Hopi, recruitment into an association is by "choice," "trespass," or "trapping." If a child has been cured by a member of an association, he may be dedicated to the association by his parents. Self-dedication may result from a dream in which an individual believes he is called to join. If an individual accidentally comes upon a society involved in ritual, he is certain to be accused of trespass and recruited. Trapping is a device employed by a society so badly in need of new members that it gets them in devious ways. For example, an ill person may be told that the only way he can recover is to join a particular society.[258] As at Hopi, initiation into a society involves a ceremony of rebirth, and abstinence or payments are also required. There are, or were, five kinds of associations or societies: medicine men, hunters, warriors, women, and clowns.

MEDICINE SOCIETIES

The use of outside medical facilities increases every year, but medicine men are still called upon to treat particular problems, and medicine associations are involved in curing certain illnesses. They combat witchcraft, hold retreats to bring rain, and, in the Keresan villages, exercise governmental control by se-

Bottom, prayer meal bowl and wooden ceremonial flute. *Top,* wooden parrot or macaw effigy with real feather tail of the type employed in the Parrot Dance. From the Museum of New Mexico collection.

lecting political officers. Medicine men assist at masked dances and are custodians of special masks, fetishes, and other paraphernalia.

Santo Domingo has four major and four minor curing societies. The major ones are the Flint, Cikame, Giant, and Bóyaka. Their power is derived from supernatural animals, and they unite to handle serious cases that affect the general good. Power to cure is gained through the use of fetishes and idols, and medicines and various items are employed for curing. Membership is either voluntary or by compulsion. Women can belong, but they are not allowed to learn all the society secrets. The minor societies are the Snake, Ant, Beraka, and Kapina. Each of these controls some ailment.[259]

As I have mentioned in reference to Isleta, witchcraft is still taken seriously by many Pueblo Indians. Lange claims that "even those who do not personally believe in witchcraft respect the danger of becoming implicated in charges of witchcraft by those who do hold such beliefs." It is believed that witches are able to assume human, bird, or animal forms. Some are little more than tricksters, "while others have the power to make one ill or even kill."[260]

HUNTING, WARRIOR, AND WOMEN'S SOCIETIES

It is not possible today to state definitely whether hunting, warrior, and women's societies are still in existence at all the pueblos. Bandelier found indications that at some villages, such as Cochiti, the Hunt societies were dying out eighty years ago, although White discovered they were still important there in 1935. According to Dozier, while the Keresan Opi War Society is extinct now, some War societies have remained important in modified functions, such as organizing small group War dances and races.[261]

White found the Opi War Society to be extinct at Santo Domingo, but states that it was composed of men who had killed an enemy and taken his scalp in a prescribed ritual manner. Their faces were painted black, and they wore a buckskin kilt similar to that of the Hopi Snake society. Eagle-down feathers were worn on the crown of the head. Their patron deities were the twins, Masewi and Oyoyewi.

Lange adds that, in former times, the killing of a bear, mountain lion, or eagle at Cochiti was tantamount to killing an enemy and that a man became eligible to join the Opi by so doing. Some of his informants believed, however, that the killing of animal equivalents only became a substitute when warfare began to die out, and men were still needed to perpetuate the society.[262] When one of the animals mentioned above, or an eagle, was taken, the game was brought with great fanfare into the village and elaborate rituals of treating it followed. Some of this is still perpetuated today. I learned that animal skulls were often placed in Zuñi shrines, and this is also a Rio Grande practice.[263]

A few women's societies are associated with men's societies. Their duties in former times included feeding cornmeal to the enemy scalps, washing men's hair for kiva purifications, grinding corn to make prayer meal for the cacique, and assisting the hunters with daily offerings and prayers when they were away on a hunt.

KOSHARE AND KWERANA

There are two complementary secret societies common to the Keres and Tewa pueblos. The Keresan names are "Koshare" or "Koshairi" and "Kwerana" or "Quiranina." The Tewa refer to them as "Kossa" and "Kwirana." Both are associated with weather control, fertility, and the supervision of ceremonies.

They alternate control over the annual patron-saint's-day dances. The koshare hold initiations (and occasionally a dance) in February, and the kwerana hold theirs in September. The applicant is required to undergo a period of training before the final induction, and in some instances he has to wait four years before being initiated. It is said that masks are used in initiations, but masks are not worn in the public performances. The koshare are associated with the Turquoise kiva, and the kwerana with the Squash kiva. At Santo Domingo,

Left, Santo Domingo Pueblo koshare. *Right*, San Juan Pueblo kossa. From Museum of New Mexico photos.

both groups are closely related to medicine societies: the koshare to the Flint Medicine Society, and the kwerana to the Ckame Society. All members of these curing groups are koshare or kwerana, but the latter do not cure diseases.[264]

Koshare and kwerana from one village will sometimes appear in dances at another village. They need to help one another out, because the life is demanding and initiates are hard to come by. "Crutsi," or "uncooked," koshare and kwerana may also appear in dances. These are uninitiated men who are not actually members of the society, but have been asked to help, and so they dress and dance like the koshare and kwerana.[265] Women may belong either to the Koshare or Kwerana societies, but they are only associate members. They lack the powers that men have, and they cannot perform the rituals. Their role is to bring water for mixing the medicine, to furnish food, and to help with preparations for the ceremonies.[266]

At the July 26 patron-saint's-day dances at Santa Ana, three female koshare members appear with a male koshare. This was consistently so for the dances of 1974, 1975, 1976, and 1977. Their costumes are described in detail and illustrated in the Santa Ana material that follows, but, briefly, they wear traditional women's dresses, and their legs, arms, and faces are painted in koshare style. Women koshare also appear at certain Santo Domingo koshare dances with their faces, arms, and legs painted somewhat like those of the male koshare.

Koshare and kwerana dress and act differently during public dances. Both are referred to in the literature as "clown societies," but only the koshare actually fulfill this role. The kwerana always maintain a dignified presence. The koshare are painted with horizontal black and white stripes or dots. The face is covered with white paint, and black rings are placed around the eyes and mouth. The hair or a cap is coated with white clay and formed into two "horns" with the aid of corn husks. The costumes are a scarf of black cloth, a black woolen breechclout, and a thick bandolier of rabbit fur. Rattles of deer or large cow hoofs are often tied at the waist.

The kwerana dress simply but colorfully in regular shirts and pants. Their only identification is a small tuft of blue jay or sparrow hawk feathers tied in their hair.

Since a principal aspect of the clowns role among the Rio Grande Pueblos is to reverse and invert the reality of Pueblo Culture, they reinforce socially acceptable behavior by performing what is unacceptable. They may do this with suggestive movements, comedy acts, and speech or by ridiculing an individual who has broken a Pueblo social norm. At one time, obscene acts, similar to those mentioned in discussions of the Hopi mudheads, were performed by the koshare. But for public performances, at least when non-Pueblos are present today, these have been eliminated because of pressure from the government, church, and schools. Now their actions are calculated to provoke laughter and some entertainment during a dance. This does not mean they do nothing but clown. At certain times they accompany the dancers in the most dignified and graceful manner possible, dancing with their hands held in a characteristic supplicating position. At such times they leave an impression so subliminal that the spectator never forgets it. As at Hopi and Zuñi, the koshare

Left, San Ildefonso kossa. *Right*, *chiffonetti* clowns climbing the pole on San Geronimo Day at Taos Pueblo.

clowns represent the way the world should not behave. To make their point, they perform activities backward or incorrectly, carrying on conversations backward, fighting over food, and mocking the sacred movements of animal dancers. At San Ildefonso, on January 23, 1973, I saw kossa perform a mock Holy Communion with a group of tourists.

On San Geronimo Day the Taos *chiffonetti*, who are similar to kossa or koshare, perform. They often throw children into the river, imitate dogs, engage in dirt fights, and tear down part of the cottonwood bower that houses the saint. Each year they attempt to climb a thirty-foot pole to bring down a sacrificed sheep and other food that is tied to the top. First they try to shoot the goods down with tiny arrows, then each clown attempts to climb the pole until at last one or two of them reach the top. A similar pole climb is held at Picuris each year on August 10. In 1974, the clowns were not able to reach the top, and a ladder was used to reach the sheep and bring it down.

EVIDENCES OF EXTRANEOUS INFLUENCES

Rivermen

A certain pan-Pueblo group of figures is often called a "grandfather" clown society. The society has a different name at each village. At Isleta it is called Te'en. The Tewa term is Tsave Yoh, the Cochiti call it Rivermen.

The members of Tsave Yoh are supernatural whippers impersonated by masked War captains. They are said to dwell in the caves of sacred hills. At San Juan, they appear in the Turtle Dance during the winter solstice. Tsave Yoh members can cure illnesses, and they serve as impersonal authorities of social control. It is their task to whip disobedient children or adults who have failed to measure up to their religious responsibilities during the year.[267]

Tsave yoh and rivermen differ from the Ogre Katcina types of western pueblos in that they include characteristics of the Spanish masked clowns, called "abules." The earliest borrowed characteristics include the use of a Spanish-style whip, a handshake gesture, and speaking in Spanish. Once these things were adopted, the Spanish tolerated their appearance, and as a result, the tsave yoh and rivermen still come in daylight and outside, while the Katcinas appear at night and within the kiva.[268] The white man's clothing represents an even later influence.

At Cochiti, on May 3, 1975, I saw seven rivermen come into the village about noon and go from house to house asking for gifts of food. The collection was put in enormous cloth sacks. The rivermen spoke Spanish only, and made a high-pitched "hooting" sound as they walked about. The performers wore old clothes. One man had on army boots, trousers, and an army coat. Another wore old jeans, tennis shoes, and a raincoat. Two men had padded their stomachs until they looked extremely fat. Most of the men carried whips of different kinds: some were fashioned from rope, others from braided leather. Around their necks were rope or string necklaces with large pendant crosses. Some crosses were of wood, with the crosspieces crudely bound together with string. Others were fashioned out of fry bread. Some were plain crosses of bread dough, and other crosses were cut out of the center of a circle of baked dough.

As the rivermen went from house to house they hooted loudly and chased any child they saw, while the children ran madly and screamed at the top of their lungs.

The masks of the rivermen were of canvas and roughly conical in shape, and they covered the entire head. Slits were cut for eye holes, some had

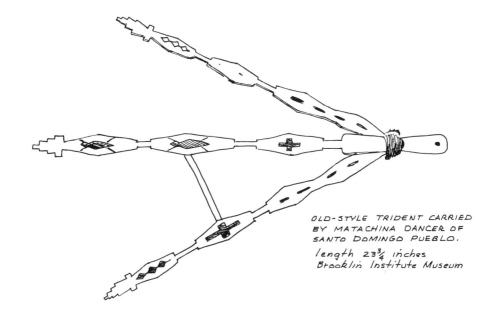

OLD-STYLE TRIDENT CARRIED
BY MATACHINA DANCER OF
SANTO DOMINGO PUEBLO.
length 23¾ inches
Brooklin Institute Museum

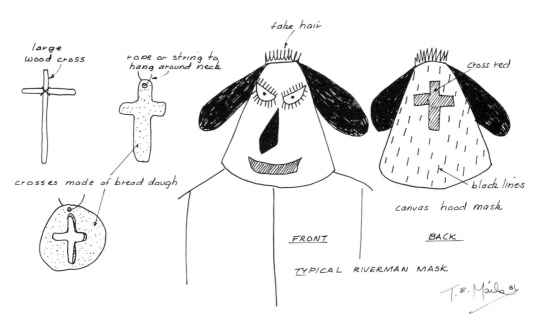

fake hair

large
wood cross

rope or string to
hang around neck

crosses made of bread dough

cross red

black lines

canvas hood mask

FRONT   BACK

TYPICAL RIVERMAN MASK

T. E. Mails 81

Top, trident carried by a matachina dancer from Santo Domingo. *Bottom*, details of Cochiti riverman's costume.

wooden noses, all had long, floppy, dog-like ears, and some had artificial hair glued or sewn on top. The masks were painted with different facial features and had a painted red cross and black rain lines on the back. A sample mask and costume is illustrated here.

About 1 P.M., a Corn Dance began. The first kiva to perform had 75 dancers, a chorus of 22 singers, and a drummer. The second kiva had a smaller group of dancers and a chorus of 17. Most of the dancers were teenagers and children. They carried fresh-cut branches, strangely not evergreen. Only 3 male dancers had parrot feathers in their hair. In both groups, the women wore print dresses under their mantas, and all wore moccasins.

It was not a well-done dance, and one wondered whether the mixing of native and Spanish customs had something to do with that. The children who danced were not as attentive as they usually are. To compound the situation, as the first kiva completed the dance and filed out of the plaza, some of the white spectators applauded, causing the Pueblo audience to grimace. One does not applaud at Pueblo dances unless, on some rare occasion, the Indians do so first.

As one can see, the rivermen and the tsave yoh are not really clowns. They are closer in role to the Hopi ogres and the Zuñi bears. The te'en members of the Tiwa are clown figures. They appear during the early spring Evergreen Dance at Isleta, and they bear no evident Spanish characteristics. The masked men remain silent, and they carry a yucca whip. Rabbits are tied to their evergreen collars. While the dance is being performed, they hand out the rabbits to women and children and in general clown with the audience. Women are teased and sometimes are chased with a threatening whip, and children bold enough to ask for rabbits are made to climb up to get one.

The argument has already been made that efforts to Christianize the Pueblo Indians were barely successful. The Rio Grande people took from Catholicism what they had to and what appealed to them, but they never allowed it to replace the native religion. Dozier describes this phenomenon as "compartmentalization." There are, however, some dances where elements of both religions are combined. The best known of these is the patron-saint's-day dance, held annually at every village on the day of the saint for whom the village was named by the Spanish. Most villages perform at this time the Tablita, or Corn Dance. San Ildefonso and San Juan do the Buffalo or Comanche Dance.

Ortiz believes that Catholic saints are an element easily understood by the Pueblos. In function, they are not very different from the Katcinas. He explains that the saints most venerated by the Indians were those compatible with the native system, for example, St. James, the patron of horsemen, and St. Raphael, the patron of fishermen.[269]

Dances held on the saint's days are at least tolerated by the missionaries. Mass is celebrated in the morning, after which there is a procession from the church to the plaza. A statue of the village saint is carried by the Pueblos to the dance plaza and placed within a temporary structure made of cottonwood boughs called a "bower." At this point the Catholic priests usually leave the area. The first dance may be done in front of the church, but the rest take place in the plaza in front of the bower. It is common to see several hundred dancers participating in a patron-saint's-day dance. In the belief that certain blessings may be obtained, Spanish and Indians may sit in the bower by the santo during the day, and sometimes the dancers will go in single file up to the santo after the first plaza dance. When the dancing ends, there is a second procession to return the santo to the church. At Cochiti, the dancers form two long lines in front of the church and kneel as the santo passes.

The Tablita Dance performed on the Catholic patron-saint's day remains

The shade bower, or shrine, for the patron saint. Green Corn Dance, Santo Domingo Pueblo.

strictly native in origin, movement, symbolism, and music. The object is the same as that of any other Tablita Dance; it is a prayer for rain, growth, and harmony. The sacred clowns or the kwerana are usually out with the dancers, and the songs are Pueblo in style. But patron saint's days are always feast days, and hundreds of Indian, Spanish, and Anglo-American visitors come to share in the event. Traders and vendors sell food, soft drinks, and crafts. Sometimes a small traveling carnival sits somewhere near the pueblo. Old friends gather to visit, feast, and watch the dances, and for families it is a time of homecoming.

MATACHINA DANCE

The Matachina Dance also has elements of Catholicism, and some of its movements resemble European dance steps. Kurath finds other indications of its Spanish origin in its performance by indigenous Spanish people living in small isolated villages of the Southwest, in the appearance of Spanish masked clowns or "abules," and in the music, which is traceable to sixteenth-century tunes.[270] Music is supplied by a Spanish violinist and a guitarist who are hired each year by the Pueblos.

Dozier states that the Matachina Dance was one of a series of pageants introduced by the early Franciscans to teach the Indians about Christianity.[271]

Matachina dancers of San Juan Pueblo.

Kurath adds that it is based upon the battles of the Christians and the Moors, and says the theme is one of good triumphing over evil.[272] The performers include a bull who represents evil; a small girl named Malinche, dressed in a white confirmation dress to represent goodness and purity; a clown, and a group of eight to twelve matachina men, including the lead male dancer known as Monanca. The matachinas sometimes dance in two parallel lines that interweave in complex figures. At other times they kneel in a random pattern. They carry a rattle in the right hand, which they often hold and shake vertically. In the left hand they hold a painted wooden trident. The bull, Monanca, and Malinche dance between the lines of matachinas. At the end of the dance the two masked abules symbolically kill and castrate the bull.

At Jemez, the moieties alternate in dancing the Matachina. One group performs it in the manner described above, and the other wears traditional Pueblo costumes and performs the dance with typical Pueblo steps. In this instance, Malinche is dressed as a Pueblo Indian maiden. A drum is used as accompaniment, and the dancers wear soft moccasins, rather than Spanish street shoes.

On December 12, 1974, I witnessed a spectacular Spanish type of Matachina Dance at Jemez. It was a cold but beautiful and cloudless day in New Mexico, perfect for dancing.

The dance began about 1 P.M., and the group comprised twelve male matachina dancers, one girl, fifteen singers, one drummer, the clown, Monanca, and the bull. The drummer and chorus wore Anglo clothing. The drum was a small hand-type, painted red.

The participants entered the dance area from a point near the kiva, the leader coming first, the girl next, the line dancers following in pairs, and finally the chorus and drummer. They walked slowly, with the drum sounding, and began to dance as they passed the square kiva. They advanced to the front of the shrine, where they formed a line. The line of dancers knelt on the ground, and the leader and girl danced, weaving as they did so in and out between them. The steps were rapid, and whenever the leader shouted the girl would turn as directed.

The matachinas' leader wore what appeared to be a canvas mask, although it could have been buckskin, since it was that color. The mask completely covered his head, and it was topped with two upright, green-painted horns or peaks. The eye slits were edged with green paint. His costume consisted of an Anglo shirt, a kilt made of a woman's flowered shawl that was fringed, white crocheted leggings, moccasins with skunk-fur anklets, and gauntlet-type gloves with fringes and a star on the cuff. In his right hand was a gourd rattle, and in his left was a small American flag on a stick.

The girl was perhaps twenty. She wore a white embroidered manta without an underdress, a woven sash, high wrapped moccasins, and skunk-fur anklets. On her upper arms were orange angora bands. On her head was a thin, blue headband. At the back of her head was a cluster of long, upright, parrot-tail feathers with shorter feathers attached at the base of the cluster. A white down feather was tied on top of her head in such a way that it hung over her forehead. She carried a Mexican-type gourd rattle in her right hand, and a blue painted wooden trident (the matachina symbol) in her left hand. The trident also had blue Christmas tinsel wrapped around it.

The other male dancers were dressed somewhat like the leader. Some wore woven sashes and over the sashes a belt with large shells hanging from it. Some wore concho belts. Two men had on black leather belts with hawkbells tied to them. All the men wore the typical matachinas miter headdress, which is illustrated. The felt fronts of these were red, maroon, green, and other colors. All were edged with black ribbons and tinsel. Gold and silver jewelry ornaments were appended to the front of the miter. A long fringe of black jet beads hung over the eyes. Sheer scarves were tied over their faces, and some scarves had gold metallic threads running through them. All the miters had three upright white feathers on top and many long ribbons hanging from them, including a broad black ribbon that covered the back of the head and hung down the back. Mexican gourd rattles were in their right hands, and wooden tridents in their left hands. All the tridents were painted, some a solid color and some varicolored with lines and dots. A few tridents had tinsel wrapped around them. There is a considerable difference between the old tridents and modern makes, and both types are illustrated. The performers are skilled in the use of the trident, and they wave it in such a graceful way that it seems supple, like a feather, rather than like a piece of stiff wood. The dancers' hands were painted white, and as they danced they at times held their rattles vertically with the gourd end down.

The clown wore a face mask that covered his head and upper body but was open in front. Its general style was like that of the leader, with horns on top and a horse's head painted on the back. He wore white clothing, buckskin gloves, and chaps and carried a braided rawhide whip.

The bull wore an Anglo shirt, a kilt, crocheted leggings, and moccasins with skunk-fur anklets. His entire face was painted red. A black-and-white cowskin was draped over his head, shoulders, and back. Steer horns were attached to it, and spruce and a small bunch of parrot feathers were tied to the hide between the horns. He held two short sticks with padded ends, like drumsticks, and walked with these touching the ground so that he moved on "four legs" as a bull does.

The bull chased the clown while the matachinas danced, charging like a bull as the clown ran, usually toward children, who would scream and scatter wildly.

BULL DANCES

Santiago (St. James), San Geronimo, and the Pecos bull are popular characters who sometimes appear at patron-saint's-day dances. They are impersonated by Pueblo dancers who wear at waist level a framework horse's body. The horse frame with its cloth cover is suspended from the "rider's" shoulders by shoulder straps. He moves the horse with quick bouncy steps that cause the horse to bobble like a trotting animal. The Pecos bull appears at Jemez in August.

At Santo Domingo the horsemen appear in late January or early February. Santiago rides a white horse, and San Geronimo a black horse. Boys who impersonate the Sandaros, or Spanish soldiers, also appear. They paint their faces black and wear false beards or mustaches. The bull is impersonated by a medicine man. The performers enter the village with great fanfare and drum music, and the bull chases the Sandaros. When the chase ends, the entire group goes to the church, where they are sprinkled with holy water, then they dance to Spanish songs, and they hold a feast. Later, the bull is ritually slain by Santiago.

On August 2, a hot, clear day in 1977, I saw the Old Pecos Bull Dance at Jemez. The "pumpkin" kiva furnished on this occasion about 175 tablita dancers, 30 singers, and a drummer. It carried no standard. There were 5 kwerana in their customary outfits. The dancers' bodies were a mustard color, and their rattles were painted to match. The women wore dresses with three-quarter-length sleeves under black mantas, tablitas, and moccasins.

The Pecos bull had a roughly representational fabric head with painted eyes, false ears, and a horsehair mane. The four-foot-long body frame had draped over it a large black cloth with many white circles painted on it. It was open in the front so that the man wearing it could see where he was going. The bearer was fully costumed, wearing an embroidered kilt, a brocaded sash, a woven belt, white crocheted leggings, and high-topped white moccasins.

Old Pecos Bull Dance.

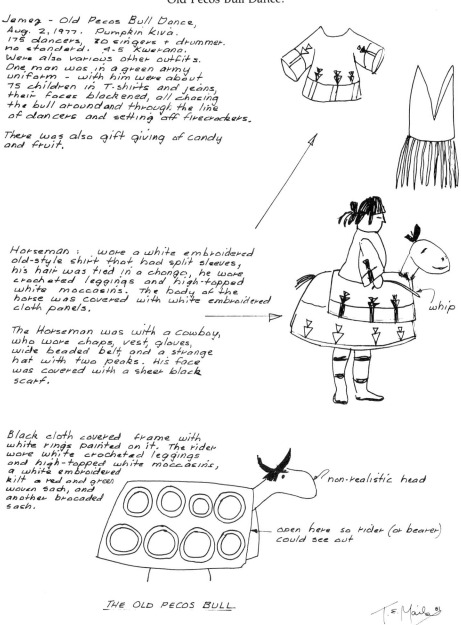

Jemez - Old Pecos Bull Dance, Aug. 2, 1977. Pumpkin kiva. 175 dancers, 30 singers + drummer. no standard. 4-5 kwerana. Were also various other outfits. One man was in a green army uniform - with him were about 75 children in T-shirts and jeans, their faces blackened, all chasing the bull around and through the line of dancers and setting off firecrackers.

There was also gift giving of candy and fruit.

Horseman: wore a white embroidered old-style shirt that had split sleeves, his hair was tied in a chongo, he wore crocheted leggings and high-topped white moccasins. The body of the horse was covered with white embroidered cloth panels.

The Horseman was with a cowboy, who wore chaps, vest, gloves, wide beaded belt and a strange hat with two peaks. His face was covered with a sheer black scarf.

whip

Black cloth covered frame with white rings painted on it. The rider wore white crocheted leggings and high-topped white moccasins, a white embroidered kilt a red and green woven sash, and another brocaded sash.

non-realistic head

open here so rider (or bearer) could see out

THE OLD PECOS BULL

T.E.Mails

The horseman's wooden-horse body frame was covered with several white embroidered mantas, and the horse had an artificial head made something like that of the bull. The man who wore the horse body had on an old-style embroidered poncho-type shirt with split sleeves, white crocheted leggings, and high-topped white moccasins.

The horseman was accompanied by a cowboy dressed in chaps, vest, gauntlet-type gloves, a wide beaded belt, and a strange hat with two triangular peaks. His face was covered with a sheer black scarf.

Other men in a variety of outfits joined in chasing the bull. One man wore a green army uniform, and about fifteen boys, their faces blackened, joined him in running the bull back and forth through the lines of dancers while they set off firecrackers.

When the chase ended, there was gift giving of candy and fruit.

At Cochiti, Santiago sometimes appears on Santiago Day, July 25. Lange says that the village people who want the "little horse" to appear must make a request to the Koshare Society in the spring.[273] Santiago is considered to be good luck, and as such is often taken to the corrals "to increase the size of the herds" and to bring luck to the horses.[274]

Spanish and other white influences have affected the Rio Grande Pueblos in varying degrees. A few villages, such as Pojoaque, have virtually no aspects of their native practices left. Others have accepted diffused elements without giving up the old ways. But there is currently a strong new interest in revival, and the young people especially are taking more pride in the ancient culture and in participating in native practices. Some instances of dances being performed after years of neglect are cited in the material to follow. There are others. In 1950, San Juan held its Yellow Corn Dance after a gap of thirty years. In 1974, Pojoaque held its first patron-saint's-day dance in over a century. Older people say the dance lines are getting longer and younger every year. The religion of the Pueblos is not a thing of the past culture. It continues to be the vital and unifying element for the individual villages, and for the Pueblos as a whole. A consideration of the ceremonial calendar and what are referred to as "public" dances strongly bears this out.

THE RIO GRANDE DANCE, "BRINGING THE BUDS TO LIFE"

Within the scheme of native Pueblo dances, two types are performed. One is the secret-association dance, which may be masked or unmasked and is closed to the public, that is, to "outsiders," although it is still "public" to the Pueblo residents of the village. The other is the public dance, which outsiders may attend. Because the public dances are open, many outsiders have the erroneous idea that they are less sacred or not sacred at all. People sometimes speak of these as "semi-sacred," which is a little like saying that a light case of the measles is not really measles. Visitors who hold to this concept treat the dances accordingly, and often without the respect they deserve.

Such people are badly mistaken. While some dances are not as momentous as others, public dances are of no less consequence in the ritual scheme than those that are secret and closed. "The (public) dances are an extension of our kiva rites, just as sacred." The dancing, in fact, begins in the kiva, and it is interrupted only while the dancers leave the kiva and proceed to the plaza. "As soon as we touch the ground the dance begins again."[275]

The sacredness of public dances is further emphasized by the fact that some dances once open to the public are closed now. The Spring Dance at Cochiti is an example. It has been closed to the public since 1947, but it is still held. The rare exceptions to this principle are the modern performances of the adaptive dances, such as those of the Comanche and the Navajo. Even dances of this type were once closely associated with rituals designed to gain power to deal with enemies. Now they are just remembrance dances to thank the gods for freedom from certain, perhaps all, "enemies" of mankind such as drought and witchcraft.

The importance of the public part of the dance is found in this: "Our dancers are talking to the people, telling them that the Katcinas are coming." Hence the public dances are vehicles used to assure the people that kiva rites are being answered by the deities. They give the people specific information as to how these supernatural blessings will be bestowed. The dances outside the kiva, "which everyone can see," make known to all the world that the promises made by the supernaturals in the closed rituals and dances are in the process of being delivered. "Our songs celebrate this, and the gestures show how it is being done."

From the foregoing it may be seen that the title "dance" is a misnomer. The performances are actually "ritual extensions," but the term "dance" is in such widespread use in the literature that I have used it also. Moreover, the dance plays a vital role in the social makeup of every village, a fact that points up graphically the foolishness of the Spanish and American officials who once thought the regimentation, toning down, or elimination of dances would be of little consequence to the Pueblos.

Ortiz, addressing the matter of the former suppression by the Roman Catholic Church of all native rituals, says, "Now the works themselves escape detection because they are held indoors (in the kiva or ceremonial room), but the mass public rituals *must* [italics his] follow. Bringing the buds to life cannot be hidden."[276] Most of what are known today as public performances were at one time carried out when there was no "public" to see them. Only the Indians were present, and they would hardly have devised nonreligious dances for an occasional priest or for a public that did not yet exist.

Proof lies in the earliest reports of dances witnessed in 1880. The form and costumes for these were, with minor exceptions, identical with those seen today. The dances have not changed with time, and we might apply this factor in a reverse direction and argue that the dances first seen in 1880 were duplications of types that were prehistoric to some undetermined date.

In summary, true appreciation for the Pueblo "dance" comes only with comprehension. One must understand first of all how the ritual life and its public dance extension works, and second what it accomplishes in the overall life of the village.

The movements of Sun Old Man govern the cycle of winter and summer ceremonies, and pueblo life conforms to a great extent, if not entirely, to the changing seasons. We have already seen that the caciques associated with the moieties control either the summer or the winter season of ritual and subsistence.

Ortiz includes in his fascinating book *The Tewa World* two instructive diagrams that show in clockwise fashion how the ritual and subsistence cycles are followed.[277] Setting these up in comparative fashion is most enlightening:

RITUAL	SUBSISTENCE
*Winter Solstice—December 21**	
Turtle	
Matachina	
Tsaveyoh	
Installation of Winter Chief	
Buffalo	Officials feed village
Eagle	
Deer	
Butterfly	
Basket	
Squash	
Gods of Middle	
Transfer Ritual	Blessing of seeds
Summer Water Giving	Winter games put away
Shinny	Reseeding of mother earth navel
Summer Water Pouring	Summer moiety feeds Winter
Summer Finishing	Cleaning of irrigation ditches
Sweet Broth, Digging Stick, Little Baskets	Planting of wheat
Summer Gods	Water is run and fishing begins
Made People Finishing	
Vernal Equinox	
Yellow Corn	Order of planting: corn, chile,
Going Between	melons, squash, all other vegetables
Rain Retreats	
It Is Raining Dance	Locust gathering
	Wild plant gathering
Corn Dance	Hunting ceases

*For comparison, see the Cochiti calendar as set fourth by Lange, *Cochiti, A New Mexico Pueblo, Past and Present*, pages 317 to 366.

Summer Solstice—June 21

Relay Racing	
Rain Standing Dance	Gathering of wild berries
Installation of Summer	Harvest of wheat
Chief	Gathering of wild fruit
	First fruits festival
	People may eat garden produce
	Squash may be stored

Autumnal Equinox

Kossa Finishing	Feeding of mother earth navel
Harvest Dance	Blessing of corn plants
Transfer Ritual	All cultigens must be stored
Winter Moiety	Irrigation canals closed and fishing ends
Scalp Chief	
Medicine Men	Cleaning of springs
Kwerana	
Hunt	Sweeping of deer earth navels
Made People Finishing	Communal rabbit hunts
All Souls	Piñon harvest
Communal Cleansing	Salt gathering
Winter Water Giving	
Winter Water Pouring	Trading expeditions
Winter Finishing	Hunting expeditions
Dance of Man	
Winter Gods	Redistribution of food
Social Dances	Winter moiety feeds Summer
Communal Retreat	

Winter Soltice—December 21

What Ortiz presents shows the elaborateness of the Pueblo ritual cycle. In briefer view there are winter rituals with dance extensions, pre-planting and planting rituals, summer ceremonies, fall rituals, and ceremonial games, all of which involve the various secret associations and in particular the Katcina Cult.

Winter Dances

After the harvest, the activities of the pueblos turn to the hunt and to the fulfilling of that aspect of subsistence needs. As we would expect, the hunting rituals and their dances are involved with vastly more than the kill itself. There is in them the recognition that man is intimately related to all living things—in this instance to the animals and birds. Within this bond of brotherhood, there is a need to express concern for the well-being of the "brothers," and for the human to do what he can to preserve, expand, and extend their life. This is not only right, it is sensible, for by preserving the game he cooperates with the gods in assuring his own future. Game-animal dances, called Buffalo dances, are traditionally performed from Christmas until early spring. Eagle dances may also be held between December and March. Frances Densmore says that Santo Domingo performs an Eagle Dance once a year to cure sickness.[278] A Tablita Dance may be held on January 1 and January 6 to honor newly chosen officers. Closed Katcina dances and maskless Katcina dances are performed at this time and continue into the spring.

Near the time of the winter solstice and the vernal equinox, sex role reversal or "transvestite" dances are held. In performing these, the women dress and act like men, or vice versa. Ortiz says they represent among other things the seasonal reversal, alternation, or disruption in the flow of time.[279] Spring comes to turn "Mean Man of the North" back. Often other Indian nations, such as the Navajo, are imitated in these dances, the purpose of which is to duplicate what the clowns seek to achieve. Through reality reversal, the dancers impress upon the minds of the people the correct or Pueblo way of living in response to nature and the deities.

Spring Dances

In a sense, the new year at the Rio Grande pueblos begins with the first day of spring. It is time now for rituals that will consider everything needed for a successful crop. These include petitions for supernatural help and irrigation rites. Pre-planting rituals, with their dances such as the Parrot, Corn Maiden, Basket, or Yellow Corn, are held as early as January and on into the spring. The planting time itself is accompanied by rituals that dramatize planting and germination and the need for rain and growth. This is also mating time, when the male-female principle is recognized in ceremonies addressed to all creation. Easter dances begin on Easter Sunday and usually include four days of dancing; Tablita dances are often performed on this occasion. Santo Domingo holds a magnificent Corn Dance at the time, and the three days of dancing after Easter are moving and spectacular, with more than a thousand dancers performing in an intricate display of ritual devotion.

Summer Dances

As Sun Father advances northward, the plants grow and mature, and the ceremonies center in fertilization and maturation. The need for rain and sufficient river water receives paramount attention. Throughout the summer the pueblos celebrate their patron saint's day with a Tablita-style Corn Dance. The fairs are held, crafts are sold, and short segments of native dances are performed for the public. Three of the largest fairs are held at Nambe Falls, Puye Cliffs, and the village sponsoring the "Annual Arts and Crafts Fair of the Eight Northern Pueblos."

Hewett says that the Corn dances seen during the summer are for the most part fragments of major ceremonies relating to the germination, maturation, and harvesting of the corn.

Fall Dances

With the arrival of harvest time, the ceremonies become vehicles of gratitude to the deities. The dance extensions are harvest dances and often are held in connection with the patron saint's day. Soon thereafter the hunting and animal dances begin, and the cycle is brought to completion.

Seasonal Games

The ceremonial calendar includes games. Ceremonial shinny games held in the spring help to insure successful planting. Foot races accompany the vernal equinox, the summer solstice, and the autumnal equinox. Chicken pulls are summer-related and held in connection with various saint's days.

Discontinuance and Revival

The Pueblos speak today of ancient dances "that are not done anymore" and of certain dances that are being revived.

Dances are discontinued "mostly because men have to work, haven't time to do the dance, since the preparations and the dance itself take many days." One discontinued dance at a certain pueblo is the Mountain Sheep Dance, in which all the performers were mountain sheep.

At another pueblo an ancient dance has recently been reinstituted. It involves the use of a traditional medicine bowl, but when the people wanted to do the dance again, they found that the old bowl had cracked. The highest medicine person in the pueblo, a woman, made a new one and taught the leaders the songs attending it. This dance is called the Go Between Dance. It has two songs, one that can be heard by the public and one that can't. It is a particularly sacred dance, and all the male performers are medicine men. The participants dance in a forward direction, with the leader carrying the bowl, and they turn back and forth as they advance. The women performers, wearing mantas, turn in rhythm with the men, but are careful never to touch them. The male costume is similar to that of the Cloud Dance, and the songs are said to be beautiful.

Public Dances in the Winter

The Buffalo Dance is one of the most important dances performed by the Pueblos. Its primary purpose is to attract the game, to increase the herds, and to moderate the weather to make hunting easier. The name can be confusing, however. On occasion the performers consist of only two men wearing buffalo headdress, and two women, but at other times an entire pantheon of game animals may be represented in the dance: buffalo, elk, antelope, mountain sheep, and deer, although Deer dances are sometimes a performance unto themselves and only deer dancers are included. In all performances the dancers hold two short sticks in their hands to serve as front legs. They walk

The Buffalo Hunt leader of San Ildefonso.

(or dance) bent over so as to proceed on four legs as the animal does. Their procession is led by a man costumed and painted as the hunt chief. Other men are dressed as common hunters to help care for the dancers. The animals are usually in two lines, and between them are one or two women known as buffalo mothers or, in the case of the Deer Dance, deer mothers.

Kurath lists five types of Buffalo dances among the Rio Grande Pueblos: Type one includes two buffalo men, one or two women, and a hunter. Type two has pairs of buffalo men and women up to six couples. Type three includes two buffalo men and one or two women, with two side lines of deer or small buffalo wearing only one horn. Type four has from two to four buffalo couples attended by game animals: deer by twos, two antelope, two mountain sheep, and two elk. Type five consists of a line of young buffalo with several "mothers." This is the fertility Buffalo Dance performed at the Puye Cliff Ceremonial.[280]

Ortiz states that two Buffalo dances are performed at San Juan today, one of which is borrowed from the Hopi (the four-person variation). Both dances are sometimes enacted in June, "unlike all other animal dances, which are performed during the autumn and winter months."[281]

Santa Clara has a Bull Dance that is sometimes performed in place of the Buffalo Dance. It represents the Pueblos' tribute to the bull for providing them with food and other needed materials. The male performers wear traditional dance outfits, plus a thick headdress of evergreen with horns, and shaped like the buffalo headdress. They carry long staffs, tipped with two eagle tail feathers, rather than the short sticks carried by game animal dancers.

At Taos, the Deer dancers are led by two men known as deer watchmen. Two other watchmen bring up the rear. All the watchmen are dressed as hunters. Two deer chiefs who follow the watchmen wear gleaming white costumes and white paint. There is a white kilt, crocheted leggings, and beaded white moccasins, and white-painted antlers are mounted on a cap on their heads. The deer mothers wear embroidered white dresses, woven belts with ribbons attached, and high-wrapped moccasins. At the back of their heads are vertically placed parrot feathers and an eagle feather. Below these hangs the iridescent skin of a wild duck. A small cluster of short parrot feathers is attached to the top of the head. Each Deer dancer wears a deer hide that covers his head and back. He also has on a black or dark-brown kilt, a leather belt, and high-topped moccasins. Two short sticks are employed as forelegs. As the deer dance, the clowns attempt to shoot them with straw bows and arrows. Now and then they will simply seize a deer and attempt to carry it away. If the deer is caught by a deer watchman or a spectator, it returns to the dance.

The Bow and Arrow Dance is a ceremony in which the entire village participates in one way or another, since it dramatizes the relationship of the people with the animals of the forest. The movements of hunters and the animals they hunt are all represented by gestures. The dance formations carry special meaning, with the dancers arranging themselves in the form of hunting parties at one time, and as large symbolic bows and arrows at another. One opportunity I had to see this dance was in late summer at the Santa Fe Indian Market,

Bow and Arrow dancers of San Ildefonso Pueblo.

where it was beautifully performed by a group of women in traditional costumes. Sometimes, though, the Bow and Arrow performers are all male and specially painted, as is shown in the illustrations.

Public Dances in the Spring

The Sun Dance was formerly engaged in by practically the entire village. Today the residents are represented by two men and two women who impersonate the village moieties. The dance celebrates the return of the growing season by dramatizing in ritual actions the planting, cultivating, and growth of the corn as a result of the return of Sun Father. At one time this ancient ceremony entirely disappeared from the pueblos, but it was revived about 1930 by the people of Santa Clara. Hewett says the performance is almost identical with the Acequia Dance, "in which the principal episode of the celebration is the turning on of the water in the ditches with the advent of the planting season."[282]

The Eagle Dance is a winter dance in some pueblos, but it is also performed in the early spring and during the summer at the Santa Fe Indian Market and at Puye Cliffs. The eagle is believed to have direct intercourse with the powers of the sky, and as such it is venerated. When its feathers are worn as parts of a costume, the bearer assumes some of the special powers of the eagle. Hence even to this day the feathers are sought, and until recent stringent government laws went into effect to preserve eagles, the birds could be seen in captivity in most of the villages. The dance costume and movements dramatize the relationship among the Spirit powers, the eagle, and man. Two men, who depict the male and the female eagle, wear costumes of cotton-covered head caps with wooden eyes and bird beaks, wings that are long strips of cloth with eagle feathers attached to the arms, a tail of eagle feathers, a breechclout or kilt, and sometimes moccasins. They imitate eagles in flight, mating, perching, and dipping to the ground to gather up the prayers of humans.

The Cloud Dance, or Spring Dance, is one of the finest performances to be seen at Santa Clara, San Juan, and San Ildefonso. The performers at San Juan include eight girls who together represent the four directions. Also, four of these represent winter, and four represent summer. Only two girls dance at a time, so as to spell one another. Male dancers wear, in addition to their traditional kilt, a thick collar of spruce and two upright golden eagle tail feathers at the back of the head. If their hair has been cut short, the feathers are held in place by a headband. The dance dramatizes the contest between the seasons, with the clouds of summer contesting with the clouds of winter for the supremacy that marks the rising of one season and the decline of the preceding one. Sometimes the dance is attended by races that trace back and forth the course of the seasonal clouds.

Public Dances in the Summer

The Basket Dance derives its name from the use of the food basket in the ceremony. The basket, with what it contains in the sequence of Basket dances, symbolizes each stage of the food that preserves the life of the tribe. One time it contains the seed that is about to be planted in the ground. Another time it contains the fruit or grain that the earth yields in response to the efforts of the people throughout the planting and growing season. At times the basket is empty, so that the dancer can wield it to describe in gestures what Mother Earth is doing to bring the crops into being. Next, the basket bears the meal that is produced when the harvest of corn is ground. Finally it bears the loaves of bread for the sustenance of the tribe.

The invocations to fertility that are offered in the Basket dances extend beyond plant life to embrace the human being, who must also multiply and transmit the gifts of life from generation to generation. Hewett believed that a complete series of the pictures presented in the Basket ceremonies "would constitute an epitome of woman's life, her consecration to child-bearing, and the sustaining of the life of the tribe."[283]

Santa Clara Cloud dancer.

The Tablita, Corn, or Harvest dances are among the best known of the Rio Grande ceremonial performances. They are called Tablita dances because the female dancers wear a tablita on the head. The Keresans describe them as Corn dances, and the Tewa describe them as Harvest dances, but they are essentially the same in form, costume, and intent. They are usually performed during midsummer and before the fall. They are a dance of gratitude for the land itself, for the moisture that has provided a bountiful crop, and to Earth Mother.

Although matched if not outstripped by the Easter and the Post-Easter Dance, the Green Corn Dance of Santo Domingo is one of the most stirring displays to be seen anywhere. It is held on August 4, and as Hewett says, "Understanding of this [dance] will make clear almost every one of the summer ceremonies of the Pueblos." He thought it was the most nearly perfect survival of the ancient religious ceremonies, a dramatization of the spiritual life, and an elaborate prayer for the maturation and preservation of the corn.[284]

> The ceremony begins with certain Christian rites held at the church. These are absolutely foreign to the main dance. They are held as a concession to the authority of the Catholic Church to which most Pueblo Indians nominally adhere. After the procession from the church to a booth at one end of the town plaza, at the head of which the image of the patron saint of the pueblo is carried, there is no further reference to anything that has been introduced by white men.
>
> The first part of the ceremony is historical in character. Emerging from the summer kiva, you see a procession of ghostly figures. These are the Koshare. It must be understood that these characters are not clowns and are not intended to amuse. They represent the Ancients, the spirits or shades of the ancestors of the people, those who still exercise a protecting influence through their mediatory office with the gods. Here is a survival of ancestor veneration as deeply rooted in the Pueblo mind as in the minds of oriental peoples.
>
> It is to be noticed that the Koshare first encircle, in their march, both halves of the pueblo, thus in symbolic movement throwing the protecting influence of the Ancients around the whole people. Meeting in the sacred precinct with another procession of Koshare that has emerged from the winter kiva there is a dramatic conference over something which is evidently the cause of great excitement. Immediately runners are sent out to the east, west, north, and south. These are seen to disappear in the kivas or into adjacent houses, and the excited conference goes on.
>
> Presently there comes running from the east the messenger who was sent in that direction. He is surrounded at once by the excited throng and his message is received with dramatic gesture and animated speeches. Then comes the runner from the west and the same dramatic performance is enacted. These are the runners sent to the frontiers who bring word of the enemy, Apache, Comanche, or Navaho, gathered for the raids upon the crops. Then come the runners from the north and south, bringing liquids of which all partake, these being for the purification of the warriors about to depart for the frontier.
>
> Then follow further dramatic performances which are readily interpreted as preparation for battle, and the procession disappears in the depth of the kiva. This closes the historical portion of the drama and discloses the motif of the ceremony.
>
> Then follows the dance proper which is an invocation to the deities that have given the corn, that have brought it to maturity, and that are now implored to protect it from the enemy.

No attempt can be made in this brief account to analyze the beautiful ceremony in full. A description of the costumes and movements would call for a discussion of the entire subject of the religion, social organization, and symbolism of the Pueblos. However, a few details may be put down.

The participants in the dance are of three classes. The Koshare have already been mentioned. The dancers in costume, numbering usually about two hundred, are male and female in equal numbers. They are in two divisions, the summer and winter people dancing alternately. Each division is accompanied by a large chorus made up of a representative group of the men of the community, among whom are noted many of the elders of the tribe. Not less than one hundred men usually are in the chorus.

The two groups of performers assemble in their respective kivas for costuming for the secret rites that are never seen in public. The summer people are usually the first to emerge from their kiva, the one at the east end of the plaza. To know when the dancers are to come out, it is only necessary to watch the great wand or standard in the center of the roof of each kiva. The taking down of this standard is the signal that the dance is to begin. The procession emerges from the door in the roof of the kiva, a man and a woman alternately coming down the ladder from the roof. As corrupted in recent years, the line proceeds to the front of the church where the dancing begins. The dancers encompass the north half of the town and enter the plaza from the west to the slow even chant of the prelude or first song. This changes to the more accentuated second song as the center of the plaza is reached. Usually four chants with the accompanying dance movements are given before this division retires from the plaza to make way for the winter people who will be seen coming out of their kiva at the west end and south side of the plaza and falling into line after encompassing the south half of the town.

At the head of each procession is carried the great wand or standard, at first by the rain priest, usually an old man, who soon turns it over to a young assistant who bears it during the remainder of the ceremony. Each division, summer and winter people, has its own wand, the two differing somewhat in symbolic ornament. This wand is a smooth pole about ten feet in length. At the extreme top is a bunch of brilliant macaw feathers, around the base of which are bunches of the feathers of the parrot and woodpecker tied with strands of colored beads and ocean shells. An embroidered banner, quite like the rain sash worn by the men in the dance, extends down the pole, secured by thongs and trimmed at intervals with eagle feathers which float out from the edge of the banner. A fox skin dangles from near the top of the wand.

This ceremonial wand is the most sacred emblem of the ceremony. Its potency in rain paraphernalia lies in the objects above-mentioned with which it is decorated, all life in nature being there symbolically represented. The wand bearer stands to one side of the line of dancers, waving the sacred emblem over them during the entire ceremony. Theoretically, all the people in the course of the day pass under it for purification. Four times each division dances back and forth in the plaza to the ever-swelling chant which increases in fervor as the day advances. Toward the end of the afternoon the two divisions combine in one grand finale.

Throughout the ceremony the Koshare, disembodied spirits of the Ancients, dance among the performers, by whom they are not supposed to be seen, with incredible grace of movement and rhythmic gesture. It will be discovered that the entire performance is under their direction. Their bodies are bare, painted in gray or red-brown earthen color representing the seasonal division to which they belong; spots or stripes and symbolic designs in black add to their mimicry, the

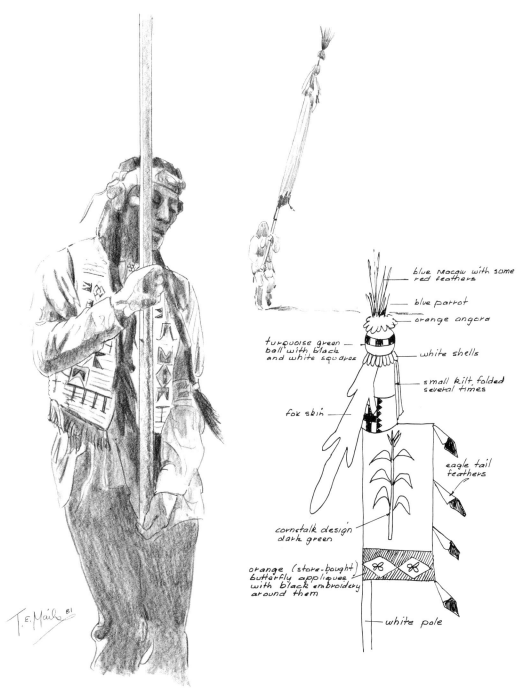

Left, the Corn Dance standard bearer at San Ildefonso Pueblo. *Top*, Green Corn Dance standard bearer at Santo Domingo Pueblo. *Lower right*, standard at Zia Pueblo, August 15, 1977.

painting of the face especially bringing out the ghostly aspect. The hair, in which tufts of dried corn husks are tied, is matted with clay of grayish color. A small black loincloth is worn, and suspended on the right hip is the buckskin medicine pouch. A girdle consisting of a roll of dry rabbit skin is worn over each ankle.

This completes the costume of the Koshare except for a few minor details. The sprays of evergreen worn and carried in the hand [by Koshare] as seen in late years are out of place. It is an indication of loss on the part of the dancers themselves of the meaning of some elements of the costume.

During the dance there is nothing but the utmost seriousness manifested by the Koshare. There is no real clowning at any time. The "horse play" indulged in outside the dance, such as chasing the children and making advances to the women, produces much laughter and has given rise to the misnomer, the Delight Makers.

The women are dressed in the simple ceremonial costume: the short black skirt of archaic weave, red embroidered belt, all the jewelry they possess—beads, bracelets, rings, etc.—the feet bare, the long dark hair flowing free. On the head is the tablita, shaped from a thin board and bearing painted symbols of sun, moon, and clouds. The costume of the men is more picturesque and significant. There is the broad sash or kilt, embroidered in symbolic designs; the white rain belt with streamers hanging down the right leg; the fox skin suspended from the belt behind; tufts of parrot and woodpecker feathers tied into the hair on the top of the head; the long hair flowing loosely down the back; a girdle of shells (conus) from the Great Sea worn over the left shoulder and crossing to the right hip; painted armbands of rawhide; on the knee a turtle shell rattle (of late years replaced by sleighbells); and on each ankle a mask made of skunk skin. The women carry sprays of evergreen, symbol of life, in each hand; the men carry in the right hand the rain rattle made from the native gourd. Much evergreen is and should be worn by both men and women.

Such is a purely mechanical description of the great Corn Ceremony of the Keres, which is seen in its entirety and at its best at Santo Domingo, but which in some form or other is still performed in every Rio Grande pueblo.

The reader will find it interesting to compare Hewett's account of the Green Corn Dance with the corn dances I have witnessed at Santo Domingo and San Felipe. These are described and illustrated in the material directly related to those pueblos.

The Butterfly Dance is a beautiful and intricate performance by a man and a woman who follow each other as they flutter through symbolic fields of corn, wheat, squash, and alfalfa. While they do this, the chorus and drummers sing for an abundance of crops, moisture, and prosperity. In one version, the male dancer wears conventional dress, but the female performer wears on her back a basic framework or plaque, which is rectangular and covered with white down feathers trimmed with red-dyed down feathers. Along the sides of the plaque, eagle wing feathers are attached horizontally to form wings that move as she dances. On top of her head she wears a vertical spike of orange and blue macaw feathers, with a cluster of different kinds of small feathers formed around the base. Hanging from these in such a way as to cover the back of the head is a cluster of eagle body feathers. She wears a white embroidered manta with no underdress, plus high-wrapped moccasins and skunk-fur anklets. In her hands are wands with wooden handles that have two eagle tail feathers attached.

The Parrot Dance is performed at San Felipe to propitiate the powers of the Bird People. In this rite the lead dancer carries a carved wooden parrot with real parrot feathers appended to make a tail. The male dancers form one line, and the female dancers another line facing them. Both lines take small steps and move sideways. At one point the lead man and woman advance to meet in the center, and then dance together down the center of the aisle formed by the two lines. When they reach the other end they separate and rejoin their lines. The next couples follow in turn until they all have performed the maneuver. As a couple dances together, the man places his right hand on the woman's left shoulder. This is one of the rare instances where male and female performers touch during a Pueblo dance. When they reach the end of the aisle, a woman standing there hands the carved parrot and a basket decorated with flowers to the female dancer, who lifts this up to the sun and returns it to the woman before rejoining her line.

The Rainbow Dance is a Tewa dance for the crops, and it requires kiva rituals of purification. Some Catholic infusion is seen when the Pueblos explain that the dance commemorates, among other things, the rainbow as a promise ending world floods. "It is still danced as a reminder of the day of the great floods." There are legends among the Pueblos that tell of a great flood that once covered the world. But the rainbow idea as a "sign" is biblical in origin.

There are usually four performers in the Rainbow Dance, two men and two women. The women wear embroidered white mantas, long-sleeved underdresses, armbands, white high-wrapped moccasins with skunk-fur anklets, and satin capes. The men wear white kilts, knitted leggings, white moccasins with skunk-fur anklets, yarn bands around the knees with hawkbells attached, a long-sleeved white shirt, painted armbands, and a buffalo-hair collar or chest plate. All four performers wear a rainbow tablita on the head with eagle tail feathers attached vertically to it. They carry a brightly painted rainbow, shaped like a large quarter moon. The modern versions are cut from plywood; the ancient models consisted of a long stick bent in a U-shape to which eagle feathers were attached to form a large fan. The illustrations clarify how these looked.

The Comanche Dance is usually seen during the summer. Although the threat of harassment by the Comanche no longer exists, the dance is still done because of its spectacular nature and in remembrance of the days when warfare was common. The female costume includes the black manta, a bright satin cape that hangs over the shoulders and down the back, white moccasins with white wrap-around leggings, necklaces, and a headband with vertical pairs of eagle side feathers. They carry in their hands two wands, each of which consists of a round wooden handle into which a pair of long feathers has been inserted. The male costumes for the dance include apparel similar to that worn by the Plains tribes: the roach and the warbonnet, beadwork, breechclouts, colored shirts, bell straps, and long angora fringes that cover the shin and moccasin top. The body paint is symbolic of war. Most men carry colored banners. As I have previously stated, I have been told that the modern dance represents the battle of the pueblos against all forces of evil that currently exist.

The War Dance of the Women had survived in only two or three pueblos when Hewett wrote about the dances in the early 1930s. He says it was performed each night by the women and children while the men were away on a war party. "It began at sunset and continued until daybreak." He also says it was performed on a circular platform. Since the dance went forward with a continuous circular movement, it came to be known as the Wheel Dance.

Finally, even the Pueblos adopted this name. Its true significance was disclosed to Hewett "only a few years ago by one of the most reliable old men of San Ildefonso."[285]

Frances Densmore describes a War Society dance held at Santo Domingo in the 1930s. Men and women took part in this, the Opi Dance. The men formed an inner circle and the women formed an outer circle behind them. Both circles moved in a clockwise direction. The women held their hands up high and motioned from side to side as the warriors imitated the "cries and calls" of the fox, bear, and other animals.[286]

The Braiding of the Peace Belt is performed today by only a few of the pueblos. At one time it was enacted when visits from one village to another were made to emphasize peace and friendship between the peoples. Such visits were usually made in the fall, immediately after the harvest, when moods were good and trading could be engaged in. The people went bearing gifts and "braided the peace belt" to express their desire for continued harmony.

My only experience with this dance was at the Santa Fe Indian Market, where it was enacted by a talented group of costumed children, some of whom wore Plains Indian-type bonnets to represent the extension of the peace wish to all peoples. At one point in the dance four or more long women's belts were stretched out between pairs of dancers, like the spokes of a wheel, the hub being formed by the place where the belts crossed. As the children danced in an intricate pattern, ducking under the belts as they moved, they literally braided the belts together and in the process drew themselves closer and closer until at last they formed a solid mass illustrating a oneness of heart and desire.

Public Dances in the Fall

The Snowbird Dance is considered to be one of the most beautiful of the late-fall ceremonies. Unfortunately, it is preserved at only a few of the villages. The name comes from the practice of weaving into the hair representations of little birds, but the name "Snowbird" is hardly descriptive of the actual purpose of the dance. It is in reality a birth ritual, through which newly born infants are introduced to life about them. Hewett states that only a fragment of the "formerly lengthy" performance is now seen. In performing, the dancers are arranged in two lines; the mother of an infant carries her child between the lines and presents it to a priest who stands at one end. He offers a prayer to all living things "in behalf of the new life that has come *to the tribe* [italics mine]."[287]

Public Dances of Undetermined Season

The Tanoan Peace Dance is described by Hewett, but I have not seen one. He classifies it as a dance performed in a religious spirit "to celebrate the close of hostilities." Supposedly, it reflects a custom employed in ancient times to settle an argument between tribes by having the two leaders meet in combat. He says the custom was practiced "down to a time within the memory of people still living in the Southwest" and that after peace was obtained its coming was celebrated by an elaborate dramatization of the episodes of war. The Peace Dance represents the chiefs of the opposing forces in mimic combat, and as such describes the battle that brought peace to the tribe.[288]

Costumes and Paint

Every part of a Rio Grande dancer's costume has symbolic meaning, although views regarding these may vary some from pueblo to pueblo.

Kilts and mantas represent the continuance of tradition.

Dance kilts with serpent designs worn by Buffalo and Eagle dancers. *Top,* canvas. *Bottom,* hide with metal cones for rattles. From the Heard Museum collection.

Mask painting tells the story of the Katcina being represented, and the brocaded sash is a symbol of the Katcina.

Every color has special associations: white for sun; yellow for butterflies or flowers, all the beautiful things; green for growth.

Eagle tail feathers represent the rays of the sun and the special power of the eagle. Breath feathers represent the "breath" of the rain and the resilience of life.

Fox skins are a reminder of the time when men were still tailed and horned. Other animal skins infuse the wearer with the power of the animal represented.

Dance paraphernalia. *Bottom,* old tablita worn by Kwan Katcina. *Top,* ceremonial bow and arrow with feathers and spruce boughs attached. From the Museum of New Mexico collection.

Gourd rattles duplicate the sound of the soft summer rains.

Douglas fir and spruce branches stand for eternal life and also make the world green.

Braided white sashes represent fertility and falling rain.

Armbands with pendant strings and feathers represent the butterfly, which is associated with germination and growth.

The combination of skunk-fur anklets and white moccasins is said to repel the evil powers that may lurk in the earth beneath the dancers' feet. This deterrent, so long as men are wearing it, extends to protect women who may be dancing barefooted at the same time. It is also said that when a woman is thus protected she is free to feel her bond with Earth Mother and to draw fertility power directly from the earth through her bare feet.

Tablita shapes and the symbols painted on them also tell the story of the deities being addressed in a dance.

All these symbolic statements are "read" by the supernaturals who have been called in by ritual to be present at the dance and who respond wholeheartedly to the petitions.

Music, Songs, and Dance Formations

Musical accompaniment for the Rio Grande dances is provided by instruments, a chorus, and the self-accompaniment of the dancers.

The musical instruments are virtually the same as those employed by the Hopi and are described in that section. Those of the Rio Grande are illustrated here. The drum is the principal dance instrument. Ordinarily only one is employed, but five or more may be used simultaneously. Rio Grande drums are fashioned from cottonwood-tree trunks, are double-headed, and are covered with horsehide or cowhide. The drumstick is usually pine, and the padded end consists of a piece of hide stuffed with deer or buffalo hair. A wrist loop is provided at the end of the handle. The drum sides are often painted and very colorful. Heads may be painted too. To make the job of holding the drum easier, some drummers use a long stick, forked at the top, on which the drum is hung. The top of the stick is held in one hand while the other hand holds the drumstick. Drummer's hands are usually painted with white clay for purification.

Densmore says that drums are sometimes given names, and that the drums are sprinkled with cornmeal during and at the conclusion of a dance.[289]

Lange, on the other hand, gives the native name for the drum and the drumstick, *o-ya-pom' potz* and *o' patz*, and says one informant told him that these were the only terms used to refer to drums, "no other designations or specific names being applied."[290]

Cochiti is famous for its drum makers, and at one time or another most Cochiti men have fashioned them. Today only a few specialize in their manufacture. The women may assist by painting the sides and heads, sometimes blackening the heads with shoe polish. The best drums have head hides that vary in thickness to give them greater tonal range. Actually, both heads are

San Ildefonso Pueblo drummer using rest stick to support the drum.

involved in the making of a tone, for when one end is struck the other also vibrates, although to a lesser degree.

When a single drum is used, the drummers may change off to give each other a rest during performances. Some drummers use different drumsticks to change the pitch. I have seen drums turned on their side so that both ends could be struck and turned upside down so quickly that the drummer did not miss a beat.

Besides the drum there are gourd rattles, turtle-shell rattles, bells, cones, rasps, flutes, and whistles. It is not known to what extent flutes and whistles are employed in secret rituals. What little is known seems to indicate they are not so extensively used as at Hopi. There is a Jemez Flute Dance that is performed by the two women's societies and the Sun Society. Since the flute is believed to make things grow better, it is played when the corn is planted. The lead dancer is the flutist and wears an embroidered black shirt of woven cotton, cut in poncho style with open sleeves, a kilt, rain sash, crocheted leggings, white moccasins, skunk-fur anklets, and a fox skin. Two eagle feather fans are attached to his shirt at the shoulders. Densmore reports that Rio Grande flutes are made of bamboo, with a carved half-gourd attached to one end as a bell. She says they are played by members of a particular society "to help the corn grow."[291]

Musical instruments. Rasping items including painted gourd, painted scapula, painted stick, set of carved wooden rasp sticks. From the Museum of New Mexico collection.

Songs accompany virtually every dance. New songs are composed for the summer dances in particular, and men with a talent for composing are called upon to create these. Variations are permitted, but they all must fit within a traditional framework. Melodies and themes may even be borrowed from another village, and on rare occasions Navajo and English words are inserted. Not all songs will be understood by the villagers, and those that adhere rigidly to traditional compositions may be understood by only the oldest people.

The songs are sung by a chorus or by the dancers. Usually only the men sing, but in some dances the women add their voices. When a chorus is involved, the songs are rehearsed for several nights, and the dancers join them for joint practices.

At the most conservative pueblos not even the villagers may record the music, but San Ildefonso, San Juan, and Cochiti have recorded some of their songs and they make records of them for sale to the public.

Dance and music at the pueblos are a unit and are not separable. Detailed investigation by Densmore,[292] Kurath,[293] and Tony Isaacs[294] has shown conclusively that the music and dance are interrelated.

Kurath has demonstrated that the dancer's speed of movement is directly connected to the tempo of the song. The dancer accelerates or slows in response to the songs and the drum. She believes that the percussive beat that underlies the melody is the guide for all steps and gestures, noting that male dancers shake their rattles in unison with the drumbeat, that the drum tremolo directs a break or wandering in the dance formation, and that certain changes in beat result in a change in the *antege* (foot-lifting) step.

Tonal patterns do not directly affect dance movements, but new phrases are often accompanied by changes in direction or formation.

Self-accompanied dances are the least complex of the dance forms and steps. The dancer can sing while dancing and can control the use of the rattle. Music is aided in such dances by bells appended to the costume and by bells and rattles strapped to the leg. The Bow and Arrow Dance is a good example of self-accompaniment in dance.

Four types of group formations are used for the larger Pueblo dances: circular, simple line, complex line, and complex mixed.

Circular, or circle, dances are usually performed in a clockwise direction, although there are exceptions. The Tablita Dance follows a counterclockwise course. Circle dances include Secret Society dances; Women's Society plaza dances; spring planting dances; and, formerly, the War Society scalp dances.

Simple line dances are commonly employed by the Pueblos. In these, the dancers remain essentially in place while they dance. Many of the simple line dances are referred to by professionals as "maskless Katcina dances," since they are performed by men only. Included in this category are the Evergreen Dance of Isleta, the Turtle Dance of San Juan, and the Bow and Arrow Dance of Tesuque. Simple line dances that involve male and female performers are the Basket dances, the Koshare Initiation Dance, and the Corn Grinding Dance.

Complex line dances involve changes in the dancer's positions. Lines move together, separate, and rejoin. Lines also move sideways.

Complex mixed dances include numerous patterns and formations, with dancers traveling in zigzag paths, lines, and circles. Included in this category are Buffalo (Game Animal) and Tablita dances.

In performing, the dancers may walk, run, jump, hop, shuffle, or do a foot-lifting step. Women do what is referred to in the literature as a "pat step," whose length is adjusted to compensate for the amount of traveling required to accomplish a choreographic pattern.

Body gestures include knee dips, torso movements, and hand signals, all employed to indicate what is in the mind of the people as each part of a dance is performed. All movements are symbolic, but some are so realistic that even an untrained observer can read them once the general import of the dance is known. By means of symbols, crops are ritually planted, cultivated, brought up from the earth, harvested, stored, and eaten. Game is called in, slain, eaten, and thanked. The Katcina are called, the rain comes with clouds and lightning, the fields turn green, gratitude is expressed. It is all there in the dance for those who have "eyes" to see it.

Feasting

The serving of food to performers and guests, commonly called "feasting," is a standard part of every private and public dance. At such times those who serve as hosts will go to amazing lengths to provide every sort of Pueblo and Anglo food. The serving will go on for most of the day. Ordinarily, a guest should be invited. But when public dances are held, any visitor can walk into a home that is serving, sit down at the table, and with no questions whatsoever will be fed. Among other things, the guest will enjoy oven-baked bread, red or green chili stew, salads, fruit, snack foods, coffee, and soft drinks. Dessert may include watermelon, cake, cookies, and pies.

When two Tablita groups are dancing alternately, the dancers from the first group are fed while the second group dances. Following instructions from the moiety leader, they may eat in the kiva, in the ceremonial house, or in their own homes.

Since no formal welfare system exists among the Pueblos, the dance days have become a means of economic stabilization. They provide ways of distributing economic wealth. Besides the feasting, the Pueblos also hold "giveaways" to allow those with surpluses to share them with the rest of the community. Housetops serve as platforms from which food and other household goods are thrown to the throngs of happy villagers who gather below. Sometimes giveaways are considered proper even if a household does not have a surplus. After namings and initiations the relatives of those so blessed are expected to show their appreciation by such gestures.

Given the overall significance of the Pueblo ritual and its dance extensions, it is easy to understand why ceremonial life has profound social implications for the Pueblo people. Dancing is a community obligation, and pressure is brought to bear by the pueblo officials, the moiety leaders, society leaders, and family upon all who are capable of performing.

Outside jobs may affect adversely the availability of an individual for practice. Those who live in Santa Fe and Albuquerque, for example, will be able to dance only one or two times a year. Some of the women must be excused to prepare food and to serve it. Pregnant women, the sick, and the very old are not expected to dance.

But faith and family pride make it essential that each family be represented in the yearly cycle. Children are encouraged at an early age to dance, and their costumes are miniature duplications of those worn by the adults. One of the most impressive things a visitor sees on a feast day is children of three and four dancing with grim determination and utter devotion. Because of this the dance becomes an important factor in the education of the child in traditional ways. As I have said, the adults are also educated in their responsibilities by the acts and lectures of the "clowns."

Some people pledge to dance a certain number of times each year and make every effort to do so. Dancers are not expected to participate without complaint. The performances are time-consuming and exhausting. The summer heat can be an awesome foe, as can the wind and the dust. Performers may experience sunburn, sore muscles, and blistered feet. No one minds or is surprised if these afflictions are commented upon during the rest periods.

Those who do not dance are at the very least expected to be in the village while a dance is going on. A few may watch television or visit, but most do not. They come to watch, or they listen from their homes. They will be so familiar with the dance that even without seeing it they will know what is happening just from hearing the drum and the songs.

It is probable that no other aspect of Pueblo life plays a more important role than the dance as a means of social integration. It establishes responsibility, supplies the essential needs, educates, and provides entertainment.

A Pueblo woman is expected to be reserved and obedient. In the dance this role is emphasized. Her steps are demure, and with few exceptions she is positioned behind the male. The Pueblo man is also expected to be reserved and obedient, but he must at the same time lead, and he is given far greater ceremonial and governmental responsibility.

As the essential teachers of the ancient ways, the elderly are able to retain a sense of pride and usefulness. They teach, and they furnish certain ritual items no one else could provide. Even in the dance itself the placement of dancers in a line is determined by age. Young men and women are placed at the head of the lines. The older dancers, including the dance leader, are usually placed in the middle. Children always bring up the rear.

Public dances are held at various times throughout the year, but unless one has a Pueblo friend to notify him or wishes to call the pueblo offices to find out when they are, the most dependable times are the feast days, which are as follows: San Ildefonso, January 23; San Felipe, May 1; Sandia, June 12; San Juan, June 24; Cochiti, July 14; Santa Ana, July 26; Santo Domingo, August 4; Picuris, August 10; Santa Clara, August 12; Zia, August 15; Isleta, August 28; Taos, September 30; Nambe, October 4; Jemez, November 12; Tesuque, November 12.

Chapter 4

BRINGING THE BUDS TO LIFE

Nowhere is the essence of the Pueblo mind revealed more clearly than in the public dances. On these important occasions careful observers find a splendid summing up of centuries of tradition. The costume, body movements, facial expressions, music, and time of year combine to reveal how Pueblos endure and prosper in their vibrant relationship with a living Heaven and Earth.

Throughout the book, color plates and drawings have emphasized this ceremonial lifeway as it has continued since earliest times. But the descriptions cover only a fraction of the public dances I have witnessed. Several more Rio Grande dances are described and illustrated in connection with their associated villages in this chapter, so that individual details, the brilliant costuming, and comparisons between villages may be fully viewed and appreciated. We leave the Pueblo people dancing and exhibiting the faith that has proven itself to them, and served them well for more than two thousand years.

By confining myself to illustrations and captions in treating these, the great variety of costuming that exists along the Rio Grande is more vividly displayed than it could ever be by word pictures alone. I also illustrate in this section certain of the already published materials concerning Katcina masks and costumes. By this inclusion a broader picture is gained of the ceremonial life of the Rio Grande pueblos as it exists in secret and in public. When this material is considered it must be borne in mind that, except for some of the data from Zia, the descriptions came originally from informants, who presented it to ethnologists without tribal sanction, and the degree of its accuracy is not known.

Among the other dances I have witnessed are the following, and a selection of these is captioned and illustrated:

Apache clowns for the San Juan Deer Dance.

Hunt leader for the Buffalo Dance at San Ildefonso Pueblo.

The male Buffalo dancer of San Ildefonso.

The Buffalo dancer of Tesuque Pueblo.

The women Buffalo dancers of San Juan.

The woman Buffalo dancer of San Ildefonso.

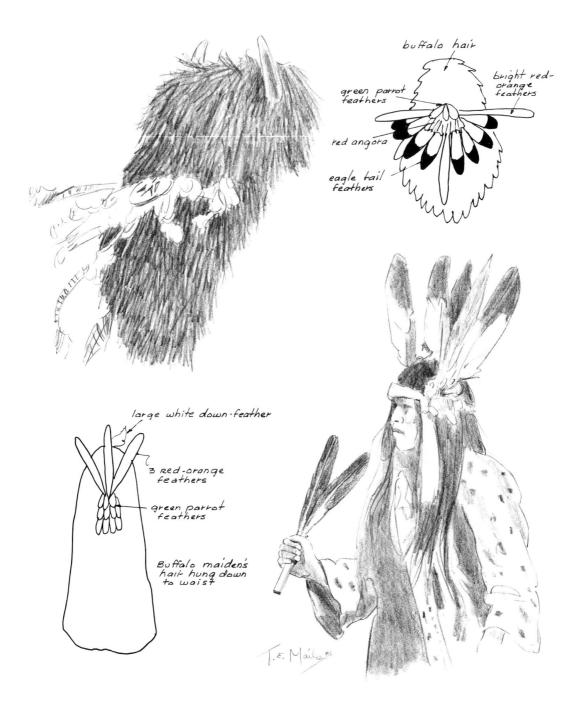

Buffalo Dance details. *Top left*, back view of buffalo headdress from San Ildefonso Pueblo. *Top right*, back of male headdress from Santo Domingo Pueblo. *Bottom left*, female dancer's hair attachment from Santo Domingo Pueblo. *Bottom right*, female Buffalo dancer from San Ildefonso Pueblo.

The Game Animal dancers of San Ildefonso.

The Antelope dancer of San Ildefonso Pueblo.

"Mountain Sheep" in the Game Animal Dance at Santa Clara Pueblo.

The Comanche dancer of San Ildefonso Pueblo.

O'shatch (Sun) Katcina mask from Santo Domingo. Width, 11½ inches; height, 25 inches. Basketry cap covered with buckskin and thick cotton. An eighty-year-old basket was used in this mask; buckskin-fringed; twenty-nine eagle feathers with tips painted white around the face of the mask; red-dyed eagle's down inside the feathers symbolize the dawn; with this is red-dyed wool yarn; the face is surrounded by white cotton symbolizing the sky after the dawn has faded. The face is predominantly blue. Red, yellow, and black cloud design at the forehead; black eyes; teeth and mouth outlined in black; white and black teeth; wool beard. The mask is used only in the big Summer Rain Dance.

Front, back, and side views of Katcina tablita mask from Jemez Pueblo. Said to be the mask from which the Hopi Hemis Katcina was adapted. Case mask is of heavy commercial leather; tablita is flanked with lightning and cloud symbols; eyeshade is of split cane. Mask diameter, 8 inches; height, 24 inches.

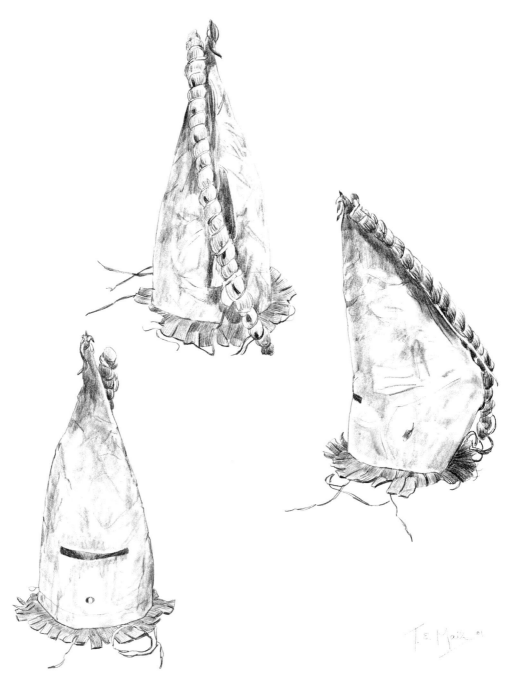

Front, back, and side views of a very old Katcina mask from Jemez Pueblo. Katcina personage not known. Made of buffalo hide with corn-husk roll on back. Painted yellow, green, and red. Height, 18 inches.

Front and side views of a replica of a Katcina mask, Santo Domingo Pueblo. Paiyatyama, said to be worn by the leader of the Koshare in the initiations of boys and girls, although Paiyatyama seldom appears at initiations today. Detail is of the corn-husk ear pendant of the mask. Height, 36 inches. Horn has black and white stripes and is tipped with corn husks. The mask is blue, with eyes and mouth outlined in black and white.

Katcina mask, Santo Domingo Pueblo, Dya'-a-nye', Deer dancer. Said to be worn by dancers in a line of as many as 150 performers. The father and mother of this Katcina were cylindrical turtles.

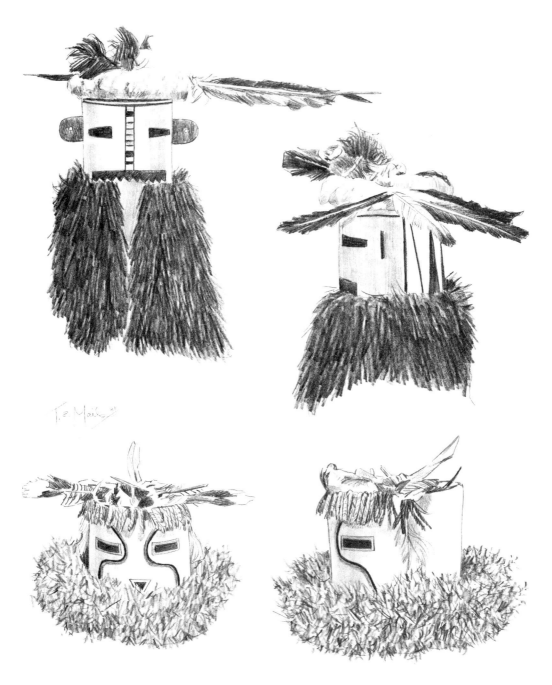

Top, front, and side views of a Rio Grande Pueblo Katcina mask. Personage unknown. *Bottom*, front, and side views of a Katcina mask said to be from the winter solstice ceremony. Height, 8½ inches; diameter of the opening for the head, 8 inches. The wreath is of dried brown pine around the base. Feathers top the mask, with bangs of red twisted yarn. Black rectangular eyes with border of blue. Inverted black triangle mouth with blue border. Face is white, with nose and mouth area yellow with blue and black border.

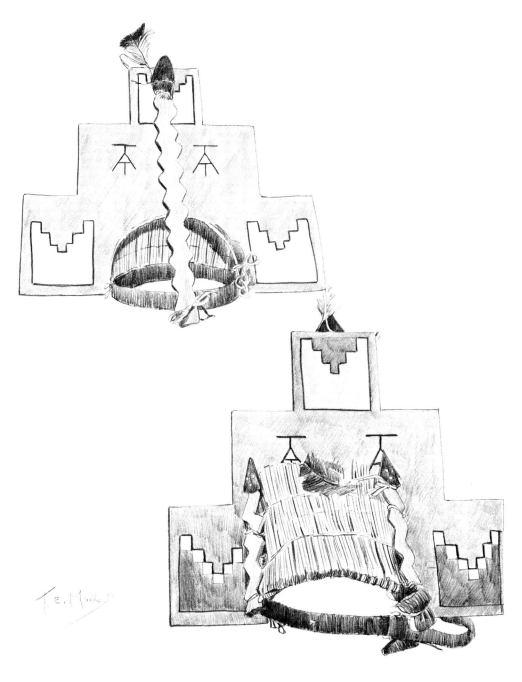

Front and back views of a Katcina tablita mask from Isleta Pueblo. The painted willow crown is flanked by lightning symbols. The cloud and rain symbols are red and yellow on a blue background. Height, 14 inches.

The Bow and Arrow dancers of San Ildefonso.

A little Corn dancer of Santa Clara.

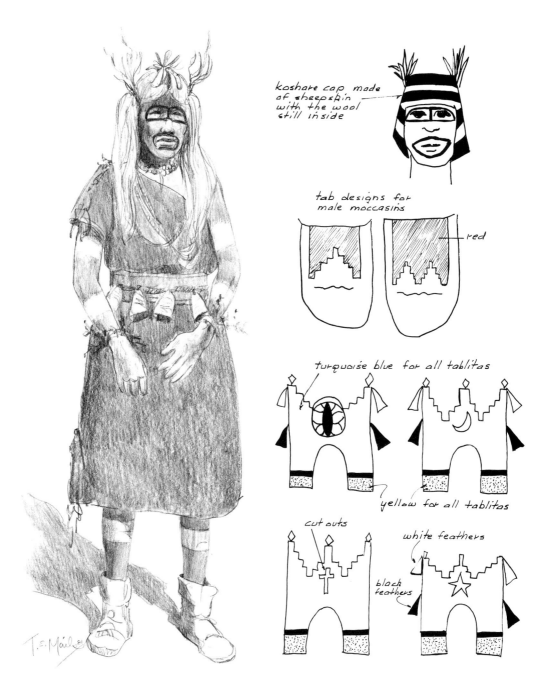

koshare cap made
of sheepskin
with the wool
still inside

tab designs for
male moccasins

red

turquoise blue for all tablitas

yellow for all tablitas

cut outs

white feathers

black
feathers

Santa Ana Pueblo Feast Day Corn Dance, July 26, 1974. Costume details: *left*, female clown; *right*, male clown cap and face paint, moccasin tabs for male dancers, tablita designs for female dancers.

San Juan Pueblo woman Cloud dancer.

A male Basket dancer of San Juan Pueblo.

A Basket dancer of San Ildefonso Pueblo.

Eagle dancer of San Ildefonso Pueblo.

War dancer on San Geronimo Day at Taos Pueblo, ca. 1920. From a Museum of New Mexico photograph.

Sun dancer, San Ildefonso Pueblo, ca. 1935. From a T. Harmon Parkhurst photograph.

Taos War dancers.

Chapter 5

CONCLUSION

The Pueblo Children of the Earth Mother was begun in 1972, and I was well into the book when I came across Charles Avery Amsden's splendid little volume *Prehistoric Southwesterners from Basketmaker to Pueblo*. What struck me most forcibly were the final paragraphs of the Introduction by Dr. Alfred V. Kidder, for it summed up precisely what I had set out to do.

Amsden, it seems, died in 1941 without completing his desire to tell "the story of one small group of people," the Anasazi, "to help to render understandable the long and painful upward struggle of all mankind." "The pity," Kidder says, "is that he could not finish it. Not so much because of the facts he would have recorded, as because of the wider meaning he would have given them . . .[1]

"Had he been permitted to finish his work he would have described the spread of farming, the gathering of population into larger groups, the development of the many-roomed Pueblo villages and cliff-dwellings with their underground ceremonial chambers that were the lineal descendants of the first subterranean dwellings. He would have taken up the Great Period of the eleventh and twelfth centuries, when Pueblo life was in fullest flower and enjoyed its greatest territorial range. Then would have come discussion of the as yet not fully explained relinquishment of large areas in the north and west, perhaps the result of a long-continued drought, perhaps caused by pressure of nomadic enemies, perhaps by a combination of the two. Next he would have treated the great new settlements that sprang up in the Little Colorado drainage of Arizona and of the Rio Grande in New Mexico; the struggles against the Navajo and Apache; and the coming of the Spaniards under Coronado in 1540. Finally he would have pictured the Pueblo Indians of today, the Hopi and Zuñi and the dwellers in the eastern villages, people who have clung so tenaciously and so successfully to their old ways of life through nearly four centuries of alien domination that, as Charles Lummis used to say, they let you catch your archaeology alive."[2]

Amsden got only as far as the Basketmakers, only to the dawn of the civilization, and it was Kidder's opinion that if Amsden had been able to treat the rest, "no one could have done it better." That is probably true, for Amsden could see deeply into the nature of people. He could record the anthropological facts, but he could also endow them with life.

I have sought also to trace this extraordinary people from their earliest known beginning two thousand years ago to the present day, and in so doing to turn archaeological remnants into living testimonies that speak of a creative, adaptive, resilient, and uniquely persistent culture. Their perseverance stands alone in the New World cultural scene, and more amazing still is the fact that they continue to defy those who at regular intervals predict their disappearance, or full merger, into the American mainstream. Diffusion and infusion have made their inroads, but the Anasazi-Pueblos live on much as they always have.

Most of those who come to know them as friends and as a culture have no wish to witness their disintegration. The loss to them, and to us, would be too much. The price would be too high. Beyond our sheer appreciation of their complex lifeway, there are many valuable lessons to be learned from it, and it is a source barely tapped. An encounter with any aspect of it is an inspiration and, at the very least, stimulating. I suspect that one day soon many of us will go to this well of wisdom, and we may even find that it contains what Ponce de León was seeking when he searched for the Fountain of Youth.

NOTES

CHAPTER I   THE HOPI—PUEBLO V

1. Alexander M. Stephen, *Hopi Journal of Alexander M. Stephen.*
2. Harry C. James, *Pages From Hopi History*, pp. 152–58, and Fred Eggan, Introduction to *Hopi Material Culture* by Barton Wright, p. 1.
3. Laura Thompson, as quoted by Eggan in the introduction to *Hopi Material Culture* by Barton Wright, p. 2.
4. Eggan, op. cit., p. 3.
5. Ibid., p. 6.
6. Ibid., p. 7.
7. James, op. cit., p. 158.
8. Albert Yava, *Big Falling Snow*, p. ix.
9. Ibid., p. 80.
10. Stephen, op. cit., p. 199.
11. Polingaysi Qoyawayma, *No Turning Back*, p. 94.
12. John G. Bourke, *The Snake-Dance of the Moquis of Arizona*, pp. 107 and 289.
13. Walter Hough, *The Hopi Indians*, p. 119.
14. Ibid., p. 121.
15. Robert C. Euler and Henry F. Dobyns, *The Hopi People*, p. 57.
16. Mischa Titiev, *Old Oraibi: A Study of the Hopi Indians of the Third Mesa*, p. 30.
17. George Wharton James, *Indians of the Painted Desert*, p. 71.
18. Earle R. Forrest, "The Mesa Dwellers of the Painted Desert," p. 4.
19. Barton Wright, *Hopi Material Culture*, pp. 77–80.
20. Wayne Dennis, *The Hopi Child*, pp. 48–49.
21. Ibid., pp. 49–62.
22. George Wharton James, op. cit., pp. 90–91.
23. Hough, op. cit., pp. 204–6.
24. Stephen, Southwest Museum Leaflet, No. 14.
25. Laura Thompson and Alice Joseph, *The Hopi Way*, p. 41.
26. Ibid., p. 41.
27. George Wharton James, op. cit., p. 82.
28. Thompson and Joseph, op. cit., p. 41.
29. Ibid., p. 41.
30. Ibid., p. 41.
31. Ibid., p. 99.
32. Hough, op. cit., pp. 57–58.
33. Stephen, *Hopi Journal of Alexander M. Stephen*, pp. 857–63.
34. H. R. Voth, *The Oraibi Oaqöl Ceremony*, p. 5.
35. Jesse Walter Fewkes, "A Few Summer Ceremonials at the Tusayan Pueblos," p. 157.
36. Hough, op. cit., p. 168.
37. Elsie Clews Parsons, *Pueblo Indian Religion*, Vol. 1, Part 2, p. 378.
38. Stephen, *Hopi Journal of Alexander M. Stephen*, p. 857.
39. Voth, *Brief Miscellaneous Hopi Papers*, pp. 99–103.
40. Fewkes, "Sun Worship of the Hopi Indians," p. 526.
41. Voth, *Brief Miscellaneous Hopi Papers*, p. 101.
42. Fewkes, "Sun Worship of the Hopi Indians," p. 526.
43. Ibid.
44. Louise Udall, *Me and Mine*, pp. 148–50.
45. Voth, *Brief Miscellaneous Hopi Papers*, p. 101.
46. Ibid., p. 102.
47. Ibid., p. 103.
48. Ibid., p. 103.
49. Fewkes, "Sun Worship of the Hopi Indians," p. 526.
50. Voth, *Brief Miscellaneous Hopi Papers*, p. 103.
51. Ibid., p. 103.
52. Ibid., p. 102.
53. Dennis, op. cit., pp. 29–30.
54. J. G. Owens, "Natal Ceremonies of the Hopi Indians," p. 165.
55. Udall, op. cit., p. 178.
56. Dennis, op. cit., p. 30.
57. Udall, op. cit., p. 179.
58. Ibid., p. 180.
59. Hough, op. cit., p. 114.
60. Owens, op. cit., p. 166, and Hough, op. cit., p. 115.
61. Dennis, op. cit., p. 30.
62. Owens, op. cit., pp. 169–70, and Hough, op. cit., p. 116.
63. Pliny Earle Goddard, *Indians of the Southwest*, p. 100.
64. Hough, op. cit., p. 48.
65. Goddard, op. cit., pp. 100–1.
66. Barton Wright, op. cit., pp. 47–48.
67. Ibid., pp. 46–47.
68. Owens, op. cit., p. 173.
69. Hough, op. cit., p. 118.
70. Owens, op. cit., p. 175.
71. Dennis, op. cit., pp. 186–90.
72. Owens, op. cit., p. 163.
73. Ibid., pp. 164–65.
74. Ibid., p. 165.
75. Titiev, op. cit., pp. 30–31.
76. Ibid., p. 35.
77. Ibid., p. 36.
78. Yava, op. cit., pp. 87–88, and Udall, op. cit., pp. 153–65.
79. Titiev, op. cit., p. 119.
80. Ibid., p. 37.
81. Goddard, op. cit., p. 102.
82. Titiev, op. cit., p. 37.

83. Ibid., p. 37.
84. Goddard, op. cit., p. 103.
85. Wright, Barton, op. cit., p. 69.
86. Goddard, op. cit., p. 103.
87. Wright, Barton, op. cit., p. 20–21.
88. Titiev, op. cit., p. 38.
89. Hough, op. cit., p. 127–28.
90. Titiev, op. cit., p. 43.
91. George Wharton James, op. cit., p. 38.
92. Frederick Monsen, "Pueblos of the Painted Desert," p. 27.
93. Udall, op. cit., p. 54.
94. George Wharton James, op. cit., pp. 38–39.
95. Ruth DeEtte Simpson, "The Hopi Indians," p. 58.
96. Ibid., p. 59.
97. Bourke, op. cit., p. 115.
98. Victor Mindeleff, "A Study of Pueblo Architecture: Tusayan and Cibolo," pp. 119–22.
99. George A. Dorsey and H. R. Voth, "The Mishongnove Ceremonies of the Snake and Antelope Fraternities," p. 171.
100. Bourke, op. cit., p. 105.
101. Ibid., p. 128.
102. Hough, op. cit., pp. 175–76.
103. Ibid., p. 178.
104. Simpson, op. cit., p. 52.
105. Hough, op. cit., pp. 61–62.
106. Simpson, op. cit., p. 52.
107. Ruth Underhill, *Workaday Life of the Pueblos*, pp. 41–44.
108. Simpson, op. cit., p. 53.
109. Ibid., p. 53.
110. Ibid., p. 54.
111. Hough, op. cit., p. 64.
112. Ibid., p. 66.
113. Ibid., p. 172.
114. George Wharton James, op. cit., pp. 74–75.
115. Underhill, op. cit., p. 65.
116. Ibid., p. 65.
117. Ibid., p. 65.
118. Hough, op. cit., p. 173.
119. Ibid., pp. 173–74.
120. Underhill, op. cit., p. 69.
121. Ibid., p. 71.
122. Hough, op. cit., p. 169.
123. Ibid., pp. 169–70.
124. Ibid., p. 171.
125. Voth, *Brief Miscellaneous Hopi Papers*, p. 107.
126. Ibid., p. 108.
127. Ibid., p. 108.
128. Hough, op. cit., p. 172.
129. Voth, *Brief Miscellaneous Hopi Papers*, p. 108.
130. Underhill, op. cit., p. 71.
131. Voth, *Brief Miscellaneous Hopi Papers*, p. 108.
132. Ibid., p. 109.
133. Titiev, op. cit., pp. 155–56.
134. Ibid., pp. 159–60.
135. Ibid., pp. 158–59.
136. Ibid., pp. 160, and Parsons, *Pueblo Indian Religion*, Vol. 1, Part 1, p. 98.
137. Titiev, op. cit., pp. 161–63.
138. Hough, op, cit., pp. 83–84.
139. Ibid., p. 84.
140. Ibid., p. 85.
141. Virginia More Roediger, *Ceremonial Costumes of the Pueblo Indians*, pp. 52–53.
142. Hough, op. cit., pp. 85–86.
143. Ibid., p. 86.
144. Nancy Fox, *Pueblo Weaving and Textile Arts*, pp. 32–33.
145. Ibid., p. 33.
146. Simpson, op. cit., p. 64.
147. Underhill, op. cit., pp. 111–12.
148. Hough, op. cit., pp. 73–74.
149. Underhill, op. cit., pp. 113–14.
150. Ibid., p. 113.
151. Ibid., p. 113.
152. Ibid., p. 114.
153. Ibid., p. 122.
154. Hough, op. cit., pp. 77–82.
155. Fewkes, "A Few Tusayan Pictographs," pp. 10–11.
156. Simpson, op. cit., p. 76.
157. Ibid., p. 77.
158. Ibid., p. 77.
159. Ibid., p. 78.
160. Ibid., pp. 79–80.
161. Gene Weltfish, "Preliminary Classification of Prehistoric Southwestern Basketry," pp. 26–27.
162. Ruth Underhill, *Pueblo Crafts*, p. 12.
163. Hough, op. cit., p. 90–95.
164. Simpson, op. cit., p. 72.
165. Underhill, op. cit., p. 16.
166. Ibid., p. 14.
167. Simpson, op. cit., pp. 74–75.
168. Margaret Wright, *Hopi Silver*, p. 8.
169. Ibid., p. 11.
170. Underhill, op. cit., p. 106.
171. Ibid., p. 107–8.
172. Ibid., p. 108.
173. Fewkes, "A Few Tusayan Pictographs," p. 11–12.
174. Ibid., p. 13.
175. Parsons, "Hopi and Zuñi Ceremonialism," p. 25.
176. Fewkes, "The Walpi Flute Observance: A Study of Primitive Dramatization," p. 265.
177. Fewkes, "Fire Worship of the Hopi Indians," p. 607.
178. Titiev, op. cit., p. 44.
179. Hough, op. cit., p. 38.
180. Titiev, op. cit., p. 45.
181. Thompson and Joseph, op. cit., p. 37.
182. Ibid., p. 34.
183. Parsons, "Hopi and Zuñi Ceremonialism," pp. 36–37.
184. Titiev, op. cit., p. 44.
185. Thompson and Joseph, op. cit., p. 137, fn. 10.
186. Titiev, op. cit., p. 53.
187. Parsons, "Hopi and Zuñi Ceremonialism," p. 38.

188. Titiev, op. cit., p. 241.
189. Parsons, "Hopi and Zuñi Ceremonialism," pp. 25–35.
190. Titiev, op. cit., p. 44.
191. Thompson and Joseph, op. cit., pp. 34–36.
192. Titiev, op. cit., p. 109.
193. Bertha Dutton, *Indians of the American Southwest*, p. 46.
194. Frederick J. Dockstader, *The Kachina and the White Man*, pp. 10–11.
195. Titiev, op. cit., p. 109, and Watson Smith, "Kiva Mural Decorations at Awatovi and Kawaika-a," p. 293.
196. Watson Smith, op. cit., p. 293.
197. Parsons, "Hopi and Zuñi Ceremonialism," pp. 40–41.
198. Dutton, op. cit., p. 58.
199. Dutton, op. cit., p. 42.
200. Titiev, op. cit., p. 110.
201. Ibid., pp. 109–10.
202. Stephen, *Hopi Journal of Alexander M. Stephen*, pp. 1037–38.
203. Ibid., p. 1040.
204. Fewkes, "Hopi Katcinas Drawn by Native Artists," p. 22.
205. Ibid., pp. 23–25.
206. Dutton, op. cit., p. 61.
207. Fewkes, "A Few Summer Ceremonials at the Tusayan Pueblos," p. 24.
208. Byron Harvey III, editor, The Henry R. Voth Collection at Grand Canyon, Arizona, p. 13.
209. Titiev, op. cit., p. 195.
210. Barton Wright, op. cit., p. 14.
211. George Wharton James, op. cit., pp. 80.
212. Roediger, op. cit., p. 107.
213. Barton Wright, op. cit., p. 100.
214. Harold S. Colton, *Hopi Kachina Dolls*, p. 16.
215. Bourke, op. cit., pp. 120–21.
216. Fewkes, "A Few Summer Ceremonials at the Tusayan Pueblos," p. 40.
217. Barton Wright, op. cit., p. 99.
218. Ibid., p. 99.
219. Parsons, *Spanish Elements in the Kachina Cult of the Pueblos*, p. 588–97.
220. Watson Smith, op. cit., p. 309–10.
221. Parsons, "Hopi and Zuñi Ceremonialism," p. 36.
222. Personal communication.
223. Clara Lee Tanner, *Southwest Indian Craft Arts*, p. 173.
224. Underhill, op. cit., p. 127.
225. Tanner, op. cit., p. 174, and Underhill, op. cit., p. 127.
226. Thomas E. Mails, *The People Called Apache*, p. 413.
227. Underhill, op. cit., p. 128.
228. Ibid., p. 128.
229. Parsons, *Pueblo Indian Religion*, Vol. 1, Part 2, p. 379.
230. Ibid., p. 380.
231. Underhill, op. cit., pp. 125–26.
232. Parsons, *Pueblo Indian Religion*, Vol. 1, Part 2, p. 377.

233. Thompson and Joseph, op. cit., p. 138.
234. Dockstader, op. cit., p. 128.
235. Ibid., p. 130.
236. Yava, op. cit., p. 138.
237. Ibid., pp. 134–36.
238. Ibid., p. 135.
239. Walter Fewkes and J. G. Owens, "The La-lakon-ta: A Tusayan Dance," p. 105.
240. Fewkes, "A Few Summer Ceremonials at the Tusayan Pueblos," p. 46.
241. Titiev, op. cit., p. 103.
242. Fewkes, "The Owakulti Altar at Sichomovi Pueblo," p. 214.
243. Fewkes, "The Walpi Flute Observance," p. 280.
244. Titiev, op. cit., p. 103.
245. Parsons, *Pueblo Indian Religion*, Vol. 2, Part 1, p. 781.
246. Parsons, "Hopi and Zuñi Ceremonialism," p. 48.
247. Titiev, op. cit., p. 104.
248. Parsons, "Hopi and Zuñi Ceremonialism," p. 37.
249. Fewkes, "A Few Summer Ceremonials at the Tusayan Pueblos," p. 110.
250. Titiev, op. cit., p. 104.
251. Ibid., p. 107.
252. Ibid., p. 130.
253. Ibid., p. 130.
254. Ibid., pp. 131–33, and Fewkes, "Fire Worship of the Hopi Indians," pp. 589–610.
255. Titiev, op. cit., p. 131.
256. Fewkes, "Fire Worship of the Hopi Indians," p. 594.
257. Ibid., p. 601.
258. Fewkes, "The Lesser New-Fire Ceremony at Walpi," p. 96.
259. Titiev, op. cit., p. 135.
260. Jesse Walter Fewkes and Alexander M. Stephen, "The Na-ac-nai-ya: A Tusayan Initiation Ceremony," p. 199.
261. Titiev, op. cit., p. 138.
262. Ibid., p. 139.
263. Ibid., p. 171.
264. Fewkes, "The Prehistoric Culture of Tusayan," pp. 161–62.
265. Fewkes, "The Walpi Flute Observance," pp. 267–68.
266. Titiev, op. cit., p. 141.
267. Ibid., p. 104.
268. Fewkes, "A Few Summer Ceremonials at the Tusayan Pueblos," p. 26.
269. Stephen, *Hopi Journal of Alexander M. Stephen*, pp. 1271–72.
270. Qoyawayma, op. cit., pp. 87–88.
271. Titiev, op. cit., p. 104.
272. Parsons, *Pueblo Indian Religion*, Vol. 1, Part 1, p. 113.
273. Titiev, op. cit., p. 105.
274. Ibid., p. 105.
275. Fewkes, "The Owakulti Altar at Sichomovi Pueblo," p. 215.
276. Titiev, op. cit., p. 105.

277. Stephen, "Hopi Tales," p. 13.
278. Titiev, op. cit., p. 105.
279. Ibid., p. 105.
280. Ibid., p. 241.
281. Ibid., p. 106.
282. Parsons, *Pueblo Indian Religion,* Vol. 1, Part 2, pp. 457–60.
283. Titiev, op. cit., p. 106.
284. Ibid., p. 106.
285. Ibid., pp. 109–41.
286. George A. Dorsey and H. R. Voth, "The Oraibi Soyal Ceremony," p. 42.
287. Ibid., p. 55.
288. Titiev, op. cit., pp. 111–12.
289. Ibid., p. 112.
290. Ibid., p. 113.
291. Parsons, *Pueblo Indian Religion,* Vol. 2, Part 1, pp. 828–39.
292. Ibid., p. 831.
293. Yava, op. cit., p. 42.
294. Roediger, op. cit., pp. 229–30.
295. Ibid., p. 230.
296. Ibid., p. 230.
297. Yava, op. cit., pp. 41–43.
298. Titiev, op. cit., p. 114.
299. Ibid., p. 115.
300. Ibid., pp. 115–16.
301. Udall, op. cit., p. 25.
302. Ibid., p. 26.
303. Ibid., p. 27.
304. Titiev, op. cit., p. 116.
305. Ibid., pp. 117–18.
306. Ibid., pp. 118–19.
307. Ibid., p. 119.
308. Ibid., pp. 119–20.
309. Ibid., p. 121, and Fewkes, "A Theatrical Performance at Walpi," pp. 605–29.
310. Titiev, op. cit., p. 121.
311. Ibid., p. 122.
312. Ibid., p. 123.
313. Hough, op. cit., p. 144.
314. Titiev, op. cit., p. 123, and Parsons, *Pueblo Indian Religion,* Vol. 1, Part 2, p. 322.
315. Titiev, op. cit., p. 124.
316. Ibid., p. 125.
317. Ibid., pp. 125–26.
318. Ibid., pp. 127–28.
319. Barton Wright, op. cit., p. 212.
320. Fewkes, "A Few Summer Ceremonials at the Tusayan Pueblos," pp. 91 and 100.
321. Titiev, op. cit., p. 235.
322. Voth, *Brief Miscellaneous Hopi Papers,* preface.
323. Fewkes, "Sun Worship of the Hopi Indians," pp. 493–525.
324. Fewkes, "A Few Summer Ceremonials at the Tusayan Pueblos," p. 138.
325. Ibid., p. 139.
326. Ibid., p. 140.
327. Ibid., p. 140.
328. Ibid., p. 141.
329. Titiev, pp. 146–49.
330. Fewkes, as quoted by Hough, *The Hopi Indians,* pp. 151–53.

331. Ibid., p. 307.
332. Titiev, op. cit., p. 152.
333. Parsons, *Pueblo Indian Religion,* Vol. 1, Part 2, p. 577.
334. Titiev, op. cit., p. 153.
335. Ibid., p. 164.
336. Ibid., p. 164.
337. Voth, "The Oraibi Oaqöl Ceremony," p. 6.
338. Voth, "The Oraibi Marau Ceremony," p. 29.
339. Stephen, *Hopi Journal of Alexander M. Stephen,* pp. 921–22.
340. Titiev, op. cit., p. 165.
341. Ibid., p. 165, and Voth, "The Oraibi Marau Ceremony," p. 51.
342. Parsons, *Pueblo Indian Religion,* Vol. 2, Part 1, p. 864.
343. Titiev, op. cit., p. 168.
344. Parsons, *Pueblo Indian Religion,* Vol. 2, Part 1, p. 830.
345. Fewkes and Owens, "The La-la-kon-ta: A Tusayan Dance," p. 106.
346. Parsons, *Pueblo Indian Religion,* Vol. 1, Part 1, p. 142.
347. Parsons, *A Pueblo Indian Journal,* p. 110.
348. Voth, "The Oraibi Oaqöl Ceremony," p. 11.

CHAPTER II ZUÑI, ACOMA, LAGUNA

1. Elsie Clews Parsons, "Hopi and Zuñi Ceremonialism," p. 62.
2. Edward P. Dozier, *The Pueblo Indians of North America,* p. 134.
3. Parsons, *Pueblo Indian Religion,* Vol. 2, Part 1, p. 872.
4. Ibid., p. 872.
5. Ibid., p. 874.
6. Charles F. Lange and Carroll L. Riley, eds., *The Southwestern Journals of Adolph F. Bandelier, 1880–1882,* p. 47.
7. Luke Lyon, "Michelangelo of the West," p. 25.
8. S. D. Aberle, "The Pueblo Indians of New Mexico: Their Land, Economy and Civil Organization," p. 47.
9. Matilda Coxe Stevenson, "The Zuñi Indians," pp. 349–50.
10. Henry Craig Fleming, M.D., "Medical Observations on the Zuñi Indians," pp. 39–47.
11. Stevenson, op. cit., pp. 369–70.
12. Ibid., pp. 370–71.
13. Ibid., pp. 371–72.
14. Jesse Walter Fewkes, "A Few Summer Ceremonials at Zuñi Pueblo," p. 5.
15. Bertha P. Dutton, *Indians of the American Southwest,* p. 36.
16. Fred Eggan, *Social Organization of the Western Pueblos,* p. 177.
17. Ibid., p. 177.
18. Fewkes, op. cit., p. 3.
19. William Webb and Robert A. Weinstein, *Dwellers at the Source,* p. 122.
20. Ibid., p. 122.
21. Fewkes, op. cit., pp. 5–6.

22. Dorothea C. Leighton and John Adair, *People of the Middle Place*, p. 48, and Dutton, op. cit., pp. 53–54.
23. Ruth L. Bunzel, "Introduction to Zuñi Ceremonialism," p. 512.
24. Dutton, op. cit., p. 53.
25. Leighton and Adair, op. cit., pp. 46 and 51.
26. Bunzel, op. cit., p. 526.
27. Dutton, op. cit., p. 54.
28. Leighton and Adair, op. cit., p. 46.
29. Ibid., p. 46.
30. Ruth F. Kirk, "Introduction to Zuñi Fetishism," p. 9.
31. Ibid., p. 11.
32. Frank Hamilton Cushing, "Zuñi Fetishes," pp. 9–35.
33. Kirk, op. cit., pp. 22–23.
34. Fewkes, op. cit., p. 7.
35. Ibid., p. 8.
36. Anna Wilmarth Ickes, *Mesa Land,* p. 149.
37. Fewkes, op. cit., p. 54.
38. Ibid., p. 9.
39. Ibid., p. 10.
40. Bunzel, "Zuñi Katcinas," pp. 604 ff.
41. Ibid., p. 844.
42. Parsons, "Hopi and Zuñi Ceremonialism," p. 41.
43. Bunzel, op. cit., pp. 879–80.
44. Ibid., pp. 876–77.
45. Ibid., p. 877.
46. Ibid., p. 870.
47. Ibid., p. 868.
48. Ibid., pp. 948–49.
49. Leighton and Adair, op. cit., p. 49.
50. Kathleen Whitaker, "The Zuñi Shalako Festival," p. 141.
51. Parsons, "Winter and Summer Dance Series in Zuñi in 1918," p. 171.
52. Lange and Riley, op. cit., pp. 51–52.
53. Fewkes, op. cit., p. 12.
54. Parsons, "Hopi and Zuñi Ceremonialism," pp. 62 and 85–90.
55. Ibid., pp. 62–63.
56. Ibid., p. 67.
57. Ibid., p. 64.
58. Walter Jarrett, "Acoma, New Mexico Sky City," p. 48.
59. Parsons, *Pueblo Indian Religion,* Vol. 2, Part 1, p. 881.
60. Frederick W. Hodge, "Ascent of the Enchanted Mesa," pp. 15–31.
61. Edgar L. Hewett and Adolph F. Bandelier, *Indians of the Rio Grande Valley,* p. 108.
62. Aberle, op. cit., p. 46.
63. Leslie A. White, "The Acoma Indians, People of the Sky City."
64. Eggan, op. cit., p. 223.
65. Ibid., p. 223.
66. Ibid., p. 224.
67. White, op. cit., pp. 41, 94, 139.
68. Ibid., p. 140.
69. Ibid., p. 64. See also Matthew W. Stirling, "Origin Myth of Acoma and Other Records."
70. Ibid., p. 87.
71. Forence H. Ellis and Laurens Hammack, "The Inner Sanctum of Feather Cave," p. 32.
72. White, "New Material from Acoma," p. 318. See also Matthew W. Stirling, "Origin Myth of Acoma and Other Records," Plate 15, for face painting.
73. White, "The Acoma Indians, People of the Sky City."
74. Ibid., pp. 135–36.
75. White, "The Pueblo of Santo Domingo, New Mexico," pp. 198–99.
76. White, "The Acoma Indians, People of the Sky City," pp. 137–38.
77. White, "New Material from Acoma," p. 322.
78. Eggan, op. cit., pp. 253–55.
79. Hewett and Bandelier, op. cit., p. 107.
80. Parsons, *Pueblo Indian Religion,* Vol. 2, Part 1, pp. 888–89.
81. Hewett and Bandelier, op. cit., p. 105.
82. Ibid., p. 106.
83. Eggan, op. cit., p. 255.
84. Ellis, op. cit., p. 32.
85. Aberle, op. cit., p. 47.
86. Ibid., p. 49.

CHAPTER III   RIO GRANDE REGION
1. D. Bruce Dickson, "Settlement Pattern Stability and Change in the Middle Northern Rio Grande Region, New Mexico: A Test of Some Hypotheses," p. 167.
2. Fred Wendorf, "A Reconstruction of Northern Rio Grande Prehistory," pp. 206–8.
3. Edward P. Dozier, *The Pueblo Indians of North America,* p. 38.
4. Ibid., p. 38.
5. Ibid., pp. 143–44.
6. Dickson, op. cit., p. 168.
7. Dozier, op. cit., p. 144.
8. Laurance C. Herold and Ralph A. Luebben, *Taos Archaeology,* and Wendorf, op. cit.
9. C. B. Cosgrove, "Caves of the Upper Gila and Hueco Areas," pp. 1–181.
10. Ibid., p. 164.
11. Ibid., p. 166.
12. Ibid., p. 168.
13. Ibid., p. 170.
14. Florence H. Ellis and Laurens Hammack, "The Inner Sanctum of Feather Cave, a Mogollon Sun and Earth Shrine Linking Mexico and the Southwest," p. 39.
15. Ibid., p. 25.
16. Ibid., p. 25.
17. Ibid., p. 25.
18. Ibid., p. 39.
19. Ibid., pp. 39–42.
20. Hubert G. Alexander, "The Excavation of Jemez Cave," p. 97.
21. Bertha P. Dutton, *Let's Explore Indian Villages Past and Present,* p. 49.
22. Alexander, op. cit., pp. 101–2.
23. Ibid., pp. 104–5.
24. Frank W. Eddy, "Excavations at Los Pinos

Phase Sites in the Navajo Reservoir District."

25. Jesse D. Jennings, "Glen Canyon: A Summary," p. 53.
26. Paul S. Martin and Fred Plog, *Archaeology of Arizona,* p. 197.
27. Herold and Luebben, op. cit., pp. 18–22.
28. Ibid., p. 19.
29. Ibid., p. 19.
30. Jeancon, as quoted by Herold and Luebben, op. cit., p. 19.
31. Herold and Luebben, op. cit., p. 20.
32. Edward Twitchell Hall, Jr., *Early Stockaded Settlements in the Governador, New Mexico. A Marginal Anasazi Development from Basketmaker III to Pueblo I Times.*
33. Alfred V. Kidder, "Pecos, New Mexico: Archaeological Notes," p. 42.
34. Ibid., pp. 5–48.
35. Ibid., pp. 50–51.
36. Alfred V. Kidder, *The Artifacts of Pecos,* p. 1.
37. Ibid., p. 2.
38. Ibid., p. 3.
39. Kidder, "Pecos, New Mexico: Archaeological Notes," pp. 133–36.
40. Ibid., p. 218.
41. Ibid., p. 143–226.
42. Ibid., pp. 307–8.
43. Kidder, *The Artifacts of Pecos,* p. 4.
44. Ibid., pp. 6–7.
45. Ibid., pp. 86–91.
46. Ibid., pp. 91–99.
47. Ibid., pp. 104–9.
48. Ibid., pp. 156–82.
49. Ibid., pp. 288–304.
50. Stanley Stubbs and W. S. Stallings, Jr., "The Excavation of Pindi Pueblo, New Mexico," p. 145.
51. Kidder, *The Artifacts of Pecos,* p. 4.
52. Dutton, *Sun Father's Way,* p. 41.
53. Ibid., pp. 41–42.
54. J. A. Jeancon, "Excavations in the Chama Valley, New Mexico," pp. 4–6.
55. Ibid., p. 8.
56. Ibid., p. 4.
57. Ibid., p. 11.
58. Bainbridge Bunting, *Early Architecture in New Mexico,* pp. 11–12.
59. Jeancon, op. cit., p. 11.
60. Ibid., p. 13.
61. Ibid., pp. 14.
62. Ibid., pp. 14–15.
63. Ibid., p. 15.
64. Ibid., pp. 16–17.
65. Ibid., pp. 17–24.
66. Ibid., p. 20.
67. Ibid., pp. 24–31.
68. Ibid., p. 33.
69. Ibid., p. 34.
70. Ibid., p. 68.
71. Ibid., pp. 66–67.
72. Ibid., p. 67.

73. Ibid., p. 68.
74. Ibid., pp. 68–69.
75. Ibid., pp. 69–70.
76. Ibid., p. 70.
77. Ibid., pp. 71–72.
78. Ibid., p. 76.
79. Stubbs and Stallings, op. cit., p. vii.
80. Ibid., pp. 2–8.
81. Ibid., pp. 24–25.
82. Ibid., p. 26.
83. Ibid., p. 26.
84. Ibid., pp. 29–31.
85. Ibid., pp. 32–46.
86. Ibid., p. 47.
87. Ibid., pp. 48–91.
88. Ibid., p. 143.
89. Ibid., pp. 143–45.
90. Edgar L. Hewett and Adolph F. Bandelier, *Indians of the Rio Grande Valley,* pp. 234–36.
91. Dozier, op. cit., p. 82.
92. Oakah L. Jones, *Pueblo Warriors,* p. 153.
93. Dozier, op. cit., p. 96.
94. Joe S. Sando, *The Pueblo Indians,* pp. 74–75.
95. Elsie Clews Parsons, *Isleta Paintings,* p. 2.
96. Sando, op. cit., p. 4.
97. Charles H. Lange, *Cochiti, a New Mexico Pueblo, Past and Present,* pp. 40–41.
98. Dozier, op. cit., p. 167.
99. Florence H. Ellis, "Big Kivas, Little Kivas, and Moiety Houses in Historical Reconstruction," pp. 290 ff.
100. Parsons, *Isleta Paintings,* p. 170.
101. Ibid., p. 176.
102. Alfonso Ortiz, *The Tewa World: Space, Time, Being and Becoming in a Pueblo Society,* pp. 112–14.
103. Esther Schiff Goldfrank, "The Social and Ceremonial Organization of Cochiti."
104. Charles H. Lange, *Cochiti, a New Mexico Pueblo, Past and Present,* pp. 125–28.
105. Gertrude Prokosch Kurath with Antonio Garcia, *Music and Dance of the Tewa Pueblos,* p. 284.
106. Parsons, *Isleta Paintings,* p. 262.
107. Ruth Underhill, *Workaday Life of the Pueblos,* pp. 66–68.
108. Lange, op. cit., p. 133.
109. Ibid., pp. 162–63.
110. Underhill, op. cit., p. 128.
111. Dozier, op. cit., pp. 108–9.
112. Parsons, *Isleta Paintings,* p. 186.
113. Ibid., p. 198.
114. Ibid., p. 206.
115. Underhill, op. cit., p. 128.
116. Ibid., p. 128.
117. Ortiz, op. cit., p. 113.
118. Elsie Clews Parsons, "The Social Organization of the Tewa in New Mexico," pp. 82–88.
119. Lange, op. cit., p. 386.
120. Ibid., pp. 374–72.
121. Ibid., p. 385, and Goldfrank, op. cit., p. 10.
122. Dozier, op. cit., p. 167.

123. Ortiz, op. cit., pp. 47–48.
124. S. D. Aberle, "The Pueblo Indians of New Mexico: Their Land, Economy and Civil Organization," p. 46.
125. Goldfrank, op. cit., pp. 25–27, and Father Noel Dumarest, "Notes on Cochiti, New Mexico."
126. Lange, op. cit., pp. 191–99.
127. Leslie A. White, "The Pueblo of San Felipe," pp. 14–19.
128. White, "The Pueblo of Santo Domingo, New Mexico," pp. 35–79.
129. White, "The Pueblo of Santa Ana, New Mexico," pp. 105–9.
130. Aberle, op. cit., p. 49.
131. Kidder, "Pecos, New Mexico: Archaeological Notes," p. 278.
132. Bertha P. Dutton, as quoted by Hewett and Bandelier, *Indians of the Rio Grande Valley*, pp. 101–4.
133. Stanley A. Stubbs, *Bird's-Eye View of the Pueblos*, p. 71.
134. Parsons, *Pueblo Indian Religion*, Vol. 2, Part 1, p. 898.
135. Hewett and Bandelier, op. cit., pp. 110–11.
136. Ibid., p. 111.
137. Stubbs, op. cit., p. 75.
138. Dutton, *Let's Explore Indian Villages Past and Present*, pp. 42–43.
139. Stubbs, op. cit., p. 67.
140. Parsons, *Pueblo Indian Religion*, Vol. 2, Part 1, pp. 891–92.
141. Hewett and Bandelier, op. cit., pp. 109–10.
142. Parsons, *Pueblo Indian Religion*, Vol. 2, Part 1, p. 903.
143. Anna Wilmarth Ickes, *Mesa Land*, p. 197.
144. Ibid., p. 198.
145. Ibid., p. 198.
146. Hewett and Bandelier, op. cit., pp. 111–12.
147. Dutton, op. cit., p. 43.
148. Stubbs, op. cit., p. 63.
149. Parsons, *Pueblo Indian Religion*, Vol. 2, Part 1, p. 901.
150. Hewett and Bandelier, op. cit., p. 109.
151. Charles H. Lange and Carroll L. Riley, eds., *The Southwestern Journals of Adolph F. Bandelier, 1880–1882*, p. 153.
152. John Peabody Harrington, "The Ethnogeography of the Tewa Indians," pp. 418–20.
153. Dutton, *Indians of the American Southwest*, p. 16.
154. Ibid., p. 17.
155. Kidder, op. cit., p. 270.
156. Parsons, *The Pueblo of Isleta*, p. 263.
157. Ibid., p. 208.
158. Ibid., p. 209.
159. Aberle, op. cit., pp. 47 and 50–51.
160. Stubbs, op. cit., fig. 6.
161. Aberle, op. cit., p. 47.
162. Hewett and Bandelier, op. cit., p. 82.
163. Ibid., p. 220.
164. Ibid., pp. 78–82.
165. Kidder, op. cit., pp. 269–70.
166. Hewett and Bandelier, op. cit., p. 78.
167. Stubbs, op. cit., p. 27.
168. Ibid., p. 27.
169. Ibid., p. 27.
170. Aberle, op. cit., p. 47.
171. Florence H. Ellis and J. J. Brody, "Ceramic Stratigraphy and Tribal History at Taos Pueblo," pp. 323–24.
172. Ickes, op. cit., p. 209.
173. Kidder, op. cit., p. 268.
174. Ibid., p. 268.
175. Ibid., p. 269.
176. Aberle, op. cit., p. 47.
177. Parsons, *Pueblo Indian Religion*, Vol. 2, Part 1, p. 933.
178. Hewett and Bandelier, op. cit., pp. 74–75.
179. Parsons, *Pueblo Indian Religion*, Vol. 2, Part 1, p. 932.
180. Stubbs, op. cit., p. 23.
181. Parsons, *Pueblo Indian Religion*, Vol. 2, Part 1, p. 932.
182. Ibid., pp. 932–33.
183. Hewett and Bandelier, op. cit., p. 77.
184. Ibid., p. 78.
185. Stubbs, op. cit., p. 59.
186. Aberle, op. cit., p. 46.
187. Parsons, "A Pueblo Indian Journal, 1920–1921," pp. 56–57.
188. Parsons, *Pueblo Indian Religion*, Vol. 2, Part 1, pp. 905–6.
189. Parsons as quoted by Kidder, "Pecos, New Mexico: Archaeological Notes," pp. 270–71.
190. Miller as quoted by Hewett and Bandelier, *Indians of the Rio Grande Valley*, pp. 96–98.
191. Harper as quoted by Hewett and Bandelier, *Indians of the Rio Grande Valley*, pp. 98–100.
192. Hewett and Bandelier, op. cit., p. 94.
193. Dutton, *Let's Explore Indian Villages Past and Present*, p. 25.
194. Aberle, op. cit., p. 47.
195. Parsons, *Pueblo Indian Religion*, Vol. 1, Part 1, p. 123.
196. Hewett and Bandelier, op. cit., p. 93.
197. Aberle, op. cit., pp. 47 and 49.
198. Hewett and Bandelier, op. cit., p. 94.
199. Aberle, op. cit., p. 46.
200. Parsons, "The Social Organization of the Tewa in New Mexico," p. 107.
201. Ickes, op. cit., p. 208.
202. Hewett and Bandelier, op. cit., p. 208.
203. Stubbs, op. cit., p. 47.
204. Kidder, "Pecos, New Mexico: Archaeological Notes," p. 278.
205. Aberle, op. cit., p. 40.
206. Ibid., p. 49.
207. Parsons, *Pueblo Indian Religion*, Vol. 2, Part 1, p. 911.
208. Ibid., p. 911.
209. Aberle, op. cit., p. 46.
210. Parsons, *Pueblo Indian Religion*, Vol. 2, Part 1, p. 912, and Vol. 1, Part 1, p. 123.

211. Hewett and Bandelier, op. cit., p. 95.
212. Stubbs, op. cit., p. 43.
213. Dutton, op. cit., p. 56.
214. Aberle, op. cit., p. 47.
215. Hewett and Bandelier, op. cit., p. 45.
216. Leslie A. White, "The Pueblo of Santo Domingo, New Mexico," pp. 80–81.
217. Ibid., p. 81.
218. Lange, *Cochiti, a New Mexico Pueblo, Past and Present*, pp. 398–408.
219. Alfonso Ortiz, *The Tewa World: Space, Time, Being and Becoming in a Pueblo Society*, pp. 46–47.
220. Ibid., pp. 46–49.
221. Ibid., p. 50.
222. Lange, *Cochiti, a New Mexico Pueblo, Past and Present*, p. 418.
223. Ortiz, op. cit., pp. 50–56.
224. Ibid., p. 52.
225. Lange, *Cochiti, A New Mexico Pueblo, Past and Present*, p. 419.
226. Ortiz, op. cit., p. 56.
227. Ibid., p. 55.
228. White, "The Pueblo of Santo Domingo, New Mexico," pp. 148–49.
229. Ellis and Hammack, op. cit., p. 30.
230. Harrington, op. cit., p. 41.
231. Ibid., p. 42.
232. Ibid., pp. 42–43.
233. Ibid., p. 43.
234. Ibid., p. 46.
235. Ibid., p. 47.
236. Ibid., pp. 50–51.
237. Ibid., pp. 567–68.
238. Ibid., p. 569.
239. Ibid., pp. 57–58.
240. Ibid., pp. 59–60.
241. Parsons, "The Social Organization of the Tewa in New Mexico," pp. 264 ff.
242. Harrington, op. cit., pp. 61–62.
243. Ibid., p. 194.
244. Ibid., p. 339.
245. Ibid., p. 222.
246. Ibid., p. 249.
247. Ibid., pp. 294–95.
248. Ibid., p. 308.
249. Ibid., p. 376.
250. Ibid., p. 389.
251. Fewkes, "A Few Summer Ceremonials at the Tusayan Pueblos," pp. 33–38.
252. Ibid.
253. Ellis and Hammack, op. cit., p. 34.
254. White, "The Pueblo of Santo Domingo, New Mexico," p. 88.
255. Dozier, op. cit., p. 156.
256. White, "The Pueblo of Santo Domingo, New Mexico," p. 175, and "Zia, the Sun Symbol Pueblo," p. 236.
257. White, "Zia, the Sun Symbol Pueblo," pp. 238–49, and Lange, *Cochiti, a New Mexico Pueblo, Past and Present*, pp. 470–508.
258. Ortiz, op. cit., pp. 86–87.
259. White, "The Pueblo of Santo Domingo, New Mexico," pp. 60–70 and 120–32.
260. Ibid., pp. 120–21.
261. Dozier, op. cit., p. 158.
262. Lange, *Cochiti, a New Mexico Pueblo, Past and Present*, p. 134.
263. Ibid., pp. 134–37.
264. White, "The Pueblo of Santo Domingo, New Mexico," p. 54.
265. Ibid., pp. 53–54.
266. Ibid., p. 54.
267. Ortiz, op. cit., pp. 74–75.
268. Ibid., pp. 161–62.
269. Ibid., p. 156.
270. Gertrude Prokosch Kurath with Antonio Garcia, "Music and Dance of the Tewa Pueblos," p. 266.
271. Dozier, "Rio Grande Ceremonial Patterns," p. 33.
272. Kurath, op. cit., p. 266.
273. Lange, *Cochiti, a New Mexico Pueblo, Past and Present*, p. 355.
274. White, "The Pueblo of Santo Domingo, New Mexico," pp. 149–55.
275. Personal communication.
276. Ortiz, op. cit., p. 117.
277. Ibid., pp. 104 and 116.
278. Frances Densmore, "Music of Santo Domingo Pueblo, New Mexico," p. 34.
279. Ortiz, op. cit., p. 170.
280. Kurath, op. cit., pp. 199–205.
281. Ortiz, op. cit., p. 172.
282. Hewett and Bandelier, op. cit., pp. 53–54.
283. Ibid., p. 127.
284. Ibid., pp. 49–53.
285. Ibid., pp. 56–57.
286. Densmore, op. cit., pp. 125–33.
287. Hewett and Bandelier, op. cit., p. 132.
288. Ibid., p. 57.
289. Densmore, op. cit., p. 45.
290. Lange, *Cochiti, a New Mexico Pueblo, Past and Present*, p. 175.
291. Densmore, op. cit., pp. 34–38.
292. Ibid., p. 49.
293. Kurath, op. cit., pp. 86–113.
294. Tony Issacs, "American Indian Music and Dance," *Focus on Dance*, Vol. 4, p. 13.

CHAPTER V CONCLUSION

1. Charles Avery Amsden, *Prehistoric Southwesterners from Basketmaker to Pueblo*, with introduction by Alfred V. Kidder, p. xiii.
2. Ibid., p. xiv.

A GUIDE TO HOPI PRONUNCIATION

In most cases, Hopi consonants are as in English. A number of consonant sounds must be represented by two or three letters: *p, t, ky, k, kw, q, qw, ', m, n, ngy, ng, ngw, ts, v, r, s, l.* Hopi distinguishes six vowels: *a, e, i, o, ö,* and *u.* The following sounds are a few of those not common to English:

ñ   not as Spanish *ñ.* It is peculiar to Hopi
and is similar to the *ng* in the English word "si*ng*ing,"
with a harder *g* sound.

ä   a very weak *a.*

ö   short *o,* similar to French *eu* in *fleur.*

q   sounds like a soft *k* sounded far back in the throat.

û   short *u,* with a slight expelling of breath.

GLOSSARY OF TERMS

FOR BOOKS I AND II

ANGLO AMERICANS Americans of European extraction.

APOCYNUM A plant related to milkweed.

ATLATL An Aztec word meaning "spear-thrower." Atlatls are short, sometimes weighted, throwing-sticks with a finger-loop handle on one end and on the other a spur, which engages a pit or cup drilled into the basal end of the arrow-like dart shaft. When the dart is thrown, the atlatl remains in the hand.

CACIQUE The supreme village or town priest under the native governmental and ceremonial organization. The Pueblo cacique is considered the primary authority in all matters. A word of Arawakan (Caribbean Indians) origin, the term was applied by Spanish officials to indigenous religious leaders.

CALICHE A crust or succession of crusts of calcium carbonate that forms within or on top of the soil of arid or semi-arid regions.

CELT A prehistoric tool of stone or bronze resembling a chisel or ax.

CHONGO The hairstyle created by forming an elongated, vertical bob of hair on the back of the head. The hair is pulled together, folded, and then wrapped with yarn.

CÍBOLA The early Spanish name for the Zuñi district.

CIST An oval or circular pit, often slab-lined, used primarily for storage. Cists also served a secondary purpose as depositories for the dead.

CLAN Clans are unilineal descent groups traced through the mother's side. They are exogamous units, and among the western Pueblos each clan controls its share of the land, ceremonial associations, and ceremonies.

COMPOUND WALLS Building walls consisting of more than one course placed side by side—a double or triple wall.

CONTIGUOUS WALLS Building walls in which there are no broken joints. All portions run together and overlap.

CORRUGATED POTTERY Pottery with alternate ridges and depressions formed on the exterior surface by a coiling-and-pinching technique.

COURSED MASONRY Masonry constructed of successive rows of stones beginning with an approximately level bed.

CROSS-BEDDED Describes stratified rock that contains irregular laminations oblique to the main beds.

DEFLECTOR An upright stone slab placed on the floor between the fireplace and ventilator shaft in a pithouse or kiva. Its purpose is to deflect the inrushing air away from the fire.

DIFFUSION The spread of elements of culture from one society to another in a chain-reaction form.

ENDOGAMOUS A rule of marriage that requires its members to marry within the group.

EXOGAMOUS A rule of marriage that requires its members to marry outside the group.

EXTENDED CORPSE A burial in which the body was stretched out full length in the grave—as opposed to a flexed burial.

FETISH A relatively small object usually of stone or bone, most often carved but sometimes natural in form, ordinarily resembling a bird or animal, and believed by the Indians to have specific powers to be used for accomplishing prescribed ends. For example, an animal fetish would be used either to help the hunter find that animal or to bring the animal close to the hunter. A ritual fetish placed on an altar would invoke certain needed powers during a ceremony.

FIRE DRILLS A set consisting of a round, pointed drill stick and a hearth stick. The fire maker placed the point of the stick on the hearth and spun the stick between his hands to generate friction. Used hearth sticks are easily recognized by the small cup-shaped depressions formed in them by the spinning drill.

FISCALES Members of the secular council as set up by the Spanish. They now serve as councilors for the governor, although they once functioned as church wardens.

FLESHER A scraper usually made of bone. It was used for cleaning hides, preparing various vegetal materials for food, and for certain other household needs.

FLEXED CORPSE A method of burial used to conserve space. The legs of the corpse were drawn up until the knees almost touched the chin, the feet were also bent, and sometimes the arms were folded as well, so that a fetal position was assumed.

HESHI A semiprecious stone, used by the modern Pueblo Indians for making what they refer to as a heshi necklace. The necklace stones are fashioned like a flat-surfaced button but are smaller, with a single hole drilled in the center for the string to pass through. Ancient Anasazi used heshi stone for various kinds of personal ornamentation.

HISTORIC A term generally applied to the era of recorded history. In the case of the Pueblos, it begins with the coming of the Spanish.

HORNO An oven shaped like the top half of a beehive. It is made of stone and adobe, and has a vent opening at the top and a side doorway through which the items to be baked are passed on a spatulate-formed wooden shovel.

IMPERSONATOR In Anasazi and Pueblo usage one who impersonates a god or spirit power by wearing the mask and costume traditionally associated with the god or spirit.

INCISED In pottery, the term applies to lines grooved into soft clay with a sharp tool.

IN SITU An object still in place in its original site.

JACAL A type of construction in which walls are made of a mat of upright poles lined with branches and reeds, then heavily plastered over with mud or clay.

KATCINA A spirit being and the masked (or rarely unmasked) human who impersonates the spirit in a ceremony. Some Katcinas have always existed, others are deceased humans who return in season to bring blessings needed for human survival. There are also Katcina dolls made for teaching aids for children.

KELEHOYA A novice being initiated into a Hopi society. The word means "little chicken hawk."

KIHUS Rectangular surface ceremonial rooms with some or all of the features common to kivas.

KILLED POTTERY Pottery buried with a deceased owner in which a hole has been punched or drilled in the bottom of the vessel in order to release its soul or spirit, since the vessel is considered a part of the owner.

KISI A small cottonwood shelter used during a dance. In particular, the Hopi use one during the Snake Dance.

KIVA Pueblo ceremonial chamber. As a rule, it is wholly or partly underground, or else designed to give the effect of a subterranean room. It is circular or rectangular. Religious rites are performed here. But it is also used by the men as a "clubroom" and a workroom for their crafts.

KOSHARE/KOSSA Secret societies common to the Rio Grande Keres and Tewa pueblos. The Keresan name is Koshare. The Tewa refer to them as Kossa. Both are associated with weather control, fertility, and the supervision of ceremonies.

KOSHARE The name used at Hano for the ritual clown.

KOYEMSHI The Hopi and Zuñi name for their sacred clowns.

KWERANA/KWIRANA The secret society of the Keres and Tewa pueblos complementary to the Koshares. The Keresan name is Kwerana, the Tewa is Kwirana. They are associated with weather control, fertility, and the supervision of ceremonies.

LAMBDOID FLATTENING Flattening of the back part of the skull. In the case of the Anasazi, this was usually caused by the use of a straight wooden cradleboard.

MACAW A type of parrot with exceptionally long and colorful tail feathers which have always been prized by the Anasazi and Pueblos for use in religious ceremonies.

MANO An oval or oblong handstone used for grinding corn and other foodstuffs on a metate.

MAUL A large stone, sometimes with a hand groove, used for pounding seeds and similar items.

MEALING BIN A rectangular box made of stone or wood that contained stones used in the manner of metates for grinding meal. The ground meal was then stored in jars or pits.

METATE The grinding stone on which the mano is used.

MOIETY A dual division of the village or Pueblo.

OLLA A pottery jar with a flared neck, used for carrying or storing water and other foodstuffs.

PAHO A prayer stick. There are many different kinds and shapes, but they are usually 6 to 12 inches long, made of cottonwood sticks, and decorated with paint, corn husks, and feathers.

PETROGLYPH A rock drawing pecked into the wall surface by using another and harder rock as a pecking tool.

PICTOGRAPH A drawing painted on a rock surface.

PI-GUMME OVEN An earth oven very similar to ones used by the Hopi to bake sweet-corn mush wrapped in corn husks.

PIKI Hopi term for "paper bread." This bread is made from a cornmeal batter, colored gray with wood ashes, dexterously spread very thinly with the hand over a heated slab of stone. After baking it is rolled up like a scroll, and in time becomes so crisp that it crackles like paper.

PILASTER A square masonry column set on top of a kiva bench, upon which the ends of the roof beams are rested.

PITHOUSE A neatly excavated earthen pit ranging from 10 to 20 feet in diameter and 2 to 5 feet deep, over which walls and a roof of beams, poles, brush, and mud were constructed to form a dwelling enclosure.

PLAZA A public square.

POLYCHROME POTTERY Painted pottery with three or more colors.

PROTOKIVA The forerunner of the kiva. It was a subterranean chamber with several features common to later Pueblo ceremonial structures.

RAMADA A canopy-like shelter made of brush, used for outdoor cooking and craftwork of various kinds. Its sides were usually left open to let breezes pass through while it protected the occupants from the hot sunshine.

RHOMBUS A long, thin, sometimes pointed, stick tied near its center on the end of a cord. The stick is swung like a propeller and makes a sound like thunder. As such, the using of one is a prayer for rain.

SHERD (OR SHARD) A fragment of a broken pottery vessel.

SIPAPU A small round hole of shallow depth dug in a pithouse or kiva floor midway between the firepit and the wall. It symbolizes the mythical place of emergence through which the Anasazi ancestors passed in their journey from the Underworld, or place of creation in the inner earth, to the surface of the world. It is also the opening through which the souls of the dead return to the Underworld, and at specified times of the year Katcinas come and return through the sipapu as they bring blessings to the Pueblo people.

SLASH-AND-BURN AGRICULTURE The farming technique whereby fields are cleared, burned, and planted over and over until yield decreases. Then the fields are allowed to lie fallow for several years until they regain fertility.

SLIP A coating of especially fine clay applied to a vessel before firing to give a smooth finish.

SPALL A chip or flake removed from a larger piece of stone. Spalling is the technique of filling in the gaps between large wall stones with the small chips of stone.

TABLITA A headdress consisting of an upright flat board of varying size which is usually carved and painted, and has feathers attached. Some tablitas are complete in themselves, and others are attached to masks.

TALUS A term that usually refers to rocks that separate from the cave roofs and fall to the cave floor to form the slopes in front of cliff dwellings.

TENIENTE Lieutenant governor in the secular council.

TIPONI A fetish made up of an ear of corn, feathers, corn seeds, vegetable seeds, piñon seeds, and a variety of outer strings. Each society has its own.

TUHUPBI Gourd smoothers.

TUMPLINE A narrow woven carrying strap passed over the forehead while carrying a burden on the back.

TUSAYAN The early Spanish name for the area occupied by the Hopi.

TWILLING A system of weaving in which the woof thread is carried over one and under two or more warp threads in such a way that it produces diagonal lines or ribs on the surface of the fabric or basket.

TWINING A system of weaving in which splints or threads are intertwined and wrapped around a foundation of radiating rods or threads.

UNILINEAL The reckoning of kinship relations through a single line of descent, either the mother's or the father's side.

VIGAS Ceiling beams which project beyond the exterior wall of a building for a distance of several feet.

WHIP The ailment for which a secret society holds the ''whip'' or power to cure by using its specific ritual in connection with the patient.

WUYE The clan ancestors. The nonhuman partner related to each clan. It consists of an animal, plant, or a natural or supernatural phenomenon. This gives the clan its name, its whip, and its protection in return for certain related services.

BIBLIOGRAPHY

FOR BOOKS I AND II

Aberle, S. D.
  1948   The Pueblo Indians of New Mexico: Their Land, Economy and Civil Organization. *American Anthropologist*, Vol. 50, No. 4, Pt. 2, Oct.
Adair, John
  1944   *The Navajo and Pueblo Silversmiths.* University of Oklahoma Press, Norman.
Alexander, Hartley Burr
  1953   *The World's Rim.* University of Nebraska Press, Lincoln.
Alexander, Hubert G.
         The Excavation of Jemez Cave. *El Palacio*, Vol. 38, Nos. 18–19–20.
Ambler, J. Richard
  1977   *The Anasazi.* Museum of Northern Arizona, Flagstaff.
Amsden, Charles Avery
  1949   *Prehistoric Southwesterners from Basketmaker to Pueblo.* Southwest Museum, Los Angeles.
Anderson, Douglas and Barbara
  1976   *Chaco Canyon.* Popular Series No. 17. Southwest Parks and Monuments Association, Globe, Ariz.
Anderson, Keith M.
  1969   Tsegi Phase Technology. Doctoral dissertation, University of Washington, Seattle. University Microfilms, Ann Arbor.
Anton, Ferdinand
  1968   *Pre-Columbian Art: And, Later Indian Tribal Arts,* by Frederick J. Dockstader. Harry N. Abrams, New York.
Arizona Highways
  1951   Vol. 27, No. 5.
  1953   Vol. 29, No. 7.
  1972   Vol. 48, No. 1.
  1973   Vol. 49, No. 6.
  1974   Vol. 50, No. 2.
  1975   Vol. 51, No. 7.
  1978   Vol. 54, No. 3.
Atkinson, Mary Jourdan
  1963   *Indians of the Southwest.* 4th ed. Naylor Company, San Antonio.
Austin, Mary
  1924   The Days of Our Ancients. *Survey Magazine*, pp. 33–38. Oct. 1.
Bahnimptewa, Cliff
  1971   *Dancing Kachinas.* Heard Museum, Phoenix.
Baldwin, Gordon C.
  1938   Excavations at Kinishba Pueblo, Arizona. *American Antiquity*, Vol. 4, pp. 11–21.
  1939   Material Culture of Kinishba. *American Antiquity*, Vol. 4, pp. 314–27.
Bandelier, Adolph F. A.
  1910   *Documentary History of the Rio Grande Pueblos of New Mexico.* Papers of the School of American Archaeology No. 13. Santa Fe.
  1966   *The Southwestern Journals of Adolph F. Bandelier, 1880–1882.* Charles H. Lange and Carroll L. Riley, eds. University of New Mexico Press, Albuquerque.
Baxter, Sylvester
  1882   The Father of the Pueblos. *Harper's New Monthly Magazine*, Vol. 65, pp. 72–91.
Beck, Peggy V., and Walters, A. L.
  1977   *The Sacred Ways of Knowledge, Sources of Life.* Navajo Community College, Tsaile, Ariz. Navajo Nation.
Beck, Warren A., and Haase, Ynez D.
  1969   *Historical Atlas of New Mexico.* University of Oklahoma Press, Norman.
Bedinger, Margery
  1973   *Indian Silver.* University of New Mexico Press, Albuquerque.
Billingsley, M. W.
  1971   *Behind the Scenes in Hopi Land.* Privately printed.
Bohrer, Vorsila L.
  1968   Paleoecology of an Archaeological Site Near Snowflake, Arizona. Unpublished Ph.D. dissertation, Department of Botany, University of Arizona, Tucson.

Bourke, John G.
  1884   *The Snake-Dance of the Moquis of Arizona.* Charles Scribner's Sons, New York.
Branson, Oscar T.
  1976   *Fetishes and Carvings of the Southwest.* Treasure Chest Publications, Santa Fe.
Brew, John O.
          The First Two Seasons at Awatovi. *American Antiquity,* Vol. 3, pp. 122–37.
Bunting, Bainbridge
  1976   *Early Architecture in New Mexico.* University of New Mexico Press, Albuquerque.
Bunting, Bainbridge; Booth, Jean Lee; and Sims, William R., Jr.
  1964   *Taos Adobes.* Publication No. 2, Fort Burgwin Research Center. Museum of New Mexico Press,
          Santa Fe.
Bunzel, Ruth L.
  1929   *The Pueblo Potter.* Columbia University Contributions to Anthropology, Vol. 8. Columbia Uni-
          versity Press, New York.
  1932a   Introduction to Zuñi Ceremonialism. Smithsonian Institution, Bureau of American Ethnology,
          47th Annual Report, pp. 467–544. Washington, D.C.
  1932b   Zuñi Katcinas. Smithsonian Institution, Bureau of American Ethnology, 47th Annual Report,
          1929–1930, pp. 837–1086. Washington, D.C.
Burroughs, Carroll A.
  1959   Searching for Cliff Dweller's Secrets. *National Geographic Magazine,* Vol. 116, No. 5.
Bushnell, G. H. S.
  1968   *The First Americans.* McGraw-Hill Book Company, New York.
Buttree, Julia M.
  1930   *The Rhythm of the Redman.* Ronald Press Company, New York.
Capps, Walter Holden (editor)
  1976   *Seeing with a Native Eye.* Harper & Row, New York.
Clemmer, Richard O.
  1978   *Continuities of Hopi Culture Change.* Acoma Books, Ramona, Calif.
Coe, Michael D.
  1962   *Mexico.* Frederick A. Praeger, New York.
Coe, William R.
  1975   Resurrecting the Grandeur of Tikal. *National Geographic Magazine,* Vol. 148, No. 6, p. 792–98.
Collier, John
  1949   *On the Gleaming Way.* Sage Books, Denver.
Colton, Harold S.
  1939   *Prehistoric Culture Units and Their Relationships in Northern Arizona.* Museum of Northern Ari-
          zona, Bulletin 17. Flagstaff.
  1959   *Hopi Kachina Dolls.* University of New Mexico Press, Albuquerque.
  1960   *Black Sand.* University of New Mexico Press, Albuquerque.
Cosgrove, Cornelius Burton
  1947   *Caves of the Upper Gila and Hueco Areas in New Mexico and Texas.* Papers of the Peabody Museum
          of American Archeology and Ethnology, Vol. 24, No. 2. Harvard University, Cambridge, Mass.
Crane, Leo
  1925   *Indians of the Enchanted Desert.* Little, Brown & Company, Boston.
Curtis, Natalie (editor)
  1907   *The Indians' Book.* Harper and Brothers Publishers, New York.
Cushing, Frank Hamilton
  1882   My Adventures in Zuñi. *Century Magazine,* Vol. 25, No. 19, pp. 191–207; Vol. 25, No. 47, pp.
          500–11; Vol. 26, No. 4, pp. 28–47.
  1883   Zuñi Fetishes. Smithsonian Institution, Bureau of American Ethnology, 2nd Annual Report,
          1880–1881. Washington, D.C.
  1974   *Zuñi Breadstuff.* Indian Notes and Monographs Vol. 8. Reprint edition, Museum of the Ameri-
          can Indian, Heye Foundation, New York. (Originally published 1920.)
Davies, Nigel
  1979   *Voyagers to the New World.* William Morrow & Co., New York.
DeHarport, David L.
  1959   An Archaeological Survey of Canyon de Chelly, Northeastern Arizona: A Puebloan Community
          Through Time. Unpublished Ph.D. Dissertation in Anthropology, Harvard University, Cam-
          bridge, Mass.
Dennis, Wayne
  1965   *The Hopi Child.* University of Virginia Institute for Research in the Social Sciences, Monograph
          26, 1940. Science Editions. John Wiley & Sons, New York.

Densmore, Frances
1938   *Music of Santo Domingo Pueblo, New Mexico.* Southwest Museum Papers No. 12. Southwest Museum, Los Angeles.
Dickson, D. Bruce
1975   Settlement Pattern Stability and Change in the Middle Northern Rio Grande Region, New Mexico: A Test of Some Hypotheses. *American Antiquity,* Vol. 40, No. 2, pp. 159–71.
Di Peso, Charles C.
1979   Prehistory: O'otam. Smithsonian Institution, Handbook of North American Indians, Vol. 9, Southwest, pp. 91–99. Washington, D.C.
Ditzler, Robert E.
1967   *The Indian People of Arizona.* Vantage Press, New York.
Dockstader, Frederick J.
1954   *The Kachina and the White Man.* Bulletin 35, Cranbrook Institute of Science. Bloomfield Hills, Mich.
Dorsey, George A.
1899   The Hopi Indians of Arizona. *Popular Science Monthly,* Vol. 55, pp. 732–50.
1903   *Indians of the Southwest.* Passenger Dept., Atchison, Topeka & Santa Fe Railway System.
Dorsey, George A., and Voth, Henry R.
1901   *The Oraibi Soyal Ceremony.* Publications of the Field Columbian Museum Anthropological Series, Vol. 3, No. 1, pp. 1–59. Chicago.
1902   *The Mishongnove Ceremonies of the Snake and Antelope Fraternities.* Publications of the Field Columbian Museum Anthropological Series, Vol. 3, No. 3, pp. 159–261. Chicago.
Douglas, Frederic H.
1953   Material Culture Notes for the Denver Art Museum. No. 22. Denver Art Museum, Denver.
Dozier, Edward P.
1957   Rio Grande Ceremonial Patterns. *New Mexico Quarterly,* Vol. 27, pp. 27–34.
1966   *Hano, a Tewa Indian Community in Arizona.* Holt, Rinehart and Winston, New York.
1970   *The Pueblo Indians of North America.* Holt, Rinehart and Winston, New York.
Dumarest, Father Noel
1919   *Notes on Cochiti, New Mexico.* Memoirs of the American Anthropological Association, Vol. 6, No. 3. Lancaster, Pa.
Dutton, Bertha P.
1963a   *Friendly People: The Zuñi Indians.* Museum of New Mexico Press, Santa Fe.
1963b   *Sun Father's Way: The Kiva Murals of Kuaua, a Pueblo Ruin, Coronado State Monument, New Mexico.* University of New Mexico Press, Albuquerque.
1970   *Let's Explore Indian Villages Past and Present.* Museum of New Mexico Press, Santa Fe.
1970   *Navaho Weaving Today.* Museum of New Mexico Press, Santa Fe.
1975   *Indians of the American Southwest.* Prentice-Hall, Englewood Cliffs, N.J.
Earle, Edwin, and Kennard, Edward A.
1971   *Hopi Kachinas.* Museum of the American Indian, Heye Foundation, New York.
Eddy, Frank W.
1961   *Excavations at Los Pinos Phase Sites in the Navajo Reservoir District.* Museum of New Mexico Papers No. 4. Museum of New Mexico Press, Santa Fe.
1964   *Metates & Manos.* Popular Series Pamphlet No. 1. Museum of New Mexico Press, Santa Fe.
Eggan, Fred R.
1950   *Social Organization of the Western Pueblos.* Chicago University Publications in Anthropology, Social Anthropology Series. University of Chicago Press, Chicago. Reprinted 1970.
Ekstrom, M. A. and J. O.
1973   *How to Read and Write Hopi.* Hopi Action Program, Oraibi, Ariz.
Ellis, Florence H.
1950   Big Kivas, Little Kivas, and Moiety Houses in Historical Reconstruction. *Southwest Journal of Anthropology,* Vol. 6, pp. 286–301.
Ellis, Florence H., and Brody, J. J.
1964   Ceramic Stratigraphy and Tribal History at Taos Pueblo. *American Antiquity,* Vol. 29, pp. 316–27.
Ellis, Florence H., and Hammack, Laurens
1968   The Inner Sanctum of Feather Cave, a Mogollon Sun and Earth Shrine Linking Mexico and the Southwest. *American Antiquity,* Vol. 33, No. 1, pp. 25–44.
Erdoes, Richard
1976   *The Rain Dance People.* Alfred A. Knopf, New York.
Euler, Robert C., and Dobyns, Henry F.
1971   *The Hopi People.* Indian Tribal Series, Phoenix.

Farb, Peter
    1968   *Man's Rise to Civilization.* E. P. Dutton & Co., New York.
Fell, Barry
    1976   *America B.C.* Pocket Books, New York.
Fergusson, Erna
    1971   *New Mexico: A Pageant of Three Peoples.* Alfred A. Knopf, New York.
Fewkes, Jesse Walter
    1891a   A Few Summer Ceremonials at Zuni Pueblo. *A Journal of American Ethnology and Archaeology,*
            Vol. 1, pp. 1–62. Houghton, Mifflin Company, Riverside Press, Cambridge, Mass.
    1891b   Reconnoissance of Ruins in or near the Zuni Reservation. *A Journal of American Ethnology and
            Archaeology,* Vol. 1, pp. 93–133. Houghton, Mifflin Company, Riverside Press, Cambridge,
            Mass.
    1892a   A Few Summer Ceremonials at the Tusayan Pueblos. *A Journal of American Ethnology and Ar-
            chaeology,* Vol. 2, pp. 1–160. Houghton, Mifflin Company, Riverside Press, Cambridge, Mass.
    1892b   The Mam-zrau-ti: A Tusayan Ceremony. *The American Anthropologist,* Vol. 5, pp. 217–46.
    1892c   A Few Tusayan Pictographs. *The American Anthropologist,* Vol. 5, pp. 9–26.
    1892d   A Report on the Present Condition of a Ruin in Arizona Called Casa Grande. *A Journal of
            American Ethnology and Archaeology,* Vol. 2, pp. 179–93. Houghton, Mifflin Company, Riverside
            Press, Cambridge, Mass.
    1893a   A-WA-TO-BI: An Archaeological Verification of a Tusayan Legend. *The American Anthropologist,*
            Vol. 6, pp. 363–75.
    1893b   Central American Ceremony Which Suggests the Snake Dance of the Tusayan Villagers. *The
            American Anthropologist,* Vol. 6, pp. 285–306.
    1894   The Walpi Flute Observance: A Study of Primitive Dramatization. *The Journal of American Folk-
            Lore,* Vol. 7, No. 27, pp. 265–88.
    1895   The Oraibi Flute Altar. *The Journal of American Folk-Lore.* Vol. 7, No. 31, pp. 265–84.
    1896a   Preliminary Account of an Expedition to the Cliff Villages of the Red Rock Country, and the
            Tusayan Ruins of Sikyatki and Awatobi, Arizona, in 1895. Smithsonian Institution, Bureau of
            American Ethnology Report, 1895, pp. 557–88. Washington, D.C.
    1896b   The Tusayan Ritual: A Study of the Influence of Environment on Aboriginal Cults. Smithsonian
            Institution, Bureau of American Ethnology Report, 1895, pp. 683–700. Washington, D.C.
    1896c   The Miconinovi Flute Altars. *The Journal of American Folk-Lore,* Vol. 9, No. 35, pp. 241–56.
    1896d   *The Prehistoric Culture of Tusayan. The American Anthropologist,* o.s., Vol. 9, No. 5. Washington,
            D.C.
    1897a   The Sacrificial Element in Hopi Worship. *The Journal of American Folk-Lore,* Vol. 10, No. 36, pp.
            187–201.
    1897b   Tusayan Snake Ceremonies. Smithsonian Institution, Bureau of American Ethnology, 16th An-
            nual Report, 1894–1895, pp. 267–311. Washington, D.C.
    1898a   The Growth of the Hopi Ritual. *The Journal of American Folk-Lore,* Vol. 11, No. 42, pp. 174–94.
    1898b   Preliminary Account of an Expedition to the Pueblo Ruins Near Winslow, Arizona in 1896.
            Smithsonian Institution, Bureau of American Ethnology Report, 1896, pp. 517–41. Washington,
            D.C.
    1898c   Archeological Expedition to Arizona in 1895. Smithsonian Institution, Bureau of American Eth-
            nology, 17th Annual Report, 1895–1896, pp. 519–744. Washington, D.C.
    1899   Hopi Basket Dances. *The Journal of American Folk-Lore,* Vol. 12, No. 45, pp. 81–96.
    1900a   The Lesser New-Fire Ceremony at Walpi. *The American Anthropologist,* Vol. 2, No. 1.
    1900b   A Theatrical Performance at Walpi. Washington Academy of Sciences, Proceedings, Vol. 2, No.
            33. Washington, D.C.
    1901   The Owakulti Altar at Sichomovi Pueblo. *The American Anthropologist,* Vol. 3, No. 2.
    1902   Sky-God Personations in Hopi Worship. *The Journal of American Folk-Lore,* Vol. 15, No. 56, pp.
            14–32.
    1903   Hopi Katcinas Drawn by Native Artists. Smithsonian Institution, Bureau of American Ethnol-
            ogy, 21st Annual Report, 1899–1900. Washington, D.C.
    1904   Two Summers' Work in Pueblo Ruins. Smithsonian Institution, Bureau of American Ethnology,
            22nd Annual Report, 1900–1901, Part 1, pp. 3–195. Washington, D.C.
    1911a   *Preliminary Report on a Visit to the Navaho National Monument: Arizona.* Smithsonian Institution,
            Bureau of American Ethnology Bulletin No. 50. Washington, D.C.
    1911b   *Antiquities of the Mesa Verde National Park: Cliff Palace.* Smithsonian Institution, Bureau of Amer-
            ican Ethnology Bulletin No. 51. Washington, D.C.
    1915   Prehistoric Remains in Arizona, New Mexico, and Colorado. Smithsonian Miscellaneous Col-
            lections, Vol. 66, No. 3, pp. 82–98. Washington, D.C.
    1916   Prehistoric Remains in New Mexico, Colorado, and Utah. Smithsonian Miscellaneous Collec-
            tions, Vol. 66, No. 17, pp. 76–92. Washington, D.C.

1917a *Archeological Investigations in New Mexico, Colorado, and Utah.* Smithsonian Miscellaneous Collections, Vol. 68, No. 1. Washington, D.C.

1917b A Prehistoric Mesa Verde Pueblo and Its People. Smithsonian Institution, Bureau of American Ethnology, Annual Report, 1916, pp. 461–88. Washington, D.C.

1919a *Prehistoric Villages, Castles and Towers of Southwestern Colorado.* Smithsonian Institution, Bureau of American Ethnology Bulletin No. 70. Washington, D.C.

1919b Designs on Prehistoric Hopi Pottery. Smithsonian Institution, Bureau of American Ethnology, 33rd Annual Report, 1911–1912, pp. 207–84. Washington, D.C.

1919c Archeological Field-Work in Southwestern Colorado and Utah. Smithsonian Explorations, 1918, Smithsonian Miscellaneous Collections, Vol. 70, No. 2, pp. 68–80. Washington, D.C.

1920a Sun Worship of the Hopi Indians. Smithsonian Institution, Bureau of American Ethnology Report, 1918, pp. 493–526. Washington, D.C.

1920b *Field-Work on the Mesa Verde National Park.* Smithsonian Miscellaneous Collections, Vol. 72, No. 1. Washington, D.C.

1921a Excavating Cliff Dwellings in Mesa Verde. *Scientific American Monthly,* Jan. 1921, pp. 9–13.

1921b Field-Work on Mesa Verde National Park. *Smithsonian Explorations, 1920,* Smithsonian Miscellaneous Collections, Vol. 72, No. 6, pp. 75–102. Washington, D.C.

1922a Fire Worship of the Hopi Indians. Smithsonian Institution, Bureau of American Ethnology, Annual Report, 1920, pp. 589–610. Washington, D.C.

1922b Ancestor Worship of the Hopi Indians. Smithsonian Institution, Bureau of American Ethnology, Annual Report, 1921, pp. 485–506. Washington, D.C.

1922c Archeological Field-Work on the Mesa Verde National Park. *Smithsonian Explorations,* Smithsonian Miscellaneous Collections, Vol. 72, No. 15, pp. 64–83. Washington, D.C.

1923 Archeological Field-Work on the Mesa Verde National Park, Colorado. *Smithsonian Explorations, 1922,* Smithsonian Miscellaneous Collections, Vol. 74, No. 5, pp. 90–115. Washington, D.C.

1924 The Use of Idols in Hopi Worship. Smithsonian Institution, Bureau of American Ethnology, Annual Report, 1922, pp. 377–97. Washington, D.C.

1925 The Hovenweep National Monument. Smithsonian Institution, Bureau of American Ethnology, Annual Report, 1923, pp. 456–80. Washington, D.C.

1926 *An Archeological Collection from Young's Canyon, Near Flagstaff, Arizona.* Smithsonian Miscellaneous Collections, Vol. 77, No. 10. Washington, D.C.

1927a The Kacina Altars in Hopi Worship. Smithsonian Institution, Bureau of American Ethnology, Annual Report, 1926, pp. 469–87. Washington, D.C.

1927b Archeological Field-Work in Arizona. *Smithsonian Explorations, 1926,* Smithsonian Miscellaneous Collections, Vol. 78, No. 7, pp. 207–32. Washington, D.C.

Fewkes, Jesse Walter, and Owens, J. G.
1892 The Lā-lā-kōn-ta: A Tusayan Dance. *The American Anthropologist,* Vol. 5, No. 2, pp. 105–30.

Fewkes, Jesse Walter, and Stephen, Alexander M.
1892 The Nā-ác-nai-ya: A Tusayan Initiation Ceremony. *The Journal of American Folk-Lore,* Vol. 5, No. 18, pp. 189–221.

1893 The Pá-lü-lü-koñ-ti: A Tusayan Ceremony. *The Journal of American Folk-Lore,* Vol. 6, No. 23, pp. 169–84.

Fleming, Henry Craig, M.D.
1924 *Medical Observations on the Zuñi Indians.* Contributions from the Museum of the American Indian, Heye Foundation, Vol. 7, No. 2. Museum of the American Indian, New York.

Folsom, Franklin
1973 *Red Power on the Rio Grande.* Follett Publishing Company, Chicago.

Forrest, Earle R.
1961 *The Snake Dance of the Hopi Indians.* Westernlore Press, Los Angeles.

1921 The Mesa Dwellers of the Painted Desert. *Travel Magazine,* Vol. 37, Aug., pp. 3–8.

1923 The Snake Dance in the Painted Desert. *Travel Magazine,* Vol. 40, Jan., pp. 16–20.

Fox, Nancy
1978 *Pueblo Weaving and Textile Arts.* A Museum of New Mexico Press Guidebook, No. 3. Museum of New Mexico Press, Santa Fe.

Frazier, Kendrick
1980 The Anasazi Sun Dagger. *Science 80,* Vol. 1, No. 1, pp. 56–67.

Fundaburk, Emma Lila, and Foreman, Mary Douglass
1957 *Sun Circles and Human Hands.* Emma Lila Fundaburk, Luverne, Ala.

Gilman, Benjamin Ives
1891 Zuni Melodies. *A Journal of American Ethnology and Archaeology,* Vol. 1, pp. 63–91. Houghton, Mifflin Company, Riverside Press, Cambridge, Mass.

Gladwin, Harold S.
1945 *The Chaco Branch Excavations at White Mound and in the Red Mesa Valley.* Medallion Papers No. 33. Gila Pueblo, Globe, Ariz.

1957   *A History of the Ancient Southwest.* Bond Wheelwright Company, Portland, Maine.
Goddard, Pliny Earle
    1928   *Pottery of the Southwestern Indians.* American Museum of Natural History, New York.
    1931   *Indians of the Southwest.* Handbook Series No. 2. American Museum of Natural History, New York.
Goldfrank, Esther Schiff
    1927   *The Social and Ceremonial Organization of Cochiti.* Memoirs of the American Anthropological Association, No. 33.
    1967   *The Artist of "Isleta Paintings" in Pueblo Society.* Smithsonian Press, Washington, D.C.
Gonzales, Clara
    1966   *The Shalakos Are Coming.* Reprint from *El Palacio.* Museum of New Mexico, Santa Fe.
Gordon, Dudley
    1972   An Early Fiesta at Laguna. *The Masterkey,* Vol. 46, No. 1. Southwest Museum, Los Angeles.
Grant, Blanche C.
    1925   *Taos Indians.* Privately printed, Taos, N. Mex.
Grant, Campbell
    1978   *Canyon de Chelly: Its People and Rock Art.* University of Arizona Press, Tucson.
Graybill, Florence Curtis, and Boesen, Victor
    1976   *Edward Sheriff Curtis: Visions of a Vanishing Race.* Thomas Y. Crowell, New York.
Gumerman, George J.
    1970   *Black Mesa: Survey and Excavation in Northeastern Arizona.* Prescott College Press, Prescott, Ariz.
Gumerman, George J., and Skinner, S. Alan
    1960   Synthesis of the Prehistory of the Central Little Colorado Valley. *American Antiquity,* Vol. 33, No. 2, pp. 185–99.
Gumerman, George J.; Westfall, Deborah; and Weed, Carol S.
    1972   *Black Mesa: Archaeological Investigations on Black Mesa: The 1969–1970 Seasons.* Prescott College Press, Prescott, Ariz.
Hack, John T.
    1942   *The Changing Physical Environment of the Hopi Indians of Arizona.* Papers of the Peabody Museum of American Archeology and Ethnology, Vol. 35, No. 1, Reports of the Awatovi Expedition, No. 1. Harvard University, Cambridge, Mass.
Haeberlin, H. K.
    1916   *The Idea of Fertilization in the Culture of the Pueblo Indians.* Memoirs of the American Anthropological Association, Vol. 3, No. 1.
Hall, Alice J., and Spier, Peter
    1975   A Traveler's Tale of Ancient Tikal. *National Geographic Magazine,* Vol. 148, No. 6, pp. 799–811.
Hall, Edward Twitchell, Jr.
    1944   *Early Stockaded Settlements in the Governador, New Mexico: A marginal Anasazi Development from Basket Maker III to Pueblo I Times.* Columbia University Press, New York.
Hargrave, Lyndon L.
    1931   Excavations at Kin Tiel and Kokopnyama. Smithsonian Miscellaneous Collections, Vol. 82, No. 11, pp. 80–120. Washington, D.C.
Harlow, Francis H.
    1970   *Historic Pueblo Indian Pottery.* Museum of New Mexico Press, Santa Fe.
Harlow, Francis H., and Young, John V.
    1965   *Contemporary Pueblo Indian Pottery.* Museum of New Mexico Press, Santa Fe.
Harrington, John Peabody
    1916   The Ethnogeography of the Tewa Indians. Smithsonian Institution, Bureau of American Ethnology, 29th Annual Report, 1907–1908, pp. 29–636. Washington, D.C.
Hart, E. Richard
    1973   *The Zuñis: Experiences and Descriptions.* Pueblo of Zuñi.
Harvey, Byron, III
    1970   *Ritual in Pueblo Art.* Museum of the American Indian, Heye Foundation, New York.
Harvey, Byron, III (editor)
    1967   *The Henry R. Voth Collection at Grand Canyon, Arizona.* From a catalogue prepared for the Fred Harvey Company in 1912. Arequipa Press, Phoenix.
Hassrick, Royal B.
    1960   *Indian Art of the Americas.* Denver Art Museum, Denver.
Haury, Emil W.
    1945   *The Excavation of Los Muertos and Neighboring Ruins in the Salt River Valley, Southern Arizona.* Papers of the Peabody Museum of American Archeology and Ethnology, Vol. 24, No. 1. Harvard University, Cambridge, Mass.

1962   The Greater American Southwest. In Robert J. Braidwood and Gordon R. Willey, eds., *Courses Toward Urban Life,* pp. 106–31. Viking Fund Publications in Anthropology, No. 32. Wenner-Gren Foundation for Anthropological Research Inc., New York.

1976   *The Hohokam.* University of Arizona Press, Tucson.

Haury, Emil W., and Hargrave, Lyndon L.

1931   *Recently Dated Pueblo Ruins in Arizona.* Smithsonian Miscellaneous Collections, Vol. 82, No. 11. Washington, D.C.

Hawkes, Jacquetta

1976   *The Atlas of Early Man.* St. Martins Press, New York.

Hayes, Alden C., and Lancaster, James A.

1975   *Badger House Community.* U.S. Department of the Interior, National Park Service, Washington, D.C.

Hegemann, Elizabeth Compton

1963   *Navaho Trading Days.* University of New Mexico Press, Albuquerque.

Helfritz, Hans

1970   *Mexican Cities of the Gods.* Praeger Publishers, New York.

Henderson, Palmer

1893   The Cliff Dwellers. *The Literary Northwest,* Vol. 3, May, pp. 79–86.

Herold, Laurance C., and Luebben, Ralph A.

1968   *Taos Archaeology.* Fort Burgwin Research Center, Publication 7. Taos, N. Mex.

Hewett, Edgar Lee

1936   *Chaco Canyon and Its Monuments.* Handbooks of Archaeological History, No. 2. University of New Mexico Press, Albuquerque.

Hewett, Edgar L., and Bandelier, Adolph F. A.

1937   *Indians of the Rio Grande Valley.* University of New Mexico and School of American Research. University of New Mexico Press, Albuquerque.

Highwater, Jamake

1976   *Song from the Earth.* New York Graphic Society, Boston.

1977   *Ritual of the Wind.* Viking Press, New York.

Hill, James N., and Hevly, Richard H.

1968   Pollen at Broken K Pueblo: Some New Interpretations. *American Antiquity,* Vol. 33, No. 2, pp. 200–10.

Hodge, Frederick W.

1898   Ascent of the Enchanted Mesa. *The Century Magazine,* Vol. 56, May, pp. 15–25.

1918   Excavations at Hawikuh, New Mexico. Smithsonian Explorations, 1917, Smithsonian Miscellaneous Collections, Vol. 68, pp. 61–72. Washington, D.C.

Hofmann, Charles

1967   *American Indians Sing.* John Day Company, New York.

Hofmann, Charles (editor)

1968   *Frances Densmore and American Indian Music.* Contributions from the Museum of the American Indian, Heye Foundation, Vol. 23. Heye Foundation, New York.

Holien, Elaine Baran

      Kachinas. *El Palacio,* No. 76, No. 4. Museum of New Mexico, Santa Fe.

Holmes, William Henry

1899   *Ancient Ruins of Southwestern Colorado.* 10th Annual Report, U.S. Geological and Geographic Survey of the Territories (Hayden Survey) for 1876. Washington, D.C.

Hough, Walter

1903   Archaeological Field Work in Northeastern Arizona, Expedition of 1901, Museum-Gates Expedition. Report of the U.S. National Museum of 1901, pp. 279–358. Washington, D.C.

1915   *The Hopi Indians.* Torch Press, Cedar Rapids, Iowa.

1917   Archeological Investigations in New Mexico. Smithsonian Explorations, 1916, Smithsonian Miscellaneous Collections, Vol. 66, No. 17, pp. 99–111. Washington, D.C.

1920   Explorations of a Pit House Village at Luna, New Mexico. Proceedings of the U.S. National Museum, Vol. 55, pp. 409–31. Washington, D.C.

1929   Explorations in a Great Secret Cave in Eastern Arizona. *Art and Archeology,* Vol. 28, Oct., pp. 117–25.

Hunter, C. Bruce

1974   *A Guide to Ancient Maya Ruins.* University of Oklahoma Press, Norman.

Ickes, Anna Wilmarth

1933   *Mesa Land.* Houghton Mifflin Company, Riverside Press, Cambridge, Mass.

Irwin-Williams, Cynthia

1973   *The Oshara Tradition: Origins of Anasazi Culture.* Eastern New Mexico University, Contributions in Anthropology, Vol. 5, No. 1. Portales.

Ivers, Louise Harris
    1977   Early Photographs of Indian Pueblos in New Mexico. *The Masterkey*, Vol. 51, No. 3. Southwest
             Museum, Los Angeles.
Jackson, William H.
    1876   *Ancient Ruins of Southwestern Colorado.* Report of U.S. Geological and Geographic Survey of the
             Territories (Hayden Survey) for 1874. Washington, D.C.
James, George Wharton
    1919   *The Indians of the Painted Desert Region.* Little, Brown & Company, Boston.
    1974   *Indian Blankets & Their Makers.* Dover Publications, Inc. (Originally published 1914, by A. C.
             McClurg & Company, Chicago.)
James, H. L.
    1970   *Acoma, the People of the White Rock.* Rio Grande Press, Glorieta, N. Mex.
James, Harry C.
    1974   *Pages from Hopi History.* University of Arizona Press, Tucson.
Jarrett, Walter
    1978   Acoma, New Mexico Sky City. *Mankind Magazine*, Vol. 3, No. 6.
Jeancon, J. A.
    1923   *Excavations in the Chama Valley, New Mexico.* Smithsonian Institution, Bureau of American Eth-
             nology Bulletin No. 81. Washington, D.C.
Jennings, Jesse D.
    1956   The American Southwest: A Problem in Cultural Isolations. In Robert Wauchope, ed., *Seminars
             in Cultural Isolation*, pp. 59–127. Memoirs of the Society of American Archaeology, No. 11. Salt
             Lake City.
    1966   *Glen Canyon: A Summary.* University of Utah Anthropology Papers, No. 81 (Glen Canyon Series
             No. 31). Salt Lake City.
    1968   *Prehistory of North America.* McGraw-Hill Book Co., New York.
Jernigan, E. Wesley
    1978   *Jewelry of the Prehistoric Southwest.* School of American Research, Santa Fe. University of New
             Mexico Press, Albuquerque.
Jett, Stephen C., and Bohn, Dave
    1977   *House of Three Turkeys: Anasazi Redoubt.* Capra Press, Santa Barbara.
Jones, Louis Thomas
    1967   *Indian Cultures of the Southwest.* Naylor Company, San Antonio.
Jones, Oakah L., Jr.
    1966   *Pueblo Warriors and Spanish Conquest.* University of Oklahoma Press, Norman.
Judd, Neil M.
    1916   Archeological Reconnoissance in Western Utah. Smithsonian Miscellaneous Collections, Vol.
             66, No. 3., pp. 64–71. Washington, D.C.
    1917   Archeological Reconnoissance in Western Utah. Smithsonian Miscellaneous Collections, Vol.
             66, No. 17, pp. 103–8. Washington, D.C.
    1919   Archeological Investigations at Paragonah, Utah. Smithsonian Miscellaneous Collections, Vol.
             70, No. 3, pp. 1–37. Washington, D.C.
    1922   Archeological Investigations at Pueblo Bonito, New Mexico. Smithsonian Miscellaneous Collec-
             tions, Vol. 72, No. 15, pp. 106–17. Washington, D.C.
    1923   Pueblo Bonito, the Ancient. *National Geographic Magazine*, Vol. 44, pp. 99–108.
    1924   Two Chaco Canyon Pit Houses. Smithsonian Institution, Bureau of American Ethnology, An-
             nual Report, 1922, pp. 399–413. Washington, D.C.
    1925a   Everyday Life in Pueblo Bonito. *National Geographic Magazine*, Vol. 48, pp. 227–62.
    1925b   Archeological Investigations at Pueblo Bonito, New Mexico. Smithsonian Miscellaneous Collec-
             tions, Vol. 77, No. 2, pp. 83–91. Washington, D.C.
    1926   Archeological Observations North of the Rio Colorado. Smithsonian Institution, Bureau of
             American Ethnology Bulletin No. 82. Washington, D.C.
    1927   Archeological Investigations at Pueblo Bonito and Pueblo Del Arroyo, New Mexico. Smithson-
             ian Miscellaneous Collections, Vol. 78, No. 1, pp. 80–88.
    1940   *Progress in the Southwest.* Smithsonian Miscellaneous Collections, Vol. 100. Washington, D.C.
    1954   *The Material Culture of Pueblo Bonito.* Smithsonian Miscellaneous Collections, Vol. 124. Washing-
             ton, D.C.
    1959   *Pueblo del Arroyo, Chaco Canyon, New Mexico.* Smithsonian Miscellaneous Collections, Vol. 138,
             No. 1. Washington, D.C.
    1964   *The Architecture of Pueblo Bonito.* Smithsonian Miscellaneous Collections, Vol. 147, No. 1. Wash-
             ington, D.C.

Keegan, Marcia
    1972   *The Taos Indians and Their Sacred Blue Lake.* Julian Messner, New York.
Kidder, Alfred Vincent
    1924   *An Introduction to the Study of Southwestern Archaeology.* Yale University Press, New Haven & London.
    1932   *The Artifacts of Pecos.* Robert S. Peabody Foundation for Archaeology, Phillips Academy, Andover, Mass. Published for Phillips Academy by Yale University Press, New Haven.
    1958   *Pecos, New Mexico: Archaeological Notes.* Papers of the Robert S. Peabody Foundation for Archaeology, Vol. 5. Phillips Academy, Andover, Mass.
Kidder, Alfred Vincent, and Guernsey, Samuel J.
    1919   *Archeological Explorations in Northeastern Arizona.* Smithsonian Institution, Bureau of American Ethnology Bulletin No. 65. Washington, D.C.
King, Dale S. (editor)
    1945   *Arizona's National Monuments.* Southwestern Monuments Association. Popular Series, No. 2. Santa Fe.
King, Patrick
    1975   *Pueblo Indian Religious Architecture.* Patrick King, Salt Lake City.
Kirk, Ruth F.
    1943   *Introduction to Zuñi Fetishism.* Papers of the School of America Research, Archaeological Institute of America, Santa Fe, N. Mex.
Kurath, Gertrude Prokosch, with Garcia, Antonio
    1970   *Music and Dance of the Tewa Pueblos.* Museum of New Mexico, Research Records No. 8. Museum of New Mexico Press, Santa Fe.
Lange, Charles H.
    1968   *Cochiti: A New Mexico Pueblo, Past and Present.* Southern Illinois University Press, Carbondale.
Lange, Charles H., and Riley, Carroll L. (editors)
    1966   *The Southwestern Journals of Adolph F. Bandelier, 1880–1882.* University of New Mexico Press, Albuquerque.
Laski, Vera
    1959   *Seeking Life.* Memoirs of the American Folklore Society, Vol. 50.
Leighton, Dorothea C., and Adair, John
    1966   *People of the Middle Place.* Behavior Science Monographs. Human Relations Area Files Press, New Haven.
Lindsay, A. J., Jr.
    1969   The Tsegi Phase of Kayenta Cultural Tradition in Northeastern Arizona. Unpublished doctoral dissertation. University of Arizona, Tucson.
Lister, Florence C. and Robert H.
    1968   *Earl Morris & Southwestern Archaeology.* University of New Mexico Press, Albuquerque.
    1969   *The Earl H. Morris Memorial Pottery Collection.* Series in Anthropology No. 16. University of Colorado Press, Boulder.
Lister, Robert H. and Florence C.
    1978   *Anasazi Pottery.* Maxwell Museum of Anthropology, University of New Mexico. University of New Mexico Press, Albuquerque.
Litto, Gertrude
    1976   *South American Folk Pottery.* Watson-Guptill Publications, New York.
Lockett, Hattie Greene
    1933   *The Unwritten Literature of the Hopi.* University of Arizona Bulletin, Vol. 4, No. 4. Social Science Bulletin No. 2. University of Arizona, Tucson.
Longacre, William A. (editor)
    1970   *Reconstructing Prehistoric Pueblo Societies.* A School of American Research Book. University of New Mexico Press, Albuquerque.
Lummis, Charles F.
    1892   The Indian Who Is Not Poor. *Scribner's,* Vol. 12, pp. 361–71.
    1925   *Mesa, Cañon and Pueblo.* Century Company, New York & London.
Lyon, Luke
    1977   Michelangelo of the West. *New Mexico Magazine,* Vol. 55, No. 6, pp. 20–25.
McCluney, Eugene B.
    1975   The Eastern Pueblos, in Donald E. Worcester, ed., *Forked Tongues and Broken Treaties,* pp. 425–48. Caxton Printers, Caldwell, Idaho.
McIntyre, Loren
    1973   The Lost Empire of the Incas. *National Geographic Magazine,* Vol. 144, No. 6, pp. 729–87.
Mails, Thomas E.
    1972   *The Mystic Warriors of the Plains.* Doubleday & Company, Garden City, N.Y.

1974   *The People Called Apache.* Prentice-Hall, Englewood Cliffs, N.J.

1978   *Sundancing at Rosebud and Pine Ridge.* The Center for Western Studies of Augustana College, Sioux Falls, S. Dak.

Marriott, Alice

1949   *These Are the People.* Laboratory of Anthropology, Santa Fe.

Martin, Paul S.

1936   *Lowry Ruin in Southwestern Colorado.* Field Museum of Natural History Anthropological Series, Vol. 23, No. 1. Chicago.

1940   *The SU Site: Excavations at a Mogollon Village, Western New Mexico, 1939.* Field Museum of Natural History Anthropological Series, Vol. 32, No. 1. Chicago.

Martin, Paul S.; Lloyd, Carl; and Spoehr, Alexander

1938   *Archaeological Work in the Ackmen-Lowry Area, Southwestern Colorado, 1937.* Field Museum of Natural History Anthropological Series, Vol. 23, No. 2. Chicago.

Martin, Paul S.; Longacre, William A.; and Hill, James N.

1967   *Chapters in the Prehistory of Eastern Arizona, III.* Fieldiana: Anthropology, Vol. 57. Field Museum of Natural History, Chicago.

Martin, Paul S., and Plog, Fred

1973   *The Archaeology of Arizona.* American Museum of Natural History. Doubleday & Company/Natural History Press, Garden City, N.Y.

Martin, Paul S.; Rinaldo, John B.; and Antevs, Ernst

1949   *Cochise and Mogollon Sites: Pine Lawn Valley, Western New Mexico.* Fieldiana: Anthropology, Vol. 38, No. 1. Chicago Natural History Museum, Chicago.

Martin, Paul S.; Rinaldo, John B.; and Bluhm, Elaine

1954   *Caves of the Reserve Area.* Fieldiana: Anthropology, Vol. 42. Chicago Natural History Museum, Chicago.

Martin, Paul S., et al.

1962   *Chapters in the Prehistory of Eastern Arizona, I.* Fieldiana: Anthropology, Vol. 53. Chicago Natural History Museum, Chicago.

Maxwell, James A. (editor)

1978   *America's Fascinating Indian Heritage.* Reader's Digest Association, Pleasantville, N.Y.

Mera, Harry Percival

1975   *Pueblo Indian Embroidery.* William Gannon, Santa Fe.

Metcalf, Willard L.

1924   Zuñi: Leaves from a Sketch Book. *Survey Magazine,* Vol. 53, pp. 29–32.

Meyer, Karl E.

1973   Teotihuacan. *Newsweek.*

Mindeleff, Cosmos

1897   The Cliff Ruins of Canyon de Chelly, Arizona. Smithsonian Institution, Bureau of American Ethnology, 16th Annual Report, 1894–1895, pp. 73–198. Washington, D.C.

1898   Navaho Houses. Smithsonian Institution, Bureau of American Ethnology, 17th Annual Report, 1895–1896, pp. 469–517. Washington, D.C.

Mindeleff, Victor

1891   A Study of Pueblo Architecture: Tusayan and Cibola. Smithsonian Institution, Bureau of American Ethnology, 8th Annual Report, 1886–1887, pp. 3–228. Washington, D.C.

Monsen, Frederick

1907a   Pueblos of the Painted Desert: How the Hopi Build Their Community Dwelling on the Cliffs. *Craftsman,* Vol. 12, Apr., pp. 16–33.

1907b   The Primitive Folk of the Desert: Splendid Physical Development That Yet Shows Many of the Characteristics of an Earlier Race Than Our Own. *Craftsman,* Vol. 12, May, pp. 164–78.

1907c   Festivals of the Hopi: Religion the Inspiration, and Dancing an Expression in All Their National Ceremonies. *Craftsman,* Vol. 12, June, pp. 269–85.

Montgomery, H.

1894   Prehistoric Man in Utah. *The Archaeologist,* Vol. 2.

Mooney, James

1895   Recent Archeologic Find in Arizona. *The American Anthropologist,* Vol. 6, pp. 283–84.

Morgan, L. H.

1881   Houses and House-life of the American Aborigines. Contributions to North American Ethnology, Vol. 4.

Mori, Joyce and John

1972   Modern Hopi Coiled Basketry. *The Masterkey,* Vol. 46, No. 1, pp. 4–17. Southwest Museum, Los Angeles.

Morley, Sylvanus G.
   1956   *The Ancient Maya.* 3rd rev. ed. Stanford University Press, Stanford.

Morley, Sylvanus, and Kidder, Alfred V.
   1917   The Archaeology of McElmo Canyon, Colorado. *El Palacio,* Vol. 4, No. 4. Museum of New Mexico, Santa Fe.

Morris, Ann Axtell
   1978   *Digging in the Southwest.* rev. ed. Peregrine Smith, Santa Barbara & Salt Lake City.

Morris, Earl H.
   1919   Preliminary Account of the Antiquities of the Region Between the Mancos and La Plata Rivers in Southwestern Colorado. Smithsonian Institution, Bureau of American Ethnology, 33rd Annual Report, 1911–1912, pp. 155–206. Washington, D.C.
   1925   Exploring in the Canyon of Death. *National Geographic Magazine,* Vol. 48, No. 3, pp. 263–300.
   1927   *The Beginnings of Pottery Making in the San Juan Area: Unfired Prototypes and the Wares of the Earliest Ceramic Period.* Anthropological Papers of the American Museum of Natural History, Vol. 28, Part 2. New York.
   1939   Archaeological Studies in the La Plata District: Southwestern Colorado and Northwestern New Mexico. Carnegie Institution of Washington, Publication 519. Washington, D.C.

Moseley, Michael E., and Mackey, Carol J.
   1973   Chan Chan, Peru's Ancient City of Kings. *National Geographic Magazine,* Vol. 143, No. 3, pp. 318–55.

Moskowitz, Ira, and Collier, John
   1949   *Patterns and Ceremonials of the Indians of the Southwest.* E. P. Dutton & Co., New York.

Muench, David, and Pike, Donald G.
   1974   *Anasazi: Ancient People of the Rock.* American West Publishing Company, Palo Alto, Calif.

Nagata, Shuichi
   1970   *Modern Transformations of Moenkopi Pueblo.* University of Illinois Studies in Anthropology No. 6. University of Illinois Press, Urbana.

Neeley, James A., and Olson, Alan P.
   1977   *Archaeological Reconnaissance of Monument Valley in Northeastern Arizona.* Museum of Northern Arizona, MNA Research Paper No. 3. Flagstaff.

Nequatewa, Edmund
   1936   *Truth of a Hopi.* Museum of Northern Arizona, Bulletin No. 8. Flagstaff.

Nettl, Bruno
   1954   *North American Indian Musical Styles.* Memoirs of the American Folklore Society, Vol. 45.

Newberry, J. S.
   1876   *Report of the Exploring Expedition from Santa Fe, New Mexico, to the Junction of the Grand and Green Rivers of the Great Colorado of the West, in 1859.* U.S. Engineering Department, Washington, D.C.

Newman, Stanley
   1965   *Zuni Grammar.* University of New Mexico Publications in Anthropology, No. 14. University of New Mexico Press, Albuquerque.

Nordenskiöld, Gustaf
   1893   *The Cliff Dwellers of the Mesa Verde, Southwestern Colorado: Their Pottery and Implements.* English translation by D. Lloyd Morgan. P. A. Norstedt and Soner, Stockholm and Chicago.

Nusbaum, Deric
   1926   *Deric in Mesa Verde.* G. P. Putnam's Sons, New York & London.

O'Kane, Walter Collins
   1950   *Sun in the Sky.* Civilization of the American Indian Series, Vol. 30. University of Oklahoma Press, Norman.

Oliver, Marion L.
   1911   The Snake Dance. *National Geographic Magazine,* Vol. 22, No. 2, pp. 107–37.

Ortiz, Alfonso
   1969   *The Tewa World: Space, Time, Being, and Becoming in a Pueblo Society.* University of Chicago Press, Chicago.

Ortiz, Alfonso (editor)
   1972   *New Perspectives on the Pueblos.* A School of American Research Book. University of New Mexico Press, Albuquerque.
   1979   *The Southwest.* The Handbook of North American Indians, Vol. 9. Smithsonian Institution, Washington, D.C.

Owens, J. G.
   1892   Natal Ceremonies of the Hopi Indians. *A Journal of American Ethnology and Archaeology,* Vol. 2, pp. 161–75. Houghton Mifflin Company, Riverside Press, Cambridge, Mass.

Pagden, A. R. (editor)
   1975   *The Maya: Diego de Landa's Account of the Affairs of Yucatán.* J. Philip O'Hara, Chicago.

Parsons, Elsie Clews

    1922   *Winter and Summer Dance Series in Zuñi in 1918.* University of California Publications in American Archaeology and Ethnology, Vol. 17, No. 3, pp. 171–216. University of California Press, Berkeley.

    1925   Introduction and Notes to Crow-wing, *A Pueblo Indian Journal, 1920–1921.* Memoirs of the American Anthropological Association, No. 32.

    1926   *Tewa Tales.* Memoirs of the American Folk-Lore Society, Vol. 19.

    1929   *The Social Organization of the Tewa of New Mexico.* Memoirs of the American Anthropological Association, No. 36.

    1930   Spanish Elements in the Kachina Cult of the Pueblos. International Congress of Americanists, 23rd Session, Proceedings, pp. 582–603.

    1933   *Hopi and Zuñi Ceremonialism.* Memoirs of the American Anthropological Association, No. 39.

    1936   *Taos Pueblo.* General Series in Anthropology, No. 2. George Banta Publishing Company, Menasha, Wis.

    1939a   *Pueblo Indian Religion.* Vol. 1, Part 1. University of Chicago Press, Chicago.

    1939b   *Pueblo Indian Religion.* Vol. 1, Part 2. University of Chicago Press, Chicago.

    1939c   *Pueblo Indian Religion.* Vol. 2, Part 1. University of Chicago Press, Chicago.

    1939d   *Pueblo Indian Religion.* Vol. 2, Part 2. University of Chicago Press, Chicago.

    1962   *Isleta Paintings.* Esther S. Goldfrank, ed. Smithsonian Institution, Washington, D.C.

    1974   *The Pueblo of Isleta.* University of Albuquerque, Calvin Horn Publishers, Albuquerque.

Peckham, Stewart

    1965   *Prehistoric Weapons in the Southwest.* Museum of New Mexico Press, Popular Series Pamphlet No. 3. Santa Fe.

Pendleton, Mary

    1974   *Navajo and Hopi Weaving Techniques.* Collier Books, New York.

Pepper, George H.

    1920   *Pueblo Bonito.* Anthropological Papers of the American Museum of Natural History, Vol. 27. New York.

Powell, Mayor J. W.

    1972   *The Hopi Villages.* Filter Press, Palmer Lake, Colo.

Prudden, T. Mitchell

    1896   A Summer Among Cliff Dwellings. *Harpers New Monthly Magazine,* Vol. 93, No. 556, pp. 545–61.

    1903   The Prehistoric Ruins of the San Juan Watershed of Utah, Arizona, Colorado, and New Mexico. *The American Anthropologist,* n.s. 5, No. 2, pp. 224–88.

Qoyawayma, Polingaysi

    1964   *No Turning Back.* University of New Mexico Press, Albuquerque.

Quam, Alvina (translator)

    1972   *The Zunis: Self-Portrayals.* University of New Mexico Press, Albuquerque.

Radlauer, Ruth S.

    1977   *Mesa Verde National Park.* Children's Press, Chicago.

Reno, Phillip

    1963   *Taos Pueblo.* Swallow Press, Chicago.

Ritzenthaler, Robert E., and Johnson, Leo

    1979   The Artistry of Sumner W. Matteson. *American Indian Art Magazine,* Vol. 5, No. 1, pp. 60–67.

Roberts, Frank H. H., Jr.

    1929   *Shabik'eshchee Village, a Late Basket Maker Site in the Chaco Canyon, New Mexico.* Smithsonian Institution, Bureau of American Ethnology Bulletin No. 92. Washington, D.C.

    1930   *Early Pueblo Ruins in the Piedra District, Southwestern Colorado.* Smithsonian Institution, Bureau of American Ethnology Bulletin No. 96. Washington, D.C.

    1931   *The Ruins at Kiatuthlanna, Eastern Arizona.* Smithsonian Institution, Bureau of American Ethnology Bulletin No. 100. Washington, D.C.

    1932   *The Village of the Great Kivas on the Zuñi Reservation, New Mexico.* Smithsonian Institution, Bureau of American Ethnology Bulletin No. 111. Washington, D.C.

    1939   *Archeological Remains in the Whitewater District, Eastern Arizona.* Smithsonian Institution, Bureau of American Ethnology Bulletin No. 121. Washington, D.C.

    1940   Archeological Remains in the Whitewater District, Eastern Arizona. Smithsonian Institution, Bureau of American Ethnology Bulletin No. 126. With appendix by T. D. Stewart, "Skeletal Remains from the Whitewater District, Eastern Arizona." Washington, D.C.

Roberts, John M.

    1956   *Zuni Daily Life.* Note Book No. 3, Laboratory of Anthropology, University of Nebraska, Lincoln.

Rodeck, Hugo G.

    1976   Mimbres Painted Pottery. *American Indian Art,* Autumn, pp. 44–53.

Roediger, Virginia More
    1961   *Ceremonial Costumes of the Pueblo Indians.* University of California Press, Berkeley and Los Angeles.
Rohn, Arthur H.
    1971   *Mug House.* Archeological Research Series No. 7-D, National Park Service, U.S. Department of the Interior, Washington, D.C.
    1977   *Cultural Change and Continuity on Chapin Mesa.* Regents Press of Kansas, Lawrence.
Sanders, William T., and Marino, Joseph
    1970   *New World Prehistory.* Prentice-Hall, Englewood Cliffs, N.J.
Sanders, William T., and Price, Barbara J.
    1968   *Mesoamerica: The Evolution of a Civilization.* Random House, New York.
Sando, Joe S.
    1976   *The Pueblo Indians.* Indian Historian Press, San Francisco.
Saunders, Charles Francis
    1973   *The Indians of the Terraced Houses.* Rio Grande Press, Glorieta, N. Mex. (Originally published 1912.)
Schroeder, Albert H.
            Puerco Ruin Excavations, Petrified Forest National Monument, Arizona. *Plateau,* Vol. 33, No. 4, pp. 93–104. Flagstaff, Ariz.
    1975   *The Hohokam, Sinagua and the Hakataya.* Occasional Paper No. 3, I.V.C. Museum Society Publication, El Centro, Calif.
    1977   *Of Men and Volcanoes.* Southwest Parks and Monuments Association, Globe, Ariz.
Schroeder, Albert H. (editor)
    1973   The Changing Ways of the Southwestern Indians. Rio Grande Press, Glorieta, N. Mex.
Schultz, J. W.
            Why the Moquis Perform the Snake Dance. *The Pacific Monthly,* date uncertain, pp. 161–66.
Scully, Vincent
    1975   Pueblo: Mountain, Village, Dance. Viking Press, New York.
Scully, Vincent, and Current, William
    1971   *Pueblo Architecture of the Southwest.* Published for the Amon Carter Museum of Western Art, Fort Worth, by the University of Texas Press, Austin & London.
Sedgwick, Mrs. William T.
    1926   *Acoma, the Sky City.* Harvard University Press, Cambridge, Mass.
Sergeant, Elizabeth Shepley
    1928   Crisis in Sia Pueblo. *Scribner's Magazine,* Vol. 98, July, pp. 27–32.
Seton, Julia M.
    1939   *The Pulse of the Pueblo.* Seton Village Press, Santa Fe.
    1962   *American Indian Arts: A Way of Life.* Ronald Press Company, New York.
Sides, Dorothy Smith
    1961   *Decorative Art of the Southwestern Indians.* Dover Publications, New York. (Originally published 1936).
Simmons, Marc
    1974   *Witchcraft in the Southwest.* Northland Press, Flagstaff, Ariz.
Simpson, Ruth DeEtte
    1953   *The Hopi Indians.* Southwest Museum Leaflets No. 25, Southwest Museum, Los Angeles.
Smith, Anne M.
    1966   *New Mexico Indians.* Museum of New Mexico, Research Records No. 1, Museum of New Mexico, Santa Fe.
Smith, Watson
    1952   *Kiva Mural Decorations at Awatovi and Kawaika-a, with a Survey of Other Wall Paintings in the Pueblo Southwest.* Papers of the Peabody Museum of American Archeology and Ethnology, Vol. 37, Reports of the Awatovi Expedition, No. 5. Peabody Museum, Cambridge, Mass.
    1972   *Prehistoric Kivas of Antelope Mesa.* Papers of the Peabody Museum of Archeology and Ethnology, Vol. 39, No. 1. Harvard University, Cambridge, Mass.
Smith, Watson; Woodbury, Richard B.; and Woodbury, Nathalie F. S.
    1966   *The Excavation of Hawikuh by Frederick Webb Hodge, Report of the Hendricks-Hodge Expedition, 1917–1923.* Contributions from the Museum of the American Indian, Heye Foundation, New York.
Snodgrass, O. T.
    1975   *Realistic Art and Times of the Mimbres Indians.* O. T. Snodgrass, El Paso.
Snow, Dean
    1976   The Archaeology of North America. Thames and Hudson, London.
Spinden, Herbert Joseph (editor and translator)
    1976   *Songs of the Tewa.* Sunstone Press, Santa Fe.

Stephen, Alexander M.
  1929 Hopi Tales. *The Journal of American Folk-Lore,* Vol. 42, No. 163, edited by E. C. Parsons.
  1936 *Hopi Journal of Alexander M. Stephen,* edited by Elsie Clews Parsons. Columbia University Con-
        tributions to Anthropology, Vol. 23. New York.
  1940 *Hopi Indians of Arizona.* Southwest Museum Leaflets No. 14. Southwest Museum, Los Angeles.
Stevenson, James
  1891 Ceremonial of Hasjelti Dailjis and Mythical Sand Painting of the Navaho Indians. Smithsonian
        Institution, Bureau of American Ethnology, 8th Annual Report, 1886–1887, pp. 229–85. Wash-
        ington, D.C.
Stevenson, Matilda Coxe
  1894 The Sia. Smithsonian Institution, Bureau of American Ethnology, 11th Annual Report, 1889–
        1890, pp. 3–157. Washington, D.C.
  1904 *The Zuñi Indians.* Smithsonian Institution, Bureau of American Ethnology, 23rd Annual Report,
        1901–1902. Washington, D.C.
Steward, Julian H.
  1941 Archeological Reconnaissance of Southern Utah. Smithsonian Institution, Bureau of American
        Ethnology Bulletin No. 128, Anthropological Papers No. 18, pp. 275–356. Washington, D.C.
Stirling, Matthew W.
  1935 *Origin Myth of Acoma and Other Records.* Smithsonian Institution, Bureau of American Ethnology
        Bulletin No. 135. Washington, D.C.
  1940 Indian Tribes of Pueblo Land. *National Geographic Magazine,* Vol. 78, pp. 549–96.
  1955 *Indians of the Americas.* National Geographic Society, Washington, D.C.
Stuart, George E., and Stuart, Gene S.
  1969 *Discovering Man's Past in the Americas.* National Geographic Society, Washington, D.C.
Stubbs, Stanley A.
  1950 *Bird's-Eye View of the Pueblos.* Civilization of the American Indian Series, Vol 31. University of
        Oklahoma Press, Norman.
Stubbs, Stanley, and Stallings, W. S., Jr.
  1953 *The Excavation of Pindi Pueblo, New Mexico.* Monographs of the School of American Research,
        No. 18. Laboratory of Anthropology, Santa Fe.
Supplee, Charles; Anderson, Douglas; and Anderson, Barbara
  1971 *Canyon de Chelly: The Story Behind the Scenery.* KC Publications, Las Vegas.
Swanson, John R.
  1952 *The Indian Tribes of North America.* Smithsonian Institution, Bureau of American Ethnology Bul-
        letin No. 145. Washington, D.C.
Tamarin, Alfred, and Glubok, Shirley
  1975 *Ancient Indians of the Southwest.* Doubleday & Company, Garden City, N.Y.
Tanner, Clara Lee
  1968 *Southwest Indian Craft Arts.* University of Arizona Press, Tucson.
Thompson, Laura, and Joseph, Alice
  1965 *The Hopi Way.* Russell & Russell, New York.
Titiev, Mischa
  1944 *Old Oraibi: A Study of the Hopi Indians of the Third Mesa.* Papers of the Peabody Museum of
        American Archeology and Ethnology, Vol. 22, No. 1. Harvard University, Cambridge, Mass.
  1972 *The Hopi Indians of Old Oraibi.* University of Michigan Press, Ann Arbor.
Twitchell, Ralph E.
  1911 *Leading Facts of New-Mexican History.* Torch Press, Cedar Rapids, Iowa.
Tyler, Hamilton A.
  1964 *Pueblo Gods and Myths.* University of Oklahoma Press, Norman.
Udall, Louise
  1969 *Me and Mine: The Life Story of Helen Sekaquaptewa.* University of Arizona Press, Tucson.
Underhill, Lonnie E., and Littlefield, Jr., Daniel F. (editors)
  1976 *Hamlin Garland's Observations on the American Indian, 1895–1905.* University of Arizona Press,
        Tucson.
Underhill, Ruth
  1944 *Pueblo Crafts.* U.S. Department of the Interior, Bureau of American Ethnology—Division of Ed-
        ucation. Washington, D.C.
  1946 *Work a Day Life of the Pueblos.* Indian Life and Customs, No. 4, U.S. Indian Service, Phoenix
        Indian School, Phoenix.
  1953 *Red Man's America.* University of Chicago Press, Chicago.
  1976 *First Penthouse Dwellers of America.* William Gannon, Santa Fe.

Vivian, Gordon, and Reiter, Paul

1960   The Great Kivas of Chaco Canyon and Their Relationships. Monographs of the School of American Research and the Museum of New Mexico, No. 22. Santa Fe.

Von Hagen, Victor Wolfgang

1950   Frederick Catherwood Arch'. Oxford University Press, New York.

Voth, H. R.

1901   *The Oraibi Powamu Ceremony.* Publications of the Field Columbian Museum Anthropological Series, Vol. 3, No. 2, pp. 60–158.

1903a   *The Oraibi Summer Snake Ceremony.* Publications of the Field Columbian Museum Anthropological Series, Vol. 3, No. 4, pp. 262–358.

1903b   *The Oraibi Oaqöl Ceremony.* Field Columbian Museum Anthropological Series, Vol. 6, No. 1, Publication 84.

1912a   *The Oraibi Marau Ceremony.* Field Museum of Natural History Anthropological Series, Vol. 11, No. 1, Publication 156.

1912b   *Brief Miscellaneous Hopi Papers.* Field Museum of Natural History Anthropological Series, Vol. 11, No. 2, Publication 157.

Waters, Frank

1963   *Book of the Hopi.* Viking Press, New York.

1969   *Pumpkin Seed Point.* Sage Books, Chicago.

Watson, Don

1961   *Indians of the Mesa Verde.* Mesa Verde Museum Association, Mesa Verde National Park, Colo.

Weaver, Muriel Porter

1972   *The Aztecs, Maya and Their Predecessors.* Seminar Press, New York.

Weaver, Thomas (editor)

1974   *Indians of Arizona.* University of Arizona Press, Tucson.

Webb, William, and Weinstein, Robert A.

1973   *Dwellers at the Source: Southwestern Indian Photographs of A. C. Vroman, 1895–1904.* Grossman Publishers, New York.

Weltfish, Gene

1932   Preliminary Classification of Prehistoric Southwestern Basketry. Smithsonian Miscellaneous Collections, Vol. 87, No. 7, pp. 1–47. Washington, D.C.

Wendorf, Fred

1954   A Reconstruction of Northern Rio Grande Prehistory. *American Anthropologist,* Vol. 56, pp. 220–27.

Wheat, Margaret M.

1967   *Survival Arts of the Primitive Paiutes.* University of Nevada Press. Reno.

Whitaker, Kathleen

1974a   The Zuni Shalako Festival. *The Masterkey,* Vol. 48, No. 3, pp. 84097. Southwest Museum, Los Angeles.

1974b   The Zuni Shalako Festival. *The Masterkey,* Vol. 48, No. 4, pp. 136–47. Southwest Museum, Los Angeles.

White, Leslie A.

1932a   *The Pueblo of San Felipe.* Memoirs of the American Anthropological Association, No. 38.

1932b   *The Acoma Indians, People of the Sky City.* Smithsonian Institution, Bureau of American Ethnology, Annual Report, 1929–1930.

1935   *The Pueblo of Santo Domingo, New Mexico.* Memoirs of the American Anthropological Association, No. 43.

1942   The Pueblo of Santa Ana, New Mexico. *American Anthropologist,* Vol. 44, No. 4, Part 2.

1943   New Material from Acoma. Smithsonian Institution, Bureau of American Ethnology Bulletin No. 136, Anthropological Papers, No. 32, pp. 301–59. Washington, D.C.

1974   *Zia: The Sun Symbol Pueblo.* University of Albuquerque, Calvin Horn Publishers, Albuquerque. (Reprint of 1962 Bureau of American Ethnology Report.)

Willey, Gordon R.

1966   *An Introduction to American Archaeology: Vol. 1, North and Middle America.* Prentice-Hall, Englewood Cliffs, N.J.

Winship, George Parker

1896   The Coronado Expedition, 1540–1542. Smithsonian Institution, Bureau of American Ethnology, 14th Annual Report, 1892–1893, pp. 339–615.

Wissler, Clark

1921   Unearthing the Secrets of the Aztec Ruin. *Harper's Monthly Magazine,* Vol. 143, No. 853, pp. 43–56.

Wormington, H. M.
    1947   *Prehistoric Indians of the Southwest.* Denver Museum of Natural History, Popular Series, No. 7. Denver.
Wormington, H. M., and Neal, Arminta
    1978   *The Story of Pueblo Pottery.* Museum Pictorial No. 2, Denver Museum of Natural History, Denver.
Wright, Barton
    1973   *Kachinas: a Hopi Artist's Documentary.* Northland Press, Flagstaff, and Heard Museum, Phoenix.
    1975a *Kachinas: The Barry Goldwater Collection at the Heard Museum.* W. A. Krueger Company with the Heard Museum, Phoenix.
    1975b *The Unchanging Hopi.* Northland Press, Flagstaff, Ariz.
    1976a *Pueblo Shields: From the Fred Harvey Fine Arts Collection.* Northland Press, Flagstaff, Ariz.
    1976b Anasazi Murals. *American Indian Art Magazine,* Vol. 1, No. 2.
    1977   *Hopi Kachinas.* Northland Press, Flagstaff, Ariz.
    1979   *Hopi Material Culture: Artifacts Gathered by H. R. Voth in the Fred Harvey Collection.* Northland Press, Flagstaff, Ariz., and Heard Museum, Phoenix.
Wright, Barton, and Roat, Evelyn
    1962   *This Is a Hopi Kachina.* Museum of Northern Arizona, North Arizona Society of Science and Art, Flagstaff.
Wright, Margaret
    1972   *Hopi Silver.* Northland Press, Flagstaff, Ariz.
Yandell, Michael D. (editor)
    1972   *Rocky Mountain and Mesa Verde National Parks.* National Parkways, Vol. 3/4. World-Wide Research and Publishing Co., Casper, Wyo.
Yava, Albert
    1978   *Big Falling Snow.* Edited by Harold Courlander. Crown Publishers, New York.
Zubrow, Ezra B. W.; Fritz, Margaret C.; and Fritz, John M. (compilers)
    1974   *New World Archaeology. Readings from Scientific American.* W. H. Freeman and Company, San Francisco.

INDEX